RICH
RELATIONS

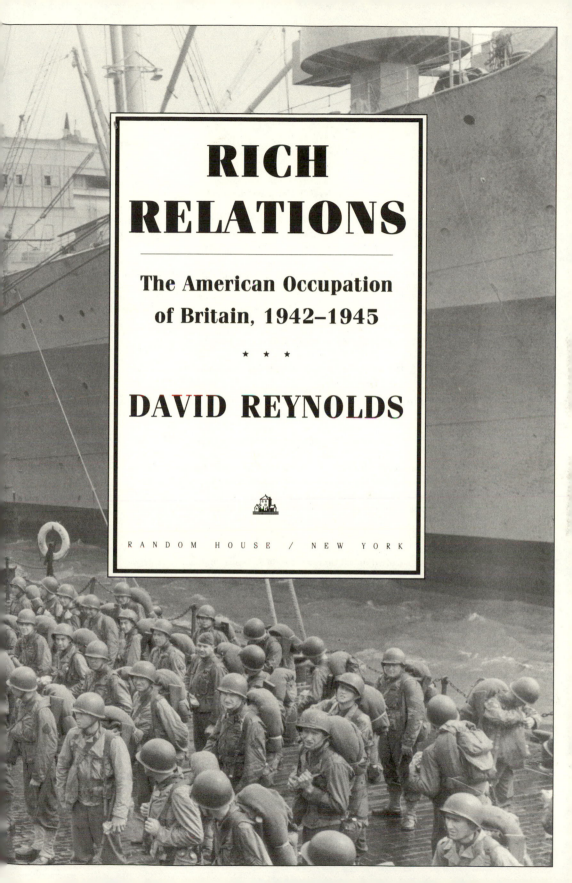

RICH RELATIONS

The American Occupation
of Britain, 1942–1945

★ ★ ★

DAVID REYNOLDS

RANDOM HOUSE / NEW YORK

Permissions acknowledgments for both published and unpublished material can be found on
pp. 553–555, which constitute an extension of the copyright page.

Photo credit for pages iv–v: National Archives

Maps rendered by Robert Bull Design

Library of Congress Cataloging-in-Publication Data
Reynolds, David
Rich relations: the American occupation of Britain, 1942–1945 /
David Reynolds.
p.   cm.
Includes bibliographical references and index.
ISBN 0-679-42161-0
1. World War, 1939–1945—Social aspects—Great Britain. 2. Great
Britain—Social life and customs—20th century. 3. United States—
Armed Forces—Great Britain—History—20th century. 4. United
States—Relations—Great Britain. 5. Great Britain—Relations—
United States. I. Title.
D744.7.G7R48   1995   940.53′1—dc20   94-13810

Manufactured in the United States of America on acid-free paper
24689753
First Edition
Book design by Jo Anne Metsch

In memory of my father,
who knew war and loved peace;
and in gratitude to family and friends
all over the United States
who showed a Brit "their" America
and taught him to like, respect, and, maybe, understand.

People go to the *movies* instead of *moving*! Hollywood characters are supposed to have all the adventures for everybody in America, while everybody in America sits in a dark room and watches them have them! Yes, until there's a war. That's when adventure becomes available to the masses!

> JIM O'CONNOR, "The Gentleman Caller," in
> Tennessee Williams's *The Glass Menagerie*,
> set in St. Louis during the Depression

It is difficult to go anywhere in London without having the feeling that Britain is now Occupied Territory. The general consensus of opinion seems to be that the only American soldiers with decent manners are the Negroes.

> GEORGE ORWELL, *Tribune*,
> 3 December 1943

Yankee Doodle came to Europe just to whip the Germans,
Stopped a while in England, before he took on Hermann.
Yankee Doodle keep it up, Yankee Doodle Dandy,
Mind the music and the step, and with the girls be handy.

> GI marching song, 1944

Inside every army is a crowd struggling to get out. . . .

> JOHN KEEGAN, *The Face of Battle*

Acknowledgments

★ ★ ★

I BEGAN RESEARCH FOR THIS BOOK IN ICY ABILENE, KANSAS, IN JANUARY 1981 and finished the writing at Christmas 1993. Work on it during that period was not continuous, because *An Ocean Apart* and *Britannia Overruled* absorbed most of my spare time between 1985 and 1990, but a project spanning thirteen years has inevitably accumulated a great many scholarly debts. The archival groundwork was done in 1981–83 thanks to research fellowships from the American Council of Learned Societies; Gonville and Caius College, Cambridge; and the Mellon Fund of Cambridge University. The first of those fellowships was held at the Charles Warren Center at Harvard in 1980–81, where I was also a visiting associate in 1990, and I appreciate the help of successive center administrators Pat Denault and Susan Hunt and the keen interest of director Bernard Bailyn. The later stages of research and writing were greatly assisted by fellowships from the Nuffield Foundation and the Leverhulme Trust, and smaller grants were provided by the British Academy, the U.S. Army Military History Institute, and the Master and Fellows of Christ's College. My Cambridge colleges, Caius and Christ's, have been hospitable intellectual homes, and the history faculty and general board of Cambridge University have been supportive about sabbaticals and unpaid leave. To all these, my grateful thanks.

Over the years I have given a number of papers or lectures on aspects of my work: in Britain at the universities of Cambridge, Oxford, London, and Hull; in the United States at the Eisenhower Centers in Abilene, Kansas, and New Orleans, at UCLA, Rutgers University, and the University of Kansas. Those audiences all helped me to clarify my ideas. I am particularly grateful to Professor Theodore A. Wilson (Kansas), to the reader for HarperCollins, and to my American editor Robert D. Loomis, who all read through a bulky draft with enthusiasm and critical insight. David Harkness in Belfast saved me from some of my misconceptions about Ulster; Harry Crosby on his hilltop in Maine, likewise, about the lives of B-17 crewmen; and Bill McAndrew and Barbara Wilson in Ottawa offered useful comments on my discussion of the Canadian Army. Barbara was also a generous guide into the excellent, ever-open Canadian archives. Among the many "survivors" of the Occupation who have spared time for my questions, I should particularly like to thank Bob Slaughter, both for his own interest and for arranging for me to meet so many 29ers. Throughout, my agent, Peter Robinson, has offered valued encouragement and advice.

Archivists and librarians are, as any research historian knows, an essential resource. In times when the volume of materials grows exponentially, while extra funds and space diminish at the same rate, their ability to attend to any one scholar's concerns is necessarily limited. I am therefore all the more grateful for their help and a few should be mentioned by name. At the National Archives in Washington, D.C., the ever-patient William G. Lewis helped me through the military maze. Marion Smith, historian of the Immigration and Naturalization Service in Washington, brought to an end my long search for statistics of war brides. In the Manuscripts Division of the Library of Congress the assistance of Fred Coker, Gary Kohn, and especially Ruth S. Nicholson was much appreciated. At the U.S. Army Military History Institute in Carlisle Barracks, Pennsylvania, Archivist-Historian Richard J. Sommers and his staff, notably David Keough, were invaluable. In the library at the other end of the same building, John J. Slonaker and Dennis Vetock embody the Platonic ideal of reference librarians. In my visits to the Roosevelt Library at Hyde Park, New York, in the early 1980s, William G. Emerson and his staff extended a warm welcome. In Abilene, Kansas, I benefited from David Haight's encyclopaedic knowledge of the Eisenhower Library, as well as from the interest and hospitality of Director Dan Holt and his wife Marilyn. Down in Appalachian Virginia, Marti Gansz and Larry I. Bland helped me exploit the riches of the George C. Marshall Library, and David Wrenn and Peter Combee enabled me to see material in the 116th Infantry Regiment museum at Staunton. At the Eisenhower Center in New Orleans, Stephen E. Ambrose generously made available the fascinating D-Day oral histories he has accumulated. In London, Rod Suddaby, Penelope Goymer, and other staff at the Imperial War Museum were very helpful. I am also grateful to Dorothy Sheridan of the Mass-Observation

Archive at Sussex University and the hard-pressed staff of the Public Record Office at Kew. In Cambridge, the University Library still manages to combine the facilities of an international research collection and the accessibility of a local public library. Without that resource, this book would have been almost impossible.

As with any book, family and friends provided the greatest sustenance. My father's death in May 1993, after six weeks in hospital, gave me new sensitivity to the interplay of life and death—a theme that informs this work. Margaret, my wife, has lived with the special relationship all our married life. From her own expatriate experience she also understands something of what the GIs felt. Although she has occasionally wondered if this project would prove more than a fading gleam in the authorial eye (and a growing mound of notes and photocopies), her support for my work and her readiness to read and criticize it have been indispensable. My gratitude also extends to numerous in-laws and friends around the United States, especially John and Judy Ray for the use of their house in the fall of 1990. Whether or not they find this book adequate recompense for my frequent absences (both physical and mental), I hope it will give them some idea of where I have been all these years.

Cambridge
June 1994

This volume is itself a venture in Anglo-American cooperation, being a single text produced for two publishers on two continents. In preparing the manuscript for publication we have collided frequently with the barrier of a common language, necessitating compromises in style, spelling, and punctuation. I am grateful to my American and British editors, Bob Loomis and Stuart Proffitt, for their collaboration; to the editorial staff at Random House in New York, who carefully oversaw the book's progression from typescript into print, notably Gail Bradney and Dennis Ambrose; and to Philip Gwyn Jones and his colleagues at HarperCollins in London for their energetic work on the British edition.

Contents

★ ★ ★

List of Tables and Charts

★ ★ ★

List of Maps

★ ★ ★

Introduction

★ ★ ★

TWO AMERICAN SOLDIERS STATIONED IN ENGLAND WERE PLANNING WHAT to do with a weekend's leave. "We gotta see Coventry," one of them said. "They tell me a naked woman rides through the streets on a horse." His buddy was impressed. "Yeah, let's go. I ain't seen a horse for years."

That exchange may be apocryphal, but the story amused Winston Churchill in May 1943 and it encapsulates the British stereotype of the wartime Americans—hedonistic, materialist, and high-tech. According to the contemporary cliché, the "Yanks" were "oversexed, overpaid, overfed, and over here." (Less familiar is the GIs' riposte, that the British were "undersexed, underpaid, underfed, and under Eisenhower.") This stereotype has passed into legend. "I like to say the Victorian era in England ended when we arrived," quipped former GI Sandy Conti fifty years later. A British newspaper, the *Daily Express*, reminisced in 1979:

> The G.I.s . . . came with saunter and swagger, with brashness and boisterousness. They came with five times the money of the British Tommy and with friendly charm which conquered the heart of many a British maiden or otherwise. . . . One joke heralded a new brand of knickers: "One Yank and they're off."

Here is *Time* magazine in similar vein on the fortieth anniversary of D-Day in 1984: "Residents of Somerset still remember G.I.s tossing chocolate bars and gum out of passing trucks to goggle-eyed children. . . . And the walls outside American barracks were lined every night with panting couples twined in a last embrace before bed check."[1]

Popular histories have taken the same line. In his swashbuckling book *Vie et moeurs des G.I.s en Europe, 1942–1947*, Marc Hillel asserted that it was "impossible to find, in the romantic annals of the armies engaged in World War Two, a soldier more obsessed with sex than the GI." The Wehrmacht enjoying four years of occupation in France, or the Red Army exacting its revenge on Germany, was, he claimed, but "the pale reflection of this unparalleled sexual appetite which possessed millions of GIs disembarking in Europe." Likewise, in his history of the U.S. Army during the war, Geoffrey Perret talked of how, in England, young women

> greeted GIs with a gratifying liberality that left rosy glows for years afterwards. American soldiers had enough unfair advantages to make even Don Juan blush. To begin with, most of the able-bodied young men of these parts had been sent to other parts. That eliminated the competition. Then came the GIs, with plenty of money, free-spending habits and a dress uniform whose sole function was to make the wearer look good off duty. Tommies . . . had to socialize in what amounted to their work clothes.[2]

While not totally inaccurate, these vignettes are simplifications of reality. About three million American service personnel visited Britain between January 1942 and December 1945.[3] Their experiences varied enormously. The 29th Infantry Division lived in southwest England for over a year and a half before landing on Omaha Beach on 6 June 1944, but most combat units stayed only a few months or even weeks. The 8th Army Air Force put down deeper roots, particularly in the villages of East Anglia. And whereas ground troops were only waiting for war in 1942–43, the aircrews were waging war every day they flew a mission. Backing up both combat soldiers and airmen were the unsung heroes of the Services of Supply—the drivers, cooks, and construction workers who kept the fighting troops armed, fed, and housed. Most service units suffered from low morale and motivation, particularly black soldiers who endured the additional miseries of abuse and segregation.

Three million Americans, engaged in a multiplicity of tasks. Clearly broad generalizations cannot tell the whole story. Consider a few biographical sketches of these "Yanks."

Bob Raymond, the son of a furniture-store owner from Kansas City, volunteered for the British Royal Air Force (RAF) in November 1940, more than a year before the United States entered the war. He trained as a pilot and served on Wellington bomber raids over Germany and

Italy until he transferred to the U.S. Army Air Force in June 1943. During those two and a half years he saw a good deal of England and grew to like the English for their courage and kindness. He felt constantly overwhelmed by small personal courtesies. When traveling in London, bus conductors refused to accept his fare and tobacconists produced packages of cigarettes from under the counter when their shelves were bare. Yet he never overcame his frustration at English inertia and "Old School Tie" class consciousness. He complained in May 1942: "The force of tradition and precedent is so strong that thinking in politics, business, religion, etc., seems to have congealed. These are the most economically backward people I've ever encountered. Labor-saving devices and short-cut, direct business methods are heartily resisted. . . . Too much tea drinking, Friday-to-Monday weekends, holidays, etc."[4]

Payne Templeton was a fifty-year-old schoolteacher from Helena, Montana. He had never been outside North America before January 1944 when he sailed for England as one of the civil affairs officers preparing for the occupation of continental Europe. But in another sense Templeton knew England—or *an* England—very well. As he wrote later, it "had been in my mind and in my dreams ever since my saturation in Scott, Dickens, Wordsworth and many others during boyhood. It was my far-back homeland whence many of my ancestors came, late in the 18th century. Here it was, just outside the barracks gate!" Every weekend, leave, and holiday of his five and a half months in England he toured historic sites, in his imagination populating Kenilworth, Blenheim, or Salisbury with characters from the literature and history in which he had steeped himself. For Payne Templeton 1944 was a sort of intellectual homecoming.[5]

Robert W. Coakley from Virginia was also a student of history and literature. Yet his experience of wartime Britain was largely confined to views from a train window in August 1944 as he journeyed from Liverpool, his port of arrival, to Southampton Docks. Britain was simply a transshipment point en route to France. After the war he married a Parisian and settled back in the United States, where he worked for the U.S. Army as one of the historians of the American war effort. It was nearly forty years before he returned to Britain.[6]

Joseph O. Curtis grew up in a black middle-class family in Washington, D.C. He had graduated from teacher's college four years before he was drafted in 1941. After training as an engineer officer he served in England from December 1943 until August 1944, mostly in Army camps in the southwest. He found the British less racist and "stiff-necked" than he had expected from movies and novels and became

close friends with one family in Chacewater, near Redruth in Cornwall. He called Mr. and Mrs. Barnes "Pop" and "Mom" and cherished
the memory of the birthday cake they made for him out of their meagre
rations. They kept in touch for several years after the war.[7]

Private John ____ was also an engineer, drafted in 1941, with an
excellent record. There, however, the parallels with Joseph Curtis end.
White, aged thirty-eight, married with one child, but separated from
his wife for thirteen years, he had an English girlfriend in 1943 who
worked in a small tailor's shop in Henley-on-Thames, upriver from
London. But, as a U.S. Army report put it, the woman "had a reputation in the community for looseness in sexual matters" and the two of
them quarreled frequently. On the afternoon of 14 July 1943 the
soldier went to the tailor's and demanded that the woman go out with
him that evening. She refused, turned on heel, and disappeared into
the workshop. He followed, drew his pistol, and killed her with three
shots at close range. He then shot himself under the chin, causing
serious brain damage. The soldier was found guilty of murder by an
Army court-martial and hanged on 10 February 1944.[8]

Other Anglo-American liaisons had happier endings. Jackson M.
Amsbaugh, from Danville, Virginia, a twenty-three-year-old GI in the
Signal Corps, was based near Newport in South Wales in the autumn
of 1943. There he met Doris Norley, a telegraphist at the local post
office. They dated for eighteen months and eventually married in
March 1945. Her parents were dubious, but they gave their daughter
the best possible wedding, with a service in the Baptist chapel where
she had grown up and a reception afterwards in a local hotel. Not long
after a week's honeymoon in Torquay, Jack was off across the Continent, ending up in Austria, from where he was transferred directly
home in October 1945. Meanwhile, Doris gave birth to their first child
in December and lived with her parents until she was able to get
passage across the Atlantic. The couple were reunited in New York on
27 March 1946 and settled in Virginia, where Jack put his wartime
skills to good use working for the telephone giant AT&T.[9]

John Ray was not a draftee but a regular Army officer. A graduate
of West Point in 1939, he had two spells in Britain—in the summer
of 1942, prior to the invasion of North Africa, and then again from
September 1943 until 7 June 1944. Though captured twice by the
Germans during the war, Lt. Col. Ray was not a combat soldier but a
staff officer, in charge of ammunition for II Corps in 1942 and then for
Gen. Omar Bradley's 1st Army in 1944. He was among a small group
of American military invited to a Thanksgiving Day reception in November 1943 at Buckingham Palace, where he was presented to the

king and queen and their daughters. Like Jack Amsbaugh, John Ray met his future wife in wartime Britain. She, however, was American—Tova Schwartz, a physiotherapist from the suburbs of Boston, who was then working at a U.S. Army hospital near Oxford.[10]

As these vignettes suggest, the experience of Americans in wartime Britain fitted no single pattern. How you judged the British depended on your basis of comparison—Bob Raymond's America was very different from that of Joseph Curtis. It also depended on how long you stayed—only a few days in the case of Bob Coakley—and what you chose to see: Payne Templeton's odysseys were not those of a young, single GI on a pub-crawl around Piccadilly. Off duty a soldier could mix with high society or lowlife, as the stories of Lt. Col. Ray and Private John ____ remind us. His "date" might be American rather than British, because not all the Yanks serving in wartime Britain were male. And, each time, what shaped the story were the person's character, education, and background as much as some essential "Americanness." Despite the uniform, there was no uniformity about the GI experience—for these seven, or for three million of their countrymen. The "oversexed, overpaid" image tells us as much about British stereotypes of the Americans as it does about the soldiers themselves.

How, then, can one write about the GIs' collective experience? Is it possible to encapsulate such diversity without gross distortion? One reason for trying lies in the cornucopia of archival material now available on both sides of the Atlantic, which has lain virtually untouched, except for some research on black GIs in Britain. The popular histories of the American presence, though readable and interesting, rely mainly on reminiscences and make little use of the archives, especially in the United States.[11]

Yet history depends not only on documents but on the questions asked of them. To go beyond conventional wisdom about the American presence in Britain we need a frame of reference that transcends the normal subdivisions of historical scholarship—diplomatic, military, social, cultural. This is, therefore, a study in international history in the broadest sense, embracing power and culture, policy and society, high politics as well as real life.[12]

To begin with we must examine the underlying clash of cultures by looking at America and Britain as societies—how they compared, and how they *thought* they compared. On the British side, that means paying particular attention to the glittering cinema images that shaped preconceptions about America. For many British people, the GI was the man from the movies. But Hollywood was not reality. The

Depression had ravaged America psychologically as well as economically. Recovery was slow and painful, and the triumphs of World War Two were essential therapy. The GIs' odysseys were part of the Americanizing of Britain, but they also contributed to the Americanization of the United States.

But why call the American wartime presence an "occupation"? Partly because commentators like George Orwell did so at the time. They were using the word polemically, but it also suggests similarities with other armies on foreign soil, friendly as well as hostile, who are all, to some extent, "oversexed and over here." In other words, we must take the GIs seriously as *soldiers* and not just as *Americans.* How do you hold an army of unwilling conscripts together, especially when it is not fighting? To that conundrum, Gen. George C. Marshall had a distinctive answer. The relative opulence of the U.S. Army was not simply a mirror of American abundance but also Marshall's deliberate strategy for dealing with the morale problems of inactive but articulate troops who were far from home. The pressures that could build up in a discontented army of occupation were illustrated by the tragic experience of the Canadian Army in Britain in 1942.

The social history of soldiering is a relatively novel idea. As Omer Bartov has observed of Hitler's Wehrmacht,

> while social historians have probed into civilian society, military historians have concerned themselves with tactics, strategy, and generals. . . . Consequently, once conscripted, the social historians' protagonists were passed over to the military historians who . . . treated them as part of a vast, faceless mass of field-grey uniforms devoid of any civilian past. Conversely, once the war was over, those soldiers who had survived it were, so to speak, delivered back into the hands of the social historians, only to continue their civilian existence with very little reference to the fact that for years they had served as soldiers.[13]

That gap reflects the larger gulf between traditional politico-military history and the new social history—the former tending to leave out ordinary people, the latter, in reaction, ignoring the dimension of power in human life.[14] Yet soldiers are ordinary people placed in extraordinary situations by those with power over them. Only by taking seriously high politics *and* real life can their experiences be understood.

High politics means looking at the GIs as objects of official policy. The prospect of a million or more young American males kicking their heels in Britain alarmed both the British government and American Army commanders. The biggest headaches were sex and race—relations between free-spending GIs and British women emancipated by wartime, and the management of a segregated army in a society unused to segregation or indeed to nonwhites. Underlying all the official activity was a debate about two alternative approaches to the problems posed by the GIs: the negative approach, meaning an attempt to avoid friction by minimizing contact, and, on the other hand, active efforts to promote friendship and good feeling. Churchill and the British Foreign Office were particularly keen on the positive approach, hopeful that the mixing up of GIs and Britons would nurture at the grass-roots level the "special relationship" that they deemed essential for Britain's future.

But what officialdom called "problems" were people in real life. If we examine the same issues from the bottom up rather than from the top down a different impression emerges. This change of perspective is, I think, particularly revealing in the case of so-called minorities who were the main victims of official policies made by white males, namely British women and black GIs, and it suggests how such groups can be incorporated into traditional international history.[15] To do this one must move away from the official memoranda that document high policy, and instead use letters, diaries, interviews, and poll data in a more imaginative reconstruction of daily living—what it meant to be a British woman in the emancipated conditions of wartime, or an underpaid and frustrated British Tommy, or a commuter-combatant American flyboy. Above all, what was life like in Britain for the average GI, a regimented tourist waiting for war?

Until June 1944 the airmen were the only Americans in Britain doing any real fighting. This was a basic British gripe about most GIs. In the final year of the war, however, Americans finally became soldiers, crossing the Channel and slugging their way into Germany. The new respect and affection they won in Britain can be measured not only in opinion polls but also in the spate of marriages they contracted in 1944–45. In the process, too, the U.S. Army came of age, with significant consequences for the balance of the Anglo-American relationship. At the centre of that story is the man from Abilene, Dwight D. Eisenhower.

The encounter of Yanks and Limeys is, then, a fascinating story in itself, but much more. It illuminates Britain and America at a turning point in their modern histories. It reveals the hidden side of the special relationship, at the level of "ordinary" people. It exposes the human, crowdlike realities inside any army. It is a story about young people going away and growing up, about making love and making war. And it is also about old people grasping at wisps of youthful memory—vivid, even painful, yet tantalizingly elusive.

Part I

SOCIETIES AT WAR

1

"Never Again"

★ ★ ★

THEY HAD COME ONCE BEFORE. DURING WORLD WAR ONE AMERICAN SOL-
diers had visited Britain in strength. What happened then established
lessons—both positive and negative—for any future war. But it was a
brief encounter. The "doughboys" soon went home and the next two
decades saw growing American disenchantment with Europe and
strained relations with Britain. In 1939–41 a reluctant America was
manoeuvred cautiously closer to war by Franklin Roosevelt, and only
unforeseen disaster in the Pacific made the country a full belligerent.
These historical legacies were part of the GIs' heritage in 1942–45.

War began in Europe in August 1914 with the United States studi-
ously neutral, and it was not until 2 April 1917 that the German
U-boat campaign in the Atlantic obliged President Woodrow Wilson to
ask Congress for a declaration of war. In his war message Wilson also
called for a draft of the nation's young manpower. This itself was
controversial: Conscription had been used by both sides in the Civil
War but never before in a *foreign* conflict. Even more disquieting were
reports that the War Department was planning to despatch troops to
France. "Good Lord!," exclaimed Senator Thomas S. Martin of Virginia. "You're not going to send soldiers over there, are you?"[1] Wilson
was indeed. By July 1917 the commander of the American Expeditionary Force (AEF), General John J. Pershing, was established in Paris and
the first U.S. combat division was disembarking at French ports. By
Armistice Day, 11 November 1918, almost four million Americans
were in uniform and half of them were "over there."

Of these, 1,027,000 passed through Britain, together with some seven thousand Army nurses. In the spring of 1918, when thousands were arriving every day, Minister of Information Lord Beaverbrook created a special "Department of Hospitality to American Forces" to ensure that the doughboys had "the time of their lives." Over 700,000 were entertained with concerts and sporting activities. The climax came on 4 July 1918 when American Independence Day was celebrated officially in Britain for the first time. The U.S. Navy beat the U.S. Army two to one in a special baseball game at Chelsea Football Ground, on the southwest edge of London. The game was played in the presence of the king and queen and some forty thousand others, many of them completely bemused by what they saw. That evening all the London theatres were thrown open to the American servicemen and some two thousand availed themselves of free tickets. Throughout the city the two national flags were widely in evidence and thousands of people wore them in miniature. In one of many speeches to note the day the government minister Winston Churchill, himself half-American, took the Declaration of Independence as his text, claiming that its sentiments now animated the war effort of the British Empire as well. In short, observed *The Times*, "it was not so much Independence Day as Interdependence Day."[2]

Yet it is easy to be misled by the Fourth of July 1918. More than one million Americans visited Britain in 1917–18 but only a small fraction lived for any length of time in the country. Between April and December 1918 the daily average was 38,423, with a maximum of 70,000.[3] Most of the Americans spent only three or four days in Britain en route to France. Shipped from Hoboken, Boston, Newport News, and other East Coast ports, most of them landed at Liverpool, in the northwest of England. After perhaps a night at Knotty Ash camp on the edge of the city they would be taken south by train to other camps around the cathedral city of Winchester before transport from Southampton over to Le Havre. A few, attached to British divisions, were despatched through Dover and Folkestone to Calais and Boulogne. Thus, for most of the Americans, their acquaintance with Britain was limited to a few days in ports, trains, and transit camps. Here was the most fundamental contrast between the American presence in Britain in World War One as against World War Two. In 1914–18 there was always a Western front in France; Britain served mainly as a training and hospitalization area. Between June 1940 and June 1944, however, France was occupied territory and Britain the Allies' front line in Europe. The American occupation of Britain in World War Two was necessarily more extensive and intensive than a quarter century before.

Those who did stay in Britain for any length of time in 1918 were mainly medical, supply, and construction personnel, and also trainees—pilots, mechanics, and tank crews, often assigned to British bases. Nearly all were white. An Army report noted: "Only one experiment was made in England with Colored Labor Battalions and this was soon given up owing to the objections of the [British] Labor Unions." The conduct of the troops in general was "remarkably good," in the view of the Army's judge advocate in Britain. Even the transients seem to have been well behaved. The Southern Provost Area—which included the major camps around Winchester and Southampton—made a total of only 1,507 arrests, despite the fact that some 800,000 troops passed through its jurisdiction in 1917–18. The record, in reality, is further evidence of the lightness of the Americans' touch on Britain. The long-stay troops were usually fully occupied in training and even they only stayed a few months, while the transit troops had little time or opportunity to escape military supervision.[4]

Despite the brevity of the American presence, World War One set some important precedents. Admiral William S. Sims, head of U.S. Naval Forces in Europe, placed his vessels under British command, viewing his role as support of the British in convoy escorts and anti-submarine warfare. Sims was an ardent Anglophile who had declared in London in 1910 that "if the time should ever come when the British Empire is menaced by a European coalition, Great Britain can rely on the last ship, the last man, and the last drop of blood from her kindred across the sea." Sims was unusual, however. The Chief of Naval Operations in Washington, Admiral William S. Benson, took a much more nationalist line. Benson was determined to use America's fleet independently for its own interests, not least in watching the Japanese. And a similar philosophy dominated the thinking of Pershing and the AEF in France. Pressed repeatedly by the French and British to commit his units piecemeal to the critical battles of 1917 and 1918, the general insisted on preparing them for action en masse as an American army, when and where his government required. At a desperate moment during the last German offensives in May 1918 the Supreme Allied Commander, Marshal Foch, asked, "You are willing to risk our being driven back to the Loire?" Pershing responded: "Yes, I am willing to take the risk." No such disaster occurred but the issue of cooperative or independent action was to be at the heart of Anglo-American debate in the next war. Significantly, Pershing's aide-de-camp from 1918 to 1923 was a devoted young colonel, George C. Marshall, who kept the controversy very much in mind some two decades later.[5]

Pershing's attitude was shared by his Commander in Chief. Woodrow Wilson personified the ambivalence of many Americans, even of English stock, towards the British Empire. He loved England and had spent several cycling holidays there when in his forties. He was steeped in English literature and his political thought was rooted in the liberal tradition of Cobden, Bright, and, above all, Gladstone—his great hero. But Wilson was also deeply suspicious of Britain as an imperial power, judging that it was partially responsible for the war. In April 1917 he insisted that the United States was not an "Allied" but an "Associate" power, indicating that its cooperation with Britain and France was for the immediate purpose of eradicating German militarism and did not betoken an identity of aims. He made his point most dramatically at the grand state banquet at Buckingham Palace on 27 December 1918. The tables in the great dining room were resplendent with gold plate. The guests, from all parts of the triumphant British Empire, were arrayed in jewels, medals, and dress uniforms, celebrating a victorious end to four years of war. But Wilson, the guest of honour, appeared in an ordinary black suit, without adornment—almost a moral judgement by the New World on the follies of the Old. His speech of thanks was clipped and formal, making no reference to the British role in winning the war. Afterwards he warned the king:

> You must not speak of us who come over here as cousins, still less as brothers; we are neither. Neither must you think of us as Anglo-Saxons, for that term can no longer be rightly applied to the people of the United States. Nor must too much importance in this connection be attached to the fact that English is our common language. . . . No, there are only two things which can establish and maintain closer relations between your country and mine: they are community of ideals and of interests.[6]

His words were apt. They were a reminder that the "Anglo-Saxon" sentiments of Churchill and his colleagues in Britain were much less evident across the Atlantic, Admiral Sims notwithstanding. And they anticipated how the two countries would quickly drift apart after Germany was defeated. Instead of "The Yanks Are Coming," the motto became "Never Again."

It would be wrong to describe the United States simply as "isolationist" in the interwar years. Particularly in economic affairs the country's world role had been transformed in 1914–18. Europe's preoccupation with the war enabled Americans to expand their trade in Latin America and East Asia. And the demand for U.S. loans, especially from

Britain, not only created substantial war debts—which proved a source of controversy after 1918—but also turned American banking houses outwards as foreign investors. Although Britain remained the world's largest source of overseas investment, the United States was the principal source of new funds in the growth industries of the future such as oil, rubber, and radio. Economically, then, America was internationalist, but its underlying political stance had not changed. Wilson's dream of a League of Nations was repudiated by the U.S. Senate in 1919–20 and thereafter the country turned its back on European commitments, even the World Court. The national philosophy in the 1920s could still be summed up in the famous words of President Thomas Jefferson in 1801: "peace, commerce, and honest friendship with all nations—entangling alliances with none."[7]

Anglo-American relations became seriously strained in the decade after the war. Washington's "betrayal" of the League rankled in London and there was growing friction over America's new financial power and commercial expansion. Access to raw materials such as tin, rubber, and oil, essential for America's booming industry but often controlled by the British, was particularly emotive. In 1929 British Prime Minister Stanley Baldwin warned his successor: "The American money power is trying to get control of some of the natural resources of the Empire." Most acrimonious of all was the simmering row about the size of the two fleets. The U.S. Navy wanted equality with Britain, at least on paper, a concession that struck at the heart of Britain's traditional image as ruler of the waves. Winston Churchill, despite his American ancestry, was a leading opponent of Washington's pretensions. In 1927, when chancellor of the exchequer, he even told the cabinet that war between the two countries was not "unthinkable" and that therefore "we do not wish to put ourselves in the power of the United States. We cannot tell what they might do if at some future date they were in a position to give us orders about our policy, say, in India, or Egypt, or Canada, or on any other great matter behind which their electioneering forces were marshalled." It took until 1930 for the British to back down, obliged to do so by the ultimate threat of a naval arms race that the wealthier Americans would win.[8]

Relations between the two governments deteriorated even further in the 1930s. The booming U.S. economy turned down in 1929, accelerated by the Wall Street crash, and American investors pulled their money out of Europe, exacerbating the financial crisis there in 1931. As the Depression deepened, the world economy broke up into competing blocs, one of which centered on the dollar area and another on Britain's protectionist links with its empire and countries using sterling. The State Department became obsessed with reducing Britain's barriers against American exports while the British claimed that they were only retaliating against the soaring U.S. tariffs of the 1920s. As the two economies drifted apart, American foreign policy also sunk into a genuinely isolationist mentality. The Depression was often blamed on the failure of the Europeans to pay their debts. It became commonplace to believe that American involvement in the war had been mistaken and that the country had only been drawn in through the machinations of corrupt Wall Street bankers, wily British propagandists, and greedy munitions manufacturers—the "merchants of death." From 1935 a series of Neutrality Acts were passed by Congress, restricting American loans and trade with belligerent countries in time of war. The novelist Ernest Hemingway captured the sense of estrangement in 1935: "Of the hell broth that is brewing in Europe we have no need to drink. . . . We were fools to be sucked in once in a European war, and we shall never be sucked in again."[9]

By the late 1930s transatlantic distrust was mutual. Even Sir Robert Vansittart, permanent undersecretary at the Foreign Office and a keen advocate of cooperation with the United States, was bitter by 1934 as he listed a decade and a half of rebuffs from America. "It is we who have made all the advances, and received nothing in return. It is still necessary, and I desire as much as ever, that we should get on well with this untrustworthy race. But," he continued wearily, "we shall never get very far; they will always let us down." He spoke for most British leaders in the 1930s; indeed some were even more cynical, notably Neville Chamberlain, prime minister from 1937 to 1940, who believed that it was "always best and safest to count on *nothing* from the Americans except words." When Britain went to war again, its main ally was France.[10]

On each side of the Atlantic policies did not change fundamentally with the coming of war in September 1939. The Neutrality Act was amended to place all trade with belligerents on a "cash and carry" basis, meaning no American loans or ships were to be involved. For their part, the British, anxious to conserve scarce gold and dollars, did not purchase heavily in the United States that winter. In January 1940 Chamberlain, with Woodrow Wilson in mind, went so far as to declare: "Heaven knows I don't want America to fight for us—we should have to pay too dearly for that if they had a right to be in on the peace terms."[11]

The turning point in Anglo-American relations came with the fall of France in May–June 1940. London (and Washington) had assumed that the French would act as a front line, giving them time to rearm and mobilize. Unlike most of the continental European states, Britain (again like America) did not impose on its citizens the obligation of peacetime military service, first in the armed forces and then in the reserves, which would have ensured a large pool of more or less trained military manpower. In Britain, conscription had been enacted in World War One, but it was quickly abolished afterwards and not reimposed until May 1939. At the start of war, therefore, the British relied on small regular forces totaling less than half a million men. While the Royal Navy was still second to none and the RAF was being equipped with modern monoplane fighters, particularly the Spitfire and Hurricane, the Army remained the Cinderella service. Only ten British divisions were in France and Belgium in May 1940, compared with 104 French divisions and twenty-two Belgian. As Sir Orme Sargent, a senior member of the Foreign Office, acknowledged (privately) in 1938, "we have used France as a shield . . . since our disarmament." The French were more blunt: The British, they said, would fight to the last Frenchman.[12]

France's surrender after only forty days of fighting was therefore a catastrophe for Britain. Hitler now controlled most of continental Europe, from the Bay of Biscay to the Black Sea. France was defeated and partly occupied, while Britain's other ally of World War One, Russia, was now bound by treaties of friendship and economic cooperation to Nazi Germany. Italy had entered the war, threatening Britain's position in North Africa; and Japan, though still neutral, was increasing its pressure on the European empires in Southeast Asia. For a while it seemed that Britain itself might be invaded. About a quarter of a million British troops were evacuated from Dunkirk, without most of their equipment, hardly adequate for defence against invasion. Although Britain survived the summer of 1940, thanks to the fortitude of the RAF and the unreadiness of the Luftwaffe, future prospects seemed grim. The French collapse had left British strategy and diplomacy in ruins.

Strategically, there was now no obvious way to defeat Germany. The traditional weapon of starving the enemy through naval blockade was blunted, because Hitler controlled most of Europe and had Russia as a willing supplier. Nor was the British Army likely to prove the agent of victory. The government's goal in September 1939 had been to raise, train, and equip fifty-five divisions by the autumn of 1941 but that had to be abandoned because of the need for industrial workers in the crisis of 1940. In any case, regardless of how manpower was distributed, a small country of some 40 million could hardly hope to take on the whole of Hitler's Fortress Europe. *Faute de mieux*, therefore, the government pinned its hopes on airpower, regarded by many of that generation as having the potency ascribed to nuclear weapons in our own age. For years the leaders of the RAF had saturated politicians and the public with their claims for strategic bombing as the decisive weapon of the future. Now, of necessity, their faith became the government's credo. The new prime minister, Winston Churchill, told the cabinet in September 1940:

> the bombers alone provide the means of victory. We must therefore develop the power to carry an ever-increasing volume of explosives to Germany, so as to pulverise the entire industry and scientific structure on which the war effort and economic life of the enemy depend, while holding him at arm's length from our island. In no other way at present visible can we hope to overcome the immense military power of Germany . . .

This fixation with strategic bombing in 1940–42 was to have lasting consequences for British policy throughout the war.[13]

The new "strategy" was less a programme for victory than a boost to morale. In reality, with France defeated and Russia an unfriendly neutral, there was little chance of Britain winning the war alone. Whatever their previous scepticism, the British therefore had no choice but to look to the United States. The Chiefs of Staff warned the cabinet bluntly in May 1940 that, without "full economic and financial support" from America, *"we do not think we could continue the war with any chance of success."*[14] The new readiness to look across the Atlantic was accentuated by Churchill's accession to the premiership in May 1940. Despite his antagonism towards the United States at times during the 1920s, he had no doubt in 1940 that an alliance with America was essential for Britain's future. Churchill assiduously cultivated a direct correspondence with Roosevelt and pressed him for the fullest possible material and moral assistance, including an immediate declaration of war.

Of course, Britain still had other allies. The dominions of Canada, Australia, New Zealand, and South Africa had committed troops to the British cause, becoming important elements in the defence of the United Kingdom and the Middle East in 1940–41. Hitler's European conquests also turned Britain into a refuge for other Allied contingents and their governments—Czechs, Poles, French, Dutch, Belgians, Danes, and Norwegians. Yet none of these actual Allies compared with the vast potential of the United States. As we shall see, the British consistently treated the American government and its armed forces with much greater solicitude than it did any of its other Allies.

Roosevelt's response to the crisis was typically complex. "I am a juggler," he once remarked. "I never let my right hand know what my left hand does." He had always been internationalist by inclination and the crisis of 1940 enabled him to make new gestures of support to Britain, including the transfer of fifty old destroyers. But the president was keenly sensitive to isolationist opinion in Congress and outside, even after his reelection in November 1940. And he also shied away from the ultimate horror of committing his country to war, if it could be avoided. For both political and personal reasons, then, he moved slowly and cautiously throughout 1941. The Lend-Lease Act of March enabled him to provide war matériel to Britain, leaving the form of payment to be decided later. But on the issue of naval support in the Battle of the Atlantic Roosevelt avoided Congress and moved covertly, gradually pushing U.S. naval patrols farther east across the Atlantic. Only Hitler's invasion of Russia in June 1941 eased the pressure on both Churchill and Roosevelt, but few in London and Washington at this stage were optimistic about a protracted Russian resistance against the Nazi juggernaut. When the two leaders met for the first time during the war off Newfoundland in August (the Atlantic Meeting), the president tried to jolly the premier along with predictions of an early "incident" that would enable him to ask Congress to declare war. But the occasional sinkings of U.S. vessels that autumn did not arouse an outcry at home, where opinion polls continued to register American desire to aid Britain but to keep out of war. In October 1941 Roosevelt told the British ambassador bluntly "that if he asked for a declaration of war, he wouldn't get it, and opinion would swing against him."[15]

The president's anxieties centred on the question of sending American troops overseas. As a precaution in the summer of 1940, Congress had enacted a peacetime Selective Service Act and on 16 October over 16 million young Americans registered for the draft. This gave the Republicans ample ammunition during the concurrent election campaign. Roosevelt was denounced as a warmonger and Republican newspapers reminded their readers that in November 1916 another Democratic president had campaigned on a peace platform, only to take the country into war five months later. Thrown onto the defensive, Roosevelt had been obliged to assure the "mothers and fathers" of America in a speech in Boston on 30 October 1940 that "your boys are not going to be sent into any foreign wars." Though an act of political expediency, this pledge also reflected Roosevelt's own inclinations. He dreaded the moral burden of committing thousands of young Americans to their deaths and he doubted that the "never again" mentality of the American people would accept it. Back in September

1938 he had told the British ambassador that, even if America were involved in another European war, "he regarded it as almost inconceivable that it would be possible for him to send any American troops across the Atlantic," except, perhaps, if Britain were actually invaded. This still seems to have been his preference in 1941. That September, Secretary of War Henry L. Stimson found the president "afraid of any assumption of the position that we must invade Germany" and Roosevelt's closest aide, Harry Hopkins, told the British in August that FDR was "a believer in bombing as the only means of a victory."[16]

Roosevelt's inclinations for an indirect strategy therefore coincided with British preferences. They also fitted those of the U.S. Army Air Corps (in America, unlike Britain, there was still no independent air force). But these views were not shared by the Army itself, headed by Gen. George C. Marshall, the Army Chief of Staff. As a young man Marshall had been temperamental and prone to fierce eruptions of anger. But his skill as a staff officer had won him Pershing's praise and patronage and, by the time he became Army Chief of Staff in July 1939, the combined effects of a happy marriage, a belated promotion, and iron self-discipline had endowed him with new and, to many, awesome self-control. Innately sceptical of politicians, Marshall never voted in elections. Nor was his nature gregarious—if obliged to attend social dinners he usually prearranged an "urgent" phone call to facilitate an early departure. He was particularly wary of the seductive Roosevelt charm and visited the president's country home at Hyde Park only once, for FDR's funeral, because, he said, "I found informal conversations with the President would get you into trouble." Roosevelt "would talk over something informally at the dinner table and you had trouble disagreeing without creating embarrassment." By 1941 Marshall had refined his natural reserve into a persona of studied, apolitical rectitude that gave him great influence over both president and Congress. "Marshall is the most accomplished actor in the Army," observed one official who worked closely with him. "Everyone thinks MacArthur is, but he's not. The difference between them is that you always *know* MacArthur is acting."[17]

In 1940–41 the Army Chief of Staff was at odds with his Commander in Chief on two fronts. First, Marshall was acutely conscious of America's own military weakness. In May 1940 U.S. armed forces ranked twentieth in size in the world; the Dutch were in nineteenth place. There were, for instance, only 260 trained pilots available to fly its total combat-worthy air force of 160 fighters and 52 bombers.[18] In these circumstances, Roosevelt's policy of material aid to Britain took scarce equipment away from America's fledgling forces and Marshall was frequently at odds with the president on this issue. Nor did Marshall share the president's predilection for an indirect strategy backed by strategic bombing. Following the principles of Gen. Ulysses S. Grant during the American Civil War, he insisted that early invasion of continental Europe followed by a massive land offensive was the only way to defeat the enemy. The joint Army-Navy "Victory Program" of September 1941 envisaged U.S. armed forces eventually totaling eight million, up to five million of them (215 divisions) for use in Europe. These two controversies—over the husbanding of American resources and the application of overwhelming strength—were to rumble on through 1942, with Marshall on one side and Churchill on the other, and Roosevelt leaning more to the British view than to that of his own military.

What Marshall could not deny, however, was the political unpopularity of the strategy he envisaged. In October 1941 the draft would lapse, having been enacted for only one year. If that happened, Marshall's new Army would melt away. In July 1941 the Chief of Staff began to campaign for renewal, urging that this time Congress remove the time limit and also the ban on the use of draftees overseas. He was concerned about the security of key Atlantic islands such as the Azores, but, in the hands of isolationist critics, this was evidence that Roosevelt was about to send another American Expeditionary Force to Europe. "OHIO" became a ubiquitous piece of graffiti—"Over the Hill in October"—in other words, desertion. With Roosevelt characteristically circumspect in his leadership, Marshall assumed most of the burden of lobbying on Capitol Hill. Eventually the obligation to serve overseas was dropped and the renewal extended for only eighteen more months, but even so the final vote was very close. On 12 August 1941 the bill passed the House with 203 in favour and 202 against. Although defeat would not have abolished the draft itself—the vote only dealt with the length of service—it was still a sobering reminder of the power of Congress and its sensitivity to public opinion. Marshall certainly took note. For Churchill and the British military, then conferring with Roosevelt and Marshall at the Atlantic Meeting, it demonstrated the continued power of isolationism and, in Hopkins's words, had "a decidedly chilling effect."[19]

That autumn, Churchill was very much on the defensive at home. To those who doubted his optimism about American entry he could only urge them to "have patience and trust to the tide which is flowing our way and to events." In the end, events did force America into the conflict, but not in the way that Churchill or Roosevelt had expected. Instead of an incident in the Atlantic, it was the surprise Japanese

attack on the Pacific Fleet at Pearl Harbor on 7 December that pitch-
forked America into war. Even then FDR waited for Germany to declare war on the United States before enlarging American belligerency
to include Europe. The day after Pearl Harbor the president cabled the
prime minister: "Today all of us are in the same boat with you and the
people of the Empire, and it is a ship which will not and cannot be
sunk"—an ironic but apt prediction of what became the closest and
most successful alliance in modern history. Within days Churchill set
out across the Atlantic and spent Christmas in Washington, planning
with Roosevelt the strategy and structures of their combined war
effort. The prime minister stayed in the White House itself, cementing
their personal friendship in many hours of conversation with the
president. "Trust me to the bitter end," FDR promised as they parted.[20]

One of the first decisions of their extended conference, code name
Arcadia, on 23 December 1941, was to send GIs to the British Isles.
Reflecting his residual antipathy towards a full-scale American Expedi-
tionary Force, Roosevelt said that he

> thought it would be a mistake to send United States troops into
> England and Scotland. On the other hand, there was a great deal to
> be said for sending bomber squadrons to operate against Germany
> from British bases. It would greatly encourage the American people
> to hear that their bombers were in action against Germany, and the
> German people would be similarly depressed. As to Northern Ire-
> land, he thought the United States should take over its defence, thus
> freeing British troops for employment elsewhere.

These proposals were warmly welcomed by Churchill; indeed they had
originated from him. Both leaders favoured bombing as a possible
alternative to large-scale land warfare on the Continent. And the
proposed despatch of four U.S. divisions to Northern Ireland would
release British forces for the Far or Middle East, while enabling the
Americans to complete their training. Such a move had been desired
by the British War Office well before Pearl Harbor and was the logical
extension of America's takeover of responsibility for the defence of
Iceland in July 1941.[21]

Although this decision therefore grew out of previous policies, it was
to prove the first step in the great American buildup in Britain. Equally
portentous were the decisions taken at Arcadia about how the alliance
was to be run. The central strategic decisions would be the responsibility of the Combined Chiefs of Staff (CCS), reporting to the two heads of
government. Under them each theatre of operations would be run on

the unprecedented principle of "unity of command." This meant that all British and American forces, of all three services, in each theatre would be under a single commander, American or British. The idea was Marshall's; his object twofold. As Pershing's former aide, his aim was to prevent repetition of the inter-Allied rows that had plagued the American Expeditionary Force (AEF) in France in 1918. He also wished to avoid both the bitter Army-Navy feuding characteristic of Washington and what he deemed the equally unsatisfactory British alternative—loose coordination that in practice left each service free to wage its own war. This may seem mere common sense today, but "Marshall's suggestion was staggering" at the time, observed historian Mark Stoler. "Never before had the forces of two or more major powers been so fused, and never in U.S. history had such army-navy coordination been achieved." In retrospect, Marshall considered it one of his most important decisions of the war.[22]

But the years 1941–45 would show that unified command was easier to establish in principle than in practice. Controversy between the two governments and rivalry among the various services would continue, and these would centre on the issues of strategy already outlined in 1941. That debate in turn was complicated by the now-global character of the war, with Germany locked in battle against Russia, and Japan running amok across the Pacific. Henceforth the question of a "second front" would be inextricably linked with the problems of reassuring Russia and containing Japan. And, as the British and Americans argued about how to employ their armies, the balance of that argument was affected by the weight of their national contributions to the war. In the short term, the British had the advantage, because their war effort was two years ahead of the American. Soon after Pearl Harbor Churchill told his Chiefs of Staff "with a wicked leer in his eye" that it was no longer necessary to be deferential towards America: "that was the way we talked to her while we were wooing her, now that she is in the harem we talk to her quite differently!" While the British were in a much stronger bargaining position in 1942–43, in the latter part of the war superior American resources, both in matériel and manpower, would tip the balance decisively. In Europe, D-Day proved the fulcrum. Ultimately, the British needed the Americans more than the Americans needed the British. Awareness of this would colour every aspect of Churchill's policy towards the United States. He remarked after the war: "No lover ever studied every whim of his mistress as I did those of President Roosevelt."[23]

The American occupation of Britain was therefore born in an atmosphere of cooperation that stood in marked contrast to preceding years of rivalry and suspicions. For all the bonhomie of Christmas 1941, however, history could not be shrugged off overnight. What past diplomacy pointed up was the elementary but problematic fact of "a single language and a double culture."[24] As Woodrow Wilson had told the king back in 1918, for all the ties of blood and language, America and Britain were very different countries.

2

The Barrier
of a Common Language

★ ★ ★

THE MOST BASIC CONTRAST BETWEEN AMERICA AND BRITAIN IS ALSO THE most obvious: The United States is a big country. At ninety-two thousand square miles, the whole of the United Kingdom of Great Britain and Northern Ireland corresponds in area to the states of Wyoming or Oregon. England and Wales, where most of the GIs were located, comprise fifty-eight thousand square miles—equivalent to Georgia or Michigan. These two countries would fit into the continental United States about fifty times. Despite its extent, however, America is sparsely inhabited. In 1940 the continental United States had 131 million people, England and Wales somewhat over 41 million. The American population was therefore little more than three times that of England and Wales. Population density was 44 per square mile in America in 1940 as against over 750 for England. This contrast was reflected in fundamental features of daily life, such as the lack of distance between dwellings and the minuteness of most domestic gardens (if they existed at all).[1]

Moreover, the British people were more concentrated in cities and towns. The great conurbations of London, Birmingham, Liverpool, and Manchester alone accounted for nearly 20 percent of England's population. In the United States it was not until the census of 1920 that a majority of Americans were listed as urban rather than rural (meaning settlements of at least twenty-five hundred inhabitants). In England the comparable turning point (measured by settlements of over two thousand) had been reached in 1851. Indeed, that was a crucial factor in Britain's industrial revolution of the early nineteenth century, which depended not on technological innovation but on the transfer of labour from farm to factory and from countryside to town. By the 1930s only about 6 percent of Britain's population was engaged in agriculture; the figure for the United States was nearly 25 percent.[2] America was therefore much larger and less densely populated than Britain. A smaller proportion of its population lived in big cities and a significant number were still farmers.

America was also demonstrably wealthier. Indeed its wealth was in part the consequence of its size—the abundance of available natural resources. For much of the nineteenth century, Britain, the pioneer industrial nation, had the highest per capita gross national product in the world. But it was overtaken by the United States during the 1870s and on the eve of the First World War American per capita GNP was some 40 percent higher than the UK's. Subsequently the national wealth of both countries increased, but American growth always outstripped Britain's, particularly in the first quarter of the twentieth century. Between 1910 and 1950 per capita GNP in America doubled. In an age when economic power was measured largely in heavy metal, America, fortuitously, commanded a significant proportion of the planet's mineral wealth. In 1913 it produced two-thirds of the world's petroleum, more than half its copper, and over one-third of its coal, zinc, and iron ore. In all these commodities it was the world's leader. When one adds to this the prodigious output of American wheat, corn, and cotton, particularly as the prairies and Great Plains were exploited after the Civil War, it is clear that Americans were, in historian David Potter's phrase, a "people of plenty."[3]

Yet natural abundance was only part of the secret of America's wealth—resources have to be utilized and that was the achievement of the country's unique industrial system. This stemmed in part from its size, or more exactly from the fact that the vast area of the United States was effectively a single common market, without internal tariffs or trade barriers. And the growth of the railroads permitted that huge market to be exploited after the Civil War. But it took big business to capitalize fully on the economies of scale promised by the big market. Far more than in Britain, American industry became consolidated in large corporations rather than in family firms, run by professional managers and dedicated to mass production of certain basic goods. Henry Ford's continuous assembly lines and Frederick W. Taylor's rules of scientific management became bywords not merely in the United States but around the world in the 1920s—"Fordism" and "Taylorism." The British economy did see its own merger boom after World War One and by the mid-1920s the top one hundred British firms accounted for 22 percent of value added, a proportion reached in

America by 1909. But although British business became bigger, it never emulated the management methods of the United States, remaining characteristically in the hands of family firms with little research and development support. Except in brewing and some foodstuffs, these companies generally made goods for others to market, rather than producing for direct sale to the mass consumer.[4]

Apart from size and wealth, the other fundamental contrast between the two countries is that of time. Relative to Europe, America was indeed the "New World," free from the dead hand of the past. England had been settled intensely for nearly a millennium. Most major towns dated from the Middle Ages, their street patterns and many of their public buildings literally laid down in stone for centuries. Most English institutions—the monarchy, Parliament, the shire, the parish—were of similar longevity, and, although the late Victorians were prone to "invent" traditions, the antiquity of England was genuine and the appeal to precedent carried automatic authority. In particular, the orders of monarchy and aristocracy rested on an hereditary principle that was officially anathema in the democratic New World. This system of primogeniture, inheritance by the eldest son, permitted the landed aristocracy—some seven thousand families—of which the monarch was the apex, to dominate wealth, social status, and political power until the late nineteenth century.[5]

America, by contrast, was an historical novelty. The Native American Indians had their own culture, of some sophistication, but it was European settlement in the seventeenth century that began the development of the North American continent as we know it today. That era, ancient history by American standards, corresponds to what historians dub the "early modern period" in Europe. Only the eastern seaboard, spanning a few hundred miles into the interior, had been settled when independence was wrested from Britain in 1776. Nearly every state west of the Mississippi was less than a century old by the time of Pearl Harbor. Several in the northwest, such as Idaho and Wyoming, had recently celebrated their first fifty years of statehood.

Not merely was America newer than Britain, its sense of a *common* history was brief. The American Revolution had some reality to New Englanders of the 1930s, surrounded as they were by buildings and memorials of that time. For Bostonians, Old North Church, the Bunker Hill monument, or the Old State House evoked the days of John Adams and Paul Revere. For a Texan, however, "the Revolution" was as likely to mean the war of independence from Mexico in 1836, kept alive by memorials and celebrations of the Alamo and San Jacinto. To a Virginian, the historical resonances were those from the "War between the States" in 1861–65: "Stonewall" Jackson and Robert E. Lee, or Manassas and Sharpsburg (battles known by totally different names in the North). Even World War One, in which the United States participated for only nineteen months, had been too short to leave a profound impact.

The size of the country and the brevity of its shared history were reflected in profound sectional consciousness. This was most acute in the old Confederacy. Nearly one-fifth of white Southern adult males between the ages of eighteen and forty-three had died in the conflict. That carnage and the subsequent twelve-year occupation by the "Damned Yankees" had not been forgotten or forgiven even in the 1930s, and the South remained a distinctive and somewhat marginal part of the American polity. Across the rest of America primary allegiances were also to town and state. A traveler observed: "To cross the Atlantic Ocean does not give one such a sensation of change as to cross from Tennessee to Arkansas." The country was a network of regions, usually structured around a local centre, such as Chicago or St. Louis. There was, revealingly, no national newspaper and most Americans had spent little time beyond their home state, let alone visited New York or Washington, D.C. Many did not regard this as a deficiency. The interwar years saw a more self-conscious celebration of "regionalism," particularly in the South, thanks to the novels of William Faulkner and the philosophical history of Wilbur J. Cash.[6]

England had its own regional attachments, of course. Yorkshiremen were brought up to believe that the best thing that came out of Lancashire was the road to Yorkshire, and local dialects remained thick, often impenetrable, in the West Country or East Anglia. Yet its compactness made the country more centralized. London was the heart not merely of government but also of finance, trade, and culture. Even the transport network, the railways and major roads, radiated from London like spokes from an off-centre hub.

The degree of centralization in each country was reflected in its political system. At the Norman Conquest, the last fundamental break in English society, all the land had been allocated by the king. Although the balance of power between Crown and Parliament shifted fundamentally over the centuries, the dominance of the central government remained. Thus, the political system had been created from the top downward, whereas, across the Atlantic, power emanated from the bottom up. The United States had never been the feudal domain of a single ruler. It began life as a reluctant confederation of former British colonies, who concluded it was better to hang together than to hang separately. The "more perfect union" established in

1787 still left the bulk of powers with the states, creating a federal government only for certain basic purposes, notably defence and foreign policy. And powers within that national government were carefully packaged out among president, Congress, and Supreme Court, to avoid the executive branch of government replicating the "tyranny" of the British Crown. By the 1830s this federal republic had become for practical purposes a democracy. Most white American adult males enjoyed the vote, even though the exact franchise was determined by each individual state.

In consequence, for most Americans as late as the 1930s, "government" meant the local or, at most, the state authorities. The federal government touched people's lives mainly through the ubiquitous "United States Post Office." Further interference was often bitterly resented: Nineteenth-century Washington replaced late-eighteenth-century London as the threat to local liberties. "Live Free or Die" is the New Hampshire state motto but it also sums up what most Confederates of the 1860s believed themselves to be fighting for in the Civil War, namely the right to maintain their own way of life, including the "peculiar institution" of slavery, against outside interference. To European observers, such as Hegel or de Tocqueville, America seemed like a society without a state, lacking a central government with a clear sovereign power. (The "sovereignty of the people" seemed meaningless, or even anarchical.) But, as James Madison, one of the founding fathers, had perceptively observed in *The Federalist* papers, this was a system whose looseness suited a large and diverse country. The development of what to a European would be a genuine central government occurred only during the triple crises of the 1930s and 1940s—Depression, World War, and Cold War. In the words of historian Ernest May, "the American government . . . of the mid-1930s seemed designed primarily to provide modest help to people within the continental limits—chiefly business managers and farm owners but also, to some degree, consumers, nature lovers, and the elderly." At that time the Pentagon was still unbuilt, the "military-industrial complex" unimagined, and less than 5 percent of Americans paid federal income tax. Thus, the United States was a democracy that became a state; Britain was a state that was slowly democratized.[7]

The looseness of America's political structure also proved well suited to its remarkable ethnic diversity. America was the beneficiary of the largest and most diverse folk movement in recorded human history, attracting two-thirds of Europe's emigrants since 1600, and immigration has been, in the words of historian Maldwyn Jones, "the most

persistent and the most pervasive influence" on the country's development. For much of the nineteenth century the principal ethnic groups
were from northwest Europe—English, Irish, German, and Scandina-
vian. As late as World War Two some 25 million Americans, or about
one-sixth of the U.S. population, identified themselves as having a
"British heritage." This was to prove a potent factor during the American "occupation." But long before this America's immigration patterns had changed significantly. In the late nineteenth century a
mixture of depression and oppression in eastern and southern Europe
spawned the so-called new immigration, totaling some 15 million
between 1890 and 1914, particularly from Italy, Russia, and the
Austro-Hungarian empire. As a proportion of the total population the
"foreign born" accounted for about 14.5 percent. Substantial and
tight-knit ethnic communities coalesced in the Great Plains, but the
bulk of immigrants were concentrated in the industrial northeast, with
nearly half in New York, Illinois, Massachusetts, and Pennsylvania.
Although the quota acts of 1921 and 1924 ended mass immigration
from Europe, it would take decades for these recent arrivals to be
assimilated. At first they clung to their own communities for self-
protection: churches, taverns, mutual aid societies, the ethnic press.
Often their initial identification was to a region back home rather than
to a country. On New York's Lower East Side around 1900 there were
Genoese, Calabrians, Abruzzians, Sicilians, and so on. These people
only began to discover themselves as "Italians" in America.[8]

By the 1930s acculturation had progressed. There was increasing
intermarriage between ethnic groups. Ethnic associations and newspapers were on the decline: In the quarter century after 1920 the
number of German-language publications dropped from three hundred to seventy. The second generation often reacted against the ethnic isolation of their immigrant parents, trying to make their way as
Americans through the avenues of urban politics, the lower civil service (police, fire, and post office), and, for the lucky few, successful
careers in sports or the movies. The prime agent of Americanization
was the school, particularly through its inculcation of the English
language. But the process of assimilation was far from complete. For
many inhabitants of the United States in the 1930s (outside the
South), their primary sense of identification was ethnic and religious.
They were Poles, they were Jews, they were Irish Catholic. What it
meant to be American was less clear.

A major obstacle to developing a sense of Americanness was the
continued political and cultural dominance of those of British stock. It
is revealing that, in all the fuss during World War One about "hyphen-
ate Americans"—Irish-Americans, German-Americans, and so on—

there was no mention of Anglo-Americans, because *American* still meant Anglo-Saxon. For the likes of Boston "Brahmin" Henry Cabot Lodge, Sr., immigration restriction was an attempt to maintain his cultural position within America. Even for Bostonians of lower social standing, the labels Irish, Catholic, and Democrat were often taken as synonyms for political corruption and social inferiority. Conversely, anti-British feeling in both world wars was for Americans of Irish or German descent as much a matter of domestic politics as foreign policy—a way of getting at the local "Anglo-" elites. The same is true for Italian-Americans in 1940–41, as indicated by the cult of Mussolini. This, noted two Harvard opinion analysts, was an expression of Italian-American resentment at "their status as marginal Americans."[9] In both world wars, it should be acknowledged, militant supporters of Germany and its allies were a minority among ethnic communities. Most kept their heads down; many went to considerable lengths to demonstrate their loyalty, in 1917–18 often Anglicizing their names. But that again indicates where America's ethnic centre of gravity still lay. The ties of language, culture, and kinship to England remind us both of the affinity many GIs would sense, however vaguely, towards Britain, and also of the uncertainties that other young soldiers of different ethnic backgrounds felt about what it was to be truly American.

Pluralist yet prejudiced, still reshaping its society in response to mass immigration, 1930s America found it even harder to cope with the issue of race. The history of white ethnic groups showed that assimilation and acceptance could occur, given time. For African-Americans, however, skin colour seemed a permanent stigma. In 1940 about 10 percent of the U.S. population was classified as black and about three-quarters of them still lived in the states of the old Confederacy. Despite the enforced abolition of slavery during the Civil War, rural blacks endured a condition approaching serfdom, tied to the land they farmed as tenants through their indebtedness to the landowner for food, seed, and equipment. Although their right to vote was officially enshrined in the Fifteenth Amendment to the Constitution, in practice it was abridged through local devices such as literacy tests and poll taxes. In 1944, it was estimated, less than 5 percent of the adult black population in the South had voted in the previous five years.[10] And socially most Southern towns had a network of so-called Jim Crow laws and customs to keep blacks and whites apart in public—designated accommodation on trains; blacks consigned to the back of buses; separate toilets, drinking fountains, and changing rooms; even different Bibles in court and separate blood banks in hospitals.

For the minority of blacks outside the South, their condition, though different, was often not much better. The migration northwards around the era of the First World War had spawned or consolidated a number of urban ghettos—most substantial in New York, Chicago, and Philadelphia, but also evident in many other Northern cities. Here a combination of residential segregation and economic deprivation accomplished less overtly what Southern "racial etiquette" decreed below the Mason-Dixon line. Not that all blacks were impoverished. Flourishing black middle-class communities did emerge around businessmen who catered to the needs of the ghetto, and tensions between the strata of black society were evident. In Washington, D.C., for instance, the black middle class whose children attended Dunbar High School and even the all-black Howard University felt themselves a cut above the poor negroes who inhabited shacks along "the alleys" between the elegant row houses of the whites. But most blacks—poor or comfortable, in the South or North—felt excluded from being fully American because of the colour of their skin.

The United States, then, was a remarkably pluralist country, both ethnically and racially, but one in which the definition of Americanness seemed in practice to marginalize many who were neither white nor "Anglo-Saxon." In its own way British society was equally prejudiced but it was also far more homogeneous: ethnic and racial distinctions were of minor importance. The most deep-seated animosities were directed towards the Jews—particularly those who were the product of the turn-of-the-century diaspora from Eastern Europe and who settled in the East End of London. The largest immigrant group, the Irish, likewise suffered a long history of intolerance and contempt, but even they amounted to barely 1 percent of the English population. As for blacks, there were probably only about eight thousand in Britain, mostly in the ports of Cardiff and Liverpool.[11] In these and other cities violent race riots had occurred in June 1919, but they were a passing phase. Most British people in 1942 would have seen few, if any, nonwhites.

There was, of course, a nagging question about what it meant to be "British." To a significant extent "Britain" was a fabrication. Most self-conscious inhabitants of England thought of themselves as English rather than British and the "United Kingdom of Great Britain and Northern Ireland" was really the sanitized product of centuries of English empire-building. In the late nineteenth century demands for "Home Rule" in Scotland and Wales had also been vociferous, but these had died down by the 1930s, while, thanks to partition, the "Irish question" was less perplexing than in the days of rebellion and civil war in the 1910s. Since 1921 the Republic of Ireland had been a separate country, while the northeastern six counties, Ulster, were ruled through their own Parliament as part of the UK. In the 1930s, then, the "national question" lay dormant. The United Kingdom seemed more united then than it had been for several generations.

Unlike America, the deepest fault lines in British society were not those of ethnicity, race, or section, but those of class. Or, more exactly, of class and status—the former denominating economic distinctions of occupation and wealth, the latter indicating the social valuation attached to these. What most distinguished British from American society was the tenacity with which the mutually supportive distinctions of class and status served as the focus of identity for most of the population. To say that one was working class or lower middle class was more socially meaningful in Britain than in the United States. Although the landed aristocracy had declined in wealth, status, and power since the Victorian age, the new business and financial elites bought land, sought titles, and aped aristocratic values. A definable "upper class" still dominated English life and commanded deference and respect. In defence, manual workers, particularly in heavy industry, developed their own "working-class" culture, institutions, and values. Equally acute were the sensitivities of those who had graduated to the lowlier "white-collar" jobs, such as clerks and teachers, who sought to distinguish themselves from their "inferiors" through a suburban lifestyle.[12]

In British politics by the 1920s class consciousness played the defining role that ethnicity and race did in America. Its main focus was the Labour party, founded in 1906. Yet Labour in power proved highly respectable. Its objectives were reformist rather than revolutionary, and neither the monarchy nor the House of Lords was ever in danger. Society was highly stratified, yet strikingly deferential. People knew their place—the status value placed on their occupation and lifestyle—and usually cultivated it. That was the paradox of England for many Americans—a social structure at once divided yet cohesive. The writer George Orwell likened it in 1940 to

> a rather stuffy Victorian family, with not many black sheep in it but with all its cupboards bursting with skeletons. It has rich relations who have to be kowtowed to and poor relations who are horribly sat on, and there is a deep conspiracy of silence about the source of the family income. It is a family in which the young are thwarted and most of the power is in the hands of irresponsible uncles and bedridden aunts. Still, it is a family. It has a private language and common memories, and at the approach of an enemy it closes its ranks.[13]

America, of course, was no "classless society" in the strict sense of the term. There were sharp differences of occupation and wealth, and the elites of cities like Boston and Philadelphia operated their own social registers and exclusive clubs. Yet these differences were less significant than in Britain. In 1939 1 percent of Americans owned 30 percent of the country's wealth; in Britain at that date the top 1 percent's share was 55 percent. In fact, the top 5 percent in Britain owned 79 percent of all wealth. In other words, America's middle income bracket was far larger than in Britain and this was reflected in people's self-images. *Fortune* magazine, in a series of polls in 1940, reckoned that between two-thirds and four-fifths of Americans considered themselves "middle class." Moreover, the socioeconomic elites that did emerge were usually regional rather than national, unlike their British counterparts in a smaller, more centralized country. And, in further contrast with Britain, wealth and status were less closely correlated with political power, thanks again to the federal system and to the pervasive democratic principle that made numbers rather than names the key determinant of power.[14]

And so we return once more to the basic parameters of space and time. America was larger, newer, and wealthier than Britain. Its politics were more fragmented and more democratic. Its fault lines were those of section, ethnicity, and race, whereas in England people defined their status above all by reference to class. Britain in the 1930s was a tightly knit, organic society, shaped by the breadth of its history and the narrowness of its space. The United States was a "segmented society," composed of interlinked elements loosely coordinated and largely left to regulate themselves.[15] Moreover, in the 1930s, unlike Britain, it had gone through one of the greatest crises of its short history, one that undermined its economy, tested its fragile institutions, and challenged its faith and self-esteem.

It has been shrewdly observed that America's "common national history" probably begins with the 1930s Depression.[16] That was the first truly countrywide experience affecting the whole population of the United States. Moreover, it was a totally negative experience, a nightmare made all the more appalling because of the dream years that had preceded it.

Both America and Britain were afflicted by economic crisis. But for Americans this was "the Great Depression"; for Britons it was "the Slump"—the contrast in nomenclature is revealing. In Britain it followed a period of minimal growth and chronic economic instability throughout the 1920s. World trade, on which Britain was heavily dependent, was slow to recover after the war. Staple British industries, notably coal, steel, textiles, and shipbuilding, were in structural decline in the face of more competitive international rivals, and the consequent unemployment never dropped below 10 percent throughout the decade. The Slump of 1929–32, when unemployment doubled and national income fell by 13 percent, was therefore like a storm in an already dark sky. Moreover, it passed relatively quickly, with evidence of recovery apparent as early as 1933. In fact, for working people in Britain, the 1920s and 1930s exhibited much continuity, good or bad. In the old industries, concentrated in northern England and south Wales, these were uniformly hard years—part of a steady decline, with unemployment usually about twice the national average. The demoralizing experience of long-term life "on the dole" was dramatized by the former shipyard workers who marched three hundred miles from Jarrow to London in 1936. Yet in the 1920s and 1930s there had been another England, of expanding suburbs and newer industries, that enjoyed relative prosperity. The belated advent in Britain of mass-produced motor vehicles and electrical appliances gave new life to the industrial economy of The Midlands and the southeast. In the 1930s better-off Britons began to taste the first fruits of a consumer society that had already flowered across the Atlantic. And new domestic demand helped reduce the impact of the world depression.

In the United States, however, the Depression was unprecedented, ubiquitous, and unrelenting. After 1924 no more than 5 percent of the workforce were out of jobs throughout the decade. In 1929 unemployment was only 3.2 percent. Thereafter it climbed remorselessly, peaking at nearly a quarter of the workforce in 1933. Despite some improvement in 1937, almost one-fifth were still unemployed in 1938. The same pattern of sudden disaster and scant improvement can be seen in other economic indicators. Measured in real terms America's gross national product had still not returned to 1929 levels by 1939, while manufacturing output had barely done so.[17] Whatever Roosevelt's New Deal achieved, it did not solve the Depression. That was the result of the war, when Anglo-French arms orders and then those of America itself galvanized the U.S. economy.

The Depression also laid bare the limits of American wealth. The prodigious triumphs of U.S. industry in the twenties, the constructional marvels of its cities, the shrewdly advertised cornucopia of consumer society—all these had obscured the extent of American poverty. The Brookings Institution calculated that in 1930 some 60 percent of American families, at least 70 million people, enjoyed an annual income of less than $2,000 a year, a sum "sufficient to supply only basic necessities." The main reason why this poverty had been easily ignored was that it was substantially rural—a reflection of America's less urbanized society and an important contrast with Britain where the problems of poverty and deprivation were centred in the cities. A quarter of the population lived on farms and their income plummeted as commodity prices collapsed (corn and wheat to half their 1929 levels by 1931, cotton to one-third). Spiraling debts forced farmers to default on mortgages and become tenants or even homeless—the Joad family of John Steinbeck's celebrated *The Grapes of Wrath*. In 1930 Brookings found that 54 percent of the nation's farm families, about 17 million people, earned under $1,000 per year. This was half its notional poverty line.[18]

The country's fragile institutions were hard pressed to cope with this appalling crisis. America's financial "system" was characterized by unit- not branch-banking. Instead of a few banking houses with national or regional networks, as in Britain, most U.S. banks were single, independent operations. They were therefore acutely vulnerable to the vicissitudes of the local economy. Four thousand failed in 1933 alone, exacerbating the commercial collapse, particularly in rural areas. Nor did America have a welfare system to cushion the shock of the Depression. Germany had operated a social insurance system for half a century, Britain and Sweden for nearly twenty-five years. The United States, statistically the richest nation in the world, had no social security (old-age pensions), no unemployment or health insurance, no family allowances. Eleven states had introduced social security by 1929 but relief, such as existed, was mainly the responsibility of local townships.

Roosevelt strengthened some of the federal government's powers. A Federal Deposit Insurance Corporation guaranteed the assets of local banks. The Social Security Act of 1935 established systems of unemployment insurance and old-age pensions. But these were only limited reforms. Social security, for instance, was financed by employers and employees—unlike European schemes, the federal government made no contribution. Although the New Deal helped ameliorate the Depression, it transformed America much less than was suggested by contemporary political rhetoric, both for and against. Sectionalism and federalism remained deeply entrenched. Retrospectively, the New Deal's historical significance "appears as a holding operation for American society: a series of measures that enabled the people to survive until World War II opened up new opportunities."[19]

Underlying all these problems of production, poverty, and dislocation was a fundamental psychological malaise. At root the Depression was a crisis of confidence in America and in its future, made all the worse by the contrast with the boom decade of the 1920s. After 1929 the American Dream had turned into a nightmare, which no one seemed able to end. Roosevelt recognized this root problem in his 1933 inaugural address when he asserted that "the only thing we have to fear is fear itself—nameless, unreasoning, unjustified terror which paralyzes needed efforts to reconvert retreat into advance." His inspirational speeches and cosy "fireside chats" over the radio undoubtedly helped. But, just as "Doctor New Deal" could not revive the economy, so he could not cure the mental malaise. The result was not a surge of radical violence, despite the alarm caused by demagogues such as Huey Long. The national mood was one of resentful "bewilderment," a torpor and introspection that matched the isolationist tone of American foreign policy in the mid-1930s.[20]

For a majority of the GIs who served in World War Two, the Depression had been *the* formative experience of their previous life. Roughly 60 percent of those who served in the U.S. armed forces during the war had been born between 1918 and 1927. Of men born during that decade who lived to maturity, three-quarters served in the wartime military. To make the point more concretely, twenty-year-olds who registered for the draft in 1941 had been only eight when the Depression began. Their conscious life had often been one of "hard times" with little hope of anything better. Some had actually volunteered for the military as an escape. Jack Gray, born in 1921, was one of seven children on an impoverished farm in eastern Texas. He was educated in a four-room schoolhouse with no inside toilets and no running water. After a year in the Civilian Conservation Corps, one of Roosevelt's many temporary work-relief measures, he joined the Regular Army because there was no other prospect of employment. His career took him with the 1st Infantry Division through Britain to Omaha Beach on D-Day.[21]

The majority of American teenagers in the Roosevelt era did not join the Army voluntarily; they accepted the draft when called after 1940. But, for volunteers and draftees alike, the Army was often the first secure employment that these young men had known, indeed their first secure institution. Attitudes to Army life were shaped accordingly. This point is as important as the broad statistical contrasts between the wealth of "average" Americans and Britons. For the GIs who came to Britain were not merely Americans, they were children of the Great Depression.

3

Transatlantic
Reflections

★ ★ ★

RELATIONSHIPS BETWEEN GIS AND BRITISH PEOPLE MIRRORED THESE UNDER-
lying contrasts between their two societies. But in history perceptions
are as important as realities; how the other country was seen mattered
as much as how it really was. Prior to the GIs' arrival, neither people
knew much, in a systematic way, about the other. Ideas were derived
from national stereotypes, mediated above all by the cinema.

For much of U.S. history Britain had been central to the definition of
American values. Originally the United States was a series of English
colonies, whose liberal traditions and political structures were modeled
on those of the mother country. After 1776 the new nation continued
to be linked to Britain by ties of trade, migration, and culture, yet its
self-image crystallized around the idea that it was "not English." The
United States was a republic not a monarchy, a land of liberty not an
empire, a democracy rather than a country dominated by an aristocracy. These stereotyped polarities were summed up in the dichotomy
of the Old World and the New. In 1848 the Boston man of letters James
Russell Lowell exhorted his compatriots:

> Forget Europe wholly, your veins throb with blood,
> To which the dull current in hers is but mud . . .
> O my friends, thank your God, if you have one, that he
> 'Twixt the Old World and you set the gulf of a sea.[1]

At this time Britain remained a force on the American continent,
with garrisons in Canada and the Caribbean, and the two countries
were at loggerheads throughout the first half of the century about the

line of America's northern, southern, and western borders. In 1814 British troops sacked and burned the president's mansion in Washington, in retaliation for similar American depredations in Canada, and the paint used to cover the scorch marks gave the White House its subsequent name. The American Civil War was another time of tension. In 1861, after Unionist interference with shipping, British reinforcements were sent to Canada and war plans drawn up for a possible invasion of Maine. The following summer, as the appalling carnage continued, the British prime minister, Lord Palmerston, speculated publicly about the possibility of "a successful offer of mediation . . . to the two parties."[2]

By 1900 American sensitivities to Britain's culture and power were less acute. The United States had passed through its phase of adolescent self-assertion and Britain had withdrawn nearly all its garrisons from the Western Hemisphere. Indeed, America's economic power now far outstripped Britain's. Yet images of Britain still remained close to the centre of America's sense of identity. This was partly because of the struggle between WASPs and other ethnic groups for power and influence within pluralist America. Stereotypes of Britain, for or against, were ammunition in their exchanges about Anglo-America. When the Populist leader "Pitchfork" Ben Tillman cried in 1896 "America for Americans, and to hell with Britain and her Tories," his target was New York plutocrats exploiting the American farmer as much as British investors and the City of London.[3]

Even more significant in the perpetuation of official Anglophobia was the treatment of Britain in American history books and political speeches. Here Britain continued to play its negative role as the antithesis of everything American. By the 1930s, British history had virtually disappeared from school curricula as a separate subject, but literature courses were still dominated by English texts. Classics such as Dickens's *A Tale of Two Cities*, the novels of the Brontë sisters, and Shakespeare's history plays all reinforced the "Old World" image of Britain. And, in the increasingly prevalent courses in U.S. history, British hostility to American independence and power was a constant theme. The impact of such courses was enhanced by the pervasiveness in American education, unlike Britain, of mass-market textbooks "adopted" by state education boards and then used throughout the school system. As a later survey of such texts noted, they were "written to indoctrinate the young with the virtues of Americanism" and were "used by teachers who often have little professional training in history and must rely on the textbook to inform them as well as their students."[4]

In America, as in Britain, movies were even more potent than books.

Polls indicated that over a third of American adults and over half of American children went to the cinema at least once a week in the mid-1930s; another quarter of the adults and 20 percent of children attended the cinema at least once a month. Hollywood's offerings on Britain during the 1930s also focused on the themes of class, Crown, and colonies. There was a rash of film versions of British literary classics, including four by Kipling and no less than seven Dickens novels. Some of them proved enormous box-office successes in America such as *Lives of a Bengal Lancer* (1935), starring Gary Cooper. The Kipling films were essentially "Westerns" transplated to more exotic locales, with the "natives" either evil or absurd (but always primitive) and the British generally decent if somewhat reactionary. Two other money-spinners for MGM, *A Yank at Oxford* (1938) and *Goodbye, Mr. Chips* (1939), both gave stereotyped portraits of English universities and public schools (the equivalent of prep schools in the United States). The former depicted a stratified world of amiably eccentric academics, forelock-tugging workers, and students engaged in an endless round of parties, sports, and high jinks. One of the biggest hits in America in the 1930s was a British film, *The Private Life of Henry VIII* (1933), which starred Charles Laughton as England's most notorious king. Three years later the American press reveled in the antics of Edward VIII and an American divorcée, Mrs. Wallis Simpson. American press cuttings about their affair run to half a million items, and it was one of the top three news stories of the decade after the Lindbergh baby kidnapping and the Dionne quintuplets.[5]

Overall there was far more reference to Britain in 1930s America than vice versa. Older Americans, and younger college graduates, might be expected to have some acquaintance with English history and certainly English literature. They were probably also better informed about English news. It was estimated that *The New York Times*, for instance, devoted nearly 20 percent of its foreign news coverage to Britain in the period 1933–41, double that allocated by its London namesake to America in 1936–39 and nearly four times as much as in 1939–41. On the other hand, younger and less educated Americans, those who would be draftees during World War Two, were unlikely to have studied Britain in any systematic way even if they had gone through high school and the little they did glean from their American history courses was basically negative. Those from the South, where British stock remained prevalent and relatively undiluted, may well have had more positive views of Britain, but for many "hyphenates" a negative image was inextricably bound up with their family's own struggles to establish themselves within "Anglo-

America." The sense of Britain as an anachronism was encouraged by what the Office of War Information (OWI) called in 1943 Americans' "distorted impression of the British governmental system." The king and House of Lords were still widely assumed to have almost dictatorial powers and Britain's more developed system of social security was largely unknown. One interviewee told an OWI pollster that "the British are still under the King." Said another: "They should get rid of the counts and no-accounts."[6]

In the American media, Britain's reputation was enhanced by the dramas of 1940. The Fall of France, Churchill's pugnacious rhetoric about fighting on, and then the Blitz and Battle of Britain—all these conveyed a new image of British heroism after years of effete appeasement. As the Anglophile banker Thomas Lamont told the British ambassador in August 1940, "if your Government had spent a million pounds a week here on propaganda, they could not have attained 1/100th of the effect that just the actual news itself plus photos plus Churchill have been able to attain at no cost at all, and with no chance of being held up to obloquy and charges of trying to subvert American opinion." In 1940 Britain's best propagandists were in fact the American media. Most celebrated was Edward R. Murrow, CBS bureau chief in London, whose vivid radio broadcasts of the Blitz were heard by many Americans, sometimes against the background of wailing air-raid sirens, the crump-crump of bombs, and the clatter of antiaircraft fire. "You burnt the city of London in our homes, and we felt the flames," wrote the American poet Archibald MacLeish in tribute.[7]

In 1940 England's history became a positive asset. Commentators drew on 1588 and 1804, on Queen Elizabeth and the Younger Pitt, to demonstrate Britain's unity and determination in the face of a would-be invader. *The New York Times,* extreme in hyperbole but representative in sentiment, editorialized on 24 July 1940:

> It is twelve o'clock in London. . . . Is the tongue of Chaucer, of Shakespeare, of Milton, of the King James' translation of the Scriptures, of Keats, of Shelley, to be hereafter, in the British Isles, the dialect of an enslaved race? . . . It is twelve o'clock in England. Not twelve o'clock for empire—there is no empire any more. . . . Twelve o'clock for the common people of England, out of whom England's greatest souls have always come . . . the nation [is] rising, as by a single impulse, to defend "This blessed plot, this earth, this realm, this England."[8]

If 1940 was the High Noon of English history, it also seemed to many American commentators the dawn of a Brave New World. The old barriers between what one journalist called "old-school-tie England" and "cap-in-hand England" appeared to be crumbling under the solvent of total war. James "Scotty" Reston, then a correspondent in London, declared in September: "What centuries of history have not done for this country, Chancellor Hitler is doing now. He is breaking down the class structure of England every night his bombers come over. . . . Why, it has even got so now that total strangers speak to each other on the streets, a completely un-English thing to do. Many people think they are seeing the start of a great movement here."[9]

Among those people was the president himself. Roosevelt had long been critical of Britain's social system—"too much Eton and Oxford," as he liked to put it. He was also aware of the growing influence of the Labour party in Churchill's coalition and was struck by the reports of social change caused by the war. When Joseph Kennedy resigned as ambassador to Britain at the end of 1940, FDR chose John Gilbert Winant as his successor. Winant was shy, idealistic, and informal—no suave diplomat. What also commended him to Roosevelt was the fact that he was an ardent New Dealer and former head of the International Labor Office in Geneva, where he had built up good contacts with British Labour and Trades Union leaders. It was common gossip in Washington that Roosevelt had appointed Winant "because he expected a social revolution in England" and was "convinced that Labor is going to run England after the war."[10]

The positive images of Britain and Churchill formed in 1940 remained permanently etched on the American mind. But they were subsequently overlaid by other impressions resulting from the series of British defeats in 1941–42. For much of 1942, until the desert victory at Alamein in November, pollsters found only 50 to 60 percent of Americans giving a firm "yes" when asked if they thought Britain was doing all it could to win the war. Russia, by contrast, won a consistent 90 percent rating. Britain's motives in fighting the war were also questioned. Its colonial policy evoked particular criticism, with over half of those asked in mid-1942 condemning it, even though their factual knowledge about the British Empire was vague and distorted. Overall, OWI concluded that about 20 percent of Americans could be described as "definitely anti-British" and that underlying stereotypes were very durable:

> Respondents assign a number of personality traits, good and bad, to the British. Over half of them regard the British as snobbish and aristocratic, and a smaller number complain about their arrogance and selfishness. But most respondents believe that the British have

many admirable characteristics. More than one half of those interviewed regard them as courageous and loyal, and they are also
praised for their honesty and sportsmanship.[11]

Nineteen forty-two therefore revived older images of England, to set
alongside those of 1940. Class and empire coexisted with Churchill
and the Blitz. Most GIs, whatever their knowledge of and interest in
England, arrived with mixed expectations.

American images of Britain took shape as part of the debate about
American identity—about nationalism, cultural values, and ethnicity.
Similarly, images of the United States have sometimes been used in
British debates about their own society. In the mid-nineteenth century
American democracy was held up by conservatives as an awful warn-
ing of the dangers of extending the franchise in Britain. Benjamin
Disraeli, soon to be Tory prime minister, predicted in 1866 that democ-
racy and land reform on the American model would reduce England
"from being a first-rate Kingdom" to "a third-rate Republic." By the
turn of the century America's economy was supplanting Britain's.
Journalists warned of American industry buying up Britain and of
Britons being enslaved by American goods. One luridly prophesied the
"Americanisation of the World." Intellectuals were also concerned
about the cultural consequences as American goods and culture
eroded the foundations of "civilized" life. To G. Lowes Dickinson, the
Cambridge don, writing in 1914, "All America is Niagara. Force without direction, noise without significance, speed without accomplishment."[12]

Conservative elements in Britain had therefore been persistently
anxious about America as a subversive force, whether political, economic, or cultural. That was to continue, as we shall see, in reactions
to Hollywood and to the GIs. Nevertheless, overall, America had been
far more peripheral to Britain's self-image than Britain was to the
cultural identity of the United States. This pattern would be reversed
in the 1940s, with America looming ever larger for Britain as the latter
shrank in interest and significance for the United States. And the GIs
played a part in that transposition. But in 1942 all this lay in the
future.

Our impressions of British public opinion during the war are derived
from a variety of sources. Chief among these are the reports by the
Home Intelligence Division of the Ministry of Information (MOI). Some
were actually opinion polls, commissioned from the British Institute of
Public Opinion (BIPO)—Britain's offshoot of the Gallup organization.

An example was the massive survey in January 1942 about "British Public Opinion and the United States." The MOI also kept its finger on the public pulse more impressionistically through regular reports from its Regional Information Officers (RIO) and from postal censorship based on as many as 200,000 letters. Also important were the reports of Mass-Observation (M-O), a private survey organization established in 1937 to assess everyday life and reactions to it. It functioned through a panel of regular observers around the country, whose opinions were supplemented by street interviewing, as in the case of their major report about "Opinion on America" in February 1942. The BBC's Listener Research reports also made use of a nationwide panel of respondents to test opinion and reaction to radio programmes. The panel method had its defects and the representativeness of such reports has been questioned, but those by M-O, in particular, are often our only source of information on some areas of British life (such as female pub-going).[13] In general, all these sources must be used with caution, because opinion polling, never an exact science, was in its infancy. But taken in conjunction with each other and used to indicate broad patterns rather than exact measurements, they are a valuable guide to the public attitudes, giving statistical significance to individual letters and diaries.

In April 1942, four months after Pearl Harbor, a BBC survey asserted that it was "probably not an exaggeration to say that a great many people are simply without opinions of any kind, or even prejudices, about anything so remote as America." The MOI had reached a similar conclusion in January when gathering evidence for its special report:

> The majority of interviewers agreed that it was the most difficult Survey they had undertaken. The interest in the United States shown by the public was scant. Most interviewers added that they were surprised at the indifference they had encountered. . . . An interviewer of more than four years experience remarked, "I met so many 'Don't knows' that even *I* began to feel embarrassed."[14]

By *indifference* the interviewers meant a lack of factual information about America. The MOI, for instance, noted that nearly a fifth of those questioned had absolutely no idea of the total population of the United States. A BBC panel report in July 1941 found similar vagueness about the size, ethnic diversity, and federal political structure of the United States. This kind of ignorance was not surprising. Only about 6 percent of British people, it was estimated, had ever visited the United States, though the proportion climbed to 17 percent for the "upper-income group." Sixty-five percent of Britons, according to a poll in mid-1942, did not "know any Americans personally." (By contrast only 32 percent of Americans at the same time answered "no" to the question "Have you ever known any English people well?")[15]

As the MOI remarked, the prevailing British image was that of "a pre-1929 America, in which Trades Unionists are ignored or attacked, corruption is common, social legislation primitive and commercialism rampant—a cocksure country with a high standard of living and a great capacity for mass-production." The Depression had registered to the extent that "America apparently no longer figures in the public imagination as the 'land of promise.' " It had been replaced by Russia, which was, in 1942, at the height of its wartime appeal to British opinion (an enthusiasm that extended from vodka to *War and Peace*). The USSR ran ahead of the United States as the foreign country in which a child of poor parents was deemed to have "the best chance." The New Deal itself evoked little interest or understanding in Britain, except among a small minority of left-of-centre politicians and reformers who advocated economic planning or who, like the former premier David Lloyd George, used Roosevelt's reforms to critique the complacency of their Tory-dominated National Government. The only real exception to the neglect of New Deal America was the president himself, who, to quote historian John Dizikes, became a sort of Superman figure:

> [O]ut of the welter of events, clouded by distance, distorted by heightened anxieties, there emerged a vivid British image of Franklin Roosevelt, clearer and more understandable by contrast with the confusion and obscurity surrounding him, a figure greater than life-size, and one which indelibly stamped itself on the consciousness of the British public: Roosevelt, hurtling from crisis to crisis, escaping obscure disasters by the narrowest of margins, miraculously converting defeat into victory.[16]

On the other hand, this paucity of factual information did not prevent British people from having firm views about America's "national character." Mass-Observation judged that Americans were liked most for their "friendliness," a composite trait that included generosity, candour, kindness, and hospitality, and for their "vigour," whose cognate buzzwords were initiative, virility, zeal, and openness. Conversely, they were disliked most for their "boastfulness," ostentation, and a propensity for talk without action, and for their "materialism," greed, and love of money. As M-O observed, the traits for which Americans evoked dislike were the "degenerate" or negative forms of those for which they were approved.[17] This suggests a consensus about the salient features of America's "national character" but divided evaluations of whether these traits were good or bad.

Older people were usually more critical of America and Americans, as were those who voted Conservative, although there were also many Labour left-wingers for whom the United States was the epitome of capitalist oppression. Education was another important variable. Much of the British elite had long regarded Americans as incorrigibly brash and uncivilized—what author and former diplomat Harold Nicolson termed in 1930 their "eternal superficiality." And in an analysis of "younger, more intelligent people" in the autumn of 1942, the MOI found that, while not overtly "anti-American," they were "extremely suspicious of attempts to paint America as a 'modern Utopia,' " especially by glossing over problems "such as Labour, and the Colour Question." The MOI concluded that, "broadly speaking, there was a lack of *positive* admiration for either American achievements or American institutions." Although many Anglo-Soviet friendship groups had sprung up, there had been "no corresponding growth of 'Americophile' societies."[18]

These "more intelligent" young people were not, however, representative of their age group. For most young people in Britain, American fashions, music, even slang, were a source of fascination, epitomized above all in the movies. It is difficult today, in an era of cable TV and home video, to recapture the enormous appeal of the cinema in 1930s Britain. In 1939 the circulation of daily newspapers was 10.5 million and 9 million families had "wireless licenses," but 23 million cinema tickets were sold every week. Some people, of course, went several times; others not at all. Surveys confirmed that the enthusiasts tended to be young, urban, and working class, more often female than male. Forty percent of London schoolchildren in the 1930s went once a week. But the extension of the cinema into the suburbs made it into a middle-class activity as well, a pleasant outing to "a picture palace" with its organ and genteel café. Working-class audiences in particular preferred American films, deploring the more static and verbose British products that had greater appeal for the middle class. One cinema manager in the East End of London explained in 1937 that his audience was very critical: "they like good pictures, good American pictures, pictures of movement and action. They won't stand British pictures here at any price." In the mid-1920s barely 5 percent of films shown were British. The Quota Act of 1927, requiring cinemas to show a fixed proportion of full-length British films, did boost this to a quarter by the mid-1930s, but it resulted mostly in "Quota Quickies"—shoddy products that were often shown to satisfy the law before cinema cleaners as they swept up the next morning.[19]

Parliament's concern about Hollywood's appeal was only partly to protect the British film industry. The deeper issue was cultural imperialism. To teachers, intellectuals, the clergy, and other guardians of morality, American films were deeply subversive. The slang was often offensive: British film censors banned such expressions as "lousy," "nuts," and "the dirty bum." The egalitarian tone was felt by some to threaten notions of social hierarchy. Concern was also expressed about the violence in such early 1930s box-office successes as *Scarface* and *Little Caesar*. There was also nationalist sensitivity. The jingoistic *Daily Express* complained in 1927 that "the bulk of our picture-goers are Americanised. . . . They talk America, think America, and dream America. We have several million people, mostly women, who, to all intent and purpose, are temporary American citizens." In all these ways America (or Hollywood's America) seemed a threat to English values. *The Times* editorialized in 1935: "Twenty million people go to the cinema every week; and in those millions the young, the unsophisticated, the slightly educated are so many that they need protection against the evils of which they are hardly aware. . . . We make no bones about training and correcting the taste of our children; and in a sense a very great many of the cinema-goers are but children."[20] That paternalism was also apparent when America arrived in person with the GIs in 1942.

One must not, of course, imagine that all cinema-goers accepted what they saw at face value. There were many reasons for going to "the pictures," not least that it was "one of the few places suitable for courting—cheap, dark, private and, above all, away from parental observation." Sheer escapism was also a motive. Doreen Evans grew up in a mining village in south Wales, "a very dull, dark sort of place." In the cinema you were taken into a world of complete darkness, "then all the screen would light up and you'd see all these marvellous film stars. Everything was bright." Mass-Observation, in particular, played down the influence of the movies. It insisted that "comparatively few people (and mostly women) get their main ideas about America directly from the cinema," and that newspapers and magazines were the real source. In its view the public understood very well that films were entertainment, not reality, and consigned them to a "special pigeonhole" in their minds.[21]

But M-O's questions, posed to the more articulate, were likely to underestimate the subliminal effect of the movies in propagating visual "images" rather than intellectualized "ideas." And its sceptical conclusion about the influence of films probably had more validity when the public was evaluating *British* films. For in that case, they knew Britain and had their own frame of reference in which to set and correct the cinema's images. That was not true of American films, however, where direct experience and indirect information were both lacking. Hollywood presented a succession of elegant women in luxurious Manhattan apartments, drunks propped up in the doorways of the Bowery, Chicago gangsters with submachine guns under their arms, and hard-bitten sheriffs and gangsters shooting it out in the dusty main streets of the American West. Wealth, violence, and corruption were the prevailing impressions conveyed. (The 1980s analogue would be the impact of *Dallas* on the European mind.) Certainly American observers abroad had little doubt of the pernicious influence of Hollywood. Joseph P. Kennedy, the U.S. ambassador in London in 1938–40, was horrified at the way "a great many people in England believe that our home life, history, and even legal practice are typified by motion pictures" and that little happened in America "besides gangster shootings, rapes and kidnappings." He even took offence at *Mr. Smith Goes to Washington*—Frank Capra's rather laboured social comedy about an idealistic Wisconsin senator (James Stewart) who smashes Washington graft and corruption with one impassioned speech—claiming the film would do "inestimable harm to American prestige all over the world." Instead of absorbing its message of democratic reform, Kennedy argued, foreign audiences would be confirmed in their impression "that the United States is full of graft, corruption and lawlessness and contains very little in politics that is creditable."[22]

Joe Kennedy's sensitivity was ironic, considering his own career, but his basic point was apt. Foreign audiences, lacking a corrective mechanism, tended to seize on features of films that confirmed basic stereotypes. The basic problem, as Kennedy and others pointed out, was the lack of knowledge and information about the United States available in Britain. America figured scarcely at all in the school curriculum. Such study as did take place, mostly of American history, consisted of "scattered experiments, dependent on interested individuals, and limited in effect by lack of co-ordination." Only six English universities offered any courses on U.S. history, and all these were optional. As for British newspapers, the United States, in marked contrast with today, attracted little attention. One survey conducted in 1936–37 estimated that even in "the more sober morning newspapers" only 8 to 16 percent of the total space for foreign news was allocated to things

American. Of this a quarter was devoted to government and politics, 15 percent to finance and commerce, and as much again, between 30 and 40 percent, to sensation, sex, and crime. Serious news appeared sporadically, at times of crisis, without background or interpretation, and coverage was concentrated on New York, Washington, and Hollywood, where most of the news agencies and foreign correspondents were located.[23]

The early years of the war had little effect on British indifference. Until June 1940 France was Britain's principal ally; thereafter Roosevelt's radio speeches raised hopes of early American entry into the war but these were repeatedly dashed. A Mass-Observation survey in October 1940 found America at the bottom of the list of "friendly" nations in terms of popularity, with gallant little Allies like the Czechs and the Dutch at the top. Among men, "the percentage of unfavourable criticism of America—our friend—equals that of Italy—our enemy." While this survey was particularly impressionistic, there is no doubt of the general scepticism with which American professions of help were viewed in Britain by late 1940. Even Churchill complained privately: "We have not had anything from the United States that we have not paid for, and what we have had has not played an essential part in our resistance."[24]

A real stimulus to British interest in and affection for America came from Lend-Lease. The long congressional debate was widely reported in Britain and its tangible results warmly welcomed. The first shipment of goods arrived on 31 May 1941 and U.S. food aid, including bacon, beans, cheese, and canned meat, constituted about one-fifteenth of all food consumed in Britain in 1941. Although Mass-Observation detected resistance among more conservative (and penny-conscious) shoppers to American canned goods, those who consumed them were enthusiastic. And the British minister of health remarked: "I have met city children playing in the country fields wearing strong, practical American clothes, and all the more pleased because they are patterns they have seen on the movies." By early June 1941 the MOI observed that the "feeling of 'It's all talk with the Americans' seems to be slowly dying." It noted a comment from the southwest regional information officer: "Previously many people regarded America as something to be seen on the films. Now they are seeing a different kind of America, and it is one which they admire." This new interest was reflected in the media. A BBC Listener Research report judged in July that about 11 to 15 percent of the civilian public, some four or five million people, were now "tuning in" to Raymond Gram Swing's *American Commentary* every Saturday night. "By many people Swing is regarded as the 'voice of America,' " noted another report in January 1942, though other commentators, such as Alistair Cooke and Elmer Davis, were also popular.[25]

Resentment, nevertheless, lingered that America was only creeping towards war. This did not change with Pearl Harbor. One MOI analyst warned three weeks later that "contrasted with the tremendous feeling of gratitude to Russia and desire to do more to aid her," there seemed to be "a feeling of malicious pleasure that the United States should have suffered hard blows, a complete lack of any gratitude for what America has done and is doing, [and] a feeling that she was merely kicked into the war." Mass-Observation believed that Pearl Harbor brought "to a head all the latent irritation with them for being so slow in coming to our aid." One female interviewee reckoned that Americans needed "a good shaking up" and that the Japanese "should have bombed New York, not the natives on those islands." M-O also detected a sense "that the Americans had been caught napping by the Japs. This began to sow a *very important seed of doubt.* Hitherto, whatever had or had not been thought of the Americans, nearly everybody thought that they were *efficient,* but now they seemed to be more inefficient than ourselves."[26] Dissatisfaction with the American war effort was to be a theme of British opinion for much of 1942, though there were doubts about British performance as well.

Mass-Observation also developed a theory to explain the contrasts of British mood towards the United States—on the one hand, interest and growing appreciation, on the other, resentment and hypercriticism:

British people have never regarded Americans as on all fours with other foreigners. To start with, they speak the same language and this leads to an exaggerated idea of the proportion of British blood in the population of the United States. Consequently there is at the back of many British minds the idea that Americans are a rather eccentric kind of Englishman, and . . . this comes out in people's feelings that the Americans ought to have been helping us right through the early part of the war, just like the Canadians and the Australians. . . . Perhaps the best way of putting it is to say that the average British person regards the average American in the light of an overseas cousin, and treats him therefore with a sort of familiarity, slightly distant familiarity, with which cousins are treated in the family circle. There has thus always been a very large volume of friendliness towards Americans, but this is tempered with a recognition of certain defects of character. Just as people tend to criticise their relations more closely and vigorously than their friends, so do Englishmen take the liberty of criticising Americans more than other foreign nations, just because they expect a higher standard of them.[27]

This "cousins theory" became something of a hobbyhorse for Mass-Observation, but it helps conceptualize a basic British ambivalence towards America. A blend of friendliness and candour towards rich and puzzling relations was to be a mark of the years that followed.

The first GIs therefore arrived in a country that still knew little in an informed way about America and Americans, but whose interest had been rising in 1941. Most British people held certain basic stereotypes about the United States as a land of enterprise and extroverts, of wealth and materialism, and these were reinforced by the insidious imagery of the movies. But there were pronounced differences of opinion about how this stereotyped America should be evaluated. Younger, working-class people tended to be the most enthusiastic, with the older, the conservative, and the better-educated being most censorious. Among those concerned about English morals and mores, the influence of America was often regarded as socially subversive. There was a potential tension here with the Churchill government's new *political* objective of a close Anglo-American relationship as the basis of British policy in war and peace.

The movies serve to heighten and often distort the differences in wealth and lifestyle between the two countries. Hollywood made America seem more opulent and dynamic, Britain more class-bound and traditional. In particular, Depression America, the social birthmark of the wartime GIs, made little impact on the British popular consciousness. For many younger Britons the GIs were simply the men from the movies.

Yet image and reality were in fact converging by 1942. The GIs left a country that was growing richer. They arrived in a country that was becoming poorer. Such was the alchemy of war.

4

"Don't You Know
There's a War On?"

★ ★ ★

IN BOTH BRITAIN AND AMERICA THE WAR MEANT PRIVATION AND SUFFER-
ing. Foodstuffs such as sugar and butter were rationed. So was petrol/
gasoline, keeping many private cars off the roads. People cultivated
their own gardens to boost vegetable production. They clustered round
the radio for war news or entertainment. And they waited anxiously
for letters from family and friends on the other side of the world. Yet
these similar threads were, in fact, parts of very different tapestries.
From 1940 the American economy boomed, while Britain slipped
deeper into deprivation and scarcity.

In the United States the term *the good war* became popular in the 1960s
to distinguish World War Two from the controversial conflict in Vietnam. In his volume of oral histories, Studs Terkel used it in quotation
marks, because, he said, "the adjective 'good' mated to the noun 'war'
is so incongruous," but to later historians it has become almost a
factual description. This is not to ignore some 300,000 war deaths or
the pain of wounds, mutilations, and breakdowns. Nor is it to forget
the race riots in the summer of 1943, the forced deportation from
California of innocent Japanese-Americans, or the miserable shanty-
towns around many of America's booming arms factories. For individuals, suffering is an absolute. But for the historian it is a relative
concept. And weighed on the scale of global misery, World War Two
treated America lightly. In the words of scholar Mark H. Leff: "War is
hell. But for millions of Americans on the booming home front, World
War II was also a hell of a war."[1]
What distinguished America from all the other belligerent countries

was that the enemy remained remote. Unlike mainland Europe, China, or Japan, the continental United States experienced no fighting or occupation. The three-year siege of Leningrad, the extermination of the Warsaw ghetto, and the 1945 famine in Japanese-occupied Vietnam had no parallels in Boston or Chicago, in Iowa or Arkansas. The British, too, were spared war on their own soil, but they endured persistent and destructive bombing from the air. Americans did steel themselves for such horrors. Early 1942 saw numerous (false) air-raid alerts, and a "dimout" was imposed along both coasts. So alarmed were Warner Bros. in Burbank, California, at the similarity from the air between some of their film studios and nearby aircraft factories that their sign-writers painted a big arrow on the roof, with the legend LOCKHEED THATAWAY.[2] But such unpatriotic prudence proved unnecessary. In the continental United States, enemy action was confined to a few shells lobbed by two Japanese submarines onto the West Coast in February and June 1942; a Japanese airman, launched from a submarine, who dropped some incendiaries over Oregon the following November; and a spattering of balloon-bombs in the winter of 1944–45. The only evidence of the vicious U-boat campaign off the East Coast in the early months of 1942 was periodic debris along the shore and an occasional explosion within earshot of Virginia Beach or the Florida Keys.

Far from damaging America, the war was of positive benefit economically. To adapt Roosevelt, "Dr. New Deal," had given way to "Dr. Win-the-War," and the latter had finally cured the nation's Depression. In 1940 unemployment still stood at over 14 percent of the civilian workforce. That had dropped to 1.9 percent by 1943. Between 1939 and 1945 gross national product in real terms (allowing for inflation) rose 70 percent. Much of this was due to America's role as what FDR called "the arsenal of democracy." By 1944 U.S. war production was approximately double that of Germany, Italy, and Japan combined and it was providing 60 percent of the Allies' combat munitions.[3] Symbols of this effort became household names: Ford's one-mile-long bomber assembly plant at Willow Run outside Detroit; Henry J. Kaiser, whose shipyards produced nearly a third of America's naval construction programme in 1943; Andrew Jackson Higgins of New Orleans who turned a sleepy pleasure-boat business into a leading producer of landing craft.

This war boom, doubling America's industrial output, was a tribute to new capital equipment and increased productivity. But it also reflected a 60 percent increase in the manufacturing workforce as the unemployed literally moved into work. The most famous movement was Westwards. Of the thirteen states to gain population during the war, the biggest beneficiaries were California (one million) and then Washington and Oregon. People went West because Uncle Sam's money went West, to work for Douglas, Lockheed, or Boeing, to find employment in one of Kaiser's shipyards or in the naval installations of San Diego or Puget Sound. But the new Western gold rush was only part of a national movement. The South's rural population, stable at around 14.6 million during the 1930s, dropped by 3.2 million during the war. Certain war-boom cities experienced phenomenal growth: Mobile County, Alabama, grew by nearly two-thirds between 1940 and 1944, the area around Norfolk, Virginia, by about 40 percent. Nearly a quarter of the population increase around Detroit and Willow Run came from Alabama, Mississippi, Kentucky, and Tennessee.[4] These migratory tides—from South to North, from East to West, and especially from farm to city—were long established. But the war accentuated them and there were also many countercurrents. Wartime America was America on the move. And the GIs were part of that mobility.

The miracle of America's war economy was that it produced (metaphorically) butter as well as guns. Between 1939 and 1945 U.S. output of textiles and alcoholic drinks rose 50 percent and that of processed foodstuffs by 40 percent. Earnings in manufacturing and war-related industries also surged. Between 1938 and the end of 1942 average annual income per family had risen from $2,418 to $3,618 in Boston and from $2,031 to $3,469 in Los Angeles. Such figures should be read with care, of course. Much of the increased income came from working longer hours, and wartime inflation eroded the value of the extra cash. What stands out, however, is that "families with more than one wage earner often had incomes which were beyond their wildest dreams during the depression." And there were many such families in wartime. In addition to males gaining employment at last after the Depression—be it in the military, war industries, or the swollen bureaucracy—many of their wives went out to work. In 1940 nearly 28 percent of adult women were employed; by 1944 the proportion was over 36 percent.[5] The basic point is again a relative one—compared with the Depression, most American families were better off. After years of unemployment most did not mind working hard, and even in a ration-book era there were plenty of goods and services on which to spend their new income.

This improvement was apparent even before Pearl Harbor. War orders from Britain and France and then America's own rearmament in 1940–41 had already boosted jobs, incomes, and thus civilian demand. Between 1939 and 1941 real GNP rose by 20 percent and expenditure on consumer durables went up 23 percent in real terms. Automobile sales, for instance, languishing at 2 million in 1938, climbed to 3.7 million in 1940 and were sustained at that level the following year.[6] Through 1942 industry was reluctant to convert to wartime production and civilians did not curb demand until forced to do so. Gasoline was not rationed until December 1942 and food rationing began to bite only in the early months of 1943. In other words, most GIs, before they were shipped overseas, could already see a perceptible improvement in the living standards of their families. This made the contrast with what they witnessed abroad all the more striking.

To tycoons like Henry Kaiser the war boom vindicated entrepreneurial capitalism. As *The Saturday Evening Post* put it: "If Free Enterprise had not flourished here, the cause of world freedom might now be lost for centuries." In reality, however, the war economy was largely big business bankrolled by big government. Kaiser's empire was like "a huge federal public-works agency, liberally funded by taxpayers' dollars," observed historian John Blum. War contracts, ultimately totaling $240 billion, were given to eighteen thousand companies, but two-thirds of the total went to the top hundred corporations and the top ten received 30 percent. This federal war spending, more than half of it funded by borrowing, revived the Depression economy far more effectively than had the New Deal, which now seemed trivial by comparison. The most substantial of the administration's work-relief programs, the WPA, received only $9 billion in 1935–45. By contrast $50 billion was spent on Lend-Lease alone— almost equivalent to *total* federal spending between 1933 and 1939. In 1939 federal government expenditure was $9.4 billion; by 1944 it had increased tenfold. As a proportion of GNP it had soared from 10 percent to 45 percent. Richard Polenberg has justly remarked: "If the military-industrial complex reached maturity in the era of the Cold War, it just as surely was born and nurtured in World War II."[7]

Whether by Dr. New Deal or Dr. Win-the-War, the American economy was being doctored. It did not heal itself through the natural motions of the "free-enterprise system." And it is in this context that we must understand the draft, the centre of the nation's programme of wartime mobilization. A total of 16.3 million Americans served in the military at some point during the war, 10 million as conscripts. The armed forces grew from 335,000 in 1939 to 12.1 million by the summer of 1945 when they constituted about 18 percent of the total workforce. Yet the civilian labour force itself only grew by under one million between 1940–42, to 56.4 million, and then declined to less than 54 million by the end of the war. The conclusion is clear, namely that most of the growth in the *total* labour force, some 10 million between 1940 and 1944, and most of the related fall in unemployment, must be attributed to the expansion of the armed forces.[8] In employment terms the draft succeeded where the New Deal failed; "GI" was the next in the long list of Roosevelt's alphabetical agencies, following the WPA, PWA, and CCC. Such is the grim irony of war—at risk of death, it gave work to millions of Americans. And not merely work, but also better food and medical care than they had known before. One young marine from Alabama admitted he had never worn shoes before joining the service.[9]

The draft therefore epitomizes wartime America more profoundly than is often thought. It was the central element of the vast federal public-works program that bounced America out of the Depression. And it was also one of the principal instruments of migration, that other great feature of wartime America. The draft pulled young men from their farms, small towns, or city blocks, despatched them to training camps, many in the Deep South, then moved them around the country to units and manoeuvres, before shipping many off across the Atlantic or Pacific. Thanks to the draft, they saw their country and, often, the world. As we shall note later, these odysseys gave them a new sense of their own identity.

If the cliché for America is "the good war," for Britain it is "the people's war." In national myth 1939–45 is depicted as a time of consensus and hard work, with all "pulling together" in a crisis, animated by the "Dunkirk spirit." The mass evacuation of the urban poor to the countryside, for instance, has been called "one of the most significant phenomena of the war" because, "among the articulate few, [it] aroused a new sense of social concern." To politicians and pundits after the war the extension of the welfare state and the Labour party's victory in 1945 were evidence of a fundamental wartime shift in attitudes to state regulation and social responsibility. Subsequent historians have chipped away at these graven images of social consensus and political reform, arguing that "the effect of the war was not to sweep society on to a new course, but to hasten its progress along the old grooves." As in America, their aim has been to set the war years into longer-term patterns. And, like most revisionist history, their achievement has been "to show that less happened, less dramatically, than was once thought."[10]

Whether or not the changes were durable, the war was, for most

Britons, a time when normal life was disrupted, usually for the worse—unlike the American experience. The war boom in America and war deprivation in Britain exacerbated the basic contrasts in wealth and lifestyle between the two countries.

The most visible evidence of war were the bombed ruins in most British cities. The worst of the Blitz was over by the summer of 1941; the 1942 bomb load, some sixty-five hundred tons, was the equivalent of a month's bombing during the winter of 1940–41. Nevertheless, these 1942 German attacks were not forgotten by any who witnessed them, particularly the so-called Baedeker raids on Bath, York, Exeter, and other historic centres in April and May 1942. The Luftwaffe still paid regular visits over the east coast in 1943 and early 1944 saw the so-called Baby Blitz on London. Worst of all, a week after D-Day, the Germans commenced their V-bomb attacks on London and the southeast. The V-1 pilotless planes and the silent V-2 rockets killed nearly 9,000 and seriously injured 24,500 before their launching sites were overrun in the spring of 1945. Thus, German raids were still frequent when the GIs occupied Britain and, in any case, evidence of earlier visits was all around. One GI, docking at Avonmouth after twenty-eight days at sea, recalled "our first look at bomb damage—all around the area, huge craters, *fresh!* The fear ran through the ship like a shot." In autumn 1944 men from the 17th Airborne Division suddenly appreciated why they had been sent to Southampton for "city combat" training. On the rail journey down there, recalled Kurt Gabel, the mood was

> pleasant and relaxing, the obligatory dirty jokes generated the usual raucous laughter, card players yelled at one another, and groups of men sang the newest songs picked up from the limeys. But the noise suddenly died down as we entered Southampton and rolled slowly through its working-class residential area. . . . Air raids here had truly *struck home.* Row after row, street after street of gutted two-story houses and the remains of ugly, red-brick tenements told of the suffering of their former occupants. . . . We were all silent, thinking the same thing: Suppose it happened in America . . .[11]

Another feature of wartime Britain was apparent within hours of a GI's arrival, namely the blackout. Before leaving America many would have been given a twenty-four-hour pass to enjoy New York, often for the first time in their lives. But the dimout in Manhattan, the switched-off advertising signs in Times Square, bore no comparison to the stygian darkness of Glasgow or Liverpool on that first night in Britain.

Because of the Luftwaffe, blackout regulations were imposed from the start of the war and rigorously enforced. Some households painted their lightbulbs blue or put cardboard shades around them, but most preferred well-lit interiors and opted for heavy shades across all their windows. Government supplies of heavy sateen soon ran out and blankets or dyed sheets were utilized. Others fitted shutters, continental-style, across the window frames. Outside, there was only pinprick lighting around some lampposts, and hooded and dimmed headlamps on cars. Thick white paint along kerbs, around obstructions, and on bumpers and running boards of all vehicles was of limited help. When walking around, electric torches were allowed, providing the light was masked by two layers of tissue paper—*if* torches and batteries could be purchased. Blackout jokes abounded—in a raffle, the third prize was a radio, the second a bicycle, and the first a torch battery. In such darkness, road accidents were frequent and even natives got lost. Norman Longmate, a boy during the war, wrote later: "It is hard for anyone who did not experience the total darkness of these wartime nights to comprehend the sense of isolation, verging on panic, that could so easily descend if one missed one's way."[12]

More significant even than the blackout was the effect of rationing. Unlike the U.S. economy, which prospered from its vast internal market, Britain had always relied heavily on foreign trade for its wealth and, indeed, for essential food and raw materials. Shortage of foreign exchange and shipping during the war, plus the depredations of the U-boats, reduced imports dramatically. In the middle of the war these were running at under half of the mid-1930s average of 55 million tons a year. The consequence, despite increased food production at home, was a steady decline in living standards. Whereas American consumer spending on food *increased* by 8 percent and on clothing and footwear by 23 percent between 1939 and 1944, in Britain there were falls of 11 percent and 34 percent respectively.[13]

Rationing was, of course, imposed in both countries and to some extent it followed a similar pattern. All citizens were given ration books. Some foodstuffs could be purchased only on the basis of a fixed amount per person per week. For others a "points" system applied, allowing each person a total number of points to be allocated according to choice among various items. This allowed the shopper some discrimination in purchasing, while the government could raise or lower the points value of each item depending on demand. Despite these similarities, however, rationing was briefer and less severe in the United States. In Britain it was imposed from January 1940, some two years earlier than America, and it began to bite straight away. Meat, for instance, was controlled in March 1940, in the United States three years later. The points system was applied in Britain from December 1941 but not in the United States until March 1943. Moreover, in America it concentrated on canned goods and processed food whereas in Britain it covered virtually all food and clothing. Furniture, made to "utility designs," could only be obtained by newlyweds or the newly bombed, while sheets, blankets, and kitchen utensils virtually disappeared from the shops. In America food rationing generally meant shortages whereas in Britain the same foodstuffs were simply unavailable. Oranges were a rarity and bananas so unusual that some young children, given one as a treat, had no idea how to eat them and bit through the skin. In America eggs became a basic meat substitute; in Britain fresh eggs were almost unobtainable in shops. (When the British ambassador was hit by one during an anti-British demonstration in Detroit in November 1941 he was reported as saying that the Americans were lucky to have eggs to throw around, when in England people had "only one egg a month.")[14]

Appeals for conservation were endless. Even the foreign visitor to Britain, unhampered by ration books, could not fail to notice. Hotel bathrooms carried a sign requesting patrons not to exceed five inches of water "as part of your personal share in the Battle for Fuel." Railway trains were late, crowded, and, by the spring of 1944, devoid of all restaurant cars. In station buffets a solitary teaspoon was often tied to the counter and in some pubs only those who brought their own glasses would be served. Restaurants were allowed only one main course and from June 1942 a maximum charge of 5 shillings (£0.25, or $1.00) was imposed, though some luxury establishments got around this with a cover charge. Many London restaurants had run out of food by 9:30 P.M. Cigarettes and alcohol were especially hard to obtain. Although the government regarded tobacco, for morale reasons, as an essential import, most popular prewar brands disappeared and tobacconists were harassed and abused by usually mild-mannered individuals in search of their daily fix. As for drink, little wine could be imported after the Fall of France and the sugar and grain shortages made beer supplies erratic and a bottle of whisky a prized possession.

Bombed, blacked out, and rationed, the British were also an uprooted people. Even more than in America, men, women, and children were on the move, pulled from homes, families, and communities into unfamiliar places and lifestyles. The most obvious shift was conscription into the armed forces, which grew tenfold from June 1939 to reach nearly five million by D-Day. Four and a half million of these were men, 30 percent of the male workforce. Even those based in

Britain moved around and were usually quartered far from home. Civilians were on the move as well. There were 60 million *officially registered* changes of address between September 1939 and December 1945, in a population (England and Wales) of 38 million. Millions more moved without telling the bureaucrats.[15]

The most familiar category of civilian migrants were mothers and children evacuated from the big cities for fear of bombing. Overall, some four million people were relocated by government evacuation schemes in 1939–45, plus another two million who voluntarily moved themselves in 1939. But, on closer inspection, the evacuation was not a once-for-all flood in September 1939 but, rather, three great tides followed in each case by a strong ebb and connected by a steady trickle. The biggest wave, involving some 1.5 million official evacuees, occurred in the first days of September 1939 but nearly two-thirds had returned home by early 1940. The Blitz prompted another series of moves, amounting to about 1.25 million official evacuees in the year from August 1940, with, again, a tendency to return home as time went on. The final exodus, centred on London in July and August 1944, was in response to the German V-1 "doodlebug" attacks that began a week after D-Day. Nearly a million left in those two months. For the women and children caught up in these migrations what stands out is "the trauma of family separation and the culture shock of coping with a new environment." In September 1942 530,000 adults and children were living in evacuation billets (mainly rooms in private houses) around the country. Half were unaccompanied children staying in foster homes. In the winter of 1943–44 the total number of billetees had dropped to about 320,000 but it soared again to over one million in September 1944 following the German V-bomb attacks on London. A quarter of these were unaccompanied children.[16]

Apart from soldiers and mothers and young children, the other great war migrants were young women, moved around the country because of service in the military or war industries. As with evacuation, historians now tend to play down the long-term consequences of women's war work. In Britain, as in the United States, the postwar period saw a reassertion of domesticity and paternalism. But during the war itself there was no doubt about the upheavals entailed for many women. By 1943 national service was compulsory for single women between the ages of nineteen and twenty-four. And from February 1942 women aged twenty to thirty could only be employed through Government Employment Exchanges, which ensured their direction into essential war industries. It was not in itself novel for

British women to take paid employment. In 1931 three-quarters of single women between fourteen and twenty-four were employed. What changed was, first, the nature of their employment. The loss of males to the armed services necessitated a flood of women into what had previously been labeled "men's jobs." In engineering the proportion of women rose from one-tenth to over one-third between 1939 and 1943. Nearly half the workers in national and local government offices were female in 1943, by which time it was unusual to see a male bus conductor. The other great change during the war was an increase in *married* women workers, previously discouraged by convention or by the notorious "marriage bar" in most professions from continuing paid employment after entering wedlock. From 1940, official propaganda such as "war weeks" pressured married women to take on jobs outside the home. In 1943 43 percent of women over the age of fourteen in paid employment were married, compared with 16 percent in 1931. Over a quarter of them were aged thirty-five to forty-four.[17]

For most of these women, it should be emphasized, war work hardly amounted to emancipation. Single girls would have expected some kind of paid employment. They may have had more money in their pockets because of a factory job, but the hours were long and the work tedious. For married women—the main "beneficiaries" of the wartime social revolution—the effect was a double burden of running a home single-handed while also holding down an outside job.

Across the board, then, life in wartime Britain was far harder than in the United States. Both bombing and blackout were distinctively British phenomena, rationing was much tougher, and the wartime disruption of family life more extensive. The contrast is apparent in the statistics. Between 1939 and 1944 consumer purchases of goods and services *increased* in America by 12 percent. In Britain in 1938–44 they *fell* by 22 percent—a pattern typical of all the other belligerent powers. Overall, the war was estimated in 1945 to have cost Britain a quarter of its national wealth, particularly through physical destruction and the sale of foreign investments. Meanwhile America's GNP increased 50 percent in real terms.[18]

What all this meant for the people involved will be explored in part IV of this book. But two points should be underlined here. First, it is clear that the reception accorded the GIs owed much to the distortions wrought in British life by the war. The disruption of family life in Britain made a young male presence more desirable. The dark, pinched, and anxious atmosphere of wartime encouraged escapism

and the search for fun. Above all, the differential impact of the conflict
on the two countries enhanced the relative wealth of Americans—as
they got richer, many Britons felt poorer. Second, the GIs started to
arrive in 1942 when the war seemed particularly grim. The minister
of information, Brendan Bracken, told one newspaper editor in March
that "the Government is very disturbed about the low morale in the
country, and particularly in the Army, but has no idea what to do."
Nineteen forty-two saw a succession of British humiliations, notably
the surrenders of Singapore in February and Tobruk in June, which
demoralized everyone from Churchill downwards. Rationing intensified as the battle of the Atlantic squeezed imports, and the "second
front" demanded by press and public failed to materialize. This was
what novelist Elizabeth Bowen called "the lightless middle of the tun-
nel."[19]

Yet we must not attribute the "overpaid, overfed" character of the
GIs entirely to the material differences between American and British
life, even when accentuated by the scarcities and frustrations of war.
For U.S. soldiers enjoyed, in many respects, better living standards
than their civilian compatriots. Consider a few examples. Thirty percent of all cigarettes produced in the United States during the war went
to the armed forces, even though they constituted only 10 percent of
the population. Canned goods were rationed at home mainly because
about half of the American production in 1943 was shipped to troops
overseas. Annual civilian meat consumption was 140 pounds per
head during the war; each GI averaged 234 pounds. And civilians
were driven to pork or eggs because Uncle Sam cornered 60 percent
of prime beef production and 80 percent of utility grades.[20] What these
figures indicate is that, although GIs risked their life and limb for their
country, those who survived, particularly those behind the front lines,
enjoyed a basic standard of living that was often better than at home.
Certainly it stood out against the deprivations of the Depression. This
reflected a deliberate policy of the U.S. government and it contrasted
with the treatment of British soldiers by their own leaders.

In other words, this is a story of armies as well as nations. The GIs
were soldiers as much as they were Americans. To understand their
reaction to Britain and their reception by its people we must turn to
the sociology of armies in general, and the American Army in particular.

Part II

OCCUPYING ARMIES

5

Occupational
Hazards

★ ★ ★

TODAY ONE LOOKS EASTWARDS FROM THE TREES ALONG SEMINARY RIDGE
across peaceful, open farmland. In the distance the slope rises gently
towards Cemetery Ridge. Yet few can stand there without feeling that
this is not merely hallowed but haunted ground. What became known
to history as Pickett's Charge, the climax of the third day of the battle
of Gettysburg on 3 July 1863, is now almost impossible to imagine.
What could have motivated some thirteen thousand Confederate infantry—most of them hungry, many without shoes—to break cover
and march, in impeccable line order a mile in width, across the open
fields to the Union line? First into shot and canister from the enemy
artillery, then into volley upon volley from the infantry sheltering
behind the stone wall. Packs, weapons, even limbs, literally went up
in smoke. As the standards fell, they were raised aloft by new hands,
only to be shot down again. Only a few hundred men actually reached
the Union position—all of whom were killed, wounded, or captured.
Barely half those who set out eventually made it back to the Confederate line.

Pickett's Charge is one of the most breathtaking examples of almost
suicidal courage on a battlefield. There are, of course, many others,
such as the walk of eleven British divisions across a mile or more of
open country east of Amiens on 1 July 1916, which left twenty-one
thousand dead—what we know in retrospect as the First Day of the
Somme. Or, for that matter, the struggle of thousands of overloaded
GIs up a quarter mile of shore and dunes against raking fire on 6 June
1944—Omaha Beach. All these are examples of battle as an unnatural
act, flying in the face of all "normal" dictates of individual prudence

and self-preservation. In each case, admittedly, there was an element of misplaced confidence—the expectation that the enemy had already been decimated by prior bombardment. But, even when disabused, men carried on—despite the ear-shattering, brain-numbing noise, despite the all-pervasive smoke that created a terrifying sense of isolation, despite the dreadful litter of the battlefield—on to almost certain death. What impelled them to fight?

After World War Two, American analysts stressed the role of what became known as "primary groups." "I hold it to be one of the simplest truths of war," wrote S.L.A. Marshall, "that the thing which enables an infantry soldier to keep going with his weapons is the near presence or presumed presence of a comrade." According to Marshall, the soldier's immediate compatriots in the squad provided emotional and physical support and also imposed standards of behaviour to which the man might not adhere if by himself. Some of these studies judged the Wehrmacht during World War Two to have maintained its cohesion to the end because of the regional basis of its regiments and its official policy of integrating replacements as a group behind the line rather than throwing them in piecemeal on the eve of battle. Likewise, British studies often concluded that loyalty to "the regiment," which was often linked to a particular county or town, reinforced battlefield esprit.[1]

More recent analyses have cautioned against overstating this argument, however. For one thing, it seems to rest on an idealized view of the German Army in World War Two, exaggerating its regional integrity and underestimating the role of ideology in its sustained resistance. More generally, to quote sociological jargon, "primary group beliefs may be disarticulate with institutional goals." In plain English, the group may combine to avoid danger instead of obeying suicidal orders—witness the "live and let live" system of tacit truces on the Western Front in World War One or the introvertive loyalties induced by the "buddy system" among American troops in Korea.[2]

Although group spirit is one of the most important reasons why men fight, other factors play their part. What "constitutes victory for the soldier" is, "in the first instance, survival itself," but one cannot dismiss entirely idealistic motives. Patriotism is most apparent when fighting to defend the homeland—it was clearly a major factor in the tenacity of Russian resistance in 1941–42 and in German defiance in 1944–45. Often love of country is linked to hatred of the enemy, who has been reduced in propaganda to a bestial force. This was a characteristic of both sides on the Eastern Front in World War Two. By contrast, American, and even British troops except in 1940, lacked any direct sense of fighting to defend their country. And in Europe, though not against Japan, sustained, collective hatred of the enemy was the exception. Conventional wisdom was that the GI fought mostly to finish the war and get home. But, even if a strong crusading sense was lacking and war aims were articulated as vague slogans like "democracy" and "freedom," there was a general sense that "Pearl Harbor meant war, and that once in the war the United States had to win."[3]

The willingness of men to go into battle also owes much to training and leadership. Training inculcates order and cohesion. It also familiarizes the soldier with his weapons until their use becomes second nature. Indeed much training is simply drill and weapons use. Tactical preparation was often less sophisticated. In World War One, particularly in America and Britain, there was scepticism that the infantrymen of mass, conscript armies (as distinct from regulars) could be taught any subtlety of tactics. Hence the doctrine of the creeping barrage—the artillery "conquered" and the infantry "occupied." Even in World War Two the Americans and the British were slower than their enemies to move on from this linear, frontal approach and grasp the concepts of small-group action and "fire and manoeuvre." Of supreme importance in all these aspects of training—order, weapons, and tactics—were the men's officers. The American Civil War and the Great War perhaps marked the apogee of leadership as transparent, insouciant personal courage, where men gained inspiration from the sangfroid of their officers advancing, armed only with sword or even walking stick, at the head of their men. But again and again in World War Two, the cohesion and motivation of small groups was determined by the courage and resolution of their leaders.

Leadership was exerted by discipline as much as by example. British troops about to go into battle in World War One would often receive a pep talk about courage, honour, and the like from the colonel. Then his adjutant or the sergeant major would follow with "the assurance that the severest military law" would apply to any who shirked their duty. Harsh discipline was particularly apparent on the German Eastern Front in 1941–45 where it "became standard policy to terrorize the troops from evading a likely death at the front by promising them certain execution if they were caught in the act." But even if that was extreme, in all armies the main function of military discipline is to intimidate the trainee soldier into obedience. "Deference to the commands of superiors has to be automatic and unquestioning, and any signs of democratic thinking or individualism that might threaten such a response must be ruthlessly stamped out," historian John Ellis has observed. In fact, this "is one of the prime objectives of military training," arguably more basic even than weapons training. Drill and what was known to GIs as "chickenshit," to the British as "bull"—namely the Army's punctiliousness about haircuts, dress, and inspections—were essential weapons in the psychological battle to reduce a relcalcitrant civilian into an obedient soldier. As one cynical U.S. veteran observed: "The aim of military training is not just to prepare men for battle, but to make them long for it. Inspections are one way to achieve this."[4]

When all is said and done, however, assaulting an enemy position under fire is not a rational act judged by the normal standards of self-preservation. Not surprisingly, many accounts of combat suggest that the emotions took over. "Anyone who has watched men on the battlefield," wrote J. Glenn Gray, "finds it hard to escape the conclusion that there is a delight in destruction." Gray was reflecting particularly on World War Two, but the same has been said of other wars. The Union Army storming Missionary Ridge outside Chattanooga in November 1863 were described as "completely and frantically drunk with excitement." When Edward Ripley charged Confederate guns during the Peninsula campaign of autumn 1864, "it was a dream, so great was the intoxication of the excitement." *Intoxication* is a word that recurs in such accounts, literally as well as metaphorically, for, as John Keegan has noted, drinking "seems an inseparable part both of preparation for battle and of combat itself" because alcohol "depresses the self-protective reflexes, and so induces the appearance and feeling of courage." Yet the notoriety of a tot of rum before going over the top should not distort a larger truth about the metabolism of battle. Denis Winter has inferred that Tommies crossing no-man's-land in World War One were "affected by two moods successively." First was a feeling "of complete abstraction"—a dreamlike quality in which they felt detached from their surroundings. "Men were so certain that they would be hit when they got out of the trench that, when after a moment they found themselves safe, relief became euphoric. There followed logically the second mood, one of positive enjoyment," in which acts of frenzy and great courage were often done. Then the excitement wore off and a new awareness of danger set in. The impression, suggested Winter, is "that men advanced and fought in a semi-drugged state. The upset in body chemistry produced by a state of high fear long sustained gave strength to eliminate a calculating response for a limited time." This would also explain the difficulty of recalling the details and even the mood of battle afterwards.[5]

Nothing can fully prepare a soldier for battle. As Gen. Mark Clark, one of America's leading commanders in World War Two, observed, "no training school, however careful or thorough, can substitute for combat" because "a soldier is always green until he's been under fire." And leadership, discipline, or even drink cannot always restrain natural instincts, as the French Army found in the mutinies of early 1917 after the failure of yet another suicidal offensive. In the end, every soldier has his breaking point. What in the Great War was called "shellshock" and in World War Two, more euphemistically, "combat exhaustion" is "not a description of exceptional cases," wrote historian John Ellis. "It is what happened, in continuous combat, to almost all the soldiers of an infantry unit who were not killed or wounded. It happened to every nationality, on every front, in every company, battalion and regiment." And as soldiers appreciate that they are fighting something more inflexible than the sternest enemy, namely the law of averages, a kind of sleepwalking, apathetic fatalism begins to take hold—what GIs called "the two thousand year stare."[6]

In even the "best" army, then, cohesion in battle is tenuous. A classic example is the flight of Napoleon's crack Imperial Guard under intense fire on the evening of Waterloo, prompting the horrified cry "la Garde recule" and the disintegration of the French line. Pondering this, historian John Keegan observed: "Inside every army is a crowd struggling to get out." And, one might add, inside every soldier is a civilian trying to escape. This schizophrenic duality of army-crowd and soldier-civilian has been a central problem for every military commander throughout history. Yet it is particularly pressing for modern mass-conscript armies, in which soldiers are not professionals but civilians temporarily denied their civilian status and rights. And countries where there is no peacetime conscription find it even harder to habituate the civilian to the shocks of military life.

Impelling an army to fight, particularly an army of conscripts, is one problem; holding it together when not fighting is equally difficult. This aspect of war has often been ignored by military historians because it lacks the drama, heroism, and macabre fascination of battle. Yet this neglect is profoundly misleading. Even combat infantrymen spend most of their time not fighting. Asked to describe a typical day in the front line, Loren W. Gast, who served with the 1st U.S. Infantry Division in Europe in 1944–45 wrote: "it is terror, excitement and monotony. It is waiting, waiting, waiting for something that never seems to arrive." Furthermore, most twentieth-century soldiers are not combat infantrymen. In the American Civil War 93.2 percent of soldiers were engaged in combat-related tasks. But after 1914, to quote Martin Van Creveld, "the products of the machine . . . finally superseded those of the field as the main items consumed by armies." In other words, the need for heavy ammunition and motor fuel meant that most armies could no longer live off the land, and enormous supply organizations mushroomed—the "tail" behind the "teeth" of the fighting infantry. The imbalance was particularly high in the American, British, and Canadian armies in World War Two, with something like four noncombatants for every fighting soldier. (The Russians and Germans kept the tail/teeth ratio down to one or two to one.)[8]

Most soldiers, most of the time, are therefore not fighting. Yet it is danger, despite its solvent potential in extremis, that usually forms the cement to keep an army together. Under fire there is apparent safety in numbers, in obeying orders, and in following well-drilled procedures. Conversely, out of action and prone to boredom, the unnaturalness of army regimentation becomes less reasonable and therefore more intolerable. All the simmering grievances begin to boil over. The army denies your individuality, reducing each civilian to a number and a standard uniform. The sobriquet GI—"Government Issue"— was a sardonic expression of this fact. Officers seem bent on humiliating you, with sadistically imposed petty "fatigues" and sarcastic denigration in public. Privacy is minimal when living in shared tents or crowded barracks. Social comforts are at a premium, with poor food, uncomfortable beds (often none at all), scant recreation facilities, and few personal possessions. Officers, by contrast, enjoy a more privileged existence in all these respects, usually segregated from their men in separate quarters, with the perquisites (including servants) carefully graded according to rank. Armies also segregate their men from the rest of society, particularly women, creating an all-male environment that may foster intense comradeship in battle but that seems claustrophobic and repressive behind the lines. And freedom disappears, not merely because of incessant orders but because, quite literally, your time is not your own, all around the clock, even to the point of designating occasional periods of "leave" when you are allowed out— the term *liberty run* was well chosen. Whenever the cohesive force of danger is absent, an army is prone to crowdlike behaviour.

Keeping an army occupied is as great a problem as making a soldier fight. During the American Civil War, autumn mud and then winter ice drove armies into encampments for several months of the year. The boredom, privation, and squalor of these "wallow holes" of tents and huts drove many to incessant gambling and drink. Whisky, known variously as "red eye," "rot gut," and "bust skull," was "the most troublesome enemy the army had to fight" in these camps, one Pennsylvania officer asserted. By the end of such a winter soldiers often wrote home, with apt if unintentional double entendre, that they were "spoiling for a fight." The French Army faced similar problems during the Phoney War of 1939–40. "We're no longer fighting the Germans," wrote one commentator, "we're fighting *ennui.*" Its manifestations were chronic alcoholism among the troops and a propensity to disappear at weekends—what the British called "French leave" and the French "filer à l'anglaise"! And even though the troops were defending home soil, friction with civilians was apparent. In the Ardennes locals generally welcomed the French soldiers billeted on them, but they disliked the black colonial troops and there was considerable bitterness about the Army's seizure of scarce fuel and its efforts to evacuate civilians from the area.[9]

All these problems become more acute when soldiers are occupying foreign territory. When the Spanish were unable to defeat the revolt of the Netherlands in the 1560s, they settled down to an eighty-year war of attrition and sieges, punctuated by minor skirmishes. According to Geoffrey Parker, "the garrisons of the Spanish Netherlands, concentrations of bored, impoverished but well-armed young men, inevitably formed a pool of lawlessness, of gambling and vice, crime and cruelty, lechery and licence in the centre of every community." That was a premodern army, living off the land in unfriendly territory. But similar problems, though less acute, afflicted the British Expeditionary Force (BEF) in Allied France in 1914–18. Attempting to understand French feelings, one British veteran remarked that

> if three million Frenchmen squatted down in an area the size of Cumberland and Lancashire [two counties in northwest England] with the purpose of driving the Irish out of Scotland, 1 per cent of them speaking English and all of them blasting shortcuts through hedges, climbing walls, scrounging wood, draining wells and banging rickety gates, then no doubt feeling would have run high among the natives of the area.[10]

In World War Two the British "occupation" of France was briefer and less onerous—a mere ten divisions for one winter of the Phoney War. Yet the case is of particular interest because the British soldier's relation to the French civilian in 1939–40 was in many ways analogous to that between the GI and the British civilian in 1942–45. In France, it was the British who were "oversexed, overpaid, and over here."

British Tommies were assumed to come from a much wealthier country. "All classes seem permeated with the idea that we are colossally rich," remarked one British diplomat. Compared with French troops, their uniforms and pay were both superior. The "alleged opulence of the British troops and the meagre pay of the French has caused considerable bitterness and ill-feeling in this country," reported the British ambassador in Paris in April 1940. This was summed up in the quip about "les quinze francs des Anglais et les quinze sous des Français." In order to defuse resentment, the French minister of information was obliged to make a well-publicized statement noting that British soldiers had money deducted for their families and that they had to pay for their beer, whereas French *poilus* enjoyed free wine, travel, and postage. Although many British troops were well behaved, particularly when billeted in small villages, their conduct in leave centres such as Tours and Lille was a source of frequent complaint. The principal causes were alcoholism and sex. In Douai the incidence of drunkenness had become so serious by March 1940 that cafés were only allowed to sell alcohol on three days of the week, and the local epidemic of VD was primarily ascribed to the BEF "because their pay is high." German propagandists played up the image of British troops as a menace to French womanhood so assiduously that British officers feared lasting damage to Anglo-French relations. "It is impossible to exaggerate the importance of this subject," noted the BEF's Adjutant General.[11]

Sex was usually *the* preoccupation of unoccupied armies. It is a commonplace of war literature that "the front was the one wartime place that was sexless" because men there were "too scared, busy, hungry, and demoralized to think about sex at all." By contrast, "behind the lines, desire was constantly seeking an outlet."[12] Aside from the satisfaction of sexual drives, female company was an antidote to the all-male environment, an expression of personal freedom, and balm for the dehumanizing rituals of army life. For army commanders, however, the soldier's relationships with women have been highly problematic. On the one hand, most took an attitude of what they considered robust common sense, namely that "basic male urges" must be satisfied. On the other hand, they have usually regarded women as a threat to military discipline and effectiveness.

Marriage was a particularly sensitive issue. This was an elementary civilian right, yet also a distraction from soldierly duty. Most armies have tried to prohibit or dissuade their men from contracting marital relationships especially while on duty abroad. Spanish military ordinances in 1632 decreed only one man in six might marry; the eighteenth-century British Army allowed a maximum of six wives "on the strength" of a unit of one hundred living in their barracks. Controlling civilian rights in a modern conscript army was harder but most armies in World War Two obliged soldiers to secure their officer's permission in advance, which then permitted a variety of official obstacles to be placed in his way. Even more worrying than permanent relationships were the results of casual ones. Venereal disease was an occupational hazard of inactive armies and historically one of the main reasons for a soldier to be out of action, far more prevalent than wounds. In Britain in the 1860s hospital admissions for venereal diseases averaged one case to every four or five men in the Army; in British India the rate climbed to one in two in 1895. Even with the new sulpha drugs in World War Two recovery took a month. Recognizing that soldiers will have recourse to casual sex, yet seeking to minimize the risk of disease, many armies have adopted a system of controlled prostitution. In World War One the French established licensed brothels, *maisons tolerées,* under careful medical supervision and secured a striking reduction in the incidence of VD. In the late Victorian era many regiments in British India had their own regulated brothels, staffed by women who were both "clean" and "sufficiently attractive," and in wartime France the BEF set up a few of its own *maisons tolerées*—the one in Rouen having only 243 VD cases out of 171,000 men served in its first year. But in Britain and America, as we shall see, such concessions to the weaknesses of the flesh provoked outcries if discovered by moralists and they were certainly not tolerated on home soil.[13]

Even highly regimented troops suffered the same problems of ennui, indiscipline, and disease when reduced to an army of occupation. The Wehrmacht in World War Two is a well-documented example. In contrast with World War One, German military law in 1939–45 was far stricter than that of Britain or France. At least thirteen thousand German soldiers were executed during the war for offences against military law. The British Army, by contrast, carried out forty death sentences in 1939–45 and the French just over one hundred. Despite this harsh discipline, the Wehrmacht experienced a disturbing increase in offences such as insubordination, plunder, and rape in 1940–41, between the Fall of France and the attack on Russia. In the 12th Infantry Division, for instance, engaged in the occupation of France and the Netherlands, courts-martial increased from an average of eighteen per month in January to September 1940 to forty-five per month in the first quarter of 1941. The divisional commander blamed this on "the long rest period in a rich land." Numerous German soldiers established liaisons with French women. By the middle of 1943 eighty thousand French women had claimed children's benefits from the German military authorities and had requested German nationality for their offspring. The pattern was repeated in occupied Russia, despite greater efforts by the Wehrmacht. Propaganda stigmatized the enemy as *Untermenschen* and there were harsh penalties for consorting with Russian women on the grounds that they were suspected spies, but the prevalence of VD and the repetition of warnings against fraternization imply that sexual contact occurred on a large scale.[14]

Although unsuccessful, these efforts to insulate the occupiers from the occupied are themselves significant. They represent an extreme version of the military response to the virus of civilian values, namely to isolate the soldier as much as possible. The management of the German Army in Russia was, of course, particularly brutal. There the "Ostheer was . . . held together by a combination of harsh combat discipline and a general license to barbarism toward the enemy." But even in occupied France, where the racism and barbarity of the Eastern Front did not apply, the same isolationist propensity was evident. Studying German Army policy towards French civilians in the northeastern *départements* of Nord and Pas de Calais, Etienne Dejonghe found "a veritable barricade of prohibitions separating the two communities," a "*cordon sanitaire* which the regulations strove to build in order to prevent all contamination of the troops by their surroundings." In Lille, for instance, where British troops had fraternized all too freely with the locals in 1939–40, the Germans established a network of institutions intended to keep the soldier pure from the taint of civilian culture. The *Soldatenheim* was to act as his recreational focus, the *Soldatenkinos* likewise as alternatives to the local cinemas, while the *Frontbuchhandlung* served as bookshop, library, and German cultural centre. These institutions were replicated around northern France, one *Soldatenheim* in principle to every town that garrisoned a battalion of German troops.[15] As we have seen, the German *cordon sanitaire* was not ultimately successful, but this example of the isolationist approach will serve as a useful benchmark when studying the practices of the American Army.

Short of attempted quarantine, most armies have adopted a dual approach to the general problem of keeping the occupiers occupied, utilizing both the carrot and the stick. With time on the soldier's hands, the privations of army life can become obsessive. The provision of hot meals and drinks (tea for the British, coffee for the Americans) was a fundamental duty of all officers. Sports have always been valued, to keep men out of mischief and to enhance physical fitness. Even more important for the soldier was his mail. "Out here news of home is like food and drink to us, however trivial," wrote Private Noakes of the BEF from the Western Front in World War One. The mail call could make or ruin a day. The absence of letters was demoralizing; yet even a good letter was scrutinized for what it said and did not say. With time on his hands, the soldier was prey to anxiety about his family and even suspicion about the fidelity of wife or girlfriend. The GI's gnawing fear was a "Dear John" letter, telling him it was all over; German soldiers in Russia in 1942 talked sardonically about children being created apparently by remote control back home.[16]

It was therefore important, while attending to basic welfare needs, not to give the soldier too much time to complain and brood. All armies of occupation have stressed firm discipline to keep the crowd tendency in check. Training and marches were staples but perhaps the main weapon was drill. A Northern private recorded camp life during the American Civil War: "The first thing in the morning is drill, then drill, then drill again. Then drill, drill, a little more drill. Then drill, and lastly drill." This was the experience of most armies when not in combat. Among the BEF in Flanders in 1914–18 the promise of "Divisional Rest" usually evoked "a huge and sardonic guffaw." One troop newspaper glossed it as "a short term used to express endless parades, ceaseless polishings, burnishings, and 'inspections.' " The aim was always the same—behind the lines drill had to replace danger in keeping men under control. As William W. Belknap, a Civil War general from Iowa, noted: "Discipline is the basis of armies. Without it, they are but organized mobs."[17]

Striking the right balance between welfare and discipline was vital when managing an army of occupation. By itself the provision of amenities and creature comforts was not enough; indeed it could be counterproductive. Take the case of the Japanese Army in World War Two. Its tail-to-teeth ratio was minuscule compared with the Americans, possibly even on a one-to-one basis in some theatres, whereas the American ratio in the Pacific went as high as eighteen to one. Traveling light with his own rice, so that there was no need to wait for hot meals to be brought up, the Japanese infantryman was self-contained except for ammunition. When taking prisoners, the Japanese were often incredulous at the luxuries of even the GI's basic K ration, which included toilet paper, soap, and the ubiquitous chewing gum. Lt. Hiroo Onoda was one of the last Japanese to surrender in the Philippines in 1945, surviving on leaves, roots, and bark. On one leaf he found a wad of gum: "Here we were holding on for dear life, and these characters were chewing gum while they fought!" The success of the Japanese taught perceptive opponents, such as the British general, Sir William Slim, that hardship itself was not necessarily demoralizing. He found that "the highest levels of morale are often met when material conditions are lowest." This was also the view of Field Marshal Montgomery, who argued that boredom and the inequity of hardships were the real dangers. His experience was that "men dumped in some out-of-the-way spot in the desert will complain less of boredom, because they have to shift for themselves, than those surrounded by a wide choice of amenities." Montgomery claimed that men would endure considerable discomfort, providing they felt that their superiors were "living in relatively much the same way."[18]

Yet both Monty and Slim acknowledged that a basic level of creature comforts had to be provided. The former believed that for the British soldier the essentials were "mail from home, the newspapers" and "plenty of tea." And even the Japanese Army did not endure hardship indefinitely. Its initial successes in 1941–42 were due to Allied weakness and complacency and to the ferocious discipline imposed on its troops. That discipline was often internalized as part of a culture of submission and honour. Yet, as the Pacific war progressed, discipline had to be maintained by increasingly brutal punishment, as with Hitler's *Ostheer* in Russia, and even that sometimes proved unavailing. For all the notorious displays of suicidal Japanese resistance, there were also many instances where hunger, disease, and the futility of the war eroded morale and resolution—the calculations of a rational civilian gnawing away at the obedience of a loyal soldier. The last stages of the Imperial Army's fanatical defence of Okinawa in the spring of 1945 were characterized by growing drunkenness, womanizing, insubordination, and even surrenders. As Leonard V. Smith has suggested, after studying the French soldier in World War One, in the last analysis, the "willingness to follow orders cannot be coerced." Military authority, "rather than a one-directional exercise in coercive power, is a tacitly negotiated settlement between the command structure and the soldiers."[19] Clearly, there is a balance to be struck in any army between the stick and the carrot, between discipline and welfare—neither by itself is sufficient in the long run.

What stands out from this discussion is the fundamental tension between the duties of a soldier and the rights of a citizen. Loyalty to the group and obedience to one's officer are the hallmarks of military life, regarded by most armies as essential to contain the crowd and to impel their men into battle. Inculcating these values has traditionally involved some physical and psychological brutality. This was relatively easy in a hierarchical society where the soldiery were recruited from the bottom of society, what Wellington called "the scum of the earth." One British officer, writing during the Crimean War of the 1850s, insisted:

> You must not look upon the soldier as a responsible agent, for he is not able to take care of himself, he must be fed, clothed, looked after like a child and given only just enough to make him efficient as part of the great machine for War. Give him one farthing more than he really wants, and he gives way to his brutal propensities and immediately gets drunk.

Such treatment became less easy with modern mass armies, comprising much of the male population, especially as education, the media, and industrial employment eroded customary habits of deference. (In 1914 one-seventh of Britain's employed population had been servants, one-quarter farm labourers.) The ethos of their society had a profound effect on how conscripts responded to army life, and here the old distinction of "totalitarian" and "liberal" states, for all its crudity, has a broad utility.[20]

Where the prevailing ideology successfully subordinated the individual to the state, military exigencies were easier to impose. That was evident in Nazi Germany, Imperial Japan, or Stalinist Russia, where all three armies were held together, ultimately, by severe discipline, enforced or internalized. By contrast, societies in which the rights of the individual have been elevated as the central political principle found it harder to raise and maintain an army. Of course, the concept of citizenship, ever since classical times, has entailed not only rights but also duties, including that of military service. Nevertheless, in modern liberal democracies, citizenship has been understood more as a bundle of rights than as a set of obligations. This individualist gloss has been the trend in liberal countries, notably the United States and Great Britain (including its former dominions, such as Canada).

In armies of occupation it is particularly difficult to prevent soldiers from reverting to civilians, because that is the nature of the surrounding society. Soldiers are being imposed on civilians, often quite directly as when they are billeted on a household. Even indirectly the military presence will be apparent in local streets and hostelries, and the unoccupied soldier's propensity for female company has to be satisfied in some way. How far an army can be isolated from the virus of local civilians, as many commanders would instinctively prefer, depends on several factors. One is logistical—if troops can be housed and fed in their own camps, regular contact with locals is much reduced. Ideology also matters. If the locals are enemies, quarantining is easier to enforce. The Germans were most successful in Russia where the enemy was stigmatized as a subhuman race. Where the locals are allies, however, as in British-occupied France in 1939–40, it is much harder to maintain credible barriers against "fraternization." Soldiers and civilians are all on the same side and the two cultures, foreign army and local civilian, are more porous.

Yet given the crowdlike propensity of unoccupied soldiers, the consequences of unruly fraternization are particularly problematic on friendly soil. Historically, most premodern armies catered to the welfare needs of their soldiers through plunder. That, for instance, was the "military cement" of Napoleon's army from the sack of Rome in 1798 to the looting of Moscow in 1812.[21] In the modern era, armies have been logistically more self-sufficient, but depredations on civilian property (and persons, particularly in the form of rape) have usually been tolerated on enemy territory. This was infamously true on the Eastern Front in World War Two, but Anglo-American troops in Germany in 1945 were not above reproach. However, a bored army of occupation on *allied* soil cannot be permitted the same degree of misbehaviour. As the BEF recognized in France, lapses of conduct are diplomatically embarrassing and fuel enemy propaganda. Thus, on allied soil, the soldier is more open to the civilian virus yet the consequences of infection are more serious. The military's preference for isolationism is both more pressing and less plausible.

At the heart of all armies of occupation is therefore a *dual* tension between soldier and civilian. Each member of an army experiences to some degree the schizophrenic pulls of military duty and civilian rights, particularly where the absence of combat allows him time to brood on his condition. Each member of an occupying army is also a soldier in contact to some degree with civilians, and that contact is likely to accentuate the civilian tendencies within him. All armies have wrestled with these problems, but for the United States in World War Two the dilemma was particularly acute.

6

Citizen Soldiers

★　★　★

IN 1944 THE PLAYWRIGHT ARTHUR MILLER WAS COMMISSIONED AS SCRIPT-writer for a movie about the real life of "GI Joe." Traveling around army camps Miller became aware that "the American soldier is a much more complicated character than he is ever given credit for being. He cannot be written into a script as though he were a civilian wearing a brown suit with metal buttons, nor can he be regarded as a 'soldier,' a being whose reactions are totally divorced from civilian emotions." In similar vein, historian Lee Kennett has observed that the GI was "suspended between two ways of life. . . . Physically he left civilian life, yet mentally he never joined the Army; he was in the service but not of it."[1] Understanding the dual identity of these citizen soldiers is essential if we want to make sense of their conduct in wartime Britain.

The fundamental point about the GIs is that most were conscripts. Ten million of the 16.3 million Americans who served in the armed forces during World War Two had been drafted—the bulk of the draftees going to the Army, since the Navy and Marines relied on voluntary recruitment until December 1942. Yet the draft was politically contentious. It had been used, reluctantly, by both sides in the Civil War. In the North the Enrollment Act of March 1863 had created a powerful federal conscription agency, with provost marshals running the draft in each congressional district and enjoying the power to conduct door-to-door registration. In a country where the federal presence was limited to the occasional postman or customs clerk, this seemed outrageous, and the New York draft riots of July 1863 were only the most notorious of a spate of disturbances across the Northeast that summer. Overall, 79 percent of Confederates and 92 percent of the Union forces were volunteers. World War One was the first occasion when the draft was used as the main means of raising military manpower. Mindful of the lessons of 1863, however, the Army left selection to local boards and enforcement to the Justice Department. This proved much more successful and 72 percent of the doughboys of 1917–18 were draftees. But efforts by Army supporters to develop this into a European-style system of peacetime Universal Military Training proved unsuccessful. In July 1939, when George Marshall became Army Chief of Staff, the Army had 174,000 enlisted men, supplemented by 200,000 in the National Guard—both of whom were operating at roughly half-strength with equipment dating back to World War One. Even in the spring of 1940 both Roosevelt and Marshall believed that a peacetime draft was politically unwise and it was only after intense lobbying by its advocates that a bill received presidential backing and was passed into law on 16 September 1940.[2]

Thus, America, like Britain in the spring of 1939, had broken with historical precedent and adopted peacetime conscription. For each country, such a practice offended against liberal traditions of individualism and antimilitarism. Yet the British system made greater inroads into civilian rights—a reflection both of a more centralized government and of a graver national crisis. The British government developed "National Service," involving the obligation of all adults between the ages of eighteen and sixty to some form of war work, civilian or military. This was a far more comprehensive manpower policy than the American system of "Selective Service" in the military (the difference in terminology is itself significant). Around 55 percent of the British labour force was mobilized for the armed forces or war work, compared with 40 percent in the United States. The sensitivity of the Roosevelt administration and Congress to civilian norms is strikingly seen in its attitude to drafting fathers. Married men with dependent children were given protected status over single men, whatever their skills. Only one in every eight men drafted during the war was a parent at time of induction and 60 percent of all deferments were given to fathers. This was indicative of "the belief by Congress and the public that fathers were more valuable to society than single men, no matter what jobs they held."[3]

The sharpest contrast between British and American conscription was in its management. In 1939 the British government established the Ministry of Labour and National Service to coordinate and utilize all the country's human resources. But the American system of selective military service operated in a deliberately decentralized manner—as usual, carefully balancing federal and local powers. Registering and receiving a draft number was an obligation under federal law for all within the designated age range (eighteen to sixty-five after November 1942). The sequence of numbers for call-up was determined by a national lottery and the size of each total draft (and exemptions from it) by Acts of Congress. But the actual selection of persons for induction into the armed forces was in the hands of some sixty-four hundred boards of local worthies—predominantly white males, and usually businessmen and lawyers. They decided who fitted the criteria for physical or mental fitness and for deferment on specified grounds (fatherhood, civilian work, and so on). Thus, the draft was a system that balanced national obligation and local implementation: Washington set the policy, the localities chose the people. A man's fate was in the hands of his neighbours. Selective Service Director Lewis B. Hershey called it "the very essence of democracy."[4]

This procedure reflected what historian John W. Chambers has termed the "dual and quite ambiguous" nature of citizenship in the American political tradition. In most modern democracies, since Revolutionary France, "military service emerged as a hallmark of citizenship and citizenship as the hallmark of a political democracy."[5] However, the great charters of the new American nation, the Constitution and the Bill of Rights, left vague the citizens' military obligations to the *nation*, whereas Americans' local obligations via militia service were clear, at least on paper. Article II of the Bill of Rights, holy writ for those now opposed to gun control, should be understood in this way—communal obligations justify individual rights. In full, it runs: "A well regulated Militia, being necessary to the security of a free State, the right of the people to keep and bear Arms, shall not be infringed." An obligation to *national* military service was only enforced effectively for the first time in 1917–18, and 1940–45 was its first test as a durable policy. Meanwhile, the military obligations of local citizenship subsisted in the form of National Guard regiments, successor to the old militias. These units were mobilized in 1940–41 and were particularly useful in 1942, constituting eight of the fourteen divisions that the United States sent overseas that year. Even though "diluted" with draftees, they retained a distinctive regional identity. Two Guard divisions figure in our story: the 34th, from the Plains states, in Northern Ireland in 1942; and the 29th, from Maryland and Virginia, which waited twenty months in southern England for D-Day.[6]

In 1941 General Marshall was therefore trying to fuse three different elements into a new Army—the old regular cadres, the draftees, and the National Guardsmen. Among enlisted men there was particular friction between regulars and draftees. It was a familiar complaint that the old Army was full of social misfits. Ray Wax, later a real estate broker in the New York suburbs, recalled that, when drafted in 1940, "I looked upon the regular army as Cossacks. It was made up of people many of whom joined to avoid a small conviction. The judge would say, Do you want six months or a tour of the army?" Although this was something of a canard, many regulars had joined up to escape the Depression and some became hard-drinking womanisers. Certainly there were pronounced sociological differences between them and the newcomers. Forty-one percent of draftees in the Army at the end of 1941 were high-school graduates or had been to college, compared with 25 percent of the "old regulars" who had enlisted before July 1940.[7] Exacerbating the friction between the two groups was the fact that, as the Army expanded in 1940–41, many of the old soldiers were promoted to noncommissioned officers. The poorer quality among them, intimidated by educated draftees, got their own back by tough training and sadistic drills. Even the more capable, proud of their service, found the complaints of the "number men" hard to stomach and often played the martinet.

The most serious problems of integration lay at the officer level. Here the demands of quantity and quality conflicted. With only twenty thousand regular officers in 1940, the Army suddenly had to train and administer a force of millions. Guard, regular, and reserve officers were all utilized to the utmost in this pell-mell expansion. In fact, by late 1943, when the officer corps had increased thirty-fold on 1940, scarcity had turned into surplus. Despite the institution of Officer Candidate Schools (OCS) an able enlisted man had little chance of obtaining a commission in 1944–45, years when the U.S. Army gained most of its combat experience. Indeed, the great need after 1941 was to clear out the incompetent officers. Marshall was accused by National Guardsmen of discrimination against them, and it is true that, of the thirty-four general officers who commanded U.S. Army corps in battle in World War Two, twenty-three were West Point graduates.[8] But, at the time of Pearl Harbor, the Guard's officers were often overage, unfit, and untrained for modern warfare—veterans of 1918 or the politically well connected. In June 1941 nearly a quarter of 1st lieutenants ordered to active duty in the National Guard were over forty. Moreover, Marshall could deal just as harshly with his fellow regular officers, among whom was a marked "hump" of 1918 vintage. Aided by his "plucking board" of retired officers and his fabled "black book" of personal jottings, Marshall purged the Army ruthlessly, moving out the old and lethargic, pushing forward the young and capable. High on his promotion list were Eisenhower, Bradley, Patton, Hodges, and Collins—all of whom would see service in Britain.

To "dig out the leaders" seemed an unending task. "I see few if any evidences of reaching down for younger men unless I press the issue personally," Marshall complained in October 1942. Battle was the great test—wholesale purges at and above the divisional level followed the early weeks of combat in both North Africa and France. It was much harder to weed out the less able when troops were inactive, as in Britain in 1942–44. And it was always especially difficult to improve the quality of the field officers and "junior leaders"—the company, platoon, and squad commanders upon whose qualities the morale and effectiveness of the enlisted men largely depended. Postwar studies repeatedly castigated the failings of American officers and non-coms, especially compared with the German Army where officer initiative was prized and the noncommissioned officers were a distinctive class of tough professionals. It was claimed that U.S. officers were "taught how to *command,* not necessarily how to *lead.*"[9] While there were countless exceptions to these generalizations, and the U.S. Army's learning curve in battle was steep, officer deficiencies were often at the root of morale and conduct problems, particularly when units were not in combat.

The officer problem went even deeper, however. To quote historian Richard H. Kohn, the U.S. Army was "a centralized, stratified, cohesive, authoritarian institution" that bore little relationship to "a decentralized, heterogeneous, individualistic, democratic, capitalist society."[10] Soldiering was a fundamentally un-American activity.

Basic training was a deliberate process of alienation from civilian life. After being inducted locally and given two weeks to settle his affairs, the soldier traveled by train to one of the vast reception centers, such as Fort Bragg in North Carolina. Here began his initiation into the uniformity of Army life: literally so. Civilian clothes were shipped home; in their place came regulation Army undershorts, undershirts, shirts, and trousers, often ill-fitting. The new soldier also had his first sight of standard Army barracks: scrubbed wooden floors, plain dark walls, curtainless windows, steel cots with green blankets, steel lockers, and embarrassingly communal washrooms. He was shown how to make his bed or pack his footlocker—"the Army Way: there is no other way." Already losing his privacy and individuality, he then moved on to another camp for seventeen weeks of basic training. Here the main aim was to inculcate Army discipline through repeated drill and lessons in "military courtesy." Then the new soldier moved from individual to unit training, in combat, service, or air arms, with particular attention to use of weapons and physical fitness (in other words, marches, marches, and more marches). Finally came his unit's weeks of exercises and manoeuvres with other arms—completing a training schedule that took fifty-two weeks in all. But throughout, discipline and conformity were stressed. Six days a week, from reveille around 6:00 A.M. in most camps, through training from 8:00 in the morning to 5:30 P.M., right through to the officially regulated "free time" before lights out at 9:45 P.M.—the soldier's time belonged to Uncle Sam. When to eat, when to wash, when to sleep—everything was prescribed. Like his clothing and provisions, a man was simply "Government Issue"—GI.[11]

For some, this new existence was not, in fact, too traumatic. On the contrary, in a country where one in three homes in 1940 did not have running water, many GIs found it materially a definite improvement. Those used to hard manual labour also found the regime acceptable. "I like the Army fine so far," one Texan farm boy wrote home from his reception center. "They let you sleep till 5:30." And a steady job, with accommodation, food, and pay provided, was a novelty for many children of the Depression. Years later Paul Edwards could still visualize one big black soldier at Fort Riley, Kansas, soon after Pearl Harbor leaning up against a wall on payday. He kept dropping his silver dollars one by one into his pocket. "Man, I'm well off," he would say. "Hear that money clinkin' in my pocket?" In general, not surprisingly, the well adjusted managed best. Gregarious, healthy, athletic young men from stable homes had the highest chance of coping. Older married men were particularly inclined to moan about the Army, usually because they had more to lose (families, careers, and so on).[12]

But young or old, stable or unbalanced, the regimentation of Army life irritated all these citizen soldiers at times. The War Department received an early warning in the summer of 1941, when protests over the extension of the draft produced a spate of press reports of indiscipline and poor morale in the Army. As *Life* magazine admitted, the root problem was that the Army "does not know whether it is going to fight, or when or where." This uncertainty was largely dispelled by Pearl Harbor. But an unpublished analysis in September 1941 by *New York Times* reporter Hilton H. Railey, himself an officer in World War One, pinpointed a deeper problem: "Command, vintage of 1917 (pretty general), appears naively and disconcertingly unaware that its men, vintage of 1940, are *a different breed of cat. . . .* The present breed (mark well) is questioning everything from God Almighty to themselves."

The most obvious reason for this scepticism was greater education. Only 9 percent of enlisted men in 1917–18 had graduated from high school, whereas the proportion among 1941 draftees was 41 percent. Marshall's Army could be trained in more complex tasks than Pershing's, but it was also more critical of what it was doing. As important as education itself was the impact of the media. Railey found that 95 percent of the men he met knew of the *Life* article that had started the morale furore (and 90 percent judged it an understatement). Even more potent, and less thoroughly studied, were the movies. In a cinema-going generation, newsreels expanded horizons about current affairs while feature films often caricatured those in authority. Their effect as solvents of deference has still to be gauged, but it was surely as substantial as it was insidious.[13]

These questioning citizen soldiers griped above all about two things—privilege and conformity. Surveys showed repeatedly that the deprivations and physical discomforts of Army life were not, by themselves, potent grievances. They only became so when linked with the privileges of military rank. These marks of rank grated again and again—particularly the Army's insistence on saluting. In vain, official apologists maintained that saluting was not "a humiliation" but a status symbol, setting soldiers apart from civilians. For most GIs it was at best an embarrassing anachronism, at worst an infuriating imposition, especially when enforced off base by aggressive military policemen. Even more offensive were the privileges of rank, such as better accommodations, immediate access to the PX, and the separate, well-provisioned officers' club. In the words of one GI: "All we ask is to be treated like Americans once again. No 'out of bounds,' no different mess rations, and no treating us like children." This idea of the Army caste system being un-American was fundamental. As the progressive publicist Herbert Croly had observed in his classic *The Promise of American Life*, "there is no room for permanent legal privileges in a democratic state." Critics often noted that the officer corps was a European import, with U.S. Army regulations derived from those of the French royal army under the ancien régime.[14]

As disheartening for many was the relentless pressure to conform. There was the anonymous uniform, the impersonal serial number, the incessant marching, the endless "fatigues" (cleaning details), and, perhaps most distasteful, the notorious "kitchen police" (KP). As historian Ross Gregory has observed, it was hard to see how cleaning tables or washing dishes bore any relation to "learning to be a warrior," but, in the Army, anything that might otherwise "seem purposeless and boring fell into the category of discipline." Obedience, of course, was

the age-old, worldwide military instrument for turning men into soldiers. As such it seems unnatural in some measure to soldiers of all
nationalities. Yet Americans found it particularly repugnant. The
point came home to Marine Eugene B. Sledge as he watched his
comrades slaughtered day after day on the Pacific island of Peleliu. As
he sat in a swampy foxhole waiting for the next bout of fighting,
"slowly the reality of it all formed in my mind: we were expendable!
It was difficult to accept. We come from a nation and a culture that
values life and the individual."[15]

The challenge to individualism also took another form. Gradually,
corrosively, Army life could eat away at the civilian standards of
personal responsibility. Two sociologists noted in 1946:

> Over any period of time the dull, do-nothing routine stimulated
> escape reactions which, in decreasing order of frequency, were mov-
> ies, gambling, liquor, and brothels. The complete exhaustion of the
> monthly paycheck within a few days was comparatively common.
> A soldier could squander his cash with equanimity, knowing that
> next month would see him "flush" again; while, in the meantime,
> there was always the assurance of food and shelter.

War correspondent Ernie Pyle, home from Italy in 1944, shrewdly
noted another facet of the same phenomenon. "A soldier loses his
sense of property. Nothing is sacred to him. In civilian life you'd call
it stealing, but over there it's the way they do."[16]

It was at this point that the GI's anomie, as neither soldier nor
citizen, was most pronounced. His reaction to the regimentation, routine, and dehumanization of Army life pushed him off base to the local
fleshpots to assert his individuality. Yet his sense of personal responsibility, central to civilian values, had been eroded by the dependency
culture of Army life. The goal, gained or desired, of his self-assertion
and irresponsibility was often women. Drunken rowdiness and sexual
promiscuity became a problem around virtually every Army camp in
the United States. Some places were notorious as "good-time towns,"
such as Phenix City, Alabama, just across the state line from the vast
infantry camp at Fort Benning, Georgia. But an OWI report in December 1942 told much the same story about the environs of Fort Bragg,
North Carolina; Camp Shelby, near Hattiesburg, Mississippi; and Camp
Atterbury not far from Indianapolis:

> In the smaller communities, soldiers and vice are considered synony-
> mous. Prostitution has burgeoned while attempts to control vene-

real disease have contributed to the schism between the enlisted men and townsfolk. . . . All of the communities studied, with the exception of Indianapolis, blamed the soldiers for an alarming increase in drinking and drunkenness.[17]

"Oversexed and overpaid" GIs were not merely a problem in wartime Britain.

Creating the new Army was therefore a formidable task for General Marshall. The fusion of regulars, draftees, and National Guardsmen, the expansion and refinement of the officer corps, the exigencies of mass training, the conventional problems of indiscipline, and the more novel phenomenon of a critical soldiery—each was a nightmare in itself. But Marshall was equal to the challenge. His greatest strengths lay in management and training rather than as a strategist. The U.S. Army of World War Two was, above all, his creation and Winston Churchill rightly dubbed him in 1945 "the true organizer of victory."[18]

In 1939–42 Marshall oversaw a series of basic reforms that transformed the Army. Their keynote was streamlined, functional efficiency. In March 1942 he swept away the old structure of bureaucratic fiefdoms within the Army, including seven separate combat arms such as cavalry and coast artillery. The reorganization was executed with deliberate secrecy and speed to minimize opposition by what became known as Marshall's "Soviet Committee." The new structure was tripartite: Army Ground Forces (AGF) commanded by General Lesley J. McNair, mastermind of the new system of training; Army Air Forces (AAF) under General Henry H. ("Hap") Arnold, whose enhanced status was intended to quiet calls for an independent air force; and what became known as the Army Service Forces (ASF) under the empire-building ex-engineer General Brehon B. Somervell. During 1942 the War Department also moved into a purpose-built home across the Potomac near Arlington National Cemetery. This replaced over twenty separate buildings in and around the District of Columbia. The new five-sided building was billed as the largest in the world—one mile in circumference with space for forty thousand staff. Jokes about the Pentagon's maze of corridors were legion. One woman supposedly told a guard that she was in labour and needed to get to hospital. "Madam," he said sternly, "you should not have come in here in that condition." "When I came in here," she answered, "I wasn't."[19]

Under Marshall and McNair the Army's methods were a mixture of the new and the old. The system of basic training impressed British officers as characteristically American, producing "remarkably good results by mass production methods." One senior observer, Field Marshal Sir John Dill, commented that each man "goes through a most extensive course 'passing down the production line' from one specialist instructor to another and finally coming out of the 'shop' very fit and well grounded." On the other hand, Marshall had the professional soldier's faith in old-fashioned discipline, repeatedly inveighing against sloppy dress, failure to salute, and other breaches of military courtesy. He told one disgruntled private in 1943 that "the process of developing the soldierly instinct requires marching up and down and duty as K.P., etc. One of the greatest difficulties we have, and it is very apparent in Africa, is the difficulty of getting the proper disciplinary response, particularly in grave emergencies, from scattered detachments of men employed in a multitude of duties other than direct combat."[20]

Marshall wanted to create citizen soldiers. He remained acutely aware that "in this army of democracy," as he put it, "you had to feel that all of your soldiers were readers of *Time* magazine." Moreover, GIs and their families also wrote back to *Time* magazine, as well as lobbying their congressmen, whatever the Articles of War might say to the contrary. Casualties in training, for instance, always elicited a flood of mail, and McNair's radio broadcast in November 1942, when he told GIs that "it is the avowed purpose of the Army to make killers of all of you," provoked an outcry. Army living conditions were a regular grievance. In November 1940 a GI sent Marshall a complaint about bad food, enclosing as evidence a particularly tough steak. Marshall forwarded the letter to the man's commanding officer "as a possible hint toward a poorly run mess" (though, he added, the steak "had reached a point where it had to be disposed of"). The Army even established its own polling organization in October 1941 to ascertain soldiers' opinions. Although this took time to get going—anonymous comment was widely deemed to undermine discipline—by 1944 a monthly digest entitled *What the Soldier Thinks* was being distributed throughout the Army right down to company level.[21]

Most of the Army's major policy decisions were, in consequence, highly political. Marshall never forgot the lesson of August 1941, when the bill to extend the draft passed the House by only one vote. In 1942–44 he haggled with Congress for months over enlarging the Army, reducing the draft age, drafting fathers, and using eighteen-year-olds in combat. Army pay was almost entirely a function of domestic politics. Congress had cut base rates from $30 a month to $21 in 1922, and it remained at that level, despite Army lobbying, until the draft in 1940. Once citizens were again becoming soldiers, however, Congress felt that something closer to civilian standards of remuneration should obtain. Basic pay for a "buck" private reverted in 1940 to the World War One level of $30 and was raised to $50 in June 1942. Politics and public opinion, then, were facts of life for Marshall. He might fume privately about "the squeakings of democracy," but, like it or not—and (in principle) he did—this was the nature of American politics.[22]

Marshall believed that the way to placate citizen soldiers and their politicians was by the best possible material conditions. He regarded troop welfare as an essential part of modern warfare. Lavish provision of gum and cigarettes or the well-stocked PX on each base was an expression of this approach. Mothers of America were assured that the Army knew "this generation of boys had been brought up on milk as a definite item of diet" and that "ample provision has been made for fresh milk for every man at every meal while in camp." As for the GI's leisure, each regiment had its own "recreation" officer by the end of 1942, one of whom explained: "Our job is . . . to make 'em happy." Critics, such as journalist Hilton Railey in 1941, complained that the Army equated morale with "entertainment and amusement"; a private even remarked that "the Army thinks morale is a leg show."[23] Over time more emphasis was placed on motivation, with Marshall sponsoring the Frank Capra movie series *Why We Fight.* But morale as welfare remained a pronounced tendency in the U.S. Army, if only because most of the complaints from GIs and congressmen were about material conditions. In short, the GI's overpaid, overfed image in Britain reflected this sensitivity to political opinion at home as much as being attributes of the American way of life.

In dealing with black soldiers, like whites, the Army took account of a soldier's status as citizen. But the result was very different. African-Americans of 1941, to quote one black GI, "were second class citizens from the word go, whether in the army or not."[24]

Blacks had served with considerable distinction in America's earlier wars. In 1865 almost 10 percent of the Union Army were negroes. But by 1900 growing discrimination in the country at large had become institutionalized in the military. In June 1940 blacks formed about one-tenth of the population but only 1.5 percent of the Army and 2.3 percent of the Navy. The Air Corps excluded blacks entirely and the Navy accepted them merely as mess attendants. The Army had only five black officers, three of them chaplains. The two combat officers came from the same family—Benjamin O. Davis, father and son.[25]

The War Department viewed blacks as a liability. Their performance in World War One was often cited, selectively, as evidence. A regimental commander from the black 92nd Division stated: "As fighting troops, the negro must be rated as second class material, this due primarily to his inferior intelligence and lack of mental and moral qualities." This stereotype was perpetuated in officer-school studies even though, as the 92nd's commander admitted, "the Division did some very aggressive work" in the last weeks of the war and many of its problems were attributable to poor officers because it "was made the dumping ground for discards, both white and black." The prevailing Army view was reinforced from 1941 by so-called intelligence tests that regularly classified roughly three-quarters of black troops (but only one-quarter of whites) in the bottom two categories out of five. In fact these Army General Classification Tests (AGCTs) measured educational achievement and socially acquired skills. Poor scores by blacks reflected the fact that most of them came from Southern states that were among the most impoverished and discriminatory in the country. Blacks and whites of comparable education generally scored equally. But these aspects of the AGCT tests were little known at the time. For most white officers the scores simply "proved" what they had always "known"—blacks were innately inferior and made bad soldiers.[26]

In all this the Army was mirroring the prevailing values of white society, particularly in the South—where roughly 30 percent of the interwar officer corps had been raised.[27] But the citizen-soldier linkage could operate in a more radical way. Historically, service in war had been an automatic avenue to U.S. citizenship for the foreign born. Those ready to die for their country were deemed worthy to vote in it. African-American leaders and journalists took note of this reciprocity between the rights and responsibilities of citizenship. In 1917–18 and again from 1940 they demanded greater black opportunities for military service. In World War Two they were supported by some leading New Dealers, notably Eleanor Roosevelt, whose advocacy of the black cause was regarded as a particular nuisance in the War Department. The president himself was more conservative than his wife, concerned about the attitude of Southern Democrats in Congress, but in 1940 he was anxious about the black vote in the imminent presidential election and made a number of concessions to black leaders. These included the promotion of Benjamin O. Davis, Sr., to become America's first black general, the appointment of Judge William H. Hastie as the War Department's special adviser on race relations, and a directive in October 1940 that enunciated what proved to be the Army's (official) racial policies for most of the war.

In this document the War Department committed itself to greater black opportunities for military service, promising that the percentage of blacks in the Army would correspond to their proportion in the population at large—roughly 10 percent. Although this target was not reached, by late 1942 about 7.4 percent of the Army was black, a marked increase since 1940. The War Department also pledged that blacks would serve "in each major branch of the service, combatant as well as noncombatant." This at last gave blacks access to the Air Corps, and the first black fighter squadron, the 99th, was established in January 1941. In practice, however, discrimination and poor AGCT scores ensured that black GIs were grossly overrepresented in service units—forming 25 percent of the Quartermaster Corps and 15 percent of the Engineer Corps, as against 5 percent of the Infantry and 2 percent of the Air Corps at the end of 1942. The "typical" black GI was likely to be engaged in construction, cooking, or laundry, in driving trucks or handling cargoes and freight. It was also Army policy to encourage black officers, but whereas black units could be led by either black or white officers, no blacks were to command white units. In fact, there were only 817 black officers, or 0.35 percent of total black Army strength, in August 1942, even though officers comprised 7 percent of the whole Army. Most black units were commanded by Southerners, who usually regarded such duty as a humiliation and who were often rejects from elsewhere.[28]

Above all, the directive of 16 October 1940 reaffirmed the basic principle of segregation. The Army would not "intermingle colored and white enlisted personnel in the same regimental organizations." This remained official policy throughout the war, breached only during the manpower crisis during the Battle of the Bulge. To counter charges of discrimination, the War Department took its stand on the "separate but equal" doctrine adumbrated in the Supreme Court's *Plessy v. Ferguson* decision of 1896: blacks were to enjoy the same quality of facilities, supplies, and quarters as whites. Yet this was hard to achieve in practice and was exceedingly wasteful of resources—leaving aside the fact that, as the Supreme Court belatedly admitted in 1954, segregation was inherently discriminatory when the benefits of social mixing were taken into account. But the business of the War Department, as it never tired of saying, was waging war not reforming society. As Marshall put it, a policy of integration "would be tantamount to solving a social problem which has perplexed the American people throughout the history of this nation. The Army cannot accomplish such a solution, and should not be charged with the undertaking." To do so, warned Marshall, would "complicate the tremendous task of the War Department and thereby jeopardize discipline and morale."[29]

Morale here meant the morale of white GIs and civilians. For the black was regarded not merely as a liability—a second-class soldier—but as an irrelevance. The War Department did not anticipate the manpower problems that developed later in the war, and it only accepted blacks in significant numbers because of political pressure. Its treatment of them within the service according to prevailing social norms was enormously inefficient in manpower terms.[30] The quota system often meant that black units were created where military need or personnel skills did not exist. The policy of segregated units resulted not merely in a costly duplication of facilities, but also in enormous personnel problems. For, although more whites than blacks, in absolute numbers, were ranked in the bottom category of the AGCTs, illiterate or semieducated white men could be dispersed through the Army and thereby absorbed manageably in individual units. But segregation meant that low-scoring blacks were all consigned to a small number of all-black units, which were therefore often extremely difficult to discipline, let alone train, especially under inferior officers. For the Army of 1941 "negro" spelled problem not potential. Second-class citizens were regarded as second-class soldiers.

In a variety of ways, therefore, Marshall's "democratic Army" reflected the values of contemporary America. Indeed, it even accentuated them, particularly in the case of pluralism. After President Roosevelt drew the opening number in the draft lottery of September 1940, it transpired that in New York City this number—158—was held by registrants bearing such names as Chon, Cody, Faruggia, Weisblum, Stazzone, and Lichtenstein. New York was New York—a law unto itself—but the human variety of America came as a revelation for most young men from rural backgrounds. Training camps were an ethnic and regional kaleidoscope, and even National Guard divisions contained at least 50 percent replacements from all over the country. The first time Robert Rasmus from Chicago heard a New England accent was at Fort Benning, Georgia. A marine from Mississippi was puzzled when troops from Chicago kept coming up to him to make conversation. Asked why, they said they loved his accent and had never heard anything quite like it before. In newspaper articles at the time, and in subsequent novels and movies, this variety was often highlighted and celebrated. The platoon on "Anopopei" in Norman Mailer's *The Naked and the Dead* included a Pole, a Mexican migrant, a Brooklyn Jew, a South Boston Irish, and a brutalized Texan sergeant. Yet at the time the initial result of this mixing-up process was often friction rather than fusion. Jewish-Americans, few of whom lived in rural areas, became butts of anti-Semitic "humour" in most units. For Leon Standifer, a WASP from rural Mississippi, Fort Benning was his introduction to jokes about blockhead Swedes and dumb rednecks, as well as to the fact that, for most GIs from north of the Mason-Dixon line, he was automatically a "cracker" and a racial bigot. Even where amicable relations were established, men were left with a sharper sense of their ethnic and regional distinctiveness.[31]

In particular, military service introduced men to the South and Southerners. Most of the new Army training camps were in the old Confederacy, where large tracts of land were available on the cheap and the climate made year-round activity possible, though not agreeable. If, as Morton Sosna has estimated, at least half those serving in the U.S. forces during the war spent time at a Southern base and only one-quarter of these were Southerners, then up to six million non-Southerners may have crossed the Mason-Dixon line for the first time during the war. In many units the Civil War was fought and refought, its passions doubtless rekindled by the movie *Gone With the Wind*, which premiered in December 1939. One marine from New York shared a tent on Parris Island, South Carolina, with some Southerners. "Back in the Bronx we just didn't look at people as either Rebels or Yanks," he recalled, "but those Southern boys sure did." Since half the noncoms in December 1941 were Southerners (reflecting their preponderance among the old regulars), sectional tension often exacerbated the frictions of basic training. Enlisted men would get their own back by singing "Marching through Georgia" as they tramped along.[32]

To some extent, black Americans shared in the North-South divide. Overall, one-third of the one million black GIs in World War Two were Northerners and they were usually better educated than their Southern counterparts. Only 37 percent had stopped their education in grade school, compared with 67 percent of Southern blacks. Inevitably, friction developed. Timuel Black, a high school graduate from Chicago, recalled that in his quartermaster unit:

> Generally they made illiterate blacks from the South the noncommissioned officers to be over us, who had more education. Most of us were from the North. Here you have a somewhat resentful southern black guy, glad to have a chance to kick this arrogant northern city slicker around.

Overall, however, the experience of Army life left most black GIs, particularly the better educated, with a keener sense of racial consciousness. In handling blacks, the Army way was the Southern way, which to Northerners was a rude shock. Discrimination above the Mason-Dixon line was real but insidious. Now that Northern blacks had put on Uncle Sam's uniform and come South, they were physically segregated on trains and buses, confined to all-black units doing menial tasks, barred from the main PXs and cinemas, and abused by white noncoms. Treated as "niggers," they reacted accordingly. Wartime polls of black GIs cast doubt on the stereotype "of the average Negro as a happy, dull, indifferent creature, who was quite contented with his place in the social system as a whole and in the military segment of that social system." Instead polls showed "a basic racial orientation highly sensitized to evidences of racial discrimination, both real and imagined."[33]

Thus, the Army mixed up young Americans as never before in their lives, but its immediate effect was to enhance rather than blur their sense of ethnic, sectional, and racial differences. Seeing America made them more aware of its variety; it was seeing the world that made them more conscious of being American.

How this happened for GIs in Britain is a theme of the book. At this point we should simply note some general points, indicating how Marshall's basic problems with citizen soldiers became more acute when the GIs went abroad.

The first is that the imperatives of welfare became both more significant and more difficult overseas; more significant, because of the GIs' sense of cultural alienation. Many of these young men had never left their home state before, and even fewer had been outside America. In these circumstances, noted two Army psychiatrists in 1943,

> Any symbol or representation of the culture that he has left assumes exaggerated value. A visitor from home, sports scores, moving pictures, American food or drinks are extra-ordinarily important for maintaining morale in expeditionary forces.

Yet to maintain supplies of mail, Coca-Cola, magazines, and the like used up scarce shipping space and required plenty of service personnel. Add that to the fact that America had the most high-tech army in the world, with a superabundance of matériel (even after drastic slimming in 1942 it took thirty-two thousand tons of shipping to transport the equipment of each infantry division) and one begins to see why the U.S. Army had such a high tail-to-teeth ratio—2.7 million ASF personnel against two million infantrymen at the end of 1943.[34]

The operational implications of this are well known. Every one of the Army's eighty-nine combat divisions was overseas by August 1945, and all but two had seen action. "Fortunately the crisis of late 1944 was the last unpleasant surprise," noted historian Maurice Matloff. "If another had come the divisional cupboard would have been bare."[35] But the teeth-tail ratio also had deleterious effects behind the lines in places like Britain. Morale in service units, engaged in routine manual labour without much obvious relation to the war, was always hard to sustain. The fact that many of those units were black, with all the concomitant deficiencies of education, training, and officers, made the morale problem among service troops even worse. And as those black GIs experienced another society where overt racial segregation was neither legal nor normal, the difficulty of maintaining Army (and American) race policy became intense.

All soldiers abroad are homesick, of course. One U.S. Army chaplain called it "the idealization of the absent"—home and family assume a rosy glow of perfection from a muddy foxhole or drafty tent on the other side of the world. But it was particularly significant among American troops because of their difficulty in stating any lofty war aims. According to Samuel Stouffer and his fellow pollsters, the average soldier did not have a clear set of ideals "beyond the recognition of the necessity of self-defense and of getting through with a disagreeable job in order to get back home as quickly as possible." While not exaggerating the ideological commitment of other armies, the U.S. Army faced a unique problem. Its citizens were never fighting to defend their homeland. This was not true for the French, Russians, and Britons, or for the Germans and Japanese later in the war. "Our great difficulty," Marshall recalled later, "was that the men were all far from their home . . . in places they had hardly ever heard of. There was none of that tremendous spirit that comes of defending your own home, your own wife and children." One attempted remedy was through the campaign medals and ribbons given to all on overseas service, after indefatigable lobbying by Marshall. In Britain, these became the subject of much derision—the idea that the Yanks deserved a medal just for crossing the Atlantic! But Marshall was convinced that "these little penny strips of ribbon will have tremendously beneficial effect on men in isolated garrisons . . . where the morale problem is extremely difficult." In the same way, he believed that high welfare standards were vital, not merely to deflect political criticism, but also as a spur to motivation. "I was for supplying [the GI with] everything we could and then requiring him to fight to the death when the time came. You had to put these two things together."[36]

In the U.S. Army, therefore, morale was always in danger of being equated with welfare. The American way of life not merely sustained the troops, it became their surrogate war aim. Home itself had become an ideal, a metaphor—as shown in journalist John Hersey's classic story about U.S. Marines on Guadalcanal in October 1942. "What are you fighting for?" he asked them. There was a long silence.

> Their faces became pale. Their eyes wandered. They looked like men bothered by a memory. They did not answer for what seemed a very long time. Then one of them spoke, but not to me. . . . He whispered: "Jesus, what I'd give for a piece of blueberry pie."[37]

Providing troops abroad with their "blueberry pie" became a prime object of Army policy. Even more than at home, welfare seemed vital to warfare. Yet even if material comforts could be provided, they were rarely enough to dispel the ennui of an army of occupation. There had to be a sense of purpose as well. In Britain, that was particularly hard to generate because combat was endlessly postponed.

7

Marking Time

★ ★ ★

IN WORLD WAR ONE BRITAIN HAD BEEN A REAR AREA OF AMERICAN MILI-
tary operations in France. Most troops passed through quickly en route
to the front. In World War Two, Nazi domination of the Continent
gave the British Isles much greater importance as the Allies' only
European strong point, from which they could bomb and eventually
invade Hitler's Fortress Europe. But that alone would not have
spawned such a large and lengthy American occupation. In August
1942 *The New Yorker* magazine's correspondent in London caricatured
GIs there as "somewhat doubtful of being able to give the town a quick
once-over before leaving to keep a date with von Rundstedt, which
they seem to imagine will be around Thursday week at the latest." In
fact, the date was not kept until nearly two years later, thanks to the
vexed Anglo-American arguments about the Second Front. The American occupation of Britain was one result of that long wait.[1]

Simply to say this, however, does not fully convey the complexities
and confusions of Allied strategy. After the war American and British
authors wrangled over what had happened, usually contrasting a
fixed U.S. determination to cross the Channel as soon as possible with
a more deliberate British strategy of squeezing Germany while striking
first at its Italian "soft underbelly." In fact, wartime strategy was far
less clear and consistent than hindsight suggests. For each government it was usually a piecemeal response to immediate problems
around the globe rather than the unfolding of some grand vision.[2]
Only if we remember that this was a world war fought by men whose
concerns were usually short-term crisis management (particularly in
1942) can we grasp the predicament of the GIs in Britain. We need to

follow the gyrations of the strategic debate, tracing their spinoffs for deployment and command in the United Kingdom. The 1942 code name for the American buildup, Bolero, was borrowed from composer Maurice Ravel to suggest a pulsating crescendo of men and supplies. That did happen in the last months before D-Day. But for most of 1942–43 the rhythm was erratic, the orchestra ever-changing, and no one seemed sure of the tune.

At the Arcadia conference in Washington in December 1941, Roosevelt and Churchill had not envisaged an immediate buildup of American ground troops in Britain. The president wished merely to take over defence of Northern Ireland and to send "a small number of American bombers" to England because of their morale effect on France and Germany.[3] In early 1942 even these limited deployments were thrown into confusion because of the deepening crisis in the Pacific. The loss of Singapore, Malaya, and the Philippines necessitated diversion of troops and supplies to the war against Japan. The four American divisions originally earmarked for Northern Ireland (Operation Magnet) were whittled down to two—the 34th Infantry and the 1st Armored. The first shipment of troops debarked in Belfast on 26 January, with three others following in the next four months, to bring the U.S. presence there to thirty-two thousand by late May. As for the air deployment, on 20 February General Ira C. Eaker and six officers arrived in London to establish a structure for the new Bomber Command. He arranged takeover from the British of eight airfields, currently under construction for the RAF, in the area around Huntingdon, some sixty miles north of London. But because of the Pacific crisis the first combat personnel did not arrive until 11 May. Both in Ulster and England, these first Americans were heavily dependent on the British for their equipment and supplies.[4]

Behind this low-key policy for sending GIs to Britain lay a strategy that was at this stage distinctively British—drafted by Churchill, endorsed by his advisers, and adopted by a Washington still in shock from Pearl Harbor. The final document of the Arcadia conference, entitled "American and British Strategy" and known in British shorthand as WWI, affirmed that, despite Pearl Harbor, "Germany is still the prime enemy and her defeat is the key to victory. Once Germany is defeated, the collapse of Italy and the defeat of Japan must follow." But, reflecting limited British resources, the document prescribed a cautious policy of "closing and tightening the ring around Germany," through sustaining the Russian front, intensifying the naval blockade, bombing Germany from the air, and promoting resistance in occupied

Europe. "It does not seem likely," WWI stated, "that in 1942 any large-scale land offensive against Germany except on the Russian front will be possible." But "in 1943 the way may be clear for a return to the Continent, across the Mediterranean, from Turkey into the Balkans, or by landings in Western Europe itself. Such operations must be the prelude to the final assault on Germany itself."[5]

This outline never enjoyed real support in the U.S. War or Navy Departments and over the next few weeks, as the trauma of the Japanese onslaught wore off, American planners came to grips with their predicament. In the War Department the bogey word was *dispersions*—the way that U.S. forces, instead of following the Pershing principle of concentration, were being packaged out around the world in desperate last stands as the Japanese drove across the Pacific and Rommel pushed towards Cairo. In early March Secretary of War Henry L. Stimson took the matter up directly with the president. He urged "offensive measures," above all "sending an overwhelming force to the British Isles and threatening an attack on the Germans in France." Left to Churchill, Stimson believed, strategy "would have degenerated into a simple defensive operation to stop up urgent rat holes, most of which I fear are hopeless."[6]

This 5 March confrontation at the White House was the genesis of General Marshall's mission to London a month later. He arrived with detailed outlines from his Operations Division, under Gen. Dwight D. Eisenhower, who believed ardently that "we've got to go to Europe and fight—and we've got to quit wasting resources all over the world—and still worse—wasting time." Marshall pressed his case on the British in what became known in London (ironically, in view of what happened five years later) as "the Marshall Plan." Insisting that "through France passes our shortest route to the heart of Germany," this projected the buildup of one million U.S. troops in Britain by April 1943 as part of a combined Anglo-American force of some forty-eight divisions. As soon as possible thereafter, six divisions would spearhead landings along the French coast from Le Havre to Boulogne—what became known as Operation Roundup. Plans would also be made for an "emergency" five-division invasion in the autumn of 1942, to be mounted either "if the imminence of Russian collapse requires desperate action" or, alternatively, if Germany was "almost completely absorbed on the Russian front" or evidently weakened. And even if this operation, eventually code-named Sledgehammer, were not mounted, "continuous raiding" of the French coast would divert the enemy and give the troops combat experience.[7]

A few days of discussion with the British brought ostensible agree-

ment on 14 April. Churchill announced that he "cordially" accepted
Marshall's plan and Foreign Secretary Anthony Eden waxed eloquent
about the "two English-speaking countries setting out for the redemp-
tion of Europe." The conception of the American presence in Britain
had now been totally transformed from defence to attack. Instead of a
couple of U.S. divisions training in Northern Ireland and a small
bomber command in East Anglia, there were to be thirty divisions and
some 3,250 combat planes in southern England by April 1943. Hastily
two special Anglo-American Bolero committees were set up to plan the
details of the buildup—details to which the strategists had hitherto
given "only the most hurried and superficial investigation."[8]

As soon as the committees began work it was clear that the thirty-
division programme was "hardly more than wishful thinking at this
time." By mid-May analysis of available shipping necessitated reduction to half that figure. Moreover, the options for 1942 and 1943 were
found to be at odds, when logistics were taken into account. According
to the official American history, "SLEDGEHAMMER's overriding need
was for a heavy flow of combat troops during the coming spring and
summer, while for ROUNDUP an even flow of cargo over the whole
period was essential to avoid congestion at the end of the program."
Troop requirements were also in conflict. An early invasion of the
Continent meant combat soldiers, and these were given maximum
priority in midsummer, with the 1st Infantry Division arriving in early
August. But the long-term Bolero project required vast numbers of
service troops (over a quarter of the total) to build bases, depots, and
airfields and to handle the munitions and equipment needed by the
combat troops. Yet another complication was the priority attached to
the bombing campaign against occupied Europe and to air support for
Sledgehammer. That meant not merely rushing trained bomber crews
to Britain but also aviation service troops. Taking all these backup
obligations into consideration nearly half the projected one million
men would be from the Services of Supply (SOS). Yet the War Department, in planning its manpower profile for the conflict, had seriously
underestimated the proportion of service troops required for modern
warfare—alloting only 11.8 percent of the 1942 troop basis to this
category.[9]

The result of these conflicting priorities—between Sledgehammer
and Roundup, between troops and cargo, between combat, air, and
service personnel—was enormous confusion in 1942. Troops arrived
in Britain without their equipment; accommodations and facilities
were hastily patched together; service personnel, few in number and
often poorly trained, were scattered around the country in improvised

efforts to address these conflicting needs. As we shall see, many of the problems experienced in Britain during the early months of the American "occupation" were the result of this chaotic influx.

Another consequence of the chaos in Washington after Pearl Harbor was that it took six months to establish a proper command structure in Britain. The senior U.S. officer there in 1941 was Gen. James E. Chaney, an airman who headed the Special Observer Group (SPOBS) in London from May 1941. SPOBS was a clandestine military mission, operating in a low-key way during the period of U.S. neutrality. When America entered the war SPOBS was suddenly forced to assume the role of an embryonic military headquarters, without jurisdiction over the service and air contingents that began to flood across the Atlantic. On 24 May Gen. J.C.H. Lee arrived with a nucleus staff to run the SOS in Britain. By the end of July he had established his headquarters near Cheltenham. On 18 June Gen. Carl Spaatz flew in as commander of the new 8th Air Force. Spaatz subsumed Eaker's 8th Bomber Command in the 8AF and set up his headquarters at Bushy Park in southwest London. To resolve the bureaucratic turf fights and prepare for an early invasion of the Continent, Marshall eventually created a new European Theater of Operations, U.S. Army (ETOUSA or ETO) on 8 June.* Both SOS and 8AF were under its jurisdiction. By then, however, Chaney had lost Marshall's confidence and he was relieved two weeks later.

Chaney, aged fifty-six, was condemned as reserved and lethargic. But bad luck also played a part in his demise—he was an old career rival of Gen. "Hap" Arnold, chief of the Army Air Forces, and was out of touch with the strategic debate in Washington in the spring of 1942. Ill-informed about the plans for bombing and invading the Continent, which were being pushed by Arnold and Marshall, Chaney still viewed Britain as an essentially defensive theatre, with few ground troops and an air contingent that would best operate in support of the British. This belief that American aviation should be placed under British direction, without a separate headquarters of its own, was the crux of his row with Arnold, for whom the creation of a separate American air command in Britain was central to his campaign for a truly independent U.S. Air Force. When Gen. Eaker, one of Arnold's main protégés, arrived in Britain in February 1942 to take command of American bomber units, the first thing he told one of the SPOBS staff

*Newsman Ernie Pyle noted that "in 1942 ETOUSA was always pronounced 'eetoosa.' " Returning to Britain in April 1944, after eighteen months away, he found that "the pronunciation had changed to 'eetowza.' " Some British officers referred to ETOUSA, disparagingly, as "*et tout ça.*"[10]

was: "I'll never take an order from a Britisher." Likewise, Spaatz was
determined that American forces "must not be permitted to lose their
identity through integration into the British command system," noting presciently that "ultimately the American Forces in the Western
European Theater may exceed in size the force of the British Government." Marshall's 8 June directive establishing ETO settled the argument against Chaney. Not only did it give the commanding general of
ETO "unity of command" over all American Army and Navy forces in
Europe and Iceland, it also set out clearly the limits of Allied interdependence. While "directed to cooperate with the forces of the British
Empire and other Allied nations" engaged in "military operations
against the Axis powers," the theatre commander was instructed that
"the underlying purpose must be kept in view that the forces of the
United States are to be maintained as a separate and distinct component of the combined forces." The Pershing principle from 1918 had
not been forgotten.[11]

Marshall's order creating ETO was drafted by his protégé, Dwight D.
Eisenhower. Within days Eisenhower was instructed to carry out his
own directive, assuming command of ETO on 24 June 1942, at age
fifty-one. In the previous six months his rise had been meteoric. Having missed action in 1917–18 he had spun out the interwar years, like
many of his West Point classmates, in frustration on Army posts in the
United States and the Philippines. But after Pearl Harbor he was
summoned to Washington where he was soon running the new Operations Division. Eisenhower pleased the Chief of Staff with his energy,
efficiency, and readiness to accept responsibility. In turn Marshall's
apparently Olympian self-control impressed Eisenhower, whose own
fiery temper was notorious. Their relationship became avuncular, almost paternal—like that of Marshall and Pershing before—although
the Chief of Staff never allowed himself to unbend too much. On one
occasion he used the universal nickname "Ike." "In the next two
sentences," Eisenhower recalled later, "I'll bet he said 'Eisenhower'
five times just to make sure that I understood it was just a slip of the
tongue."[12]

Marshall also reinforced lessons Eisenhower had learnt from his
1920s mentor, Gen. Fox Conner, about the need for unified command
and allied cooperation in wartime. But Ike made these precepts
uniquely his own. With his gregarious manner, ready smile, and
informal ways, he was better equipped than the reserved Marshall to
put them into practice. And his conception of Anglo-American relations was less nationalistic than that of Eaker and Spaatz. Although
Ike had found the British at the Arcadia conference "difficult to talk to"

and "stiff-necked," he told his staff soon after arrival in London: "Gentlemen, we have one chance and only one of winning this war and that is in complete and unqualified partnership with the British. . . . I shall govern myself accordingly and expect you to do likewise." On his own admission he became "a fanatic" on the subject, dealing ruthlessly with any infractions. When one offender was sent home for insulting a British officer, the latter interceded: "He only called me the son of a bitch, sir." Ike replied: "I am informed that he called you a *British* son of a bitch. That is quite different. My ruling stands."[13]

But Eisenhower was only in Britain for a few weeks before the whole basis of Allied strategy changed yet again. In April the British had gone along with the "Marshall Plan" mainly to prevent the Americans veering off towards the Pacific. Sledgehammer aroused nothing but alarm in the minds of the senior British military, and the Chief of the Imperial General Staff, Gen. Sir Alan Brooke, became convinced that his opposite number, Marshall, had "practically no strategic vision" and that "his thoughts revolve round the creation of forces and not on their employment."[14] As the logistical problems of Bolero became ever more alarming, British planners isolated the operational difficulties of a proposed attack on the heavily defended Pas de Calais, noting the lack of landing craft and the hazards of autumn weather and tides in the Channel. They successfully insisted that the operation could not be mounted after August 1942. This meant that little more than one U.S. division would be combat ready, that British units would comprise the bulk of the invasion force, and, thus, that London would have the moral right to veto the operation.

Roosevelt's own thinking about Sledgehammer was mainly dictated by the need to relieve the Russians. Intelligence reports throughout the summer depicted the struggle on the Eastern Front as teetering in the balance. The president hoped to draw the Luftwaffe away from the East by landing troops under cover of massive air support. He told Churchill that this would lead either to substantial destruction of German airpower, or, if the Luftwaffe "fails to come out," to increased ground operations "with the objective of establishing permanent positions." But, as the U.S. official history of wartime planning observed, "the chance of a strategic success was directly in proportion to the risk of tactical failure—the stronger the German reaction, the more probable the result that Allied troops would once again have to be evacuated in the face of superior German forces, as earlier from Norway, Dunkerque, and Greece."[15] And, one might add, the logistical tangle underlying Bolero meant that these "Allied troops" would, as in those earlier ill-fated operations, be largely British—a further debacle that Churchill could not contemplate politically.

By June Churchill, his Chiefs of Staff and his cabinet were agreed that "there should be no substantial landing in France unless we intended to remain" and that the condition for such a landing was a weakening of Germany on a scale currently unimaginable.[16] Churchill descended on Washington in mid-June to urge the merits of an alternative 1942 operation, then code-named Gymnast, which had been under intermittent consideration for months. This would be a combined invasion of French Northwest Africa, intended to relieve the pressure on the British in Egypt by threatening Rommel's rear and eventually evicting him from North Africa.

Gymnast had few supporters among the military on either side of the Atlantic. The Americans, horrified at existing "dispersions," had no desire to open yet another front; while the British Chiefs of Staff wanted direct U.S. help against Rommel in Egypt. Even Brooke felt it would be premature until the future of Russian resistance was clear. On 21 June the Combined Chiefs of Staff recommended that "Gymnast should not be undertaken under the existing situation" and that the buildup in Britain should continue, with Roundup as the priority. But, over their heads, Roosevelt and Churchill agreed to push on with contingency planning for Northwest Africa. As Stimson noted, it had always been "the President's great secret baby."[17]

Aghast at the drift of events, Marshall made a desperate tactical move. He threw his support behind the long-standing preference of Admiral Ernest King, the Chief of Naval Operations, for a Pacific First strategy. On 10 July they jointly advised the president:

> If the United States is to engage in any other operation than forceful, unswerving adherence to full Bolero plans, we are definitely of the opinion that we should turn to the Pacific and strike decisively against Japan; in other words, assume a defensive attitude against Germany, except for air operations; and use all available means in the Pacific.

King was serious; Marshall later claimed he was bluffing—though the records of the time leave some doubt. His dedication was more to the principle of concentration than to Germany First.[18] Either way, the president quickly ended the revolt by obliging the Joint Chiefs to admit that they had no detailed plans for a Pacific strategy. Marshall's last-ditch attempt, in another visit to London in mid-July, failed to divert Churchill. Without British support, Sledgehammer was impossible to mount. And, under those circumstances, Roosevelt's wishes were clear: Gymnast, in some form, should be the Allies' preferred operation for 1942. By the end of July this was confirmed in principle. Although the scale and location of the operation were matters of further controversy, it was eventually agreed that Allied troops should land in Algeria and Morocco in the autumn. This operation, renamed Torch by Churchill, commenced on 8 November 1942.

Marshall felt betrayed by his president and Commander in Chief. But there was little doubt that Sledgehammer would have been a suicide operation—and a British suicide at that. Moreover, he failed to appreciate the urgent political imperatives requiring some kind of operation against Germany in 1942. Meeting with Churchill and Marshall back in December 1941, FDR had emphasized "that he considered it very important to morale—to give this country a feeling that they are in the war, [and] to give the Germans the reverse affect [sic]—to have American troops somewhere in active fighting across the Atlantic." Roosevelt was struggling against the formidable legacy of Pearl Harbor. The clamour for revenge against Japan was intense; by contrast, American personnel and territory had scarcely been attacked by the Nazis. During 1942 opinion polls showed that up to 30 percent of Americans inclined towards a compromise peace with Germany.[19]

Churchill, equally, needed a victory against the Germans. The previous two years of war had been a series of almost unbroken defeats for the British Army, whenever it was up against serious opposition, culminating in the ignominious surrenders at Singapore and Tobruk in February and June 1942. Confidence in generals, equipment, and, most basic of all, men, was almost nil in Whitehall. In June 1942 even the British commanders in the Middle East admitted: "We are still largely an amateur army fighting professionals" and, a month later, Churchill remarked gloomily that "[i]f Rommel's army were all Germans they would beat us." The premier therefore feared that any German army, even the twenty-odd substandard divisions currently in France, could inflict a disastrous defeat on British troops in 1942. And, after the string of humiliations, he became convinced "that his life as Prime Minister could be saved only by a victory in the field."[20]

But the logical point for that victory was Libya, where Rommel's forces were pushing, apparently inexorably, towards the Suez Canal. Roosevelt toyed with that idea periodically and in mid-June Marshall was ready to commit the 2nd Armored Division, under Gen. George S. Patton, to Egypt. His Operations Division continued to favour sending U.S. troops there right into mid-August. But, as Harry Hopkins noted, that would have raised again "the difficulty of mixing our troops with the British" in a theatre where the British were dominant and that was, moreover, regarded as the pits of British imperialism.[21]

In any case, both leaders needed a genuinely new front for diplomatic reasons. Against Marshall's advice, Roosevelt had told the Soviet foreign minister in June that the Western Allies "expect the formation of a second front this year." Churchill was more circumspect about 1942, but he also recognized the need to sustain Russian morale and in August flew on a hazardous mission to Moscow to explain the new plan to a sceptical Stalin. The probability that Germany would now be forced to occupy the whole of France, tying down additional troops, was a benefit of Torch. But the essential point was that Churchill could, as he told Stalin, "proclaim 'Torch' when it begins as the second front," whereas reinforcing Egypt, however valuable to Britain, would only be strengthening an existing line.[22]

Whatever its rationale, Torch was to cast a long shadow over Bolero. Despite the Pentagon's efforts to keep the operation within bounds, it developed into a major three-point landing, using troops and supplies designated for Britain. The borders of ETO were now enlarged to include North Africa, with both Eisenhower and Spaatz moving there, and Britain was relegated to a supply base for Torch. SOS personnel remaining in the UK devoted most of their energies in the last months of 1942 to servicing the Mediterranean. All the combat divisions already in the British Isles were also despatched to North Africa—the 1st Infantry from England and the 34th Infantry and 1st Armored from Northern Ireland. That winter only one American division remained in the country—the 29th Infantry, which arrived in October and was based at Tidworth Barracks near Salisbury. Similarly, the 8th Air Force lost twenty-seven thousand men and about 75 percent of its supplies to create the new 12th Air Force in North Africa. More than one thousand planes had been despatched from Britain to the Mediterranean by June 1943.[23]

The American presence in Britain reached 228,000 Army and AAF personnel in October 1942, but then dropped to 105,000 by February 1943 and stayed at around that level until May (table 7.1). This was only one-tenth of what the Marshall Plan had projected back in April 1942. Moreover, the character of the force had changed yet again. Having been initially defensive in the early months of 1942, then having moved to an offensive character under the Bolero program, the emphasis in winter 1942–43 was once more on the defensive: "a balanced ground force" similar to the one envisaged after Pearl Harbor under the Magnet plan for Northern Ireland. The troops in Britain were either supplying North Africa or assisting in the defence of the

7.1 U.S. ARMY TROOP BUILDUP IN THE UNITED KINGDOM, JANUARY 1942 TO FEBRUARY 1943

Year and Month	Arrivals[a]		End-of-Month Strength					Allied Force[b]
	Monthly	Cumulative from January 1942	Total	Ground Forces	Air Forces	Services of Supply	HQ ETO and Miscellaneous	
1942								
January	4,058	4,058	c	c	c	c	c	0
February	0	4,058	c	c	c	c	c	0
March	7,904	11,962	c	c	c	c	c	0
April	0	11,962	c	c	c	c	c	0
May	24,682	36,644	c	c	c	c	c	0
June	19,446	56,090	54,845	38,699	12,517	1,968	1,661	0
July	26,159	82,249	81,273	39,386	17,654	21,902	2,331	0
August	73,869	156,118	152,007	72,100	37,729	39,280	2,898	0
September	28,809	184,927	188,497	79,757	57,752	39,527	9,618	1,843
October	39,838	224,765	223,794[d]	90,483	66,317	40,974	18,509	7,511
November	7,752	232,517	170,227	5,656	32,227	31,698	17,640	83,006
December	9,322	241,839	134,808	17,480	40,117	32,466	6,313	38,432
1943								
January	13,351	255,190	122,097	19,431	47,325	36,061	5,672	13,608
February	1,406	256,596	104,510	19,173	47,494	32,336	5,507	0

[a]By ship. Excludes movements by air.
[b]Air, ground, and SOS personnel assigned to Allied Force at the time and earmarked for movement to North Africa.
[c]Data not available.
[d]The peak strength of about 228,000 reached in the UK during October is not indicated here because embarkation for Torch began before the end of the month.

Source: Rupp., 1: p. 100.

South Coast. Army planners had not abandoned hopes of attacking the Continent, but, both strategically and logistically, early action was inconceivable. With plummeting numbers, chaotic movements, and uncertain mission, morale was difficult to sustain. Eaker, who replaced Spaatz as 8th AF commander in December, lamented in February 1943: "It is a heart-breaking business to see our bomber force going downhill instead of uphill."[24] Not so much Bolero as *Pavane pour une Infante Défunte.*

There was also a command vacuum at the top. Officially Eisenhower remained commanding general of ETO. But after August 1942 he was preoccupied by Torch and he left Britain for the Mediterranean in November. Effective authority in Britain therefore devolved upon his deputy, Gen. Russell P. Hartle, commander of U.S. forces in Northern Ireland since January 1942. "Scrappy" Hartle was only a year older than Eisenhower, but he was a very different character. Marshall felt he "gave a decidedly mediocre performance in cleaning up his unit and providing adequate leadership" when in charge of the 34th Division, and vetoed him for a combat command. Hartle also lacked Ike's talent for public relations and his passion about Anglo-American harmony.[25] This must be borne in mind when looking at the problems in GI-British relations in the winter of 1942–43.

Marshall may have been slow to grasp the political preoccupations of Roosevelt and Churchill, but he had a *military* point that the two leaders, for their part, were equally slow to appreciate. Deep down, Marshall knew he had no feasible operational plan for 1942—in January 1943 Eisenhower admitted that Sledgehammer had been logistically impossible in 1942 and by May Marshall himself acknowledged that it "might have been suicidal." What they were fighting for was not Sledgehammer but Roundup. They were using the chance of invasion in 1942 to justify holding troops inactive but ready until 1943. Otherwise, dispersionitis would take hold and the shortage of shipping would prove insuperable. As Marshall and Admiral King told the president in July 1942: "Our view is that the execution of Gymnast, even if found practicable, means definitely no Bolero-Sledgehammer in 1942 and that it will definitely curtail if not make impossible the execution of Bolero-Roundup in the Spring of 1943." Even Gen. Brooke in London, who followed Churchill and backed the operation, admitted in July 1942 "that the mounting of Operation 'GYMNAST' could only be at the expense of 'ROUND-UP.'" Both Roosevelt and Churchill dismissed such warnings, but events were to prove the accuracy of Marshall's prediction.[26]

At the Casablanca conference of January 1943, with Churchill urging that Sicily be the next step, Marshall warned: "Every diversion or side issue from the main plot acts as a suction pump." Yet his ability to take control was limited by the confusion within the American Joint Chiefs of Staff. At Casablanca, the well-organized British were able to get their way to a substantial degree because of internal American arguments about the merits of the Pacific and the Atlantic. "One might say we came, we listened and we were conquered," in the chagrined words of U.S. planner Albert C. Wedemeyer. Moreover, American leverage over the British was limited because of their belated entry into the war and the consequently superior weight of the British in the alliance. Until June 1944 there were more British Empire divisions than American in combat against the Germans and Italians.[27]

All this is familiar—in Wedemeyer's words, "the Mediterranean as a trap which prolonged the war in Europe by a year." Yet one should also remember that the war against Japan acted as another suction pump. In December 1942 more U.S. troops were in the Pacific than in the Atlantic theatre. Indeed, if only troops in contact with the enemy are considered, "Army forces deployed against Japan at the end of the year numbered about 464,000, as against only about 378,000 against Germany and Italy." The balance did not tip the other way until May 1943.[28]

This was not merely because of the magnitude of the Japanese threat, at least until the battle of Midway in June 1942. It was also because of the Chief of Naval Operations, Admiral Ernest J. King—described by one of his daughters as "the most even-tempered man in the Navy. He is always in a rage." King's fixation with the Pacific was partly because the Navy would have a much grander role to play in that island-hopping conflict than in a continental war against Germany, but King also rightly calculated that "Russia will do nine-tenths of the job of defeating Germany." A further complication was the Navy's private war with General Douglas MacArthur—the prima donna Army commander in the southwest Pacific—which made it impossible to create a unified command for the whole Pacific. Thus, there were, in effect, two Pacific theatres clamouring for men and matériel, as well as the two in Europe. And, after the demise of Sledgehammer, a disillusioned Marshall did little to check the westward drift of American deployments. From mid-1942 there was a trade-off. The British got much of what they wanted in the Mediterranean, while King and MacArthur secured a good deal for the Pacific—with each side regarding the other's operations as a "dangerous political sideshow."[29] "Germany First" became a slogan not a strategy.

It was not until the second half of 1943 that the Pentagon finally pinned Churchill down about France. Unlike the previous summer, Roosevelt and the JCS were now working in harmony. At Quebec in August 1943, agreement in principle was reached with the British to mount Operation Overlord the following year. At Teheran in November, Stalin added weight to the American case and a firm commitment was finally elicited from Churchill for invasion in May 1944.

Thus, the consequences of "global coalition warfare" left the American forces in limbo in Britain even longer than Torch, by itself, would have obliged. Numbers remained virtually static until May 1943 (table 7.2). Thereafter the growth was mainly in Army Air Force personnel for the strategic bombing offensive against Germany (code-named Pointblank), agreed upon in principle by the Allies at Casablanca. *Faute de mieux*, this was the main way of striking at Hitler's Europe in 1943. Between May and December the number of operational heavy bomber groups in the ETO jumped from sixteen to nearly thirty-eight, combat aircraft strength from 1,260 to 4,242. The American air forces in the UK occupied sixty-six bases by the end of 1943. Related aviation service units in Britain, however, had not kept pace with the influx of aircrew. In fact, there were even insufficient trained personnel back in the United States. Between October 1943 and the end of March 1944 seventy-five thousand "casuals" arrived in Britain. These were service personnel, shipped as individual replacements rather than as organized units, who needed further training before they could be utilized on bases around the country.[30] Half-trained, itinerant, unitless personnel constituted the worst problems as far as Army discipline was concerned.

The decisions at Quebec and Teheran shifted the deployment pattern yet again. Bolero had, one might say, unraveled in 1942–43, but in the autumn of 1943 the buildup resumed in earnest. With Overlord scheduled for the spring of 1944 the priority became ground troops, not airmen. Up to August 1943, the 29th Infantry Division was still the only U.S. combat division in Britain until the 5th arrived at Tidworth. In September the 101st Airborne located around Newbury and the 3rd Armored in Somerset. By D-Day twenty U.S. combat divisions were in Britain—nearly a quarter of the total number overseas. The months of March to May 1944 also saw a particularly rapid influx of SOS service personnel, mostly for the invasion. By June 1944 there were 1,527,000 Army and Army Air Force personnel in the United Kingdom—40 percent Ground Troops, 30 percent SOS, and 28 percent AAF.

| Month | Arrivals[a] | | End-of-Month Strength | | | | |
	Monthly	Cumulative from January 1942	Total	Ground Forces	Air Forces	Services of Supply	HQ ETO and Miscellaneous
1943							
January	13,351	255,190	122,097[b]	19,431	47,325	36,061	5,672
February	1,406	256,596	104,510	19,173	47,494	32,336	5,507
March	1,277	257,873	109,549	19,205	51,566	34,244	4,534
April	2,078	259,951	110,818	19,184	53,561	33,886	4,187
May	19,220	279,171	132,776	19,204	74,205	34,028	5,339
June	49,972	329,143	184,015	22,813	107,413	49,444	4,345
July	53,274	382,417	238,028	24,283	132,950	73,831	6,964
August	41,681	424,098	278,742	39,934	152,548	79,898	6,362
September	81,116	505,214	361,794	62,583	168,999	120,148	10,064
October	105,557	610,771	466,562	116,665	200,287	148,446	1,164
November	173,860[c]	784,631	637,521	197,677	247,052	191,208	1,584
December	133,716	918,347	773,753	265,325	286,264	220,192	1,972
1944							
January	166,405	1,084,752	937,308	343,972	317,227	273,294	2,815
February	136,684	1,221,436	1,084,057	442,474	338,317	299,710	3,556
March	124,412	1,345,848	1,199,077	488,379	375,152	325,577	9,969
April	216,699	1,562,547	1,422,276	599,425	410,562	391,994	20,295
May	108,463	1,671,010	1,526,965	620,504	426,819	459,511	20,131

[a]By ship. Excludes movements by air.
[b]Includes 13,608 men assigned to Allied Force for this month only.
[c]A large portion of these arrivals consisted of units redeployed from North Africa.

Source: Rupp., 1: pp. 129, 232.

As for the U.S. Navy, in 1942–43 this had made little impact on Britain, except for headquarters staff in London and the bases at Londonderry (Northern Ireland) and Gare Loch, off the Firth of Clyde in Scotland, which were used in the Battle of the Atlantic. But during 1944 the U.S. Navy's presence in Britain grew significantly in preparation for Overlord—seamen, aviators, and Construction Battalions (Seabees). On 6 June 1944 it was estimated that there were nearly 122,000 U.S. Naval personnel in ETO, ashore or afloat. Most had been located at small bases along the south coast ports west of the Solent, with a strong presence around Plymouth and Weymouth, headquarters of the two U.S. naval task forces for 6 June. But the naval base at Londonderry still had several thousand sailors and marines.[31]

On the eve of D-Day there were at least 1,650,000 members of the United States armed forces in the British Isles, more than double the number at the end of 1943. Managing this frenetic buildup demanded considerable talents, but the leadership problems of 1942–43 took time to resolve. In February 1943 Marshall had created a separate North African Theater of Operations. This did something to address the command vacuum of the previous winter, because Eisenhower relinquished all responsibility for ETO and Hartle was replaced by another Marshall protégé, Gen. Frank M. Andrews—an energetic, able, and agreeable man who had something of Ike's concern for Anglo-American relations. But Andrews was an airman and his considerable leadership skills were largely absorbed by the 8AF buildup. Moreover, his tenure was tragically brief. According to Eaker, he was "probably the best blind-instrument pilot in the whole Army Air Corps." With "an undaunted belief in his ability to navigate in any weather," he flew to Iceland on 3 May 1943, ignoring warnings about near-zero visibility. Coming in "on an instrument approach with minimum navigational aids," he was on a correct line with the airfield but caught a small hill just before reaching the runway. The plane was destroyed and Andrews and all his staff killed.[32]

In less than a year, ETO had four different commanding generals: Eisenhower, Hartle, Andrews, and then Jacob L. Devers. Each newcomer naturally took time to find his feet. Devers had commanded the Armored Force in 1941–43, but his later career has been criticized. Marshall felt he became far too ambitious, believing that ETO was prelude to command on D-Day. Historian Geoffrey Perret has described Devers as "brainy, vain, loquacious," a "suave bureaucrat and operator."[33] Nevertheless, he found considerable scope for his energies in Britain in the second half of 1943. The influx of GIs created new problems and Devers sponsored significant initiatives in relations with

British troops and the management of black GIs. Yet he, like his predecessors, was operating under serious limitations with a weak staff and limited clout in Washington. In January 1944 Eisenhower returned to London as Supreme Commander of the upcoming invasion. No one else had Ike's commitment to Anglo-American relations, and his leverage in Washington by then was considerable. But, as in 1942, Ike's attention was focused on mounting an invasion. There was a limit to what he could do to manage the occupation.

As these theatre commanders came and went, one major figure remained on stage. That was Gen. John Clifford Hodges Lee, who was head of the Services of Supply in Britain from late May 1942. To many of his men he was a martinet, obsessive about spit and polish, and officiously religious. (From his initials, J.C.H., he became known as "Jesus Christ Himself.") Eisenhower had doubts about his efficiency, passing over him for deputy theater commander in September 1942 and finally giving him the title in January 1944 with considerable reluctance. Much offence was caused by Lee's socializing with English aristocrats and by his private train. This comprised ten coaches, including two sleepers, a dining car, a conference car, and two "monster box cars" each holding five automobiles and a couple of jeeps. It required eighteen staff to run, often more than the total number of passengers. Yet Lee should not be caricatured or underestimated. His unpopularity was partly because the SOS was the scapegoat for any and every supply shortage. This was not always fair since it was distributing worldwide an inventory of nearly three million items. (The mail-order giant, Sears Roebuck, handled only 100,000.) Moreover, Lee was a complex man. He took a very positive approach to Anglo-American relations. His Christianity was sincere (in retirement he became one of America's leading Episcopalians) and he did try to put it into practice. We shall see that his treatment of black GIs was unusually "enlightened" for a Regular Army officer.[34]

The deployment, logistics, and command of the GIs in Britain were all, therefore, determined by the politics of grand strategy. American combat troops were a rarity until late 1943, apart from a brief flurry in mid-1942 and with the conspicuous exception of the 29th Division. Most GIs in 1942–43 were either service troops, who had particular problems of morale and conduct in an inactive theatre, not least because many were black, or else air force personnel, for whom the war was all too active—equally a source of psychological strain. Moreover, grand strategy determined that in 1942–43 Britain was not just an inactive theatre but a distinctly minor one. The troops that were there suffered from limited resources, poor facilities, and deficient commanders. Yet the Bolero planners had operated in the summer of 1942 on the assumption that Britain would be home to over one million GIs by the following spring. The procedures hastily established in 1942 set the framework for the American occupation throughout the war.

As this chapter has also shown, the intense period of occupation was much briefer than often thought. The real buildup of American personnel—ground troops, airmen, and sailors—occurred only in the six months prior to D-Day. The special mood of spring 1944 is evoked in chapter 20. After D-Day the occupation continued, but on a smaller scale and, as we shall see in chapter 22, in a form more like that of 1918 when Britain was a base area for a kaleidoscopic succession of short-term visitors whose real war was going on across the Channel. Even in the last year of the war, the GIs in Britain were pawns of Allied grand strategy.

8

Making
Space

★ ★ ★

POSTPONEMENT OF THE CROSS-CHANNEL ATTACK FROM 1942 TO 1944
meant the American occupation of Britain would be long and substantial. The intervening oscillations of Anglo-American grand strategy
also gave Bolero its peculiar changes of tempo—from allegretto to
lento and then allegro furioso. Yet the GIs in Britain would not have
caused so many problems had there been room to accommodate them.
It was a question of making space as well as marking time.

Even in the United States, of course, there were limits to the land
available for Army use. In January 1942 Marshall grudgingly instructed that, to avoid "unnecessary expense," camps for infantry
divisions would be "limited in acreage to that necessary for sound
training and will generally not exceed 40,000 acres." But by British
standards forty-thousand acres per division was an unheard-of indulgence, equivalent to nearly half the Isle of Wight. And most GIs did
basic training in the vast camps of the old Confederacy—the biggest,
Benning and Bragg, being around 100,000 acres. Facilities there may
have been primitive in the hell-for-leather expansion of 1942, but
space for accommodation and training was not an issue. When the
War Department decided to establish a Desert Training Center to simulate conditions in North Africa, Patton and his staff flew out to California in March 1942 to reconnoitre. After surveying a barren wasteland
about the size of Pennsylvania, he selected some sixteen thousand
square miles and had the center in operation within weeks. It was as
if he had taken over one-third of England.[1]

As Patton established his empire in the California desert, Gen. Marshall was in London telling the British that they would need to find room for one million GIs by the following spring. Hastily the combined Anglo-American Bolero committee addressed the administrative nightmares this would pose. In early meetings there was even talk about the need to "evacuate towns wholesale and hand them over to the armed forces." The panic abated somewhat as it became clear that the Marshall Plan was utopian, and in 1942–43 Bolero planners struggled to make meaningful logistic projections amid the fluctuations of grand strategy. In the end there were four Bolero Key Plans. But the guidelines laid down in the early weeks set the pattern for the whole American occupation.[2]

British forces were concentrated in southeastern England, against the residual possibility of invasion. U.S. troops and supplies would arrive in the ports of western Britain—on the Clyde, Mersey, and Bristol Channel. For logistic reasons it therefore seemed sensible to assume that in an invasion of France, the British would be on the left (east) and the Americans on the right, with a dividing line around the Isle of Wight. Such thinking was also administratively convenient, because it coincided with the borderline between the British Army's Southeastern and Southern Commands. Therefore the Bolero planners quickly concluded that the U.S. Army should gradually take over Southern Command's facilities from Hampshire west to Cornwall. This would constitute the base of an American triangle. Supply and communication facilities from there towards the northwestern ports would form the other two sides of the American area, with an apex in the West Midlands.[3] Although Torch delayed execution of these plans, leaving only one U.S. combat division in Britain in the winter of 1942–43, the eventual buildup of 1943–44 followed their outline. Of the twenty American divisions in Britain at the beginning of June 1944, sixteen were in the southern triangle.

The Marshall Plan of 1942 was superimposed on and interwoven with the project of creating a vast American bomber force in England. In this case the strategic and logistic geography pointed to East Anglia. That was the area of England closest to Germany yet partly protected by the fighter screen around London and the southeast. Numerous RAF airfields were already in existence or under construction and space was available for new bases as needed. RAF Bomber Command would gradually be moved north into Lincolnshire and Yorkshire. As with ground troops, the decision to mount Torch undercut expectations of a vast buildup in 1942–43. But the eight RAF bases around Huntingdon, some sixty miles north of London, that Gen. Eaker took over in the spring of 1942 formed the nucleus of what would be a vast

Army Air Force empire by 1944. There was a significant 9th AAF presence by D-Day in Kent to provide tactical support for the invasion forces, and the huge maintenance depot at Burtonwood near Manchester constituted another AAF pocket, but the bulk of the 426,000 American airmen were located in Norfolk and Suffolk. It was as if 130 airbases had been dropped down in the state of Vermont.[4]

On a smaller scale, Northern Ireland was another important American area. This was also a legacy of decisions made early in 1942 when two U.S. divisions were sent there to complete their training and assist in its defence. Although both departed for North Africa at the end of the year, the infrastructure for an American presence had been established. When Bolero resumed in late 1943, Ulster became an essential holding area and training ground for troops awaiting space in England. Four American combat divisions (the 2nd, 5th, 8th, and 82nd Airborne) were there at the end of 1943. In addition, Londonderry remained a significant naval base; there was a major aircraft repair depot at Langford Lodge, twenty miles west of Belfast; and five AAF bases were engaged in the vital task of training replacement bomb crew for units in England. The rundown after D-Day was rapid but in early 1944 GIs seemed omnipresent in Ulster, peaking at 120,000.[5]

Maps 8A and 8B show the geography of the American occupation at Christmas 1943 and again five weeks before D-Day. Comparing them highlights two points. First, the speed of the final buildup and the brevity of an intense American presence. Total numbers had more than doubled in the three months before Christmas, but they nearly doubled again from 761,000 to 1.42 million by 30 April 1944. In December 1943 only Wiltshire and (marginally) Suffolk hosted more than 50,000 GIs, compared with twelve counties the following spring. Second, the maps highlight the geographic as well as the temporal specificity of the American presence. Some areas saw very few GIs, notably mid-Wales, northeast England, the Lake District, and most of Scotland except Clydeside and Edinburgh, a popular leave centre. The majority were concentrated in the southern triangle and East Anglia. By 1944 there was, in addition, what might called a northwest corridor through Staffordshire, Cheshire, and Lancashire—partly the result of Burtonwood depot but mainly because it linked the south to the arrival ports and served as a staging area for follow-up combat divisions and service troops. (Patton's 3rd Army was located here until D-Day freed up the southern camps.) In these areas the American presence seemed overwhelming that spring. To one visitor from Washington, Assistant Secretary of War John J. McCloy, England was almost "another segment of America."[6]

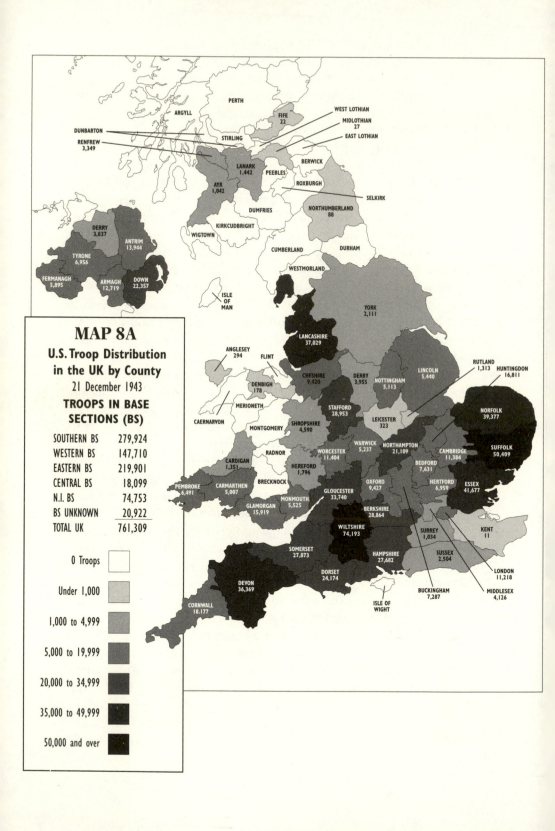

MAP 8A

U.S. Troop Distribution in the UK by County

21 December 1943

TROOPS IN BASE SECTIONS (BS)

SOUTHERN BS	279,924
WESTERN BS	147,710
EASTERN BS	219,901
CENTRAL BS	18,099
N.I. BS	74,753
BS UNKNOWN	20,922
TOTAL UK	761,309

0 Troops

Under 1,000

1,000 to 4,999

5,000 to 19,999

20,000 to 34,999

35,000 to 49,999

50,000 and over

PERTH

ARGYLL

FIFE 22

WEST LOTHIAN

MIDLOTHIAN 27

EAST LOTHIAN

DUNBARTON

RENFREW 3,349

STIRLING

BERWICK

LANARK 1,442

PEEBLES

ROXBURGH

AYR 1,042

SELKIRK

DUMFRIES

NORTHUMBERLAND 88

KIRKCUDBRIGHT

WIGTOWN

CUMBERLAND

DURHAM

WESTMORLAND

DERRY 3,837

ANTRIM 13,944

TYRONE 6,956

FERMANAGH 5,895

ARMAGH 12,719

DOWN 22,357

ISLE OF MAN

YORK 2,111

LANCASHIRE 37,029

ANGLESEY 294

FLINT

CHESHIRE 9,420

DERBY 3,955

NOTTINGHAM 5,113

LINCOLN 5,440

RUTLAND 1,313

HUNTINGDON 16,811

DENBIGH 178

MERIONETH

CAERNARVON

MONTGOMERY

SHROPSHIRE 4,590

STAFFORD 28,953

LEICESTER 323

NORFOLK 39,377

CARDIGAN 1,351

RADNOR

WORCESTER 11,404

WARWICK 5,237

NORTHAMPTON 21,109

CAMBRIDGE 11,384

SUFFOLK 50,409

PEMBROKE 6,491

CARMARTHEN 5,007

BRECKNOCK

HEREFORD 1,796

BEDFORD 7,631

HERTFORD 6,959

ESSEX 41,677

GLAMORGAN 15,919

MONMOUTH 5,525

GLOUCESTER 33,740

OXFORD 9,427

BERKSHIRE 28,864

WILTSHIRE 74,193

SURREY 1,034

KENT 11

LONDON 11,218

SOMERSET 27,873

HAMPSHIRE 27,682

SUSSEX 2,504

DORSET 24,174

BUCKINGHAM 7,287

MIDDLESEX 4,126

DEVON 36,369

ISLE OF WIGHT

CORNWALL 18,177

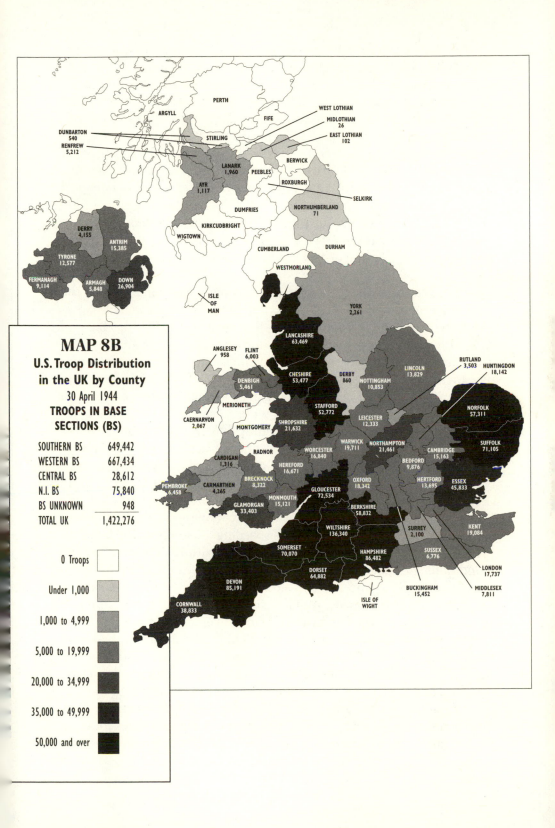

MAP 8B

**U.S. Troop Distribution
in the UK by County**

30 April 1944

**TROOPS IN BASE
SECTIONS (BS)**

SOUTHERN BS	649,442
WESTERN BS	667,434
CENTRAL BS	28,612
N.I. BS	75,840
BS UNKNOWN	948
TOTAL UK	1,422,276

0 Troops

Under 1,000

1,000 to 4,999

5,000 to 19,999

20,000 to 34,999

35,000 to 49,999

50,000 and over

PERTH

ARGYLL

FIFE

WEST LOTHIAN

MIDLOTHIAN
26

DUNBARTON
540

EAST LOTHIAN
102

RENFREW
5,212

STIRLING

LANARK
1,960

PEEBLES

BERWICK

AYR
1,117

ROXBURGH

SELKIRK

DUMFRIES

NORTHUMBERLAND
71

KIRKCUDBRIGHT

WIGTOWN

CUMBERLAND

DURHAM

DERRY
4,155

ANTRIM
15,385

WESTMORLAND

TYRONE
12,577

ISLE
OF
MAN

YORK
2,261

FERMANAGH
9,114

ARMAGH
5,848

DOWN
26,904

ANGLESEY
958

FLINT
6,003

LANCASHIRE
63,469

CAERNARVON
2,067

DENBIGH
5,461

CHESHIRE
53,477

DERBY
860

NOTTINGHAM
10,853

LINCOLN
13,829

RUTLAND
3,503

HUNTINGDON
18,142

MERIONETH

STAFFORD
52,772

LEICESTER
12,333

NORFOLK
57,311

MONTGOMERY

SHROPSHIRE
21,632

CARDIGAN
1,316

RADNOR

WORCESTER
16,840

WARWICK
19,711

NORTHAMPTON
21,461

CAMBRIDGE
15,163

SUFFOLK
71,105

HEREFORD
16,671

BEDFORD
9,876

PEMBROKE
6,458

CARMARTHEN
4,265

BRECKNOCK
8,322

OXFORD
18,342

HERTFORD
13,695

ESSEX
45,833

GLOUCESTER
72,534

GLAMORGAN
33,403

MONMOUTH
15,121

BERKSHIRE
58,832

SURREY
2,100

KENT
19,084

WILTSHIRE
136,340

SUSSEX
6,776

LONDON
17,737

SOMERSET
70,070

HAMPSHIRE
86,482

BUCKINGHAM
15,452

MIDDLESEX
7,811

DEVON
85,191

DORSET
64,882

ISLE OF
WIGHT

CORNWALL
38,833

These maps cannot fully convey the impact of the Americans, however. In terms of total numbers of GIs, Northern Ireland does not bulk
large. Yet, outside Belfast, this was sparsely populated terrain and the
American presence at its peak represented one-tenth of the 1937
population (more like one-fifth in County Fermanagh, host to the 8th
Infantry Division). In England the local impact was even more pronounced in places. At the end of April 1944 there were 71,000 GIs in
Suffolk, which the 1931 census listed as having 401,000 inhabitants.
Assuming population increase since then had been roughly balanced
by the wartime loss of males to the British forces, this suggests a ratio
of one GI to every six civilians. In Wiltshire, which hosted the largest
number of Americans in 1943–44, the English probably outnumbered
the Yanks in the spring of 1944 by not much more than two to one.[7]

Space constraints posed all sorts of problems. Take, for instance, the
increased road traffic as Britain filled up with American vehicles, particularly jeeps and 2½-ton trucks—the most distinctive products of
U.S. auto technology. In the spring and summer of 1943 there were
only about 20,000 American motor vehicles in Britain, but the number increased steadily from August to reach 104,000 by the end of
March 1944. This should be set against a total of only 2.6 million
vehicles in Britain in 1938 (most of which disappeared from the roads
during wartime because of fuel rationing). Not surprisingly there was
a commensurate increase in the number of accidents. In the period
from July 1942 through March 1944, there were nearly twenty-nine
thousand accidents in the UK involving American vehicles (372 being
fatal), but well over twenty-four thousand of them occurred after July
1943. Contrary to the image of the fast-moving Yank, only about
one-sixth of these were the result of speeding—usually in the blackout
at night. More commonly, GIs failed to cope with the cramped driving
conditions. Roughly a third of the accidents were caused by sideswip-
ing, as drivers on the "wrong side" of the vehicle tried to pass or
overtake on narrow roads. And a quarter occurred at speeds of under
5 mph, often as large trucks were being reversed or parked.[8]

Men were even harder to accommodate than vehicles in a country
one-fiftieth the size of America but with one-third of its population. As
the Bolero committee realized at an early stage, accommodation required a mixture of existing facilities and new construction. In the case
of combat troops the former meant old British Army barracks, notably
Tidworth, near Salisbury, which was home at various times for eight
American divisions. The new building was usually on smaller wartime
camps, constructed of Nissen huts and dispersed around the countryside.

Where you lived had a considerable effect on how you got on in Britain. A striking example is the experience of the 29th Division, which earned the derisory GI nickname "England's Own" because of its twenty-month stay—the longest of any U.S. combat division. (When a touring evangelist put up a sign asking "Where will you spend eternity?", one 29er supposedly scrawled underneath: "In England.")[9] From October 1942 until May 1943 the division's home was at Tidworth. Thereafter its three regiments (the 115th, 116th, and 175th) moved into battalion- or even company-sized camps in Devon and Cornwall until just before D-Day. In neither case was the accommodation agreeable. At Tidworth they lived in two-storey Victorian cavalry barracks—cavernous rooms of bunk beds with a single fireplace and one toilet and one bathtub per floor. When the men stuffed their mattresses with straw to keep warm in the winter the result was an outbreak of scabies. In the southwest some troops were based in similarly antiquated barracks, including Fort Tregantle, a relic of the Napoleonic wars. But most were in field camps such as Ivybridge and Bridestowe near Plymouth. These generally consisted of small Nissen huts—hemispherical tubes of curved corrugated iron plates over a concrete slab, with brick walls and drafty windows at either end. In wet weather the surrounding field became a sea of mud.

Winter in either setting was grim, but at Tidworth the men felt particularly isolated. There were a couple of pubs on base but few communities nearby and "we didn't get familiar with the local people," recalled Bob Slaughter of the 116th. When the troops were given a pass they descended en masse (often most of the regiment at a time) on big towns like Salisbury or Andover, where the townspeople were hardened to soldiers, having suffered the British Army at Tidworth for years. The camps in the southwest, by contrast, were purpose-built for wartime. The local villages were nearby—Ivybridge with its pubs and shops just down the hill, for instance—and the locals were less inured to soldiers, who in any case were more easily assimilated in battalions of less than one thousand men than in a division of fifteen thousand as at Tidworth. Accordingly most 29ers have particularly fond memories of Devon and Cornwall. At Fort Tregantle, Erik Juleen from Chicago found living conditions "prehistoric," but the people "wonderful." Most men soon discovered that the pub was "the neighborhood social center" and through contacts made there, according to Robert M. Miller, then commander of F Co. of the 175th, "we literally integrated into thousands of British families." In Bridestowe at Christmas 1943, the CO recalled, the 2nd Battalion of the 116th had "far more invitations from civilians for men to spend the holidays than we could possibly fill."[10]

Headquarters staff were particularly difficult to accommodate since most needed to be in or near London. Here office space was at a premium because of British demands and the effects of German bombing. The United States embassy was located in Mayfair's Grosvenor Square (on the opposite side from the current modernist embassy building), in what had been a fashionable prewar residential area. After Pearl Harbor the embassy and the U.S. Army and Navy colonized other buildings in the square. ETO headquarters were at number 20, on the northwest corner leading up to Oxford Street. By 1944 the area had become almost an American ghetto. (One parody of a popular song was entitled "An Englishman Spoke in Grosvenor Square.") At an early stage in 1942, however, it was decided that Gen. J.C.H. Lee's Services of Supply HQ could not be housed in London. In July 1942 most of its staff moved to Cheltenham, the elegant spa town about ninety miles west of London. There they could be accommodated in offices previously used by British civil servants and the move also brought SOS near the apex of the American Triangle that it was intended to service. There were, however, real drawbacks. Some SOS staff remained in London (in an annexe to Selfridges department store) and, to add to the confusion, ETO in London retained control of certain administrative and supply activities. Military police, for instance, fell between the two commands. Even more disastrous, SOS was left out of the logistical planning for Torch (because this was operational) but was then asked to help clear up the ensuing mess. Not until Eisenhower's return in January 1944 were the two HQs merged, with Lee becoming deputy theater commander for administration and supply. In Washington the Pentagon had been constructed to reduce the confusion caused by having the War Department on many separate sites. In England physical separation exacerbated the bureaucratic conflicts between SOS and ETO.[11]

In the case of the American airmen, their headquarters requirements were even more demanding. In 1942 Eaker wanted his Bomber HQ to be near London and also close to RAF Bomber Command at High Wycombe, on the edge of the Chiltern Hills northwest of London. In March 1942 he told Gen. Chaney that there was only one suitable property, in terms of position, existing buildings, and space for expansion. This was Daws Hill Lodge, a country house that had become the home of Wycombe Abbey girls' school. Eaker demanded some of the buildings immediately and the rest by 1 June. The school protested strenuously but, under British Defence Regulations, notice was served on 30 March and the buildings requisitioned on 14 April. It was an example of how quickly civilian activities could be overridden where

military needs seemed urgent. Nevertheless, the former school buildings did have their drawbacks. On the first night the officers took over
the teachers' offices while the enlisted men were sent to the girls'
dormitories. Soon the officers were roused by the ringing of bells,
which they eventually traced back to the dormitories. Above the push
buttons were signs: IF MISTRESS IS DESIRED, RING BELL.[12]

Not all American needs could be satisfied by existing British facilities. The Army's hospital programme is an instructive example of the
problems of making space while marking time. As the head of ETO's
hospitalization division, Col. Joseph R. Darnall, observed later, they
were operating "in a recurring administrative fog and on the shifting
sands of uncertainty." First they had to estimate bed requirements as
a proportion of total troop strength. In early 1942 ETO Chief Surgeon
Gen. Paul R. Hawley could only use the experience of the U.S. Army
in World War One and of the British Army in 1940–41. By 1943, in
the final Bolero planning, Hawley had direct evidence from the North
African campaign. As a result he increased his estimates of beds for
sick and nonbattle casualties from 2.25 to 4 percent of total strength,
while pushing down his ratio of battle casualties to total strength
committed from 10 percent to 7 percent. This played havoc with
planning. Hawley also had to cope with the changing strategic priorities. In the spring of 1942, assuming that within a year one million GIs
would be poised in Britain to make a hazardous invasion of France, he
was demanding ninety thousand hospital beds. In early 1943, with
North Africa the war zone and Britain a backwater, the aim was forty
thousand beds to support a total theatre strength of 427,000. In the
summer, with Overlord being planned in earnest, his target was
ninety-five thousand beds by April 1944.[13]

Obtaining these beds was even more difficult. In 1942 Hawley received a flood of offers of English country houses, their owners animated, possibly, by altruism, but more likely by the desire to avoid
taxation. Few of these were suitable, however. The Americans were
able to take over some British facilities, such as the Churchill Hospital
in Oxford, but most of the requirements could only be satisfied by the
construction of new hospitals. Hawley wanted them clustered in
groups of four or five for greater efficiency—Great Malvern and Cirencester being two of the nuclei. In all some 116 hospitals of various
sizes were constructed, including 36 station hospitals with 834 beds
and 16 general hospitals with a fixed-bed capacity of 1,082.[14]

The greatest new construction programme was for airfields. Even in
1942 cost estimates for this were running at double that for hospitals.
In this case, too, official projections rose and fell with the shifts in

grand strategy. In May 1942 127 airfields were planned. By December 1943 the AAF were using only 66, but a total of 108 was projected. In all, it has been estimated that 175 UK airfields experienced some kind of American presence during the war. Perhaps about two-thirds of the heavily used bases were taken over from the British, as the RAF vacated East Anglia much as the British Army moved out of Southern Command. But even the fighter fields needed modifications, such as steel matting on the grass runways. And bomber stations, old or new, required vast concrete runways, hardstandings, and perimeter tracks to handle the heavy American B-17s and B-24s (the Flying Fortresses and Liberators). The impact of the 8th Air Force on East Anglia will be discussed more fully in chapter 17. What should be stressed here is the overall effect. Some five hundred airfields were constructed in Britain during the war. It was one of the biggest civil engineering projects ever undertaken in the country and, according to historian Roger Freeman, the concrete alone amounted to the equivalent of four thousand miles of three-lane motorway. At the programme's peak in 1942 a new airfield was being started, on average, every three days.[15]

At every stage in the construction process for hospitals and airfields the Americans had to work through the British authorities. Col. Darnall recalled some particularly fraught negotiations in April 1944 to secure the site for a crucial transit evacuation hospital at Blandford, Dorset, for casualties from France. On a beautiful spring day he and representatives of several Whitehall government departments set off on a field trip:

Our friends, the British, pointed out the beauties of several inaccessible and unsuitable patches of waste land which we promptly rejected. The only piece of property that met all requirements was meadow land at Morton House, near a railhead and on a good road for evacuation from the debarkation ports of Weymouth and Portland. . . . The farmer who owned the land refused to release it because his eighty head of cattle would starve if deprived of their pasture. The local representative of the Ministry of Agriculture was polite but supported the stand taken by the farmer. The War Office representative regretted the stubbornness of the landowner, and again tried to persuade us to accept unsuitably located waste land. With marvelous control of temper, I expressed *my* regrets that 80 head of cattle should be given priority consideration above the lives and welfare of thousands of American wounded. The British were polite but firm and assured me that within a few weeks or months, they might induce the farmer to lease his land. I told them we *must* have a *favorable* decision within 24 hours, otherwise it would be necessary to present emergency demands at Cabinet level. Twenty-three hours later we were informed by the War Office that the farmer had capitulated and the Morton House pasture land was ours.[16]

Even when land had been obtained, the Americans usually needed the British to do the construction because of the shortage of American service troops. With most of British military labour in 1942 tied up in building ordnance depots, this meant using civilian contractors acting for the British Ministry of Works. In the winter of 1942–43 some seventy-five thousand civilians were engaged in military projects, mostly for the Bolero programme. The U.S. Army was not impressed with the results. Deadlines were missed repeatedly because of labour shortages. Workmanship was often shoddy, or at least not to American standards. Yet the latter often seemed excessive to the British. In the case of hospitals, for instance, ETO got its way on floor space per patient (seventy-two square feet as against the British norm of sixty), but the British managed to eliminate central heating and to economize on kitchens. Even the use of U.S. construction troops did not eliminate the problems. They had to get accustomed to differences in materials (particularly brick and tile rather than wood), electrical systems (British appliances operated on double the American voltage), and even language (words such as tap/faucet or lift/elevator). And everywhere there was the mud. The combination of wet weather, clay soil, and high water tables constituted an engineer's nightmare. Roads and runways required special, hand-packed rubble foundations of a sort unimagined in most of the United States. GIs constructing the base at Debach near Ipswich in the winter of 1942–43 joked that a periscope had been spotted on number two runway.[17]

For all its defects, Britain had one great advantage as a base for the U.S. Army: security. By 1942 the danger of invasion had receded and, despite occasional raids, there was no major air threat until the advent of the V-bombs in June 1944. But there was one part of the UK where security anxieties remained—Northern Ireland. There it was a matter of making space, and making it safe as well.

Under the Anglo-Irish treaty of 1921 Ireland was partitioned. Six counties in Ulster, in the northeast where the pro-Unionist Protestants were deeply entrenched, remained part of the United Kingdom. The rest of Ireland became independent, distancing itself from Britain by Catholicism, the Gaelic language, and, from 1937, a republican constitution. Nevertheless, "Eire" remained part of the British Commonwealth and London was incensed in 1939 when the Irish leader,

Eamon de Valera, refused to enter the war against Germany. When GIs started arriving in Belfast in January 1942, de Valera reiterated Eire's claim over the whole island "no matter what troops occupy the Six Counties." The Irish minister in Washington, Robert Brennan, told Under-Secretary of State Sumner Welles that the sending of American troops "was regarded by the Irish government and people as official sanction of the partition of Ireland." He added that "increasing belief existed on the part of his Government and people that these American troops were going to be used to attack the Irish forces."[18]

Roosevelt's private response was "that he only wished they would." Although Irish-Americans remained powerful within the Democratic party, their sting had been drawn by partition, which, though disliked, was formally recognized by the United States. The Roosevelt administration regarded Irish neutrality as a serious impediment to the war effort. The *Pocket Guide to Northern Ireland* issued to GIs in 1942 stated categorically:

> Eire's neutrality is a real danger to the Allied cause. There, just across the Irish Channel from embattled England, and not too far from your own billets in Ulster, the Axis nations maintain large legations and staffs. These Axis agents send out weather reports, find out by espionage what is going on in Ulster. The Ulster border is 600 miles long and hard to patrol. Axis spies sift back and forth across the border constantly.

In February 1944, with D-Day approaching, de Valera was formally asked for "the removal of these Axis representatives as constituting a danger to the lives of American soldiers and to the success of Allied military operations." In response, he put the Irish Army on alert against possible American invasion and warned publicly that "at any moment the war may come upon us." Hurriedly the Roosevelt administration backed off, but de Valera capitalized on the boost to his popularity at home by calling a general election on 30 May and winning a handsome majority.[19]

During 1942 there remained fears of direct German attack. That spring the U.S. military attaché in Dublin wrote a widely circulated memo about the possibility of a successful Nazi invasion of Ireland, quoting Irish generals to the effect that their forces were only likely to offer active resistance for forty-eight hours. When the GIs arrived in Ulster to relieve the British, they therefore had two specified roles: "to defend North Ireland against attack by the Axis powers" and "to be prepared to move into South Ireland for the defense thereof." Presidential emissary Harry Hopkins returned to Washington from a visit to the American forces in Ulster in April 1942 claiming that they "had it all taped in the event of invasion to occupy Dublin . . . in seventy minutes." At the centre of the strike force was the 1st Armored Division. In September 1942 its intelligence officer expected only "token resistance" from the "poorly equipped" Irish Army, such as would "serve to satisfy Irish honor." But he predicted that "Irish guerrillas" would offer effective resistance "of the 'knife-in-the-back' type," and urged that "military justice must be swift, certain and harsh." Catholic priests should be placed under "immediate surveillance" and "there must be no fraternization between the troops and the civil population" because "under these conditions the SOUTHERN IRISH are the most treacherous people on earth." With such planning papers in circulation, it was little wonder that, according to the U.S. consul in Belfast, it was "common talk in Northern Ireland, not only in the American Army itself, but among the general population, that the purpose of the American Army in Northern Ireland is to take over the whole of Ireland."[20]

Apart from a possible threat from Eire, there was also concern about internal security in Ulster. The Irish Republican Army (IRA) was waging a bombing campaign against British targets and in 1942 it denounced the United States for conniving in the British occupation. Soon after the first GIs arrived, the Army placed off-limits the Falls Road and other Nationalist areas of Belfast. In September 1942 the U.S. consul reported "considerable resentment" towards the IRA among GIs, "quite a number" of whom had "been brutally assaulted under cover of darkness"—Londonderry being a particular trouble spot. There was also concern about subversion. The border was largely uncontrolled. In places, such as Pettigo in County Fermanagh, it ran down the middle of the village street. GIs often crossed into County Donegal, especially on Sundays when the pubs were closed in Ulster. Some even went to Dublin for recreation. In the other direction, not only could IRA activists move to and fro, but the war industries in Ulster used workers from the south, some of whom were IRA suspects. The AAF repair base at Langford Lodge employed some sixteen hundred Irish civilian personnel by June 1943 and British troops were used to guard millions of dollars of machinery and supplies. Although little sabotage occurred, fears were intense.[21]

Establishing a safe space for the GIs was particularly difficult, therefore, in Ireland, and Irish neutrality caused offence right up to the end. In May 1945, with the newspapers full of revelations about Belsen and Buchenwald, de Valera paid a courtesy call on the German ambassador to "express condolence" on Hitler's death, just as he had visited the U.S. minister, David Gray, a few weeks earlier following the death of Roosevelt. Fence-sitting was only his public posture, however. In practice Irish neutrality had become progressively more biased towards the Allies, partly because of Eire's economic dependence on Britain but also because de Valera's "sympathies were pro-British throughout the war" though his policies were "even more emphatically pro-Irish." The Irish and British armies had secret contingency plans to cooperate in the event of a German invasion of the south. Likewise, American Army's war plans in 1942 involved what David Gray called "direct, though unavowed liaison with the Irish Army General Staff."[22]

The most striking example of such cooperation was the treatment of American aircrew who landed in Eire because of weather or mechanical failure. The Dublin government tried to avoid this happening. Using white stones the word EIRE was marked out in letters thirty feet high on sixty headlands around the coast. The Irish Chief of Staff, Gen. Daniel McKenna, personally flew in a B-17 with Gen. Edmund Hill, commander of the AAF in Northern Ireland, pointing out every sign and its identification number so they could be entered on American maps. Even so, American landings in Eire became all too frequent. In the early years of the war errant British airmen had been interned (as were all German servicemen). In December 1942, however, Gray reached an informal agreement that American airmen would not be interned if on "non-operational flights." All U.S. crews were then given strict instructions "that in the event of forced landing in Eire they should make strong claims that they were not on combat mission but were ferrying planes, transporting personnel, or on training flights." Such claims were often spurious but de Valera turned a blind eye. No American airmen were interned in Eire during the war and this arrangement was extended to RAF crews in 1943 while German seamen continued to languish in prison in the Curragh.[23]

Perhaps the most delicate of these forced landings occurred in the west of Eire on 15 January 1943. A B-17 en route from Gibraltar to Prestwick in Scotland lost its way, ran out of fuel, and was forced to crash-land near Athenry in Galway. It carried six senior U.S. officers, including Gen. Jacob Devers, then commander of Armored Forces who had been inspecting troops in North Africa. They were lucky to escape—the plane crashed through a stone wall at 70 mph before coming to rest in a field. Devers and the other Americans crawled out of the wreckage and were quickly surrounded by local people, amazed both at the plane and at the fact that its passengers were still alive. One woman rushed out with bandages. When assured that they were not needed, she said: "God bless you all. If nobody is hurt then I'll run home and get the whiskey." In turn Devers offered a crate of fruit on the plane to the locals, who, he recalled, "ate it greedily." His party was taken to a hotel in Athenry and an excellent meal provided (for which Devers insisted on paying). While there he talked on the phone to David Gray in Dublin who for obvious reasons could not explain about the agreement, but promised: "Everything is going to be all right." Deliberately leaving the people of Athenry with the impression that they were to be interned, the Americans were taken under cover of darkness by car to the border some 120 miles away, frequently getting lost en route. After another drink at the border post, they were met by Gen. Hill's staff and driven to Lurgan before resuming their journey to Britain.[24] They had discovered the answer to the wartime Irish joke: "Who are we neutral against?"

Accommodating the GIs safely in the United Kingdom was hard enough. But they were not a bunch of tourists, whose main requirements were board and lodging. This was an army, supposedly preparing to invade Hitler's Fortress Europe. Finding space for training was the toughest problem of all.

For a start, the U.S. forces were competing with the British Army, 1.7 million of whom were cooped up in Britain in January 1943, not to mention Allied contingents of whom the 170,000 Canadians were the largest. The British Army and RAF had arrogated large areas of countryside during the war. An estimate in 1945 put the figure at one-thirteenth of the total area of England, Wales, and Northern Ireland. These depredations usually conflicted directly with the needs of agriculture. Imports had been severely reduced in wartime because of the U-boat threat and the need to conserve scarce shipping and foreign exchange. Whereas home-grown food catered to about a third of national requirements prewar, the proportion had risen to 70 percent by mid-1943. The large open tracts most in demand for training, especially for tanks, were usually prime arable land, particularly in the main centres of the American occupation, southern England, and East Anglia. The land-use question was also highly politicized. As the War Office reminded ETO (with evident distaste), "democracy is now highly developed in this country and the evacuation of population or the sterilisation of any considerable area of land is a matter which usually entails public meetings in some form and a degree of publicity." The government was therefore reluctant to utilize its powers under Defence Regulation (DR) 51 to effect total dispossession. Where possible, it preferred dual use between landowner and the military under the provisions of DR 52. This was less contentious politically and allowed cultivation to continue, but both farmers and soldiers found it intensely frustrating and recriminations about damage were inevitable.[25]

It was estimated in June 1941 that damage to fences and hedges accounted for 30 percent of civilian claims against the military, crops 25 percent, and livestock 21 percent. Broken hedges and fences were the most serious because they usually led directly to the other forms of damage. In addition, troops spread animal infections, such as foot and mouth disease and, more deliberately, were prone to shoot some game or help themselves to scarce chickens and eggs. Many exercises had a tendency to degenerate into gratuitous vandalism. After the 1st Canadian Division had "attacked" the Sussex town of Horsham in April 1942, one soldier wrote home: "What with going through people's fields and hedges and cutting down big trees—the engineers actually blew up a farmer's bridge—and tearing across the country the way we did, you can bet we enjoyed ourselves."[26]

In the spring of 1943 Julia White received a requisition order from the War Office. Part of her farm at Inkpen in Berkshire, on the edge of an old rifle range, would be used by the U.S. Army as a battle training area. Miss White was a single woman in her early forties who ran the large farm with the help of two farmworkers. For her the "Yanks" were an unmitigated nuisance—years later her memoirs still bristle. "The troops would arrive in luxury coaches in the morning, leaving them to block the lane all day, walk down the hill to the battle area (apparently American soldiers don't march) and begin the battle." Firing often seemed indiscriminate, with empty cans, rabbits, or "even people walking along the top of the hill" as targets. She and her men got used to bullets whistling by them as they farmed. Once a flamethrower completely burnt up a small copse. The fields became littered with unexploded ammunition and pockmarked with slit trenches—both of which were great hazards to the tractors. For over a year the GIs paid their visits. Compensation was minimal, complaints unproductive. One officer told her "in his American drawl" that "didn't I know that the U.S. army had taken over the whole of the south of England and could do what they liked in it?"[27]

The situation was equally unsatisfactory for the U.S. Army. "It is difficult to conduct any large-unit training here," noted a Pentagon observer in February 1943, and ETO Commander Gen. Frank Andrews advised Marshall to give GIs "as much combat and amphibious training as possible in the States." Only around Salisbury Plain was unrestricted manoeuvre possible, but even there GIs had to compete with the neighbouring British units for use of the training areas and firing ranges. This was certainly the experience of the 29th Division when based at Tidworth in 1942–43. Partly in consequence (and also because of the poor physical fitness of many men) it spent much of its time that winter in long twenty-five-mile road marches around Stonehenge. According to Edwin Young, a medic, "one of our clerks figured out that we had walked over 3,000 miles, or equivalent to all the way back home, during this period." Although Gen. Devers considered the 29th's régime "highly beneficial," Gen. Hawley, ETO chief surgeon, called it an "unusually strenuous programme which broke down many soldiers." He wanted more moderate training for future units. But as 29er Melvin Sherr observed of the time at Tidworth: "What else was there to do?"[28]

When the division moved to Devon and Cornwall, large-unit manoeuvres were possible on Dartmoor and Bodmin Moor. But these were remembered with loathing by most 29ers—treeless wastes of spongey soil where the wind always blew and the only alternative to driving rain was the drenching mist. Capt. Maurice Clift, a company CO in the 115th Regiment, wrote a parody of John Masefield's poem "Sea Fever," in which the first and last verses ran:

> I want to go out to the moors again,
> To the fog and the rocks and the rain,
> To the gorse and the marsh and the muddy pools,
> Wherein the boys have lain. . . .
> Oh, I'll go out to the moors again,
> But mind you and mark me well:
> I'll carry enough explosives,
> To blow the place to hell.[29]

Away from the moors, in their camps around local villages, troops focused on weapons skills and small-unit training. There was little room for anything more ambitious.

On the moors or off, the use of live ammunition was rigorously controlled. A battalion commander in the 115th wanted to fire a machine gun over the assault course at Launceston to give greater realism to training. His CO eventually gave permission as follows: "I certify that I consider it safe to fire from the position you pointed out to me, provided of course that guards are placed to prevent persons or cattle from crossing the direct line of fire." When the Americans took over the Bodmin Artillery Range from the British Army, they discovered that the main Launceston-to-Bodmin road ran like a corridor through the middle of it. Along the road were houses in which civilian families continued to live. The guns had to fire *over* the houses to hit target areas on the other side.[30]

The 29th's experiences in the West Country were not unique. When the 6th Armored Division arrived in the Cotswolds in February 1944, its commander spent the first month trying to secure a suitable firing range. Meanwhile his men were kept occupied in road marches and close-order drills—neither of which seemed much use to tank crews. It was a far cry from Patton's Desert Training Center in California. The 90th Infantry Division, in south Wales that spring, had great difficulty finding ranges for small-arms and grenades and so concentrated on weapons proficiency and physical conditioning. "My memory of training in England," recalled Gen. William E. DePuy, then a captain in the 90th, "was that we did a lot of road marches." And about the same time, Gen. Wade H. Haislip, the new commander in Ulster, was complaining to the Pentagon about "the handicaps of limited equipment, bad weather, and almost non-existent training areas. My hope is that I can prevent the troops from going backwards." The 2nd Division, part of his command, had to concentrate on small-unit training, often in empty castles or factories, because of the weather. It was impossible to repeat the manoeuvres of army or corps strength in which they had participated in Texas and Louisiana before departure.[31]

Of course, Army commanders always want more space (and more men and equipment). But the experience of the two U.S. divisions in Ulster in 1942 was a sobering reminder of the consequences of inadequate training. Col. Hamilton H. Howze, G-3 of the 1st Armored, recalled:

> We were mostly tramping around the roads while pretending that we were fanned out across the countryside; we couldn't get onto the ground, with rare exceptions. We had the most horrible fights with landowners where we did inadvertently get on the ground, or where we had permission to bivouac and damage[d] crops, trees or grass.

Gen. Orlando "Pinky" Ward, the divisional commander, claimed that the major July 1942 exercise with the British had been "completely artificial—so artificial that the training destroyed more confidence than it built." Likewise, the 34th Infantry Division spent most of its time on weaponry and marching. Scattered across the counties of Tyrone and Fermanagh in battalion-size encampments, its men had scant opportunity to operate as regiments, let alone as a division. At the end of 1942 the 34th and 1st Armored were diverted to Operation

Torch and sent into battle in Tunisia, where they were caught up in the notorious American debacles of Kasserine and Fondouk in February and March 1943. Undoubtedly there were many reasons for these setbacks, often at higher levels, including inferior tanks, inadequate air support, and faulty dispositions. But, in Eisenhower's judicious understatement, there was "no blinking the fact that we have had certain disappointments" with the divisions themselves. They had arrived in Ulster half-trained and the situation there gave officers and men scant opportunity for improvement.[32]

Little wonder, then, that the American military were constantly trying to obtain more space. But any request, however small, entailed extensive negotiation with the British War Office and Ministry of Agriculture, as medical officer Col. Joseph Darnall discovered in April 1944. Where large acreage was involved the matter often went to the British cabinet, as when ETO requested some 190,000 acres of Wiltshire downland in autumn 1943 for armored training. The minister of agriculture warned of "a very serious effect on food production" and the cabinet agreed only after the request had been cut to 141,000 acres. It also insisted that dual use be maintained and no live ammunition fired.[33]

The most controversial demand was made in connection with amphibious training for invasion troops. In September 1943 a special Assault Training Center opened on the north Devon coast between Appledore and Woolacombe. It covered some twenty-five square miles including eight thousand yards of beach. Here amphibious and assault techniques were refined and practised by the assault divisions for Overlord. But the small size of the centre meant that training was not possible above the battalion level. Moreover, the proximity to civilian areas imposed very tight limits on live firing. Invasion planners therefore demanded an area of about twenty-five square miles on the south Devon coast, between Kingsbridge and Dartmouth, known as the South Hams. They wanted total freedom for firing and manoeuvre, including naval and aerial bombardment, so as to simulate combined operations. An additional attraction of the area, though not appreciated until 1944 when the invasion plan was enlarged, was that the central part of the coastline was strikingly similar to that of Utah Beach. Behind Slapton Sands was Slapton Ley, a shallow lake with narrow exit points, which resembled the flooded hinterland of the southeast Cotentin.[34]

The request to take over the South Hams came before the government ministers only weeks after the debate about tanks on Salisbury Plain. Moreover, the Americans wanted total control, under DR 51, and not dual use. Some 2,750 people would be displaced and seventeen thousand acres of farmland despoiled. But the case was compellingly presented. "Without training facilities of this nature," the Overlord planners warned, "it is firmly believed that the success of proposed operations would be jeopardized." And the U.S. Army enlisted Ambassador Winant to apply pressure directly on Churchill. Because of its political sensitivity and security implications, the issue was handled by an inner circle of ministers, rather than the whole cabinet, and approval was given on 3 November. The county council was then told that the area must be totally vacated by 20 December.[35]

The decision was announced at public meetings in the principal villages on 12–13 November. Although rumour had run riot over the previous few days, the news still came as an enormous shock. This was an isolated backwater of Devon and the older inhabitants rarely left their villages. They were giving up homes, farms, and livelihoods for several months, in return for minimal compensation and the hardly satisfactory promise that although American forces "would not wantonly destroy houses and churches . . . it could not be guaranteed that damage and destruction would not occur." Although people accepted the decision in principle, the U.S. consul in Plymouth reported, there was much criticism of the government's "autocratic and undemocratic methods" of implementation, particularly its speed, and on 15 December he noted "unofficial but reliable information" about "a fair number of suicides" among civilians about to be evacuated.[36]

Not only had the people to move themselves and their property, it was also necessary to strip the local churches because their safety could not be guaranteed in a target area. This meant packing up candlesticks, pulpits, and even fragile chancel screens. At Blackawton the Norman font had to be removed and an American sergeant arrived to help, chewing gum and asking, "Where's Norman's font we've heard so much about?" As a final act, a notice signed by the bishop of Exeter was pinned to the door of each evacuated church:

FROM THIS PARISH TO OUR UNITED STATES ALLIES

This church has stood for several hundred years. Around it has grown a community which has lived in these houses and tilled these fields ever since there was a church. This church, this churchyard in which their loved ones lie at rest, these homes, these fields are as dear to those who have left them as are the homes and graves which you, our Allies, have left behind you. They hope to return one day, as you hope to return to yours, to find them waiting to welcome them home.[37]

9

A Day Trip
to Dieppe

★   ★   ★

THE AMERICANS WERE NOT THE ONLY FOREIGN TROOPS MARKING TIME AND making space in Britain in 1942–44. In fact, until the middle of 1943, GIs were outnumbered by Canadian soldiers, some of whom had been in the country since 1939. They, too, had to endure cramped accommodation and inadequate training facilities. The Canadian experience in Britain serves as an instructive counterpoint to that of the U.S. Army. Moreover, it was the Canadians who mounted the first major assault on Hitler's Fortress Europe, nearly two years before the invasion of Normandy. The Dieppe raid of 19 August 1942 was, "in ratio to participating forces, the most costly Allied offensive assault of the war."[1] Its tragic story highlights the pressures within an army of occupation.

Dieppe was the climax of a series of raids on occupied Europe mounted or projected in 1942 by Britain's Combined Operations Headquarters under the command of Admiral Lord Louis Mountbatten. Bruneval in February and St.-Nazaire in March were small-scale but successful British commando raids on the French coast that boosted British morale (and Mountbatten's reputation). Determined to be in on the action after over two years of waiting in England, the Canadian command in Britain insisted on having the leading role in the next and much bigger raid, scheduled for Dieppe. Dress rehearsals in June were not impressive and on 8 July the raid, then code-named Rutter, was abandoned because of bad weather, the troops having been embarked for several days. Two troopships had been attacked by the Luftwaffe and German intelligence was alerted. Despite this, the following month the operation was remounted under a new name—Jubilee. The troops were to land at eight points along a ten-mile front, centred on the promenade at Dieppe. Of the six thousand land troops involved, nearly five thousand were from the 2nd Canadian Division under the land-force commander Gen. "Ham" Roberts. The rest were British commandos, charged with destroying German gun emplacements on the flanks, plus a token presence of fifty of their newly formed American equivalents, the Rangers. In the air above them, the Luftwaffe would be drawn into a major battle and, it was hoped, heavy fighter losses inflicted.

Churchill had characterized this as a "butcher and bolt" raid on a German strongpoint, over in a morning. In fact the butchery was all on the Allied side and few had a chance to bolt. For most, the day trip became a one-way ticket. Only one of the two commando actions was successful and the main Canadian assaults resulted in appalling casualties. Sixty-eight percent of the five thousand Canadians were killed, wounded, or captured. All the new Churchill tanks were left on the shingle, many intact, and Hitler publicly expressed his appreciation at receiving prototypes for German intelligence to examine. In addition, the RAF suffered 13 percent casualties and lost 106 planes, over double the Luftwaffe's losses. It had mobilized sixty-six squadrons and flown over twenty-one hundred sorties in what, albeit briefly, was the "the largest air battle of the Second World War." With hindsight, the disaster seems so inevitable that it has encouraged the darkest suspicions. Dwight Eisenhower's grandson, for instance, has even suggested that Dieppe was "a planned failure, a sacrificial expenditure of 3,000 lives" by the British to show Marshall "the futility of further argument" about invading France in 1942.[2]

That is to subscribe too fully to American myths about British duplicity. Dieppe was more a cock-up than a conspiracy. But it was such a costly cock-up that it required a major conspiracy to conceal it. Here, as usual, the British establishment excelled. Churchill's own post facto questions were fobbed off in 1942 and again in 1950 when he was trying to explain the fiasco in his memoirs. There he finally used an account prepared for him by Mountbatten. Dieppe, Churchill claimed, was "a reconnaissance in force," from which invaluable lessons were learned for Overlord two years later. This became the standard line. Mountbatten even told still-bitter Canadian veterans in 1973: "the Duke of Wellington . . . said that the Battle of Waterloo was won on the playing fields of Eton. I say the successful landing in Normandy was won on the beaches of Dieppe." The truth of such contentions cannot be explored here, but many of the "lessons" seem to have been fairly obvious, such as the need for air cover and naval bombardment or the dangers of attacking a well-defended port. Historian John Keegan, one of many sceptics, has remarked that it is "as illuminating to say of Dieppe . . . that it taught important lessons about amphibious operations as to say . . . of the *Titanic* disaster that it taught important lessons about passenger design."[3]

Most of the "lessons," in fact, had been noted beforehand, only to be ignored as political pressures, bureaucratic manoeuvring, and sheer incompetence emasculated the plan. It was Gen. Bernard Montgomery, involved in the early planning as head of British South-East Command, who insisted on a frontal assault, arguing that flanking attacks required too much precision for ordinary troops. But he assumed that adequate firepower would back the operation—assumptions that were negated by the Navy's unwillingness to hazard any battleships after the loss of the *Prince of Wales* in December 1941 and by the RAF's refusal to risk more than a token force of bombers when it was hoarding everything for the strategic bombing of Germany.

The list of errors runs on and on—intelligence failures, security leaks, lack of surprise. And, although Mountbatten's official biographer argues with some justice that the whole affair was a case of too many cooks, much of the blame must attach to Mountbatten himself as head of Combined Operations. Ambitious, energetic, and well-connected (he was a second cousin of the king), "Dickie" was a favourite of both Churchill and Roosevelt. At forty-one, with previous experience only in commanding destroyers, he was put in charge of Combined Operations, promoted by Churchill from commodore to vice admiral, and imposed on the irate Chiefs of Staff as a fourth member of their committee. Despite this spectacular inflation of rank, he lacked the clout to force the necessary support from the Navy and RAF or the skill to recognize the defects of the suicide mission that was left. "A very gallant sailor," observed Montgomery. "Had three ships sunk under him. *Three* ships. [Pause.] Doesn't know how to fight a battle." After Rutter had been abandoned, Montgomery, in fact, became so alarmed at the plan that he dissociated himself completely from it, and historian Brian Loring Villa has argued that Mountbatten actually remounted the operation in August without proper authorization from the Chiefs of Staff, conscious of the importance of the raiding programme for his own career—he was being tipped as deputy Allied commander in the eventual invasion of France.[4]

Mountbatten's failures—which were appalling—were, however, those of a man who had been absurdly overpromoted by Churchill. The prime minister was desperate for action, and Mountbatten's energy and verve contrasted refreshingly with the negativism of the senior military. With Britain rejecting Russian and American demands for an immediate second front in France, Dieppe became an important surrogate. Churchill was presenting it as such in Moscow just days before the operation began. While the North African invasion struck at the "soft underbelly of the crocodile," he told Stalin, the Dieppe raid would rap him on the "hard snout." And behind Churchill was British press and public opinion—equally desperate for some morale-boosting success in 1942 and dismissive of the problems surrounding their panacea slogan of "a second front." To quote a poignantly apt remark by *The New Yorker*'s correspondent in London, Mollie Panter-Downes, people were talking that summer as if "a Continental invasion was as easy a jaunt as a prewar cheap-day trip to Dieppe."[5]

Yet the shambles on the British side should not distract from the basic point for our purpose. In Villa's words, "if the Canadians had said 'No!' after the first cancellation, there would have been no Dieppe raid in 1942." British troops would not have touched the mission after Monty backed out, and the 2nd Canadian Division's commander, Roberts, was himself deeply unhappy about the plan by mid-July. He only went ahead after formally being "instructed" to do so by the commander of Canadian forces in Britain, Gen. Andrew McNaughton.[6] Why McNaughton did this, why Canadian commanders placed their own men's necks in the noose formed by Mountbatten, is the sad subject of this chapter.

As an independent "dominion" within the British Empire, Canada made its own decisions about foreign policy. Its government, under Prime Minister William Lyon Mackenzie King, declared war a week after Britain, on 10 September 1939. It quickly decided to send an expeditionary force to Britain and the first Canadian troops docked in the Clyde on 17 December 1939. During the next few weeks the whole of the 1st Canadian Division arrived in Britain and was based at British Army barracks in Aldershot, forty miles southwest of London. By May 1940 there were over twenty-five thousand Canadian troops in the country and in those critical weeks they were shuffled around the country, twice nearly being committed in France. The 2nd Canadian Division joined them in late summer and the 3rd Division in July 1941, while the 1st Tank Brigade and the 5th Armoured Division arrived, respectively, in June and October–November 1941. By the time the United States entered the war there were already 120,000 Canadian troops in Britain. In April 1942 Gen. McNaughton, who had built up the Canadian Corps in 1940–41, was designated GOC First Canadian Army.[7]

The Australian and New Zealand governments also had troops in Britain in 1940, but these were moved to Egypt at the end of the year. Other Australasian contingents were sent to reinforce Singapore. The willingness of the Pacific dominions to subsume their troops in the British war effort in North Africa and Southeast Asia, despite growing anxiety in 1941–42 about the direct threat from Japan, contrasted with the Canadian approach. McNaughton was firm on two points. He would keep the Canadian Army intact, to operate as a single entity, and it would fight the Germans in Europe and not in peripheral theatres like North Africa. This tenaciously nationalist position was rooted in memories of Britain's "colonial" attitude to the Canadians in World War One. Maintaining its integrity, the Canadian Corps had won a famous, if bloody, victory, at Vimy Ridge in April 1917 and during the great German offensives in the spring of 1918, its commander, General Arthur Currie, like Pershing for the Americans, had resisted Anglo-French attempts to throw his troops into the line piecemeal. McNaughton was convinced that this was the right policy for Canada—"the acid test of sovereignty is the control of the armed forces." He was determined to avoid the Canadian force becoming "decentralized under British command" resulting in "an inferior role in the total Allied war effort." Contradicting the claim by McNaughton's biographer that he was willing "to fight his Corps wherever it might be needed," Brian Villa has shown that informal British invitations for the Canadians to join the Australians and New Zealanders in North Africa were repeatedly rebuffed in 1940–41. For McNaughton, commented Villa, "Vimy II could not possibly exist in North Africa; it must lie in Europe."[8]

But Vimy II kept being postponed. For a year after May 1940 the Canadians' prime function was protecting Britain against invasion and they were ranged along the North Downs in Surrey and Hampshire as part of the reserve forces. In the autumn of 1941 all the Canadian troops moved into positions along the Sussex coast, from Hastings to the Hampshire border. Yet they were guarding Britain against an invasion that no longer seemed likely. A new, offensive role had to be found. In September 1941, McNaughton, an assiduous media man, had told a press conference that the Canadian Army was "a dagger pointed at the heart of Berlin." That phrase was to haunt him, echoing through 1942 and 1943 "proudly at first, then with an ironic note, and finally with a kind of forlorn and increasingly vocal resentment as British, Australians, New Zealanders, Indians, South Africans, and eventually Americans went into battle on different fronts all over the world while Canadians still languished at garrison duties in England."[9] By keeping the Canadian Army intact, McNaughton had also kept it out of action. Within his own command, General Crerar of 1st Corps was one of several senior officers who fundamentally disputed McNaughton's policy. By the spring of 1943, the Ottawa government concurred and it finally overrode McNaughton. The 1st Division and the 1st Tank Brigade were despatched to join the Mediterranean campaign from July 1943.

These were the troops who had served longest in Britain—the 1st Division had waited three and a half years for action. The other longest-serving division, the 2nd, was, however, by then incapable of action, having been decimated at Dieppe. For, in the interim between the end of the invasion threat and the abandonment of McNaughton's policy, the only way for the Canadians to get at the Germans was through raiding the Continent. Crerar badgered both Ottawa and London for a lead role in these operations in 1941–42, and pressed his case on the British with particular stridency in February and March 1942 while McNaughton was back in Canada. Writing to Montgomery on 5 February 1942, Crerar demanded that "a very high proportion of these prospective raids, if not the total, should be undertaken by detachments from the Canadian Corps." A month later, he took his case to Brooke, the Chief of the Imperial General Staff, complaining about the "galling" inaction, and McNaughton pressed the issue with Mountbatten throughout April. Their campaign was successful. Despite Mountbatten's reluctance, on 30 April the Canadians were formally offered the leading role in the Dieppe raid. The Ottawa government, reassured by vague information that this would only involve a brigade, gave its approval the next day. After the Canadians had struggled so hard for the opportunity, McNaughton seems to have been reluctant to ask awkward questions about the plans and the operation.[10]

Canadian participation in the Dieppe raid was therefore partly a consequence of McNaughton's determination to maintain his Army intact to fight the Germans. By 1942, *intact* meant untouched; the Canadians were unbowed but unbloodied. Dieppe was the "answer." But there was another explanation—less familiar, yet more pertinent for us as we seek to understand the dynamics of armies of occupation. This was Crerar's acute anxiety about the morale crisis in his divisions by early 1942 as discipline and enthusiasm had been eroded by months of stultifying inactivity.

Morale was not a new problem for the Canadians in 1941–42. The 1st Canadian Division had spent a miserable first winter in Britain in early 1940. This was the coldest winter for half a century and the division was decimated by colds and influenza. At Aldershot it was housed in a mixture of draughty Victorian barracks and unfinished new construction. The divisional commander complained that the contractors, whose pace was leisurely at best, were determined to complete the cricket pavilion before the accommodation huts. His men also came from a country where strict temperance laws were still in force, a legacy of prohibition during World War One. In 1939 Ontario, from where between a third and a half of these Canadian troops hailed, still had only "beverage rooms" in whose grim surroundings nothing but beer could be drunk and where no entertainment was provided. The English "pub" was therefore a revelation for the young Canadians, and drunk and disorderly conduct prompted numerous local protests. Soldiers, for their part, reported being "short changed" in pubs and set upon by "local roughs." Censors' reports on troop letters home indicated pervasive "boredom, homesickness and a feeling of not being really needed" but, although concerned about the situation, Gen. Crerar opined that "with the coming of the better weather . . . most of the causes for complaint will disappear."[11]

He was right. In fact, May–June 1940 saw a Canadian-British encounter that should be dwelt on because of its implications for our understanding of armies of occupation. During the early days of the Dunkirk crisis, when invasion seemed imminent and evacuation of more than thirty thousand British troops impossible, the 1st Canadian Division was moved into Northamptonshire as the main mobile reserve against the Nazi invasion. Their stay there was brief, for some regiments only a few days, but it had a lasting effect because, in the emergency, the troops were billeted (lodged) in British homes. Between 28 May and 11 June some twenty thousand Canadians were billeted for various periods of time. In return householders were paid one shilling and twopence (roughly twenty cents) per head per night. In Northampton itself, the British claims officer noted, "there were some 9,002 payments by cheque, but some hundreds of billetors are not included in these as they waived payment out of enthusiasm and appreciation of the Canadians." The Princess Patricia Regiment spent two short periods in billets in the nearby town of Kettering. Private Howard Clegg noted in his diary: "We are supposed only to sleep in our billets, between our own blankets. But the good people insist on supplying all bedding, sheets, pillow-slips, etc., and on feeding us as often as we will surrender to their insistence. Some of the fellows have been virtually adopted by their host families." By the time of the regiment's departure Clegg wrote: "Kettering has changed the fellows' opinion about the English. . . . The hospitality has been overwhelming." The general verdict now was that "The English are tops!"[12]

What we might, for shorthand, term the "Northampton Experience" can be explained in several ways. In part, the soldiers were buoyed up by the excitement of movement and action. As Private Clegg observed, "it was a welcome relief to bored troops after six months semi-confinement at barracks. . . . No wonder people liked us and talked about our cheerfulness and good manners, and all sorts of qualities of which we never suspected ourselves. The fact is we were happy." In addition, they were encountering a different brand of English people. Although there were local hospitality committees in Aldershot, that had been a garrison town since the 1850s, inured to troops and their problems. Around Northampton, by contrast, soldiers were more of a novelty and the generally working-class families on whom the Canadians were billeted responded with spontaneity and warmth. Also important was the "Dunkirk spirit." For both the Canadians and the British, the war was now in deadly earnest. The troops were needed and were made to feel needed. This mood of mutual respect continued that summer as the Canadians witnessed civilian fortitude during the Blitz and the troops, often under canvas or even sleeping in the open as they moved around the country, were invited into people's houses to take a bath. Above all, entering the Englishman's "castle" was of critical importance. Through billeting, the troops, often for the first time, met the locals in their own homes instead of at arm's length in pubs or streets. Howard Clegg considered the English water closet, still operated by a chain, a particularly good way of breaking the ice:

> Every chain has its own little idiosyncracies. Many of them simply defy the uninitiated to manage them properly. Consequently dignified hostesses, when showing you where the bath-room is and which towel is for you, have also to give a lesson in managing the chain. . . . You really get to know people when you have used their bathroom a few times.[13]

The Northampton Experience was revealing but not definitive. It showed what could happen when the chemistry worked, especially inside ordinary homes where "soldiers" and "civilians" became people. But that was still a rare occurrence. At the end of June the same 1st Division made itself very unpopular in Oxford when drunken Canadians ran amok, breaking glass, harassing women, and careering around the streets in military vehicles. As usual with such incidents, a minority was to blame but the difference with Northampton was striking. In that case, the town became their temporary home, the townspeople their hosts. "At Oxford the units were distributed under canvas in the country for miles around; Oxford was just . . . the place where one sought amusement—and booze." As hundreds of troops, in large groups, wandered from pub to pub, they had little chance to meet the locals as friends.[14]

Thus, the same troops, in changed circumstances, behaved very differently. And most of the Canadian force arrived after June 1940. Although a good many witnessed the Blitz or vivid evidence of it, those who arrived in 1941 were denied their equivalent of the Northampton Experience. The winter of 1940–41 saw a slump in morale and renewed indiscipline. In October 1940 McNaughton was receiving "many complaints" about "drunkeness [sic] and disorderly behaviour, damage to private property, slovenliness in dress, misuse of mechanical transport, dangerous driving," and a thriving black market in petrol. Prime Minister Mackenzie King himself was concerned at reports that "the men are getting out of bounds" and that there would be "great difficulty in restraining them from many wild exploits if their energies are not used up in actual fighting."[15] The summer months of 1941 reduced these problems but did not eliminate them. By the time the three Canadian infantry divisions settled into Sussex that autumn, their commanders feared that another winter of cold, blackout, and inaction could prove disastrous.

Canadian commanders in 1939–41 faced comparable problems to those confronted by Marshall and McNair in 1941–42 as they tried to forge an army. There were tensions between the hard core of regulars from the old "Permanent Force" and the newcomers. The Canadians also had their own "National Guard" problem in the form of the provincial militia units, who formed half the strength of the 1st Division in 1939. Many of these men were overage and unfit for serious action. As in the U.S. Army, perhaps the gravest weaknesses were among the regimental officers, both regular and militia, whose attitude towards training, wrote army historian Charles Stacey, was often "casual and haphazard rather than scientific; like the traditional amateur actor, they were cheerfully confident that it would be 'all right on the night' without having to exert themselves too much." Like later GIs, the Canadian also suffered from lack of space. Training in 1940 was largely a matter of weapons, fitness, and road marches, with little chance to exercise en masse above the battalion level. The first time the 1st Canadian Division manoeuvred as a unit—around the Kent town of Ashford during February 1941—the result, to quote its commander, General Pearkes, "was the most terrible traffic jam anyone ever ran into." Columns of vehicles seemed to converge simultaneously from all directions on tiny crossroads and McNaughton was "livid with rage."[16]

These problems of personnel and training were common to the

Canadians and Americans in Britain. Other difficulties were more peculiarly Canadian. Because of the rush to send the 1st Division to Britain in late 1939, "raw recruits who required individual training made up more than half" its numbers, noted historian John English. Some French-speaking troops felt alienated from the anglophonia of their officers and the English natives and this may help to explain their unruly behavior in west Sussex, which eventually prompted Montgomery, the area commander, to ask for their removal elsewhere. These problems pointed to something deeper. Unlike the American and British armed forces in World War Two, the Canadian Army Overseas was an entirely volunteer force, to avoid repeating the bitter conscription controversy that had so antagonized French-Canadians in 1917–18. Consequently, the Canadian authorities were not inclined to turn away any volunteers. Although half the 1st Division were militia men, many others, as the Division's nickname, "Breadliners," suggests, joined up to escape the Depression. "I wasn't patriotic," one recalled. "I just wanted some good clothes and hot showers and three decent meals a day and a few dollars for tobacco and beer."[17]

That motive, in itself, was not surprising—the U.S. Regular Army had been an alternative to unemployment for many in the 1930s and some Americans even volunteered for Canadian service in 1939. What was unusual about the Canadian Army in 1939–40 was that there was virtually no psychological testing of volunteers. Men's "mere act of volunteering was presumed to indicate their fitness for soldiering," commented historians Terry Copp and Bill McAndrew, adding that the "most rudimentary prudence might have detected, not marginal individuals, but mental defectives, psychotics, alcoholics, and former mental patients, whose potential usefulness to the army was questionable." Consequently, the 1st Division, and to some extent the 2nd, in Britain had not merely to turn civilians into soldiers, but also to weed out the misfits—usually only after persistent misconduct had betrayed them. Between February 1940 and March 1941 (when the Canadian strength in Britain had reached fifty-six thousand) 2,135 troops of all ranks were returned to Canada for discharge. Over one-fifth of these were classified as mental cases—"chiefly anxiety neuroses, chronic alcoholism or mental deficiency."[18]

But the fundamental Canadian problem was inaction. The German attack on Russia in June 1941 made Nazi invasion seem unlikely, the real war more remote, and their training even less meaningful. Mail censors noted in September 1941 that "many men express their desire to serve in Russia, and several mention that they are beginning to learn the Russian language." In these circumstances, their physical discomforts often became an obsession. Letters home were full of complaints about the food. Being on British ration scales was itself a grievance, but in some cases the men only got two meals a day, both of them cold. There were "mutinies" or sit-down strikes over food in at least two camps in August 1941. Accommodation was also grim. Billets, that catalyst for good relations, were usually employed in 1940 and 1941 only for troops away on detail from the main unit or in emergencies such as Dunkirk week. Most of the troops lived either in tented camps, military barracks or requisitioned houses. The camps were often devoid of recreational facilities and set in open country, miles from any town. As for the barracks, military censors in September 1941 noted that whenever "Canadian troops are moved into new stations, away from the large military centres like Aldershot, there is considerable improvement in their morale." According to one soldier then in Aldershot: "The people around this area have been used to troops for so long that they pay little or no attention to us." Yet "a meal and an evening in a soft chair with pleasant company" could make a soldier feel human again. It was, sighed another Canadian in a letter to his family, "just like a breath of Heaven to go into someone's home" and have "the sensation of being in a place where people 'live.' "[19]

In early 1942 all these problems combined in extremis to constitute what was the nadir of misconduct and indiscipline for the Canadian troops in Britain. January and February 1942 "saw the greatest shuffle in commands that had yet taken place" as McNaughton succeeded in establishing age limits for officers of the rank of lieutenant colonel and above. The problem of psychiatric cases reached "epidemic proportions" that winter, with the increase ascribed by two wartime psychiatrists who studied it to the cumulative stress of "boredom, separation from families, inactivity and indefinite waiting." And the Christmas season saw a rash of fights between British and Canadian troops that often escalated into feuds between whole units. Censors attributed these fracas to "general inaction," judging that all the men "are spoiling for a fight, and would probably prefer to expend their energies on the enemy."[20]

Such was Crerar's concern, as commander of the 1st Canadian Corps, that on 6 January 1942 he requested morale reports direct from all his units, instead of relying on censors' analyses of soldiers' mail home. Some of these reports have a formulaic quality about them— few commanders, faced with such a request, would dare admit openly that morale was bad since it reflected in part on them. But the commander of the 3rd Division, whose men were newly arrived and mostly located in east Sussex, stated that half were living in hutted camps (despite a winter even worse than 1940) and that 50 percent of these camps had only bucket latrines. A few even lacked electricity and had to subsist on hurricane lamps. Pearkes, the 1st Division commander, whose men were now spending their third winter of inactivity in Britain, was quite candid. "Facilities for recreations and amusements are totally inadequate," he reported. Men quartered away from the coastal towns, to the north of the Downs, found that the "lonely countryside and lack of amenities tends to increase any feeling of being fed up." And, said Pearkes, after two years of intensive training, it was "only to be expected that the men show little enthusiasm for these activities. . . . The majority would more than welcome an opportunity of seeing service in a more active theatre."[21]

In terms of high politics, Pearkes acknowledged the merits of McNaughton's policy of keeping the Canadian Army intact. But, as his last comment suggests, in his capacity as a unit commander, he deplored its effect on morale. Crerar himself emphatically rejected McNaughtonism. On receipt of these reports he took action on two fronts. To all his commanders on 5 February 1942 he sent a circular expressing concern at "the bearing of personnel" and stating that "definite steps require to be taken to raise the present standard." He particularly tried to stamp on the "excuse, which has been utilized to exhaustion" that "the actual fighting (which we Canadians came over here to do) has so far been denied to us and, as a result of this disappointment, it has been necessary to accept evidences of rowdyism on the part of Canadians as a reasonable psychological release from their pent-up emotions." But, while ordering subordinates to tighten discipline, Crerar also tried to secure for the Canadians a share of "the actual fighting." It was on the same day, 5 February, that he wrote to Montgomery demanding that "a very high proportion" of the future raids on France, "if not the total, should be undertaken by detachments from the Canadian Corps." At the heart of his case was this warning: "as the months go by and opportunities fail to materialize in which the officers and men of my present command can match their skill and courage against the enemy, the more difficult it will be to maintain in them the desired keenness and morale."[22]

The Canadian Army's participation in the Dieppe raid should therefore be seen not merely as the result of high politics among its senior commanders but also as their response to a crisis of morale. None of this absolves either them, Mountbatten, or British policymakers from the tragic botches that subsequently led to disaster in August. But it shows the pressures working on leaders of an unoccupied army. Lord Moran, Churchill's wartime physician, wrote a classic account of military morale, born of his observations as an army doctor in the trenches in World War One. He devoted a chapter to "monotony":

> At Armentières in the first winter I cannot remember thinking that life was monotonous. It was novel, eventful; though nothing ever happened, I kept thinking that something was about to happen. But the winter of 1917, the third out here, seemed interminable; the awful sameness of the days fastened on to the mind, till I prayed that something, that anything might happen; but nothing did happen, until at last I had given up anticipating anything.

In Moran's judgement, monotony was "a sickness of the mind." Just days before Dieppe, one Canadian wrote home: "I fear that if we don't attempt to invade very soon the boys will be hard to handle, it is very obvious that their patience has been tried to the fullest degree and [they] are on the verge of insanity through lack of action."[23]

For men who came back from the Dieppe raid, it was a shattering experience. One wounded survivor from the Essex Scottish Regiment, which had attacked the promenade itself, wrote home: "Nearly all our friends have gone and it was with heavy hearts that the few remaining fell in for roll call this morning. As yet we are in such a daze we can't seem to realize the truth." But, though sobered, he had been inspired by the experience: "The question on everyone's lips [is] can we invade the continent? Without a doubt we can and will." This was also the effect on Canadians who did not participate. In early September, postal censors reported: "After the raid, the Morale of all the troops was considerably enhanced. There is a feeling of pride in themselves, and . . . the sense of frustration has been dispersed. Confidence in their own capabilities is freely expressed" and many considered "that the great feat which was accomplished has completely vindicated the Canadians as first-class fighting men in the eyes of the British and the world in general, which was never in doubt."[24]

Ironically, newspapers in the United States initially presented Dieppe as their own national epic. The American Rangers (though actually only fifty strong) were given star billing. YANKS IN 9-HR. DIEPPE RAID exulted the New York *Daily News* in front-page banner headlines the following day. Canadians were furious. *The New York Times*, which had proclaimed on 20 August that U.S.-ALLIED TROOPS, TANKS RAID DIEPPE 9 HOURS, was obliged two days later to print a piece correcting "misapprehension in the United States regarding the size of the United States part in the attack" and noting the "embarrassment" among American Army officials in London and what it discreetly called "some disgruntlement in other quarters." As both McNaughton and Eisenhower concluded, the blame lay mainly with headline writers in America, but they were operating in a British news blackout imposed while the extent of the disaster was assessed and official excuses were concocted. Unlike the Canadian press, who accepted British direction and steered clear of details, the American media simply made the most of what information they had.[25]

This unfortunate incident, which rankled for years afterwards in Canada, was an intimation of things to come. Most GIs were not left kicking *their* heels in Britain. And those who were obliged to linger would not allow themselves to be treated like the "Canucks." The American occupation of Britain turned out very differently from the Canadian.

Part III

HIGH POLICY

10

U.S.
and Them

★ ★ ★

ALL ARMIES ARE IN DANGER OF REVERTING TO CROWDS. WE SAW IN THE
previous part of the book that this is particularly true when troops are
not fighting and there are poor facilities for housing and training. If the
soldiers are on enemy soil it is easier to maintain a certain distance
from the local population. But where the "occupied" territory belongs
to allies, moreover allies who share a similar culture and speak the
same language, then the barriers between soldiers and civilians are
especially porous. This is not necessarily a bad thing—as the Canadians found in Britain in 1940, rapport with the locals can do wonders
for troop morale. But often contact resulted only in friction. So, was it
better to try keeping troops and civilians apart, and minimize trouble,
or to orchestrate their encounters in the hope of achieving harmony?
How the American and British authorities wrestled with this dilemma
during the long wait of 1942–44 is the subject of part III.

In September 1943 the 8th Air Force commander in Britain, Gen. Carl
Spaatz, stated that there were "three crimes a member of the Air Force
can commit: murder, rape and interference with Anglo-American relations. The first two might conceivably be pardoned, but the third one,
never." That same month Winston Churchill spoke about "the frater-
nal association of our two peoples" to an audience at Harvard University: "If we are together nothing is impossible. If we are divided all will
fail." The importance of what he was already calling "the natural
Anglo-American special relationship" had become axiomatic in London and Washington.[1]

This was at the level of cliché, however. Practicing what one preached was another matter. Hard-pressed American officers were more concerned about training their men than about getting on with the locals. There was also a question of methods. At one end of the spectrum, the aim might be simply to avoid trouble by keeping Americans and Britons at arm's length through a mixture of tough discipline and generous welfare. At the other extreme, positive programs could bring GIs into friendly contact with British people, but this was more time consuming and less useful militarily than mere damage limitation. The two approaches were encapsulated by Cyril Radcliffe, director-general of the British Ministry of Information, in June 1942: "There is no limit to the harm that is capable of being done if relations between the American soldiers and the local inhabitants go awry." On the other hand, he added, nor was there "any so favourable opportunity of promoting good Anglo-American relations and a wider understanding of each other's ways than these visits afford."[2]

In official approaches to this problem, three broad patterns can be discerned. The military of each country tended to be more preoccupied with damage limitation. This was particularly true of the Americans, with the conspicuous exception of Eisenhower. The positive line was usually espoused by diplomats from both countries, together with propagandists from the British Ministry of Information (MOI) and the American Office of War Information (OWI). That said, second, the British government tended to place greater stress on positive measures than did the Americans. The Foreign Office took a growing interest, animated by the Churchillian aim of a long-term "special relationship." And, third, the emphasis of both governments shifted from the negative in 1942–43, when their main concern was to establish a fabric of law and order for the American presence, to more positive measures in the year before Overlord, encouraged by a top-level directive from Roosevelt and Churchill.

The evolution of official policy in 1942–44 is the theme of this part of the book. This chapter examines certain basic decisions taken by the American and British authorities in 1942, when, for a time, it seemed that one million GIs would be in Britain by early 1943. These decisions concerned the legal position of the soldiers, their food, housing, pay, and leave accommodation—issues central to the GI's "oversexed, overpaid, overfed" image. The effect of these decisions was to allow U.S. troops preferential treatment compared with other Allies, such as the Canadians, and to set precedents that shaped GI-British relations for much of the war.

If all armies are potential crowds, the most basic need for commanders is authority to arrest, try, and punish their soldiers. Otherwise, even deserters could not be lawfully apprehended and the army would disintegrate. This was easily arranged at home, under appropriate laws and military regulations, but overseas a host government had to concede special "extraterritorial" jurisdiction to foreign armies. By the twentieth century this principle was recognized in international law, particularly on the Continent, and both the British and American armies in France in World War One had been allowed to exercise exclusive courts-martial jurisdiction over the misconduct of their soldiers. But the position in Britain was somewhat different. The modern British concept of a sovereign state had been developed in part to rein in private armies, outside the effective control of the Crown. In the words of the Victorian constitutional theorist A. V. Dicey, it was "a fixed doctrine of English law that a soldier, though a member of a standing army, is in England subject to all the duties and liabilities of an ordinary citizen."[3] Thus, in peace or war, British troops in Britain remained liable to ordinary courts for any breaches of the civil or criminal law, such as theft from or assault on civilians. This was true in peacetime in America but *not* in war, under Article 74 of the U.S. Articles of War.

The American demand for exclusive extraterritorial jurisdiction over its soldiers therefore clashed with the British insistence on the exclusive "rule of law." In World War One the issue had been discreetly handled without abridging that principle. In March 1918, Defence Regulation 45F gave the American Army all necessary powers to enforce discipline over their troops who had contravened U.S. military law. In practice all American offenders against *British* law were also handed over to the American military, but the British government refused to make a formal concession of exclusive jurisdiction. In World War Two the British maintained their constitutional position in the case of other Allied forces in Britain. An Act of 1933 regulating British Commonwealth forces and, on the same pattern, the Allied Forces Act of August 1940 for the exiled continental forces, allowed these to operate their own military law over their forces in Britain while preserving the jurisdiction of British courts in crimes against British law.[4]

The Americans, however, would not accept that position. The State, War, and Navy Departments demanded de jure and not merely de facto acknowledgement of exclusive jurisdiction over their forces in Britain. The British were unwilling to relent. Aside from the constitutional principles at stake, the British Attorney General also feared that any concession on this point would "raise a demand from other Allied Powers for similar treatment." The Americans' authority to exercise their own military law over GIs in Britain was empowered by an Order in Council on 22 May 1942, applying to them the provisions of the 1940 Visiting Forces Act. Even that was contentious because American negotiators bristled at anything that would liken them to the small "refugee" Allied governments. But the more controversial issue was crimes committed against British law, particularly when men were off base and off duty. Here the conflict of British and American legal principles was direct. Against the British insistence on the rule of law, the American case for exclusive territoriality argued that GIs had been conscripted and sent abroad against their will. In this sense they were always "on duty" and thus should be under military law. It was also argued that American public opinion would resent foreign courts exercising jurisdiction over U.S. citizens.[5]

The emotional temperature of the issue was indicated by the case of two Americans, aged twenty-two and seventeen, volunteers in the Canadian Army, who had robbed a British car driver at gunpoint near Oxford early in 1942. Tried in an English court, they were sentenced to six months hard labour and one was ordered to be whipped with twelve strokes of the "cat." The judge added: "Gangsters are unwelcome in this country." Learning belatedly of the case, Ambassador Winant was incensed. "I did not like his inference [sic] and I disliked the order for corporal punishment more." He told the State Department: "No American soldier would want a comrade to be ordered flogged by a British judge." Winant successfully persuaded the home secretary, Herbert Morrison, to remit the whipping, but he agreed to keep his intervention secret because Morrison feared a reaction in Parliament.[6]

In the end, the British cabinet conceded the American demands and placed a special bill before Parliament exempting members of the U.S. armed forces from criminal prosecution in any UK court. This was partly because of the adamantine rigidity of the American case, and partly because of the size of the anticipated American presence, which might have strained British juridical resources. But the main reason was quite simply that the United States was a far more important and powerful Ally than, say, Canada or Poland. The foreign, home, and Scottish secretaries jointly advised that "in the paramount interest of the co-operation of the United States with us in the war we must give them satisfaction." They therefore dismissed alternatives to an Act of Parliament, such as a 1918-style "gentleman's agreement," which would have avoided publicizing what they admitted was "the privileged position conferred upon the American Forces by comparison with those of the Allied Governments established in this country." Equally, they ruled out reserving cases of murder, manslaughter, and rape to British courts, which would have reduced "the risk that public feeling might be aroused in this country if serious crimes against civilians were not tried in our courts."[7] In short, despite the possible outcry from the Allied governments and the British public, Churchill's cabinet decided that the special relationship with America dictated special treatment for the GIs.

In the event there was no serious backlash either from Allied governments or domestic opinion. Canadian soldiers, for instance, were tried in British courts for breaches of British law, usually amid lurid publicity in the British press. That autumn the Canadian Army Public Relations Officer in London started writing routinely in protest to any newspaper editor who highlighted Canadian misconduct ("you would never put 'Englishman' in the headline"). Canadian Military HQ closely monitored debate on the 1942 bill, but no formal representation was made about the special American legal position.[8]

In the British press the "revolutionary" nature of the legislation was widely noted, but commentators also felt that shared legal traditions and procedures would minimize difficulties. *The Times* was typical when it editorialized that "the practice may . . . prove a good deal less revolutionary than the form, thanks entirely to the unique relationship created by history and preserved by common ideals between Great Britain and the United States." There was some grumbling in Parliament, but this was mostly directed at the British government, not at the Americans. As one MP complained, the bill was "brought before the House as a fait accompli" and "rushed through all its stages in one sitting" on 4 August to beat the summer recess. Explaining the urgency, the home secretary told the cabinet that "serious cases had already arisen and he was having great difficulty in dealing with the matter in default of the passage of the Bill into law." Public concern about the substance was somewhat assuaged by promises that, as far as possible, trials would be held in open court, near to the scene of the alleged crime, and by assurances that American military law was at least as tough as British criminal law. To take an example that would prove of considerable future significance: under U.S. Article of War 92 the punishment for rape was death or life imprisonment—considerably harsher than in Britain.[9]

The United States of America (Visiting Forces) Act became law on 6 August 1942. There was naturally great interest in the first case tried under its provisions, that of a twenty-five-year-old airman from Texas accused of raping a sixteen-year-old shop assistant in an air-raid shelter. The British press fixated on whether the trial conformed to movie stereotypes. Its informality, lack of wigs, and absence of legal circumlocution were all noted, but the *Daily Telegraph* remarked that there was "none of the highlights which Hollywood has led us to expect in an American court of law." After four days, during which the woman was the only female in a court of forty men, the soldier was acquitted. According to *Time* magazine, as he "symbolically went free in a jeep, the townspeople cheered."[10]

Trial in an American court was but one facet of the "privileged position" accorded to an insistent United States Army by an unusually cooperative British government. The GI's diet was another instance.

In World War One American troops in Britain were initially supplied by the British to minimize the pressure on shipping and the need for special American quartermaster depots. But the doughboys soon "objected most strenuously to the British rations. . . . The British soldier wanted his tea; the American soldier his coffee." The latter "did not relish the heavy puddings, Australian rabbit, sausage, etc., served in the British messes; instead he demanded a substantial evening meal in place of the tea that seemed to satisfy the British 'Tommy.' " Quantity as well as taste was at issue. British ration scales were deemed inadequate and the "Special Ration for American Troops in England," initiated from July 1918, included not merely greater variety than the British Home Ration on which the doughboys had previously subsisted but, for example, 50 percent more meat/bacon (fifteen ounces a day). Even those Americans living on British bases, such as trainee air mechanics, ate in separate messes almost everywhere by July 1918.[11]

In 1942 the British preferred the original 1918 arrangements, whereby they supplied the GIs, to save on shipping and construction. The State and Treasury Departments concurred, agreeing in February that "so far as possible, supplies, services, and materials for the American forces in British Empire areas should be supplied by lend-lease in reverse." Initially the Army had no choice because of the logistic crisis after Pearl Harbor. In Northern Ireland, for instance, the first American rations did not arrive until 18 March, while SOS HQ staff in Cheltenham had to rely on British messes and rations for weeks after their arrival in July 1942. But although Churchill was hopeful that the GIs might be converted to tea drinking, the Army (mindful of 1918) always intended that British rations were only a stop-gap. "American soldiers could not live on British rations," Roosevelt himself said bluntly in February 1942. Eisenhower took the same view when in Britain in July, while General Somervell, head of the SOS in Washington, would have nothing to do with any British attempt "to impose their standard of living on our troops." GI complaints about insufficient beef, coffee, fruit, and vegetables and too much tea, bread, potatoes, and mutton confirmed these judgements and in August the War Department formally agreed that the feeding of American troops in England "should be done by our Army supply system." Even when this became possible, however, large quantities of meat, vegetables, and dairy products still had to be procured locally, as well as most bread until 1944. From September 1942, in deference to Whitehall's concern about civilian morale, ETO agreed to use "National Whole-meal Flour" (a mixture of wheat, barley, and oats) instead of white bread baked with specially imported American wheat. The results were not popular with the men.[12]

Despite these privations, however, GIs still enjoyed a superior diet to British soldiers, let alone civilians, with fruit and meat particularly abundant. In early 1944 the British cabinet expressed concern about the "excessive" U.S. meat ration and the consequent demands on scarce shipping space (much of the meat came from Australia). It was calculated that GIs were receiving about twelve ounces of meat, sausage, and bacon a day, three times the British civilian ration and 50 percent more than British troops in the UK. The Minister of Food, John Llewellin, who had previously headed the Supply Mission in Washington, told the cabinet that the point had been "raised informally" with the Americans "on many occasions" and that he had once discussed it with General Marshall himself. According to Llewellin's revealing account, Marshall

> admitted that the American Army meat ration was too large but it has apparently been approved by Congress. To alter it would mean publicity throughout the United States and would in Marshal[l]'s view lead to thousands of mothers writing to their Congressmen to complain that the American Army authorities were not providing properly for their sons.

(The Army Chief of Staff did, covertly, cut meat consumption by 14 percent by imposing three meatless meals per week, but this was only for troops in the United States.) Thus, the "overfed" American GI was not only a reflection of American abundance, but also testament to Pentagon sensitivity about the welfare issue.[13]

Similar considerations dictated the response to the idea of lodging GIs in British homes. The British Army did this on a large scale to mitigate the accommodation crisis, but it was ruled out in 1942 for the bulk of the American Army in Britain. Most would live on bases vacated by the British forces or in new camps of their own. Regional commissioners in the south and southwest agreed in July 1942 that billeting in civilian homes "would be only resorted to as a last measure and was being treated as a reserve of accommodation in the event of plans being altered or air raid damage." The main exception to this was for headquarters staff in London, Cheltenham, and other urban centres, but this was often in large hotels, such as the Cumberland in London. From mid-September 1942, it also was agreed that officers above the rank of major could be billeted privately.[14]

The ban suited both governments. In Britain the billeting of soldiers had always been unpopular among civilians and the government was also still recovering from the widespread "privacy" backlash engendered by the Blitz evacuations of 1940–41. Remuneration for taking in billetees was notoriously low, particularly in view of the damage often caused and the difficulty of getting prompt and adequate compensation. On the other side, the Bolero Committee received numerous reports of hoteliers and houseowners asking existing guests to leave so as to offer the accommodation to U.S. officers at higher rent. This was a persistent grievance of Americans in London (not only from the military but also journalists and civilian officials). American commanders also preferred to maintain unit cohesion and discipline by keeping the GIs on base as far as possible. There, American standards of food and housing could also be guaranteed more easily.

This policy could not have been maintained if Bolero had gone ahead according to the Marshall Plan, but the mounting of Torch and the decline in the GI numbers enabled the billeting ban to be sustained through 1943. The consequences for relations with British civilians were considerable. Where billeting did occur, it definitely helped to break down the "women and drink" image of the GIs and integrate them into the local community. The regional commissioner for the northwest cited in January 1943 an example from Bury, a town on the northern edge of Manchester, where "several young officers who are attending a technical course are living in billets. They seem to be finding their way to local churches and forming large circles of English friends."[15]

This observation is confirmed by the Canadian evidence. Although the Northampton Experience of June 1940 was an aberration, it prefigured what happened on a larger scale (albeit less intensely) later in the war. From 1942 billeting became more prevalent for the Canadians, as they were moved out of permanent barracks (partly to make room for the GIs) and were settled in Sussex. While tents were widely used in summer, the Canadians also occupied a multitude of small hotels and guest houses, particularly in winter, and thus became part of local communities. The effects were quickly observed by Canadian censors in soldiers' letters home:

> It is noticeable that when men move out into billets away from the large Military Camps, and they come into more direct daily contact with the civilians, the natural reserve of the latter is broken down and they become more interested in and friendly towards the Canadian soldiers, and invite them into their homes, and provide them with hospitality and entertainment, which action is greatly appreciated by the troops, who make frequent reference to it in their letters.

The consequence of lengthy periods of residence by the same troops in one area and in close contact with civilians was demonstrable. By the spring of 1943 censorship reports were commenting almost routinely on the good relations that now obtained between Canadian troops and British civilians; in fact the issue ceased to be a serious command problem. A soldier in the Seaforth Highlanders of Canada wrote home:

> The Canadian Army after a year of homswaggling, brimming high pressuring and generally separating the people from their collateral—have eventually settled down to fraternize with the people, marry their daughters—return their hospitality and settle down to tea-drinking with gusto. We are now English speaking and take interest in Post-War England—speak easily and unashamed of fags—blokes—Kips—darts—mild & bitter—wireless sets and winkles. It has become part of our daily system.[16]

Kept for the most part away from British home life and fed and housed according to their own standards on base, the main way that American GIs came into contact with British people was when they had a leave "pass" to go off base into the local town. It was there that their "overpaid" status became particularly contentious. In various parts of Whitehall the matter was taken up seriously in July 1942, as disturbing reports came in from across the country. The GIs were accused of buying up anything for which ration coupons were not needed. The list included combs, razor blades, pipes, watches, torch batteries (vital for the blackout), blankets, towels, and playing cards. Most offensive of all, they were drinking pubs dry, emptying fish-and-chip shops, and filling the tables of exclusive restaurants that no British private would be able to afford. The local authorities were also concerned about the GIs "turning girls' heads" with their money and plying them with drink, while the Army noted British soldiers' resentment at the GIs' ability to outspend them in pubs and with women. One British officer suggested "appealing to young women, as part of their war effort, not to encourage troops of any nationality to indulge in ostentatious expenditure in public places," but this idea was not regarded in Whitehall as a serious proposition.[17]

Comparisons between American and British pay rates were a sensitive political matter in London. Against claims that the GI was overpaid, it could reasonably be argued (and was) that the British Tommy was scandalously underpaid. Sir Edward Grigg, undersecretary of state for war, told one persistent MP in February 1942: "This is a very delicate and difficult question which I do not think it is at all desirable to discuss by Question and Answer in this House." Churchill himself became "deeply concerned" about the issue of GIs' pay in July 1942. At his request the chancellor of the exchequer, Sir Kingsley Wood, set out the basic statistics. An American private in Britain, with less than three years service, was due $60 a month ($50 base pay, plus 20 percent for overseas service). This meant a daily average of 10 shillings (50 pence) or $2.00 if he was single and six shillings and sixpence (33 pence) or $1.33 if married. An unmarried British soldier (after six months service) was left with 3 shillings a day (15 pence) or 60 cents, and his married counterpart only two shillings and sixpence (12.5 pence) or 50 cents—in other words roughly one-third of the GIs' disposable cash.[18]

Other Allied contingents in Britain, particularly the Canadians and Australians, were also regarded as overpaid. But in the Canadian case—the most numerous Allied contingent in Britain throughout 1942—special arrangements were made to reduce their spending power. As Gen. Crerar pointed out to Montgomery in July 1942, while a Canadian soldier's pay was

> considerably higher than that received by his British counterpart [in fact, double], the actual cash payment made to the individual Canadian soldier in this country is very nearly the same. The reason for this is that approximately one-half of the Canadian soldier's pay is, by regulation, either "deferred" or "assigned" (to a dependant) or both and that, as a result, he has no means of touching it while over here.[19]

Churchill and his colleagues wanted the Americans to follow the same course, holding back much of the GI's pay in credits and thereby reducing his purchasing power in Britain. This the War Department resolutely refused to do. It did agree to two palliatives, however. The first was to pay the GIs as far as possible twice a month, to reduce the cash available for a night on the town after payday. The other was to urge soldiers to buy war bonds and insurance or to make deposits under the Army's savings plan, thereby mopping up surplus capital. These measures were felt in principle to be "very helpful" by the chancellor of the exchequer. Nevertheless, the American refusal to impose compulsory savings schemes was probably one reason why the government conceded a flat-rate 20 percent pay rise to British troops in August 1942. In addition, the pay problem strengthened the desire of the American Army to provide for GI needs as much as possible on base, stocking the PX with imported U.S. goods and so minimizing the GI's need to purchase articles such as combs or batteries in British shops.[20]

It took time for these measures to have an effect, however. Shipping shortages made it hard to import not only food but also nonessentials in sufficient quantity in 1942–43. And savings schemes were vitiated by command lethargy and soldier indifference. A sample of unmarried GIs in southern England in September 1942 suggested that the "average" private was spending two-thirds of his disposable pay and that official savings schemes were little used and not well known. One-tenth of all men saved nothing at all. By the spring of 1943, the pay question was being raised again not merely by the British War Office but by both Eisenhower and Ambassador Winant—all without success. It was not until late in 1943 that the combination of PX abundance and savings propaganda had some effect. In August 1943, according to ETO, the proportion of soldiers' pay available for spending in Britain was 33 percent; by April 1944 this had dropped to 26 percent. In July 1944 Eisenhower's staff announced that in ETO "approximately 75 percent of American soldiers' pay is being sent home or spent in Army channels."[21]

The War Department's resistance to compulsory deferrals and compulsory savings was a further reminder of the politics of Army welfare. It is worth noting that in early 1942, before the Canadian deferrals had got going, the "average" GI in Britain was no better off than the Canadian soldier. This was because Canadian pay rates were high to attract recruits to an expanding *volunteer* army. It was not until the June 1942 rise, when base pay increased two-thirds from $30 to $50, that the GI was definitely overpaid compared to other Allied soldiers in Britain. It is likely that intensified British concern in the late summer of 1942 reflected the consequences of this boost to GI purchasing power.

Congress in the 1930s had been indifferent to the pay of a volunteer

Army that was widely regarded as employment for those who would otherwise be in prison. But once "our boys" had been drafted, their pay, like their conditions, were matters of intense political concern. To all British critics the Pentagon explained that it was illegal to withhold soldiers' pay without an Act of Congress, that legislation was unlikely in view of the enthusiasm on Capitol Hill for the 1942 pay rise, and that this would, in any case, be bad for morale especially if no similar restraint was imposed on the booming pay of industrial workers back home. In 1942 the congressional elections in November were cited as a reason for particular political sensitivity, but the War Department was no more willing to take on Congress the following spring, even though Marshall was told directly by his staff that "the problem of reducing the amount of surplus funds held by our personnel overseas . . . is nowhere under control" and that "in some places the problem is more acute than ever." The Chief of Staff reserved his political capital on the Hill for a few major issues, such as lowering the draft age and enlarging the Army. On issues of soldier welfare, where in any case his sympathies lay with the GI, he would not confront political and public sentiment. British government minister John Llewellin concluded that, on such issues, "my experience in Washington showed me that no one below the President has any control over the U.S. soldiers." And when Ambassador Winant raised the pay issue with Roosevelt himself in August 1942, the president left the War Department to draft a bland restatement of the voluntarist approach, which ended: "You may be sure that we shall strive for a suitable solution." Roosevelt was no keener than Marshall to let Congress accuse him of denying American boys their just reward.[22]

On food, accommodation, and pay the U.S. Army in Britain had been determined to ensure that GIs' rights as American citizens were not abridged by service overseas. This was deemed essential for morale. But the thrust of all these policies, reinforced by the underlying legal position of the Army in Britain, was towards a separate American enclave. Not only was this militarily desirable, commanders also felt it would minimize contact and thus potential friction with the locals. The same policy obtained for GIs on leave in Britain under the aegis of the American Red Cross (ARC).

In February 1942 agreement was reached between Gen. Chaney, then the ranking American commander in Britain, and the ARC authorities in London and Washington for a division of labour in Britain. The Army would take care of soldier welfare on base; the ARC would look after it off base in local towns, particularly leave centres. Specifically, this meant that the Army would provide facilities on base such as post exchanges, cinemas, athletic equipment, reading rooms, and so on. The ARC would organize and operate "clubs" in converted premises for soldiers on leave and in transit.[23]

The first of these clubs opened in Londonderry in May 1942 and by the end of the year fifty were operating, with eighty-five hundred beds or a weekly sleeping capacity of sixty thousand. In the week of New Year 1943 over 250,000 meals were served. All of the clubs had recreation rooms, an information bureau, and a restaurant, where a three-course meal with coffee could be purchased for 1 shilling (20 cents). Some were small scale with few or no beds, intended as an off-base hostelry for a few hours for men on a short pass in the local big town—for instance in Bishop's Stortford or High Wycombe. But in the large cities and resorts peacetime hotels were taken over—such as the Lansdowne Grove in Bath (375 beds) and the Palace Hotel in Southport, on the Lancashire coast (430 beds). In Norwich the medieval Bishop's Palace became the ARC club from December 1942, with the bishop retaining an office in the buildings. The most important leave area was, of course, London. There eight clubs, with a total of three thousand beds, were in operation by January 1943, mostly in former hotels such as the Washington in Curzon Street (off Park Lane). One of them, Rainbow Corner in Piccadilly, functioned as a clearinghouse for ARC activities. This included what became a nationwide booking service for GIs. In the words of the ARC director in Britain, Harvey D. Gibson:

> The Military authorities have worked out a very complete system for the assignment of our men when on furlough to make their homes at our various clubs. Whenever a man is given his furlough notice he is also furnished with a card which in effect reserves for him a room at an American Red Cross Service Club on a certain day at a certain place. Each day the Military authorities send to our Club Department at headquarters in London complete information regarding such assignments and all rooms are held until 12 o'clock midnight on the day of the expected arrival. Men on leave are not compelled to utilize our clubs to which they are assigned in this way, although they are expected to and they do in almost all cases. . . .

Although the system did not work quite as smoothly as that, by 1943 the American Army in Britain had evolved a system of controlled leave accommodation whereby passes would not be issued unless rooms had been booked in advance. The ARC, Gibson liked to claim, was operating "the largest hotel chain in the world."[24]

To understand how this had come about, we need to appreciate the Red Cross's unusual position in the United States. The International Red Cross was founded in 1864 to aid the casualties of war without regard to nationality. The United States joined in 1882 and for two decades the ARC remained a small, private philanthropic society engaged in international war relief. But in 1905 it was reincorporated to "act in matters of voluntary relief and in accord with the military and naval authorities as a medium of communication between the people of the United States of America and their Army and Navy." In 1917–18 a plethora of relief organizations offered their services to the doughboys in France—among them the ARC, the (Protestant) YMCA, and the (Catholic) Knights of Columbus—engaged at times in fratricidal rivalry of that peculiar intensity that sometimes afflicts those determined to do good. The result was very patchy provision of facilities. To prevent the same mess in World War Two, Marshall announced after Pearl Harbor that the ARC would be "the sole non-military organization to operate with an expeditionary force during the war." This confirmed the ARC in the ambiguous position it had held since 1905. On the one hand, it was a huge philanthropic organization (thirty-seven hundred chapters and 5.6 million members in 1939), raising funds through intensive solicitation of private contributions. On the other, it was officially a "governmental agency," charged with satisfying many of the welfare needs of the American armed forces.[25]

Up to a point, then, Chaney's decision in February 1942 was in line with War Department policy. But in many theatres of operations, the ARC's role as auxiliary to the Army was low key and conventional: recreation and entertainment work in hospitals, field officers to assist men with family or financial difficulties, the provision of coffee, snacks, and cigarettes to troops on the move. In France in 1917–18 the Army ran its own rest areas and this was followed in many theatres in World War Two, particularly North Africa and Italy. But things worked out differently in Britain.[26]

Gen. Chaney's decision to turn leave accommodation over to the ARC reflected the peculiar circumstances of both time and place. He was operating, it should be remembered, as a theatre HQ but without the status, staff, and resources to do so—a predicament only resolved in June 1942. He was also faced with a large influx of troops to Northern Ireland and eastern England. (This was even before he learned of the nightmare one-million scenario under the Marshall Plan.) These GIs not only had to be accommodated on bases (a headache in itself) but enabled to go on leave—Chaney was at this stage envisaging a seven-day pass every three months. Assuming, as he then did, an ultimate strength of 250,000 men, that meant space for 17,500 men on leave at any one time. Yet accommodation was very hard to acquire in a compact, urbanized society under conditions of wartime, especially for a commander lacking both funds and clout. Hence, the attractions of a well-endowed private organization on the spot and enjoying special military status. With both the War Department and the ARC in Washington slow to see the urgency of his situation, an increasingly panicked Chaney cabled on 15 March: "There is no, repeat no, space in London or other large cities to care for men on leave unless it is specially provided. Several weeks ago 800 men of Allied forces on leave had to sleep in [air-raid] shelters. Due to bombing and to growth of government offices London is much more congested in our opinion than even Washington." And even if rooms could be found by GIs privately, the cheapest bed and breakfast in London in 1942 cost the equivalent of $2.40 a night—at a time when GI base pay in Britain was still $36 a month. Chaney warned Washington bluntly: "Furlough policy for this theater [is] dependent upon adequate provision for sleeping and messing accommodations."[27]

After some persuasion, the ARC authorities agreed to take on what, for them, was the unusual and onerous burden of the Service Clubs. However, these were not intended by Chaney to be as isolationist as they did become. From the start he wanted a "modest charge" to be imposed for canteens and dormitories, even though this was against the ARC's "no charging" policy. He pointed to the bad impression that would otherwise be caused by a "free handout" to soldiers who were "receiving higher pay than any others" in Britain. He noted that service hostels for other Allied troops were making such charges—the equivalent of 50 cents being the going rate for British and Canadian troops. Furthermore, he considered it necessary that ARC clubs "offer reciprocal hospitality [in] some of our facilities to Allied troops, especially [in] Ulster, following customary practice here." If the facilities were completely free, Chaney warned, such reciprocity "would swamp us."[28]

Charges were accepted reluctantly by the ARC,[29] and the principle of Allied reciprocity was applied in some clubs in 1942. This followed pressure from the War Office in London, who emphasized that GIs were allowed to use all canteens, hostels, and recreation rooms operated for British troops on exactly the same terms as the British. On Chaney's direct instructions, and against the wishes of the ARC in London, the Londonderry club was opened on 6 May 1942 to all Allied servicemen. But after three weeks it was reported that British troops were monopolizing the place and that GIs were disgruntled. The next step was to ration the British to set hours and facilities, but even this proved inadequate. The ARC Club was simply too popular. Similar problems emerged in Salisbury—a popular leave centre for the large numbers of Allied troops training in the area. At the end of 1942 it was reported that of the last twenty thousand men to use the ARC Service Club in Salisbury, twelve thousand had been British. Given these kinds of pressures, it was not surprising that the ARC decided that the Clubs were for U.S. service personnel and that Allied troops would only be admitted as guests of GIs.[30]

As will be clear, this "Americans only" policy was in part a response to practicalities and was adopted only after the alternative had proved unworkable. On the other hand, it had always been the preferred stance of the ARC authorities in Britain. It was not merely that their fund-raising in the United States was based on the premise that donors were helping *American* boys far from home. They also believed that GIs preferred and deserved an all-American environment. This brought them into conflict with those who advocated a more positive approach to good Anglo-American relations and who accused the ARC of building barriers rather than bridges. Among these critics was the British Ministry of Information (MOI), which had principal responsibility on the British side in 1942 for coordinating relations between civilians and GIs.

The MOI ended up with this role after months of confusion in Whitehall. Since the beginning of the year various British organizations, both educational and philanthropic, had been planning what they could do to make the GIs feel at home. In March the foreign secretary, Anthony Eden, established a special committee to coordinate their activities, headed by Sir Edward Grigg, a Tory MP and until recently a junior minister at the War Office. But Grigg was gradually squeezed out by the minister of information, Brendan Bracken—Churchill intimate and wily politicker—who insisted that "primary responsibility" for all hospitality arrangements must rest with his ministry, operating through Grigg and others as it saw fit. Grigg argued that this would taint the whole operation in the eyes of GIs as British government propaganda, but he was fighting a losing battle: The MOI had the support of the Foreign Office and of Churchill himself. By November Grigg exploded angrily to Bracken that he had been completely sidelined: "What the hell, is the most modest comment I can make."[31]

That left Bracken in control of hospitality on the British side but still unsure of his exact role. Eisenhower made it clear "that he did not want to have British Welfare Officers interfering in the welfare of American troops," which, he said, was a matter for ARC field officers. Ike was equally emphatic that "the Red Cross shall act as my agent in co-ordinating outside welfare and 'get together' activities." Of these, the most pressing issue was the numerous offers, from British organizations and private citizens, to welcome GIs into British homes. Following Eisenhower's policy, this was placed in the hands of the ARC. But their British head in July 1942, William E. Stevenson, a former Rhodes scholar at Oxford in the 1920s, was highly sceptical of any home hospitality programme. He claimed from personal experience that "he knew how difficult it was for the British to accept any stranger into their homes." In any case, the ARC had its hands more than full establishing the Service Clubs, without yet more impositions. The home hospitality scheme failed to get going in 1942, except in a patchy and localized way, leaving many offers of help not taken up and would-be hosts offended to receive from the ARC only a form to fill in instead of a gracious letter of thanks. As the MOI put it later, the British "came forward with premature offers of hospitality, which the Americans were not ready and not organized to accept, and this undoubtedly led to disappointment and a feeling of frustration."[32]

The most frictional point of ARC contact with the British in the summer of 1942 was the British role in the ARC Clubs themselves. Although the ARC paid for staff and food, the cost of acquiring, renovating, and, to a large extent, equipping the Clubs was financed by the British government under Reverse Lend-Lease. Moreover, most of the staff were actually British. At the end of 1942 there were just over four hundred ARC employees in Britain but some six thousand paid British staff and thousands more British volunteers. Without these the Clubs would not have been able to function. Many of the volunteers were members of the nationwide Women's Voluntary Service for Civil Defence (WVS). Its founder and chairman was the formidably capable Stella, Lady Reading, whose favourite sayings included: "It is no good relying on the next person to do the job, she is probably relying on you." The WVS, with its distinctive green tweed suit, maroon sweater, and "schoolgirl felt hat" had "transcended its apparently basic middle classness" to do enormously valuable relief work in the streets during the Blitz. By July 1942 it needed new outlets and Lady Reading saw the GIs as a worthy cause. She told her members: "This is a wonderful opportunity to get to know the people with whom our destiny is now completely bound up. It is also a chance to repay some of the innumerable kindnesses Americans have shown to our people here and in America since the war began."[33]

The ARC insisted that all British staff or volunteers must remove their own uniforms and wear that of the ARC. Incensed, Lady Reading took her protests to Eisenhower himself, but without much success. Undoubtedly the ARC in Britain was fanatically punctilious about uniforms. Its dress regulations for staff would not have seemed out of place in the most exclusive boarding school for young ladies, with precise instructions on the colour of blouses and stockings, length of hair (no ribbons or bows), and the exact location of identity pins and patches (to the last quarter of an inch). That said, there was more involved here than obsessive propriety and organizational vanity. The ARC in Britain was budgeting for expenditure of some $13 million in fiscal year 1943 and feared that essential fund-raising back home would be damaged if it did not receive full credit for the work of the Clubs. Photos of uniformed British women catering to the GIs would be a public-relations disaster. Hence its insistence on all British staff wearing its uniforms or smocks. The British were equally keen to publicize their role in GI hospitality. Bracken told the ARC that "it must be clearly understood that it was the British people and the British government who were rendering these services."[34]

The uniform furore was indicative of a deeper problem. Many of the ARC leadership would, ideally, have preferred to run the Clubs entirely with U.S. personnel. That was not just because, as one put it, otherwise "you are going to have Lady Reading bouncing in and out on you." They also believed that "the men in these facilities we run have a right to expect to come in contact with Americans." Harvey D. Gibson, the New York banker who became ARC commissioner in Britain in November 1942, explained this philosophy the following spring when seeking permission to serve hamburgers in ARC Clubs. Although unsuccessful (the British Food Ministry, backed by SOS, cited the world meat shortage and the already generous GI meat allowances), Gibson's argument is revealing:

> It is an accepted fact both by the American people who contribute the funds to support our Red Cross operations, and the U.S.A. Military authorities, that for an American Red Cross facility to be of the most value as a morale building institution for the Armed Forces it is necessary to create a strictly American atmosphere, which is done by giving the men a comfortable place where they may spend their time off duty and enjoy a conversation now and then with American Red Cross girls, offering them American interiors by rearrangement of drapes, furniture, posters, etc., installing showers and other distinctly American comforts and amenities, and last but not least by

preparing and serving food as nearly in American fashion as circumstances make possible . . . [including] doughnuts, coca cola and coffee made in the American manner.[35]

Some Americans also disliked the ARC's attitude. James P. Warburg, the forceful head of foreign propaganda for the Office of War Information (OWI), visited Britain in August 1942 and chastised Eisenhower at length about the situation. He suggested opening the canteens, if not the dormitories, of ARC Clubs to British servicemen. And he urged him to alter the ARC philosophy, claiming that "the present attitude is that the ideal thing for the American troops would be to staff all the Red Cross clubs with American Red Cross girls in American uniforms and provide the boys with as many things as possible, such as Coca-Cola, which they are used to back home." Warburg warned Eisenhower that the "greatest danger to Anglo-American relations resulting from the presence of American troops in Great Britain appears to be the attitude on the part of some of our government or private agencies which can best be summarized as a desire to build a little America within the British Isles."[36]

As far as Ike himself was concerned, Warburg was preaching to the converted. As soon as he arrived in Britain, Eisenhower was emphatic about the need for good relations between the GIs and the civil population. This was partly damage limitation—with GI pay, food, and indiscipline causing offence in Britain, Ike was very conscious of the way this was being exploited in Nazi propaganda. In allowing such "friction to develop between ourselves and our Allies," he warned, "*we are playing entirely into the hands of our enemies.*" But his was not just a negative aim of avoiding friction; Eisenhower went out of his way to foster what he called "mutual association." He told the Pentagon:

> I consider it of the highest importance that we utilize the desire of the British citizen to offer his hospitality and to bring the U.S. soldier into touch with the British private home. My interest arises purely from a military standpoint and is directed toward the development of a common or mutual feeling of understanding and esteem which I consider will be necessary to obtain maximum effectiveness of the combined forces of the two nations.

Eisenhower personally promoted the idea of home hospitality in the summer of 1942. He felt, according to aide Harry Butcher, "that if an American soldier has the opportunity of living, say for a weekend, in the home of a British family, possibly even helping them wash the dishes, tend the garden, and be a general handy-Andy around the house, there could be developed a much greater degree of friendliness and companionship than if both are stand-offish." And, following the advice of Ambassador Winant about British privations, he insisted that each man "should carry with him a day's rations," particularly commodities difficult to obtain such as "meat, fats and sweets."[37]

But Eisenhower only stayed in Britain for five months before moving to Northwest Africa. And from August much of his energy in London was absorbed in preparing for Operation Torch. His brief if energetic engagement with the social problems of the American presence in Britain therefore had little long-term impact. When home hospitality was handed over to the hard-pressed and, at this time, reluctant ARC, momentum soon flagged. And the ARC's monopoly over GI welfare arrangements squeezed out most British efforts. Even a proposed division of labour whereby the ARC would provide "Hotels and Day Clubs in the larger towns" while British organizations under the MOI would establish "Recreational Centres in the smaller towns and villages" was not formally operated. The ARC and MOI argued out each local case individually, with the ARC anxious to provide its own services wherever possible.[38] By 1943 it was developing its own network of "Aeroclubs" on USAAF airfields and using "Clubmobiles"—converted single-decker London Transport buses—to bring a touch of America to troops on isolated bases. From each Clubmobile ARC girls in uniform dispensed doughnuts, coffee, gum, cigarettes, and American magazines to the accompaniment of "phonograph" music.

Barriers to an effective "positive" approach to Anglo-American relations existed on the British side as well. Churchill, though enthusiastic in principle, took only a sporadic interest in such matters. He, like most of Whitehall, was preoccupied with more vital problems of the Allied war effort in 1942. As for the MOI, it had only limited resources to expend on GI-British relations. In London the issue was not handled by a separate division until 1944 but was part of the wide purview of the Home Division, whose main concern was domestic morale. And in the localities each of the MOI's regional information officers was allocated only a derisory £50 ($200) a year for coordinating local hospitality programmes. Their task was made even harder by what Sir Arthur Willert, information officer for the southern region, called "the impenetrable fog of 'security' stretching across the Atlantic and far into England," which meant that "American units arrived here and there and everywhere in ever increasing numbers unannounced and unshep[h]erded." And, as Willert also noted, in the autumn of 1942 "just when everybody was keyed up to receive great masses of Americans, a large portion of those already here disappeared to North Africa and for nearly a year expected arrivals failed to materialize."[39] Not until late 1943 were conditions ripe for a joint official campaign in "positive" mode—to foster good Anglo-American relations by bringing GIs and British together rather than keeping them apart.

11

Hearts
and Minds

★ ★ ★

BY THE END OF FEBRUARY 1943 TORCH MEANT THAT AMERICAN TROOP strength in Britain had declined to little over 100,000, well under half the peak of 228,000 in October 1942 (table 7.1). Because of this and because of the negative measures taken to minimize friction, the Foreign Office felt that the GI problem was under control, at least for the moment, and that the difficulties had been "surprisingly small."[1] What followed in early 1943 was greater attention to boosting the morale of the GIs and educating Americans and Britons about each other.

One of the units sent to North Africa was the 1st Infantry Division, the "Big Red One," which had languished at Tidworth Barracks for two months from August 1942. In November, II Corps Headquarters in Algeria reported: "Since arrival in this theater, there has been a noticeable improvement in the appearance and discipline of the 1st Division." But the morale problem was more acute for those GIs who remained—Lee's SOS personnel, the 8th Air Force units in East Anglia, and the 29th Infantry Division, which, as the only combat division left, replaced the Big Red One in the spartan conditions of Tidworth. These men lacked a sense of purpose—no threat of German attack, no prospect of Allied invasion. Transport was in short supply, particularly to take SOS and AAF personnel from isolated rural bases to local towns. They had to endure the long British winter evenings, made all the more stygian by the total blackout. And the pervasive dampness chilled a man far more comprehensively than the colder but drier climate of the northern United States. (When Harry Hopkins, Roosevelt's confidant, alerted Churchill to his impending visit in April 1942, his telegram was brief and to the point: "See you soon. Please start the fire.") Commanders had no doubt that morale would deteriorate, however energetic special service officers were in organizing on-base recreational activities. Eighth Air Force commander Gen. Spaatz warned subordinates at the end of September: "We are approaching our most difficult season."[2]

GIs, like all troops overseas, longed for news from home. After visiting ETO in January 1943, Gen. Hap Arnold, AAF commanding general, reported caustically: "Mails are abominably handled. We are thinking of putting our mail in bottles and dropping in sea. Should speed up." Newspapers were equally important. From 18 April 1942 the "soldier's newspaper" *Stars and Stripes* began printing in London. Marshall wrote a statement for its first issue, recalling its contribution in France in 1918 and asserting that "the morale, in fact the military efficiency of the American soldiers in these Islands, will be directly affected by the character of the *Stars and Stripes* of 1942." The paper, though under officers' ultimate editorial control, used a wide variety of agency wire reports and photos. By August 1942 circulation was thirty-two thousand, with 80 percent remailed by GIs to the folks back home.[3]

At this stage, however, it appeared only weekly, being dependent on British presses and on the availability of newsprint, which, like the mails, took up scarce shipping space. But in October 1942 the Army's hand was forced by a request from the *Chicago Tribune* to the British MOI for a license to print a daily newspaper for GIs in Britain. Under the eccentric ownership of Robert R. McCormick, the *Tribune* had, for years, taken a vituperatively anti-British, anti-Roosevelt line. The president himself cabled Churchill asking that a licence be rejected because the paper printed "lies and deliberate misrepresentations in lieu of news." The *Tribune* was, however, in those days a very good city paper, with comprehensive sports and regional coverage, and its potential appeal to GIs, starved of news from home, was evident. As Ambassador Winant admitted, there was clearly "a demand for an American Daily Newspaper by our troops." Marshall eventually arranged that the British edition of the *Stars and Stripes* would appear every day except Sundays, subsidized initially by profits from the Army weekly *Yank*, which was edited by GIs themselves out of New York. The first issue in this new form appeared on 2 November, printed on the presses of the *Times* newspaper in Fleet Street, thanks to the intercession of Brendan Bracken, the minister of information. *Yank* started its own London edition six days later, coinciding exactly with the start of Operation Torch.[4]

GIs were strictly forbidden from bringing their own radios with

them—baggage was searched and sets confiscated. They were therefore reliant on whatever the Army provided, theoretically one radio for
every hundred men. But these were medium-wave sets, only able to
pick up the British Broadcasting Corporation (BBC), which had a
monopoly of the British airwaves. Since 1940 the BBC had run its own
"Forces Network," for British troops at home and abroad, and had
included in that some news, music, and sports programmes specially
for dominion contingents—such as "Hello Diggers" for the Australians
and "Beaver Club Party" for the Canadians. As the American presence
expanded in the summer of 1942, the BBC made some efforts to meet
the new demand. Jack Benny alternated with Bob Hope for a half-hour
on Sundays at 12:30 P.M. And, from August "American Sports Bulletins" were broadcast at 7 P.M.—five minutes during the week, ten
minutes on Sundays. These were exceptions, however. GIs found most
of the BBC's output totally unpalatable. The music was described as
lacking "oomph" and "zing." The humour seemed laboured—jokes
had "long, long time fuses." British radio was felt to be "an acquired
taste," commented one reporter, "like carrying an umbrella or washing behind the ears." The BBC privately acknowledged the problem.
One official admitted: "All information is unanimous that American
troops consider the BBC's programmes 'lousy.' . . . Even news, which
one might suppose would form common ground to all English-speaking peoples, is unacceptable to American troops when presented in the
British manner."[5]

The "manner" was not, it has to be said, so much a function of
nationality as of class. The BBC, only just breaking free of the dour
Presbyterian Director-General Sir John Reith, still saw itself as the
guardian of morals and culture. Until September 1939 radio news
bulletins were read by men (definitely not women) dressed in dinner
jackets, who related the grimmest or gladdest of tidings without a
flicker of emotion in impeccable southern English upper-middle-class
accents. One CBS commentator suggested, tongue in cheek, that if the
world ended at 3 P.M. tomorrow, the BBC would wait until the regular
six o'clock news bulletin and then announce it as follows:

> This is London calling. Here is the news and this is John Snagge
> reading it. The world came to an end at two minutes after three this
> afternoon, during a debate in the House of Commons. A summary
> of the debate will be given at the conclusion of this bulletin.

During the war "Auntie" BBC diversified in both voice and content,
but its Forces Broadcasts, particularly early on, were almost as unpopular among British troops as among GIs. BBC Cairo lamented in

May 1942: "There is no longer any doubt that practically all our troops in the Middle East habitually listen to Axis radio in preference to the BBC." Complaints, it said, were always the same: "Cut the talk. Cut all the explanations and excuses. Give us straight music, snappy variety, and hard honest-to-god news. . . . [B]eyond any shadow of doubt the most popular radio feature among the British forces in the Middle East today is the young lady who sings Die Liebe Marlene every night from Belgrade."[6]

American commanders naturally did not want their men listening to Axis propaganda. Their proposed remedy was, quite simply, an American Forces Radio Network in Britain. This was a matter on which both Marshall and Eisenhower felt strongly and they argued their case vigorously from July 1942, once it became clear that the GIs were not going to be in Paris by Christmas. Such a network would, however, be an unprecedented breach in the BBC's cherished monopoly status. There were fears that it would encourage applications from commercial stations, that British listeners would tune in to the U.S. programmes, and that the Americans might try to scoop the BBC on war news. Most of all, two major objections were raised. First, the BBC had successfully rebuffed all such proposals from the other Allied contingents in the UK. The most powerful case had been made by the Canadian Army in Britain, which, 170,000 strong at the end of 1942, was much larger than the GIs. (The BBC in fact estimated the total number of Canadians in the country, including those serving with the RAF, at nearly 300,000.) Nevertheless, the BBC hierarchy had consistently taken the line that a separate Canadian wavelength was "out of the question." Any special treatment for the Americans would therefore clearly be resented. The other main objection was, in shorthand, "separatism." The BBC's director of programme planning, Godfrey Adams, warned:

> The American Army authorities are anxious to have everything over here of their own—their own equipment, of course; their own food, their own sports kit to play their own games, and so forth. In a word, pretty well all they require from this country is a piece of land to camp on until the "second front" opens. . . . If, now, they have their own broadcasting transmitters, this separatism will be carried a stage further.

Adams suggested that these reservations were shared not only by the British War Office but by "certain civilian quarters" among the Americans, notably Ambassador Winant.[7]

All in all, the BBC felt that the U.S. Army was not "playing cricket" and that it ought to do so. "After all they are playing on our ground, and using our bats and wickets," the controller of news complained. But Adams responded sadly that although "the Americans are playing on our ground . . . baseball it is, and not cricket." Threats by ETO to create a major diplomatic row overcame government reservations and the BBC was mollified by assurances that the new network would function as "an auxiliary service" of the BBC, taking a substantial number of BBC programmes and operating "in harmony with the best interests of broadcasting in the United Kingdom." Adams continued to warn that the Canadians "cannot fail to feel sore when they find out that elaborate plans have been made for the entertainment of American troops over here." But, as in other aspects of the U.S. presence, such as the legal position of the GIs, the diplomatic importance of the United States to Great Britain proved decisive. (The Canadian forces did not get their own network until July 1945, when the rundown of its troops was well under way, and it lasted barely six months.) The American Forces Network (AFN) began operating on the Fourth of July 1943 from seven transmitters in Army camps around Britain, and by April 1944 its hours were 11 A.M. to 11 P.M., Monday to Saturday, and 8 A.M. to 11 P.M. on Sundays. To the BBC's chagrin, most of the material came from the United States, though, as part of the official agreement, all references to commercial sponsors were eliminated. The AFN was striking evidence of British recognition, albeit often reluctant, that the special relationship meant special treatment.[8]

Mail, newspapers, and radio were all conventional Army remedies for soldiers' ennui and angst. More novel was Eisenhower's method of finding out what GIs were really feeling, to pinpoint morale problems. On 5 August 1942 he had lengthy conversations with Elmo Roper, a pioneer of opinion polling in the 1930s, who had come to Britain at his request. Ike then cabled Washington asking for an officer "specially selected as an expert in the sampling of opinion." In the event two officers arrived at ETO HQ on 20 August, Capt. Felix E. Moore, Jr., and Lt. Robert B. Wallace, the son of Roosevelt's vice president. Their brief was "that continuing surveys of soldier opinion be made in order to secure information for the development of policies which will insure rapid adjustment of American troops to service in ETO. Particular attention will be paid to those factors which will insure continuance of cordial relations between American soldiers and British civilians and soldiers."[9]

In taking this action, Ike was a pioneer. Although the War Department's Research Branch had commissioned its first poll in December

1941, only two major studies had been completed by June 1942 and nothing had been done overseas. Research teams were not established in other theatres until the fall of 1943. In Britain, however, there was a major survey in September 1942 and six more the following January. ETO considered the reports "of immense value in keeping this headquarters informed as to the morale situation and the needs of troops" and "an important factor in policy determination." The ETO research branch, with a staff of fifty at its peak, included such noted postwar opinion analysts as Irving L. Janis. Though some techniques were still rudimentary, they drew on and refined methods pioneered in the Gallup and Roper organizations of the 1930s. The reports, some 150 in all, provide a unique guide to the broad pattern of GI attitudes.[10]

Immediately after their appointment, Moore and Wallace organized a survey of soldier opinion on attitudes and practices affecting Anglo-American relations. Questionnaires were completed by 3,711 white enlisted men from fifteen stations, mainly west of London and south of Cheltenham, between 14 and 26 September. On each station the random cross sections ranged from one in five to one in twenty. All the troops had been in England at least three or four weeks, many for two or three months. Their responses confirmed more impressionistic views of soldier opinion. More than eight men in ten agreed that "most of the English civilians are friendly and seem to be trying very hard to make the American soldiers feel at home." On the other hand, only one-third definitely agreed that "English soldiers are going out of their way to help the American soldiers and show them a good time." Fifty percent actively disagreed with the statement. The surveys also highlighted GI scepticism about the UK war effort. A quarter did not think that "the English are doing as good a job as possible of fighting the war considering everything." The survey concluded that GIs who had attended high school and especially college were the most sceptical and that Northerners were significantly more critical than men from the South. This indicated that "the men bring their attitudes with them and find little in England to change them." Analysts did suggest, however, that "it is possible to change the attitudes of enlisted men toward our Allies by the use of specially prepared lectures and movies."

The survey also elicited information about attitudes to British hospitality. Half the men had received invitations to British homes and, in all, some 40 percent had made visits—"many of them several times." The pattern varied, however, from place to place—the proportion of men receiving invitations ranged from only an eighth on one station to four-fifths on another. The poll made very clear the failure of official hospitality schemes. Ninety percent of the men who had received invitations said these had arisen through personal contact and only 1 percent said they had come via the Red Cross. Of the men who had not received invitations, two-thirds said they would like one, but the poll found that a hard core of one-quarter of the men, including some who had already made visits, did not wish to be invited or to visit again. Dislike of the British and a feeling of "little in common" were the most frequent reasons given for this attitude. The survey concluded that "there is some evidence which at least suggests that visiting does create a friendlier attitude," but it warned that those well disposed in advance to the British might be keenest to visit and so home hospitality simply reinforced previous assumptions. It did not, therefore, venture a "clear-cut answer" on Eisenhower's basic hypothesis—that if a GI spent "a weekend in the home of a British family" the result would be "a much greater degree of friendliness."[11]

In the first three weeks of January 1943, 2,353 enlisted men were questioned at eighty-two camps throughout the UK about their leisure and reading activities. The scale of the survey meant that the men were selected by special service officers on each base, who did not always follow instructions, with the result that the sample was considerably better educated than the Army as a whole and the answers probably excessively cerebral. But although the exact figures should be taken with caution, the broad patterns are again indicative. The overriding impression from the six surveys was the degree to which GIs kept to themselves. Two-thirds did not leave their camp on the "average day" and half the movies and stage shows they watched were on base. Over half said that they "very seldom" or "never" visited an American Red Cross Club. It was clear that on-base activities of various sorts were of major importance in keeping GIs occupied. The surveys also revealed considerable keenness to know and understand more about the world events of which they were a tiny part. Only a quarter felt they had better than "a general knowledge of 'headline' events." There was an overwhelming demand for regular talks about "what is going on in the world today, providing that they are made by competent and interesting speakers." Over two-fifths wanted them as frequently as once or twice a week and most GIs sought plenty of opportunity for discussion. Even allowing for the "overeducated" nature of the sample and the fact that most men would naturally prefer a couple of hours indoors to tramping through mud and rain, the surveys made a clear point.[12]

It was certainly not lost on Gen. Frank M. Andrews, newly arrived in London as commanding general of ETO. Indeed it probably lay behind a long dinner conversation he had on 9 February 1943 with Viscount Astor about "preventing boredom among soldiers by giving them something useful to talk about." Waldorf Astor—owner of the *Observer* newspaper—took a keen interest in the British Army as well as in promoting Anglo-American relations. His mother was American, as was his vivacious wife, Nancy, Britain's first woman MP. Astor brought to Andrews's attention the educational work then going on in the British Army.[13]

Since the start of the war the British Army had programmes of voluntary lectures, but Army education really got going only in the summer of 1941 when the War Office became concerned about the decline in morale among troops in Britain. With little prospect of invasion to gear them up, troops were "listless and lazy," in the words of Sir James Grigg, doing only what was absolutely required of them— "civilians in khaki" in the worst sense of the term. The Adjutant General of the British Army, Gen. Sir Ronald Adam, took a particular interest in the soldiers' welfare and morale problems. He oversaw the introduction of psychological selection tests in the summer of 1941 and it was he who established the Army Bureau of Current Affairs (ABCA) in September 1941. This began a programme of compulsory talks, led by junior officers and followed by group discussion, based on ABCA pamphlets entitled "Current Affairs" about various aspects of the war effort such as "Our Ally, Russia" or "The Development of Nazism." Adam took Army education particularly seriously in 1942–43: "the maintenance of morale during this fourth winter is clearly of great importance," he warned in July 1942. During a four-month trial, from November 1942 through February 1943, all British soldiers were supposed to spend four hours a week in Army education, including one on "Current Affairs" and another discussing a new series of booklets called "The British Way and Purpose," which examined aspects of British society worth fighting for. This scheme was extended through the summer.[14]

During the spring of 1943 ETO debated how to adapt the British scheme to their circumstances. The major difference was that discussions were to be restricted to the war and current affairs. This was partly justified by reference to the GI's educational level. The ETO's chief of special services, Col. Theodore Arter, noted that whereas 79 percent of GIs in Britain had completed eight years of education, only 17 percent of British troops had done so. "Therefore there is a greater need for formal education among the British than among the Americans." Col. Raymond W. Barker, ETO's G-3 in charge of training, also argued that they should not "embark on any extensive educational program which does not contribute directly to the build-up of an effective fighting machine with the least practicable delay." The conclusion was therefore that "stress should be laid on Current Affairs, British-American relations—not on cultural subjects." This also reflected the preferences of the Pentagon itself, which feared congressional criticism if it got into anything politically contentious.[15]

While ETO was finalizing its plans, it became the target of a scathing attack by the distinguished Protestant theologian and social commentator Reinhold Niebuhr. That summer Niebuhr spent ten weeks in the UK and was particularly impressed with the extensive British schemes of Army education. On returning home, he lambasted U.S. Army efforts as "piddling compared with the highly organized British system." Niebuhr's article in the weekly *The Nation* on 21 August, with highlights picked up in *Time* magazine two weeks later, attacked the basic philosophy of the U.S. Army in Britain about soldier morale and motivation:

> Compared with this British program, the United States Army is culturally and educationally poverty-stricken, though it is not poor in any other respect. . . . There are Red Cross clubs in every part of the British Isles for our soldiers. There is no lack of entertainment. Moving pictures and theatrical performances are plentiful. American soldiers can get unlimited amounts of cigarettes tax-free, while British soldiers are limited to five tax-free cigarettes a day. Naturally, chocolate bars are also more plentiful among our service men.

Niebuhr went on to denounce *Stars and Stripes*, which, he complained, "not only carries baseball box scores but has a daily photo of some glamor queen, usually a Hollywood star . . . presumably for the purpose of providing 'pin-ups' to enliven the bare walls of the barracks." He ended with a stern warning: "The American soldier has Hollywood, in both the literal and symbolic sense, to fill his leisure hours; but he lacks help in finding the spiritual and moral significance of the titanic struggle in which he is engaged. We may one day rue this neglect of the substance of democracy in democracy's army."[16]

In London an incensed Col. Arter regarded the article as totally unjustified (though the fact that his memo referred throughout to "Reinhold Wiebuhr" is perhaps partial vindication of its argument!). Arter defended *Stars and Stripes* (only one pinup a week and a third of its space devoted to the meaning of the war) and noted that Niebuhr had never inquired officially of ETO about its educational work, in particular being apparently unaware of what was in the pipeline. But the furore made the formal launch of what was called "Army Talks" a delicate public relations exercise for ETO. It wanted to avoid charges of propaganda or merely "copying" the British. The first pamphlet of "Army Talks" appeared on 29 September, to explain the scheme, and it got going in earnest from 11 October with a pamphlet on "War and the Supply Lines." The press were taken to a demonstration session, which the SOS public relations officer specified should comprise "a truly able officer" and "particularly intelligent soldiers." Reporting the launch favourably, *The New York Times* said nothing about British precedents and cited the New England Town Meeting as its model.[17]

It was one thing, of course, to establish a scheme of this sort on paper in London, quite another to make it work in isolated Army camps and air bases across Britain. The British had the same problem. ABCA's effectiveness depended on the enthusiasm and ability of the officers involved and many men were openly cynical or apathetic, snoozing at the back while a few enthusiasts chattered on. "Army Talks" was even more patchy in coverage. The hour a week was not compulsory in Air Force units, because of operational pressures, and in SOS, where supposedly it was obligatory, a survey in March 1944 found that two-thirds of units had received no instructions to hold discussions and 57 percent were not receiving "Army Talks." Under one-fifth of units were actually receiving the pamphlets *and* holding discussions. Nevertheless, the programme was a significant innovation, testifying to a growing concern in the U.S. Army in Britain by 1943 about GIs' attitudes as well as their material welfare. In the words of ETO's in-house history, it reflected the novel concept of "treating the soldier as something more than a rude mass of appetites and genitals."[18]

One of the main aims of U.S. Army education in Britain was to foster better attitudes towards the British, particularly soldiers—who, as Wallace's original survey had indicated, were much less popular than British civilians among GIs. By August 1942 all arriving GIs were being issued *A Short Guide to Great Britain*, a thirty-eight-page, pocket-size pamphlet in a series produced by the War Department's Special Service Division for troops going overseas (following British Army example). The author was the Yorkshire-born American novelist Eric Knight. He provided a variety of useful information about daily life—such as pubs, sports, and the arcane currency—and even included a glossary of problematic terms (cookie/biscuit, vest/waistcoat, and so on). There were warnings against bragging or getting into arguments, especially about British customs ("NEVER criticize the King or Queen"). In similar vein, the *Guide* to Northern Ireland warned GIs to avoid any discussion of sectarian problems: "Don't argue religion. Don't argue politics." The information and advice in these handbooks followed the central themes of U.S. government publicity about Britain after Pearl Harbor. Of these the most important was that the two countries were both democracies. Aristocratic privileges were played down as comfortable rituals, the monarchy equated with the Stars and Stripes as the symbol of nationhood. "The important thing to remember is that within this apparently old-fashioned framework the British enjoy a practical, working twentieth-century democracy which is in some ways even more flexible and sensitive to the will of the people than our own." Thus, the basic argument of the British *Guide* was that "in their major ways of life the British and American peoples are much alike. They speak the same language. They both believe in representative government, in freedom of worship, in freedom of speech." But each country had "minor national characteristics which differ" that German propaganda would try to exploit.[19]

Yet those men who read and heeded these *Guides* would have been a small proportion of the three million Americans who passed through the United Kingdom during the war. More significant were the indoctrination lectures GIs received onboard ship and on arrival at their first base. Instructions to 8th Air Force service personnel in September 1943, for instance, specified in some detail the content of such lectures. They should "emphasize the paramount importance" of "proper relations" with British civilians and soldiers and the ways in which GIs "may carelessly create ill-will between the forces of the principal Allies." In particular, soldiers should be "informed that the sale of beer and spirits is strictly limited" and cautioned against "excessive drinking." They should be "made to realize generally that stringent rationing prevails throughout all fields of British life, to conduct themselves accordingly and to avoid being indiscreet in the matter of excessive spending, due to the comparatively high standard of pay received."[20]

The most imaginative effort at indoctrination was the fifty-minute film *A Welcome to Britain* made in 1943 by the British Ministry of Information with the cooperation of OWI to show to GIs on arrival. Gen. Adam at the War Office also took a keen interest, appearing himself at the beginning. With the movie actor Burgess Meredith as a friendly GI guide, the film took soldiers through some typical or embarrassing situations in Britain. In a country pub a GI was shown chatting up the barmaid, throwing his money around, and insulting a Scottish soldier about his kilt. Invited into a British home for supper, he cleans away a week's rations while his hosts look on, silent and glum. Later in the film he takes a train, getting out of the compartment with a black GI. Both are invited by an elderly English lady to her house for tea. While the black GI buys some cigarettes, Meredith confides to the camera that this sort of thing was not unusual in Britain. It might not happen at home, he said, but then the point is that we're not at home.[21]

The need for education in Anglo-American relations was mutual. If GIs needed to respect the customs of their hosts, the English had to appreciate that their visitors were not transplanted Englishmen. That was the burden of the material issued by ABCA to British troops in 1942. In July, September, and December the United States was the subject of "Current Affairs" pamphlets, all of which tried to promote awareness and respect for distinctive American traits by rooting them in the unique history of the United States. Like the GIs' *A Short Guide to Great Britain* the dual aim was to highlight basic similarities and then to expose minor contrasts between the two countries, so as "to defeat Goebbels' attempt to sow discord between us." Although the detailed material, mostly by academics in the MOI's wartime employment, was more cerebral than the chatty style of *A Short Guide,* ABCA's editorial comment rammed home the basic message—on all the essentials, like democracy and freedom, "Americans and English think alike," but what the often "trivial points" of difference showed was that the "Americans are not Englishmen who are different, but foreigners who are rather like us."[22]

In mid-March 1944 "Current Affairs" and "Army Talks" published the same article for simultaneous discussion in both armies. Entitled "The Yank in Britain," its author was the American anthropologist Margaret Mead, best known for her writings on the South Pacific and on American culture. Mead was keenly interested in Britain. Her third husband, Gregory Bateson, was English and in the spring of 1943 they had been exploring possible projects about Anglo-American similarities and differences with both *Time* magazine and CBS radio. From July through October 1943 Mead toured Britain under the auspices of OWI, principally to assess wartime welfare programmes, but she was quickly drawn into the business of interpreting the GIs to the British, and vice versa. The result was this specially commissioned piece for the two armies. Like other official education material Mead asked her readers to respect the cultural relativities rather than to judge the other country by one's own standards. She addressed the basic differences of time and space, focusing on the propensity of young American males to think about today and tomorrow ("the past is for girls only"—women, claimed Mead, constituted the majority of prewar American visitors to England) and on the American tendency to equate "bigness" with "greatness" (so how could Britain be "Great" when one can fly from coast to coast in a couple of hours?). These contrasts, argued Mead, helped to explain GI-British misunderstandings. History and tradition translate into respect for one's elders and a tendency to understatement, not the outspoken pushiness that fits a culture in which children are often more socially adept than their (immigrant) parents and in which "man, not 'history' made America." As for the GI's reluctance about home hospitality and his tendency to cry off at the last minute, remember, said Mead, that back home there would be a porch, a yard, or even a car for getting acquainted with young people of his own age, before having to enter the cramped space of the family circle on its best behaviour.

Mead's pamphlet was one of several pieces that she produced while in Britain, most of which were stitched together in a booklet called *The American Troops and the British Community.* Victor Weybright of OWI, London, praised her "extraordinary influence in Britain," and Lady Reading—who "managed to nobble a largish number of copies" of Mead's earlier work, *The American Character,* for WVS staff—had "a stream of letters back saying what a tremendous help" it was. The Foreign Office felt that her piece for ABCA, though underrating British interest in the future, "could scarcely be improved . . . as a description of the background of the American soldier, designed to promote better understanding on the part of the British army." Her ideas were widely taken up in official circles, particularly her analysis of "dating," which will be discussed in chapter 16.[23]

How much of this came to the attention of ordinary soldiers is a different matter, though. Many GIs paid little attention to indoctrination lectures; likewise many British soldiers dozed through ABCA sessions. And we shall see in chapter 19 that relations between the two armies were always tense. But the American occupation of Britain also saw a much more extensive attempt at education, using the presence of the GIs to influence the views of the British public as a whole about America and Americans. The effects of this campaign were to be seen in British schools and cinemas.

In Whitehall, the roots of this campaign dated back to 1941. The tangible evidence of American aid provided by Lend-Lease aroused new public interest in the United States. One BBC Listener Research Report in July 1941 "detected a genuine realisation on the part of ordinary people that, despite all the output of Hollywood, they know very little about the American as a human being, and they want to know more." In the spring of 1941 the Ministry of Information therefore mounted a publicity drive about the United States, with warm support from the Foreign Office who stressed "the vital need for the sake of future Anglo-American relations of a more widespread comprehension of America in this country." Together they spurred the Board of Education, the government department with oversight of schools, into an unprecedented effort to promote American studies.[24]

In July 1941 and February 1942 the board issued guidance memoranda about the teaching of U.S. history in elementary and secondary schools. These contained general advice about methods of instruction and short booklists. The line, as with ABCA, was "to make children realize that Hollywood, hot music and slang are not the most important features of the life of the U.S.A.; they should come to appreciate the great American leaders and the generous idealism actuating this nation, that speaks the same tongue as we do but is otherwise different in tradition and outlook." To fill the gap in suitable reading material for British children, special texts were also published. With the help of Ambassador Winant, himself a former history teacher, Allan Nevins of Columbia University, the Civil War historian, was commissioned by Clarendon Press in Oxford to produce a forty-thousand-word survey for use in all the secondary schools in Britain. This volume, to which Winant contributed a foreword, was published early in 1942 under the title *A Brief History of the United States.* Clarendon was delighted and asked Nevins and his Columbia colleague Henry Steele Commager to write a longer history, which appeared in December 1942.[25]

The basic problem, however, was that most British teachers knew as little about the United States as the general public. The Board of Education therefore arranged a series of week-long training courses for teachers around the country—an initiative that the board punningly claimed would "make history." By the time the series of eighteen courses ended in autumn 1942 more than three thousand teachers from England and Wales had participated. The board concluded that, whereas in mid-1941 not more than a dozen secondary schools undertook any systematic study of U.S. history, the figure by early 1943 ran into hundreds if not thousands and it appeared "now the rule rather than the exception for some emphasis to be given to the study of the U.S.A. at some stage of the senior school curriculum."[26]

Because of the constraints of the examination syllabus and the shortage of suitable books and teachers, America was often studied not through a sustained, formal course but by short interdisciplinary projects. For instance, Blackley Senior and Junior Schools, in a working-class area of Manchester, made contact with schools in some of Manchester's namesake cities across the United States and used such everyday items as coins, postage stamps, and the labels from American canned goods. The Board of Education also utilized the GIs. The poet Louis MacNeice was commissioned to write a twenty-four-page illustrated booklet, *Meet the U.S. Army,* about America, its customs, and its Army. One hundred thousand were printed in July 1943 and a copy sent to every school for use in preparing lessons or talks for pupils. MacNeice's theme was the usual one—to transform the GIs from a vague stereotype and "set them in a perspective from where they will appear as human beings—like us *and* unlike us, but more the former than the latter." The most successful educational opportunities often occurred when children had a chance to meet "real Americans" and hear them talk about "real America." Some soldiers who had been teachers in civilian life gave special lessons to schools near their bases. Others simply came to talk informally to schools and youth clubs about their hometown and its way of life. Even so, what children wanted to hear was often more about the America of the movies. In the autumn of 1942 children in High Wycombe in Buckinghamshire particularly enjoyed talks given in two schools by an AAF captain attired in full Indian costume and singing traditional Indian songs.[27]

Whitehall's big push on American studies was in 1941–42. But as the Board of Education activism waned, America's image in Britain became a matter of concern for agencies of the U.S. government. The complaints about Hollywood made before the war by the likes of Ambassador Kennedy became more insistent in wartime because the main markets for U.S. films had now contracted down to the UK, the British Empire, and Latin America. The big studios therefore pushed harder than ever in Britain, their major outlet, aided by the British government's relaxation from 1942 of quota laws requiring a proportion of British films to be shown.[28] Official concern was not just about Hollywood's influence on *British* audiences; as the opinion polls for ETO indicated, most GIs arrived in Britain with images already set by the movies.

Early in 1943 U.S. consuls around Britain were asked by the State Department to report on "motion pictures" in their district.[29] They found that audiences had increased significantly since the beginning of the war—up one-third in Birmingham, maybe doubling in Manchester—and the general consensus was that on average adults now went to the cinema at least once a week, although the most avid moviegoers were "workers," women, and teenagers. In the Midlands, for instance, Birmingham had eighty cinemas, Leicester had thirty, and Coventry twenty-two. Most of the movies shown were American—at least 85 percent, the Birmingham consulate reckoned. Gangster movies, Westerns, and horror films were no longer very popular; nor were war stories, with exceptions such as *Wake Island*—a box-office hit about U.S. Marines holding out against the Japanese. What audiences wanted above all were the "technicolor" musicals—light-hearted and entertaining—though short Disney cartoons were also well liked.

Not all reports assumed glibly that British audiences equated Hollywood's America with the real thing. As the U.S. consul in Manchester noted, the cinema was a form of escapism for hardworking people living under difficult conditions. Nevertheless, even he had no doubt that America was generally "regarded as a fabulous country of glitter and glory." Others were concerned about the corrupting effect of Hollywood's America on the young. The consul in Birmingham stated that the "local public is particularly critical of many of the shorter American films which are often shown with the feature, more especially those typifying the seamier side of American life and dealing with divorce, gangster activities and child precocity." There had been much correspondence about this in the local press, speculating on possible correlations with wartime teenage delinquency. He concluded that there were "many who feel that the distorted or 'Hollywood' impression of American life conveyed by certain types [of films] is likely to prove inimical in [sic] a better Anglo-American understanding."

"Can nothing be done about the movies?" moaned the head of OWI in London in March 1943. Any answer clearly lay at the American end and by 1943 OWI had mounted what has been called "an intensive, unprecedented effort to mold the content of Hollywood's feature films." In the 1930s the movie industry had imposed its own self-censorship, but its production code was a response to criticism from the Catholic Church and mainly regulated scenes of sex and violence. After Pearl Harbor, censorship became political in content and governmental in operation. By 1943 staff from the OWI office in Los Angeles issued broad guidelines, sat in on story conferences, reviewed screenplays, rewrote scripts, and pressured studios to scrap whole pictures. The Office of Censorship could withhold export licenses for unacceptable films. The basic criterion of the *Government Information Manual for the Motion Picture Industry* was "Will this picture help win the war?" This meant highlighting the struggle ideologically as a crusade for "democracy," embodied by America at home and assisted by its Allies abroad.[30]

In films about the United States, treatment of organized crime, political corruption, and rampant violence was discouraged. OWI even took exception to the delightful Frank Capra film of the black comedy *Arsenic and Old Lace*—in which two lovable spinsters administer mercy doses of arsenic in elderberry wine to lonely old men. It was "not recommended for special distribution in liberated areas" because of "its presentation of lawlessness and police inefficiency." OWI also wanted Westerns explicitly dated in a foreword ("our story takes place in 1870, when the American West was a turbulent frontier . . .") so that "audiences abroad will not be led to think that the action they see is taking place in present-day America." Good movies, on OWI criteria, included such 1944 hits as *Since You Went Away* (David O. Selznick's classic in which Claudette Colbert holds an Ohio family together while "Pop" is away at war) and the Judy Garland musical *Meet Me in St. Louis* ("a refreshing and wholesome picture of the American family")—both of which, significantly, were set in "real America." This was crucial, in the view of the head of OWI's British Division in Washington, Ferdinand Kuhn. He wanted "to get accurate representations of ourselves into the ordinary Hollywood film," to satisfy what reports from Britain showed to be the "great and unsatisfied curiosity about American institutions that we take for granted." His pitch mingled business and patriotism. He argued "that the American public has an extension of perhaps 20 million film-goers in the British Isles, that these films are the most potent of all influences in determining British attitudes towards America, and that we are all sunk unless we keep the common people of Great Britain on our side during the war and after the war."[31]

Apart from projecting favourable impressions of America, OWI tried to alter movie stereotypes about Britain, which reinforced GI prejudices as well as offended British audiences. Kuhn was fighting what he termed the "castles and castes" image, seeking instead to present "the picture of progressive, true-to-life England." He and his staff believed that Britain was, belatedly, becoming more democratic and thus more like America. One of its reviewers asserted in March 1944: "The British today feel that caste relations are relics that are vanishing." Thus, OWI welcomed *Spitfire*, the 1943 movie by Sam Goldwyn, Sr., about R. J. Mitchell, the designer of the famous British fighter plane. "The British caste system is shown as a diminishing survival. All of the people shown illustrate the growing democracy in England, and seem to be the kind with whom we have much in common." By contrast, OWI's particular bête noire, with regard to Britain, was MGM, whose *Yank at Eton* (1942), starring Mickey Rooney, was judged "poisonous from start to finish" by Kuhn because it took Eton as typical of English education and pictured the country as "a land of stately homes, butlers, and stiff-necked snobs and sissies."[32]

American propagandists were also active in Britain itself. Ambassador Winant's special assistant, Herbert Agar, told OWI in November 1942 there was "now intense curiosity about America all over the British Isles." His letter helped prompt OWI to set up not only a British Division in Washington but an office in London, incorporating various existing publicity operations, which started in January 1943. This had three branches—a newsroom, a reference library, and a "slow media section" concentrating on cultural and educational work. One of the latter's most successful projects was the "Young America" exhibition that opened amid great fanfare in London in April 1944 (even gaining a mention on BBC news bulletins). This aimed to give an unvarnished account of the life of children and young people in "real" America, featuring scrapbooks compiled by some thirty American schools. The exhibition, OWI reported, was "a visible demonstration that a concept of America based on Hollywood was false—almost everyone commented on this." After three weeks in London a modified version of "Young America" traveled the country in a U.S. Army truck. By March 1945 it had stopped in 194 places, from Bridlington to Barnstaple, and had been seen by more than thirty-seven thousand people.[33]

But there were very definite limits to what OWI could achieve. In August 1943 its British staff totaled forty-four (thirteen officers and thirty-one clerks). It noted sadly that the British Ministry of Information maintained 347 personnel in the United States. Moreover, much of its work centred on "hot news" and propaganda on the Continent, working closely in these areas with the MOI, BBC, and the Political Warfare Executive. Most cultural relations activities were left officially to the State Department, whose Division of Cultural Relations dated only from 1938 and whose wartime priorities were Latin America, China, and the Middle East. Early in 1942 the department's European Division had supported calls for action "without delay" to satisfy the unprecedented British interest in the United States, but it made few concrete suggestions and little ensued.[34]

Under the circumstances much depended upon the actions of individual American consuls around the British Isles. Their response varied greatly. Some took little interest in cultural relations, believing it would involve them in "political" activity outside their official brief. In February 1942 the consul in Belfast sent a curt rejection when asked to preside over the first of nine special lectures on America to be given for local schoolteachers. Yet the following August he was scathing in complaints to Washington about British ignorance of the United States and their failure to remedy this in schools. At the other extreme was his colleague in Manchester, George Armstrong, an avuncular widower who loved children. Armstrong gave numerous informal talks on American history and life to schools in his district, which ran as far afield as Sheffield, Nottingham, and Derby. He also encouraged pen-pal correspondence with American schools, liaised with American Army units about GI visits, and arranged prizes for school essay competitions about America. Armstrong was a fanatic about cultural diplomacy, however, and became highly critical of how little was being done. Most U.S. consuls did what they could sporadically, without his single-minded passion.[35]

In 1942–43, therefore, the problems caused by the American presence in Britain inspired a variety of attempts to change hearts and minds. On the British side, they reflected the unprecedented public interest in the United States and the importance attached to good Anglo-American relations by the British government. On the American side, OWI and other diplomatic personnel shared this concern, but some U.S. Army innovations, such as the American Forces radio network and the on-base educational programme, still embodied the "little America," damage-limitation philosophy. By autumn 1943, however, events made such a policy almost untenable.

12

Friends and
Relations

★ ★ ★

AT CASABLANCA IN JANUARY 1943 ROOSEVELT AND CHURCHILL GAVE PRI-
ority to a major bombing offensive against Germany. This led to a new
influx of American airmen into Britain that summer. At Washington
in May and at Quebec in August the two leaders firmed up plans for
invading France the following spring. From late summer the combat
divisions started arriving, supported by service personnel. On 31 May
1943 U.S. troops in Britain numbered 133,000. They passed the half-
million mark in November, exceeded one million during February
1944, and peaked at 1,527,000 on D-Day (table 7.2).

One result was an accommodation crisis. Although the billeting of
GIs in private homes had hitherto been avoided except for some officers
(chapter 10), in June 1943 it was agreed that from the New Year it
would be necessary on a large scale for enlisted men. The billets were
only for sleeping purposes—meals would be taken in unit messes—
but, even so, both the Home Office and the Ministry of Information
hoped that the scheme would not be compulsory, in view of the
unpopularity of billeting among civilians. But the War Office, requiring
billets for up to 100,000 GIs, rejected any idea of a voluntary scheme.
Responsibility for finding billets was handed over to the local police
and it caused great ill-feeling that autumn. The number of beds required was large—5,575 in Hampshire, for instance, and 3,800 in
Dorset. And the unlucky householder would be left with kitchen and
bathroom plus one room per family member, the rest being turned
over to GIs. In Bristol the U.S. consul reported in November that the
issue "has, in my estimation, aroused more interest and discussion
than any development since the heavy bombing of 1941 . . . discussion

that was highly tinged with acrimony and showed a fairly general dislike of the idea on the ground that the proposed billitees [sic] were Americans." Little wonder the British authorities regarded the whole idea as a "dangerous experiment."[1]

More GIs, almost inevitably, meant more incidents with the British. And it was hard to "indoctrinate" the rush of new troops into the nuances of British life. By midsummer this was apparent in East Anglia, where the bulk of the airmen were concentrated. In July 1943 Gen. Eaker told his subordinates in the 8th Air Force that the relationship between the Americans on the one hand and British troops and civilians on the other was "not as good as it was a few months ago when our force was smaller." The British authorities in East Anglia agreed that relations had "recently deteriorated rather sharply." In America, the press began publicizing the problems. A long piece in *Time* magazine in December, entitled "Poor Relations," noted that "in recent months it has become increasingly obvious that the people of Britain are annoyed by the free-spending, free-loving, free-speaking U.S. troops." Although *Time* likened the problems to those caused by troops everywhere, not least the British Tommies in France in 1914–18, it suggested that "the British are understandably short of temper" and that many had "now come to think of the U.S. soldier as sloppy, conceited, insensitive, undiscriminating, noisy."[2]

In 1942–43 the British press had, with government encouragement, been practising what one OWI official called "almost complete self-censorship" on any stories about friction with GIs. The U.S. embassy in London noted in December 1943 that "generally, only favourable articles are published, and unfriendly feeling is only rarely and indirectly mentioned in news articles." Not until a series of frank articles in the *Daily Mirror* at the turn of the year was the silence broken. The *Mirror* invited Britons and Americans to voice their mutual grievances, and it printed special pieces on American homesickness and the difficulties of GI brides. The writer George Orwell also spoke out. "Discussion of inter-allied relations is still avoided in the press and utterly taboo on the air," he complained, arguing that the failure to voice and answer mutual criticisms only stored up problems for the future. "No sensible person wants to whip up Anglo-American jealousy. On the contrary, it is just because one does want a good relationship between the two countries that one wants plain speaking."[3]

But words were no longer sufficient. The pressures mounted for a more "positive" policy to promote friendly relations—especially from the War Office and the Foreign Office in London.

★ ★ ★

The initiative came particularly from Col. Brian Rowe, who since 1942 had been responsible for War Office liaison with ETO over the GI presence. Rowe was enthusiastic, energetic, and well informed about American affairs—until shortly before the war he had been in public relations work in New York. In August 1942 he had drawn attention to the problems that would be posed by a million or more GIs in Britain for months or even years. "Even relations and friends are often better liked when their stay is short," he noted. "And these Americans are not relations, or even friends." But his calls for a positive campaign went unheeded, as numbers tailed off and the problems diminished during the winter. In May 1943, with the GI influx resuming, Rowe returned to the charge. Writing to the Foreign Office, he distinguished between two targets. If the aim was "to ensure that there are no incidents so untoward that questions get asked about them in the House" [of Commons]—what he called "the generally accepted target"—then "we are not doing too badly." This, he said, "appears to be the official attitude of the War Office, the Ministry of Information and the Air Ministry." But, he continued, there was a more elevated target: "the one thing which means most to the world in the after-war—a real friendship between the common men of the two nations." If one asked "Are we making good use of this opportunity?" the answer was an unqualified "No." Rowe identified two basic problems. One was the "lack of a strong lead from above," akin to that given by the Anglo-American duumvirate of Eisenhower and Alexander in North Africa. "The other reason is that there is no common policy between Ministries, no plan, no drive; and, inside Ministries, it seems to be no one's business in particular." Rowe sought a directive from the very top, from Roosevelt and Churchill, to encourage fraternization between the two armies. He also proposed an interdepartmental committee in Whitehall (with American representation) to ensure its implementation.[4]

Rowe's memoranda were the familiar products of any able staff officer, eyes fixed on his own brief. As such they could have been buried but for the concern now felt at senior levels of Whitehall. In the summer of 1943 the War Office established a special subcommittee, including Rowe, to review relations between British and U.S. troops in all theatres and to advise on "methods of promoting mutual understanding and friendly relations." Nothing of this sort had been done for the Canadians or any other Allied force in Britain. At its opening meeting on 4 August the committee "agreed that the first thing to be done was to arouse the U.S. authorities to a sense of the importance and urgency of the problem." Equally significant was the vigorous interest of the Foreign Office's American Department, by then deeply dissatisfied at the MOI's diffidence. It agreed with Rowe's calls for a top-level directive and a coordinating committee and, moreover, was ready to push the matter onto the diplomatic agenda in a way that Rowe could not. Enlisting the backing of Foreign Secretary Anthony Eden, the department prepared a briefing note for Churchill to take with him to his meeting with Roosevelt in mid-August at Quebec. This received warm endorsement from Gen. Adam, Adjutant General at the WO, who observed that although the U.S. officers he met were "always willing to make pleasant noises about the desirability of fostering and cementing Anglo-American friendship," in practice they rarely did anything. He also deplored the monopoly by the American Red Cross of welfare arrangements. The basic problem, said Adam, was that "no lead is given from Washington and all American Generals are frightened to do anything on their own." Therefore "nothing short of intervention on the highest possible political level on both sides will have any effect."[5]

Most of the Quebec conference was spent in planning for Overlord and other future operations in the Mediterranean and Burma. By contrast, relations between American and British troops occupied only one sentence of the State Department's minutes for 22 August:

> It was agreed between the President and Prime Minister that all possible steps should be taken to promote fraternization between the U.S. and British forces in the British Isles and, with a view to accomplishing this end, Mr. Eden should speak to General Marshall, to General Devers and to Norman Davis [Chairman of the American Red Cross] as to methods for its accomplishment.

In fact, Churchill had not even discussed the matter with Roosevelt; as the British minutes make clear it was Eden who "had indicated the difficulties which had arisen and obtained the President's authority to discuss the matter" further. The lack of extended discussion did not, in fact, matter. That single sentence in the official minutes was strictly all the Foreign Office needed to galvanize the U.S. Army—its Commander in Chief had spoken. But the impact of Roosevelt's instruction was undoubtedly enhanced by the furore that the British unwittingly unleashed after the conference.[6]

On 24 August, Eden conveyed the gist of the Foreign Office briefing paper to Sir John Dill, head of the British Joint Staff Mission in Washington, for Dill to take up with Marshall. The officials who drafted the original brief did not want it passed verbatim to the Americans, because of its critical tone, but that caveat was lost as the paper ascended the FO hierarchy. In his letter Eden stressed to Dill that his request was "no reflection" on Gen. Devers, ETO commander in London, who had been "consistently helpful and friendly," but he retained some of the unvarnished Foreign Office prose:

> We had hoped that the presence of large numbers of American troops in the United Kingdom, North Africa and other theatres of war, training or fighting side by side with our own men, would have done much to develop mutual understanding between the two peoples. Eisenhower, of course, fully understands its importance from the military angle and he has worked hard to promote it, but very little has been done in England. The principal reason seems to be that the American military authorities in England tend to discourage fraternization as a waste of time that ought to be devoted to purely military purposes; and the American Red Cross, which is responsible for social amenities, concentrates on reproducing the American atmosphere and deliberately discourages any intrusion of British friendliness.

Dill simply passed Eden's letter to Marshall and a paraphrase was sent to Devers and Davis in London. Although its author was identified only as "a high British diplomatic source," such blunt criticism of ETO and the ARC, coming via the U.S. Army Chief of Staff himself, provoked what Marshall called "quite violent" reactions. The ensuing controversy served to ram home the bland conference minute.[7]

Devers circulated the criticisms to subordinate commanders, all of whom naturally defended themselves strenuously. Eaker, for instance, called it "a base slander against Eighth Air Force Officers and men" and demanded that the "nameless diplomatic source" be "removed from anonymity and be asked to prove his charges." Devers's own reply to Marshall described the accusations as "completely without foundation and contrary to the policies and practices of this theater." Among measures taken to foster fraternization, he instanced various joint activities between GIs and British troops, such as dinners, dances, and athletic meetings.[8]

His response was passed via Marshall and Dill back to the Foreign Office, where officials, though embarrassed, were unrepentant. Their own back channels indicated that the American authorities had received a "salutary" shock. Privately the SOS Chief of Staff, who drafted

Devers's reply to Marshall, admitted to Col. Rowe of the War Office that it was "an eye-wash cable" setting out "various small but definite things which have been done." Rowe believed from his sources that Devers, Lee, and their staffs "would certainly welcome a directive." They were all keen to get something done but realized that "they might make themselves politically unpopular if they initiated strong action without covering authority from above." When Devers saw Sir Ronald Adam at the end of September he was still "considerably shaken at the whole episode," and "expressed the keenest desire to know what he could do next in order to improve relations between the British and American armies."[9]

As a result ETO representatives started attending the War Office's subcommittee on relations between British and U.S. troops and on 19 November it was formally reconstituted as a joint "Anglo-American (Army) Relations Committee," with Gen. Abbott, Devers's G-1, as the U.S. co-chairman. Its terms of reference were "to keep under constant review the problems arising out of the association of British and U.S. troops in the European theatre" and to make policy recommendations, particularly on "methods of promoting mutual understanding and friendly relations between the two forces." The committee's main achievement was a very successful programme of troop exchanges between American and British units—known by the clumsy War Office title of "inter-attachment." What these exchanges revealed at the grass-roots level about the two armies will be examined in chapter 19. Suffice it here to say that between November 1943 and May 1944 some nine thousand American and British soldiers spent an average of twelve days living and working with units of the other army. In addition, over forty-six hundred 8th Air Force personnel paid visits averaging twenty-four hours to British units over the same period; similarly some thirty-six hundred men from the 9th Air Force visited for an average of six hours. Thousands more were affected by contact with the visitors. First U.S. Army HQ judged the scheme "the best means yet attempted to create a better understanding between soldiers of the two armies," while, for the British, Gen. Adam called it "a 100 per cent success."[10]

The exchanges were launched by the formal directives from ETO and the WO that Rowe had long been demanding. Their emphasis was not on technical or tactical training, but on "the intermingling of American and British soldiers" in preparation for the campaign in France. "Soldiers who fight together must understand each other and have complete confidence in each other's abilities," wrote Devers. "They must know and appreciate each other's qualities, methods and weapons." Reflecting the greater British emphasis on a long-term special relationship, the War Office also alluded to "the obvious benefits which must result after war from better understanding and mutual esteem between the armed forces of the two peoples."[11]

The new committee, the interattachment scheme, and the joint directives were major innovations, all of which could be attributed in large part to the ripples caused by Eden's letter. By the middle of October Nevile Butler, head of the the FO's American Department, felt that "matters have turned out much better than might have been expected as far as United States Army co-operation is concerned." But, he added, "it is too much to hope for any great change of American Red Cross policy." The ARC had fiercely defended itself against the claim in Eden's letter that it "deliberately discourages any intrusion of British friendliness." Norman Davis, the ARC chairman then in London, told the War Department that he and Devers were "amazed at the gross inaccuracy and unfairness of the charges." He claimed that the British "had been misled and misinformed" as to Red Cross policy. On 3 September a furious Davis phoned Richard Law, a junior Foreign Office minister, to protest about the cable from Marshall. Davis said Law had "agreed that the statement made in Quebec was incorrect and unfortunate, that it evidently originated from a memorandum made at a time when the matter was not thoroughly understood, that our policy was unassailable and that he would write me a letter to that effect." Law's own account of his talk with Davis indicates no such agreement with ARC policy—merely acceptance that "there was very little progress to be made on this line"—but he felt it politic to send a soothing letter telling Davis "how much we admire the magnificent work which the American Red Cross is doing."[12]

The furore about Eden's letter, therefore, had little effect on the ARC. By the winter of 1943–44 its critics were numerous and varied. One official at the British embassy in Washington claimed the ARC's goal was "to cater for American nostalgia by providing the nearest possible approximation to home and hominy, Coca Cola and drug stores." Leaders of British women's organizations including Lady Reading and Pamela Churchill (the premier's daughter-in-law) were also much exercised. On the American side the ARC's most impassioned critic was Herbert Agar, special assistant to Ambassador Winant and from September 1943 the director of OWI in London. In January 1944 these complaints found their way to the White House after the lawyer and civil libertarian Morris Ernst, an associate of the president, wrote a vehement attack on what he called the "shocking job" the ARC was doing in Britain. There were even some sceptics within the ARC itself.

Although Harvey Gibson, the commissioner in Britain, resented any criticism, Richard F. Allen, the vice chairman in Washington, was more open-minded and was considered by the British embassy to have "departed a long way from rigid isolationism." Allen periodically nudged Gibson in a discreet way about adverse comment, though the response was usually a blockbuster letter in self-defence.[13]

The criticisms of the ARC dated back to the summer of 1942 (chapter 10) and fell into two main categories. One was the insufficient recognition supposedly given to British assistance. British Reverse Lend-Lease continued to pay for most of the premises and equipment, to the tune of some $16 million in 1943–44, and it was widely felt that this was not properly acknowledged by the ARC. In May 1944 Gibson called such a charge "entirely incorrect," explaining that every club posted a notice about British aid in a prominent place. Like many of Gibson's responses, this was strictly true but disingenuous. According to Allen, writing on 7 April, the notices had only been displayed "within the last two months." Gibson was equally casuistical in handling the allegation that the ARC glossed over the role of British staff in its clubs. Numbers peaked in May 1944 at nearly twenty-nine thousand, when American personnel amounted to only two thousand. Of the British roughly half were volunteers, the rest carefully vetted employees. Gibson and the ARC feared that publicity for British helpers would damage fund-raising at home, the ARC's main source of money. Although he therefore did acknowledge British help, this was largely in private letters or in speeches to British audiences, such as an English-Speaking Union luncheon in Leicester in May 1944, which was picked up by some British newspapers but not the American press. In striking contrast were two lengthy articles in *The New York Times* on 16–17 March 1944, inspired by the ARC as part of its annual fund-raising drive and based on one of Gibson's memoranda. These said virtually nothing about the British role, but dwelt on how the ARC was running a huge "hotel chain" of 170-plus service clubs whose main objective was "to furnish home-minded Americans with a little touch of home abroad." Not until a week later did the paper print a piece lauding the British staff (ranging from "nobility to factory girls") and giving precise numbers. Without them, it said, the ARC "could not approach the job it is doing in Britain." This corrective was apparently inspired by the Ministry of Information, not the ARC![14]

The second major grievance against the American Red Cross was its policy of banning British and Allied personnel from the service clubs, except when mealtime guests of GIs, thereby helping to create a purely "American" atmosphere. On the latter point, Gibson was not merely unrepentant but "proud." The Army, he reiterated, "from the very first have urged us to provide a home away from home for our American soldiers and that was the No. 1 purpose for which we were over here." On the exclusion of all but GIs, the fund-raising aspect was again relevant. Allen was fearful of creating any impression "that we were asking for funds to finance welfare and recreation centers for all the Allied armies rather than just for the American army." Practical considerations also bulked large. Gibson and Davis cited the 1942 open-house experiments in Londonderry and Salisbury, which led to the ARC being overwhelmed by British soldiers. In March 1943 Brendan Bracken, the British minister of information, had admitted to Gibson "that we do not think it fair to expect your Clubs to offer unrestricted entry to British troops," who had their own homes to go to when on extended leave. And, as Richard Allen commented in August 1944 "the real difficulty lies in the fact that our U.S. forces abroad and at home live on a higher standard than our Allies. Our men demand more wherever they are. The American Red Cross standard in Great Britain and in all other countries," he added, was "far below the standards maintained for service-men here in the United States."[15]

Faced with such ARC arguments, the Foreign Office made little progress. One junior official commented: "Everyone has had a go at the ARC: but like Uncle Joe Stalin they're impervious to argument and sentiment." Senior figures admitted that "more harm than good would be done if artificial efforts at mixing up resulted in overcrowded canteens, etc." The root problem was that in 1942–43 the ARC seemed the main (blocked) conduit for British contact with the GIs. But by the spring of 1944, the growing size of the American presence and the widely acknowledged need to address the problems created meant that the "mixing up" of GIs and British civilians was advancing along other channels.[16]

In the confusions of 1942 the Ministry of Information had assumed responsibility for coordinating British hospitality for GIs, but its efforts were hamstrung by lack of funds and personnel (chapter 10). In late 1943, however, as Bolero at last gathered momentum, the American presence became a government priority. Brendan Bracken, the MOI's head, remarked at the end of the year: "These American soldiers are going to be a great trouble until the fighting starts." On 8 January 1944 the MOI announced the formation of a separate American Forces Liaison Division (AFLD). In April it had eight full-time staff. At the local level, Deputy Regional Information Officers (RIOs) were appointed to handle Anglo-American affairs full-time in the eastern, southern, and southwestern regions, where the bulk of the GIs were to be found, supplemented by thirteen civil liaison officers around the country, usually part-time. The RIOs coordinated "Hospitality Committees" of community leaders and representatives of voluntary organizations in towns across the country. Some committees had been created in 1942, only to collapse in most cases after Torch, but they were resurrected with renewed official encouragement in 1944. By the end of March, 176 were in existence and a peak of 329 was reached just before D-Day. Most important of all, the MOI finally prised money out of the Treasury. From 1 March 1944 the MOI secured a budget of £500 per month ($2,000) for each RIO (instead of the previous £50 a year). As the Midlands RIO noted, this gave the Ministry new clout with the voluntary bodies "when we were in a position not only to call the tune, but also to pay the piper."[17]

In parallel with these MOI initiatives, action was taken on the American side. In November 1943 staff at the U.S. embassy in London, led by Herbert Agar, proposed a joint Anglo-American committee to help smooth relations between GIs and British civilians. Their overture was warmly welcomed in the FO, but Ambassador Winant was more cautious because of opposition within ETO. Some senior officers, including Gen. Lee, feared that this would be "equivalent to [political] agitation." The situation was transformed, however, by Eisenhower's return to England from the Mediterranean in January 1944 as Supreme Commander for Overlord. When the idea of a special committee was broached, Ike was "enthusiastically in its favour." On 14 February Winant, Law, Bracken, Adam for the WO, and Lee as ETO deputy commander agreed to act as the "British-American Liaison Board" (BALB). In practice they would be represented by lower-level officials, but Lee promised that instructions would be given to subordinates that would ensure respect for BALB's recommendations. The board was to deal with GI-civilian relations as a counterpart of the Anglo-American Relations Committee, whose brief was relations between the two armies. Its working members met formally for the first time on 3 March 1944 and thereafter fortnightly through the summer. BALB spent much of its time on cases of local friction but it also addressed general policy problems such as hospitality and race relations.[18]

The new arrangement was, however, vitiated by rivalry between the head of the MOI's new American Forces Liaison Division (AFLD), Sir Godfrey Haggard, and his stand-in, Gervas Huxley, who ran things until late February when Haggard returned from being consul general in New York. The MOI wanted to retire Huxley from its service but he had powerful backers among the voluntary societies with which MOI had to work, including the formidable Lady Reading. When Haggard took over, Huxley was therefore "kicked upstairs" and given the title "Adviser on Relations with American Forces." He was also made the MOI's representative on BALB, who elected him chairman on 17 March. Haggard, for his part, was unable to secure a seat on BALB and complained that Huxley, as "adviser," kept receiving inquiries on the work of his own division. In October 1944 Haggard brought matters to a head, complaining that his staff were "defeated and defeatist. I can give them neither leadership nor inspiration nor initiative until the situation is cleared up." He won a seat on BALB, but Huxley remained as adviser though supposedly confining himself to chairing the board.[19]

Huxley's anomalous situation reflected the MOI's antagonism to BALB. Its minister, Brendan Bracken, viewed the board as a potential challenge to the MOI's monopoly, certainly in the grand policymaking form envisaged by Col. Rowe, whom he succeeded in excluding from membership. He wished it to have no secretariat, offices, or even phones, and said that the AFLD would provide whatever administrative functions were needed. Although a joint secretariat was established, it had only one member from each side, it was based in the AFLD, and its British secretary was the division's second-in-command, Henry Maxwell. (His American counterpart was Janet Murrow, the wife of CBS bureau chief Ed Murrow, whom Winant appointed despite State Department opposition.) Consequently, BALB remained a largely consultative body, doing useful work but having strained relations with Haggard and the AFLD where the main task of liaison with the U.S. Army was taking place.[20]

Compared with this bureaucratic feuding, a smoother system for official hospitality evolved in Northern Ireland. There, the American presence had a political sensitivity that was absent on the mainland because of the tendency of the Catholic and Nationalist minority to interpret it as endorsement of partition. Moreover, Northern Ireland was a small, tightly run state, with its own devolved government. In September 1942 a committee on troop welfare and hospitality had been established under Sir Basil Brooke, the most energetic member of the cabinet, and he continued to preside after his elevation to the premiership the following May. This top-level body kept firm control over all aspects of the American presence, to a degree never achieved in Britain by the MOI. In Ulster the MOI operated, as its own internal history admitted, as "an adjunct" of the Unionist government. There was also less of a problem with conflicting voluntary agencies than in

England. The local hospitality committees established in Ulster in the autumn of 1942, on the initiative of Brooke's committee, were organized by the WVS, under its chairman, Lady Gladys Stronge, whose husband was a senior government minister. Again, MOI officials collaborated but did not lead. Although these committees became autonomous, WVS influence remained strong. The MOI's regional officer in Belfast noted that the committees included "very few members of the Catholic-Nationalist minority." Despite "a small number of honourable exceptions," as he put it, the "welcome given to the Americans has been overwhelmingly on the part of the Unionists and Protestants—those loyal to the British Crown and resolved to maintain the British connection."[21]

By the end of 1942, therefore, Northern Ireland had a bureaucratic structure for dealing with the Yanks that was more coordinated and higher-powered than its counterpart in Britain. Although falling into disuse in the quiet winter of 1942–43, it was quickly activated by Brooke in October 1943 when the second American invasion began. Both the government and the U.S. Army concentrated on minimizing the American presence in Belfast, where the potential for trouble was greatest. Passes were given only to those who had confirmed overnight accommodation, and transport was laid on to encourage GIs to visit the city on a day trip. "We are going to do all we can to keep our officers and men out of Belfast," Gen. Leroy P. Collins, the SOS commander in Ulster told the Brooke committee. "That falls in very well with this Local Hospitality Committee programme. With your help the smaller places can be made attractive." The local committees, numbering forty-five at their peak, arranged a variety of activities for GIs, ranging from fishing to factory visits, with regular dances and home hospitality the most popular.[22]

Comparison with Ulster highlights the bureaucratic tangles that entrapped official hospitality programmes on the British mainland. Nevertheless, the creation of the American Forces Liaison Division and the British-American Liaison Board in early 1944 did at last provide institutional mechanisms for fostering relations between GIs and British civilians. The network of information officers and hospitality committees across the country ensured grass-roots support and the U.S. Army was now under instructions to treat the whole matter as a priority. Through Gen. Lee orders were issued to unit commanders arriving in an area that one of their first tasks was to make contact with the RIO, local officials, clergy, and heads of voluntary societies, using the Hospitality Committee wherever possible, and that these initial meetings were not to be delegated to subordinates.[23]

Where these arrangements worked on both sides, the results could be impressive. In Birmingham, for instance, a Hospitality Committee was active from early 1944, and in July nearly three thousand GIs were entertained in local homes through officially fostered contacts alone. The committee made strenuous efforts to interest GIs in the surrounding area, arranging shows, speakers, historical tours, and factory visits. The Midlands RIO reported proudly that, although U.S. Army interest was initially limited, "in almost every instance, once they had heard one of our speakers, they came back for more, and, in fact, at one time the demand for speakers exceeded the supply." This work was greatly assisted from the American side by Col. James A. Kilian, commander of the 10th Replacement Depot at Lichfield, which was the biggest unit in the region. Among GIs, Kilian's depot became notorious for its brutality to offenders imprisoned in its stockade. But, as far as Anglo-American relations was concerned, he was a great success—because his unit was a fixity in the area, because he was its CO right through the war from late 1942, and because he took an obsessive personal interest in good community relations.[24]

On arriving at Lichfield Kilian made contact with the locals that mattered within a thirty-mile radius, right down to pub landlords and regular customers. Local societies were invited to the base and their events faithfully patronized by Kilian or his representative. Requests from schools, clubs, and churches for speakers were honoured by carefully selected GIs and the depot's band and variety show performed to great acclaim at local factories during the meal breaks. Some 200,000 British workers were entertained in the twelve months from April 1943 and, said Kilian, "the factory managers have continuously assured us that production has jumped after each showing." In 1944 his Tuesday lunches for civic and business leaders from all over the Midlands became celebrated. So impressed was BALB that a summary of Kilian's "Methods for Promoting Anglo-American Relations" was distributed to RIOs and U.S. officers in the spring of 1944.[25]

The attention attracted by Kilian indicates, however, that he was the exception not the rule. Interest from the American side in local contacts could not be presumed. But the new funds available in 1944 allowed the MOI to promote its own "British Welcome Clubs" for GIs to meet locals in the smaller towns. The Foreign Office considered this an "admirable initiative," not least because it bypassed the American Red Cross. The clubs were largely run by the Women's Voluntary Service in local church halls, social clubs, or even private homes, but the MOI donated up to £30 to cover costs such as crockery and chairs. In a few exceptional cases larger sums were provided for renting premises, such as in Colchester in Essex where "no adequate Hospitality Committee" existed or the Suffolk town of Bury St. Edmunds where GI-civilian relations had been strained and the local authority was regarded as "unhelpful." But in all cases the MOI acted as facilitator rather than as provider. Lady Reading told Eleanor Roosevelt that this was the scheme's great virtue—instead of the previous tendency for such initiatives to be "directed centrally," they were being "done on a local basis with local understanding of the problem and of the people concerned."[26]

In all, 206 such clubs received MOI financial support, most of them operating in the peak period of March to July 1944. The MOI did not regard them as an unqualified success. Although intended as a "bridge between British civilians and American soldiers," in many cases "the British troops far outnumbered the Americans." This was sometimes because the word *British* in the title proved misleading and the MOI eventually succeeded in having the word dropped. In other cases, "the personality of the organiser" or "the existence of counter-attractions," especially in large towns, acted as deterrents. In general, however, the MOI felt that the experiment was "well worthwhile" and that "the successes were greater than the failures." The southern RIO, Sir Arthur Willert, believed that "the only valid criticism" of the scheme was that it "started a year too late." It would have been "invaluable," he claimed, for dealing with SOS and other units "marooned" in England in 1943. In general the Welcome Clubs served their dual function of circumventing the ARC and bringing GIs into amicable contact with British civilians. The MOI felt that "many lasting friendships were made through this channel," cemented subsequently in people's homes.[27]

Getting the "Yanks" into British homes had, after all, always been the underlying objective of exponents of the "positive" approach to GI-British relations, from Eisenhower downwards. In 1942 home hospitality had been yet another task delegated by ETO to the ARC, who lacked both the will and the resources to cope. By late 1943, however, the ARC Club network was well established and the new ETO lead on Anglo-American relations evoked a response from Commissioner Gibson. ARC publicity started to highlight its work in this area and by June 1944 even longtime critics such as Alan Dudley in the FO acknowledged that the ARC "has recently done a good deal to encourage mixing" with British civilians, and that they "do not seem to be anything like as anxious as they were to claim that they, and they alone, are concerned only with providing the American boys with a home from home." He concluded that "the pressure exerted at Quebec and Washington" had "done some good."[28]

In November 1943 the ARC created a separate Home Hospitality Division at its London HQ, directed by Agnes de Paula, to oversee hospitality supervisors in local Service Clubs. The latter kept lists of British people offering hospitality and GIs seeking it, endeavouring to match people of similar interests so that, in de Paula's words, "a square peg is not put into a round hole." One American fan of the novels of Thomas Hardy was even able to spend a weekend with a family who lived in the author's former house. Particularly before D-Day British hosts were encouraged to act as "foster parents" and "adopt" a GI. According to de Paula, 95 percent of the soldiers returned "again and again to their 'second' homes." Not all such visits resulted from formal ARC "pairings"—of nearly 100,000 GIs who visited British homes in the first four months of 1944, 61,000 did so as a result of personal invitations by British staff and volunteers. Nevertheless, formally or informally, in 1944 the ARC Clubs were acting much more as a channel for contact between GIs and British civilians. By January 1945 more than one million home visits by GIs had taken place under the aegis of the ARC.[29]

Another, albeit rather different, channel of "home hospitality" was the practice of billeting GIs in rooms in British homes. Some 100,000 GIs were accommodated in this way in south and southwest England in the winter of 1943–44. Billeting, it will be remembered, had been accepted most reluctantly by officialdom as a "dangerous experiment." But, as the War Office admitted in April 1944,

> these misgivings had proved completely unfounded. Excellent relations had prevailed throughout between hosts and guests, and the system had evidently led to a much friendlier attitude on both sides than had previously existed. A census showed that complaints had been received in the case of only one out of every thousand men billeted.

Credit was given to ETO's meticulous instructions, and above all to the GIs themselves who, to quote Willert, the southern RIO and originally an opponent of the scheme, ensured "by their behavior that we should be wrong."[30]

The success of billeting—like that of the Welcome Clubs, home hospitality, and the Army interattachment scheme—seemed to show that properly managed "mixing" of GIs and British could have positive and rapid effects. There was particular official satisfaction at a survey of U.S. Army mail from Normandy in July 1944. A quarter of the letters written by GIs were addressed to British homes.[31]

★ ★ ★

All these programmes commenced before Eisenhower returned to London in January 1944, but they maintained momentum because of his (by then celebrated) enthusiasm for Anglo-American relations. He told one English correspondent in January 1944 that "maintaining a firm Anglo-American partnership for the purpose of winning this war lies close to my heart. There is no single thing I believe more important to both our countries." His message of 19 February, "To Every American Serving Under My Command," reiterated warnings about drink, bad language, and "discourtesy to civilians," and reminded every GI he was "a representative of our country." These were no platitudes as far as Ike was concerned. He told senior staff that he expected "every officer throughout your Service to make it his own, burning it into his mind so that it becomes part of his military character." Whatever the impact of such exhortations lower down, they made each U.S. officer aware of his ambassadorial responsibility.[32]

Nevertheless, Ike's main task was to get a huge Allied army established in France in less than six months, and that limited the time and energy he had available for Anglo-American relations. Beneath him, many of the institutional arrangements established in the winter of 1943–44 were short-lived. The British-American Liaison Board and the Anglo-American (Army) Relations Committee had lost most of their vitality by the autumn of 1944. This was partly because leading activists such as Col. Rowe and Alan Dudley had moved on to other duties, but mainly because the urgency of the issue had diminished with Overlord and the rapid contraction of the American presence from its D-Day peak of 1.65 million to under 700,000 during the following autumn and winter. This dramatic change was also reflected in hospitality arrangements at the grass-roots level. The MOI reported that as of 31 October 1944 a total of 199 Welcome Clubs had been established with its financial support, "but in view of the recent considerable exodus of American troops from this country, 122 Clubs have either closed down or temporarily suspended their activities."[33]

In other words, the energetic, top-level campaign for "positive" Anglo-American relations only got going in the spring of 1944 and was running down by late summer. Moreover, even at its peak, results were patchy and depended enormously on local circumstances. Visits by Gervas Huxley of the MOI to various troop centres in February and March 1944 made this very clear. In Oxford, for instance, there was a large and well-run ARC Service Club in the Clarendon Hotel, which worked closely with the English-Speaking Union in arranging college tours and home hospitality. Week-long special courses for American and British soldiers at Balliol College were particularly popular. In Northampton, too, Huxley found the situation "very good indeed," with a "strong" Hospitality Committee, enthusiastic interest from the local newspaper, and a "really admirable" ARC director. Southampton, by contrast, seemed to be "not a particularly happy centre for Anglo-American relations." The city centre had been devastated by bombing and there was an acute shortage of accommodation and amenities. The civic hospitality committee was only just getting going in March and seemed to lack direction.[34]

Just after D-Day, the MOI's Home Intelligence report noted that "the public's increasingly kindly feeling towards U.S. troops" had continued over the previous month, which it attributed particularly to "the fact that people are getting to know the Americans better," for example through billeting. Yet the report also pointed to abiding points of friction, which even well-run official schemes could not resolve. Top of the list was the relationship between GIs and British women.[35] As far as the two governments were concerned, the root of all evil during the American occupation was "sex."

13

Male and Female

★ ★ ★

NOT ALL THE AMERICANS IN WARTIME BRITAIN WERE MALE. ALTHOUGH only the Russians used women in combat (mostly in the Air Force), the United States forces accepted female volunteers in ancillary roles, particularly for clerical work and nursing. Some 350,000 American women served in the military during World War Two, 140,000 of them in the Women's Army Corps (WAC). Only a fraction of these servicewomen, however, came to Britain. By D-Day there were 10,500 female nurses out of 133,000 U.S. Army medical personnel in the UK. The first WAC battalion (destined for the AAF base at Stone in Staffordshire) did not arrive until July 1943. There were only 1,200 WACs in Britain by the end of the year and 3,700 just before D-Day. At that time, well under 1 percent of the American presence in Britain was female.[1]

Moreover, their social life tended to revolve in American circles. Most WACs were entertained in British homes but few visited those homes more than once or twice. American women were rarely seen dating non-GIs; all but eight of the 323 WAC marriages in ETO were with Americans. Nor did these women pose many disciplinary problems. Nurses held the rank of officers and were therefore not supposed to mix with enlisted men. And despite the "Wackies" being the butt of endless bawdy jokes and rumours, their VD rate was usually around 10 percent of that among male GIs in Britain. The official Air Force history noted that "the disciplinary problem was so negligible that its very absence is worthy of favourable comment." It concluded that the "WACs proved much less of a problem than the male military mind envisaged."[2]

What really preoccupied the "male military mind" (and its British civilian counterpart) was the relationship between American males and British females. Apart from disciplinary problems, this raised two very sensitive issues of public policy that form the subject of this chapter—venereal disease and soldier marriages. Not only did these provoke controversy in Anglo-American relations, they also reveal important contrasts between the laws and mores of the two English-speaking peoples. These contrasts helped give the "universal" problem of soldiers and sex its distinctive character during the American occupation of wartime Britain.

The persistent advances of amorous GIs were notorious. In January 1943, Gen. Russell P. Hartle, acting theatre commander in Britain, ordered his subordinate commanders to take action "promptly and forcefully" about the spate of complaints concerning GIs accosting British women—including wives in the presence of their husbands. Even women indoors were not immune. One young mother on a Birmingham housing estate recalled that nearly every evening she and her friends

> would hear a knock on the front door and on opening it would find a GI who stated that a Greg So-and-So had sent him. When one flatly denied knowing his friend, he would calmly say, "Come on baby. I know your husband is away in the forces." One would have to slam the door in their faces to keep them out.

Almost as offensive were the condoms regularly found littering churchyards, school playgrounds, and other secluded places. They were known to the Americans as "rubbers," to local kids as balloons, and to the British middle-class as "French letters." Clarence Roesler, an American military policeman in the West End of London, never forgot the night he was approached by a "very starchy lady"—she "was at least a grandmother, and boy, was she angry"—who insisted he come into her house. She pointed to the mail slot in the door, telling him it was for "letters of the Royal Mail variety . . . not these," and then presented him with "a shiny brass waste-basket at least half full of used condoms."[3]

The prevalence of GI promiscuity and of what today would be called sexual harassment cannot be doubted. But the fault was not all on one side. It was a commonplace that many British females were as "oversexed" as American males. The locus classicus for this was Piccadilly Circus, on the edge of London's theatre district, where the statue of Eros, though boarded up against bombs, remained very much the genius loci. Few who visited Piccadilly during the war forgot the experience. The ARC's Rainbow Corner club was right there, at the bottom of Shaftesbury Avenue. GI Robert Arbib recalled the Americans surging in and out of it like "a never-ending tide," in search of food, friends, dancing, and above all girls. "The girls were there—everywhere," setting their price according to the soldier's rank. "At the Underground entrance they were thickest, and as the evening grew dark they shone torches on their ankles as they walked, and bumped into the soldiers, murmuring, 'Hello, Yank,' 'Hello, soldier,' 'Hello, dearie!' " Around the dark edges of the Circus "the more elegantly clad of them would stand quietly" in their furs and silks, awaiting officer clientele.[4] Once a deal had been struck, the act usually followed quickly—in shop doorways, dingy alleys, or the courtyard of nearby Shepherd Market. Even for GIs not wishing to avail themselves of sexual services, Piccadilly was a "must" when visiting London, a tourist attraction akin to the Changing of the Guard at Buckingham Palace.

Although the "Piccadilly Commandos" (and their sylvan sisters, the "Hyde Park Rangers") became notorious, more or less casual prostitution occurred wherever GIs were based. As the SOS provost marshal in Cheltenham lamented in February 1943: "Even if a most efficient military police force is operating, law enforcement is most difficult under blackout conditions." Joan Blewitt Cox, then a young woman in the Devon resort of Torquay, recalled that two days before the arrival of GIs in January 1944 "*swarms* of strange girls and smart young women *invaded* the town." Such itinerant "camp followers" were familiar sights around any American base, but they were not the main problem. In February 1943 the ETO's provost marshal general (PMG) reported: "Most British women over 18 are in the Services or have work to do. The only ones who have little to do but play are the youngsters under 18. As a natural result, a great deal of our trouble has been caused through the association of our men with very young girls; a few cases have involved girls as young as 13." Sexual relations with girls under the age of sixteen constituted the criminal offence of statutory rape. The PMG added: "Most cases of statutory rape start with the soldiers buying drinks for the girl." Under British licensing laws it was unlawful to sell or give alcohol to anyone under eighteen or to enter a bar or pub if under fourteen.[5]

To the American and British authorities, the male-female problem was therefore the combined fault of promiscuous soldiers, predatory women, and unruly teenagers. What it meant for the men, women, and families involved will be addressed in chapter 16; this chapter concerns itself with official perceptions and responses. To a large degree those responses were local. Much depended on the leadership skills of unit commanders, the vigilance of military police (MPs), and the cooperation of the British constabulary. Where matters got out of hand, standard remedies included a curfew for GIs, restricted sale of bottled liquor, and intensified use of American MPs and British women police. But there were limits to what such measures could achieve. The VD epidemic among GIs in Britain by 1943 required action at the highest level. After touring Britain that summer, Dr Joseph E. Moore told the Pentagon: "In the public health and medical fields . . . there is no other factor so disturbing to Anglo-American relations as the venereal disease problem."[6] VD was not a peculiarly British affliction, of course. The United States also suffered a VD crisis in 1942–45, but the response there was strikingly more vigorous than that in Britain.

Back in the nineteenth century both countries had experienced great spasms of evangelical religious revivalism, with which were associated movements of moral reform. These included antislavery, temperance, and "social purity." In America moral reform reached its peak in the Progressive Era before and during World War One—nationwide prohibition and the campaigns to clean up the army camps being notable examples. Even when the momentum of reform had waned on the national level, America's federal structure helped keep laws against liquor and prostitution on the books of many states and cities. In New York, for instance, merely to be caught soliciting could result in a six-month prison sentence. And as VD rates soared during 1941–42, cities embarked on energetic campaigns of "social protection" to root out prostitution and disease, encouraged by passage of the May Act in July 1941 that made illegal any kind of prostitution within "reasonable distance" of military installations. By 1944 nearly seven hundred red-light districts had been closed down. Moreover, in July 1942 a ruling from the Arkansas Supreme Court paved the way for local ordinances to apprehend, examine, and treat VD suspects. Most large city governments had divisions of VD control by the end of the war. This dual programme—antiprostitution laws and compulsory treatment of VD suspects—was an indication of how far, in "liberal" America, the constitutional police power could be invoked in certain circumstances to override private rights in the interests of the "public good."[7]

America's nineteenth-century reformism had its parallel in Britain's Contagious Diseases (CD) Acts of the 1860s. This legislation, passed because of the soaring rates of VD among British troops, enabled police in specified garrison towns to inspect regularly "common prostitutes" and intern those with VD in "lock hospitals" for up to nine months. An 1885 act also suppressed organized brothels, driving prostitution underground behind a cover of massage parlours and the like. But the CD Acts provoked their own backlash among women's groups on account of their one-sided emphasis on women and their intrusion into physical privacy. A vigorous campaign led to their repeal in 1886. Thereafter, the campaigns for "social purity" subsided. Although brothels were illegal, neither prostitution nor the transmission of VD was a crime. Prostitutes could only be arrested if they indulged in indecent behaviour or caused a public nuisance by loitering or obstruction. In World War One the VD epidemic prompted the commanders of Canadian, Australian, and New Zealand troops in Britain to demand tougher action against prostitutes and compulsory treatment, but the government resisted for a long time, fearful of women's organizations. Eventually another one-sided measure—Defence Regulation 40D— was introduced in March 1918 making it an offence for an infected woman to have intercourse with any member of HM Forces. But no government department wanted the opprobrium of enforcing it and the threat of a backlash in the upcoming election from six million newly enfranchised women made it a dead letter even before it was rescinded after the Armistice in November 1918.[8]

By World War Two, British attitudes to prostitution and VD had therefore evolved very differently from the American. In Britain both issues were regarded primarily as matters not of public health but of personal privacy, into which the state dared not intrude very far. The CD Acts and Regulation 40D had become notorious warnings to that effect. To the U.S. Army, however, such an attitude was unacceptable as VD rates soared in the autumn of 1942 to a peak of fifty-eight cases per thousand troops per annum in December. (The annual rate for GIs back home was 39 per thousand men per year.) ETO demanded action on prostitution and treatment. But a meeting with government officials at the end of October drew a blank. Frank Newsam, deputy undersecretary at the Home Office, expatiated at length on the delicacy of the police's position. They could only take action if the woman was proven to be "a common prostitute" and if she was observed by an officer to be loitering or soliciting to the annoyance of inhabitants and passers-by. Any amendment of those laws, he said, would be "highly controversial and therefore impractical." Instead, he suggested that the U.S. Army might do more by lecturing the troops, freezing part of their pay, and imposing a curfew on GIs in London—attempts to put the onus on the Americans, which did not go down well in ETO.[9]

The political sensitivity of the issue was underlined by the overwhelming rejection on 15 December 1942 of a Commons private member's motion for a system of compulsory notification of VD suspects, patterned on that in existence in some thirty American states. The debate was reported in *Time* magazine, which quoted the complaint of the bill's sponsor, Dr. Edith Summerskill, that the minister of health had "approached this problem like a Victorian spinster reared in a country parsonage and sheltered from the facts of life."[10]

Summerskill's strictures were not entirely fair. The Home Office was petrified about prostitutes, but the Ministry of Health was beginning to take action to confront Britain's VD epidemic. A few discreet notices in public toilets about a few treatment centres were clearly not sufficient. In October 1942 the taboo was partly lifted by a radio broadcast from the government's chief medical officer, and a newspaper publicity campaign commenced early in 1943. A new Defence Regulation (33B), which came into effect in January 1943, required the compulsory examination and treatment of suspected carriers when named by a VD patient whose testimony was corroborated by two independent reports. Unlike 40D this applied to men as well as women and the offence was not to have sexual intercourse if infected but to refuse treatment. Among working-class people in London, the survey group Mass-Observation found overwhelming approval of both 33B and the public education campaign—indicating what it called "a minor social revolution." People were "ready and waiting for a further lead by those in authority," M-O added, not least because of the "welter of half knowledge and superstition" about how VD could be contracted.[11]

Nevertheless, public education did little to address the problem in the short term. And the stringent conditions attached to 33B meant that in practice it proved of little medical value. As in World War One it was pressure from the Allied armies in Britain that acted as a spur on the British authorities. Approximately 30 percent of American Army VD cases were contracted in London; the figure for the Canadians was 40 percent. Like ETO the Canadian command favoured a system of compulsory notification and treatment, following that in all Canadian provinces. In February 1943 the Americans returned to the issue, pointing out to the War Office that "very definite steps" were being taken by ETO "to discourage the accosting of decent British women in the streets" and suggesting that "this was the time for the British to take reciprocal action by preventing the accosting of American soldiers by prostitutes." Col. Rowe of the War Office produced a supportive memorandum, pointing out the potential damage that stories about Piccadilly could cause to Britain's image in the United States, and this helped to enlist the support of the Foreign Office.[12]

This combined pressure forced a roundtable meeting between the

U.S. and Canadian armies and the British military, police, and health authorities on 16 April 1943. The defensive Newsam was at pains to "brand as mischievous any suggestion that the present state of affairs was in the nature of a scandal." But there was general recognition by this time that the issue of prostitution was neither soluble nor central to the VD crisis. The principal American representative, ETO Chief Surgeon Gen. Paul Hawley, adroitly shifted the terms of the debate. "There was no more moral laxity in this country than in the United States," he said. "The problem was one for the public health authorities." On his suggestion, a Joint Committee on Venereal Disease was established in June, comprising representatives of the American, British, and Canadian forces and of the Ministry of Health, to cooperate in treatment. Although the Americans and Canadians were still at odds with the British on compulsory notification (the Ministry of Health arguing that this would drive VD underground), the committee endorsed the North American practice of "contact tracing." In a trial scheme in six East Anglian counties in 1943, specially trained U.S. Army nurses would question an infected soldier, try to elicit detailed information about his sexual partners, and then would approach these women to encourage them to have a medical examination. The consultations were voluntary and the emphasis throughout was on "tactful" and skilled questioning. Despite doubts, the scheme proved very successful, with over three-quarters of the five hundred women approached going for examination, and the practice was thereafter adopted by many local medical officers with the warm encouragement of the Ministry. In September 1943, the Joint Committee on VD expressed itself "convinced that a voluntary system of tracing and following up of contacts is, in general, the most effective basis for action."[13]

Although the VD debate had shifted away from prostitution, national morals remained a sensitive topic in Anglo-American relations. The Foreign Office was greatly alarmed by a long piece in *The New York Times* on 2 June 1943, written by its London correspondent Milton Bracker, that was headlined U.S. ARMY STARTS LONDON VICE FIGHT. Bracker reported that VD rates among GIs in Britain were at least 25 percent higher than those at home and that between one-third and one-half of cases were traced to the Piccadilly area. Conditions there, he said, "literally startle many Americans from such cities as New York, Chicago, and San Francisco, to say nothing of Middle Western towns and Southern farms." As for the atmosphere in Shepherd Market, that could be "compared only to the red light districts of Genoa and Marseilles." The impression given by the article, which was clearly derived from ETO sources, was that the U.S. Army's anti-VD campaign was being frustrated by the failure of British police to crack down on the Piccadilly commandos. This was reinforced by another article by Bracker two days later, which noted that Newsam had refused to talk to him, and was headlined INTERVIEW BARRED ON VICE IN LONDON. Supreme Court Justice Felix Frankfurter, a Roosevelt intimate, warned the embassy in Washington that the pieces were "political dynamite." But, to the relief of the Foreign Office, they were not picked up in the American press and by late July the embassy had received only one letter of complaint.[14]

By late 1943, however, the problem was far wider than Piccadilly. The influx of GIs from the summer prompted expressions of alarm from the regional commissioners in the south and southwest, Sir Harry Haig based in Reading and Gen. Sir Hugh Elles in Bristol. Both pointed to by-then familiar problems—GIs with too much time and money, "good-time girls" freed from home discipline, the stimulus of drink, and the effect on transatlantic relations if Britain became typed as "a nation of prostitutes," to quote one GI's letter home. They enlisted the support of concerned local VIPs such as Viscount Astor, lord mayor of Plymouth. The remedies proposed were also familiar—tighter licencing laws, improved base facilities for GIs, increased use of American MPs and British women police. But there was also growing recognition that better recreational facilities were needed for GIs and British women workers to keep them out of pubs. "The best way of dealing with the problem," the MOI observed at a meeting of regional commissioners in December 1943, "was to find means of introducing American troops to the better type of English girl." Although not stated publicly, this was the main motive behind institution of the "British Welcome Clubs" early in 1944 (chapter 12). As Lady Reading put it to Eleanor Roosevelt, local girls would apply for membership and those selected could "invite their friends there for a snack, a game and perhaps a dance."[15]

Although Britain's VD crisis was exacerbated by official reticence about sexual mores, there were failures on the American side as well. The Army's own preventative measures were slow to get going because it feared appearing to encourage promiscuity by providing condoms and drugs. There were also practical problems. In 1942 GIs relied on the British not only for bread but also for condoms. These proved "totally unsatisfactory" because they were too small! Not until early 1943 were American condoms generally available, for sale in PXs and also for free distribution under a new War Department ruling. Another problem was establishing enough prophylactic stations, because of British unwillingness to release scarce buildings or to advertise their function. Even the conventional green light fell foul of black-out restrictions. Eventually that problem was solved when the long-suffering American Red Cross agreed to operate prophylactic stations in their clubs—an ideal arrangement since many VD cases occurred while the GIs were on leave and they were virtually obliged to stay in ARC hostels. Most important of all, it also took time to develop and mass-produce adequate drugs. It was not until April 1944, with the PRO-KIT cream combining sulfathiazole and calomel, that an effective and acceptable chemical treatment was available. Army medical historians called PRO-KIT "the most important venereal disease preventative measure developed during the war."[16]

The biggest official British grievance against the U.S. Army was the number of GIs who arrived in Britain already infected with VD. In August 1943, the War Office formally complained that when the *Queen Mary* docked on Clydeside at the end of July with its latest consignment of GIs, there were twenty-five VD cases on board. In the three months from 1 November 1943, 910 soldiers arriving in the UK had to be hospitalized immediately for VD at an infectious stage. There was a danger of such men spreading the disease in Britain and the British wanted no VD cases to be shipped. The Pentagon, however, argued that if that became public policy, men would contract the disease to avoid overseas service. Furthermore, the incubation period for VD could be up to four weeks, and so the consequences of a GI's final fling in the fleshpots of Manhattan might not be detected until after his arrival in Britain. Both Ambassador Winant and Gen. Eisenhower took up British complaints personally with Marshall in Washington in 1944, but the Pentagon continued to insist that improved inspection before and during shipment was the answer.[17]

Nevertheless, the spring of 1944 saw a gratifying decline in incidence of VD in all the main Allied forces in Britain. The U.S. Army average in Britain for 1943 had been forty-three cases per annum per thousand men (compared with twenty-six for troops in the United States) but in the weeks before D-Day it was running at little over twenty. The Canadian Army's experience in Britain was similar: VD down from an annual rate of over forty in 1943 to 22.4 per thousand per annum in the second quarter of 1944. The medical staffs of both armies explained the decline as the cumulative result of improved efforts at education and treatment, intensified training in anticipation of the invasion, and the cessation of most leave from early May.[18] Not that the problem disappeared; it became serious again in the autumn and winter of 1944–45 (chapter 22). But as a potential threat to Anglo-American relations, it had been contained.

★　★　★

The other great "sex" problem for the American and British authorities was what to do about GI marriages to local girls. Not all Allied armies regarded such marriages with disfavour. Of the Poles stationed in Scotland, never more than thirty thousand in all, nearly eleven hundred had Scottish brides by the end of 1943. By then over fourteen thousand Canadian servicemen had married British women.[19] At that date GI brides were numbered in hundreds rather than thousands. This was only partly because GIs were late arrivals in Britain. More significant was the distinctive attitude of the British government and especially the U.S. Army to GI-British marriages. Explanations for this reveal much about the two countries and their relationship.

Most armies have regarded sex as a necessity but marriage as an impediment to their soldiers' performance. In France in 1917–18 officers often tried to discourage weddings between doughboys and local girls, but the official policy was summed up by the AEF Judge Advocate General in 1919:

> While it was desirable that soldiers should not contract marriages during the period of hostilities, nevertheless marriage was always regarded as a personal right and privilege of the individual with which military headquarters had nothing to do. Following this policy, these headquarters declined to give express consent to marriage or to refuse the same.

The onus was on the soldier to furnish the local authorities with an affidavit that he was not already married. His commander merely certified that he had "knowledge of no information contrary" to this.[20]

During the Depression the Regular Army adopted a tougher policy. Fearing that the War Department would become another welfare agency, it ordered that married men could only enlist or reenlist if able to prove that they could support their dependents on their pay or other income. For similar reasons, an enlisted man who wished to marry needed the permission of his commanding officer. These impositions could be justified when the Army's budget was tight and soldiers were volunteers. They were less tenable under conditions of the wartime draft, when military service became a matter of obligation not choice and when the number of soldiers affected soared from thousands to millions. A War Department circular of 26 February 1942 therefore stated that "instructions requiring enlisted men to obtain permission of their superiors to marry are rescinded."[21]

GIs started arriving in Northern Ireland on 26 January 1942 and within two months the first marriages were taking place. According to the commander in Belfast, Gen. Hartle, GIs had been told before leaving the States that Army Regulations were being amended to allow them to marry without permission and were "using it as their authority to marry." Hartle protested strongly against any such liberalization, but the Army's judge advocate in London pointed out that it had never been within the power of the commanding officer to prohibit a marriage. *Permission* in previous directives only implied that the CO was willing to accord the soldier the privileges allowed by the Army to married men of their class. Failure to secure permission would result in disciplinary action or even discharge from the Army, but it could not invalidate the marriage.[22]

On 8 June 1942, however, the War Department reinstated the old marriage rule for troops overseas. Circular 179 stated: "No military personnel on duty in any foreign country may marry without the approval of the commanding officer of the United States Army forces stationed in such foreign country or possession." This volte-face was prompted by the situation in Trinidad where an American base had been established on land leased from the British under the Destroyers Deal of 1940. To quote one ETO officer, the circular "was designed to protect soldiers from hasty marriages in countries where the bulk of the population was negro and socially and mentally inferior to the average American soldier." More generally, its aim was to prevent marriages of calculation by overseas prostitutes.[23] In Britain, however, it became the cornerstone of a widespread Army policy to discourage GI marriages to British women by almost all means possible.

ETO Circular 20, promulgated by Eisenhower on 28 July 1942, took the War Department's policy much further. It stipulated that officers and men could only marry with their commander's permission and after written notice of three months. Violation of these procedures would be a court-martial offence under the 96th Article of War—"conduct of a nature to bring discredit upon the military service." The appropriate superior had to affirm that the marriage was "in the interests of these [ETO] forces in particular and the military service in general." An applicant was to be told that marriage would entitle them to no special treatment in living arrangements, in rental, subsistence or travel allowances, and in medical or PX privileges. His wife would not be transported at government expense, either within the ETO or to the United States on his return. And he should know that "she will not become a United States citizen by virtue of marriage to him. She will be subject to applicable immigration and naturalization laws."

The draconian provisions of Circular 20 provoked discontent within ETO, both at the staff and enlisted levels. They were somewhat relaxed in Circular 66 on 22 October.[24] This reduced the notice period to two months. A new form of words obliged the appropriate commanding officer to judge, in negative rather than positive vein, that the marriage "would not bring discredit to the military service." The circular also dropped the tendentious statements about allowances and migration rights, noting that the spouse would be "entitled to all the allotments, insurance, and other benefits" authorized to military wives and that, although marriage conferred no automatic citizenship, spouses would "be exempted from immigration quotas and are entitled to speedier naturalization."

In the first eight weeks of the new circular there were only 116 marriages in ETO. At least seventy of these (and probably ninety-seven), were "because of a condition of pregnancy or illegitimacy." In other words, marriages were usually being permitted only where the existence of an "illegitimate" child would otherwise "bring discredit upon the service." During the winter of 1942–43, some commanders recognized that Britain might be a long-term station for their men and that the denial of marriage was both unrealistic and bad for morale. This seems to have been the case in the 8th Air Force, for instance.[25] But in the SOS, the moralistic J.C.H. Lee took the toughest possible line. As his Chief of Staff admitted privately in November, "the only applications to marry which are being approved at this headquarters are those in which pregnancy is shown. . . . The SOS appears to be the only [ETO command] in which all requests, except those involving pregnancy, are arbitrarily denied." But Lee claimed the support of both Eisenhower and Hartle, and even glossed Circular 66, misleadingly, to justify his pregnancy-only criteria. He claimed in January 1943 that theatre policy authorized "approval of requests for permission to marry only where such exceptional circumstances exist as to require approval in the best interests *of the Service*. No further explanation of disapproval will be given."[26]

By the spring of 1943 senior ETO staff officers were concerned at the situation. They felt that to grant permission only in cases of pregnancy was both "untenable" and an invitation to immorality. (Cases had been reported of couples deliberately contriving a pregnancy to force the issue.) Now that a separate North African Theatre had been created and Britain was no longer Ike's responsibility, ETO pressed the new commander, Gen. Frank M. Andrews, for a clear statement of policy. Although Andrews chose to reaffirm Circular 66, he told his subordinates "as a rule of thumb" that "marriages which ordinarily would be approved by appropriate military authorities in the Continental United States may be approved in the European Theater of Operations." In reply, Hartle admitted that his own policy on marriage had involved "interpreting and perhaps extending that of the Theater," but he explained that marriage had been "one of my greatest concerns and problems" and that his object had been to "discourage it to the maximum." Methods of discouragement included "advice on the part of all echelons of command as well as the chaplains, convenient transfer of personnel, consultation with civil registrars with an arrangement for the non-issuance of licenses and, in some cases, disapproval." Hartle's defence forced Andrews to reaffirm the legal position:

> I recognize the many disadvantages in local marriages; however, my point is that there is no legal or moral justification for prohibiting them. On the grounds of common sense you may consider it advisable to discourage marriages, but you cannot do so officially or prevent them by any official act unless they reflect discredit on the military service.[27]

Andrews's death in May 1943 ended this brief attempt to produce a more liberal and consistent theatre policy on marriages. Although Hartle moved on, Lee remained. The "discredit on the service" clause usually proved sufficiently flexible, but, if not, red tape could be used to enmesh the applicants. Transferring GIs who wanted to marry was, as Hartle indicated, a frequent practice: Peter Hettinga was packed off to Northern Ireland for three months after he had applied to be married. Even more common was simply deliberate delay in processing of any application. Beverley Schoonmaker of Edinburgh was interviewed at her fiancé's camp in Peterborough a full year after they had filed an application. Such practices had the support of the Pentagon. In November 1943 the Adjutant General in Washington, concerned that "the problems resulting from the overseas marriages of military personnel are increasing daily," issued a "list of pertinent facts" that, if known, "would operate greatly to discourage the overseas marriage" of GIs. These included the absence of automatic citizenship, the termination of dependents' allowances six months after the end of war, the ban on transport to the United States at public expense throughout the war and for six months thereafter. These were to be made known to all military personnel by whatever means seemed appropriate to commanders, as long as these did not "result in political repercussions or inflammatory propaganda." In Lee's SOS, for instance, the "pertinent facts" were read and explained to troops but the memo was not posted on bulletin boards "or otherwise disseminated to civilians."[28]

It is instructive to compare the U.S. Army's policy with that of the Canadian Army overseas. Canadian soldiers also required official permission and two month's notification before they could marry but, in the words of the Registry Office in Edinburgh, "no disciplinary action is taken if a soldier marries without permission." In the Canadian case, and most others, the only action taken against the soldier would be to deny him the allowance for his wife and any children. The gulf between American and Canadian policy was exposed by a formal protest from the Canadian government in January 1944 about the American base commander at Argentia in Newfoundland who was preventing all GI marriages to local women, even in cases of pregnancy. Responding, the War Department expressed its "considered view" that "marriages by United States military personnel in foreign countries should be discouraged in the interests of the persons concerned." The Canadians were equally blunt, noting that there were no restrictions on their service personnel marrying Americans: "In general, marriage is regarded as a civil right, which should not be interfered with by military regulations."[29]

ETO's reasons for its deterrent policy were partly military. It did not want wives living near base and distracting soldiers' attention. Since men were not allowed to bring over their families from the States, local marriages were deemed "unfair" and a "detriment to morale." The policy was also a recognition of the higher material standards of the U.S. forces. Like GI pay, dependents' allowances compared favourably with those of other armies and with civilian pay rates. By 1944 a GI's wife received $50 a month plus $20 a month for the first child. As Hartle put it: "Gullible men are readily seduced by British girls, whose ulterior motive may be that of extra remuneration on the part of our Government as well as that of the soldier."[30] This extension abroad of the Army's antidependents policy of the 1930s also reflected the U-turn in American immigration policy between the wars. The quotas imposed from 1921 were designed to maintain the Anglo-Saxon predominance, but during the Depression attitudes hardened into a general antipathy to foreigners jumping on the faltering American bandwagon. American general officers seem to have taken on the burden of keeping the huddled masses at arm's length. The U.S. Army had become an agent of social control.

On the British side, the tough American policy on soldier marriages enjoyed official support. There was a natural concern to prevent bigamous unions and by the autumn of 1943 the Home Office had persuaded all Allied contingents to adopt the American requirement for a certificate of official permission. This, and the imposed waiting period, permitted checks to be made about the marital status of both partners. But bigamy was not the only issue; the British establishment was anxious to deter legal marriages with Americans in particular. Many British officials shared the ETO belief that girls saw a GI husband as their passport to the American dream. In 1942 Sir Hugh Elles, the southwestern regional commissioner, felt that "wide publicity" should be given to the U.S. Army's "very stringent regulations" about GI marriage, particularly the fact that it did not guarantee American citizenship or ensure a free passage across the Atlantic. The Ministry of Information also wanted to publicize the American marriage circulars, but the Foreign Office judged that this would seem too obviously like official deterrence. Instead, following hallowed British practice, questions were "planted" in Parliament in October 1942 allowing ministers to "respond" by drawing attention to the regulations. The press then dutifully picked up the Commons exchange. The *Birmingham Post*, for instance, in an editorial entitled "A Timely Warning," called the position of GI brides "extremely uncomfortable" and concluded that "the risks are greater than prudent women will care to face." These concerns were shared by the churches. In May 1943 the archbishop of Canterbury, Cosmo Gordon Lang, told Gen. Devers that there was need for "a more careful scrutiny" of GI marriages on both sides. He cited "cases where the girl is of bad character and is looking out for what she can get" and also concern "that decent English girls may be taken in by an exaggerated picture of their prospects which a rather expansive American soldier may give."[31]

What emerged, then, was a joint official effort to deter Anglo-American marriages. British registry offices were instructed by the government not to issue a marriage licence to a GI unless the soldier had received official permission. This, and the antipathy of many American commanders, was enough to put off most couples. But it was privately acknowledged that, if any soldier insisted on being married without the certificate, "the Registrar-General would have no option but to instruct the Superintendent Registrars to proceed with the marriage provided there was no lawful impediment in any other respect." And although the soldier would be liable to court-martial, the ETO Judge Advocate admitted that "his wife would be entitled to all the benefits of the Servicemen's Dependents Allowance Act."[32]

There was, then, an element of bluff in official policy on both the American and British sides. And, of course, not all U.S. commanders were martinets like Hartle and Lee. Gen. Ralph Pulsifer, a senior ETO staff officer, took offence if he was not invited to the marriage of any member of his "official family."[33] In 1942–43 the American command was improvising policy: GIs were being trained for war in semipeace-time conditions of unknown duration. In these circumstances, marriages were undesirable but inevitable. In early 1944, with combat beginning in earnest, the tough line was easier to maintain. But it broke down completely in the last months of the war, with consequences for soldiers and brides that will be examined in chapter 23.

14

Black and White

★ ★ ★

AS FAR AS OFFICIALDOM WAS CONCERNED, SEXUAL RELATIONS WERE MOST worrying when the males were not only American but also black. Racial friction over British women was the most frequent cause of fracas among GIs. It also raised larger policy issues—notably whether to impose a "colour bar" in Britain and the rights and wrongs of "miscegenation."[1]

The War Department continued to regard black GIs as a liability and confined them largely to service units. But in 1940 President Roosevelt had imposed a quota target of 10 percent blacks in the Army in general and also in each theatre. Furthermore, there were to be no geographical restrictions on the use of blacks, at home or abroad. The War Department reiterated that its task was not social engineering—Secretary Stimson referred in his diary to "the insoluble problem of the black race in this country"—but it enforced the new official policy. Stimson resisted pressure from congressmen (mainly in the South but also on the West Coast) to keep black units out of their districts. He took a similar line about sending black GIs abroad: "Don't yield," he ordered his staff when the British authorities on the Caribbean island of Trinidad were reported "strongly opposed to the assignment of colored units."[2]

The black British community probably numbered no more than eight thousand in 1939, mostly concentrated in the ports of Liverpool, Cardiff, Newcastle, and London. Britain was thus overwhelmingly a "white" country and the British government intended that it should remain that way. Although in 1941–42 one thousand foresters were brought from British Honduras to the Edinburgh area and some 350 engineering and electrical technicians came to Merseyside, these schemes were only for the wartime emergency. As a Foreign Office official noted in January 1942 after discussions with other government departments, "the recruitment to the United Kingdom of coloured British subjects, whose remaining in the United Kingdom after the war might create a social problem, was not considered desirable."[3]

Nor did the British government want black GIs. Although American construction units were needed to help build the air bases scheduled under the Bolero programme, the British Chiefs of Staff asked in April 1942 for the maximum number of *white* engineer units that were available. They were supported by Gen. Chaney, the U.S. Army commander in Britain, who cabled Washington on 17 April: "Colored units should not, repeat not, be sent to British Isles." But the War Department instructed on 25 April that "in planning for shipment of troops to the British Isles, including Northern Ireland, Colored Troops may be included in reasonable proportion for any type of Service Units."[4]

What, Whitehall wondered, did a "reasonable proportion" of black troops mean in practice? As with so many of the GI issues that summer, the question was discussed in an atmosphere of anxiety created by strategic confusion. By 12 May 1942 there were only 811 black GIs in Britain. But putting together the Marshall Plan target of one million GIs in Britain by April 1943 with the Pentagon's quota of 10 percent blacks in the Army and in every theatre, British policymakers were sure they would be hosting 100,000 black GIs by the following spring. Their concerns were partly practical: Segregation meant that even more space would have to be found in an already crowded island—an extra thousand hospital beds, for instance. The Home Office also feared racial friction, only to be told in May by Col. Edward Betts, ETO Judge Advocate, that the "American negro was now integrated on a basis of complete equality in the economic and political life of the country" and he "did not therefore expect that there would be serious trouble in this country." This astonishing claim went unchallenged, but it was certainly not believed. The cabinet wanted the Americans to "reduce as far as possible the number of coloured troops . . . sent to this country." The Foreign Office raised the issue repeatedly while Marshall and Hopkins were in London in July and pressed them again through the embassy in Washington during August. Foreign Secretary Anthony Eden even represented British policy as altruistic, telling Ambassador Winant that "our climate was badly suited to negroes." But Marshall simply reiterated that politics (black pressure) and practicality (the need for service troops) left the Army no alternative. The president confirmed that policy in a letter, drafted by Marshall, to Winant in September.[5]

Unable to keep black GIs out of Britain, both ETO and Whitehall devoted an inordinate amount of time in 1942 to managing their presence. It was initially hoped to cluster black units in areas where there was already a black population, as was the policy back home. That was the advice of visitors to Britain in the summer of 1942 such as Arthur Sulzberger, the publisher of *The New York Times*, who suggested that "they be moved out of rural areas and concentrated in ports like Liverpool . . . where people are used to all kinds of foreigners, including negroes." This policy, endorsed by Gen. Spaatz of the 8th Air Force and by Stimson in Washington, was practised as far as possible. But geographical concentration could never be a panacea because many black units were fulfilling essential tasks outside port areas— driving supplies, moving ammunition, and constructing bases. In doing so, they came into contact with all levels of British society.[6]

Eisenhower explained the problem in a letter to Washington on 10 September 1942:

> here we have a very thickly populated country that is devoid of racial consciousness. They know nothing at all about the conventions and habits of polite society that have been developed in the U.S. in order to preserve a segregation in social activity without making the matter one of official or public notice. To most English people, including the village girls—even those of perfectly fine character— the negro soldier is just another man, rather fascinating because he is unique in their experience, a jolly good fellow and with money to spend. Our own white soldiers, seeing a girl walk down the street with a negro, frequently see themselves as protectors of the weaker sex and believe it necessary to intervene even to the extent of using force, to let her know what she's doing.[7]

How to maintain the "separate but equal" policy in a society unused not only to segregation but to nonwhites preoccupied Eisenhower during his short stay in Britain in mid-1942.

In doing so, he and his staff were under constant political scrutiny from back home, from white liberals and black pressure groups. The National Association for the Advancement of Colored People (NAACP) complained to the ARC on several occasions about "segregated recreation centers in London and other English cities for Negro soldiers" and its executive secretary, Walter White, cabled Churchill in November about reports that the British government had asked Washington to send no more black troops to Britain. (After long consultation the Foreign Office decided discreetly to ignore the telegram because it was doubted "whether we could honestly give a categorical denial.") The NAACP also had the support of Eleanor Roosevelt, regarded by the Pentagon as a persistent troublemaker on racial issues, who noted stories that "young Southerners were very indignant to find that the Negro soldiers were not looked upon with terror" by British girls and suggested to Secretary Stimson that "we will have to do a little educating among our Southern white men and officers." When he heard that Mrs. Roosevelt was to visit GIs in Britain in October 1942, Stimson asked Roosevelt personally to caution her against "making any comment as to the different treatment which Negroes receive in the U.K. from what they receive in the U.S." The president was "very sympathetic to our attitude," noted Stimson, "and told me that he would pass the word on to Mrs. Roosevelt."[8]

One of Ike's first acts on arrival in Britain was to loosen the censorship restrictions imposed on the American press there. Hitherto Army policy in London had been "to avoid passing stories dealing with racial difficulties, especially those dealing with local women." The Navy took a similar line. In June 1942 Frederick R. Kuh, London bureau chief for the *Chicago Sun*, wrote a long piece about American naval personnel in Londonderry, focusing on relations between black messmen and white sailors. Naval censors wanted to ban the whole article but Kuh appealed to a sympathetic Ambassador Winant and the case went all the way to Admiral Harold L. Stark, commander of Naval Forces Europe, who censored the text himself. A passage reporting the blacks' satisfaction with their conditions, officers, and local hospitality caused no problems, but Stark cut references to segregation and to a fracas when a black messman was caught with a local woman. "Too many of your nationality over here," a white sailor cried. When the negro protested, "I'm an American," he was told: "For me you're a nigger and always will be a nigger."[9]

Ike considered this kind of censorship pointless. He lifted the ban on U.S. correspondents visiting black camps and told them in August that it was best to "let the American public know what the problems are and the success or failure in meeting [them]." Some American pressmen actually favoured the restrictions. Led by Raymond Daniell, head of *The New York Times* bureau in London, they urged him to reconsider, claiming that reporters like Kuh were intent on "trouble-making" about the race question. Admiral Stark was also afraid that this new liberal policy would leave the Navy out on a limb, but Ike stuck to his guns. He told Daniell, in a letter intended for all American correspondents, that "so far as I am concerned news involving negroes is no more subject to censorship by military authorities than is any other type." He would only intervene if a story would "tend to create and magnify racial difficulties within this command," for example by attempting "to take an isolated case of friction between white and colored soldiers and make it appear that this was typical." This still left scope for official censorship but it was a major advance on previous policy and it reflected Ike's extremely open approach (for an Army officer) to press relations.[10]

Ike also issued two firm statements of racial policy. The first, dated 16 July 1942, stated "the desire of this headquarters that discrimination against the Negro troops be sedulously avoided." It then tried to adapt the "separate but equal" doctrine to British conditions. Where possible, welfare and recreation facilities should be segregated. But "the Red Cross has been informed that wherever it is not possible to provide separate accommodations, the Negro soldiers will be given accommodations in the clubs on the same basis as White soldiers." Around local camps, commanders were enjoined to avoid "discrimination due to race," while "at the same time minimizing causes of friction." Ike suggested as an example the rotation of leave passes (to avoid having blacks and whites in the same town on the same night), but "always with the guiding principle that any restriction imposed by Commanding Officers applies with equal force to both races."[11]

On 5 September Eisenhower issued a further circular to his commanders. It made clear that an overt colour bar was unacceptable in Britain. "Undoubtedly a considerable association of colored troops with British white population, both men and women, will take place on a basis mutually acceptable to the individuals concerned. Any attempt to curtail such an association by official orders or restrictions is unjustified and must not be attempted." The rest of the circular was devoted to racial epithets, often the cause of fistfights. Ike stated categorically: *"The spreading of derogatory statements concerning the character of any group of United States troops, either white or colored, must be considered as conduct prejudicial to good order and military discipline and offenders must be promptly punished."* Ike also insisted that the circular "must not be handled in a routine or perfunctory manner" but *"brought to the attention of every officer in this theater."*[12]

How *were* such directives handled within ETO? The 8th Air Force was not substantially affected at this stage. Its black strength peaked in 1942 at just under fifteen hundred on 26 October, and at the end of

January 1943 only eleven officers and 573 men were not white. Despite some racial incidents, for example drunken brawls in and around Sheffield in early September, the problem was not given special attention. In Northern Ireland, Gen. Hartle tried to shift the problem down to the soldiers who would have to implement any race policy. On 3 August, after his first black trucking unit had arrived, he had its CO and those of neighbouring white units select a few noncoms "of the substantial representative type" to form a joint "Good-Conduct Committee." After a briefing by him, outlining the racial situation in Britain as against America, they were given "some subjects for discussion" and, under the guidance of a special service officer, encouraged to draw them up into "rules of good-conduct." These were then accepted by the command and members of the committee shared them with incoming units. The rules included segregation where possible (dances, accommodation, private parties, etc.) but otherwise mutual respect in mixed facilities such as washrooms and Red Cross clubs. "Neither race must interfere with or 'cut in on' soldiers of the other race in company with girls."[13] Hartle's was a covert way of getting official policy adopted at the grass-roots level. He believed it would have greater credibility and therefore effect if ostensibly established by the white and black GIs themselves.

The bulk of the black troops in Britain in 1942 were under the command of the Services of Supply and it was Gen. J.C.H. Lee who devoted the most time and ingenuity to implementing Ike's memoranda. In August 1942 Lee appointed a special officer to address the problem—Capt. Edwin R. Carter, Jr.—an Army chaplain from Virginia. The following month Carter visited "every negro unit and many white units in [SOS] Southern and Western Base Sections." Lee also worked closely with Gen. Benjamin O. Davis, Sr., the Army's only black general, when he toured Britain on an inspection trip in the autumn. Lee's complex personality made a deep impression on Davis. On the one hand, there was his notorious luxury: the special train, for instance, or a dinner at his Cheltenham HQ of "banquet proportions"—five courses with two kinds of wine. On the other hand, Davis was struck by Lee's sincere concern about race relations: "He is a very fine gentleman" who "stands for equal fairness." Lee's line, Davis told his wife, was that "the white soldier doesn't have to go where he doesn't like the scenery" but that "he has no right to force his opinions on the British people." Although Davis had power only to recommend, he was pleased to find that his recommendations were acted upon promptly. On a personal level, it did not pass unnoticed that Lee "kindly let me use his shower."[14]

One of Davis's recommendations dealt with the "committee" approach to race relations. On 30 September 1942 black and white troops under Hartle's command had clashed in Antrim, leaving one black dead and a white GI wounded. Reporting on this, Davis concluded that reliance on the "Good-Conduct Committee" of NCOs had resulted "in small unit commanders feeling a lack of a sense of responsibility and this may have contributed to the unwarranted assumption of authority by enlisted men." SOS staff fully agreed. Lee had no doubt that commanders had to command. Whenever possible, a new black unit in SOS was "quarantined" on base, to allow time to "indoctrinate" it about British conditions and to coordinate arrangements with local officials. This happened, for instance, in Somerset in July 1942, where SOS liaison officers working with British Southern Command made arrangements in towns like Yeovil and Chard for separate blocks of cinema seats or separate rooms in pubs for black troops. The aim, noted Col. Murray Montgomery, Lee's personnel officer, was to prevent "white and colored soldiers from attending the same activities simultaneously," while giving each race "an equal opportunity of attending the same [kind of] functions as the other." But, to avoid imputations of racial discrimination, everything was to be done "on an organizational basis"—in other words, a dance would be held for a company of the "98th Engineer Regiment" (which happened to be black) or for a company of the 16th Infantry Regiment (which happened to be white). As Lee himself put it: "While color lines are not to be announced or even mentioned, entertainments such as dances should be 'by organization.' The reason, if any, given for such an arrangement should be 'limitation of space and personnel.' "[15]

Apart from covert racial segregation, the other prong of Lee's policy was more positive: "to foster organizational pride, coupled with a sound educational and recreational program." Unit commanders were told to establish libraries and athletic programmes, show movies, and promote concerts and theatricals. Col. Montgomery admitted that equipment for some of these activities was lacking—"at present we have plenty of films but no projectors"—but the overall aim was clear: "making the men happy in their own camps and thus reducing the number on pass privileges." Again, this was conventional Army policy, reflecting the general "cocoon" approach adopted for most social problems created by the GI presence in Britain. But Lee and his associates also recognized a deeper personnel problem. Chaplain Carter's brief from Lee was to help develop "measures designed to instil into the negro a pride in his organization and [make him] a better soldier." Davis stated at the end of his tour: "The trouble which has developed between the white and colored soldiers has invariably been found to be due in an important degree to inefficiency by small unit commanders in controlling their men. . . . Emphasis should be placed on assigning the most experienced and able officers to colored units." Davis also persuaded Lee to increase the number of black enlisted men admitted to Officer Candidate School (OCS) and he headed a special board to assess candidates. Fifteen black nominees were approved in October.[16]

A recurrent concern for the Army was the lack of black women in Britain. In August Eisenhower asked for several thousand black members of the Women's Army Corps (WACs) to staff special clubs for blacks, but this was regarded by WAC commanders as a demeaning use of their personnel and Ike dropped the idea. Instead, ETO again turned to the hard-pressed Red Cross for special clubs and facilities. As usual, some ingenuity was required to avoid public imputations of racial discrimination. Harvey Gibson, the ARC commissioner in Britain, announced in September 1942 that white and black troops were "welcome at all American Red Cross clubs, canteens or recreation centers" but that, since the Army was tending to concentrate black troops in certain areas where they would therefore be the main users of ARC facilities, "colored male and female personnel are now about to begin to arrive from America to staff these centers." Officially the ARC took the line: "We have no negro clubs. We have no white clubs. We have negro staff clubs and we have white staff clubs. Any negro in this Theater is welcome to any club we have." While this did happen on occasions, in reality colour lines were generally observed and internal ARC and Army documents referred to such clubs simply as "negro."[17]

The way these clubs fitted into the pattern of "organizational" segregation can be seen in the case of Tewkesbury, a market town midway between Cheltenham and Worcester. Tewkesbury had a population of under six thousand, but less than three miles away was the huge general depot at Ashchurch that in August 1942 already had three thousand personnel (many of them living in bell tents). Managing the troops' impact on the nearby town was difficult enough in purely numerical terms, but it was complicated, as far as the Army was concerned, by the substantial black presence at the depot. That autumn the SOS gave passes for Tewkesbury to three or four hundred white troops every Tuesday, Thursday, and Saturday, and to some two hundred black GIs every Monday, Wednesday, and Friday. Sundays were alternately black and white. The Special Service Section of SOS proposed "a day club for colored troops at Tewkesbury. . . . It was felt that the service club recommended at Worcester together with the one at Cheltenham would serve white troops, the one at Tewkesbury colored troops." This was approved, though publicly SOS avoided saying that the Tewkesbury club was "for colored troops."[18]

Officially, the British government distanced itself from what was happening. On 4 September 1942 the Home Office wrote to all chief constables:

> It is not the policy of His Majesty's Government that any discrimination as regards the treatment of coloured troops should be made by the British authorities. The Secretary of State, therefore, would be glad if you would be good enough to take steps to ensure that the police do not make any approach to the proprietors of public houses, restaurants, cinemas or other places of entertainment with a view to discriminating against coloured troops. If the American Service authorities decide to put certain places out of bounds for their coloured troops, such prohibition can be effected only by means of an Order issued by the appropriate American Army and Naval authorities. The police should not make themselves in any way responsible for the enforcement of such orders.

Informed of the circular, Eisenhower's staff moved quickly to counter its implications. "The policy of non-discrimination is exactly the policy which has always been followed by the United States Army. . . . With reference to the question of placing certain places out of bounds, we do not make any restrictions of that kind on the basis of color."[19]

In fact both the Home Office circular and the ETO response were equally disingenuous. The U.S. Army was operating a policy of de facto racial segregation, but it could not have done so without cooperation or at least acquiescence from the British authorities. This issue caused more debate at the top of Churchill's government in 1942 than any other aspect of the American "occupation."

Those most concerned on the British side were the military. At a meeting at the War Office on 5 August it was agreed that, although segregation arrangements were a matter purely for the U.S. Army, British officers should lecture their troops, including women soldiers of the Auxiliary Territorial Service (ATS), on the need to minimize contact with black GIs. The War Office preferred to put nothing on paper because of the delicacy of the subject, but two days later Gen. Arthur Dowler, the senior administrative officer in Southern Command, issued "Notes on Relations with Coloured Troops" to district commanders. He was sympathetic to the principle of discrimination, claiming that the "generality" of blacks were "of a simple mental outlook" and lacked "the white man's ability to think and act to a plan." But his main point was the need to avoid friction with white GIs. While showing sympathy to blacks, therefore, British soldiers "should not make intimate friends with them, taking them to cinemas and bars." And "white women should not associate with coloured men" at all: they "should not walk out, dance, or drink with them." Dowler wanted "the British, both men and women, to realize the problem and adjust their attitude so that it conforms to that of the white American citizen."[20]

This document was intended for British soldiers, but there were also official demands to "guide" civilian behaviour as well. In July the GOC of British Army Western Command complained to the city of Chester that black GIs stationed nearby had been walking around with white women: "this sort of thing is not customary in America and . . . we do not want to infringe American customs." The lord mayor replied that Indians and West Indians, who were British subjects, could be described as coloured, and asked what the GOC was proposing to do about them. An interdepartmental meeting about black GIs in Whitehall on 12 August discussed whether to "discourage British women from such associations by an open statement on the danger of venereal disease" or else "to foster a whispering campaign on the same lines." Both ideas were strenuously opposed by the Foreign Office because of their effects on "progressive elements in the United States." But "whispering campaigns" of a less-pointed character were undoubtedly promoted. Discussing the issue on the same day, the MOI's advisory committee for the Bristol area felt that "probably the best means of approach is that individual and unofficial warnings should be spread about" using the WVS, Housewives Committees, and the like. This was also the view of the local regional commissioner. This discussion presumably explains why the wife of the vicar of nearby Worle in Somerset proposed to local women a six-point code of conduct. She suggested crossing the street if a black soldier was coming towards her, moving immediately to another seat in a cinema if he sat next to her, and leaving a shop as quickly as possible if he entered.[21]

Inevitably, intimations of official policy soon leaked out. On 6 September the *Sunday Pictorial* publicized the story of the vicar's wife. The following day the *Daily Herald* reported a ban on black GIs attending dances in the town of Eye in Suffolk—blaming the U.S. Army, though it transpired that the decision had been taken by the local council. The weekly *New Statesman* carried details of how a British Army unit was told on no account to eat or drink with black GIs and also reported "on fairly good authority that the ruling in one area is that if an A.T.S. girl is seen walking with a coloured soldier 'she should be removed to another district for another reason.' " The whole issue of a "colour bar" was raised in the House of Commons at the end of September by back-bench MPs. Responding, Churchill regretted the "unfortunate question" and expressed the hope that "without any action on my part the points of view of all concerned will be mutually understood and respected." Most significant of all, Gen. Dowler's "Notes" fell into the hands of the Colonial Office, which had special concern both for the British colonies and for colonial subjects in Britain. One official called the document "puerile and prejudiced stuff." Forced out into the open, the secretary of state for war, Sir James Grigg, decided to request cabinet sanction for the policy he and his officials had been discreetly pursuing. Without written instructions, he said, officers should be allowed to "interpret" the "facts and history of the colour question" in America to British Army personnel "and so educate them to adopt towards the U.S.A. coloured troops the attitude of the U.S.A. Army authorities."[22]

The issue came before the cabinet on 13 October, after five other cabinet ministers had submitted papers. The main opposition came, predictably, from the colonial secretary, Lord Cranborne, who rejected the idea of "educating" British troops. They should be told the reasons for the U.S. attitude but "left to draw their own conclusions as to their behaviour." Equally, he said, British thinking "should be explained to the Americans, and the American Army should be asked to respect our attitude to British coloured Colonial people in this country." Churchill, however, was not sympathetic. When Cranborne raised the case of one of his own black officials—barred from his regular restaurant to avoid offending U.S. officers—Churchill quipped: "if he takes a banjo with him they'll think he's one of the band." In fact, the prime minister had not read the relevant papers and while he did so during the cabinet meeting there was a "wild discussion" in which "everyone spoke at once."[23]

On most major issues, the War Office got its way. Ministers accepted that the American Army's attitude was "a factor of great importance" when determining British policy towards the black GIs and, that "it was desirable that the people of this country should avoid becoming too friendly with coloured American troops." The cabinet also agreed that information and guidance about American race policies should be given to British troops, both via their officers and through an ABCA "Current Affairs" pamphlet. The cabinet did go some way towards Cranborne by noting that "it was equally important that the Americans should recognize that we had a different problem as regards our coloured people and that a *modus vivendi* between the two points of view should be found." But no specific action on this point was mentioned in the cabinet conclusions and the War Office used this lacuna to justify not making any approach on the matter to Eisenhower and ETO HQ. Senior figures in the Colonial Office agreed privately that pressure to have the British attitude explained to GIs would get the government "into very deep water indeed." Nor was there any objection, even from the Colonial Office, to the double-standard policy of covertly supporting U.S. Army segregation as long as the British authorities were not implicated in its enforcement.[24]

The only major modification to Grigg's paper was on the question of whether troops should not merely be informed but "educated" into adopting U.S. Army attitudes to black troops. Richard Law, a junior Foreign Office minister, agreed with Grigg, arguing that "the really important thing is that we should not have avoidable friction between the two armies and that the [white] American troops should not go back to their homes with the view that we are a decadent and unspeakable race." But Eden's private secretary Oliver Harvey was more concerned about liberal opinion in the United States than about Southerners. Eden himself thought Grigg's proposal went "much too far" and most of his cabinet colleagues concurred. A revised version of Dowler's guidance notes was duly prepared for circulation to senior officers. On Churchill's instructions this was shown to Eisenhower before it was discussed and approved by the cabinet on 20 October. Its presentation of the racial situation in the United States was more nuanced than in the original, and the patronising image of negro character was omitted. But British troops (especially women) were still advised to avoid contact with black GIs. Although the official line now was that there was "no reason" for British soldiers to "adopt the American attitude" they were told that "they should respect it and avoid making it a subject for argument and dispute." As the related ABCA pamphlet put it: "One of the responsibilities of a host is to avoid embarrassing his guests."[25]

During the winter of 1942–43 what the British government called "the colour problem" remained latent, because of the diversion of troops to North Africa. There were only 7,315 black GIs in the British Isles at the end of 1942, under 7 percent of the total American military presence. But, as Bolero gathered pace, the issue became pressing again. At the end of 1943 about 65,000 black GIs were in Britain; by D-Day the total was around 130,000—far above the 100,000 bogey that had so exercised Whitehall in 1942. In consequence, racial problems increased. There were some particularly serious clashes in

1944 in Leicester between black GIs and white paratroopers from the 82nd Airborne Division, veterans of the Sicily campaign. Relations with local women were the prime cause. In Ulster, preoccupied with the Protestant-Catholic divide, black-white issues assumed an Orange hue. One Unionist MP in County Londonderry complained that the girls going out with black GIs were "mostly of the lowest type and belong to our 'minority.'" In April 1944 an ETO censorship report on soldiers' mail throughout the UK found that where white or black GIs referred to the other race, 90 percent of the comments were unfavourable. The report, dated 29 May 1944, concluded that "if the invasion doesn't occur soon, trouble will."[26]

As the buildup began in earnest, there was discussion of whether to "educate" civilians as well as British service personnel about "American" racial thinking. This had been explicitly rejected by Bracken for the MOI in October 1942, but it was mooted informally by various ETO officers a year later. Their concern was the growing number of racial incidents in which British civilians were taking the side of the black GIs, but Grigg at the War Office supported the idea in the hope of reducing miscegenation. Citing morale reports from Army units abroad, he told Churchill: "I expect that the British soldier who fears for the safety or faithfulness of his women-folk at home would not feel so keenly as the B.B.C. and the public at home appear to do in favour of a policy of no colour bar and complete equality of negro troops." Again Grigg was in the minority, however. Sir Harry Haig, the southern regional commissioner, for all his concern about wayward girls, considered that the incidents that worried ETO really arose from what British civilians regarded as "unfair and bullying treatment." He argued that the U.S. Army had imported the problem and that they had to control it. This was also the view of officials in the American Department of the Foreign Office. One minuted: "Apart altogether from the ethical aspect, even to attempt to proceed as the Americans suggested would obviously be political dynamite for ourselves in most parts of the Colonial Empire."[27]

But the head of the American Department, Nevile Butler, was "not quite happy" with this. Having previously served at the Washington embassy, he was conscious that some of Britain's staunchest supporters on Capitol Hill were die-hard white Southerners (such as Congressman Nat Patton of Texas). Butler noted that "the way in which our public have received the coloured troops has not altogether pleased our Southern friends who think it may lead to trouble for them after the war" through black militancy. He therefore favoured disseminating the guidance given to British servicemen "by a discreet distribution to selected users in our civilian population"—code for an MOI-inspired whispering campaign. Even if this was ineffective, he believed it important to let the Americans "know we have tried to do something." Butler's proposal was not taken up, but the priorities behind it help explain why the FO tried to keep at arm's length Walter White, Secretary of the NAACP, when he visited Britain in early 1944. It did not want any meetings between White and Churchill or Eden to be featured in the American press.[28]

Intensive efforts *were* made discreetly, however, to guide the conduct of British women. In the case of service personnel, military discipline was invoked. Local police forces routinely reported women soldiers found in the company of black GIs and, by January 1944, there even appears to have been an ATS order "forbidding its members to speak with coloured American soldiers except in the presence of a white." Even against civilian women, the law could also be used. In July 1943 the Derbyshire police were prosecuting racially mixed couples on account of the damage they were doing to growing crops! Most common was vigorous use of the wartime Defence Regulations, especially prosecutions for trespass against women found with black GIs on U.S. military premises. Five who were so caught at Melton Mowbray in Leicestershire were each sentenced to one month's imprisonment in June 1943. In Leicester the following January, two factory workers from Preston, aged twenty and twenty-two, were found sleeping in a hut where black GIs were stationed. They were prosecuted under the Defence Regulations for trespass on a military camp and given three months hard labour.[29]

Nor were blacks included in the various schemes to promote good GI-British relations in 1943–44. These carefully respected the principle of tacit racial segregation. In June 1943 the War Office noted that "it had definitely been agreed with U.S. authorities that no coloured troops should be billeted," and this remained ETO policy when billeting got going in the New Year. Black GIs did not participate in the exchanges with the British Army. On 16 February 1944 the ETO and War Office agreed that there were "obvious difficulties about arranging inter-attachments with coloured units" and that nothing should be done "until the matter had been referred to high level on both U.S. and British sides." That was the cue to drop the whole idea. And, to quote the MOI's internal history, the "kind of contact which the M.O.I. sought to foster through the Welcome Club scheme was not altogether applicable in the case of coloured soldiers." To avoid accusations of discrimination, the British-American Liaison Board welcomed the WVS offer "to run additional or alternative facilities in localities where

. . . supplementary provision for the convenience of coloured soldiers was required." In fact only three of these "Silver Birch" Clubs appear to have been established (in Birmingham and at Bala and Penarth in Wales), because of the mobility of the black SOS units. In short, the official campaign to improve GI-British relations in 1944 largely ignored black GIs. In their case, the official philosophy remained largely the negative one of damage control.[30]

This is not to say that the U.S. Army was immovable in its racial policies. As we shall see in chapter 18, growing numbers and greater trouble prompted important experiments that were made in 1943–44, notably creation of the 8th Air Force's Combat Support Wing. Increased use was made of mixed black and white military police patrols. ETO called for black units to have 25 percent more officers than whites, and special officers were appointed to handle racial issues full-time, not only in SOS and 8AF but also in all-white combat divisions. All these moves reflected a recognition within SOS that "broad scale segregation of these troops" could "no longer be effected if serious interference of the mission of these troops is to be avoided" and also that "the colored problem is created largely by the white man," especially white officers. Gen. Lee, the SOS commander, agreed, and his own reasoning went considerably beyond military imperatives. He told his staff in September 1943: "Our basic law and our professed policy is to give him [the negro] a fair chance to make the best of himself. He has a better chance in England to enjoy himself than he has ever had before." And, he added, "we must face the fact that the majority of the people on this earth are not white people. They are colored. In our own self-interest, we must treat them fairly if we expect similar treatment from them. They can come to power."[31]

But command decisions, however "enlightened," depended for their implementation on junior officers. Take, for instance, the "indoctrination" about British conditions given to new units on their arrival. Pfc. Thomas J. Farrell, newly arrived from the States at a camp near Salisbury on 4 November 1943, was informed that it was "not uncommon to see colored soldiers with white girls," and that "we were to overlook these things and not to start fights or brawls." The line was that "the colored soldier was fighting for his country just the same as we were." But when Cpl. Charles A. Leslie arrived at Stone in Staffordshire in mid-September 1943, "we were told by the Chaplain that there was no distinction made as to color in the U.K., and that we would see some negroes with beautiful white girls, and they always get the best . . . and that he did not personally like it." After making his feelings clear, the chaplain "told us to keep our tempers in check, and take no action whatever." That kind of "spin" distorted the official message.[32]

For most white officers, like enlisted men, the most emotive racial issue was sex. Gen. William A. Weaver, the SOS Chief of Staff, went on record that

> God created different races of mankind because he meant it to be so. He specifically forbade inter-marriage. Our Lord Jesus Christ preached the same tenet, the grounds for which were that such unions would make the blood of offspring impure. It is a biological and historical fact that racial mongrelization results in the progeny acquiring the bad habits of both sides with very few of the good attributes of either.[33]

Sharing this social Darwinist philosophy, most white officers took an even tougher line on black GI marriages than on white. Added to the list of official "discouragements" where black GIs were concerned was the sobering fact that mixed-race marriages were illegal in thirty out of the forty-eight states of the Union. Furthermore, where this was the law in the state of domicile of either party, then the marriage was also invalid everywhere in the United States.

As with white GIs, none of this was strictly an impediment to a legally contracted marriage in the UK. The couple could, in theory, choose to live in Britain or to accept a common-law status in America. And on paper, as the ETO inspector general put it in January 1944, "the policy seems to be to permit marriage of colored soldiers to white women when [a] soldier applies for permission with admitted paternity or prospective paternity." But, even in pregnancy cases, it appears that black GIs were often quickly transferred and their partners counseled against marriage by British welfare authorities. In 1947 the black journalist Ormus Davenport, himself a wartime GI, claimed that there had been a "gentleman's agreement" to prevent mixed marriages.[34]

In the 8th Air Force Service Command where most of the AF blacks were concentrated, a total ban on such marriages was quite explicit. The commander, Gen. Hugh J. Knerr, routinely dismissed all requests for black GIs to marry British women as being "against public policy." The 8AFSC's judge advocate, Col. J. L. Harbaugh, warned in August 1944 that this was "not strictly in accord with the directives of higher authority and would prove embarrassing in the event a disgruntled negro soldier should complain to the Theater Command under the provisions of A.W. 121." He argued that the "discredit on the service" rubric and Gen. Andrews's "rule of thumb" in 1943—namely to approve marriages that would be approved by the Army in the United States—justified giving official sanction where such marriage did not breach the laws of the GI's home state and where it seemed "probable" that he could "support his wife in the United States and prevent her becoming a public charge after his discharge from the Army." Knerr was persuaded to use a broader form of words—"such marriages are considered against the best interests of the parties concerned and of the service"—but the blanket prohibition remained.[35]

On one occasion at least, Gen. Knerr was challenged on grounds of civil rights. In April 1944 Pfc. Jack ____, a divorced black GI from Dallas, Texas (where mixed marriages were illegal), applied for permission to marry Celia ____, from a town near Sheffield, who was expecting his child. The application went forward with the notation "Soldier is colored" and was rejected by Knerr as "against public policy" on 17 May 1944. The woman and her father lodged various complaints with War Department and U.S. Strategic Air Forces command, Celia calling the decision "a denial of civil liberty." The family also protested to their local member of Parliament. He, in turn, raised the matter with the Foreign Office and it was discussed at the British-American Liaison Board in September. There the ETO representative explained with studied vagueness, that in such cases, "there was no general rule or principle involved. The decision rested with the Commanding Officer, who gave or witheld permission at his discretion and according to all the circumstances of the case." Thereafter the FO dropped the matter and in December the 8th Air Force Service Command sent a terse letter to the family reaffirming the decision. To avoid continued argument no additional explanations were given. What happened to the woman and her child is not recorded, being of no concern to the U.S. Army.[36]

Illegal sex was even more emotive than lawful marriage. Of 121 rape convictions at U.S. Army General Courts-Martial in wartime Britain, black GIs accounted for one-third (forty-one) even though they were numerically less than one-tenth of the total American presence. This was a general pattern for the U.S. Army in Britain and on the Continent—black GIs had a disproportionate share of convictions for crimes of sex and violence. To Sir James Grigg of the British War Office, such statistics revealed "the natural propensities of the coloured man." But Walter White of the NAACP put it down to racial prejudice. After touring ETO in early 1944, he noted that "great unhappiness among Negro soldiers has resulted because of their belief that they are punished more quickly and more severely than white soldiers in Special and General Courts Martial." Most GI rape cases in Britain, unlike those on the Continent, stemmed from earlier acquaintance or even intercourse before the woman tried to draw the line. In such situations, the court was usually left adjudicating between the stories of the two people involved. In weighing up the probability of consent or coercion, prejudice against the word of a black could affect the issue. Certainly this was true in the American South. As Gunnar Myrdal noted in 1944: "Greater reliance is ordinarily given a white man's testimony than a Negro's. This follows an old tradition in the South, from slavery times, when a Negro testimony against a white man was disregarded."[37]

This issue became a matter of public controversy in Britain in the spring of 1944. On 29 April 1944 a U.S. Court-Martial convicted two black GIs of forcibly raping a sixteen-year-old girl at Bishop's Cleeve in Gloucestershire the previous month and sentenced them to death. Alerted by brief press notices, a number of Labour and Independent MPs raised the matter in the Commons on 10 May and pursued it vigorously through the summer. The Foreign and Home Offices were greatly embarrassed by the furore and the British Information Services were kept informed, lest they had to counter any American backlash. Three issues exercised the critics. The first turned on yet another basic legal difference between America and Britain. In the United Kingdom rape was not a capital crime; it was in most of the American South and in the U.S. Army. The MPs found it "an anomaly," in the words of Labour member Rhys Davies, "that a person can be sentenced to death on British soil, for an offence to which the same punishment would not apply under our own law." This was a reminder, second, of the unprecedentedly wide legal powers accorded to the U.S. forces in Britain—reviving bitterness created by the government when it rushed through the Visiting Forces Act in 1942. In the case of other Allied armies in Britain, a death sentence on one of its soldiers could only be carried out with the concurrence of the British government, whereas the U.S. Army had been accorded exclusive jurisdiction over its own troops. Third, there were imputations of racial discrimination. Although, under duress, the home secretary stated in June that seven GIs had been executed in Britain—all but one for murder, the other for murder and rape—he and the FO stonewalled requests for information on whether the soldiers were black or white.[38]

Despite the efforts of these MPs, agitation on the issue might have been confined to Parliament, but for a case that hit the headlines just before D-Day. Both because of the furore it caused and its revealing character, the twists and turns of the story are worth close examination.

A thirty-year-old black GI truck driver from St. Louis was accused of raping a thirty-three-year-old British woman (wife of a truck driver and mother of two children) in Combe Down, a village on the outskirts of Bath, around midnight on 5 May 1944. Arrested following identification by the woman soon afterwards, the soldier signed a confession late the following day admitting rape at knifepoint. He was tried and convicted by General Court-Martial (GCM) at Knook Camp in Wiltshire on 25 May. In accordance with orders of Gen. Devers the previous December, all GCMs involving a black GI had a black officer as a member of the court. In this case it was a 1st lieutenant, new to the command. Apart from one white officer of similar rank, the rest of the twelve-man court were all whites of much greater seniority—captain or above. The court unanimously found the accused guilty of rape and sentenced him to be "hanged by the neck till dead."[39]

There was no dispute that intercourse had taken place—in a field a few minutes from the woman's house. Despite a search, no knife was found to confirm the woman's story and the defence produced several witnesses who testified that they had never known the accused to possess a knife. The issue therefore turned on the two stories. The GI claimed he had first met the woman at a local pub on 27 April, propositioned her outside, and then had sex with her in the nearby field, for which he paid £1. On 3 May they met again, with the same results. When they met at the pub on the 5th, he claimed that she told him to knock on her window later and, when he did so, she put on her clothes and accompanied him to the field. After intercourse this time, however, she demanded £2 and when he refused she told him "I will get you in trouble." He had no previous convictions, denied possession of a knife, and claimed that his "confession" had been signed under duress, without knowing what was in it, after a day without food. He had been told he had better sign if he knew what was good for him. For her part, the woman denied all previous acquaintance with the GI, and her husband more or less confirmed her alibis for the nights in question. On the 5th, she claimed, she had been in bed with her husband when she heard a knocking on the door below. Opening the window, she saw a black GI who asked the way to Bristol. He seemed unable to understand her directions, so she told her husband she would go and help him. Dressing hurriedly, she went downstairs and let him in. When further instructions proved unavailing, she agreed to accompany the GI and set him on the right road, but after she had done so he forced her at knifepoint to go into the field where, she said, paralyzed with fear, she allowed him to have intercourse.

On 2 June the trial record was routinely reviewed by the judge advocate of XIX Corps. He accepted the statements of the investigating officers that the confession was signed voluntarily, and argued that, "in view of the many discrepancies between the testimony of the accused" and those of the investigators and the woman, "I believe the accused's credibility is substantially discredited." He therefore "recommended that the sentence be approved" but, "inasmuch as this is not an aggravated case of rape, it is believed that the sentence should be commuted to life imprisonment." This followed the pattern of similar cases.[40]

While the record was awaiting the final routine review by ETO HQ itself, news of the case had appeared in the British press. *The Daily Mirror* published an account on 30 May under the headline U.S. SOLDIER IS SENTENCED TO DEATH, adding that the woman "went 100 yards in nightdress to direct him." In an editorial on 2 June, the paper appealed for clemency, noting that the evidence might have inspired an element of "reasonable doubt" in a British jury. The *Mirror*'s editorial director, Cecil King, believed "the evidence would certainly have resulted in acquittal in an English court"—a view shared privately by the Foreign Office's legal adviser, Patrick Dean. The *Mirror*'s coverage unleashed a storm of protest. Two hundred locals submitted a petition on 2 June, insinuating that the woman was regarded as having loose morals and a record of association with black GIs. On 8 June Eisenhower received another petition signed by the mayor of Bath and some thirty-three thousand residents of the city. There was reaction, too, in the United States. On 7 June Thurgood Marshall, counsel for the NAACP, cabled Eisenhower asking for a stay of execution, and on the 12th the *Mirror*'s account was summarized in *Time* magazine. On 9 June the British left-wing newspaper *Tribune* actually published substantial extracts from the trial transcript, including the GI's claim about a forced confession and the woman's story of going out to direct the GI. *Tribune* also quoted the prosecuting officer's (apparently serious) remark that the story showed how helpful the English were to GIs: "they go out of their way to do things."[41]

When the ETO's assistant staff judge advocate, Capt. Frederick J. Bertolet, reported on 17 June, he disapproved the guilty verdict. His judgement was promptly upheld by Eisenhower himself. Bertolet concluded that the confession had not been voluntary. It was made by "an ignorant soldier," with only seven years primary schooling and in the lowest category of AGCT scores, "after a long period without food," and in the intimidatory presence of a captain specially brought in for the purpose. He believed that the evidence showed that the accused did not understand the significance of the statement or the gravity of the crime. With the "confession" out of the way, the case became "largely a question of whether the accused or the prosecuting witness should be believed." Bertolet had no doubt that the woman's "remarkable conduct in going out with the accused at midnight cast doubt on her credibility" and that it was "impossible to say with any certainty that a conviction would have resulted had the confession been excluded."[42]

ETO's decision to reverse the original judgement was surely influenced by the public outcry, which coincided most embarrassingly with D-Day. That was certainly the view of the XIX Corps judge advocate, in a vehement dissent from the ETO review. Of course, he was trying to protect his own reputation, but a similar interpretation was implied by Col. Ganoe, the ETO representative on the British-American Liaison Board, who observed that "many factors came into his [Eisenhower's] realm as reviewing authority which the court cannot take into consideration."[43] But simply to say that the reversal was an act of diplomacy is not sufficient. It seems likely that the 25 May court acted according to conventional U.S. Army attitudes towards black conduct and testimony—which one token, junior black officer, easily overawed by his superiors, could not offset. The 2 June review operated similarly. What the furore had done was to force a more scrupulous, colour-blind examination of the evidence in the light of a basic presumption of innocence and not guilt.

That, of course, was not how ETO saw it. Col. Jock Lawrence, ETO public relations officer, complained that the "*Daily Mirror* and certain other papers of that nature, constantly make us look as if we are some uncivilized nation, having come here to invade them, to rape their women, etc." He felt that such papers "do more harm than Mr. Goebbles [sic] himself." The theater provost marshal wanted the British press to "accept censorship in rape cases" but it was pointed out that press reports of GI trials in Britain could not be censored because of the provisions of the Visiting Forces Act. Instead stories were planted stressing that careful reviews were routinely undertaken and that no GIs had been executed "merely" for rape. ETO also decided in November 1944 that GI crime statistics furnished to British officials should no longer include the designations "white" or "colored" because "these reports reach such high levels that they may eventually be discussed in Parliament and ultimately reach the press."[44]

Lawrence also proposed that, because the Bath case had left "a doubt in the minds of the British people and possibly American people as to the judicious approach of Courts Martial, in ETOUSA, in Negro cases," the theater judge advocate, Gen. Edward C. Betts, should take on a special black counsel. But Betts insisted that "to the extent that there is a negro problem of ETOUSA, it is a command problem rather than a sociological one"—requiring the usual skills of military leadership not special measures for particular social groups. To request a special counsel would, he said, "constitute a confession of inadequacy" by ETO and encourage charges of previous partiality. So wary were ETO staff officers about creating this impression that they kept papers on the matter away from Eisenhower and the Pentagon.[45]

The storm about the Bath rape case blew over. Ike's timely action defused public anger and the war news soon preoccupied the press. The hanging on 11 August of the two black GIs convicted of the Bishop's Cleeve rape attracted relatively little attention. Nevertheless, the Bath case has been worthy of lengthy discussion. Whatever Gen. Betts might say, the problem *was* sociological, in a double sense. It reflected the failure of American society to eradicate racial discrimination *and* the delicacy of exporting Jim Crow practices into a society with very different mores and laws.

Above all, what the case highlights are the complex human stories behind the official statistics and memoranda. In this part of the book I have considered the GIs as "problems" for American and British officialdom. It is now time to look at the American "occupation" not from the top down but the bottom up, through the experience of ordinary men and women. To explore this we need to move away from the official documentation, though not discarding it entirely, into a more imaginative reconstruction of the human side of Anglo-American relationships. What was life like, behind the stereotypes, in wartime Britain? For the "Yanks" themselves? For the "Gals" they met and dated? For the American airmen who, unlike most GIs, were waging a real war? What did it mean to be a "Negro" in such a different society? And how did American soldiers get on with their British counterparts? These are the themes of the next five chapters as we shift the focus from high policy to real life.

Part IV

REAL
LIFE

15

Yanks

★ ★ ★

THE SCENE IS A TOBACCONIST'S SHOP. TWO AMERICAN SOLDIERS ARE sprawled across the counter, one of them just sober enough to make unwanted advances to the two shopgirls, the other fighting drunk. Enter novelist George Orwell in search of matches. The pugnacious GI lurches to his feet:

SOLDIER: Wharrishay is, perfijious Albion. You heard that? Perfijious Albion. Never trust a Britisher. You can't trust the b____s.
ORWELL: Can't trust them with what?
SOLDIER: Wharrishay is, down with Britain. Down with the British. You wanna do anything 'bout that? Then you can ____ well do it. (Sticks his face out like a tomcat on a garden wall.)
TOBACCONIST: He'll knock your block off if you don't shut up.
SOLDIER: Wharrishay is, down with Britain. (Subsides across the counter again. The tobacconist lifts his head delicately out of the scales.)

This encounter, or, allowing for literary licence, something like it, was what made George Orwell complain in December 1943 that "Britain is now Occupied Territory."[1] As he observed, such an episode was not exceptional in London, or other towns. It encapsulated the stereotype of the "Yanks" as oversexed, overpaid, and over everything. This chapter looks behind that stereotype, at what it was like to be a GI in wartime Britain.

Of course, GI John Doe did not exist. The three million Americans passing through Britain each had an experience as distinctive as his own personality. Inevitably young single GIs in their early twenties saw things very differently from middle-aged staff officers like Capt. Ted Fossieck, with wives and families of their own. At the other end of the spectrum from Orwell's drunken "friends" in the tobacconist shop was Leland D. Baldwin, an academic historian turned intelligence officer, whose spare time during his three months in Britain in 1942 was largely spent finding a publisher for his next book. Age, rank, education, and family background were among the many factors that differentiated GIs' experiences of Britain. What each person found depended on who he was and where he came from. That said, however, some broad common features may be discerned.

For almost all GIs their journey to Britain and to their first station left an indelible impression. The experience was both profoundly exciting and deeply alienating. It marked the end of the familiar, and established Britain, for all its similarities, as irrevocably foreign.

The voyage was an epic in itself. Most GIs had never left the United States before, let alone sailed the Atlantic ocean. They would embark, bleary-eyed and the worse for wear, after a final night on the town, usually Manhattan itself. Many were carried in old troop transports, but about a quarter of the GIs who arrived in Britain in the thirty months prior to D-Day (nearly 425,000) traveled on the eighty-thousand-ton British liners *Queen Mary* and *Queen Elizabeth*. (Such was their size and grandeur that many GIs assumed they *must* be American.) The great advantage of the *Queens* was that they could do the trip in five or six days; a Liberty ship in convoy might take a couple of weeks. Yet whether it was a *Queen Mary* or, at the other extreme, HMS *Franconia*, a converted banana boat, the voyage was devoid of luxury. For most GIs, the memories that endure are those of food, sleep, and nausea. Food meant only two meals a day but several sittings, so that there always seemed an endless chow line. Since many of the vessels were British, food also meant an introduction to a foreign diet—sticky oatmeal in the morning, leathery mutton at night. William E. Jones, on the *Franconia* in January 1944, never forgot the sight (and smell) of the "old sheep" in the "butcher shop" in the hold. As for sleep, that was also a euphemism. The *Queens* and other liners were "double-bunked"—hot beds operating on twelve-hour shifts. In lowlier vessels men were reduced to hammocks, strung in any empty space, or even blankets in the corridors and stairways. Every vessel was packed. The *Queens* carried fifteen thousand GIs compared with two thousand prewar passengers. Seven or eight times usual capacity was normal.

Compounding the bad food and overcrowding was the effect on inveterate landlubbers of the rolling Atlantic and the incessant zigzagging to evade U-boats. For many the voyage became a continuous, mind-numbing bout of seasickness. If you wanted to clean up, the showers ran only saltwater. Those still healthy had little to do. Physical training was often impossible in force-eight gales. Men gambled, bickered, and fought in the closed, fuggy environment. In those circumstances, rumour thrived. Officially no one had been told their destination. Iceland? England? Somewhere more exotic? Everyone had an answer. Planes overhead?—probably the Luftwaffe. Remember that shuddering roll last night? Maybe they were dropping death charges.[2]

Little wonder the first sight of land came as a huge relief: England's *green* and pleasant land (even greener in Ireland). Then there was the first close-up of the port—be it Belfast, Liverpool, or Glasgow, the bomb damage was a chilling novelty. A city skyline leering at you like a mouth with half its teeth knocked out. Endless delays to get to the quay. Maybe a brass band and an inaudible speech of welcome from some local worthy.

The first GIs in Belfast in January 1942 were interviewed by the BBC. One said bluntly, "I sure wish I was back home again," but most were more diplomatic:

"Well, Sergeant, is this country anything like what you expected it to be?"

"It's a lot better, sir."

"In what way?"

"Well, we always heard that Ireland was a land of potato famines and that a lot of people left Ireland because there wasn't enough to eat, to come to the States, but on the contrary I'm quite surprised to find that it's a land of plenty—plenty of food and plenty of attractive girls. This is rather important."[3]

Weighed down with kit, jollied along with some Red Cross coffee and doughnuts, the men were soon out of the docks and into the next great alienating experience—a British train. To anyone used to the open coaches on American railroads (and most British trains today) it was a shock to experience what one GI called "those curious little European compartment cars." From a narrow side corridor, clogged with men and baggage, sliding glass doors (usually requiring the application of brute force) opened into constricted compartments. For GIs the sense of imprisonment was made worse by the blackout blinds, round which only an occasional peek was possible at night, and the lack of heat or food in many cases. What should have been "a tourist's dream turned out to be a subway ride." And a long one at that. Like all troop trains, progress, to quote novelist Evelyn Waugh, was "a series of impetuous rushes between long delays."[4]

At last, GIs uncoiled stiffly onto stations. "Somewhere in England."

(The station name-boards had been taken down to fox German invaders, and many GIs were convinced initially that they had arrived at Hovis. Only later did they discover that Hovis was what "Best Bakers Bake.") Off the station and into waiting trucks. After a bumpy ride, eventually a first sight of their new home. Maybe some bell tents glimpsed through the mist in a chill Devon dawn. Or rows of Nissen huts—like tin semicircles—on a new air base such as bleak Greenham Common in Berkshire. Perhaps the grim brick barracks of Tidworth or some other old British Army camp, each building named for battles long ago and "heated" by an occasional fireplace. More inedible food. A handout of local funny money—large bills, many sizes of coin—multiples of twelve and not a sensible decimal system. Try a nearby phone box: What's this "PRESS BUTTON A" and "PRESS BUTTON B"? Welcome to Britain. Ha!

Not every GI arrived direct from the United States. The 9th Infantry Division reached Liverpool on Thanksgiving Day 1943 after a twenty-eight-hundred-mile voyage from the battlefields of North Africa. The divisional history records that onboard ship the news "that the United Kingdom was to be their eventual destination brought grins to even the seasick. The Ninth's soldiers had spent the past year amongst sub-standard living conditions, without normal pleasures." In contrast with Algeria, England promised to be much more like home. Yet the culture shock was still real. Gen. Omar N. Bradley and his staff flew into Scotland from Sicily in September 1943 to prepare for D-Day. In Glasgow they took breakfast at the Grand Hotel. The Scottish waitress offered them, in heavy brogue, a choice of two main dishes—neither comprehensible. "Let me have the second," Bradley replied nonchalantly. She returned with boiled fish and stewed tomatoes. He had turned down sausages. They asked for a pitcher of water, but the waitress looked startled. She returned with a silver teapot of hot water. It took several more minutes to obtain a jug of cold water. Bradley's aide, Chet Hansen, then requested some glasses. Her face suddenly brightened: "Oh, you want to drink it, do you?" Thankfully completing their meal, they went to pay, in Hansen's words,

> holding dumbly in our hands the collection of coins given us by the Finance Officer in Algiers. The Scottish girl at the cashier's desk looked on the General amusedly as she picked from his hands the proper price of his breakfast. We then asked her delicately what was the proper coin for a tip. She pointed it out and we carried our tips back to the table feeling somewhat strange in this country that was already stranger in many respects than either Africa or Sicily.

Hansen thought this sense of strangeness was "because in England we mingled with and learned to know the people" whereas "in Africa the American Army was a self-contained unit and our associations were restricted to the Americans in our units. Furthermore, much of our time there had been devoted to combat operations and we had little opportunity to meet the civilian populus."[5]

Whether one came from "civilized" America or the "primitive" Mediterranean, the culture shock was both real and abiding. The accommodation, the money, the accents were among many reminders that this was not America. And, in comparison with combat theatres in more backward parts of the world, you rubbed shoulders more frequently and on more equal footing with the natives. So Anglo-American contrasts were regularly being forced to your attention. In time, most Americans in wartime Britain found their own modus vivendi. But how they did so was significantly shaped by that other culture of which they were a part—the United States Army—and by what it was doing (or not doing) in Britain.

By the time they reached Britain, most GIs had been in the Army for well over a year. But that did not mean they were entirely at home in such an un-American institution, which continued to offend against basic principles of equality and individualism. The privileges of rank, for instance, became even more infuriating overseas, to all but their beneficiaries. The front line itself was a great leveler: officers shared the hardships, and women, liquor, and entertainment were largely unobtainable. But in rear areas, where the desirables were available but not abundant and where officers pulled rank to secure them, GIs could become irate. "I would like to know where all the beer is going that they send over hear [sic]," wrote an artilleryman based near Cheltenham in September 1942. "I seen a lot of empty cans in back of the officers quarters."[6] The perks of rank were also evident in less overt ways, such as mail censorship. Officers read the letters of their men, using scissors to clip out unit names, locations, and other details of possible use to the enemy. The fact that for most officers this was a boring chore did not affect the basic principle as GIs saw it. Many deeply resented this intrusion into their privacy, especially since officers were trusted to censor their own correspondence.

As aggravating as inequality was the Army's denial of one's individuality. The apparently petty regulations, the routines of cleaning, inspection, and fatigues, the demand for mindless, often demeaning conformity ("chickenshit") continued overseas. Again, near the front, much of that went by the board in the struggle for survival. In an inactive theatre such as Britain, 1942–44, however, it became a standard way to keep men occupied. Service troops were at least engaged in work that had some plausible utility. Unloading supplies, trucking ammunition, constructing huts and landing strips—you could see some kind of relevance to the war effort. But it was boring, monotonous, and often wearisome. A survey of over three thousand SOS troops at twenty-eight different British bases in July 1943 found 30 percent ready to admit dissatisfaction with their jobs. As for combat troops, they were training for action that never seemed to come. Once basic weapons training was accomplished there was a limit to what more could be done, especially with so little space to train. Hence the endless round of drill and marches.[7]

Like any soldier, the GI found solace from his officers and the daily grind in communion with his buddies. Gripes, gossip, rumours were all aired and eased in unit solidarity. Yet most units also had their internal frictions, their personality clashes, which proximity and purposelessness only exacerbated. Living cheek by jowl day by day, night by night, in, say, the confines of a Nissen hut, men got on each other's nerves. It might be as simple as the other guy's singing, or as incorrigible as his body odour. Perhaps it was Joe's cigar smoke, or Charlie's distinctive whistling, or Pete's tinny phonograph—at times anything could grate. Ethnic or regional differences were the source of more fundamental problems. Many units had their own Mason-Dixon line. Walter Gordon of Mississippi, a private with the 101st Airborne, thought that when many Northerners heard a Southerner drawl, their "first inclination is that he's a field hand." Jewish-American GIs learned to develop a particularly thick skin. Harold Baumgarten from New York, a replacement with the 29th Division in 1944, was referred to as "the Jew," deliberately given guard duty on a Jewish holiday, and "singled out for details (dirty ones) on all occasions." It probably did not help that Baumgarten was a smart, premed college student. Even where it did not cause friction, the turnover of men could erode solidarity, particularly given the Army's replacement policy. Unlike the Germans (at least in the early years of the war), the U.S. Army fed in replacements piecemeal, rather than rotating whole units who therefore arrived with some sense of esprit. Individual, green GIs, sent as replacements into a close-knit rifle squad, were often cold-shouldered until they proved themselves. In combat, where the results of this policy became notorious, matters resolved themselves quickly: integration or death. In inactive units, the process could take much longer. Baumgarten recalled that replacements joining the 29th Division at its camp in Ivybridge near Plymouth in late 1943 were placed in tents, while "the regulars were living in Nissen huts."[8]

Most men needed breaks from Army life. Its inequalities, regimentation, and personal incompatibilities infuriated everyone at times. Officers, of course, were well aware of this and special service programmes were supposed to give the men the outlets they needed. On camps in the United States the facilities were often better than men had ever seen before—for sports, movies, and games. In Britain, however, that was not the case, especially in small isolated camps and during the first year or so of the American presence. The lack of radios, phonographs, magazines, and even baseball equipment was, for instance, a constant complaint of the 8th Air Force in 1942. The BBC's dominance of the airwaves and the difficulty of importing American papers, magazines, and movies also meant that many GIs found little to their taste from the media. Surveys in September 1942 consequently detected a significant contrast in leisure activities for GIs at home and abroad (table 15.1). In the United States soldiers were said to be more likely "on a typical evening when not on duty" to write letters, listen to the radio, read magazines, or see a movie, whereas men stationed in England were more likely than those at home to drink beer or liquor, play cards, or date a girl. In England there was also a greater propensity to drink something stronger than beer (partly because the beer was so weak): one-third of the drinkers "on a typical evening" in mid-1943 as against one-fifth back home. Forty-four percent of this sample of GIs in Britain complained that they had trouble "much" or "most" of the time in finding interesting things to do on free evenings.[9]

The problems were exacerbated by the culture of irresponsibility that army life fostered. Although often hated for its regimented, conformist ethos, most armies have an inclusive, insulating effect on their men as the provider of all daily needs. As suggested in chapters 6 and 10, this was particularly true for the GIs, children of the Depression, under leaders who hoped that generous welfare provisions might substitute for the absent motivation of defending hearth and home. By the time he arrived in Britain, the GI's sense of individual responsibility had already often been dulled within Uncle Sam's cocoon. Even if he had not completely lost his "sense of property," to quote Ernie Pyle's euphemism, he could easily lose his sense of propriety. With "right" and "wrong" prescribed at every turn on-duty by Army regulations, going off-duty and especially off base could easily mean irresponsible behaviour—the term *liberty run* is symptomatic. David K. Webster, a Harvard English major and somewhat detached member of the 101st Airborne in Aldbourne in Wiltshire, noted in his diary in October 1943: "Although I do not enjoy the army, most of the men in this outfit find it a vacation. Boys who have been working steadily at home enter the army and are relieved of all responsibilities. It is unanimously

15.1 OFF-DUTY ACTIVITIES OF ENLISTED MEN IN ENGLAND
COMPARED WITH ENLISTED MEN IN THE UNITED STATES, 1942

In England

MORE MEN . . .

. . . DRINK BEER OR LIQUOR

ENGLAND 36%
U.S. 28%

. . . PLAY CARDS

ENGLAND 25%
U.S. 8%

. . . DATE A GIRL

ENGLAND 21%
U.S. 13%

FEWER MEN . . .

. . . WRITE LETTERS

ENGLAND 49%
U.S. 60%

. . . SEE A MOVIE

ENGLAND 24%
U.S. 33%

. . . READ A MAGAZINE

ENGLAND 21%
U.S. 43%

. . . TAKE PART IN SPORTS

ENGLAND 15%
U.S. 21%

. . . LISTEN TO THE RADIO

ENGLAND 11%
U.S. 53%

. . . READ A BOOK

ENGLAND 10%
U.S. 14%

. . . GO TO A DANCE

ENGLAND 8%
U.S. 10%

Source: ETO-2, "Off-Duty Activities of Enlisted Men in
England," based on survey 14–26 September 1942,
RG 330/94, box 1014 (NA).

agreed that they never pitched such glorious drunks back home." Or, as a more censorious American civilian observed of the GIs in March 1943, "it would not be an exaggeration to say that if many of them got up to half the antics at home that they do in England they would spend most of their time in gaol."[10]

The irresponsibility spilled over into personal ethics. The Army was a ruthlessly male institution. It encouraged and glorified stereotypically masculine "virtues"—courage, toughness, aggression.[11] One's private parts came under communal scrutiny every morning in the showers, rival virility was constantly being appraised, scatological language was de rigueur. For some in this male body shop, sexual instincts were suppressed or sublimated, for others they were expressed in powerful homosexual ties. For many, however, the "maleness" at times cried out for an escape in female relationships, made all the more urgent by long absence from wives and girlfriends. And the sense of unreality created by being abroad made it easy to slide over normal standards of monogamous loyalty, especially where local women seemed wild about you (or your money). This was England; "it" didn't quite matter.

Even those who felt it did matter found separation a testing experience. Take, for instance, Capt. Ted Fossieck, who arrived in Northern Ireland just before Christmas 1943 as an intelligence officer with XV Corps. Fossieck was a reservist from Michigan, married since June 1940, who wrote to his wife nearly every day. An English teacher by profession and regular churchgoer by avocation, he was soon appalled at how soldiers were taking "disgusting" advantage of the blackout. One member of his section—a husband and family man back home who would not miss a day's Bible-reading even when abroad—was running after girls "like a single man." This prompted Fossieck to suggest ways for him and his wife to maintain some kind of social life even though apart, such as filling in at dinner parties and going in a mixed group to dances. The criterion, he said, was to do nothing that might harm their marriage.[12] Such arrangements, agreed or tacit, were evolved by countless couples in wartime.

Many soldiers who were in no sense promiscuous craved and enjoyed female company and understanding. Another staff officer, a devoted family man in his fifties with teenage children, was posted to an air base in Cambridgeshire in the fall of 1943. Like Fossieck he was soon appalled at "the drinking and playboy attitude of 90% of the men in this outfit"—with the CO a prime offender. For one Saturday night party on base, thirty-three British women were brought in by bus but only twenty-two went back on it; the rest spent the night in officers' rooms. In January 1944 he went so far as to report the "drunkenness and licentiousness of officers of this wing" to headquarters. But then, hospitalized for a month in Oxford for a hernia operation, he developed a crush on an elegant and thoughtful American Army nurse, taking her out for dinner (with orchids), writing her long letters, and blowing off steam to her as an "outlet for my feelings." She eventually put a tactful but firm stop to the friendship. Significantly, all this occurred in February and March 1944, at a time of acute ennui and homesickness for him. By May, with D-Day imminent, he threw himself back into operations plotting, working long days but with a sense of achievement as June 1944 unfolded. His story was probably repeated on numerous occasions. The conjunction of alienation, loneliness, and boredom prompted men to form friendships of varying sorts with "other women," American or British.[13]

The most celebrated was Eisenhower himself. His liaison with his British driver-secretary, Kay Summersby, was hot gossip among ETO staff officers by 1944 and a source of bitter resentment to his wife, Mamie (whom he kept calling "Kay" by mistake when back in Washington on leave in January 1944). Yet even in Summersby's colourful account, written while dying of cancer thirty years later, theirs was not a heavily sexual relationship. The only time they tried to make love, she claimed, Ike was unable. All through the war Eisenhower wrote regularly to his wife, 319 letters in all, and the aging Harry Truman's claim that Ike wanted a divorce in 1945 has never been substantiated. But Mamie was remote and Ike had no one with whom to share his lonely burdens. What the vivacious Kay provided was sympathy, companionship, and help in relaxing—whether on horseback or around a bridge table. The closeness was real but ephemeral. As Ike's biographer, Stephen Ambrose, observed: "He loved Mamie for half a century. But loving Mamie did not necessarily preclude loving Kay" under the peculiar and intense conditions of wartime. One senior officer and family friend told gossips: "Leave Kay and Ike alone. She's helping him win the war."[14]

While often feeling free to "kick over the traces" abroad, GIs fretted about the loyalty of "their" women back home. Sometimes their fears were well founded. In one remarkable case, two U.S. sailors, swapping stories in an English pub, each pulled out photos of his wife back in Norfolk, Virginia, only to find themselves staring at the same woman. After the shore patrol had separated them and tempers had cooled, they discovered that the problem was not adultery but bigamy. Their wife Elvira turned out to be an "Allotment Annie" maintained by Uncle Sam for no less than six sailor-husbands—all of them snared in the night club where she worked near the vast Norfolk naval base.[15] This case was extreme, but most GIs dreaded a "Dear John" letter telling them that wife or sweetheart had found someone else. "Don't Sit under the Apple Tree with Anyone Else But Me" was one of the top hits of 1942. This proprietorial attitude was partly a reflection of a male double standard about sexual ethics; monogamy was for her not me. But it also expressed the homesickness and, more, the idealization of home to which GIs, like most soldiers abroad, were prone.

Wife, girlfriend, home all assumed an aura of perfection from across the ocean. They had to, for, in large measure, this was what the men were fighting for. They embodied abstractions such as "America" and "the democratic way of life." Take food, for instance, around which, to a notable extent, soldiers' letters revolved. That was in part because censorship prevented them saying much about work, partly because the food was often so dire. But also involved here was the "blueberry pie" complex that John Hersey described among marines on Guadalcanal (chapter 6). Three months into his time in Ulster, Ted Fossieck and his colleagues found a rare "real" egg (rather than the powdered norm) served at Sunday breakfast. As he wrote to his wife that afternoon, "we fell to talking of breakfasts at home and we all spoke of the things we'd be having—in my case I pictured one of your lovely, fluffy omelets complete with a couple of strips of crisply fried bacon and some real sweet rolls with nuts, raisins, and sugar icing and real hot coffee— even now I drool to think of it, and I did at the time."[16]

Such feelings were particularly acute at holiday times, such as Thanksgiving or Christmas. Dick Murray was a twenty-two-year-old steelworker from Pittsburgh who was in the Army in Northern Ireland. This letter to a friend dated 15 May 1944 captures the oscillations of mood that afflicted young soldiers abroad:

> I had a weekend pass to Belfast. Saturday night I got pretty drunk with a nice lieutenant. . . . Sunday morning I remembered it was Mother's Day, and I got very lonely, so I went to the Red Cross and asked them for a mother to take to church. They telephoned one for me and I went on a tram to pick her up. She was a very sweet lady of about 60, and we went to the Presbyterian Church where we met her husband who had just finished teaching Sunday School. However, they have no such thing as Mother's Day in Ireland and there was no mention of the day in the service.[17]

The main connection with home, and all it represented, was through letters such as these. Letter writing was the most frequent off-duty activity for GIs in Britain. Among the cross section surveyed in September 1942, half said they wrote letters in the evening; on average every GI wrote one letter a day.[18] Yet few GIs had experience of expressing their inner selves in this way. Most, indeed, were not particularly literate. And what they wanted in return was not worrying detail (about which they could do nothing), or too rosy a picture, which was equally demoralizing. Letters from home needed to tell you that things were basically okay—except for *your* absence. But since letters were also an outlet for worried parents, harassed wives, or confused girlfriends, they often failed to provide the comfort GIs craved. Home ought to be perfect, but was it? That, too, was part of the insecurity for which soldiers tried to compensate.

Aside from simple tourism, then, many GIs sought from Britain and the British an escape from the regimented conformity of Army life and an alternative to its oppressive masculinity. At a deeper level, many also craved and found surrogates for "home."

Yet these varied and complex desires for escape and consolation were not always easy to satisfy in wartime Britain. Locally, there was little chance of an exciting night on the town. For many GIs the English pubs were a turnoff, with their bizarre customs, inconvenient hours, and, worst of all, unpotable drinks. Unlike American varieties the beer was warm and weak. Jokes about it were legion: "if this is beer, you can pour it back in the horse" conveys the general flavour. Down in the southwest the local brew was cider. Capt. William S. Weston recalled how his men, from an antiaircraft battery attached to the 29th Division, would descend each evening on the pubs of Buckfastleigh in Devon:

> the Yankees drank cider whether they liked it or not. It was pastime, an easy way to kill an evening and spend some money. Then too, it helped a man forget his troubles. The cider tasted like a mild vinegar and had about as much kick, but an evening's consumption could make a man so sick that the daily irritations of army life disappeared in a tidal wave of overwhelming misery.

The GI's preference for hard liquor was also difficult to satisfy, except at black market prices. Whisky usually cost £5 ($20) a bottle that way—the story was told of a GI who refused to buy from an honest publican at the proper price of £1 because he wanted "the real stuff." Many were the GIs who bought from a street vendor and found themselves with local "hooch" or even cold tea. In most towns and villages around Army camps sex could also be had at a price, but, as the story of the black GI in the Bath rape case suggests, the price tended to rise with demand. In fact, some GIs believed the price of everything went up when they came into sight. Two disgruntled GIs in Chester complained: "The only thing that is cheap in England is the women."[19]

Even for those whose leisure preferences were more moderate than "booze and broads," there was often little off base to entertain them. This was even true of the larger towns, on which they would descend on summer evenings or Sunday afternoons. In 1942 the U.S. consuls in both Birmingham and Manchester, around which large numbers of GIs were being stationed, warned repeatedly about the lack of facilities. "Manchester has the appearance of a very grim town," reported Consul George A. Armstrong in July 1942. "It is particularly lonely on Sundays when the soldiers come in." His Birmingham counterpart, James R. Wilkinson, told the embassy:

> Outside of two very expensive and relatively small restaurants operated by the leading local hotels there is in cold fact not a good eating place in town. Moreover, aside from cinemas and a limited number of cheap but rigidly regulated dance halls, there is virtually nothing to interest the average soldier.

By December 1942 Wilkinson was reporting that the "spectacle of troops wearing the American uniform being forced to choose between loitering in public places and taking what low dance halls have to offer is continually evoking contemptuous comment" among locals. The lord mayor of Birmingham was even threatening to put the city out of bounds to GIs.[20]

GIs propping up walls or ambling aimlessly were a familiar sight in many British towns in 1942. The problem was partly solved as the American Red Cross "hotel chain" spread around the country. Yet that had consequences of its own. The GI on pass would, in Wilkinson's words, "go directly to what may be compared to a piece of American territory" where his basic needs would be met in an Americanized environment. Food, drink, music, and decor were deliberately as similar to "home" as possible. Occasional sallies into the native hinterland would continue to seem unreal, as well as unsatisfying compared with the relative comfort of the ARC. Moreover, even though both the British and American authorities improved GIs' leisure facilities in 1943–44, loitering with discontent remained a familiar pastime. English towns still offered little entertainment for the average GI. In many, for instance, cinemas and other places of entertainment remained firmly closed on Sundays. Yet this was the day of the week when many GIs "hit town." After the 9th Infantry Division settled around the ancient cathedral city of Winchester at the end of 1943, it took all the persuasive talents of Gen. Manton S. Eddy and his staff before "the city fathers finally decided to break with custom and allow Sunday movies in Winchester."[21]

Nor had officially sponsored hospitality—on which the British government and its auxiliaries expended so much time, thought, and money—a great deal to offer the "average" young, single GI. After her four-month tour of Britain in 1943 Margaret Mead summed up "the various formal efforts which are made to entertain Americans" under the three headings: "Tradition, the Countryside and the Home." The majority of GIs had little enthusiasm for tours of Oxbridge colleges and Gothic cathedrals, she remarked. Imagine their reaction to a similar promenade around Harvard or Yale. "All this interest in the past seems to him merely a premium on bad plumbing and crooked staircases." As for the delicate varieties of the English countryside, this was "not nature as the young American knows it," full of space and size. "To him the country is where you can do something"—drive, hike, swim, fish, or ski—rather than "a place to be in." And home hospitality—centrepiece of official efforts to welcome the GI—was anathema to many American soldiers. Off-duty for a precious few hours, they had little desire to put on their best manners and venture into the social minefield of an English teatime. The fact that many accepted and then chickened out at the last moment left ill-feeling among the hosts and made the whole venture counterproductive on both sides.[22]

For pleasure pure and unadultered (or impure and adulterous), London was the best bet. An ETO survey in September 1942 indicated that of men who had been in England at least four weeks, about half had been given a pass of twenty-four hours or more and that most of these—more than one-third of the total—had used it to visit London. (The whole 1st Infantry Division was given permission to visit London on its first weekend in Britain in August 1942 and most of its fifteen thousand GIs did so, crowding into trains, taxis, pubs, and hotels.) Although there were periodic official mutterings about restricting GI access to London, on the whole it suited both the British and American authorities to funnel GIs there. Socially it was the city best equipped to act as a safety valve, with something for every taste (or lack of taste). Every GI gave the "sights" at least a cursory tour. For the studious, there were museums, concerts, and theatres; for the gregarious, London offered pubs, night clubs, and even the Piccadilly experience (as participant or spectator). Economically, too, it was convenient. The

ETO survey in 1942 indicated that of the "average" GI's net disposable pay of $40 a month, between half and two-thirds would be spent on a one-day pass in London. The survey commented: "It is clear that the major share of the burden of absorbing the excess spending power of the American soldier falls on London. To the extent that London furnishes facilities for absorbing this excess with least detriment to the English economy, this may be a fortunate circumstance."[23]

But there were unfortunate side effects. More than anywhere else, London gave the GIs their bad name. The metropolis offered not merely escape but anonymity. Officers in particular could let their hair down more easily than in towns near to base. In mid-1943, for instance, Gen. Devers was greatly exercised about the "increase in disorderly conduct in London by officers" and the leniency of punishments imposed. From the GI's vantage point, London helped give the British an equally bad name. Curtis Moore, from Virginia, was drinking in a pub, but came to in a police station. Someone had put a "knock-out drop" in his drink and relieved him of £7 (nearly $30). This was typical of the petty crime and rip-offs that GIs experienced in the metropolis. Stung by press criticism, one GI spoke for many when he wrote to the *Daily Mirror* at the end of 1943. "We agree that Johnny [Doughboy] is far too liberal with his pay," but "who sets the prices on commodities?" such as whisky, or services such as cabbies' tips. As for American morals, he went on, "we have been accosted by painted women more times in one night on Piccadilly than in our life previously"— often by "girls who should have been off the streets after dark because of their extreme youth." Remember, he added: "We have no homes or loved ones to go to over here; hence we choose London" and "we go up there after weeks of camp life."[24]

London seemed decadent in more than a moral sense. In August 1942 Gen. George S. Patton recorded his impressions in a letter to his wife:

> London looks like a dead city in that there are no motor cars except military and a very few taxies on the streets and very few people. It is always black out and realy black. . . . I bought a pair of shoes for $30.00, but there is nothing else for sale. The coffee is artificial and one is always hungry. . . . The only thing they seem to have lots of is smoked salmon and decayed grouse. On the other hand, they take long weekends and get to the office at ten.

Patton, of course, was no Anglophile and his stay in Britain in 1942 was very brief. But similar impressions can be gleaned from the diary of Leland D. Baldwin, a student of English history who spent much time in London while based at Greenham Common in Berkshire in 1942. Touring the city in a taxi in October, he found the debris of the Blitz cleared, "but the walls and the gaping cellars of thousands of houses and office buildings remain like the ruins of a city just excavated. At one place there was a sweep of perhaps a mile, down which one could look across the remains." Like Ted Fossieck in Northern Ireland, Baldwin noted that at Greenham Common "already a favorite pastime is concerned with talking about what we are going to have to eat when we get home," but, unlike Gen. Patton, Baldwin had time to find decent restaurants in London. Indeed, that became one of the main reasons for a visit—to escape the powdered eggs, boiled cabbage, and the coffee—"perish the name!" At Frascatis or the Cumberland Grill, he found, you could still get a good meal at a good price.[25] Baldwin was a staff officer, but any GI who wanted could also easily afford some of the best restaurants in London. The fact that his patronage was often tolerated with ill-concealed disapproval and that no British private could either afford or would dare to enter, gave the meal added spice. The socially subversive effects of the GI's money was a major grievance among what today would be called the English "establishment."

Educated officers like Patton or Baldwin would acknowledge, of course, that bomb damage, blackouts, and rationing were all features of a London distorted by wartime. But even on them, the subliminal effect was immense. For Patton, it was "a dead city," for Baldwin a sort of latter-day Pompeii. And for the average GI, not prone to studious reflection, the effect must have been even more powerful. Educated or not, they had heard of London, the heart of the great British Empire. Yet where was the greatness? Evidence of physical and moral decay was everywhere. All this fitted with the traditionalism and primitiveness of English daily life, as glimpsed in pubs and local towns. And the absence of a second front confirmed the general American view that, overall, the British were doing little to help win the war.

Moreover, wartime London was being viewed from Americanized Red Cross clubs and with the advantage of wealth that enabled them to buck "the class system." Likewise, on base, whatever the privations, it was clear that the quality of the American's life was much better than that of the native—that was surely why the Limeys were so anxious to cash in. And if being Government Issue in Uncle Sam's Army was so much better than being a civilian in "Great" Britain, then real America was clearly even more superior. In April 1943 a Mass-Observation survey of GIs found "that Britain was looked upon not only as backward compared with the U.S.A., but as being definitely impecunious and without much of what even the poorest people in America would take as a matter of course," such as automobiles and central heating. Even the dreaded powdered egg contributed to such assumptions. "Is it on account of the war you never have eggs?" asked one surprised GI. "I had grown to suppose that England had always been an eggless country."[26]

Such perceptions of superiority were encouraged by the way the British lumped all GIs together. On base, it still mattered if you were a Cracker, a Yankee, a Jew, a Polack, and so on. Most American platoons were ethnic potpourris. But off base, to the British you were all "Yanks." And you began to realize that, comparatively speaking, you *were* all Yanks—that the similarities outweighed the differences in a foreign situation. Whereas initial Army training back in the United States had served, for many young GIs, to highlight the variety of American life, service abroad was creating a sharper, prouder sense of what it meant to be American.

What did GIs make of the British people? When they spoke of the British, most meant the English—the two terms were used interchangeably, and relatively few GIs penetrated Wales or Scotland. The principal exception is Northern Ireland, where a distinct set of reactions can be discerned.

In Ulster, GI-civilian relations had first to cope with the sectarian divide. Irish-American GIs were often vehemently anti-British. In September 1942, the senior Catholic chaplain with the U.S. forces bluntly told the consul in Belfast, Parker Buhrman, that "the British should get out of Northern Ireland." But most GIs were not partisan. Buhrman reported "considerable resentment on the part of American troops" about the IRA. "Individual American soldiers have been subjected to threats by IRA partisans ever since they arrived in the North of Ireland. Quite a number of them have been brutally assaulted under cover of darkness." Among civilians, too, the sectarian divide shaped reactions. Tom Harrisson, the head of Mass-Observation, visited Ulster in May and June 1942. He found the Protestant majority "favourable, often enthusiastic about the Americans," welcoming them "not only for themselves and for the war," but also, "almost unconsciously, as a strengthening of the forces of order against the constant fear of Catholic (Nationalist) trouble." The Catholics, on the other hand, he judged "largely antagonistic, though it is only a minority who are strongly so, and many individual Catholics are thoroughly in favour of the Americans."[27]

Where sectarianism could be negotiated, GIs seemed to have felt most at home in Ulster. That was the conclusion of Iphigene Bettman, an OWI official, who toured the UK in 1943–44. Many GIs told her that hospitality in Ulster was second to none, even in America. "The strain is obviously here in England," she wrote, "where reserve, formality and trace of 'superior race' feeling makes the difference of our customs a greater cause of friction." Observers in England agreed with her. "The real tragedy," wrote Consul Armstrong from Manchester in April 1944, "is that the American does not really understand the British, that he often lives here months without any natural association, and that while successful attempts are made to break down this separation, a sufficient number of the visitors are not reached." Armstrong was an enthusiast for Anglo-American relations, but his judgements squared with those of anthropologist Margaret Mead, who wrote in March 1944 that "as Johnny thinks of home he learns little in England." She, too, noted that the GI had "practically no contact with English people in groups, with family groups, or clubs, or discussion groups."[28]

These observations were reinforced by official reports. After an intensive survey of the whole command, the provost marshal of the 8th Air Force concluded in November 1943:

> In general, the American soldier is imbued with a "Limey" complex and has not the desired respect for the British. His feeling towards the British does not amount to an active dislike, but is passive and apathetic. Because of this lack of feeling towards the British, he makes no attempt, generally speaking, to get to know them better.

The report stressed that these opinions "do not manifest themselves in public and, with the exception of a lack of comradeship, from outward appearances and for practical purposes the relationship is good. During the entire survey not one unpleasant incident was observed." But the provost marshal had no doubt of the underlying attitudinal problem:

> This noticeable apathy of American troops towards the British is due primarily to one cause: Nostalgia. The average American soldier is not interested in Britain or the British. He is only interested in the day the war will end, so that he may return home. During the interim, he remains close to his own fellow Americans and seeks diversions in pubs and other public places of amusement. The British home, the one instrument through which a stronger bond between

British and Americans could be forged, is not being entered as much as would be desired. Only two per cent of American troops are accepting existing hospitality.

This he ascribed to two main reasons: "Being a guest demands a certain amount of discipline from which the soldiers are trying to get away on their free time" and "many homes are now devoid of their daughters, which lessens the attraction for young men."[29]

Similar conclusions are to be found in two reports from the ETO opinion pollsters, one based on a representative cross sample of nearly three thousand GIs in November 1943, the other derived from a similar sample who filled in anonymous questionnaires during "Army Talks" sessions in March 1944. Although 73 percent and 83 percent respectively indicated a "favorable opinion" of the English, the "softness" of that statistic is suggested by the fact that 62 percent in March 1944 expressed themselves, more precisely, as "fairly favorable." Of those whose opinions of the English had improved since arrival, half indicated that it was "due to getting to know the English people better." On the other hand, 43 percent in November attached little or no importance to Anglo-American relations—a statistic that horrified Gen. Devers. The March survey confirmed that official hospitality was rarely successful in fostering close personal contacts. Less than one GI in twenty said he had met most of the English people he knew that way; twelve out of twenty said these contacts were the result of a "chance meeting." And in both surveys, the men who said their opinions had become "more favorable" since arriving in the UK were balanced by an equal proportion who said that these had become "less favorable"—a third in the first survey, a quarter in the second.

In other words, closer contact could be detrimental as often as beneficial. Part of the reason may have been the nature of those contacts. For perhaps the most striking finding of the second survey was the proportion who indicated that they had "gotten to know no English families." This was 34 percent in the case of GIs who had been in the country less than six months, 20 percent for those in England between six and twelve months, and 11 percent even in the case of veterans of over one year. As for the "oversexed" image, it is worth noting that the proportions saying they had "gotten to know no English civilian girls" were, respectively, 25 percent, 17 percent, and 11 percent.[30]

These various reports remind us that effusive wartime letters about British hospitality and nostalgia from veterans about their time in Britain do not tell the whole story. Many GIs passed through wartime Britain without any deep and informed awareness of its inhabitants. As Gen. Eisenhower, Lady Reading, and many others observed, spending time in a British home was perhaps the most revealing experience and many GIs never crossed the threshold. Although most of them became less overtly critical over time and established a modus vivendi with the natives, this was frequently a matter of pulling punches. Taught by experience, as well as by periodic indoctrination lectures, they learned not to speak their minds when asked the recurrent pub question, "Well, Yank, what do you think of it over here?" As one GI in Cambridge groused (to an American civilian) in March 1943: "If you want to get along with them, don't knock their country because they can't take it. Just tell them you think everything here is great." Or, to quote another American soldier in late 1944, when asked by a British officer how he liked the country: "Sir, we like you and you like us and that's our orders, sir."[31]

In May 1943 the Canadian journalist Graham Spry, who was then doing advisory work for the British government on Anglo-American relations, propounded his own theory about how GIs acclimatized to Britain. He suggested that they were not unlike ordinary tourists and that, in general, there were

> three stages which visitors pass through—the antiquities, old cottage, sight-seeing stage (a brief period dominated by garrulous guides); the anti-coffee, anti-climate, anti-slowness stage (a longer period punctuated with rude encounters in trains and buses, and for the lighter-headed or stronger-armed perhaps a fight or two in a pub); and finally the adjusted stage when friendships begin to form.[32]

As Spry admitted and we have seen in this chapter, many GIs did not get beyond the second stage. They remained resentful and anti-British, keeping country and people at arm's length. Personal contact was often skin deep and left painful scratches. Furthermore, the premiss behind official thinking about home visits, welcome clubs, and the like was that getting to know individual British people would lead to a favourable view of their country. In the jargon of wartime sociologists, improved "interpersonal relations" with the local inhabitants should mean better "intergroup relations." As we have also seen, this was not automatically true: "friendly interpersonal relations and hostile intergroup relations may coexist" or, in plain English, liking Brits did not necessarily mean liking Britain.[33]

I shall return to this point in chapter 24 when considering the legacies of the GI's service abroad. But, though important, it does not negate the equally important fact that many GIs *did* break through to "stage three," forming close, affectionate, and often intimate relations with individual Britons.

16

Gals

★ ★ ★

THE *DAILY MIRROR* PUT IT *ALL* DOWN TO HOMESICKNESS. NOT JUST THE MIS-
conduct of GIs, but that of the British as well:

> Home's not a place. It's a combination of people you know, doing
> jobs you know, places that look the same, familiar faces, familiar
> food, familiar laws, and so on. . . . And now what's happened? Even
> those remarkable few who live in the same house find it another
> world. Steak and kidney pie isn't every Wednesday any longer.
> There's a hole in the ground where the Snooks lived. The Grey Lion
> got blown up. Laura's in the WAAF and George is over Genoa in a
> Lancaster.[1]

The *Mirror* had a point. The GIs were uprooted by war, but so were
the British. To understand their mutual interaction we need to see
things through British eyes as much as American. Anthropologist
Margaret Mead aptly observed that many Britons reacted to every GI
"as a stereotype," but the same was true in reverse.[2] Many GIs had
their own "Limey" stereotype about their hosts. And those stereotypes
have endured. Next to the caricature of the "oversexed" GI, the image
of the "ever-ready" British female is probably the most durable myth
of the American occupation. Yet it does not (thankfully) require a long
aside on Foucault to suggest that "sex" is not an unchanging and
uncontrollable essential force (whatever army commanders might believe). The British woman of World War Two was not a mere "gal";
like the GI, she had her own individuality and history, her own culture
and attitudes, her own family relations and wartime problems. Only by

first exploring these can we understand the rich relations between the GIs and British civilians in general.

As we have seen, officialdom on both sides tried to control and channel male-female contacts. The British Welcome Clubs, for instance, aimed to introduce GIs to selected "nice" British girls. Hostesses for the American Red Cross clubs were also carefully vetted. But, for the most part, contacts were made more casually. Bridget Goodlace, of the Women's Auxiliary Air Force (WAAF), was based in Cambridge in 1942 and went with a girlfriend to the fair on Midsummer Common. "We decided to see if we could find a couple of Americans to take us on the rides as we had very little money and Americans always appeared to have plenty. We saw two standing by a ride so we went and stood behind them. Naturally, they started talking and we spent the evening with them." She later married one of them.[3]

A particularly common meeting place was the local cinema. Moviegoing, as U.S. consuls found in 1943, became even more frequent among the British in wartime. There were one billion admissions in 1940, 1.49 billion in 1942, and 1.58 billion in 1944—the equivalent of nearly forty tickets a year for each member of the population. "Going to the pictures" was particularly popular for British women and many encountered GIs in doing so. Avice Wilson, a fifteen-year-old in Chippenham, Wiltshire, when the 2nd Armored Division arrived in 1943, recalled that "queueing was an ideal way to strike up an acquaintance and sever it if necessary as one reached the top of the line." From the GI's point of view, the movies were often better on base, particularly the larger ones, but hanging around the local cinemas was a good way to pick up local girls.[4]

The place where GIs most frequently met British women was at a dance. With cinemas, dance halls were the main venue for an evening out in the 1930s, their appeal enhanced by popularized jazz music on the BBC. They offered a socially acceptable place for young women to enjoy themselves and meet men—an advance on the careful chaperoning of upper- and middle-class girls pre-1914 but where girl still met boy in a group situation, usually as part of a gaggle of friends on both sides, where coupling could be flexible and not necessarily too intimate. Most of all, the dancing was energetic and good fun. In wartime it became a cathartic escape from worries and weariness. Famous London dance halls such as the Lyceum and the Hammersmith Palais flourished during the war with American clientele. But dances went on all around the country—in church halls, town halls, even marquees—to phonograph records if there was no band, with partners of the same sex if the men were in short supply. Most villages had one a week. In rural areas the Women's Land Army served as a useful reservoir of females for U.S. Army dances. "Land girl" Shirley Joseph, then living in a hostel at Shrivenham in Berkshire, felt "like one of several cows being sent to an auction sale" as they were "herded into a truck" and driven to the nearby American base, where "we were shepherded out of the truck and dutifully filed past the M.P. on duty at the entrance of the hall, presenting the little slips of paper which entitled us to admission."[5]

Of course, the GIs were only one of several Allied armies in wartime Britain. An Ipswich girl who "adored dancing" partnered Czechs ("oh, those marathon Viennese-style waltzes"), Dutchmen, Scots, Americans, Poles, French, and even a New Zealander, not to mention men from all over the British Isles.[6] But for many the Yanks offered something special. There was the excitement of new dances like jitterbugging (jiving), which involved a few dance steps, performed vigorously at some distance from one's partner, punctuated by close encounters when the girl might be lifted off her feet or swung around with skirts flying. And there was the "big band sound"—associated with Artie Shaw, Tommy Dorsey, and above all Glenn Miller—brassy (in contrast with the frequent use of violins in British bands), sometimes ebullient, but often dreamily romantic "smooth music." For many British women of that generation the surest way to evoke the GIs remains tunes such as "Stardust" or Miller's signature "Moonlight Serenade." The atmosphere they created was unique and indelible.

The GIs offered money as well as music. The soldiers may not have felt themselves particularly wealthy on base, with primitive accommodation and unpalatable food, but compared with most of the other Allied servicemen, especially the British, they had a large amount of disposable income that was mainly expended on leisure and amusement, not to mention the resources of a well-stocked PX. The indirect beneficiaries of the U.S. Army emphasis on soldier welfare were British friends of GIs, especially women, for whom gifts of chocolates, cigarettes, and the coveted "nylons" were almost incredible in a country seriously rationed for years. (Such was the shortage of silk for stockings that many girls habitually painted their legs with pancake makeup or even gravy powder, using eyebrow pencils to draw the "seams.") One woman in Bristol was puzzled at what her friend saw in a rather wooden GI. When asked where they went for dates, the friend finally admitted that they visited Clifton College, a boy's school that was HQ for Gen. Bradley's 1st U.S. Army in 1943–44. The GI was a chef in civilian life and worked in the HQ kitchens, where she dined out free on steak, beef, and other wartime unimaginables.[7]

It was not merely in matters material that GIs made a fuss of their British girlfriends. Another woman, in wartime a teenager working in an aircraft factory in Leicester, later reflected on the contrast in styles: "A British soldier would take a girl for a drink, bore her to death talking about cars or sport, etc. If he saw any 'mates' he abandoned the girl except to buy her a drink now and then until it was time to go home. With the GIs it was very different. The GI would buy me a drink and entertain me as though I were the only person in the room." GIs were widely regarded as not only more solicitous but more forward than British men. Harry Crosby, an 8th Air Force navigator who was based in wartime Norfolk, observed that back home American adolescents were expected to make a pass on a date; the test for the girl was her adroitness in saying no. In Britain, he reckoned, girls expected the men to show restraint. A man's kiss was therefore regarded as a much more serious token of affection than the American might have intended.[8]

These contrasts were developed into a full-blown theory of "dating patterns" by the anthropologist Margaret Mead after her visit to Britain in 1943. She set it out for both American and British audiences— notably in an article printed simultaneously for the two armies in their education pamphlets "Current Affairs" and "Army Talks" in March 1944, which must have produced considerably more animated discussion than usual in such gatherings. The initial reserve of the English, the preponderance of single-sex schools, and the surplus of women to men were all grist for Mead's mill. She argued that the Americanism "to date" indicated that the main point was a social event rather than a personal relationship. Dates were "a barometer of popularity"—the boy boosted himself by big talk, sounding as if the girl was bound to fall into his arms, whereas the girl "proves her popularity by refusing him most or all of the favours which he asks for. . . . If she kisses him back, he'll take as much as she will give and despise the girl, just as she will despise him if he doesn't ask for the kiss. A really successful date is one in which the boy asks for everything and gets nothing, except a lot of words, skilful, gay, witty words." Mead went on to suggest that "this game is confusing to the British." Girls might be put off by the GI's wisecracking, speed, and assurance. Or they might confuse "dating" with "wooing" and kiss back "with real warmth" or even "think the Americans were proposing when they weren't and take them home to father."[9]

Mead's theory was an attempt to explain why GIs seemed oversexed to many English people and why local girls seemed cheap and forward to many GIs. It was reinforced by the contrast between the attitude of most American enlisted men to British girls as against WACs of their own armed forces. One GI womanizer reminisced that "we would never have got away with behaving with a WAC as we did with the English girls. I don't know a guy who tried." Another "felt a little uneasy in the company of a WAC. It was like being with a sister who might tell Mom." This was partly because most of the WACs were well educated and very responsible, having been carefully screened for service overseas. But a cultural difference was apparent to many observers. One ARC organizer in London reported WAC resentment of British girls, because of their "attitude toward the male. . . . The British girls are ready to come just as soon as the American crooks his little finger." Put less shrewishly by a GI from South Carolina, English girls "went out of their way to make a man feel more comfortable and wanted." Another recalled being stood up by a WAC with whom he made a date when they first came to London, whereas "I never had an English girl fail to show up on a date."[10]

Underlying all these sources of GI appeal—be it dancing, dress, largesse, or even cultural confusion—lay the impact of movie stereotypes. To WACs or Army nurses, GIs were just guys from Virginia, Ohio, or whatever—more diverse, perhaps, than the men they had known back home, but recognizable and each to be taken on his merits. For most British girls, a "Yank" was someone encountered hitherto only on the cinema screen and thereby surrounded by an aura quite absent for any WAC. He evoked the whole range of stereotypes about American wealth, abundance, and excitement. Many GIs exploited this shamelessly, talking up their homes back in the United States and even insinuating they had Hollywood connections. What made the impact of this all the greater was that some GIs were *literally* men from the movies. It was an open secret that Clark Gable—Rhett Butler of *Gone With the Wind*—was on an air base near Peterborough in the spring of 1943 (making a training film for air gunners). James Stewart arrived in Norfolk in November 1943 and stayed till VE day, first flying Liberators and then working as a staff officer. Glenn Miller, also in the U.S. Army, toured all over England from his base in Bedford until killed in an air crash in December 1944; he gave seventy-one live concerts before nearly a quarter of a million listeners. And one woman remembered hearing Bing Crosby in person singing "White Christmas" one December, while standing atop an air-raid shelter at the huge 8th Air Force service depot at Burtonwood near Manchester. "It was snowing heavily and he stood there singing in a long white mac. It was pure silence, there were many tears."[11]

For many young British women, the GIs were seen in this way—as exotic creatures who stepped out of the silver screen, or, more mercenarily, as sources of food, gifts, and fun. Others were probably swept off their feet and bruised in the process. (If only they had read their Margaret Mead!) Yet these rather patronizing images of British "gals," true though they may have been in part, are not credible as a complete account of the reactions of British women to the GIs. We must look more closely at the impact of war.

Official reports and soldiers' letters commented repeatedly on the enthusiasm of mid-teenage girls for the GIs. These children were some of the prime victims of wartime disruption. They might be evacuees, moved away to foster homes, and forced into a premature and precocious adulthood. There were 236,000 unaccompanied children in this position in September 1942. In his novel *Put Out More Flags*, Evelyn Waugh caricatured them as the appalling Connolly trio, led by the "ripely pubescent" Doris, whose "figure was stocky, her bust prodigious, and her gait, derived from the cinematograph, was designed to be alluring." Or they might be latchkey kids, left to their own devices after school because their mothers were in the factories. The female labour force had risen from 5 million in June 1939 to a wartime peak of 7.25 million four years later. By then 43 percent of them were married—compared with 16 percent in 1931—and one-third had children under fourteen.[12]

The effect of the GIs on such teenagers is summed up in a Home Office report in 1945:

> To girls brought up on the cinema, who copied the dress, hair styles and manners of Hollywood stars, the sudden influx of Americans, speaking like the films, who actually lived in the magic country, and who had plenty of money, at once went to the girls' heads. The American attitude to women, their proneness to spoil a girl, to build up, exaggerate, talk big, and to act with generosity and flamboyance, helped to make them the most attractive boy friends.

Probation reports also indicated the social context of war and deprivation. One from the London docklands commented on

> the way in which girls of about fourteen seem to attract them [GIs]—all that seems to be necessary is for the girl to have a desire to please. . . . Those girls who are misfits at home or at work, or who feel inferior for some reason or another, have been very easy victims. Their lives were brightened by the attention . . . and they found that they had an outlet which was not only a contrast, but was a definite

compensation for the dullness, poverty and, sometimes, unhappiness of their home life.[13]

The phenomenon of mid-teenage promiscuity was of particular concern to the authorities. But the most common companions of GIs were young working women in their late teens and early twenties. Before the war roughly three-quarters of single women in that age bracket were in paid full-time employment, but they usually lived at home and contributed their weekly wages to their parents as the equivalent of work within the house. For women of this age the big change was not outside employment but work away from their hometown. Nearly half a million were conscripted into the womens' branches of the armed forces. Thousands more were directed into war work or often volunteered to avoid the services. Others helped on farms in the Womens' Land Army. These young women, living in hostels or "digs," were able to create a new social life for themselves, without parental restraints and with far more money than prewar. As an example, take the case of an eighteen-year-old daughter of a building craftsman in Andover in Hampshire, who in 1941 volunteered to give up her job as a draper's assistant to work in munitions production. Within a few weeks she had left home and was living in "digs" in Reading, working in a factory making Sten guns and shells. She was up before 6 A.M., left the house at 6:30, and had a long walk to catch the special factory bus at 7:10. She and her friends worked an eleven-hour day in unpleasant conditions. "To be shut in for hours on end, with not even a window to see daylight, was grim. The noise was terrific and at night when you shut your eyes to sleep all the noise would start again in your head. . . . The work was very monotonous, often on very tiny component parts. . . . I think boredom was our worst enemy." Little wonder that, outside work, as she said, "we were . . . thinking only of fun." They would take the 7:30 P.M. bus back to the digs, have a quick meal, and then wash and change to go out to dances or to the cinema.[14]

The "good-time" girls, about which so much was written during the war, were often reacting to the bad time they had at work. Wealthy Americans offered the chance to enjoy themselves after a monotonous and wearying day. But none of this would have been possible without the more general emancipation of young women that occurred during the war. Mulling it over in 1945, newspaper editor Cecil King and his wife agreed "that the main change since 1939 had been in the position of women. . . . Everywhere one sees women either in slacks or with bare legs. Smoking in the street by women is general, and we are both struck by the way women are determined to claim in every way the same freedom as men." Or, as Mass-Observation put it in February 1944: "Many of these girls [aged sixteen to eighteen] today are leading more or less adult lives; they work in factories and offices, doing jobs with much responsibility. As a corollary to this new responsibility they demand the right to live adult lives in their spare time."[15]

One striking sign of these social changes was female pub-going—the subject of several studies by Mass-Observation (M-O) in 1943. Before the war pubs had been largely a male preserve—a place to "get away from the missus" during the week, with women usually found there only on weekends and, even then, in male company. In rural districts this remained the pattern during the war—in Devon pubs surveyed by M-O only 8 percent of customers were female—but those in urban and industrial areas witnessed a marked increase in the number of unaccompanied young women. This was true not merely in Central London pubs around the railway stations, but also in the suburbs where women made up 25 or 30 percent of customers on a weekday evening. Often a quarter of them were under twenty-five and many were in their mid-teens. Similar patterns were found outside the metropolis in industrial towns such as Bolton and Liverpool. Mass-Observation concluded that "the initiative seems to lie considerably more with the women than the men." Its reports did "not suggest that the men take the women to the pubs with a view to making them drunk and seducing them. If anything the boot would seem to be on the other foot; but many of the young women, though they may indulge in promiscuity on occasion, seem mainly out to have an exciting evening at the expense of American and Canadian soldiers."[16]

Less public but no less extensive were relationships between GIs and married British women. Again these should be understood in the context of wartime pressures. The surge in paid employment for *married* women meant greater burdens rather than greater independence. They had to combine the demands of employment with those of the home. Shopping meant visiting not a single supermarket (as today) but a series of specialty shops, many of which had little to sell because of wartime shortages. And if you started work at 7:30 and finished at 5:00 or later, then the only time to shop was during the lunch break, which meant that many women skipped their main meal in order to buy groceries (assuming the shops had not closed for their own midday break). Laundry was another grind. It usually started Sunday night and involved twenty-four hours of soaking, boiling, rinsing, wringing, and ironing—all hard physical tasks in an age before automatic washing machines and driers.

For many women the strain was hard to bear. Female rates of absenteeism in the munitions industry were double those of men, and married women's absenteeism was significantly higher than that of single women. Although menstrual cycles were a factor, women often took time off simply to catch up with the accumulated household chores. One Mass-Observation investigator described the efforts of "Mrs. B.," whose household included two school-age children and a married daughter and son-in-law. At lunchtime she rushed home from the factory. "When I arrived with her," wrote the investigator, "the whole house was in a complete mess. Two days' washing up is piled high in the sink; a great bundle of washed but unironed clothes lie on the floor beside the sink; odd shoes and socks belonging to the children are scattered about on chairs; and the table is a mass of crumbs and dirty crockery. Mrs. B. seems at a complete loss where to begin." Hardly had she got started before it was time to return to the factory. "If I could have just a couple of days to get straight," Mrs. B. said wearily, "then it would be all right . . . but I can't manage like this."[17]

Mrs. B. at least had some extra money coming in. Another set of pressures was experienced by those women with very young children who had to stay at home. In 1944 nursery places were available for little over 6 percent of children under the age of four. Although others were cared for by child-minders or grandparents, many mothers looked after their children and therefore did not earn extra income. If their husbands were in the services, then their financial position was often grim. In 1943 base pay for a British private was 21 shillings a week (£1.05, or a little over $4.00). From that three shillings and sixpence was deducted as an allotment to his wife and the government added twenty-one shillings and sixpence to make a weekly family allowance of 25 shillings ($5.00). If, say, she had two young children the additional allowance of 18 shillings made a weekly total of 43 shillings (£2.15). Only in April 1944 was this raised substantially to £3 (roughly $12.00) a week. As the historians of wartime social policy observed, "the wives of the lowest ranks of the Services . . . who had small children and no other income but their allowances and their husbands' compulsory allotments, must have lived until the last year of the war in conditions that certainly were near to hardship even if they did not topple over the borderline." Many became dependent on credit from landlords and shopkeepers and fell heavily into debt. One way out was to live with parents or in-laws. This relieved the financial pressure by creating new social stress. As a study of soldiers' families in London in 1943–46 noted: "However amicable both parties are, the situation is a difficult one. Inevitably there is some friction between the two families, and each makes the other fidgety with hints, interferences and criticism. Children are a nuisance to those who are not their parents, and the parents themselves have the strain of trying to keep them quiet for the sake of others."[18]

Whether in paid employment or working at home, most married women with menfolk in the services (some two and a half million wives) faced the added strain of separation and loneliness. The burden of managing the family finances and worrying about the children fell totally on their shoulders and most tried to keep their anxieties out of their letters to their husbands. Leaves were brief and infrequent, allowing little time to address problems and rebuild relationships. Emergency "compassionate leave" from the forces (or "passionate leave" as it was known colloquially and more accurately) often came too late to help. One Army medical officer in the Middle East said that in his experience the fidelity of wives usually stood two years' separation but that in the third year an increasing percentage lapsed. One-third of all illegitimate children born in Birmingham in the last two years of the war were offspring of married women. Wartime marriages proved particularly brittle. Weddings increased dramatically at the beginning of the war, from 362,000 in 1938, to 440,000 in 1939, and 471,000 in 1940—figures never matched again throughout the conflict. One such wife in London, married for six years by the end of the war but whose husband had been abroad for three of them, called their marriage "a honeymoon on the instalment system." As a London probation officer noted, "Hasty war marriages, on embarkation leave, sometimes between comparative strangers, with a few days or weeks of married life, have left both parties with little sense of responsibility or obligation towards one another."[19]

It was into this situation of overwork and anxiety, hasty marriages, and extended separations that the GIs and other Allied servicemen came. Mrs. G., a Londoner of twenty-six, married with a boy of two, was discovered by her husband to have had affairs with two Canadian soldiers. Her husband was well behaved, helpful but fussy, boring and not "a good mixer." Looking back, she admitted, "it was marriage instead of the services"; she didn't want to be conscripted. Not only Allied servicemen were involved. C.M., a teenager from a respectable, church-going family in the Midlands, married her forces sweetheart, John, early in the war. Later she met a young British Fleet Air Arm pilot and soon they were deeply in love. Then she found that she was expecting his child.

> I knew then that I had to make a very hard decision. I knew that if
> I told him I was expecting his child, he would never let me go, so I
> decided I must not tell him. Instead, cruelly, I wrote and told him our

relationship must end and we must just remain friends. . . . I was heartbroken. But, above all, the guilt and torture of deceiving John was unbearable. I don't know how I survived. In those days divorce and all that sort of thing was such a disgrace. I just couldn't face up to my father, or going away from home to somewhere strange.

Her son was born and her husband assumed it was his own. They had two more children and, on her own admission, "a happy married life" for forty years, but she never told him of her secret (though she believed that her mother guessed). Only after his death could she begin to talk of her anguish and guilt.[20]

Some husbands forgave their wives, a few even accepted the off-spring as their own. But, in the period 1945–47, 60 percent of divorce petitions were filed by husbands (compared with a more normal 45 percent by the early 1950s). Two-thirds of all petitions in 1945–47 cited adultery (unlike 40 percent in 1949–54). To quote one study of divorce in England, these statistics "reflected the working-out of war-time conditions when husbands had relatively few opportunities for desertion and wives extended opportunities for adultery." That, of course, is an unbalanced judgement. Husbands in the forces also had extended opportunities for adultery, but a visit to a Cairo brothel or a fling with an Italian teenager was somehow placed in a different category. This was partly because evidence was hard to come by, but also because of a double standard about sexual fidelity. This came out very clearly in the columns of womens' magazines where agony aunts such as Leonora Eyles and Evelyn Home took a stern line with wives who wrote in about their affairs. One was firmly scolded in July 1943 for her disloyalty:

Your husband has gone overseas. Do you realise what this means— danger, privation, loneliness, possibly pain and death? Do you realise that he and all those with him are facing all this cheerfully and for your sake so that you, and all of us here at home, can live in safety and comfort? . . . Can you believe that you, and others like you, who have no idea of remaining loyal to their marriage vows, who talk lightly of "being in love" with another man, are worth the lives of all our gallant men?

Many husbands and wives remained faithful to each other despite long separations. But a considerable number did not. For wives the infidelity was harder because it was usually more public or else required greater efforts at concealment. Their sense of guilt was an added wartime burden.[21]

★ ★ ★

Uprooted adolescents, young women away from home, and lonely war wives—all these were particularly susceptible to the GI's charm, wealth, and image. It is the conjunction of American invasion with wartime disruption that made the GI's impact so powerful. To many commentators the combined effect was a serious moral decline, a wartime sexual revolution. Petitions for divorce rose dramatically towards the end of the war, from 8,357 in 1941 (slightly less than the 1939 figure), to 25,789 in 1945. Illegitimate births showed a similar pattern: fairly stable at the beginning of the war—about 26,500 in 1939 and 1940—but then rising steadily to over 64,000 in 1945.[22]

Yet all statistics have to be interpreted with care. The increase in divorce since the late 1930s owed a good deal to the Matrimonial Causes Act of 1937, which for the first time included desertion and cruelty as well as adultery among grounds for divorce, and to changes in legal procedure that allowed cases to be heard outside London. Similarly, the registrar general (Britain's equivalent of the U.S. Census Bureau) noted that the rise in illegitimacy should not be taken as a simple indicator of "loosening of restraint in the sexual behaviour of people during the war." The revolution was as much statistical as sexual. New legislation required that, from July 1938, when new parents registered the birth of a child, they had to enter their date of marriage on the certificate. As a result it was possible for the first time to discover how many children were conceived out of wedlock.[23]

The result was what even the registrar general, in his judicious prose, called a "revelation . . . sufficiently startling to render the matter of more than statistical significance." In 1938 and 1939, one-seventh of all the children born in England and Wales were conceived outside marriage. Nearly 30 percent of all mothers conceived their firstborns out of wedlock. The registrar general noted that "the births of 1938 and 1939 were all products of peace-time conceptions, and there was no reason to suppose that these proportions, astonishing as they may have seemed, were other than representative of the prevailing peace-time conditions." Significantly, these prewar statistics were not published until 1947. Only then was it evident just how many "legitimate" births had actually been conceived "in sin."[24]

What happened is shown in table 16.1. Column 6 indicates that, in 1938–39, 70 percent of the children conceived outside marriage were legitimized before birth by their parents' marriage. After 1940 the percentage of children conceived out of wedlock actually *declined* until 1945 (column 5). Only in 1945, too, was the total number of children conceived out of wedlock greater than in 1938 (column 4). What also

16.1 PREMARITAL PREGNANCIES AND ILLEGITIMATE MATERNITIES IN ENGLAND AND WALES, 1938–50

| Year | Illegitimate Maternities | Premaritally Conceived Legitimate Maternities | Total Maternities Conceived Out of Wedlock | | Percentage of Irregularly Conceived Maternities Regularized by Marriage of Parents before Birth of Child |
| | | | Numbers | Percentage of All Maternities | |
1	2	3	4	5	6
1938	28,160	66,221	94,381	14.6	70.2
1939	26,569	60,346	86,915	13.8	69.4
1940	26,574	56,644	83,218	13.7	68.1
1941	32,179	43,362	75,541	12.7	57.4
1942	37,597	40,705	78,302	11.8	52.0
1943	44,881	37,271	82,152	11.8	45.4
1944	56,477	37,746	94,223	12.3	40.1
1945	64,743	38,176	102,919	14.9	37.1
1940–1945	262,451	253,904	516,355	12.9	49.2
1946	55,138	43,488	98,626	11.8	44.1
1947	47,491	59,633	107,124	12.0	55.7
1948	42,402	62,304	104,706	13.4	59.5
1949	37,554	59,185	96,739	13.1	61.2
1950	35,816	54,188	90,004	12.8	60.2
1946–1950	218,401	278,798	497,199	12.6	56.1

Source: *The Registrar General's Statistical Review of England and Wales, 1946–1950, text, civil* (London, 1954), p. 90.

declined in wartime, however, was the proportion of premarital conceptions that were regularized by marriage before the child's birth (column 6). By 1944–45 this was down to 40 percent (compared with 70 percent in 1938–39). The period 1946–50 showed a partial return to prewar patterns, though not at the same level, so that by 1948–50 only 60 percent of premarital conceptions resulted in illegitimate births. In other words, what increased dramatically during the war years was illegitimacy rather than "immorality."

What do all these statistics mean in human terms? As the registrar general observed, the explanation for the decline in legitimization "is almost unquestionably to be found in the enforced degree of physical separation of the sexes imposed by the progressive recruitment of young males into the Armed Forces and their transfer to war stations at home and abroad." It was likely that "many children were thus inadvertently transferred from the legitimate to the illegitimate class by the imposition of war obstacles to the timely marriage of their parents."[25] This seems a reasonable assumption since the legitimization rate reverted to close to prewar levels once the war was over. Among those "wartime obstacles" was, as we have seen, the antimarriage policy of the U.S. Army, where even pregnancy was dismissed by some commanders as sufficient grounds for allowing a marriage.

Yet it should not be thought that prenuptial pregnancies are always a mistake, to be rectified in normal times by a hasty shotgun marriage. Historians of bastardy over the centuries, notably Peter Laslett, identify two other types of conception outside wedlock (leaving aside those resulting from rape). One might be termed the "coercive," where one partner, usually the woman, seeks pregnancy in order to induce the other to accept marriage as inevitable. This undoubtedly happened to GIs in wartime Britain. An occasional variant of it, as noted in chapter 13, was pregnancy agreed by both partners in an attempt to coerce the U.S. Army into approving the marriage. But this takes us into the other and, more common, type of premarital conception—namely that arising from an engagement or understanding to be married. Historically, sexual relations have been an accepted part of courtship, particularly in rural areas. Although conventionally supposed to have become taboo because of the spread of "middle-class morals" in Victorian England, Laslett's "courtship model" holds up, with some modifications, into the twentieth century and there is considerable evidence that it continued to be common around the time of the Second World War. Consecration followed consummation, and not the other way round.[26]

The 1938–39 statistics can be read in this way, and surveys of

English women who came of age during the war years suggest a similar story. Eustace Chesser's sample of some six thousand women from across the country in the mid-1950s, for instance, revealed that some 40 percent of married women born in the decades 1914–24 and 1924–34 had had premarital sexual intercourse, and that this had often been with their present husbands—evidence of what Chesser called "the fairly extensive practice of sexual intercourse during the engagement period."[27] Of course, it is impossible to say what proportion of wartime pregnancies were the result of courtship, as against coercion or misjudgement. But the evidence of sexual mores before the war suggests that many may have grown out of a steady relationship that both sides intended would blossom into marriage, and were not just the unfortunate result of teenage folly or spinsterish despair.

In other ways, too, wartime male-female relationships may not have been as exceptional as some moralists believed. Gaggles of GIs and women hanging around cinemas, pubs, dance halls, and street corners—the highly public forms of encounter that officialdom deplored—in fact mirrored prewar patterns, especially for the working class. Take the industrial town of Preston in Lancashire, which during the war was a local centre for thousands of GIs. In the 1930s young working men (and soldiers, for Preston was a British garrison town) had also clogged its streets, particularly on weekends, and this was the main way to meet a future partner. Certain parts of town were what locals called "the monkey rack," the most celebrated being Fishergate, near the railway station. On weekends, one old man reminisced in the 1970s, "it was a mass of boys and girls that used to walk up and down"—many of them no more than sixteen. Boys "used to put their new suits on" and "if they saw anybody they fancied, they'd whistle, you know, er say 'ello and try and pick up a conversation. . . . It were a mass, weren't it? wi' young people. No owd uns were there. It was just a mating place, you know? not a meeting place, on'y a mating place."[28]

What happened in Preston in wartime was not greatly different, especially for working-class girls. This kind of oral evidence, and the statistics examined earlier, suggest that the difference was one of degree rather than kind. There were more young men walking the towns—more evident because they wore strange uniforms, spoke with different accents, and had money to throw about. The disruption of family life, especially for females, meant that there were more unaccompanied women on the streets and in the pubs, all through the week, while sexual encounters could be more public because of the privacy of the blackout. And the tragic consequences of sex were more evident because many relationships failed to develop into marriage thanks to the War Office or Uncle Sam. The statistics suggest that such increase in promiscuity as did occur was mainly in the last year of the war—a point to which I shall return in chapter 22. But the claim that 1939–45 saw a precipitous decline in British sexual morals is difficult to prove.

Avice Wilson from Chippenham recalled that, after the GIs arrived in 1943, "the town girls began to be divided as Officers' girls, Serge[a]nts' girls and the others. They were sub-divided into those that did and those that didn't." Many women discovered, sometimes to their surprise, that being one of "those that didn't" was no barrier to fun and enjoyment. A British woman journalist, who spent three years surrounded by Americans in the U.S. Navy's Public Relations Office in London, found that "once you put up the respectability sign you had no more trouble with the Americans than you had with the British. . . . I still had a perfectly wonderful social life. 'Yes' or 'No,' you were still good for a dinner and a movie and they always took you home afterwards." One suspects that many female encounters with GIs were more social than sexual—at the most fleeting romances and not passionate affairs. A Bournemouth girl in her late teens had a succession of wartime dances and dinners with foreign soldiers. "They came and went without tiresome farewells, and we did not wonder or worry too much about being stood up on a date. There was always a fresh face to take over, another whirl of gaiety before they, too, moved on." The sense of fun is captured in this story about Mary Churchill, the prime minister's youngest daughter, later Lady Soames, who was a nineteen-year-old sergeant in the ATS in the summer of 1942. At a dance in a London suburb, she encountered GI Bill ("Feets") Adams, a huge truck driver from Grand Rapids, Michigan, who wore 14EE boots, the largest size issued by the U.S. Army. Small, vivacious, and forthright, she started to tease him about his feet. According to *Time* magazine, which told the tale with relish, "Private Adams turned Sergeant Churchill over his knee, [and] gave her about 30 good-natured whacks." His buddy said afterwards: "She's a regular guy and, like her old man, can take it."[29]

For most British girls, dates with GIs gradually revealed the variety behind the uniform. Take the case of one young woman from Gloucestershire. Before the war most of what she knew about Americans was gleaned from the movies, but this changed rapidly after she started as a volunteer in an ARC Club. GIs often insinuated that they were film directors, or something big, but it took little acquaintance to discover that most did not fit the oversexed, overpaid stereotype. Certainly not Glen, a schoolteacher from Kentucky, with whom she went out for a few walks. When once he bought her a cup of coffee, it was a major event. On their visit to the local Christmas pantomime, *she* had to buy the tickets. Another tightwad was George, a post-office sorter from New York, who seemed to accept her parents' hospitality as his right. On the other hand, Joe proved a real gentleman. He often visited her home, but never took more than a cup of tea or coffee, insisting that he had plenty to eat and that he would not deprive British people of their scarce rations.[30]

This Gloucestershire woman was doing what Margaret Mead had recommended, namely turning the American from "an anonymous soldier" into an individual human being, with a name, personality, and history of his own.[31] Instead of "Yank" it was Glen, George, or Joe. Not just for young women, but for their families too. Their mothers and fathers often wanted to meet GI boyfriends, partly to satisfy the usual parental anxieties but also because congenial young Americans helped relieve the tedium of those grim middle years of the war.

For other women, getting to know the GIs was more harrowing, though ultimately no less rewarding. Joan Blewitt Cox lived in Torquay, on the Devon coast, with her widowed mother who ran a small hotel. In January 1944 two police officers hammered on the door with papers commandeering the hotel as billets for American soldiers. They advised Joan and her mother to live on the ground floor and leave the troops the upstairs bedrooms. One of the policemen then turned to Joan and said that the Yanks were "overpaid, oversexed, and would be right here," adding, with a horrible laugh, that she was in for the time of her life. In fact, as they later discovered, the authorities could not have forced two lone women, without a man in the house, to take in troops, but at the time their representations had no effect. The most helpful advice they got, from one British officer, was to move out as much furniture as possible and keep their own doors locked. Joan was "truly scared." Although at work, she was an only child and her father had died when she was a baby, so she had no experience of men in the house—let alone Americans. The two women moved the furniture into one bedroom, took up the carpets, and waited.

The night of 29 January 1944 was as quiet as usual in their peaceful neighborhood. Then suddenly, at precisely midnight, dozens of trucks roared up their lane, all crammed with American troops. In a moment, she wrote, "there seemed to be hundreds of them" (in fact only twenty) with "expressionless poker faces" who were "stampeding up the stairs in heavy army boots," piled up with kit "like human snails." And "I shall never, never forget the stench they brought with them—tired, hot, unwashed men." All night she and her mother hardly slept as the shouting and crashing went on above and around them, reverberating off the bare boards. At first the GIs were "highly suspicious of us—they never smiled, and would meet us round a corner as though ready to attack. None of them had any idea where they were, and several asked us 'Where the enemy was.' " Some apparently thought they were in Germany. At night the curfew was no restraint. "Behind locked doors, we listened to the drunks trying to scale up the drain pipes and wall" before being dragged in, amid more crashing, through the windows. The electricity regularly fused—one GI swung from the ceiling on a light flex.

Yet Joan Blewitt Cox never needed her emergency hat pin. In time she and her mother discovered that most of their unwelcome guests were "simple at heart"—worried about wives or girlfriends back home and, most of all, fearful of the Germans. "We began to feel almost 'motherly' towards these men, and finally my mother asked the Sergeant in charge if he thought any of the lads would like to come down in the evenings for an hour—about a couple of evenings per week— just to sit by the fire and listen to the radio in a comfortable chair." The following evening, two embarrassed men duly knocked on the door. "They sat silently and awkwardly, as though they weren't used to sitting in an easy chair. I got on with some sewing and turned on the radio for the 'News' in order to avoid having forced conversation." Their hospitality hardly seemed to have been a success but, to their surprise, two other GIs came down the following evening. Gradually the ice thawed.[32]

The story of Joan and her mother shows clearly why the authorities were so fearful of billeting and why their fears proved unfounded. An American journalist who toured Devon in April told Lady Astor: "The billetting [sic] seemed really to be a success in Torquay; some of the women in the little houses they were in were quite touching, they were almost having a fight at one place over which had the 'best boy,' and were saying how much they would miss them." But billeting in 1944 involved only about 100,000 GIs. Most got to know British homes and families in more casual ways—through acquaintance with ARC volunteers or through what many GIs considered the most distinctive English institution, the pub. Many, especially in rural areas, came to appreciate the social qualities of "the local" and, where they showed a modicum of tact, were often warmly welcomed. John Warren served as a Red Cross field director in England in the spring of 1944. He wrote his wife:

Our principal recreation here is visiting the pubs of an evening. Our favorites are the small neighborhood pubs, which presumably have been serving son, father, and grandfather, and so on back to the dawn of time. . . . We are all practising "darts." Some of the British are surprisingly good; many are no better than most of us. I've played quite a few games, a native and a Yank pairing up against one or more similar pairs. We are always careful to have some of the natives playing—unless they insist our playing among ourselves—in order that they will not feel we have preempted what must be, for many, their sole pastime. Without exception everybody has been very friendly. It is soon Bill, and John, and Alf.[33]

For other GIs, their entrée into English family life came through children. Kids had suffered greatly from the war. Ice cream manufacture was banned from September 1942 until March 1945 and after July 1942 sweets were rationed—the norm was eight ounces every four weeks. Despite ingenious home recipes for such delicacies as substitute peppermint lumps or wartime toffee, some kids resorted in desperation to indigestion tablets or cough lozenges. Birthdays and Christmas were austere occasions, with candles in short supply and sugar for icing tightly rationed. The social deprivation was even more serious than the material. The basic supports of home, family, and friends had all been called into question. Many youngsters, as we have seen, were evacuated and had to live in overcrowded homes with hosts or foster parents. Those who stayed at home were frequently without fathers or older brothers for much of the war, while their mothers were less available because of war work. Most children of working mothers were therefore left much more to their own devices, particularly after school hours. One young mother of two, who had gone out to work in a factory in Wiltshire to stop her worrying about her RAF husband in the Middle East, eventually decided to quit her job. Her sister was looking after the children very well, but, she said, "I sort of feel they'll forget I'm their Mummy. . . . Starting at six in the morning and getting back at nine, all I see of them is when they're asleep."[34]

In any local town the GIs were often surrounded by kids. "Any gum, chum?" became a notorious catchphrase (to which the ritual response was "Gotta sister, mister?"). Some middle-class children had a more refined opening gambit: "My mother says that I shouldn't ask American soldiers for gum, so I'm not." Either way, the effect was the same: GIs deluged kids with surplus candy, peanuts, and chewing gum. Parties for the local children, particularly at Thanksgiving and Christmas, were also routine. In just over two years from 1 July 1942, AAF units alone gave 379 parties for over fifty-eight thousand British kids. On 25 December 1943 Clinton Reams, a Pennsylvanian in the 1st Infantry Division, helped to entertain kids from an orphanage in nearby Dorchester. There was a Christmas present for each child and a meal of "mash potatoes, turkey, and cranberries, and the works." Even oranges—one per child. "They were really happy with the dinner and everything."[35]

For the kids, there was the pleasure of sweets and food amid the rationing. They were also entranced by the glamour of America and the excitement of war. But for many the appeal was more fundamentally human: young men in a world from which fathers and older brothers seemed to have vanished. Soldiers' attitudes to all this varied. For some GIs, handing out gum became little more than an amusing ritual. Others got peeved at the amount of orchestrated "begging" they encountered, finding it symptomatic of what one called "this attitude that's about now among the English, of 'The Americans are rich: let's rook 'em all we know.' " As for the parties, these were obviously good public relations for the Army, and many men were simply doing what they were told. Yet there is no doubt that numerous GIs showed warm and spontaneous generosity to kids, way beyond the call of duty. On the afternoon of 20 October 1943 a bus carrying officers of the 66th Fighter Wing based at Sawston Hall near Cambridge hit a small boy of six or seven. It was entirely the child's fault because he ran right out in front of them. He was knocked under the bus, and fractured his skull. The bus was emptied and the boy rushed to Addenbrooke's Hospital in Cambridge, but he was pronounced dead on arrival. Although the inquest exonerated the Americans, the officers and men at Sawston Hall raised £64 (about $250) for the mother, attended David's funeral, wrote to his father out in the Middle East, and made a point of sending the family a Christmas parcel.[36] No one seeing David's body on the road could fail to transpose the events into his family back home—*my* son, *my* kid brother. At such moments, a child becomes a universal.

Through various channels—girlfriends or kids, billeting or pubs, home hospitality or casual meeting—the American invasion finally penetrated the Englishman's castle. Although a significant number of GIs never befriended English people and never entered their homes, there is a wealth of stories to show how mutual homesickness made many GIs into adopted family members. The experiences of George McIntyre, a thirty-four-year-old engineer in the Devon town of Totnes in 1944, encapsulate many of the themes of this chapter.

"Mac" and his friends soon got to know the local pubs—he counted nineteen in a town of about five thousand people—and they became adept at cribbage and darts. But he felt he only began to really "live" in England when he got to know a few of the local families through evenings at The White Horse. He was eventually adopted by the Prince family and spent most of his off-duty time at their home, including Sunday dinner. At first Mac felt embarrassed eating their food, in view of the rationing, but then he found he could repay them with surplus from the company kitchen. George Prince, an inveterate smoker, appreciated the cigarettes and his wife almost cried when Mac arrived with ten pounds of raisins. He was allowed to go with daughter Irene to the cinema and nearby historic towns. Sure, he kissed her "good-night" occasionally, but the relationship was entirely proper. Not only was Mac married and Irene fifteen years his junior, but his affection for her was matched by special relations with each of the Princes, whether it was shopping in town with "Mum," hunting or hiking with "Pop," playing cards or fishing with the sixteen-year-old twins, or talking about the war with George Junior, a British soldier. He had become an honoured member of the whole family.[37]

Few GIs enjoyed an Anglo-American relationship that was as rich as this one, but George McIntyre's story was not unique. Through getting to know English families, a large number of American soldiers did more than observe Britain from an American cocoon. Though no less American because of that—as we have seen, time in Britain usually made GIs more conscious and more proud of being American—it taught them some understanding of the country and some appreciation of its people. Yet even for GIs like Mac, the experience was ultimately unreal. None of them truly "lived" in Britain. At root, this is because of what it meant to be in the Army.

For readers too young to have experienced the draft or conscription, a rough contemporary analogy would be the experience of tourism. Your basic needs for room and board are taken care of in an environment similar to your own. You see the foreign country through a glass, darkly—from your hotel window or tour bus. Occasional visits to a local restaurant, historic site, or even showpiece home offer only impressions of what ordinary life might be like, from which you can always retreat to your own tourist bubble and, eventually, to your own country.

Yet the experience of tourism, though a helpful analogue from life today, is only of limited use. That is partly because of the privations and squalor of army life—in 1942 the cruise liners had been stripped of every luxury, the hotels were Nissen huts, and brussels sprouts seemed to come with every meal. A more important difference is that tourists travel because they wish to, soldiers because they have to. Most of the grousing GIs interviewed in Cambridge in March 1943 admitted that "their feelings would have been different if they had come to England of their own free will, as tourists, rather than soldiers."[38]

What can evoke this experience of *regimented* tourism for those who have never known it? Perhaps novels about strict English public schools in the Victorian era. Maybe, in yet paler reflection, being a student at college, where even today there are institutional constraints on one's freedom of action, not to mention crummy food and cramped accommodations. Yet none of these parallels capture the essence of what makes an army fundamentally different from any other social institution. And that is killing.

Soldiers were being trained to do what was most rigorously forbidden in "normal society"—to take life. And in doing so they risk their own lives, whose preservation was the most basic individual instinct. Part of what made wartime Britain agreeable for many GIs is that, despite occasional bombs, the war seemed far away. For service troops that was particularly the case; even for combat units the routine of drills and marches could be a narcotic. Yet there were frequent intimations of mortality, whether it was an ammunition truck exploding or men being killed in a live-fire exercise. And who knew when the real fighting would start and what horrors it would bring? Death remained the GI's raison d'être and it touched all his human relations, in the Army and with the British.

For one group of GIs, moreover, Britain was in *no* way an inactive theatre in 1942 and 1943. American airmen were not waiting for war; most working days death was waiting for them. Theirs is a very special story.

17

Flyboys

★ ★ ★

ESTIMATED TIME OF ARRIVAL IS 1530. AS IT GETS NEAR, THE BASE BEGINS to come alive. Out they come, from the operations room, the mess hall, or the Aeroclub; officers and men, medics and ARC staff. Field ambulances and mobile control vans pull out onto the edge of the field. Ground crews reappear, having slept off their all-night exertions to get the B-17s ready for takeoff. Some men stand chatting or smoking. Others toss a baseball idly to and fro. But all keep glancing at the eastern sky. Suddenly a shout goes up from an officer with binoculars on the control-tower roof. Following his outstretched arm, straining eyes locate the first tiny specks on the horizon. A fuselage glints in the sunlight. The counting begins. Had they all come back? The specks get nearer and the familiar outline of a Flying Fortress takes shape. The lead plane is clearly damaged. Its landing gear is still not down. The one behind fires a double red flare—casualties on board. The ambulances rev up. In the Forts come, just clearing the church and the big trees by the farm. Along the village street, women stop chatting and gaze upward. Kids point at the smoke pouring from one of the planes.

This kind of scene was enacted almost daily in East Anglia for nearly three years from the summer of 1942. Its impact on those who flew and those who watched is the theme of this chapter. American airmen suffered unique stresses from their job as commuter combatants. And they forged particularly special relations with their host communities.

All the belligerents in World War Two bombed the enemy's home front to some degree. But most governments treated airpower more as a tactical than as a strategic weapon, to be used in support of ground troops or, particularly in the case of Japan, the Navy. To quote historian Richard Overy, "only Britain and the United States intended from the outset to pursue a bombing strategy and to devote large resources to it in the face of all the arguments for diverting such resources to other purposes." In the British case, Churchill was pushed along by the advocacy of "Bomber" Harris and others after France fell, because there seemed no other way to achieve victory, or even to strike back against Hitler. The diversion of resources that ensued was enormous. In consequence, tanks, transport aircraft, and landing craft—all vital to any invasion and ground war on the Continent—had to be bought largely from the United States. Even so, the results in 1940–41 were not impressive. Daylight raids incurred heavy losses while the hope of precision bombing at night proved chimerical. In desperation, Bomber Command shifted to a strategy of "area bombing," a euphemism for saturation attacks on industrial regions in the hope of undermining civilian morale as much as military production. Even this had limited effect. As Max Hastings has observed, "only America possessed the industrial resources to embark on strategic air warfare on the necessary scale to have decisive results within an acceptable period."[1]

The Americans were distinctive not merely in resources but in doctrine, namely daylight high-altitude precision bombing applied to strategic objectives and practiced in large, dense formations. Unlike the RAF, the Americans did not abandon the concept of daylight bombing. They believed that new technology made it possible to fly too high for enemy retaliation. Self-regulating oxygen systems for the crew and a turbo supercharger to keep the engines at maximum power enabled planes to operate at twenty-five thousand feet and more. Yet even at these heights the fabled Norden bombsight—an electromechanical computer—would permit remarkable accuracy and enable the enemy's key industrial targets to be singled out again and again. When enemy fighters proved more effective at great altitude than anticipated, the AAF increased the defensive armament on the planes, with several crew members acting as full-time operators of the revolving gun turrets. And flying in large, closely packed formations would maximize firepower and minimize fighter penetration.

That, at least, was the theory. In fact, strategic bombing proved less effective than its advocates believed and the costs were appallingly high for the young men who crewed the B-17s or the B-24 Liberators. In the two infamous raids on the Schweinfurt ball-bearings factories on 17 August and 14 October 1943, the 8th Air Force lost 36 bombers out of 230 despatched on the first occasion and 60 out of 320 on the second. The standard tour of duty for the members of a bomb crew was twenty-five combat missions. Conventional wisdom was that you had a one-in-three chance of going the distance, but for many airmen the odds seemed even worse. The 94th and 95th Bombardment Groups flew their first combat missions on 13 May 1943. A month later, on the evening of 13 June after a disastrous raid on Kiel, nearly half the original crews and planes had been lost and only nine missions had been completed. The 381st Bomb Group, flying out of Ridgewell, southeast of Cambridge, entered combat on 22 June 1943 with thirty-six crews. Ken Stone, a survivor, recalled: "We were a well-trained unit, our morale high." Even so, by 9 October, a little over three months later, the 381st had lost twenty-six of the original crews, a 72 percent loss. "Of the nine original crews in our squadron," Stone observed, "only two crews completed twenty-five missions."[2]

The biggest threat came from the enemy fighters that swarmed around the heavy bombers as soon as their own escorts dropped away because of their limited range. The Me-109s and FW-190s, often piloted by crack aces such as Goering's personal squadrons ("the Abbeville Kids"), would circle the bombers, steering well clear of their well-defended tails and picking off crews that were too green or too damaged to hold close formation. Their threat was not blunted until early 1944 when the new P-51 Mustang fighter, with long-range disposable fuel tanks, offered the prospect of fighter escort for the whole mission. Even the Mustang, however, did not eliminate the other great danger—flak from the German antiaircraft guns, which proved far more accurate than had been expected. John Butler of the 93rd Bomb Group wrote in his diary: "I can say with truth that I'd rather face fighter than flak. A fighter you can do something about, but flak you can't."[3] A pilot could not even take evasive action because he had to hold the plane on even course through its bomb run, making it an easier target for the German gunners.

Fighters and flak were not the only hazards. Numerous planes limped home only to crash and explode on landing. Others "bought the farm" on takeoff, when failure to get airborne in time meant almost certain death for a crew whose B-17 carried twenty-seven hundred gallons of fuel and fifty hundred-pound bombs. Just flying at high altitude carried its own dangers. A fault in the oxygen supply could render a man unconscious in a couple of minutes. Frostbite was commonplace at temperatures of fifty or sixty degrees below freezing, even with heated flying suits. Sometimes crew members had to don emergency oxygen packs and climb out onto a narrow catwalk above the open bomb doors to dislodge unreleased bombs into the English Channel far below. Even if nothing went wrong, ten or eleven hours in a tiny ball turret—knees pulled up, hanging into space—left one cramped, shocked, and exhausted. And it was never prudent to drop one's guard. At dusk on 7 June 1944, as the 34th Bomb Group was landing at its base at Mendlesham, near Stowmarket, after a mission, four B-24s were shot down in as many minutes by Me-410s. (Ironically, the group lost no planes to German fighters over *enemy* territory in all its 170 operations from Mendlesham!)[4] Little wonder that, after debriefing from a mission, many of these young, fit men in their early twenties collapsed onto their beds and slept without undressing.

What made danger and fatigue much worse was the uncertainty. Though ordinary crew members received their first official intimation when the operations officer snapped on the lights in their hut at 2:00 or 3:00 in the morning, telltale signs could be observed beforehand. For Harry Crosby, a navigator with the "Bloody Hundredth" at Thorpe Abbotts in Norfolk, it was when the red light flashed on during a movie in the base cinema, indicating that field orders had arrived, and the "bigwigs" in row seven trooped out amid a grim silence. John Comer, with the 381st at Ridgewell, used to scan the mess in the evenings for the armorers. If they were absent en masse, then it was a fair guess that they were at the bomb dump—sometimes known as "Boom Town"—preparing the next day's loads.[5] Once a mission was in the offing, many found it hard to sleep that night. Until the briefing, no one knew whether it would be a suicide mission into the Ruhr, or a "milk run" over the Belgian coast (and everyone quickly learned that there were no milk runs). Even after a 4 A.M. breakfast—real eggs and other delicacies for the men about to be hanged—and you were into the aircraft, you might have to fret around for an hour on the hardstanding before being given clearance for takeoff.

At any stage in the whole process, even when airborne, the mission might be aborted on account of bad weather—usually heavy cloud over the base or the target. During the 8AF's time in Britain, a quarter of all days were nonoperational because of weather. Hiram Drache of the 457th Bomb Group reckoned that "the frustrations of weather probably caused as much suspense as enemy action." G. W. Pederson, a gunner with the 306th, was briefed for at least forty missions more than he flew.

> I'd get all that adrenaline flowing and tension built up, and go through the work of getting the guns ready. Then we'd be told the mission was delayed an hour. This compounded the tension. We'd wait the hour and then they'd come around again to say it's delayed another hour. This sometimes went on for several hours. Then,

finally, the mission would be scrubbed. It was always a great letdown. . . . [6]

The AAF had its own ways of trying to minimize the sense of danger
and insecurity. A dead crewman became a nonperson almost instanta-
neously. In some cases his belongings were cleared out of the hut
before the other crew members came back from their debriefing. Billeting officers did the same thing for the crews of overdue planes. Medical
reports acknowledged that heavy casualties had a serious effect on
men's morale: "the sight of one of our airplanes blowing up in mid-air,
the presence of dead crew personnel in the returning airplane, or the
presence of mutilated and wounded crew members . . . are the most
harrowing phases of their experience." Internally, the stress built up
and men coped with it in different ways. Some spent hours evolving
their own probability theories about the chances of survival. Many
became intensely superstitious, taking special coins, love letters, or
baby shoes on missions. One pilot always wore the same sweatshirt.
Not even heavy smoking and drinking could provide relief. A navigator at Grafton Underwood stopped eating in the flying officers' mess: "I
didn't know any of them anymore. I ate with the ground crew instead.
They were still the same men as when I'd arrived." Others went numb.
After Robert Bieck at Old Buckenham in Norfolk had been "hit hard"
by the loss of his closest friends, he "elected to be as distant as possible"
short of "being a jerk."[7]

Near the end of a tour, the tension became almost intolerable. John
Comer developed intense neck pains. He went to the flight surgeon
who gave him a thorough examination and then asked how many
missions Comer had flown.

"Twenty-four, Sir."

"Are you getting nervous about the twenty-fifth?"

"Oh, not much—some men sweat it out, but it doesn't bother me."

"All right, Comer. I think I know what your problem is. I'm going
to give you some pills. Take one when the pain bothers you and before
going to bed at night."

He went into the next room, but Comer caught sight of him in a
mirror on the wall. He was laughing. An orderly handed him a bottle
and he came back, serious-faced again.

"Here you are. Now take these and I'm sure you will be okay in a
week or two."

Comer threw the placebos in the first trash can he passed. On his
twenty-fifth mission he was in excruciating pain and had hardly slept
the previous night. Yet within ninety minutes of landing safely he

suddenly realized that the pains had gone. "Never before had I any conception of what effect tight nerves can create in an otherwise healthy body."[8]

This struggle for physical and mental survival was usually waged in the grimmest surroundings. A few groups did enjoy relatively palatial accommodation. The 91st was transferred to Bassingbourn, southwest of Cambridge, in October 1942, supposedly as a temporary measure while the runway at Kimbolton in Huntingdonshire was being lengthened. Bassingbourn was an RAF airfield opened in 1938, which had been constructed to prewar standards. The barracks were two-storey brick buildings with steam central heating—a far cry from the damp Nissen huts of Kimbolton. Legend has it that the 91st's commander, Col. Stanley Wray—a well-known humourist who once told his men that any crash landing should take place in a field of brussels sprouts— actually moved his men to Bassingbourn without permission, so impressed was he with the facilities. Certainly, most air bases were more like Kimbolton: Nissen huts moored in a sea of mud. (The 384th Bomb Group quickly renamed their base, at Grafton Underwood in Northamptonshire, Grafton Undermud.) The stove in the middle of the Nissen hut was inadequate except in summer, and showers were usually some distance away—"four walls and no roof," as John Pendleton recalled at Attlebridge.[9]

Jammed together in a small hut, the men tended to get on each other's nerves, particularly during the frequent spells of bad weather. In the second half of November 1943 John Comer's crew took off from Ridgewell eight times without getting in a mission.

> That was hard on morale. Being confined too much of the time to the small metal quarters, we became irritating to each other. Sometimes Lancia's noise became abrasive and Wilson's disorderly bunk was always revolting to a person like me, who wanted things neat and shipshape. There were days when Rogers withdrew into a morose silence and ignored the rest of us. When he was in those moods it was better to leave him alone. Tedesco's continual harping on Brooklyn and New York got on my nerves. Hadn't he been anywhere else before he was drafted into the service?[10]

Danger, stress, and privation were not peculiar to airmen. At Alconbury near Huntingdon, on the evening of 27 May 1943, ground crew were loading bombs on to a B-17 when a five-hundred-pounder suddenly detonated, setting off several others. Eighteen men were killed and twenty-one injured by the blast (and four B-17s completely destroyed). Ground crews also struggled with their own psychological tensions. Most were dedicated to the planes they serviced, which were often flown by the same aircrews. Carl Gjelhaug of the 446th, a young replacement pilot of twenty, was fussing around his Liberator when the crew chief—an "old-timer" of thirty—came over and said quietly, "Lieutenant, there's one thing you don't have to worry about and that's the condition of this aircraft. It's been preflighted for you and always will be. You take my word on it." (Gjelhaug did, and lived never to regret it.) Like airmen, many ground crew had to develop a façade of professional detachment. Cleaning up after a raid could involve blood, clothing, even pieces of a body. The 100th crew chief Clarence Schroepfer, who arrived at Thorpe Abbotts in 1943, admitted: "We had gotten close to the early crews, but so many were lost we didn't want to know the later ones." The long, repetitive work also drained their physical and mental stamina, without the release enjoyed by aircrew after a successful raid and, eventually, a completed tour of duty. No twenty-five missions for them. An 8AF report in August 1944 found that the morale of ground crews

> was at a low ebb. Most of the ground crews and ground staff have been in this theater for from one to two years. Ground crew work is arduous, tedious and monotonous. The crews often work night after night and consequently they suffer from as much or more fatigue than the combat crews. Their activities are more restricted than combat crews, they have less time to themselves and fewer opportunities to leave their stations.[11]

The same stories could be told of the growing number of fighter bases in ETO—both those engaged in escort duty with the 8th and those of the 9th Air Force, established in autumn 1943 to provide tactical support for ground troops in the forthcoming invasion of Europe. Their ground crews experienced the same pressures of hard work, long hours, and suppressed loss. For fighter pilots, the target was three hundred combat hours, which might mean anything from sixty to eighty missions. Particularly at long range over Germany, the demands on Mustang pilots in 1944–45 could be even worse than on bomb crews because they were alone in the aircraft. As well as flying and firing, they had to act as their own navigators—a tough task in cloud-covered Europe—and no one was there to help if there was a problem with the oxygen supply.

For all concerned, in the planes and on the ground, there was no escape from the excitement, tension, and uncertainties. No escape—

Mess call on board a troopship bound for Northern Ireland, February 1942. Some men are wearing life belts.

Inside their cramped Nissen hut, men from a U.S. Navy aircrew while away an evening in March 1944.

A typical wartime base: Nissen huts at Lopcombe Corner Camp on the Wiltshire-Hampshire border, 13 July 1943.

Construction on an air base in Essex, April 1944. The U.S. censor has blanked out the unit markings on the planes.

U.S. ARMY MILITARY HISTORY INSTITUTE

Crews of the 97th Bomb Group mount their bikes on leaving the briefing room at Grafton Underwood in Northamptonshire in the summer of 1942.

In the Dove Inn at Burton
Bradstock, Dorset.

A dance at a British
Women's Land Army camp
at Culford, Suffolk.

An American airman and his British date at a London cinema in March 1944, under the gaze of Errol Flynn.

Men from the 100th Bomb Group rehearse Handel's *Messiah* with local women in Dickelburgh Church, Norfolk, late 1943.

In the entrance hall of the American Red Cross Club in Norwich (the Bishop's Palace), unemancipated GIs wait while British volunteers sew on their buttons.

Anticipation in a West Country village as GIs unload a truck for a Christmas party in 1944.

In Bath U.S. military police pose with four-year-old Billy Hobbs—adopted as their mascot after he had broken his leg.

At a pub near Hemel Hempstead in Hertfordshire, black GIs from an American trucking company relax with the landlord and a local "bobby" after a training march, 17 June 1942.

From a "black-staffed" American Red Cross Clubmobile (a converted London bus), Clarice Brooks of New York dispenses coffee and doughnuts to black GIs in the field.

Black GIs parade through Trafalgar Square during the "Salute the Soldier" week,
30 March 1944.

Making strategy at Quebec in August 1943. From right to left: Churchill, Roosevelt, and Mackenzie King of Canada; behind them, Adm. William D. Leahy, Adm. Sir Dudley Pound, Gen. George C. Marshall, Field Marshal Sir John Dill, Adm. Ernest J. King, Gen. Sir Alan Brooke, Air Marshal Sir Charles Portal, Gen. "Hap" Arnold.

Gen. Dwight D. Eisenhower reviews men of the 29th Infantry Division at Tavistock, Devon, on 4 February 1944. To his right is their commander, Gen. Charles H. Gerhardt.

Slapton Sands from the air, with inland lagoon, after exercise Fox, 14 March 1944. Naval gunfire has pockmarked the beach and completely destroyed a former hotel.

Landing on Slapton Sands during one of the Fabius exercises, May 1944.

As GIs await
embarkation for
D-Day near a South
Coast port, life goes
on for the locals.

Loading for D-Day at Brixham in Devon.

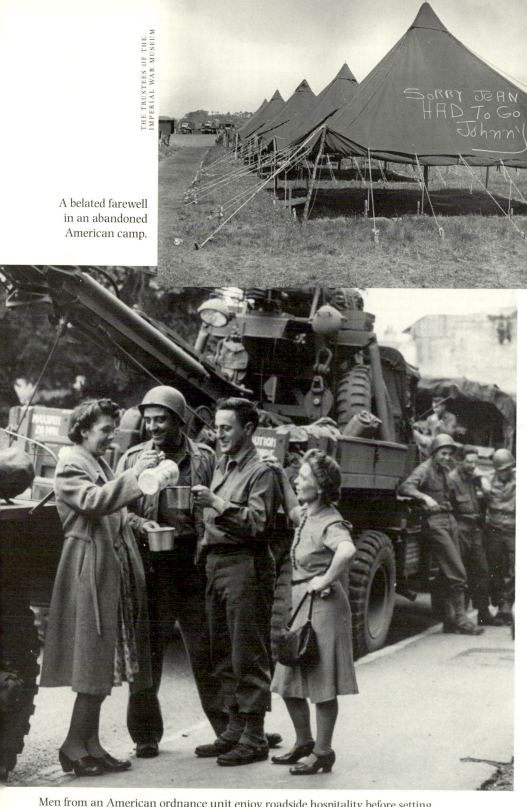

A belated farewell
in an abandoned
American camp.

Men from an American ordnance unit enjoy roadside hospitality before setting
out for France, 24 July 1944.

Madingley Cemetery near Cambridge with some of the first American dead to be interred there—a picture released for Memorial Day, May 1944.

GIs and other soldiers perched atop the boarded-up statue of Eros in Piccadilly Circus on VE Day, 8 May 1945. The Stars and Stripes hang from the balcony of the ARC's Rainbow Corner club a little way up Shaftesbury Avenue on the right.

In the bombed-out shell of Coventry Cathedral, GIs from a nearby convalescent hospital attend a Mother's Day service on 13 May 1945.

Andrew and Irene on
their wedding day in
June 1945.

Brides, some with babies, at Tidworth Station en route to the nearby
staging camp, February 1946.

but certainly safety valves. Such were the pressures on base that AF medical officers considered it "essential that 48-hour passes be granted every two weeks with seven day leave after 15 to 20 missions." This kind of statement would have evoked a hollow laugh from most men. A survey in May 1944 indicated that, of those with more than fifteen missions, only one-third had been given a furlough since they started combat flying. Of those who had been flying combat missions for a month or more, about a quarter had not had even a twenty-four-hour pass. May 1944 was, admittedly, a busy time, in the buildup to D-Day, but the figures were not atypical. What upset men as much as the infrequency of passes was their unpredictability. They were often told only just beforehand and did not have time to plan. This was because command was loath to let fliers off base, given the hazards of the weather, and, when they were released en masse, it was usually because bad weather was certain or the men were exhausted.[12]

In the last week of July 1943, for instance, a predicted few days of high pressure permitted Gen. Eaker to mount a frenetic series of raids on Germany—what became known as Blitz Week. By its end, 8AF operational strength was down from 330 aircraft and crews to under 200. The effect on the survivors was evident. Although 31 July "dawned warm and clear," the 100th's group history records that its men were "fast going stale" due to "so many hard missions in quick succession and not enough relaxation." Then "someone broke down and lifted pass restrictions." Half the combat crews were given immediate passes and, to help the rest relax, about 150 English women from Norwich and Bury St. Edmunds were bussed in that evening for a dance in the officers' club. Those GIs with passes were hastily summoned back from London on 2 August, only to sit around fuming on base the following day because bad weather over the Continent ruled out the anticipated mission.[13]

The psychological function of passes to London is best indicated by John Comer's story of the 381st after the first Schweinfurt raid on 17 August 1943. From twenty-six planes the group despatched, eleven were lost and 101 crew were missing. Next morning few men turned up for breakfast. Those who did ate silently and quickly. Comer found that "the long rows of empty tables took away my appetite. Only yesterday men were crowding in line waiting for seats." On the 19th, much to the men's surprise, they put up a squadron for a raid over Holland, but morale remained low. On the 20th, in the middle of the morning, the loudspeaker on base started blasting: "All combat personnel report to Operations." On the way over there was much bitching and in the Operations Room "gloomy silence until we were all assembled." Then came an amazing announcement—every combat man would receive a four-day pass. Personnel trucks would leave at 1:30 P.M. and take men to the outskirts of London where they could catch the underground into the centre. When the cheering died down, the officer continued: "This pass will be mandatory unless excused by the Flight Surgeons." A voice shouted out: "But some of us are broke. Hell, we can't take off for London with no money!" The answer came back: "We thought of that. The Finance Officer is standing by to issue an advance on your next pay, for all those who need it." As Comer reflected later:

> The whole thing was organized superbly. The Command obviously wanted all of us away from the base, away from the empty tables at the combat mess, away from the empty bunks in the huts. They wanted us to rid ourselves of whatever tensions had built up inside. Someone at headquarters was smart enough to know that the best therapy was a big blast—a wild weekend that would let it all come out.

That is what happened. On their last night in London Comer and his buddies did not get back to their hotel till 4 A.M. By the time they woke up it was too late for breakfast. They set off around the pubs in a "superbender" that ended with Comer being carried senseless onto the train back to Ridgewell.[14]

Wartime Britain was therefore not merely the backdrop against which the airmen's drama was played out, it was also a part of the action. As Harry Crosby of the 100th observed, "at nine o'clock in the morning we could be bombing Berlin and at midnight at a fancy dance in London."[15] Even if there wasn't a pass at the end of the mission, the sense of schizophrenia was still acute—a morning's hell over Hitler's Reich, then back to the rural tranquility of an East Anglian afternoon. Noise and silence, war and peace, death and life. For some, the contrasts only added to their inner tension. For others, they offered essential release from the pressures of an all-male struggle for survival. The result was often a very special relationship with the local communities.

To many GIs the countryside of Suffolk, Norfolk, and Cambridgeshire seemed the epitome of "Merrie Olde England"—with their churches, pubs, and manor houses, their winding lanes, thick hedges, and thatched cottages that seemed to stretch back into the mists of time. Not merely antiquated but positively primitive—cars were a rarity, the horse still did much of the ploughing, and outside privies and water pumps seemed the norm. In fact, the East Anglia they knew was a product of recent history. Its backward character owed much to the steady collapse of grain prices since the 1870s, in part the result of an earlier American invasion—cheap grain. Although there had been a respite in World War One, the Slump of 1929–32 was "almost unparalleled in its severity" with a price fall of over one-third. People moved away and some of the best arable soil in England deteriorated into parkland and grazing. Chronic poverty was the fate of those who remained. Unlike the bulk of American farmers, who were owner-occupiers, those in East Anglia were predominantly tenant farmers and farm labourers, working the estates of larger landowners. Income for everyone declined and there seemed little incentive for modernization. East Anglia in the 1930s might be considered England's equivalent of America's "Deep South," not in its race problem but in the preponderance of tenant farmers and rural poverty. Jamie McIver, who, like a number of energetic lowland Scots, came down to farm in Suffolk during the Slump, was appalled at what he found. "Dereliction. The fields were wet, the hedges like forests. The East Anglian farmer had lived with his decline so long that he couldn't move, he couldn't think. There he was bogged down in the best corn area of England with ruin right up to his farmhouse door."[16]

In retrospect, it is clear that World War Two marked the start of a revolutionary transformation in English agriculture, particularly in East Anglia. Faced with Nazi blockade, the government paid high, subsidized prices for grain and offered hefty financial incentives to turn grassland back to the plough. By the end of the war the total arable acreage had almost returned to that of the halcyon days of the 1860s. Higher prices also encouraged greater efficiency. Tractors, milking machines, and even combine harvesters became more common. And the conveniences of modernity came as well. By the end of the war much of rural East Anglia had electric lighting and mains sewerage. "A degree of modernization had occurred in six years of war which might have taken decades in peacetime."[17] It was the beginnings of the mechanized, labour-intensive, heavily subsidized modern era of English farming.

In 1942, however, this second agricultural revolution was only beginning to take off in East Anglia. The region remained overwhelmingly rural. Even Norwich boasted only about 125,000 people in the 1930s; Ipswich had barely 90,000, and Cambridge 80,000. In the villages and small towns, few of which numbered more than three thousand people, the old ways still prevailed. To an outsider like Jamie McIver, the traditionalism seemed a product of geography as much as history. "The big skies leave the East Anglians empty. . . . There is nothing for a man to measure himself by here. In Scotland you have the hills, the mountains. They diminish a man."[18] Nineteen forty-two saw something against which to measure oneself—the air bases. For many villages, they were the biggest event for centuries.

All over England, of course, new military bases and depots sprang up during the war. But often this entailed an expansion of existing facilities, as in the Salisbury area. What was distinctive about East Anglia was the extent and scale of totally new construction. This region was the prime site for the bomber offensive against Germany: flat land, few big towns, and close proximity to the Continent. In 1942–43 a vast "U" of bomber and fighter bases was etched out around the fens, stretching from the vicinity of Peterborough in the northwest past Cambridge and down to Chelmsford in Essex before thrusting northeast via Ipswich to end in a thick wedge around Norwich (map 17A). Although RAF Bomber Command moved the centre of its operations north to Lincolnshire and Yorkshire, it continued to operate out of local airfields such as Bourn and Mildenhall, so the American occupation was compounded by a continued British presence as well. By 1943, as one Whitehall memo had predicted, East Anglia had become "a mosaic of aerodromes five miles apart." That, in itself, was a huge intrusion into small, quiet, rural communities. What made the American impact even greater was that their bases were largely for heavy bombers. Even where the 8th took over RAF airfields, the grass or metal-meshed strip had to be replaced by a concrete main runway well over a mile in length. In addition, two subsidiary runways and several miles of concrete perimeter track and hardstanding had to be laid. A typical base such as Ridgewell in Essex also required thirty miles of drains, five hundred separate buildings, and a sewerage plant for twenty-five hundred people.[19]

Most of these bases took six months to construct and none of those nearby would forget the noise, the technology, and the invasion of Irish navvies or black GIs to build them. But the finished product was even more remarkable. The "Aeronautical Correspondent" of *The Times* visited some of the early American bases, taken over from the RAF, in August 1942. His article, headlined U.S. AIR FORCE SETTLE IN ALL-AMERICAN AIRFIELDS, caused some offence in Whitehall, where its image of the Yanks' self-sufficiency was deemed undesirable, but it gives a vivid sense of the novelty of the American presence. The visit, he wrote, was like making

an impossibly fast journey to America. At one moment one is driving along a typical English country road, and the next, as if by magic,

MAP 17A

8TH Air Force Bases
in East Anglia
June 1944
(Based on C&C 2: p. 647)

- ✪ COMMAND HQ
- ❸ BOMBARDMENT DIVISION HQ
- ◇ FIGHTER WING HQ
- ◆ FIGHTER GROUP AIRDROME
- ● HEAVY BOMB GROUP AIRDROME
- ○ TRAINING AIRDROME
- ⊠ RECONNAISSANCE AIRDROME
- ▲ STRATEGIC AIR DEPOT (SAD)
- ■ CITIES/TOWNS

N

The Wash

WENDLING
ATTLEBRIDGE
HORSHAM ST. FAITH
SHIPDHAM
RACKHEATH
NORTH PICKENHAM
DEOPHAM GREEN
Norwich
❷ KETTERINGHAM HALL
NEATON
BODNEY
HETHEL
WATTON
Great Yarmouth
OLD BUCKENHAM
SEETHING
E. WRETHAM
HARDWICK
BUNGAY
SNETTERTON HEATH
TIBENHAM
METFIELD
ELVEDEN HALL ❸
KNETTISHALL
THORPE ABBOTTS
HALESWORTH
HONINGTON
EYE
HORHAM
TROSTON
GREAT ASHFIELD
BURY ST. EDMUNDS
MENDLESHAM
FRAMLINGHAM
RATTLESDEN
LAVENHAM
WATTISHAM
DEBACH
LEISTON
RIDGEWELL
▲ HITCHAM
MARTLESHAM
SUDBURY
Ipswich
RAYDON
WORMINGFORD
BOXTED

WALCOT HALL
KINGS CLIFFE
DEENETHORPE
POLEBROOK
GRAFTON UNDERWOOD
GLATTON
MOLESWORTH
ABBOTS RIPTON
HARRINGTON
ALCONBURY
CHELVESTON
❶ BRAMPTON GRANGE
KIMBOLTON
PODINGTON
THURLEIGH
Cambridge
BOTTISHAM
MILTON ERNEST ✪
VIII SERVICE COMMAND HQ
SAWSTON
BASSINGBOURN
Bedford
DUXFORD
STEEPLE MORDEN
FOWLMERE
SAFFRON WALDEN
NUTHAMPSTEAD
DEBDEN

○ CHEDDINGTON (BOMBER)
✪ VIII COMPOSITE COMMAND HQ

○ BOVINGDON (BOMBER)
✪ VIII FIGHTER COMMAND HQ
BUSHEY HALL

✪ 8TH AIR FORCE HQ
HIGH WYCOMBE

BUSHY PARK ✪
USSTAF HQ

River Thames

London

one is transported 3,000 miles across the Atlantic. . . . All trace of British occupation has disappeared so completely that it is difficult to believe that the aerodromes were ever the homes of R.A.F. squadrons. The aircraft are American, and so are the petrol trailers, lorries, mobile workshops, bomb-trolleys, "jeeps" (powerful little passenger cars), salvage vehicles, and all the thousand and one pieces of equipment without which an air force could not function. . . . The Americans are not relying on this country for even the smallest items; they have actually brought with them their own dustbins—garbage cans, they call them.[20]

A bomber base might cover as much as five hundred acres and serve as home for two or three thousand GIs. They would outnumber even a reasonable-size town such as Oundle in Northamptonshire, whose fourteen hundred population were barely two miles from AAF Station 110 at Polebrook. There were other vast U.S. installations around Britain, of course, but even the biggest supply depot, such as Ashchurch near Cheltenham, lacked the drama and awesome technology of Polebrook or Ridgewell. Rows of jeeps, forklifts, and 2½-ton trucks simply could not compare with a squadron of B-17s lined up, engines roaring, ready for takeoff. Any day the "big birds" could be readily seen by the locals. Unlike airfields back in America, where thousands of remote acres could be set aside and fenced in, British bases seemed wide open. On the 490th's airfield at Eye in Suffolk, one set of hardstandings had to be built on the other side of the main Ipswich-to-Norwich road. A permanent guard and gates were required to stop traffic whenever aircraft taxied to and fro. On the 100th's first Sunday at Thorpe Abbots in June 1943, "dozens, if not hundreds of people," jammed the narrow lanes around the base, eager to look at the planes, some of which were parked only a few feet from the road. The hamlet of Upper Billingford actually lay within the airfield perimeter. One house, the Taylor's, was next to the petrol store, and Lodge Farm lay a few yards from the perimeter track. (On 26 November 1943 one of Farmer Draper's outbuildings was partly demolished by the aborted takeoff of a B-17 appropriately named *Hang the Expense*.) Even for those at safer distances, the noise made the air base an unforgettable part of daily life. One woman, a wartime teenager in Oundle, recalled:

Every morning about 5 A.M. we would be awakened by the "preflight"—the warming up of the engines of squadrons of giant B-17s across the fields at Polebrook. By breakfast they would be taking off, low over our roofs, climbing in threes to gather in vast formations, high in the sky. . . . In the afternoon they would return, we'd hear the thunder of their engines and pause in our games as they limped back, now in two's and three's, low over the Northamptonshire fields. . . .

On any clear day the B-17s left their signatures for hours in white contrails scrawled across the blue sky.[21]

Despite their striking air of Americanized self-sufficiency, no base was an island, entire unto itself. Many of them had very poor recreational facilities, particularly in 1942–43. Even the larger ones later in the war, equipped with movie theatres and ARC Aeroclubs, could not keep most of the men on base during free evenings—the need to get out of the tense, militarized environment was too great. What helped them to do so was the prevalence of bicycles, more evident on air bases than on other U.S. installations because of the size of the base and the lack of public transport in these rural areas. As soon as they arrived, newcomers were advised to go into a nearby big town, such as Cambridge or Norwich, and purchase a secondhand bike. (Some "borrowed" them from RAF bases.) Mastering their new mounts was not always easy. Some GIs had never ridden a bike before and those who had were often used to coaster brakes, whereby one slowed down by reversing the direction of the pedals, rather than lever brakes on the handlebars. There was also the English perversity of keeping to the left of the road—many GIs omitted to do so and paid the penalty—and the blackout was an added hazard, especially after an evening in the pub.

Apart from their independence, what also helped to bring airmen into the local community was their longevity in the area. Even aircrew could be around for a half year or more—the first 8AF twenty-five-mission tour of duty lasted from September 1942 until April 1943. Three-month tours were largely a phenomenon of the easier days of 1945. Ground crew, who outnumbered airmen something like twenty to one, had no term of duty and were often at the same base for a year or more. This made them far more settled than most combat or service troops. Some units were a fixity for several years. The record was held by the 306th Bomb Group, which was based at Thurleigh near Bedford from September 1942 until December 1945, during which time it flew 342 missions, but the 91st enjoyed the pleasures of "Country Club" Bassingbourn from October 1942 to June 1945, and the 351st was at Polebrook from April 1943 until June 1945.[22]

For all these reasons the U.S. bases made an enormous impact on the nearby communities—their size and technology, their proximity and audibility, the independence and continuity of many of their residents. Most of all, they were at war. This set the airmen in East Anglia apart from GIs in the rest of Britain.

What grated most about the American occupation for British people in 1942–44 was the Yanks' inactivity. The high jinks, loud mouths, and heavy spending would have been forgiven more readily if there had seemed some point to their presence. One can capture the mood in the diary of *Daily Mirror* director Cecil King, which, in 1942–43, was full of gossip and jokes against the GIs. Here are some examples:

On 6 October 1942 King reported an encounter with two "very drunk" GIs on the train home the previous evening. "They expressed some admiration for Hitler, contempt and dislike for England" but "the only subject on which they got very animated was negroes. If they could have a chance of shooting their own American negroes over here, then their journey would indeed have been well worth while. They may have been a particularly poor pair, but they didn't look it, and on their performance yesterday I should say their morale was at zero and their military value very near nil." On 19 March 1943 he was recording the gossip from North Africa, namely that "the Americans are at present useless, rather like the Italians. They can organize transport well and repair tanks well, but as fighters they just don't compete." The entry for 23 September 1943 was devoted to a third-hand anecdote about "two very sloppy American soldiers" in a London park who encountered a British general and, instead of saluting, called out: "Well, skirty-pants who's winning the war now?" And on 26 November King noted some stories about recent unprovoked assaults by GIs and wrote that: "Anti-American feeling is still a burning subject. It appears that though we see Americans at every street corner, this is nothing to what is in store. If there are to be three times as many Americans, I reckon we can look to an increase of nine times in the intensity of anti-American feeling."[23]

Cecil King was an acidulous observer (the published version of his diaries is disingenuously mistitled *With Malice Toward None*) but the truth and representativeness of these stories are not relevant here. What they illustrate is London gossip of the time, noted by someone with a keen anti-American ear. In London, or in provincial centres such as Salisbury or Bristol, the GIs seemed to be over here and underemployed.

Even in East Anglia relations were far from perfect. Some airmen loathed the squalor of their surroundings. A few called England "Goatland" because of the strong unwashed smell emanating from some of the rural natives. The end-of-month payday often spelled trouble as tense men with money to burn spilled into the nearby towns on liberty runs. Drunken escapes from the mounting losses or a riotous celebration of a completed tour were commonplace and these often occurred in local pubs. Many women at a base party sensed an air of sexual aggression, particularly after a mission. VD rates were also consistently higher in the AAF than for ground combat forces in Britain. The Army Medical Department's history adds that there was little difference between the experience of the SOS and AAF, but, "in general, the highest rates for any of the three groups were among troops of the Air Forces, the only troops then actively engaged in combat." Although the high AAF VD rate is often ascribed to ground crews, this was by no means always the case. "The worst incidence in the 8th Air Force for several months in 1944," noted Roger Freeman, "was the [379th] bomb group stationed at Kimbolton which also had the best operational record of all similar organisations in the Command." This coincidence was also apparent in the RAF, where, for most of the war, "VD was more prevalent in Bomber Command than in any other RAF command." A forty-eight-hour superbender around Piccadilly by a frazzled combat squadron could have dramatic consequences for the station's VD rate.[24]

Such violence and promiscuity, however understandable, could alienate the local people. Yet, more often than not, the air war seems to have brought GIs and civilians closer together. The spectacular drama of takeoff and the oft-time tragedy of homecoming were almost daily events for the local villages. Ten B-17s and ninety-eight men from Bassingbourn were lost on the Schweinfurt raid on 17 August 1943, but locals didn't need access to the classified statistics to know that something had gone dreadfully wrong. Michael Bowyer watched the Flying Fortresses take off over Bassingbourn that morning. That evening, he saw them come back very late, the Bassingbourn contingent "within a gaggle of 36 with nine trailing behind, two of which could be seen with engines out of action." Next morning, there were only three B-17s out on the hardstandings and "it was common knowledge locally that the 91st had suffered very badly." In the pubs, landlords and regulars would mark the absences. An ATS woman stationed near Bedford recalled how "when we used to call in at the pub and enquire 'Where's Tex?' or 'Where's Pennsylvania?' they would just say that they hadn't made it back." Likewise Ruby Kranz, then a teenager: "Since we counted the planes out and back, we knew how many were missing . . . we always wondered who they were. Then we'd hear about how, on base, this man or that man cried, because mates were gone."[25]

In these circumstances, the positive bonds, where they formed, were all the stronger. For local boys the GIs' attractions were deeper than gum. A huge propeller aircraft nearing takeoff seemed like a living thing, a great dragon, clawing the air to pull itself off the ground in a frenzied roar. Many kids spent hours hanging around the base perimeters, fascinated by the spectacle, and some became devoted mascots of the local units. For some GIs the local pubs were their recreation; others might find their outlet in a church choir. In either case, the welcome was usually warm and the affection mutual. "They were far more uninhibited than the British," recalled one Suffolk woman, then an ARC volunteer. "They *talked* about homesickness. They *admitted* fear. . . . There was no stiff upper lip. If it had been a good raid with few lost there was a happy atmosphere, but if it was a bad one a terrible air of depression hung over the whole place." And for an airman adopted by an English family, the bond often had a special strength and value. At Christmas 1943 Saul Kupferman of the 306th accepted a blind invitation from the Nicholls of nearby Bedford. "It was one of the best things I've ever done in my life!" he wrote later. "They became 'my' family for the nearly eight months I was in England." Looking back, he felt that "the love and friendship they offered me during those trying times, as well as the home atmosphere, played an important part in my survival."[26]

At first glance, it would seem that equally special relations were forged between AAF commanders and their RAF counterparts. The advocates of strategic bombing on both sides quickly combined in 1942 to advance their common cause—Gen. Eaker of the 8th AF and his counterpart at RAF Bomber Command, Air Chief Marshal Sir Arthur Harris; and their superiors Gen. Arnold and Air Chief Marshal Sir Charles Portal, chief of the air staff in London. Harris and Eaker are "in each other's pockets," Portal observed in January 1943. In February 1943 Portal sent Arnold arguments to strengthen his hand in the battle for greater resources for the 8th AF. The outcome of this cooperation was, on the face of it, highly successful. The Casablanca conference of January 1943 sanctioned the "heaviest possible bomber offensive against the German war effort." Moreover, this was to take the form of an Anglo-American "Combined Bomber Offensive" (CBO) aimed at "the progressive destruction and dislocation of the German military, industrial and economic system, and the undermining of the morale of the German people to a point where their capacity for armed resistance is fatally weakened." Arnold and Portal joined forces at the Washington conference in May to push through more detailed plans and in June 1943 the directive for the CBO (code-named Pointblank) was approved.[27]

Yet, on closer inspection, overlap between the two air wars was strictly limited. The Casablanca bombing directive was part of the usual Anglo-American fudge at such conferences. Phrases from rival documents were patched together in the final policy directives to give everyone something of what he wanted. Casablanca left the U.S. Navy much leeway to prosecute its war in the Pacific, it gave Churchill and Brooke authority to push on with operations in the Mediterranean, and it retained for Marshall and the U.S. Army their cherished aim of "the decisive defeat of Germany in 1943." The bombing directive had the same air of compromise about it. The clause about fatally weakening Germany's capacity for armed resistance enabled the two armies to argue that bombing was not totally autonomous, but the emphasis on destroying Germany's "military, industrial and economic system" left Eaker free to get on with "precision bombing" of selected industrial targets, while the words "undermining of the morale of the German people" sanctioned Harris's campaign of area bombing of population centres. In short, agreement on paper legitimized divergence in practice.[28]

This is what happened. Pointblank became largely an American operation, aimed at destroying the long-term Luftwaffe threat through targeting the German aircraft industry on the ground. The RAF's role, in deference to Harris, was left vague: "as far as practicable to be complementary to the operations of the Eighth Air Force." The year from March 1943 marked the apogee of his philosophy of area bombing, aimed at the Ruhr, Hamburg, and Berlin. Likewise, Arnold's hopes for an integrated command for the CBO, akin to Eisenhower's in the Mediterranean, resulted only in a loose advisory committee under Portal. The divergent strategies were partly to blame, but there were also larger diplomatic reasons. Max Hastings has observed that "Bomber Command was Britain's last entirely independent contribution to the Allied war effort, gripping the imagination of the British people and much of occupied Europe. As the enormous build-up of American air power developed in 1943 and 1944, the British were determined to ensure that Harris's forces were not submerged."[29]

The official British history of strategic bombing concluded that "for most of 1943 there was no combined offensive, but, on the contrary, a bombing competition."[30] Although the air war could bring Americans and Britons very close on the ground, it remained divisive among commanders. Once again, "real life" and "high policy" operated in separate compartments.

18

Negroes

★　★　★

"I MUST TELL YOU SOMETHING INTERESTING," WROTE A YOUNG WOMAN student from southeast London to a friend in April 1943. One day various GIs and white British soldiers were at a canteen for Allied troops, as well as a coloured airman from one of the British Dominions. Then

> an American airman walked in, and seeing the coloured airman quietly sitting at a table, strolled up to him and slashed [slapped] him across the face! Of course everyone jumped up ready for a fight but the proprietress managed to stop it. Someone said "send for the U.S. police" but the Americans tried to pass it off, and said that if the coloured man would go, everything would be all right. The British said if anyone ought to go it was the American. A schoolmistress who was helping at the back, dashed out and slashed [slapped] the American's face, and her language was very choice! Anyway, they smuggled him out, but our men said if they saw him again they'd kill him and all the rest of it. Meanwhile, the coloured man sat there as if dazed, it was unexpected and so unwarranted. It seems amazing that the Americans are fighting on our side, when you hear things like that.[1]

This was one of many such incidents around Britain in 1942–45. To a degree that may seem surprising today, British people transcended the stereotypes about "negroes" and welcomed nonwhite GIs. The nature of that welcome and its effect on black Americans are the themes of this chapter.

★　★　★

In the eighteen months from December 1942 to D-Day, the number of nonwhite GIs in Britain grew from 7,000 to 130,000. The 844th Engineer Aviation Battalion, engaged in aircraft construction in Suffolk in the summer of 1943, consisted largely of "Spanish-speaking Mexicans" from around the California-Mexico border,[2] but most of the nonwhite GIs were what would now be called "African-American." This recent designation owes a little to the events described in this book, but it was certainly not a term used or understood in wartime Britain. Most Englishmen referred to "coloured people," or, gradually adopting American racial terminology, to "negroes." What the words actually meant, however, many had no real idea, since the tiny non-white population of prewar Britain—perhaps eight thousand—was clustered mainly in Liverpool, Cardiff, London, and a few other ports. It is clear that many English people, particularly in rural areas, had never seen a nonwhite before. Stories were frequent of black GIs who represented themselves as "Red Indians" and of white GIs persuading British people that the blacks had tails. Even where such credulity was lacking, many English people were simply fascinated by physical appearance—dark faces offsetting white teeth, and the strikingly pink palms—and their responses to black GIs were often somewhat naïve and superficial. In East Anglia in March 1943 the MOI's regional information officer reported that "black troops in the district where they are stationed seem popular with the inhabitants—regarded as children and liked for their singing, their smiles and their kindness to children." Although a slightly patronizing attitude of this sort was frequent, it reflected a sense that black GIs were preferable to whites. A woman in Marlborough, Wiltshire, wrote in March 1943: "Everybody here adores the negro troops, all the girls go to their dances, but nobody likes the white Americans. They swagger about as if they were the only people fighting this war, they all get so drunk and look so untidy while the negroes are very polite, much smarter and everybody's pets." Or, in the oft-quoted words of one countryman: "I don't mind the Yanks, but I don't care much for the white fellows they've brought with them."[3]

Higher up the social scale expectations and prejudices were more sharply defined. On 26 September 1942 the weekly *The New Statesman and Nation* printed the story of "the grand lady" who thought she would do her bit for Anglo-American relations by writing to the commander of the local American base and inviting six of his men to Sunday lunch. But, she added, "No Jews, please." On Sunday there was a knock at the door and she opened it to find six black Americans standing there. Horrified, she gasped that there must be some mistake.

"Oh no, ma'am," one of them replied, "Colonel Cohen no make any mistakes." The story was apocryphal but apposite. That same day Capt. Leland Baldwin and the AAF chaplain from Greenham Common called on a Baptist minister in nearby Newbury, who, Baldwin scribbled later in his diary, "was worried because he had to baptize some negroes and a white Am[erican] in the same pool at the same service. Talk, talk, talk in the precise and pompous English manner, then decided to hold two services." Not all churchmen took this view. The vicar of Haughley, a village near Stowmarket in Suffolk, had a letter published in the local paper in September 1942 announcing that he and his wife would "welcome visits from coloured troops. . . . The Vicarage rest room—so long as we can afford to keep it open—will be for their use. It has comfortable furniture, writing-table, and free materials, papers and books, a wireless, and a good piano."[4] But the vicar was unusual, not least in having grown up in a mixed-race situation in British Guiana. As the British government's "whispering campaigns" suggest (chapter 14), most "opinion leaders" within local communities were ready to accept American segregationist policies and the stereotypes of black sexuality and violence that underpinned them.

It was the policy of de facto segregation that evoked particular protest in Britain and tended to divide the governors from the governed. As early as August 1942 the regional commissioner for East Anglia, Sir Will Spens, was warning Whitehall: "Restrictions imposed on coloured troops by American Officers in regard to their admission to places of entertainment and in general the attitude of white to coloured American troops are already arousing some criticism, both among civilians and among our own troops. It seems desirable," Spens advised, "that consideration should be given to preventing such criticism being advertised by the Press." An MOI Home Intelligence report in mid-September 1942 noted that the "only strong feeling" about GIs reported in the southwest region was

one of indignation at an attempt at Weston-super-Mare to impose a colour bar. The Weston-super-Mare Information Committee passed a resolution indignantly demanding that the Ministry of Information should take effective measures to stop a "Whispering Campaign" in favour of a colour bar. . . . The opinion has been expressed from many quarters that we should not allow American views on this matter to be imposed on this country. A contrary view appears to be held by certain leaders of women's organisations whose views differ to those of the rest of the community and who would welcome greater segregation. It is the attempts by these leaders of women's opinion to bring their views into practice which has led to considerable irritation.[5]

The term *colour bar* fails to convey adequately what many English people found so outrageous. It was not merely that the authorities were trying to keep black GIs apart from whites, but that the whites were acting in a unilateral and often unprovoked manner—as in the incident described at the start of this chapter. Many were the occasions when a white GI tried to evict a black from a pub, or ostentatiously smashed the glass from which the black had been drinking and then flung down some coins as contemptuous compensation. Often English girls who associated with blacks were abused because, for many Southern GIs, this was proof of British moral decadence. "I have not only seen the Negro boys dancing with white girls, but we have actually seen them standing in doorways *kissing the girls goodnight,*" wrote one incredulous lieutenant. Even when walking the streets by themselves blacks could be attacked. A Blackpool aircraft worker recalled seeing "American troops literally kick, and I mean kick, the coloured soldiers off the pavement." If questioned, he said, their response was "always more or less the same: 'Stinking black pigs,' 'black trash' or 'uppity nigger.' " Where British people did get involved, the trouble could escalate dramatically—as in Cosham, near Portsmouth, on 24 July 1943. At closing time that Saturday night, black GIs spilled out from the pubs and gathered on the road, impeding traffic. White military police (MPs) told them to move on, but one argued back. Soon he was surrounded by English civilians, commenting loudly on the action: "Why don't they leave them alone?" "They're as good as they are," and "That's democracy!" In the words of the southern regional commissioner, "the situation eventually developed into one of mass insubordination" and a black sergeant told the MPs, "we ain't no slaves, this is England." Only the arrival of the company commander got the troops back to barracks, but further trouble occurred there and both the private who argued back and the sergeant were court-martialed. Disturbances like this, where the presence of sympathetic bystanders emboldened black GIs, led senior U.S. officers to urge "indoctrination" of British civilians.[6]

As historian Graham Smith has observed, the evidence "points overwhelmingly to the conclusion that the blacks were warmly welcomed in Britain, and the action of the white Americans in furthering a colour bar was roundly condemned." The issue became even more sensitive where *British* subjects were the victims of racial abuse or assault. The Dominion airman mentioned at the beginning of the chapter was one of several thousand West Indians and Africans who served in Britain during the war. The RAF was felt by the Colonial Office to have been "quite magnificent" when "compared with the 'blimpish' attitude hitherto shown by the Admiralty and the War Office on the colour question." By November 1944 there were some four thousand West Indians serving as ground staff on RAF bases around the country and a number of coloured airmen had been decorated for gallantry in combat. Other British colonials came to fill gaps in the civilian workforce. At the beginning of 1943 about one thousand foresters from British Honduras were working in Scotland and 350 West Indian technicians and trainees were engaged in munitions work on Merseyside. If, as seems likely, the black British community doubled during the year, it was not surprising that there were numerous run-ins with white GIs.[7]

The SOS commander in London, Gen. Pleas B. Rogers, admitted privately that in the capital "the negro British nationals are rightly incensed. They undoubtedly have been cursed, made to get off of the sidewalk, leave eating places and separated from their white wives by American soldiers." On Merseyside a West Indian technician was beaten up by GIs when he refused to leave a cinema queue. (He was later visited by "the American authorities" in the hope of hushing up the affair.) This incident and others were reported by the government welfare officer for the technicians, Learie Constantine, a West Indian test cricketer and Lancashire resident for most of the 1930s, who had himself been the victim of harassment by white GIs. He wrote: "I cannot lay sufficient emphasis on the bitterness being created among the Technicians by these attacks." In another case Sgt. Arthur Waldron, a West Indian who volunteered for service with the RAF and became a gunner on a Stirling bomber, was set upon at a dance in Bury St. Edmunds town hall on 23 June 1943. An American sergeant told a white girl not to dance with Waldron and, when she took no notice, he and another GI beat up the airman. Waldron wanted to prefer charges and wrote a dignified letter of complaint to the colonial secretary, but the matter went no further because, a week later, he was shot down and killed over Germany.[8]

Even those government ministers and senior officials who were most unhappy about the black presence wanted to see "fair play" on civil rights. Where they drew the line was over sexual relations and here, it is clear, American racial stereotypes were little different from those prevalent in Britain. In Scotland, where the British Hondurans were located, the Duke of Buccleuch told the Colonial Office that "improper

intercourse with decent young women should be strongly discouraged." Cornish Member of Parliament Maurice Petherick warned
the foreign secretary that the "blackamoors" would "obviously con-
sort with white girls and there will be a number of half caste babies
about when they have gone." He suggested the black GIs be sent to
"fertilize the Italians who are used to it anyhow." Many British women
of social standing were particularly agitated. According to the MOI, the
"considerable whispering campaign" in the summer of 1942 "against
the association of white women with coloured men" had emanated "to
some extent from Lady Reading's organisation of the W.V.S." Novelist
Ann Meader, in the hothouse atmosphere of Weston-super-Mare in
October 1942, was appalled to see two black GIs with two fair-haired
white girls. She felt for a moment that the girls should be "shot" for
risking "coloured blood" in their children.[9]

It would be wrong, however, to treat these attitudes as peculiarly
"upper class." Although many British people at the lower end of the
social scale welcomed black GIs and condemned discrimination
against them, it seems likely that there was a general predisposition
against miscegenation. Historian Graham Smith suggested that "the
British ceased to view the black soldiers' relations with the local girls
with equanimity" in "about March or April 1943," but in fact the
distinction between civil rights and sexual wrongs had been apparent
in British attitudes from the start. An overview of MOI home intelligence reports from August to October 1942 noted that "the British are
characteristically against discrimination, though association between
these [black] troops and British girls [is] regarded with disapproval."
It seems probably more accurate to say that the gradual increase in
black numbers and in sexual incidents brought into the open latent
attitudes. These rested on the prevailing social Darwinist stereotypes
about distinct races of differing attributes and quality.[10]

Anthony Richmond, in his study of West Indian workers in Liverpool in the 1940s, found that even before the war there was "a
widespread conception of the Negro as a person of low social status,
little skill and doubtful moral habits." Sociologist Kenneth Little, surveying the "coloured community" of Tiger Bay around the Cardiff
docks in 1941 (before any GIs arrived), concluded that "colour aver-
sion" was "very strong." Only three of eleven hotels or boarding-
houses he approached would accept coloured guests. In a national
overview, published in 1943, Little judged that there was "a substantial body of antipathy, more evident in London and a number of
seaport cities, against coloured people" that was based largely on
"rationalizations justifying the inferior status of coloured people in our

society." These were "transmitted as part of the cultural heritage" and centred on the idea that contact with nonwhites could bring sexual "contamination" or at least the "lowering" of social status. Little did not believe these attitudes were confined to the "middle" or "upper" classes. As one boot operative explained, when asked why he would not let a coloured person live in his house: "It may be thought that to working people like ourselves living in a working-class locality, such things as social status would be of little value, but to be cut or ignored by one's acquaintances is felt just as much here as in any other place." Likewise, the West Indians in Liverpool frequently complained that, if they were seen with a white woman, it was immediately believed that she was of bad character. As one put it: "If I was seen walking down Lime Street with the Queen of England and nobody recognized who she was, it would be assumed that she was a street girl. But as soon as it was discovered that she was the Queen, it would be at once assumed that I must be the King of somewhere or other."[11]

As Little suggested, these attitudes were more apparent in London and the seaports where Britain's small prewar black population was concentrated. But in areas of the country where nonwhite had not penetrated before, it seems likely that the same stereotypes existed, if only through books and films. Little suggested that the "warmth with which the cause of the coloured American was taken up in a number of rural areas" should be understood in relative terms. Enthusiasm for the "better-mannered" blacks was an initial reaction to the more pushy and "aggressive" white invaders, and, as social relations developed, he judged, "epithets seem to have become modified to a type more usual to the pattern of white-coloured contacts in this country." Again and again Little's interlocutors expressed no objection to non-whites *"in their place"*—a key phrase that indicates the threat they seemed to pose.[12] After the war, that sense of threat was often economic: immigrants taking "our" jobs. During the war, when most nonwhites (American or British) were visitors, the threat was defined in sexual terms. That is where most British people drew their colour line.

It is likely, then, that many British people felt a sense of hospitality and social justice towards nonwhites (often conceived in the abstract) and also a keen dislike of too close association in the flesh (both metaphorically and literally). In the latter, they were no different from many GIs. The crucial Anglo-American contrast is captured in these observations by the 8th AF provost marshal in his survey of troop attitudes to the British in November 1943:

The British have a policy of public social equality which permits all races to associate in public places without unfavorable notice, as long as they behave respectably. However, this democratic spirit does not apply to private social equality. British society never permits a situation to arise whereby any white woman would be placed in a position that she would have to be escorted along by a person of a different race.

As for GIs, he said, "irrespective of the section from which American troops come, most of them do not wish negroes to frequent the same places as they do."[13]

This distinction between attitudes to public and private space is fundamental, but, as sociologist Anthony Richmond observed, drawing the line between the two arenas was often problematic. There was no segregation or discrimination in Britain on public transport or in public places such as banks and post offices. A hotel might be deemed a public place, but often nonwhites would find they were turned away because "no rooms were available" or "non-residents were not welcome for meals." A Colonial Office survey in May 1946 had no doubt that a "colour bar in hotels, boarding houses and public houses" was "very frequent but only the most outstanding cases are brought to public notice." The most celebrated of these involved Learie Constantine when he came down to London in July 1943 to play cricket only to be barred from the room he had booked in advance at the Imperial Hotel in Russell Square. The manageress allegedly told him she wanted "no niggers in our hotel." Constantine successfully sued for damages and, because of his celebrity status, the case aroused considerable publicity. In 1946 the Colonial Office judged that, in consequence, "hotels are very much more cautious now in refusing accommodation to coloured people" but that there was "still a great deal of discrimination," for instance, in dance halls. An example cited was the Paramount Dance Hall, in London's Tottenham Court Road, where "at various times a colour bar is imposed."[14]

The Paramount was a GI favourite throughout the war. The ban on Constantine at the Imperial Hotel was, apparently, the result of the management's concern not to offend its clientele of some two hundred white Americans. What these examples suggest is not that the arrival of white GIs prompted racial discrimination, but rather that it sharpened it. In particular, the American presence and pressure helped determine where the line between public and private should be drawn. To examine this in more detail requires a brief pub-crawl around England.

* * *

The pub was one of the principal arenas of Anglo-American contact. As we have seen, it was, variously, a place where soldiers could pick up girls (and vice versa); where tense or bored men found release through getting drunk; and where locals and Americans played darts, swapped stories, and made friends. It was also where friction between black and white GIs often flared into open conflict, because women, drink, and local bystanders made a combustible mixture.

The U.S. Army's response was its system of de facto segregation. Smaller towns often had "white nights" and "black nights" for passes. In larger towns, capable of absorbing many troops, the Army established a network of black and white pubs and dance halls. Take the example of Ipswich—a centre for white airmen and black support and construction troops in East Anglia. In the autumn of 1943, an internal SOS document designated a number of pubs as "exclusively for colored troops," particularly in the area around St. Peter's Street where the ARC Club for black GIs was located. But such segregation often reflected British preferences as well. In Leicester in January 1943, there had been a black-white clash at the canteen at the railway station and various brawls in local pubs. The landlord of *The Three Cranes* formally complained to the city's chief constable after a number of evenings when black GIs had brought in underaged girls whom he refused to serve, or, if alone, had persistently chatted up women already there until he asked them to leave. In both cases, his actions led to disturbances and threats against him. In general, the chief constable reported that "reputable licensees" felt that "the white troops are the cause of the trouble and that they begin the taunting of the blacks." Whoever was responsible, however, he wanted official American action—either alternate black and white nights or banning Leicester entirely to troops of one colour and insisting that they use Northampton or Nottingham instead. In other words, the local police as much as the U.S. Army favoured a system of segregation.[15]

Official patterns of segregation often grew out of local circumstances. The western port of Bristol had a large number of black troops in the vicinity, particularly those working at Avonmouth docks. In mid-September 1942 English dockers walked out when black GI stevedores were used to unload two U.S. vessels. Although racial antipathy may have been an element, this was part of a larger battle by the docker's union against the use of Army labour in general. By January 1943 a Mass-Observation survey found considerable praise in Bristol for black GIs. "It's skilled work on the docks and not to be picked up in a day," said one dock official, "but these negroes have done their best and have been a great help." Dockworkers with whom M-O spoke were impressed by their politeness and education: "They are not like we've seen them on the films . . . not stupid and dull . . . they are educated, some of them." On the other hand, there seemed to be relatively little social mixing with English men and it was "rare to see a negro walking with a white woman during the day." After dark, however, according to one middle-class Bristolian, "every open space in Bristol is full of black Americans with their white girls," usually with one soldier keeping lookout for white GIs. In mid-December 1942 some Southerners decided to take concerted action. There was a rash of fights and stabbings in the Old Market area, after which alternate passes were instituted and the black stevedore unit was temporarily banned from the city. By then, the same Bristolian noted, informal segregation had developed in local pubs:

> If a negro does go into a pub that has been adopted by the whites, he runs the risk of being beaten up, but there are other pubs where no white American will go. The Bristol people leave certain pubs to the Americans. It is funny in some places to find pubs that Bristol people have used regularly for years, now completely empty of them except for a few dazed ones who don't seem to have taken in what's happened to them, and spend their time sitting in corners and staring at the Americans.[16]

The same local patterns are apparent in the segregation of that other sensitive social institution, the dance hall. Cambridge was a small market town whose main wartime function was not the education of students (almost all men had gone) but the entertainment of thousands of Allied troops marooned in the surrounding countryside. In mid-January 1944 the SOS deputy theater provost marshal, Gen. George M. Alexander, visited Cambridge and worked out a plan "to avoid mixed dances," namely that "future dances will be arranged for organizations [i.e., by unit] so as to avoid [racial] mixing." This systematized informal arrangements that had been established over the previous months. In February 1944, however, Cambridge figured in a list of complaints about racial discrimination submitted by the NAACP. Col. James Day from the ETO Inspectorate General was sent to inquire into the situation. The manager of the Dorothy Dance Hall in the town centre told him that, after a meeting with the Cambridge chief constable and a member of the U.S. Army provost marshal's staff, "we were advised, not in writing, by the Chief Constable about June or July of last year that Colored Troops were out of bounds here." This was "owing to five other places in the town being in bounds" for them. But, when turning blacks away, the manager gave as his reason that "our floor is not suitable for jitterbugging." Since, as he put it, this was "the dancing life of the colored troops," the ban proved perfectly effective. The chief constable himself admitted to Col. Day that "we came to a general agreement" that the hall "should be kept free from Colored Troops." His explanation was that it was an up-market venue for ballroom dancing, popular with British and U.S. officers. Choosing his words carefully, he said: "I do not remember that the American Military Police contacted me about it" and that "I do not know of any occasion where Colored Troops have been barred because of color." Neither Alexander nor any American MP officer was interviewed, and the Army report given to the NAACP stated that where black GIs were barred in Cambridge, "as at the Dorothy Cafe Dance Hall, it is because of the wishes of the local manager or of the Chief Constable."[17]

The combination of official pressure and local circumstances can be seen with particular clarity in Liverpool. This was close to the vast AAF repair depot at Burtonwood, where many black and white GIs were stationed, and also home for many of the West Indian technicians recruited to work in wartime Britain. In some cases, such as the Grafton Dance Rooms, a colour bar was gradually imposed because of trouble with West Indians. On the other hand, the dance hall at the Aintree Institute was closed to all nonwhites after a shooting and stabbing incident involved drunken black GIs, and it does seem that the widening colour bar was largely the result of the increased American presence. The West Indians themselves had no doubt that white GIs were the main reason why their social opportunities had contracted by 1943. One complained:

> We the Negroes had to suffer quite a lot of bars when we came here first but now it's worse. The Americans have got some power over things that I can't understand. There used to be a few dance halls that we could go to after a week's work, or whenever one feel [sic] like dancing. . . . Now when we enter these halls all one can hear is "No Negroes." When we ask why, this is always the answer, "Well, the Americans don't like the Negroes in the same place where they have fun."

At Reece's Dance Hall the manager admitted that he had imposed a colour bar for essentially commercial reasons, because white U.S. officers had objected to any black presence and he regarded their custom as essential. And at the Casino dance hall in nearby Warrington,

American pressure was official. The manager received a written request from a local U.S. officer: "It is not our intention to dictate the policies of privately owned establishments, but in the interests of eliminating trouble in which our troops may be involved, we will appreciate your co-operation in prohibiting Negroes from attending dances." When the manager refused, the American and British military authorities declared the ballroom out of bounds to all their servicemen.[18]

Of course, white GIs did not have a uniform attitude towards blacks. To capture the range of diversity, here are two anonymous comments entered on an ETO questionnaire in September 1942. The authors were on the same base, probably the supply depot at Ashchurch near Cheltenham, where blacks were also stationed and where off-base passes were carefully rotated. One wrote:

> Negro troops have the girls coming down to camp and call for them. If anything will make [a] Southern's Blood run hot it is to see this happen. . . . If it keeps on going as it is we will have a nice negro lynching down here and then things will be better.

The other, however, felt that

> The Negro problem has been very poorly handled here by our officers. . . . Rather than lessen the friction between the white and colored troops our officers have, through their actions & statements, definitely increased the friction . . . [and] have managed to give official sanction to the anti-Negro group in my outfit. This has tended to make others (who normally might have accepted working & associating with Negroes) equally as antagonistic. In my outfit is now "The thing" to hate the negros [sic]. . . . Actually what is taking place in our army today is nothing more disgraceful than what Hitler is doing to minorities in Germany. I joined the American Army to fight against the persecution of minorities. I resent that our Army actually practices the same type of persecution.[19]

Only 10 percent of troops on the base were Southerners, and the second man probably came from north of the Mason-Dixon line. But we should not assume that all Southerners were rednecks. Some probably had close if paternalistic relations with black tenants or maids, whereas many rural Northerners had never seen a black face before entering the Army. Growing up in Clinton, a college town in Mississippi, GI Leon Standifer had played with kids from "nice" black families. ("The term *black*, of course, was not used then. We always spoke of 'colored people.' *Negro* was not a polite term, and *nigger* meant you needed to have your mouth washed out with soap—it was a word trashy people used.") Nor were all Northerners opposed to segregation. On the contrary: In many Northern cities this was practiced less blatantly than in the Jim Crow South through residential segregation, which rested on income differentials and was enforced by zoning laws and real estate agents. It seems likely, as a rule, that most white GIs in Britain were uncomfortable in the presence of blacks and vexed by "the negro problem." An American civilian interviewing GIs in Cambridge in March 1943 found that if a man came from a Northern,

> or, as the phrase goes, more enlightened state, he is angry with the southern soldier for bringing his bigotry . . . into a foreign country where enough misunderstandings exist already, with the American authorities for not having enough sense to work out some discreet system of segregation similar to that which operates in the northern cities of the United States, and with the English people, who have never had to face the problem, for daring to take sides in a dispute about which they know nothing. . . .[20]

Similarly, black GIs did not conform to a single stereotype, but this was often hard for British people to appreciate because of the restrictions on social contact. Nor were they helped in their understanding by some of the initiatives by ETO. In the summer of 1943, for instance, the Public Relations Office in London decided to establish a special "negro chorus," formed around an existing choir in the 923rd Engineer Aviation Battalion. This would tour the country, accompanied for part of the time by the noted black tenor Roland Hayes, in the hope "that the resulting publicity would be of tremendous value in the handling of the Negro problem, both here and in the United States." The chorus duly sang all around Britain in the winter of 1943–44, beginning with two concerts in London's Albert Hall at the end of September—parts of which were broadcast on the BBC and the AFN and relayed to the United States. As far as ETO was concerned, the chorus hit all the right notes. But, at the same time, the (black) head of the War Department's special Negro Press Section, Maj. Homer B. Roberts, was trying to combat this kind of musical Sambo image. What he wanted was "that type of material which shows the Negro performing his duties as a soldier." Scenes such as "a Negro quartet, jazz bands, Negroes eating watermelon and fried chicken are never used."[21]

Numerous black GIs were people of education—as the Avonmouth dockers had discovered to their apparent surprise. George Goodman, a professional social worker with bachelor's and master's degrees to his name, came to Britain with the ARC and was director of the black club in Bristol in 1942–44. Like anyone from the United States he was struck by the basic contrasts of geography and history, appreciating for the first time what it meant to be a small island that had been settled for centuries. To his mind, English privacy and conservatism made sense in a new way. William H. Simons, a teacher's son from Washington, D.C., was a social studies major in a local college when he was drafted in February 1943. He arrived in Britain in July 1943 as a corporal with the HQ of a Quartermaster battalion and was stationed near Worcester. He, too, was struck by the traditionalism (typified by the rigid adherence to "teatime") and the often primitive conditions in rural areas. Like many educated GIs, he also found that England made English literature come to life. After visiting some nearby towns and pubs, he wrote home in September, "one can readily see how the subjects of the Great English writers were picked. I can really appreciate the writings of Chaucer, Shakespeare, Ben Jonson, Samuel Johnson and the others."[22]

In other words, many black GIs reacted to Britain as *Americans,* and not just as blacks. Nevertheless, none of them failed to notice the absence of formal segregation in Britain or the attempts by the U.S. Army and white GIs to impose it. As Simons put it, the contrast between "the attitude of the English people" and those of many white GIs was like "a star[r]y sky upon a cloudy night." An ETO survey of 422 black GIs in November 1943 found them significantly more likely than a control sample of whites to have a favourable opinion of English people (80 percent to 68 percent). There was also repeated criticism of the whites for, as one put it, "doing everything they can to convince the British people that is as regards the colored fellows being just about the lowest form of human beings." Experience in Britain sharpened their grievances about life in the United States. A Northern black, with a grade school education, commented that "we are treated better in England than we are in a country that is supposed to be our home." Not surprisingly 52 percent of black GIs in the survey (compared with 30 percent of whites) confessed to "sometimes" or "very often" feeling "that this war is not worth fighting." A Northern black with a high school education wrote: "I am an American negro, doing my part for the American Government to make the world safe for a democracy I have never known."[23]

Such inferences were drawn by most black Americans in Britain (and other parts of Europe). But reactions to the situation varied. As naval steward Ray Carter observed: "Some of our men were broken by racism in the United States armed forces. There are always a small number of real Uncle Toms." Others kept their opinions to themselves but developed strategies of evasion and minimal cooperation, reminiscent of covert black resistance on slave plantations before the Civil War. For one, "it became a game of seeing just how much we could avoid doing. We found out that one of the most effective little gimmicks was to take a clip board, pad, and pencil and go up to the headquarters area and just walk around. No one ever bothered to ask us what we were doing up there."[24] A few were pushed into open violence by white taunts and harassment, or deliberately provoked a fight by flaunting their social freedoms. Most, however, were obliged to get on with their work, with varying degrees of enthusiasm, and store up experiences and grievances for the future. Army discipline left them little choice.

Perhaps the most politicized group of black Americans were the American Red Cross staff—in a freer yet ambiguous position of educated civilians operating as Army auxiliaries. George Goodman at the Bristol ARC Club told Walter White of the NAACP that "the chief complaint against us is the fact that we are too bright intellectually, which only means that we do not brook any foolishness." Many keenly resented being part of a system of segregation covered by a smokescreen of ARC/Army disinformation. When the SOS instituted pass restrictions in Bristol after the troubles of December 1942, Goodman wrote a courteous but firm letter of protest direct to Gen. Lee about "excluding Negro soldiers from Bristol." In early 1944 there was friction in Winchester between black SOS troops and white GIs from the 9th Infantry Division. The 9th's commander, Gen. Manton S. Eddy, was critical of the director of the ARC black club in Winchester, Elizabeth McDougald, whom he described as "a highly educated negress with very definite ideas on race equality" and "an agitator of the worst sort." Among the evidence he cited against her were her protests that white soldiers were not allowed to patronize her club ("she was very clever in trying to trip me into statements that might prove that I was discriminating against the colored soldiers") and the interest she took in a court-martial case involving two black officers stabbed by a white paratrooper from the 101st Airborne Division when he saw them with a white girl in a pub. After she complained formally to SOS that the 9th was trying to prejudice local people against blacks, both Eddy and the local SOS commander recommended her replacement by "a person of tact." In April, however, the tension exploded in a series of racial clashes. The Army closed the black club in Winchester and redirected coloured troops to Basingstoke. But the woman sent there to be director of the black ARC Club, Camille K. Jones, soon resigned in protest. As she told the ARC in July 1944, watching the "infiltration of prejudices" and the "consternation" they created among local people had brought to a head nineteen months of frustration. "I see us fighting fascists but not fascist principles for in our midst we continue to harbor doctrines of racial supremacy which belie the course [cause] for which we are fighting."[25]

The majority of black Americans in wartime Britain were not, however, educated nor particularly articulate. Three-quarters of black GIs were ranked in the bottom two categories out of five in the Army General Classification Tests (AGCTs), and segregation meant that low-scoring blacks were parceled together in a few units, unlike whites. Some of the consequences can be illustrated by the case of three hundred black GIs who were suddenly dumped in the village of Wortley in Yorkshire in the late summer of 1942. They belonged to an ordnance unit working at a local 8th AF bomb depot. In general, relations with English civilians were good—some blacks had visited people's homes and sung in a local church. But in Wortley, and in the nearby city of Sheffield, there were a number of incidents. Women going home from night shifts in local factories were accosted and attacked; several local men were also the victims of assault. Some of these affairs were totally unprovoked; many involved drunken GIs. But two threads ran through the majority of cases. First, the black GIs often carried sheath knives ("a weapon completely foreign to British tradition," according to the chief constable of Sheffield). The other factor was the prevalence of racial insults, real or imagined, as a stimulus to many of the attacks. The case of a thirty-year-old man threatened by a black sergeant with a knife outside the Adelphi Hotel, Sheffield, on 3 September 1942 is fairly typical. He was accused by the sergeant and a crowd of six other black GIs of having insulted them in the pub earlier in the evening. The sergeant, later traced, was "the worse for drink and used obscene language to the police," who eventually concluded that "an unknown person made derogatory remarks about the coloured soldiers in the public house that evening, but there is not the slightest evidence to suggest that such remarks were made by the victim of this attack."[26]

Clearly some black violence around Sheffield was a response to racism, real or imagined. Equally clearly, its worst excesses could have been corrected had the soldiers not been armed. Both the chief constable of Sheffield and the 8th AF investigators urged strongly that all troops going on pass should be checked first by their commanders for knives and other weapons. Significantly the unit commander was a twenty-two-year-old officer, short of staff and with only two years' experience. Speaking generally, many of the problems faced and caused by black GIs could have been ameliorated by commanders who were both firmer and more sensitive. But command of a black unit was widely regarded as a stigma and many blacks were under poor or inexperienced officers. What made this worse was the prevalent Army philosophy of fixed black inferiority. A medical officer dealing with Wortley depot considered that "the majority of the men are below normal intelligence," describing them clinically as "high-grade morons."[27] Yet this language was an example of the Army's propensity to treat AGCT scores as a measure of innate intelligence rather than of acquired skills. To classify someone as "moron" implies an irremediability that is not suggested by the words *poorly educated* or even *backward*. Faced with large groups of unskilled men of a different race, many white officers regarded their task as impossible—at best a disagreeable exercise in damage control.

These attitudes were particularly apparent in the handling of venereal disease. In America and Britain black GI rates were much higher than white. Among AAF personnel in Britain in 1943–44 the annual VD admission rate per thousand troops was 27.19 for whites and 168.71 for blacks—over six times larger. Statistics for all U.S. commands in Britain in early 1944 show that black units reflected the general decline in VD cases just before D-Day, but the black VD rate was still around five times that of whites.[28]

Neither tough punishments nor the Army's prophylactic campaign in 1943–44 achieved more than temporary success among black GIs. For many white field officers that simply confirmed their underlying racial stereotypes. The commander of one black unit, who was rebuked in March 1943 about its high VD rate, replied with some asperity that he was

> at a loss how to control a people who are more or less indiscriminate in their sex relations in their home country, with their own colour; are highly sexual in their natural impulses and are in a country where they may indulge in sexual relations with white women without resentment. . . . Naturally any white woman with pride will not have intercourse with a coloured man, and it is therefore—with possibly a few exceptions—probably only those generally diseased with whom the coloured man comes in contact.

In his opinion the only sure way to reduce the VD rate would be "to completely isolate the coloured soldier, allowing him no passes" and therefore no contact with British women.[29]

In retrospect, however, the situation looked different. As the Army Medical Department's official history put it in 1960, the failure to control the VD rate "was, at least in part, a reflection of the failure of [American] society through individual and governmental efforts to develop a satisfactory race relationship between the white and Negro populations."[30] This was written fifteen years after the war, when the civil rights movement was beginning to change racial attitudes profoundly. What is interesting is that by late 1943 the buildup of black troops in Britain and the growing racial violence this caused were forcing some U.S. commanders in Britain to similar conclusions. This can best be illustrated by the effect on the 8th Air Force of one of the most violent racial incidents in wartime Britain, near Preston in June 1943. The shake-up in command and policies it produced showed clearly that the "problems" caused by black GIs could be dramatically ameliorated when the men's "potential" as soldiers was properly acknowledged.

On the night of 24 June 1943 some black GIs got involved in an argument with white military police in the village of Bamber Bridge, four miles south of Preston. The incident involved the same ingredients as many others around the country at pub closing time: attempts to arrest some drunk or disorderly soldiers, resentment by other black GIs that grew into open argument, and the presence of British bystanders who took the side of the black GIs. But this incident escalated into outright violence. Stones and bottles were thrown at the MPs, who retaliated with nightsticks and eventually firearms. Two black GIs were wounded. They were taken back to their camp, in the grounds of nearby Adams Hall, where feelings ran high. Some men left the camp immediately in search of revenge; most gathered in high indignation. The CO was away and his deputy and some other officers (all but one of them white) tried to restore calm. Their efforts enjoyed some success until, around midnight, a dozen MPs roared up to the camp in two jeeps and a makeshift armored car on which was mounted a machine gun. Although officers got the MPs to leave, rumours now spread that the latter were out to kill the black GIs. The gun rooms were broken into, rifles and ammunition taken, and order broke down completely. In the words of the official report, "officers were held up by armed men, and rifle fire was discharged throughout the camp." Black noncoms proved unable or unwilling to control their men, some taking a lead in the mutiny. A number of GIs left the camp in trucks and drove through Bamber Bridge, shooting at MPs, Army vehicles, and even civilian property, doing considerable damage. It took until 5 A.M. to

bring things under control and get the men back to camp. A white
officer and three black GIs were shot (one of the latter fatally), and
several blacks and MPs were injured.[31]

The black troops came from two battalions of the 1511th Quartermaster Truck Regiment (Aviation), whose HQ was at Adams Hall. As
air support troops they were part of the 8th AF Service Command
(8AFSC), under Gen. Henry J. Miller. Miller and his superior, Gen.
Eaker, immediately took action of the sort by then routine in such
cases. Charges were preferred against all who had violated military
regulations. At the same time, deficient officers were removed and
black MPs introduced into the area. But Miller's detailed report, submitted three weeks later, took a rather different line. In his view "the
alleged mutiny was primarily caused by the racial problem and was
not created by any failure of command." He doubted whether, "with
the state of mind ascribed to the colored soldiers, any officer, regardless of experience level, could have handled the situation differently."
He attributed their frenzy to three main factors. One was the effect of
racial equality in Britain in exacerbating white-black tension and
violence. The second was their "extremely low level of intelligence"
as measured by the AGCT scores—roughly half being in categories
four and five, compared with about 20 percent in an average company. This, said Miller, made them susceptible "to the slightest
rumor or outward influence that bears on the race problem." And,
third, because their work as truck drivers took them across much of
Britain, they were not only harder to discipline but also more at-
tuned to every such rumour of discrimination through their "grape-
vine."[32]

Miller's proposed remedy was to create a special "Composite Command" within 8AFSC to oversee black trucking, ordnance, and other
supply units. A strong staff, dedicated full-time to these problems
among black troops, would be better able to control their relations
with white GIs and British civilians and to improve their discipline and
performance. Privately Miller had no doubt that

> one of the basic reasons for the current racial troubles is the unrealis-
> tic manner in which these problems are handled. So long as the
> natural fact is ignored that all races are not endowed with the same
> intelligence and therefore the same standards could not be de-
> manded of them, trouble will multiply. On the other hand when a
> policy of firm control within the limitations of intelligence is adopted
> trouble decreases. In the present instance the fostering of a weak
> apologetic attitude to a dependent race can have disastrous results.[33]

The 8th AF commander, Gen. Eaker, took up Miller's proposal for a special command, but in a distinctly different spirit. On 10 July, Eaker told his staff that "he felt that 90 per cent of the trouble with Negro troops was the fault of the whites." He also believed that, instead of protesting at official policy, "we should stop arguing as to the reasons why they [the blacks] were sent here and do our best to cooperate with the War Department in making their employment here satisfactory to all concerned." Eaker agreed with Miller that small trucking and ordnance units, dispersed across the country, needed a proper structure to ensure discipline and efficiency. But he also believed this could boost their morale, and he personally chose the name "Combat Support Wing" because it would assist "the build-up among colored troops of a definite feeling that they are contributing to the combat effort."[34]

With the approval of Gen. Devers the Combat Support Wing (CSW) was activated on 27 August 1943, under the command of Col. George S. Grubb. In his previous capacity as 8AF provost marshal, Grubb had spent much time weeding out bad officers from black units and he treated this as one of his priorities in CSW. In some cases he requested officers by name from Washington, such as one who, in civilian life, had been president of a refrigeration company in Birmingham, Alabama, where he had managed a fleet of trucks with black drivers. Also important were careful training and improved on-base facilities—to reduce grievances and the desire to go into the local town. Touring the units assiduously, Grubb took particular pains to explain to their men how their tedious work played an important part of the larger war effort. He went beyond the usual platitudes about officers knowing their men by instructing company commanders to "take time out each day" to learn about the background and family circumstances of two of his soldiers, giving at least fifteen minutes to each and showing solicitude for particular obstacles and worries. By December his efforts were already bearing fruit. Despite the fact that black strength in 8AFSC had increased from a monthly average of fourteen hundred between January and July to nearly four thousand in the autumn, misconduct had declined and performance had improved. The court-martial rate had dropped by 60 percent and the VD rate by more than a quarter. At the same time, the ratio of men per truck had been halved, as had been the monthly percentage of unserviceable vehicles (to 8 percent).[35]

This improvement continued. In July 1944 Grubb said he had no doubt that "negro soldiers can do a first-class job when properly led and handled." He rated the truck companies particularly highly: "in many instances they have done work superior to that done by white troops." Like Eaker, Grubb felt that "the majority of incidents between white and colored troops are provoked by white troops" and he considered that his men had generally

> been well received by the communities which they habitually visit. Many of them have been entertained in the homes of British civilians. Generally speaking, they have made a good impression wherever stationed. In general, the negro troops are more courteous and better mannered than the white troops.

Grubb's successor, Col. Robert M. Goodall, concurred in his own report in October 1944. Despite having what he called "a remarkably low I.Q. on army intelligence tests," black GIs in the CSW had, he said, "made a major contribution to the war effort. They have demonstrated an enormous capacity for work under pressure. No matter how weary these soldiers may have been, they have unhesitatingly responded to the demand whenever called on to load or deliver a cargo of bombs or ammunition required on a combat station." Equally, their accident, crime, and VD rates had "responded quite definitely to intelligent efforts." Goodall felt that the name "Combat Support Wing" had proved "a remarkable stimulus to unit and individual morale," facilitating successful appeals to the men's pride whenever there was a temptation to revolt.[36]

This was only a small experiment. Even at its peak in December 1943 the CSW included less than five thousand black GIs. But it showed that, with skilled officers, thorough training, and attention to morale, great improvements in black performance and conduct could be achieved. It also showed how fallacious was the assumption among white officers that AGCT scores indicated irremediable defects in intelligence. When treated as potential soldiers rather than as command problems, black Americans had much to offer their Army and their country.

Wartime Britain therefore proved something of a sociological laboratory for black GIs, with regard to military performance and to civil rights. In both cases, however, conventional wisdom was tested and broken only through violence. The Combat Support Wing was the 8th Air Force's response to a temporary mutiny. Some blacks asserted their civil rights by mixing with white women, to the anger of whites, and by fighting back against insults and abuse. A few took advantage of the freer situation in gratuitous attacks, which served to reinforce negative stereotypes.

Yet a picture of unmitigated racial violence would not be accurate. The novelty of blacks for Britons and the outrage of many white GIs at British mores combined to magnify every rumour of misconduct. One gets a whiff of this in the diary of Ann Meader in Weston-super-Mare in October 1942, who reported local gossip that in Bristol white women were "waiting in queues of as many as 50 for the blacks to come out at night." The British-American Liaison Board was informed in July 1944 that around the East Anglian towns of Diss and Eye, where there had been much fuss about black babies, less than a dozen coloured illegitimate children had been born, despite the fact that some fifteen thousand black GIs had been stationed there over the previous eighteen months.[37]

Stories of the oversexed GI were probably even more overblown in the case of blacks than whites. After all, even at the D-Day peak, only one in every thirteen GIs in Britain was black. The 8th AF provost marshal, Maj. William H. Dribben, judged in November 1943 that

> the association between colored troops and white women in England is not as common as barrack and public house gossip would have it. Most of the public houses patronized by negro troops were investigated, and it was found that white women were very much in the minority. The streets in the center of towns and in the areas where colored troops are quartered were closely watched, and by far the majority of colored troops were unaccompanied by women.

Even where dances were not segregated, it did not follow that the races mixed. At one such dance, Dribben reported, there were between seventy-five and one hundred black GIs.

> Despite the fact that there were many women and girls present, and that many attractive girls were dancing together, only fifteen colored troops were dancing. The remainder stood or sat by themselves on one particular side of the dance floor. From people who frequently attend this dance hall, it was learned that the colored troops will only ask those women to dance who are known to associate with them. During the intermission only a few women remained on their side of the hall.[38]

Many black GIs, despite the relative social freedoms of England, were as homesick as their white counterparts. Perhaps even more so, because of the lack of black men and particularly black women in Britain. (The first black U.S. nurses did not arrive until August 1944.) In a few cities such as Liverpool it was possible to organize weekly dances with coloured girls, but this was because the city "had a certain permanent coloured population on which to draw." As one black GI commented in a letter home in December 1942: "It sure is lonesome over here." Another wrote that "I miss the colored people, my people, more than anyone in the world."[39]

Yet even the latter went on to say that the locals were "exceptionally good to us. Most of the people don't know no color line or discrimination." Most black GIs, even if they were homesick and made no close British friends, must have noted the absence of *public* discrimination in Britain. This was perhaps the overriding impression taken home by all of them, regardless of education or political sensitivity.

Take the case of Joseph O. Curtis, a lieutenant in an engineer regiment, who was stationed at various bases in England, mostly in the West Country, from December 1943 until August 1944. The first few weeks were grim: "no movies, no papers, no women—way out in the middle of nowhere." Christmas was spent in a tent in the corner of a field. From films and reading, such as the novels of P. G. Wodehouse, and from the American negro press, he had expected to find snobbery and racial prejudice. Instead, English people proved friendly and approachable. In Cornwall he had several long discussions in the home of a local schoolmaster and was "adopted" by the Barnes family of Chacewater, near Redruth, who baked a cake for his birthday from their meagre rations with sugarless frosting on top. "You know," he wrote to a friend in March 1944, "the more I see of the English, the more disgusted I become with Americans. After the war, with the eager and enthusiastic support of every negro who will have served in Europe, I shall start a movement to send white Americans back to England and bring the English to America."

That may have been hyperbole of the moment, but, for Joseph Curtis, as for many black GIs, service in Britain opened their eyes and expanded their sense of the possible. On August 1944, just before leaving for France, he visited the theatre at Stratford-on-Avon to see Shakespeare's *As You Like It*. His wartime photo album begins with pictures of the production together with a quotation from the duke's opening speech in Act Two: "Sweet are the uses of adversity, which like a toad . . . wears yet a precious jewel in his head." That, said Curtis, "sums up my attitude to the Army."[40]

19

Allies

★　★　★

IN THE SUMMER OF 1942 A BRITISH SOLDIER WROTE ABOUT HIS RECENT encounter with some GIs in a pub:

> One of them turned to one of our Lance Corporals and said: "Say, Tommy, what do they pay you a day?" Fred replied: "Three and six." At this he laughs loud and calls to all his gang . . . says that British soldiers would work for a dime if the big shots paid it to 'em. When we came outside after the place had closed there was an army lorry waiting for the Yanks. We stood there and watched them pile in. Then the one who had been doing all the shouting put his hand in his pocket and as the lorry pulled away, threw about a bob's worth of coppers at us and shouted above the others' laughter "Get y'self a cup of tea each of you poor little ____." If I could have laid my hands on him, I, like many more, would have busted his pan. I think they *stink*.

The War Office mail censorship report that reproduced his letter (expletives deleted) commented: "Such incidents do little to inspire respect and friendship for U.S. Troops."[1]

Yet these soldiers were supposed to be allies in the greatest amphibious operation the world had ever seen. How the GIs got on with British troops and with those of other Allied armies in Britain, notably the Canadians, is one theme of this chapter. Again it takes us deep into the conditions of Britain at war. The other theme is how British commanders viewed Marshall's "army of democracy." Their doubts help explain London's hesitations about the Second Front in 1942–43 and also the rows in 1944–45 about strategy and command, which will be explored in the next part of the book.

It was a wartime commonplace that GIs got on better with British civilians than with British troops and that the disparity in pay was the root of the problem. As we have seen, the "average" GI had around three times as much pay as his British counterpart. The U.S. Army, unlike the Canadian, refused to impose compulsory deferrals, and voluntary savings schemes did not begin to bite until late 1943 and 1944. Moreover, British troops were paid weekly and GIs monthly. This meant that at the end of the month GIs could hit the town with a much larger amount of money to burn. Indeed they tended to keep on base when they were short of cash. Although bimonthly paydays were encouraged, these did not eliminate the problem and, in any case, were not universal (for instance in the AAF). A further problem was that the British Tommy had to pay more for "extras." Comparing the American PX with the British NAAFI, cigarettes were often one-tenth of the price (and superior in quality), while razor blades, polish, and other cleaning materials would also be much cheaper. A cup of tea and two buns midmorning would set a Tommy back 3 pence, whereas coffee and doughnuts could usually be obtained free or at nominal cost from the American Red Cross Club, Clubmobile, or Donut Dugout.[2]

The Tommy's inferiority complex was increased by the contrast in dress. The British soldier wore an all-purpose "battledress" made of thick wool, which served, as its title suggested, for both "battle" and "dress" purposes. Although its functional utility was admired by some senior American officers, such as Gen. Omar Bradley, on social and aesthetic grounds it was definitely not a winner. GIs, by contrast, had three outfits: fatigues, field service dress, and service uniforms. The latter was the result of reforms back in 1926, which replaced the World War One choker-collar uniform with a service jacket, shirt, and tie. These were an enormous social asset for the GI in Britain, making them look like officers to the British eye. Cases were reported of Tommies who accidentally saluted American privates on account of their uniforms. Enhancing the well-dressed look were the GI's rubber-soled shoes with leather uppers, instead of the British hobnailed boots, which betrayed his soldierly status wherever he walked.[3]

Most British troops only encountered GIs in off-duty situations. In the pub or dance hall the GI's wealth and appearance enhanced his appeal to female company. This setting also heightened the GI's notorious tendency to "talk big." Particularly resented were the taunts about British military failures. Standard lines (heard or reported) included: "Gimme a beer as quick as you guys got out of Dunkirk," and "I hear the British flag has four colours: red, white, blue—and yellow." Fights were common between troops the worse for drink. Even friendly contact was difficult for impoverished Tommies. As one remarked ruefully: "It is our country and half the time we cannot even afford to buy the Americans a drink. It is a case of our guests treating us—and paying in bank notes." British troops therefore found it hard to get to know Americans. Instead they would deride GIs for being pampered— "as many dresses as a debutante"—and for their casual manners. An ATS woman soldier in Norwich wrote caustically in the spring of 1943:

> I quite agree that their uniforms are snappy, but from a military point of view a bunch of boy scouts could give them points and a bad beating. They are slovenly, untidy, and quite undisciplined. They can't march or drill and to see them salute would make a cat laugh. Don't think I'm prejudiced against them. I know some swell chaps in the U.S. army but they aren't soldiers.

There were many jokes about the array of ribbons on American chests. "Heard of the three Yanks who went to a war film? Well, one immediately fainted and the other two got a medal for carrying him out." And there was considerable malicious pleasure at news of the Americans' reverse at Kasserine in February 1943. "The Yanks Are Running" was widely sung, putting new words to the old World War One tune.[4]

The fact that the GI was better paid and better dressed than his British counterpart was undoubtedly central to the ill-feeling between them. But the insults about Dunkirk and Kasserine remind us that national pride was also at stake. And, as more detached British observers admitted, instead of blaming the overpaid GI, one could as well say that the Tommy was underpaid.[5] The resentment of British soldiers towards the GIs in 1942–44 can only be understood by reference to the morale and welfare problems of the *British* Army in the dark middle period of the war.

In May 1942 there were over 1.5 million *non-American* soldiers in the United Kingdom, most of them British. At a time when there were only two American divisions in Northern Ireland, there were thirty-four British divisions and five Canadian in the UK, as well as four other Allied brigade groups (Dutch, Belgian, Czech, and Norwegian).[6]

Creating a large army had been just as difficult for the British as for the Americans. Both countries had small professional forces in 1939 and conscription only took effect in Britain in October 1939, a year before the American draft. The Fall of France forced a massive expansion of the British Army—the so-called fifty-five-division scheme—and a rethink of tactics and training, which, during the Phoney War, had presupposed a repetition of trench warfare. The Army also had to be almost totally refitted, since most of its modern equipment had been left in Belgium. The crisis of 1940 kept everyone busy and occupied, and spirits were raised by easy victories against ill-trained Italian troops in Libya. The year 1941 was a very different matter, however. The inertia of the winter and the diminished threat of invasion after Hitler turned against Russia left troops at home bored and apathetic. The desertion rate in the year from October 1940 averaged ten per thousand men—double the previous year and the peak for the whole war. Courts-martial likewise tripled in incidence to one per thousand, which the Adjutant General, Sir Ronald Adam, attributed to the expansion of the Army to include "men who were not so readily subject to discipline" and to the "boredom resulting from enforced inactivity."[7]

Interviewing soldiers in the spring of 1941, Mass-Observation found that "aimlessness" and "loneliness" were the two perennial complaints. Men were bored with their job and with the lack of action; they missed home, family, and a normal sex life. Poorly paid and lacking friends of both sexes, the British soldier found little to amuse him off duty. M-O concluded that "while the service man usually has more leisure on his hands than he had in his peacetime job, his choice of methods of employing it are severely limited." One bombardier in the AA Command summed up the Army sardonically as a

fine introduction into monastic life with the emphasis on poverty, chastity and obedience. The soldier's poverty was created by rates of pay kept deliberately low in order to restrict him socially. The demand for total obedience resulted in the issuing of lunatic orders by men who had little idea of the consequences of carrying out those orders. The unnatural demand for chastity was enforced by locating men in wildernesses, deserts and jungles, sometimes for years at a time.[8]

The other great morale problem was persistent defeat. The disasters in Greece and Crete in April and May 1941 were followed by a stream of reverses in the North African desert once Rommel's command and a leaven of German troops stiffened the Italian armies. At the end of May 1941 Sir John Dill, then Chief of the Imperial General Staff, warned Churchill that "we started the war without an army. Although we are getting on, our army is not an army, except in name." In 1942 things got worse. February saw the surrender of Singapore and June the capitulation of Tobruk—in both cases to inferior forces. "Our army is the mockery of the world," scribbled Sir Alexander Cadogan of the FO in his diary in February. "We are out-generalled everywhere," he wrote in June. The effect on policymakers' confidence in the Army was devastating and we have seen how it contributed to Churchill's reluctance to risk a second front in 1942. But these debacles also contributed to an equally serious morale crisis in the Army itself. In North Africa the British had the advantage in men and matériel, yet they kept falling back. Although superior German equipment was often blamed, particularly the dreaded 88mm guns, most criticism was reserved for training and leadership. "Amateurs" against "professionals" was the refrain in London and Egypt. The commander in North Africa, Gen. Sir Claude Auchinleck, was the main target, but the problem went deeper than that. "Half our Corps and Divisional Commanders are totally unfit for their appointments," wrote the weary CIGS, Gen. Sir Alan Brooke, on 31 March 1942. Yet, he added, "if I were to sack them I could find no better! They lack character, imagination, drive, and power of leadership."[9]

Churchill entirely agreed, but he could not say so in public. He therefore tried to make defeat less bitter by making the enemy more awesome. After Rommel had captured Benghazi on 29 January 1942 he told the Commons: "We have a very daring and skilful opponent against us, and, may I say across the havoc of war, a great general." Brooke, in private, explained defeat very differently as "nothing less than bad generalship on the part of Auchinleck." Hitler, a master propagandist, appreciated what Churchill was up to. In July 1942 he remarked:

> People frequently ask how it is that Rommel enjoys so great a world-wide reputation. Not a little is due to Churchill's speeches in the House of Commons, in which, for tactical reasons of policy, the British Prime Minister always portrays Rommel as a military genius. Churchill's reason for doing so, of course, is that he does not wish to admit that the British are getting a damned good hiding from the Italians in Egypt and Libya.[10]

It is only in this atmosphere of boredom, alienation, and defeat that the impact of Gen. Bernard Montgomery on the British Army can be properly understood. As the American soldier-historian Carlo D'Este has observed, "American opinion of him has, over the years, evolved into a stereotyped image of a pretentious, egotistical general whose achievements never matched an inflated reputation." Undoubtedly, Montgomery was often his worst enemy—vain about himself, condescending about the Americans, and ready to embroider the record to his own benefit. Yet he was enormously important to the revival of the British Army in 1941–42. First, he was an outstanding trainer of troops. With missionary zeal after Dunkirk, he set about creating efficient, purposeful soldiers—rising through divisional and corps appointments to head South-Eastern Command in November 1941. He rooted out incompetent officers, instituted year-round training, and excelled at large-scale, realistic exercises. He loved to descend unannounced on units and to speak directly to the men—"a tough, stringy bird-like little man" determined to make his impact not merely on senior officers but on ordinary soldiers. From an early stage, he developed an unrivaled rapport with his men.[11]

Montgomery not only trained troops, he also led them to victory. Taking command of the 8th Army in Egypt in August 1942, he galvanized commanders, men, and training. His triumph at El Alamein in November was preeminently an infantry victory—a bloody slogging match that tested training and stamina to the limits. Many have subsequently disparaged his achievement, noting that he enjoyed substantial logistic and intelligence advantages over Rommel. Also played down at the time was the fact that over half the tanks and artillery and 60 percent of the infantry in the Axis Army was Italian, and that only thirty-six of Montgomery's eighty-six infantry battalions were actually British. But even if Alamein was almost a victory of the Empire over the Italians, none of this mattered at the time. It was represented as the first occasion on which the British had beat the Germans. Churchill ordered church bells to ring out across the country in celebration. They had been silent since 1940 in readiness for warning of possible invasion. And when Montgomery returned to London on leave in May 1943 he was mobbed wherever he went. At the theatre the audience stood to applaud *him* not the cast; outside, crowds massed ten deep to see or even touch him. Undoubtedly "Monty" was an inveterate self-promoter, but nothing succeeds like success. His cult status in Britain was at the root of many Anglo-American command wrangles later in the war.[12]

Victory gave the British forces new pride, but basic problems remained. In the British Army no less than the American, troop morale and conduct were always worse behind the front lines. Just as British troops seemed "oversexed, overpaid, and over here" in France in

1939–40, so their misconduct aroused resentment in rear areas of the Middle East in 1942. British diplomats in Teheran warned that "we are being adversely compared to Bolsheviks" (the Russian soldiers were very strictly disciplined) and suggested that British troops should be clearly told that "they are here as allies and friends and are not in military occupation." In places like Teheran and Cairo, the problems were particularly acute. Men languished there for years without home leave and an element of racism undoubtedly coloured their relations with the civilian population. Yet "occupational hazards" were also evident in Britain. The GOC of Eastern Command warned his troops in East Anglia in November 1942 that their "looting and damage to property" were a "legitimate cause of reproach to the Army in civilian eyes." And the aimlessness identified by Mass-Observation in 1941 remained prevalent. War poet Kenneth Neal exclaimed:

> Let us have some clean killing at the last!
> We're tired of waste and muddle and the mind
> Perpetually and helplessly confined
> To barracks and parades upon a tidy square.[13]

In 1942–43 a few of those confined in England got their chance for some killing, in Northwest Africa, Sicily, and Italy. But many units remained in Britain for years. Sword Beach on 6 June 1944 was the first time the 3rd British Division had been in action since Dunkirk, four years before. Most of its men had served only on the Home Front. (Histories of its component regiments, such as the South Lancs, pass over these intervening years almost without comment.) The 15th Scottish Division, heavily mauled in the battle for Caen in June 1944, was an amalgam of territorial regiments—equivalent to the National Guard—none of which "had ever smelt powder in earnest," historian John Keegan has noted. "For four and a half years they had guarded the coasts against invasion and the inland counties of England against parachute descent, trained in endless divisional 'schemes' and regimental manoeuvres, and fired their weapons at paper targets and squares on the map." The occupational blues of the GIs were nothing to this—even the 29th U.S. Division was only in Britain for twenty months prior to D-Day.[14]

Of course, British troops were at home, whereas GIs were not. As Gen. Marshall liked to say, it was peculiarly hard to convince GIs that victory or defeat in the war would have much effect on their home and loved ones. But this was true, albeit to a lesser extent, in Britain in the middle of the war. By 1942 the threat of German invasion was no longer real and, apart from the "Baedeker Raids," German air attacks had largely abated until the "flying bombs" of summer 1944. Inaction encouraged apathy about the war effort among many soldiers and this could not be dispelled even through the more realistic training developed in 1941–42 by Montgomery and others. Of course, many British soldiers enjoyed periods of home leave denied to GIs. Wally Littlewood from the northern city of Sheffield was serving with the Royal Engineers down in Sussex in 1941–42. The "southerners" in his unit were able to go home on weekends or even overnight. Capt. Harold Foster, a grenadier guardsman attached to the 3rd Division on the south coast after Dunkirk, recalled: "Many Officers and Men had their wives in the Battalion area and soon permission was given for these men to live out so that normally, after the day's work and training was over, men could be with their families." While they felt it boosted morale, Montgomery ruthlessly evicted wives and families from the area of all his home commands on the grounds "that in war a soldier could not concentrate on his military training if half his mind was concerned with domestic problems." (The result was an inversion of conventional morality whereby sexual promiscuity caused less offence than connubial virtue.) But Monty was exceptional. The practice of having families nearby continued and, together with the availability of periodic home leave, was probably, on balance, deleterious to troop morale. Contact was insufficient to replicate "normal" family life, but enough to reinforce the part-time attitude to soldiering that Monty so detested.[15]

Perhaps the root problem was the fundamental alienation of many of the troops from the Army. A damning War Office morale report in July 1942 diagnosed two grave ailments. One was *lack of pride in the Army*—the growing evidence "that the ordinary soldier suffers from a lack of respect for himself as a member of the Army." Poor pay was a symbol. "The feeling that he is the worst paid of the Services, worse paid than other soldiers, and worse paid than the average civilian worker—facts which are brought home to him every time he enters a public house and almost every time he seeks female society—is most damaging to his self-respect." The other problem was the soldier's *lack of solidarity* with his military and political leaders. "The morale and fighting spirit of the Army as a whole would be enhanced if the ordinary soldier could be reassured that differentiations due to social tradition and the subordination involved in military discipline do not imply a fundamental conflict of interests." Put bluntly, this was a "them and us" mentality, which manifested itself particularly in anger at officer privileges and at the sham of formal inspections. The report argued that "the most powerful factor in creating or impairing a sense of solidarity in the Army is the regimental officer" and it lamented the "deplorably large proportion of officers who fail to care properly for their men's welfare and to inspire their respect."[16]

Animosity towards officers is, of course, a feature of every army and, as we have seen, the U.S. Army had enormous problems of its own in trying to root out the incompetent and unfit. Yet the British case was extreme. This was partly because the Great War's carnage had left a far greater mark on Britain than on America, both at the time and later. As Gen. Sir David Fraser has observed, the men who composed the British Army of 1939–45 came from "a profoundly unmilitary— indeed anti-military—generation," having imbibed the "vague pacifi-cism" of the interwar years and the general idea "that life in the army was nasty, brutish and probably short." Even more important was the fact that the normal army polarity of "them" and "us" was compli-cated by what Americans called the English "class system."[17]

Nomenclature itself betrayed the difference in attitude. In the U.S. Army the divide was between "officers" and "enlisted men"; the Brit-ish Army referred to "officers" and "other ranks." At the beginning of the war officers remained overwhelmingly "gentlemen" in the British Army—in 1939 84 percent of entrants to Sandhurst (Britain's West Point) had been to "public school." Some believed it should stay that way. Lt. Col. Bingham wrote to *The Times* in January 1941 to insist that officers should be drawn only from "the aristocratic and feudal" classes who knew how to look after "their people." In 1940–41 Bing-ham and his ilk were satirized in papers like the *Daily Mirror* as "Colonel Blimps"—the prewar creation of cartoonist David Low and embodiment of fossilized, upper-class jingoism. They, and the caste system they represented, became scapegoats for Britain's defeats. It was, like all caricatures, often unfair. There were numerous examples of how the studied sangfroid of an "Eton and Oxford" officer inspired men under fire. Even Americans were not immune. One imperturbable officer at Anzio in 1944 was dubbed by GIs "Typical Englishman No. 1." According to a journalist, he was "a reservoir of strength and his clipped English and stylised public-school attitude to every situa-tion helped to create the legend that nothing could 'rattle' him. It was impossible to believe that an exploding shell held any menace when the captain remarked in his quiet drawl, 'God, that landed only a mashie shot away.' "[18]

Nevertheless, the debacles of 1941–42 helped democratize officer recruitment, with special selection boards and psychological testing. Again Montgomery was symbolic of the change. His concern for his men and his informal dress (the beret became as much a trademark as Churchill's cigar) were emblematic of a new approach to command in a democratic army. Nor was he obsessed about the uniforms of his troops. He claimed to have issued only one order on dress to the 8th Army in North Africa, after a naked Canadian soldier had leaned out of a truck to doff a top hat in salute as his commander went by. Even Monty felt that this was too much and issued a one-line order: "Top hats will not be worn in the Eighth Army." As Angus Calder has put it, Monty "was by way of being the People's General of the People's War."[19]

Like so many English institutions, however, this was a case of new wine in old bottles. The officer corps was broadened in composition, but its ethos remained much the same. The Army continued to reproduce the manners and hierarchies of an English public school, aided by the deeply rooted regimental system with its atavistic loyalties fostered in separate "messes." As an American OWI report observed in March 1942, although only a quarter of cadets at Officer Cadet Training Units were from public schools, the rest seemed happy to become "gentlemen by proxy for the duration of the war," adopting the polished cross straps, swagger canes, long haircuts, and "Mayfair moustaches" of the "traditional British military gentleman." What made matters worse, the report argued, was that these men "were leading an Army run on machines, though often they know less about the mechanics than the men they command. As a result considerable dissatisfaction has spread through the ranks, expressing itself chiefly in inter-class friction."[20]

The most serious consequence of this social-cum-technological divide was in the armoured divisions. All armies in the 1930s were slow to abandon the horse, but the problem was particularly acute in Britain where a tactical divide was reinforced by class distinctions. The "professionals" were in the Royal Tank Corps, equipped with slow, heavily armed Infantry tanks to support the foot soldiers. The cavalry remained an "exclusive and expensive club" for scions of the landed elite. When the cavalry units were eventually mechanized in the late 1930s they were simply converted into armoured regiments within a separate Royal Armoured Corps and equipped with lighter, faster Cruiser tanks. The result, to quote historians Shelford Bidwell and Dominick Graham, was to hand "the new, decisive arm of the future over to the most mentally inert, unprofessional and reactionary group in the British army." Despite the fusion of the two corps and their enlargement during the war, the cavalry ethos remained dominant. Most tank men conceived of their role in traditional cavalry terms, as reconnaissance and shock troops, and this attitude was reinforced by early successes in the Western desert. The idea that tanks should work closely with infantry was abhorrent—socially as much as militarily. Before Alamein a cavalry officer tried to refuse the attachment of a regiment of the Royal Artillery: "We only accept support from the Royal *Horse* Artillery." The cavalrymen were slow to learn their lesson—as the carnage of the tank charge outside Caen in July 1944 was to show. Aptly, that operation was code-named Goodwood—for one of England's major horse-race meetings.[21]

The GIs, it should now be clear, were a symptom more than a cause of the morale problems in the British Army. For the Tommy, being underpaid was but one facet of being an underemployed underclass. Yet the Americans provided a yardstick against which British soldiers could measure their predicament, being the most numerous and best treated Allied contingent in Britain by late 1943. And the "inter-attachments" between the two armies in the winter of 1943–44 provided opportunities for informed comparison on both sides.

The idea for these exchanges was derived from North Africa where, it was found, "British and American troops evidently get on better when they are out side by side on the same job than when they are side by side in the same bar." In the winter of 1943–44 some ten thousand British and American troops in Britain were involved in official exchanges. Small groups, usually one officer and ten men, lived with a similar unit of the other army for up to two weeks. The effects were generally beneficial. One group of GIs, attached to a British transport company in Belfast, was "unanimous in saying that their attitude to the British Army in general and toward the individual soldier, was changed completely by their exchange tour of duty." A U.S. officer who took some GIs to a British signals unit in Buckinghamshire reported that his men were

> told very frankly about a week after they arrived that the [British] soldiers had not looked forward to our being attached. They said that most Americans they had observed were very rowdy and loud and seemed only intent on bragging about what they were doing to win the war. They then qualified this by saying that their opinion had been changed completely after living so closely together with our men.[22]

But exchanges also provided a chance for more critical analysis. U.S. officers were struck by the British class divide. One of them, attached to a British Army hospital in Southampton in the summer of 1943, wrote home that at dinner

> I mentioned how beautiful Ingrid Bergman was. "Be careful, sir," someone said. "There is a fine of drinks all around if you mention girls in this Mess, simply not done." . . . Other topics which are taboo are religion and money, which limits the discourse to polo, cricket, dogs and the war. You may tell jokes, but they must be from Punch and you must always quote Punch as your authority. This morning I dunked my toast and the chappie alongside said "I remember so well 8 years ago seeing a man who had been to America doing that in the mess—bit of a shock you know!" He hadn't gotten over it yet.

The more technological RAF seemed just as hidebound. One AAF officer dined with an RAF Training School in November 1943— "drinks, blessing, service, menu, toast to the King all were in striking contrast to our Services."[23]

Most soldiers did not penetrate an officers' mess. For them the difference in hierarchies was most evident in the place of the noncommissioned officer (NCO to the British, noncom to the Americans). By early 1944 nearly 40 percent of enlisted men in the U.S. Army were noncoms—about 2.5 million out of 6.5 million—and by the end of the war nearly half. In the British Army the proportion of NCOs to privates was much less, and they were also quartered and messed separately from their men, unlike American noncoms. Thus, the British NCO had a status and a role that was distinctive. One report from the 5th U.S. Infantry Division in Northern Ireland noted that he was "highly trained, commands great respect and performs many of the duties normally done by a commissioned officer in the U.S. Army." Gen. Marshall certainly thought that the segregation of British NCOs was better for discipline and leadership. On the British side, some soldiers took a similar view, but others commented favourably on the general lack of "class distinction" in the U.S. Army. Judgements among GIs also varied, but the dominant note was that British practice stifled initiative: "The [men] rely too much on the NCOs."[24]

Another difference was that the British Army operated on a more relaxed timetable. Not only was the working day shorter, but there was a half-hour break mid-morning and the lunch hour was ninety minutes not sixty. Most British units also had "tea" late afternoon and "supper" in the early evening. The British predilection for tea was a subject of amusement to GIs both in camp and on the battlefield. One anonymous American poet penned this caricature:

The General sat on the anxious seat
Watching his troops in the battle heat
When a courier drove up the shell torn street
With a message grave that spelled defeat
Unless the General could stem the retreat.
So the General called for his battle map
And figured a plan to escape the trap
He jumped in his jeep and buckled his strap
But his batman placed a tray in his lap
And his adjutant said, "I say old chap
You cawn't do it now, it's tea time."[25]

For many American soldiers, "teatime" became the metaphor for a languid, almost indolent approach to warfare that seemed peculiarly British. The contrast was especially striking to those who served in both forces. Bob Raymond from Kansas volunteered for the RAF in 1940 but transferred to the AAF in June 1943. He found that GIs differed greatly from the men with whom he had been associated during the previous three years:

> Every one of them has a light-hearted, happy-go-lucky expression as though they were enjoying life. They talk and laugh loudly at work and wear the most oddly assorted clothes. Their headgear is especially varied—from something that looks like a baseball cap to the regular military peak cap. . . . This is a most democratic Army too in a thousand small ways. I had forgotten that my fellow citizens were like that, or rather I guess I've been too long used to the more class-conscious British way. . . . The Yankee energy here displayed is infectious. It makes me feel like I've been sleep walking.[26]

On material conditions, comparisons were overwhelmingly in the Americans' favour. British soldiers were able to see firsthand the abundance and cheapness of goods in the PX. In the messes the fruit, fruit juices, and sweets were matters of comment. Capt. Ted Fossieck in Ulster provided extra cookies for one of his men who had not "been able to get enough to eat after spending two weeks with the British." Bob Raymond found AAF food "so good and plentiful that I can scarcely believe I'm still in England." Across the board, the U.S. Army seemed to have more material resources. Tom Tateson, a Yorkshireman, retained a vivid memory of Hampshire just before D-Day, where his signals unit shared washing-up facilities with the Americans: "In the British Army in those days a single bin full of luke-warm greasy water was all we had to dip our mess tins in. The Yanks had a row of three bins of hot water to be used in sequence, so that the third one remained perfectly clean and clear. A simple and common-sense refinement," said Tateson, "but one which made a great difference and seemed to us a luxury."[27]

Many British soldiers, even if they did not experience interattachments, had glimpses like Tateson's. Although instinctively patriotic, they were left with images of an army that was less stratified than their own and that used more of its superior wealth and technology to the benefit of the "poor bloody infantry." It was a powerful cultural message—on both sides. Contact with the downtrodden and apparently sluggish British Army could only strengthen the GI's sense of material and cultural superiority. British soldiers may not have been the recipients of gum or nylons, but for them, no less than British kids or women, the GI contributed to the process of creeping Americanization. I shall return to these themes in the penultimate chapter.

The GIs also encountered other Allied soldiers in Britain, especially Canadians. In January 1943, the Canadian Army in Britain amounted to some 170,000 men. By comparison, the Polish contingent numbered about 25,000, the Czechs 3,200, the Belgians and Dutch each around 2,000, and the Norwegians 1,750. Most of the 35,000 Free French were in England at this time, but they departed for the Mediterranean later in 1943. Canadian strength peaked at just over 200,000 in mid-1943, when it was still larger than the American, but then, with dispersals to Sicily and Italy, it declined to 170,000 at the end of 1943 (when GI numbers had reached 773,000) and stayed at this level to D-Day. Even so, the Canadians remained culturally significant for the GIs. They were the only other major English-speaking foreign contingent in Britain and they occupied a delicate position as both a former British colony and an uneasy neighbour of the United States. The relationship between Tommies, Yanks, and Canucks is therefore of especial interest.[28]

After the crisis of 1942, described in chapter 9, reports on Canadian discipline and morale indicate a steady improvement in 1943. This was partly because Gen. McNaughton's policy of not packaging out his troops in peripheral theatres under British command was overridden by Ottawa. Canadians were finally sent into action in the Mediterranean theatre. But the nature of the Canadian presence in Britain was also significant. For eighteen months from autumn 1941, three Canadian infantry divisions had been on anti-invasion duties in Sussex and many of their men were billeted in local houses, particularly during winter. A British liaison officer with the Canadian Army reported in May 1943 that in southeast England there now exists a kind of joint communal life between residents and troops, and no civic function is held in which the Canadians do not actively participate. There is the same participation in the home life of the communities and to date over 10,000 Canadian soldiers have been welcomed into British families as sons in law. The Mayor of Guildford, whose son in law is a Canadian corporal, cannot speak too highly of him.

(The Canadian Army, as noted in chapter 13, took a much more lenient attitude to soldier marriages than the American Army.) After training in Scotland, the 3rd Division settled into Hampshire in a similar way from September 1943. Although morale sagged as usual during the winter, the indiscipline and fights of 1941–42 were a thing of the past. A survey of over ten thousand letters from Canadian soldiers over the period 6–20 April 1944 concluded that "relations between British civilians and Canadian troops continue to be very cordial, and not one adverse comment has been seen." The war diary of one regiment from the 3rd Division contains this remarkable entry for 31 August 1944, during fierce fighting in France: "We who have spent so many years in England think and speak constantly of England and our friends there . . . even to the point of appearing disloyal to Canada. The thought of returning there on leave sometime soon alone makes life supportable at times."[29]

Not everyone was pleased to hear that Canadian troops were making themselves at home in England. The figures for Canadian marriages, for instance, were deliberately played down because of resentment by British troops that the "colonials" were grabbing local girls. In British units overseas the most extravagant rumours about Canadian adultery, promiscuity, and VD were rife. The commander of one infantry battalion in Persia, most of whose men came from Sussex, reported to the War Office in May 1943 that there was "more bitter feeling against the Canadians at present than against the Germans." (The charges were investigated by Canadian Military HQ who found them greatly exaggerated and noted that the record for offences against women by British troops in Sussex was much worse!) This British unit was abroad and inactive; consequently men were prey to all the worst morale problems. But it was generally true that British soldiers got on less well with Canadian troops than did British civilians—the same pattern as with GIs and for the same "overpaid, over-sexed" reasons.[30]

Nevertheless, relations with British troops did improve steadily over time. In January 1943 one Canadian censorship report stated that the "mutual dislike and distrust of each other, notable in the earlier days, have disappeared." The Canadian Army's compulsory savings scheme was undoubtedly a factor, but what helped most was that, unlike the Americans, the Canadians were not a self-contained force. Their doctrine and equipment were British, and they trained and exercised regularly with British units. McNaughton commanded a mixed corps of Canadian, British, and New Zealand troops in 1940; conversely Montgomery had the two Canadian corps under his Army command in southeast England in 1941–42. As historian John English remarked in 1991, although "no formal alliance existed between Britain and Canada, the forces of the two nations were more closely integrated than those of the NATO allies today. Canadian and British formations were completely interchangeable and their artillery and staff systems perfectly gloved." In consequence, Canadian and British troops saw much more of each other in working hours. There was nothing comparable to the formal Anglo-American inter-attachments of 1943–44, because they were happening all the time. Although never reaching the harmony of Canadian-civilian relations, contact between the two armies caused much less friction in 1943–44 than earlier in the war.[31]

There was another important reason for the improved relations—the arrival of the GIs turned the Anglo-Canadian polarity into a triangular relationship. One report in February 1943 noted that the "bonds of friendship between Canadian and British troops seem to have been strengthened by the arrival of the Americans, who occasionally get disliked by making some initial mistakes, as did the Canadians." To the British, the GIs seemed brasher, wealthier, and rowdier than the Canadians, whose conduct became more acceptable in consequence. Canadian troops, for their part, resented the superior food and conditions of the GIs. "Why they live like Kings compared to the Canadian Army," groused one Canadian signalman in June 1943, "and mind you they were complaining." The quality of the ARC Service Clubs and their "GIs-only" policy were frequent grievances, as was the fuss British officialdom made about hospitality for GIs. One Canadian soldier complained in August 1942:

> The papers are full of them. M.P.'s [members of Parliament] organize drives to get people to invite them out to tea and all such things. Canadians are thus maddened for they have been here over 2½ years and nothing like that was ever done. . . . The typical piece in the papers is—Remember these boys are 3000 miles from home etc. etc. Wonder where we come from.

"It appears that wherever Canadian and American troops meet there is trouble," wrote the British regional information officer in Manchester in July 1942.[32]

These kinds of comments recurred in 1943–44, but, as Canadians became used to the American presence, so a more complex pattern emerged. Some continued to grouse about GIs, others warmed to them. Even in August 1942 one censorship report considered that "Canadian soldiers seem to have much in common with the U.S. soldiers—more so than with the British soldiers." The same sentiments were sometimes voiced at the top. Gen. Frederick F. Worthington, commander of the 4th Armoured Division, depressed about the war, opined in the same month "that we will have to look to the Americans to win it. He says they are so far ahead of the English in ideas and equipment that he thinks Canada should adopt their organization and plan to do our fighting as part of their army." Canadian tank-enthusiasts like Worthington had worked particularly closely with the Americans, but the sense of North American identity was widespread. One officer wrote at the end of 1943 that Englishmen

don't seem to realise that we are much closer to the Americans than we are to them. And that is particularly true of the boys from the West. There are a bunch of B[ritish] C[olumbia] boys here . . . and they seem to have stronger ties with the U.S. than they have even with Eastern Canada.[33]

Overall, Canadian reactions to the GIs remained ambivalent, with much depending, as ever, on individual temperament, background, and experiences. Charles Murphy, editor of *Fortune* magazine, judged in January 1944 after a visit to Britain that the arrival of the U.S. Army had cast the Canadians in a new role as Anglo-American interpreters—"trying to explain the Americans to the British, and the British to the Americans whom they meet in the pubs." That perhaps smacks too much of the fashionable wartime metaphor of Canada as "linchpin" in the Anglo-American alliance. What one can conclude, however, is that being in Britain in company with Americans forced many Canadian soldiers to think hard about their own sense of identity. Canada was moving away from a British past towards an increasingly Americanized future. Some welcomed this, others did not; their reactions to Yanks and Limeys were bound up with these feelings.[34]

Whereas many Canadians had complexes about the United States, most GIs couldn't give a damn about Canada and its people—except American blacks. Unlike the U.S. Army the Canadians did not operate segregation. Of course, the Canadian black population was minuscule by comparison with the American—officially twenty thousand out of a population of 11 million in 1931—and it was concentrated in Halifax, Nova Scotia, and a few towns in southwest Ontario. But the difference in treatment was noted by American blacks. One wrote in April 1944:

> I'd say that England is a grand country, mainly because the Englishman does not look at a coloured person the way an American does, you know what I mean, you are not looked on as a dumb native, or something worse, as you are in the States. This mainly was one of my reasons for coming to Canada and fighting with the Canadian army with boys of all colours, from all walks of life. I wouldn't be in any other army.

The point was also taken by black U.S. Gen. Benjamin O. Davis. In October 1942 he visited the Canadian Army hospital at Cliveden in Berkshire, where he talked to a coloured private from Chatham, Ontario, just across Lake St. Clair from Detroit. After the visit Davis recorded sadly in his diary: "No color prejudice there. He is with his white comrades. A border line makes so much difference."[35]

The GIs set off complex reactions among British and other Allied troops, acting as catalysts for their own cultural chemistry. But their most important impact, as far as the war effort was concerned, was on British commanders.

British appraisals of the first GIs to arrive were distinctly unflattering. The British commander in Ulster reported in May 1942 "that not only is the standard of the American troops pretty low, but worse still they appear to be quite complacent about it." When the 1st Infantry Division arrived in England in August 1942, its initial indiscipline also made a bad impression, particularly since it was an old division, largely composed of regulars for whom the excuses about National Guardsmen or draftees could not be invoked. The head of British Southern Command considered the men "untrained, unhardened, and very raw and amateurish. Not fit to fight for a very long time—twelve to eighteen months."[36]

In Washington Gen. Marshall was well aware of British scepticism and of the need to counter it, if he wanted an early attack across the Channel. (After the war he reckoned that British doubts that the U.S. could produce "workmanlike divisions" had been a major reason for their opposition to a second front in 1942–43.) In May and June 1942 he therefore staged a series of special visits to Army camps for British VIPs, including Churchill. All responded with fulsome letters of praise. Churchill wrote Stimson that "I have never been more impressed than I was with the bearing of the men whom I saw" and told his aide, Gen. Ismay, that the troops were "wonderful material and will learn very quickly." Churchill had been particularly struck by the 77th Division—a draftee division that had been organized only in April. This was one of Marshall's showpiece units. After seeing it two weeks earlier, Mountbatten told Marshall: "the fact that this state of efficiency can be reached in eight weeks has completely revolutionised my ideas of the future." Both Churchill and Mountbatten had latched onto something very important—the Americans were quick learners. But they knew that the 77th was not representative of the U.S. Army as a whole in 1942. And the British military, in particular, were very alert to present deficiencies. Gen. Sir Alan Brooke, Marshall's British counterpart, who accompanied Churchill, noted afterwards: "The American systems of individual and elementary training seem excellent, but I am not so certain that their higher training is good enough, or that they have yet realised the standard of training required." This was also the opinion of Field Marshal Sir John Dill, head of the British staff mission in Washington.[37]

The U.S. Army's first taste of action against the Germans only reinforced British doubts. The defeats inflicted on the 1st Armored Division around Kasserine in mid-February and on the 34th Division at Fondouk at the end of March shocked Americans in Tunisia and back home. Tactics had been faulty, command indecisive, and some troops fled under fire. In fact, these two divisions were unready for battle—training had suffered while they were cooped up in Ulster. The debacles also reflected faulty intelligence and dispositions, for which the British shared the blame. And under Gen. George S. Patton and his successor, Gen. Omar N. Bradley, II Corps in Tunisia was hammered into shape. But there was no denying the fact of defeat, or the way it reinforced British prejudices. For Eisenhower's aide, Harry Butcher, "the outstanding fact" after Kasserine was "that the proud and cocky Americans today stand humiliated by one of the greatest defeats in our history. This is particularly embarrassing to us with the British." Montgomery told Brooke that apparently "the Bosche does just whatever he likes with the Americans." On 4 April he felt that "the American contribution to the party up to date has been very disappointing."[38]

The most damning indictment came from Gen. Sir Harold Alexander, commander of all Allied ground troops in North Africa. On 3 April

1943 he sent a six-page, handwritten letter to Brooke, heading it "most secret." According to Alex, the Americans were "very nice, very matey," but

> they simply do not know their job as soldiers, and this is the case from the highest to the lowest, from the General to the private soldier. Perhaps the weakest link of all is the junior leader, who just does not lead, with the result that their men don't really fight. . . . a few bombs and they all go to ground and call for air support. . . . In fact, they are soft, green and quite untrained. . . . If this handful of Divisions here are their best, the value of the remainder may be imagined.

Alexander allowed that "the Americans have the human material for a first class army. After all, these same men's grandfathers fought like heroes in the Civil War." But he felt it would require enormous work, particularly with the officers. Apart from sacking the failures ruthlessly, he said, they "must attach their best and most promising young potential commanders to our best units and go into battle with them— so that they may see how we do it."[39]

Brooke copied the letter to Dill in Washington, only to be reprimanded by Churchill, who did not think that anything so sensitive "should have been sent out of this country to anyone." Brooke warned Dill that he "should on no account communicate any version, whether bowdlerised or not" to Marshall, and Dill assured Churchill that he had not done so. But, according to one of his aides, Dill *did* show a copy to Marshall. The latter brushed it off, saying "Do not worry, they will learn in their own way and I think very quickly," but he did not forget or forgive. A decade after the war Marshall was still saying that "Alexander did us great harm by his statement that our troops were not battle worthy."[40]

Both sides drew lasting lessons from Tunisia. For the British, the most important was the idea of Americans under British tutelage. Although U.S. troops were less numerous than the British in North Africa, Eisenhower was placed in charge of Torch because both governments agreed that, given the continuing Anglo-French recriminations about 1940, a British commander would be more likely to antagonize the French and thus elicit armed opposition. (Marshall admitted after the war that this promoted Ike "further than would have been done normally.") When operations in Libya and Tunisia were fused, the British were happy for Eisenhower to continue as Supreme Commander, even though their troops were still preponderant. This was partly because he ran an harmonious Allied Force Headquarters (AFHQ), but also because, in counterbalance, Alexander would be in charge of the actual battle. Brooke wrote later that the elevation of Ike was "flattering and pleasing" to the Americans and

> they did not at the time fully appreciate the underlying intentions. We were pushing Eisenhower up into the stratosphere and rarified atmosphere of a Supreme Commander, where he would be free to devote his time to the political and inter-allied problems, whilst we inserted under him one of our own commanders to deal with the military situations and to restore the necessary drive and co-ordination which had been so seriously lacking. . . .

Harold Macmillan, British political adviser at AFHQ, explained the philosophy to a new member of his staff:

> you will always permit your American colleague not only to have a superior rank to yourself and much higher pay, but also the feeling that he is running the show. This will enable you to run it yourself. We . . . are Greeks in this American empire. . . . We must run AFHQ as the Greek slaves ran the operations of the Emperor Claudius.[41]

This condescension was understandable. While GIs were learning the hard way in Tunisia, the victory at Alamein and Rommel's retreat had turned Montgomery and the 8th Army into international celebrities, not least in the United States. Hard-won victory made British officers even more patronising about the neophyte Americans, many of whose commanders had come to North Africa virtually unbloodied. Even the dynamic Patton had only been in battle for a total of three days before he landed in Morocco; Alexander, though six years younger, had ten years of service in combat theatres and had been wounded three times. Brooke and Montgomery were particularly contemptuous of Eisenhower, most of whose career had been spent as a staff officer. Monty told Brooke in April 1943 that Eisenhower was "a very nice chap. I should say he is probably quite good on the political side. But I can also say, quite definitely, that he knows nothing whatever about how to make war or to fight battles; he should be kept right away from all that business if we want to win the war."[42]

The British were happy to follow the same "stratosphere" approach for the invasion of Sicily in July 1943, with Alexander in charge of ground forces under Eisenhower's overall command. Although Alex praised the improvement in U.S. troops (especially to Americans), his doubts remained. He assigned a supporting role to Patton's 7th Army because he deemed it inferior to Monty's British 8th Army. But Sicily was "the proving ground where the U.S. Army came of age," in the words of historian Carlo D'Este. As Marshall told Dill, the GIs *were* quick learners. Compared with Tunisia, troop performance and staying power were excellent, and both Patton and Bradley proved themselves as leaders, albeit in different moulds. Ike cabled Marshall: "The Americans here have established themselves as a completely worthy teammate for the famous British Eighth Army." Especially impressive was American mobility, as Montgomery himself recognised. While his units were tied down in the east, Patton's troops slipped Alexander's leash and raced across the west and north of the island. The contrast was not due simply to Monty's caution. With new Sherman tanks instead of inferior Grants, and ample numbers of trucks, the Americans were equipped to move more quickly than the British. Sicily was an early intimation of how American technology would rewrite the conduct of warfare in 1944–45.[43]

This was one reason why American commanders had no intention of accepting British tutelage—they had much to teach as well as to learn. In any case, they had drawn their own lessons from North Africa. The Kasserine fiasco was partly because the 1st Armored was packaged in small detachments under overall British command. In the future, U.S. officers believed—reiterating the Pershing principle from 1918—their troops must fight as organic divisions under American command. Otherwise the Limeys would steal all the credit, as when entering Tunis in triumph in May 1943. British gibes like "how green was my ally" and references to the U.S. Army as "our Italians" were deeply resented. "The British have gypped us out of everything," a disgusted Gen. McNair told Ike's deputy, Mark Clark, after visiting the Tunisian front. Patton fumed in his diary in April 1943: "God damn all British and all so-called Americans who have their legs pulled by them. I would rather be commanded by an Arab."[44]

Patton, however, was fuming at everyone, regardless of nationality. Eisenhower, Devers, and especially Clark were also victims of his anger. What Patton had in acute form was a disease afflicting most senior U.S. officers in 1942–43: promotionitis. All professional soldiers suffer from it in war, because that is the only time they can prove themselves. But the Americans were infected even more than the British, because the interwar period had been so barren of opportunity and because the United States had entered the war so late. In 1942 it mattered more than ever to be in the right place at the right time, because windows of opportunity opened spectacularly and closed abruptly, playing havoc with normal patterns of promotion. Clark, two years Eisenhower's junior at West Point but a protégé of both Marshall and McNair, won his first star in August 1941, when Ike had only just been made full colonel. In 1938–39 Ike asked Clark to help him get out of the Philippines, where he had languished for all the 1930s; in 1940 he was eager for a staff job under Patton when the latter took command of an armoured division. As late as April 1942 Ike told Patton that by the time he got out of "this slave seat" in the War Department, "you'll be the 'Black Jack' [Pershing] of the dam [sic] war." Yet working for Marshall proved Eisenhower's ticket to stardom. Within six months he was a lieutenant general, outranking Patton, seven years his senior, and pulling Clark into *his* orbit. Patton was left fuming about Ike and Clark, the "boy wonders." His hatred of Clark cooled in 1943 once he had outstripped him: "Looking back, men seem less vile," Patton observed in a telling diary entry. He remained bitter at Ike, but knew that his career now depended on the man he called "Divine Destiny" Eisenhower.[45]

The rivalry among these three is a reminder of how much was at stake for senior American officers and how easily British commanders could become the all-purpose scapegoats for their frustrations. For Patton and Clark, in fact, the Mediterranean war became an exercise in personal and national vindication. In Sicily Patton was emphatic that "the U.S. must win—not as an ally, but as a conqueror." He told the commander of the 45th Division: "This is a horse race, in which the prestige of the U.S. Army is at stake. We must take Messina before the British." They did, with almost a day to spare, but the strain on Patton was partly responsible for two notorious occasions when he slapped shell-shocked GIs—nearly ending his career but for Ike's continued support. In fact, the rivalry was much more on Patton's side than that of Monty, who, for all his vanity, genuinely admired Patton's dash and mobility. The story repeated itself in Italy. In May 1944 the publicity-conscious Clark convinced himself that Alexander and the British were engaged in a conspiracy to deny him and his Army a fair share of the glory. Clark's suspicions, "amounting to paranoia," were so strong and his ambition so consuming that he defied Alexander's orders in his headlong rush "to be first in Rome and to be there before *Overlord*." He enjoyed his Roman triumph for two days before the Normandy landings pushed everything else out of the headlines.[46]

Eisenhower, alone, stood above this personalized nationalism. That was partly because, as Supreme Commander, his own career was now tied to the success of the alliance. But it was also a matter of temperament. His affable, informal manner (and his ability to get others like

Clark and Bedell Smith to do his dirty work) made him hard to dislike. Only Brooke and Monty continued to doubt his abilities; his British naval and air subordinates in the Mediterranean, Cunningham and Tedder, became good friends, and Churchill was an enthusiastic admirer. Ike also had a unique vision of alliance cooperation. There was no historical precedent for Allied Force HQ and he devoted most of his energies to making it work. According to a disgusted Patton, Ike said he "did not consider himself as an American but as an ally." He told Marshall that his method was to drag all disputes "squarely into the open, discuss them frankly, and insist upon positive rather than negative action in furthering the purpose of Allied unity." In staff discussions he refused to "deal with our military problems on an American vs. British basis," despite the natural instinct of each side. Although he denied being "ambidextrous in attitude," this was in fact an excellent description of the Allied two-handedness that he achieved. It was Churchill who said that "there is only one thing worse than fighting with allies, and that is fighting without them!" But Ike alone made virtue out of necessity.[47]

Allied Force HQ was a unique achievement, but biographer Stephen Ambrose has pointed out "how often and how seriously Eisenhower botched things in North Africa" as a military commander. He was cautious in his use of troops, hesitant in judgement, slow to remove inept commanders, and often bogged down in detail. Undoubtedly he had improved by September 1943, when his forces invaded Italy, but his future remained unclear. At root, he had been a caretaker for Marshall, who was expected to take command of the invasion of France. By November Ike was resigned to replacing Marshall as Army Chief of Staff. But Roosevelt baulked at such a move. Marshall had made himself indispensable: "I didn't feel I could sleep at ease if you were out of Washington," FDR told him. The transfer would also place Eisenhower in command of his former patrons—a relationship that would be difficult in the case of Marshall and impossible in the case of MacArthur. Moreover, Ike had now three major amphibious landings under his belt, he was popular with Americans and Britons, and he was unparalleled at managing an Allied team. Although Marshall agreed with Ike's philosophy, as Ambrose has noted, he lacked "the patience to work smoothly and efficiently with prima donnas, especially British prima donnas." In short, it had become not merely logical but almost inevitable that, as Roosevelt told him in person on 7 December 1943: "Ike, you are going to command Overlord."[48]

Part V

MAKING WAR
AND
MAKING LOVE

20

Countdown to
D-Day

★ ★ ★

THE 6TH OF JUNE 1944 SAW THE GREATEST AMPHIBIOUS OPERATION IN military history. In America and Britain it is widely viewed as the inexorable application of Allied superiority, the decisive event of the war, and the beginning of the end for Nazi Germany. Not only does this ignore the Red Army, which bore the brunt of the land war against Hitler, and whose operation Bagration of June 1944 won a quicker and more devastating victory than the battle of Normandy. It also glosses over the doubts and anxieties at all levels of Eisenhower's command about the likelihood of success. Despite two years of preparation, the Allies were not ready for invasion. And many, even at the top of the U.S. Army, were still unsure whether the GIs were up to the task.

By 1944 the Second Front had become known as "the Secondhand Front"—such was the boredom among many Britons at the recurrent delays. But the formal announcement on 17 January of Eisenhower's arrival at what the *News Chronicle* called "the new invasion H.Q. in Britain" started months of mounting excitement. During April and May rumours of imminent invasion ebbed and flowed like the Channel tides. According to a Ministry of Information report on 11 May, "comment on any other war topic is almost at a standstill. . . . While the majority expect to wake up any morning to find invasion has started, the minority who think it will never take place is growing." Two weeks later the OWI office in London reported that "the general mood could be described as one of depression, anxiety and restlessness." Despite strict instructions against press speculation, so-called military correspondents pontificated quite openly on likely invasion scenarios. In early May, for instance, the *Daily Telegraph* featured reports that the Germans would attack the assault force with "radar-controlled bombs," U-boats, and two-man midget submarines, "while electrically-controlled minefields are blown up." Although meteorological forecasts were banned because of their possible use to the enemy, many British papers carried prominent daily accounts of the previous day's weather in the Straits of Dover. And on 5 June the popular *Daily Mail* devoted much of page three to "apologies to the world" from a twenty-three-year-old London girl, an Associated Press teleprinter operator, who had "set five continents shaking" the previous day when she inadvertently transmitted a practice message that the invasion had started. According to the *Mail,* the media, police, and government offices had all been deluged with inquiries from the public.[1]

One of the most bizarre leaks of information occurred in the *Daily Telegraph* crossword. Between 2 May and 1 June its clues elicited five invasion code words, including Overlord itself and the names of the two U.S. invasion beaches, Omaha and Utah. On 1 June British MI5 officers questioned the crossword's compiler, Leonard Dawe, a schoolteacher from Leatherhead in Surrey. He stuck to his explanation that it was all a "fantastic coincidence." But forty years later one of his ex-pupils, Ronald French, claimed that Dawe would regularly assemble pupils in his study to fill in blank crosswords and write clues. That spring French and his pals were spending much time hanging around American and Canadian army camps in the area, where soldiers used code words freely without always knowing their significance. The boy had entered some of these on Dawe's blank forms. After his release by MI5, Dawe interrogated French, discovered what had happened, and swore him to secrecy.[2]

The vast American presence, peaking at 1.65 million, was now an open secret. On 10 April, Eisenhower's HQ issued an order confining all U.S. troops in the country to camp from 0001 to 2400. The Third U.S. Army's provost marshal called it an "all-UK showdown on AWOLs" because, he claimed, "there were thousands [of] soldiers roving around without passes or furloughs." Journalists were candidly reporting the problems. "Scotty" Reston, *New York Times* correspondent in London, wrote at length in February on "the increase in divorce, bigamy and venereal disease" following the American "invasion" of Britain. Reston claimed the GIs had caused a "social revolution." Sir Basil Liddell Hart, the distinguished British military commentator, toured what he called "occupied England" the same month for his weekly column in the *Daily Mail.* He noted cases of "rude and inconsiderate behaviour" by GIs and "spiteful criticism from English people." He also felt that, among GIs, Army divisions had the best discipline and esprit de corps. "It was where non-divisional elements were quartered, and in the larger towns where the military element was more mixed, that the atmosphere was not so good." Overall, however, Liddell Hart's verdict, both in private and in print, was favourable. He could not "think of any case in history" where relations between occupiers and occupied had been so good. "Still less can I recall any case where two great allied armies have got along so well."[3]

If this great buildup, its purpose, problems, and even code names were matters of public discussion, then there was little hope of concealment from German intelligence. On 18 May German radio quoted a statement from Rommel, the German commander in northern France, that "the invasion will begin at any moment now." In these circumstances, anything to conceal the exact invasion point was invaluable. Since 1943 Anglo-American planners had agreed that the Normandy beaches north of Caen should be the main target, because the Pas de Calais, only twenty-one miles from Dover, would inevitably be heavily defended by the Germans. But, to cover the real thrust, an elaborate deception operation was formulated in February 1944, code-named Fortitude. Its aim was to sow doubt in German minds that an early invasion was going to be attempted and, more important, to convince them that substantial thrusts would be made at Norway (from a fictional British Army in Scotland) and, in the south, at Calais from a dummy U.S. 1st Army Group located in Kent. Patton, still in disgrace from the Sicily slapping incidents, was a convenient high-profile figurehead for this latter ploy. Using spurious radio traffic and messages from German double-agents in Britain, Fortitude South proved particularly successful. By June 1944 Field Marshal Gerd von Rundstedt, overall German commander in the West, believed that there were over eighty Allied divisions in Britain—a 50 percent exaggeration—and that the attack on Normandy, preparations for which were so evident, would only be precursor to a main assault on the Pas de Calais in July. German dispositions along the French coast were made accordingly.[4]

A whole battery of security measures introduced that spring sought to safeguard the Fortitude plans. The one that bore hardest on the British people was the reintroduction of a ban on visitors along the coast. This had originally been imposed from the Wash to Hampshire in 1940–42 as an anti-invasion measure, but was lifted in 1943 because of protests from would-be holidaymakers and the like. The War Office still wanted it "to safeguard our preparations for offensive operations," especially after the Fortitude plan was drawn up, but the

Home Office pointed out the difficulty of police enforcement and the many loopholes—it would not exclude residents, visits to relatives, or phone calls. Churchill sided with the civilians and there ensued what Brooke called "a royal scrap." When told by the Chiefs of Staff that the ban would prove to the Americans that Britain was serious about the invasion, Churchill responded sharply: "We do not wish to knock our people around in order to impress the United States." Eventually Eisenhower himself appealed to the cabinet, warning that "it would go hard with our consciences if we were to feel, in later years, that by neglecting any security precaution we had compromised the success of these vital operations or needlessly squandered men's lives." Although Churchill still doubted that the ban "would contribute materially to security," he accepted the force of Ike's argument. The cabinet agreed to a visitors' ban from 1 April, covering the coastline ten miles deep from Land's End to the Wash, plus the Forth estuary in Scotland.[5]

The security measures and the deception plan were all welcome assistance. But Eisenhower and his subordinates did not place much faith in Fortitude.[6] After all the publicity and preparation, the chances of surprise seemed slight. The invasion would be a frontal assault on prepared enemy positions, which, it seemed, could succeed only through skilled troops in overwhelming numbers and, particularly, through devastating firepower. But in early 1944 it was far from clear whether these essentials could be provided, because of arguments between the Allies and among the rival services.

The basic plan, as it had evolved by February 1944, was to land five Allied divisions on five invasion beaches along a fifty-mile stretch of coast west of the Orne estuary near Caen (map 20a).[7] At Supreme Headquarters Allied Expeditionary Forces (SHAEF), Eisenhower would direct all land, naval, and air forces assigned to his command. As land commander for the assault, Montgomery would command the 21st Army Group (AG), comprising the First U.S. Army (FUSA) led by Bradley and the 2nd British Army under Gen. Miles Dempsey. The latter was responsible for the three eastern beaches, Sword, Juno, and Gold, where respectively the 3rd British Division, the 3rd Canadian, and the 50th (Northumbrian) Division would land. The next beach west, Omaha, was the target for elements of the 1st and 29th U.S. Divisions, while GIs of the 4th Division would assault Utah, across the Vire estuary on the southeastern base of the Cotentin Peninsula.

The allocation of the western beaches to the Americans was the outgrowth of both history and logistics. Canadian and British divisions had been concentrated in Kent and Sussex since the invasion scares of

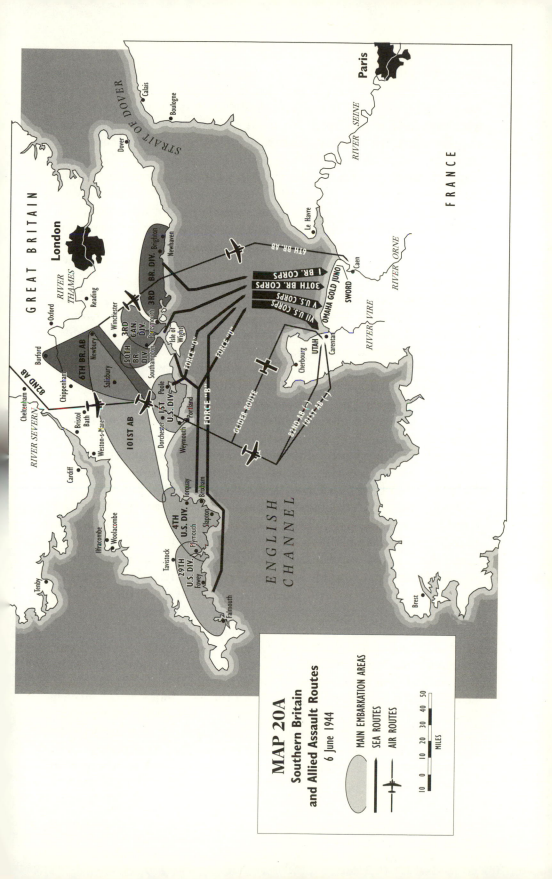

MAP 20A
Southern Britain
and Allied Assault Routes
6 June 1944

MAIN EMBARKATION AREAS
SEA ROUTES
AIR ROUTES

MILES
0   10   20   30   40   50

1940–41. The 29th Division, sole survivor from the 1942 buildup, and the new American divisions that arrived in 1943–44 were all in western England, close to the Avon and Mersey ports from which they were supplied and reinforced. To avoid nightmare swaps of troops and supplies across the country, the invasion planners simply accepted the status quo. Only once established on the Continent would the significance of that decision become apparent, with the weaker army on the decisive northern flank of the drive into Germany. In 1943–44, however, the planners were mainly concerned to secure a safe beachhead.

They had problems enough with the detailed Normandy invasion plan, code-named Neptune (strictly, Overlord referred to the whole campaign in northwest Europe). Earlier Anglo-American planners under the acronym COSSAC (Chief of Staff, Supreme Allied Commander) had proposed attacking the Caen area but in what Ike, Monty, and Bradley all agreed was insufficient strength. COSSAC, operating in mid-1943 without a Supreme Commander and under impossible logistical constraints from the Combined Chiefs of Staff, calculated that it had been allocated only enough landing craft for three divisions on a thirty-mile front. Once Ike and Monty were appointed, they were able to exercise much greater leverage on the Combined Chiefs of Staff and secure the increased logistics for a more powerful assault. Thus, the invasion front was extended, the assault force enlarged, and three airborne divisions were included to secure the flanks—the 6th British around Caen and the American 82nd and 101st to protect the Utah beachhead and seal off the Cotentin.

Yet the use of paratroops was a matter of vexed debate. On the one hand Eisenhower faced mounting scepticism from his air force commander, Air Chief Marshal Sir Trafford Leigh-Mallory, who predicted grave losses of troops and pilots, especially in daylight. With Bradley equally adamant, Leigh-Mallory told him formally: "if you insist on this airborne operation, you'll do it in spite of my opposition." At the other extreme, Ike had to fend off Marshall and Arnold in Washington who repeatedly urged a much more ambitious airborne landing around Evreux, some seventy-five miles *east* of Caen, to capture airfields and threaten Paris! It was a rare case of interference by the Army Chief of Staff, but it showed how out of touch the desk warriors could be with anxieties of those responsible for the invasion. On 19 February Ike told Marshall firmly that the airborne forces had to be used in close support of the amphibious assault. "The resistance to be expected by our landing forces at the beaches is far greater than anything we have yet encountered in the European War." Even so, it took another round of correspondence before Marshall desisted.[8]

On 22 March Eisenhower composed a secret memorandum "for the record" about his problems over the previous two months. He reported "satisfactory progress" on those to do with planning, training, and logistics for the invasion. The "matters that have really caused us trouble," he noted, were "those in which only the Combined Chiefs of Staff can make final decisions."[9] Overlord was, in fact, the supreme test of the principles of unified command that Roosevelt and Churchill, under the tutelage of Marshall, had established in the weeks after Pearl Harbor in an effort to handle both interservice and international arguments. In 1944, as in 1942, both sets of arguments involved two entangled strands—conflicts of interest and differences over strategy.

The landings would depend in large part on superiority at the point of attack. Part of the problem was securing the necessary vessels to support the desired five-division lift. The U.S. Navy maintained a jealous control of all landing craft and Ike fought a war of attrition with Washington in early 1944 to divert craft to Neptune from what he called "the Navy's private war" in the Pacific. But men alone were inadequate if not backed by overwhelming firepower. Early planning had given the Royal Navy responsibility for naval bombardment of the beaches. By January 1944, however, British planners calculated that to drench the beaches and neutralize all known strongpoints would require about twenty cruisers and one hundred destroyers—a figure far in excess of what the Royal Navy could or would make available. In April and May Eisenhower gradually secured additional American warships, including three battleships, to strengthen the bombardment forces. Even so, these seemed far from adequate for the task at hand.[10]

Air support was even more problematic. The U.S. 9th Army Air Force was created specifically in October 1943 to support the cross-channel attack. But not until a month before D-Day was it made available to practice with the troops in ground-support operations. By then the GIs had completed their training and were about to move into the preinvasion areas. In consequence, Bradley noted, "we went into France almost totally untrained in air-ground cooperation." Ike had even greater difficulty in bringing the "bomber barons" under his control. Leigh-Mallory was a hesitant figure whom neither Spaatz of the U.S. 8th Air Force nor Harris of RAF Bomber Command took seriously. They would only work with Air Chief Marshal Sir Arthur Tedder, Ike's trusted British deputy. Personalities aside, both Spaatz and Harris had their own strategies for winning the war through strategic airpower and remained convinced that Overlord was an irrelevance. Harris was still obsessed with area bombing of German cities to break morale, while Spaatz focused on key industrial targets in a campaign of greater precision (in theory if not always practice). Senior U.S. airmen were saying in early 1944 that they only needed another twenty or thirty clear operational days to "finish off the war on their own."[11]

Ike fought a dual battle with the bomber commanders. One was to bring them, at least temporarily, under his "direction." This was not achieved until 14 April, after weeks of haggling over a form of words. The other was to agree on an operational plan. Ironically, by this stage, Spaatz had finally found a winning strategy. The "oil plan," targeting fourteen synthetic oil plants that produced about four-fifths of German production, achieved dramatic success that spring. But by this time the advocates of strategic airpower had lost their credibility because of the bombast of the past. And, as shown at a conference of senior airmen on 25 March, the "oil plan" could not make a decisive difference before the invasion began. The alternative was the "transportation plan" drawn up by Tedder's staff, which targeted the nodal points of the French rail network. Although also exaggerated by its advocates, this would clearly have greater bearing on German troop movements and Ike put his weight behind it. Both he and Bradley averred later that it was one of his greatest contributions to the success of Overlord. Even so, internecine battles continued and it was only thirty-six hours before the invasion began that the targeting for D-Day and after was finally confirmed.[12]

The governments as well as the services were arguing about the transportation plan. For most of April Ike had to battle against Churchill and the British cabinet, who feared opprobrium for causing heavy French civilian casualties. Only when Churchill referred their argument to Roosevelt did Ike get his way. On 11 May the president replied that he was "not prepared to impose from this distance any restriction on military action by the responsible commanders that in their opinion might militate against the success of OVERLORD." It was a characteristic answer. Although Commander in Chief, FDR usually left operations and even strategy to his commanders: the decision for Torch in 1942 being a rare if momentous exception. Churchill, by contrast, was an inveterate meddler in matters military and Ike was subject to constant inquiries and suggestions, often delivered late at night in those after-dinner harangues at which the prime minister (fortified by an afternoon nap) usually wore down his opponents. Marshall became seriously concerned that his protégé was succumbing to "localitis." Anxious to reduce the British pressure, in March Eisenhower moved SHAEF headquarters out of central London to Bushy Park in the southwestern suburbs (code-named Widewing). That was, he told Marshall, "closer under the noses of the London authorities than I desire," but a move right down to the coast would have required "too much expense in signal equipment and troops."[13]

Churchill's interference was a matter of calculation as well as temperament. By 1944 the British were struggling to maintain equality in the transatlantic alliance—as many of the arguments over Overlord bear witness. The tenacious battle to keep Bomber Command out of Eisenhower's control, for instance, was partly because it was now the only truly independent great weapon left in British hands. Similarly, Churchill's vehement opposition to landings in southern France (Anvil) reflected an element of "sheer chauvinism" in his strategic thinking: Anvil would divert resources from Italy where the British were still a powerful partner. In an effort to break the Italian stalemate, Churchill impetuously masterminded the Anzio landing of 22 January 1944. But this was half-baked and underresourced; its outcome was only another deadlocked front, established at great cost. As Churchill wrote Gen. MacArthur, instead of throwing "a wild cat on the shore" he had landed "a beached whale." For most Americans outside the Mediterranean theatre, Italy had become a dead end. Marshall and Eisenhower saw Anvil as a way to support Overlord, by opening up Marseilles and other southern ports, and to utilize all the American (and Free French) divisions that had been trained for war. Although they accepted in March that there would be insufficient landing craft in June for simultaneous landings in southern and northern France, the argument was resumed, with increased bitterness, in the summer.[14]

In the command structure for Overlord, too, the British tried to maximize their influence. By 1944, unlike 1942, it was clear that the United States would be the preponderant partner once the Allies were established on the Continent, and an American Supreme Commander was therefore inevitable. But British scepticism about Eisenhower had not abated. On 15 May Brooke confided to his diary that Eisenhower was "no real director of thought, plans, energy and direction! Just a co-ordinator, a good mixer, a champion of inter-Allied co-operation," though, he acknowledged, "in these respects few can hold a candle to him." The British were keen to perpetuate the "stratosphere" policy that had worked well for them in the Mediterranean, with Ike as Supreme Commander and British subordinates (in this case Montgomery, Leigh-Mallory, and Admiral Sir Bertram Ramsay) conducting land, air, and sea operations. Since the invasion was being launched from Britain, it seemed both sensible and appropriate to give Britons operational command of the assault. Once in France, as we shall see in the next chapter, the balance of the alliance shifted rapidly.[15]

As with the interservice arguments, those between the two governments were rooted in basic differences about strategy. The British remained wary of invading France, at least until Germany was about to collapse. Although the prime minister sometimes predicted the Channel running with blood, his real anxiety was not the landing itself but the breakout. In October 1943 he had spoken privately about a "disaster greater than that of Dunkirk" and in early 1944 Anzio, on which he brooded frequently, served as a haunting lesson "about how not to do it." His official biographer suggested that his lassitude that spring, on which many commented, was not merely the aftermath of pneumonia but a mental fatigue born of worry about Overlord. Publicly he put the best face on matters, telling the final conference of Overlord commanders on 15 May, "I am hardening toward this enterprise." While some historians have played down this remark, Ike rightly took it as a sign of Churchill's basic doubts. A few weeks earlier, the premier had told Pentagon emissary John J. McCloy that, though "completely committed," he would ideally "have liked to have had Turkey on our side, the Danube under threat as well as Norway cleaned up before we undertook this." Brooke, who had fought in Normandy in 1940, never overcame his deep reservations. On the eve of D-Day he was still "very uneasy about the whole operation. At the best it will fall so very very far short of the expectation of the bulk of the people, namely all those who know nothing about its difficulties. At the worst it may well be the most ghastly disaster of the whole war!"[16]

The doubts of Churchill and Brooke are a familiar part of the Overlord story. What should be underlined is that they were shared to some degree by most of the senior commanders, American as well as British. On 29 May Leigh-Mallory, concerned about the movement of German reinforcements into the Cotentin, deliberately went "on record" in a letter to Eisenhower about the dangers of the airborne drop, predicting "at the most 30 per cent of the glider loads will become effective for use against the enemy." The ground commanders had to radiate confidence, but they too expressed serious doubts in private. Bradley made very clear to McCloy on 17 April "the need of a greater quantity of naval support" and the fact that he was "uneasy about the air," at both the tactical and strategic levels. At the end of the month, Gen. Leonard T. Gerow, the Corps commander for Omaha and an old friend of Eisenhower, laid out at length his own fears, particularly about underwater obstacles and naval cooperation. Chastised by Ike, Gerow claimed he "wasn't pessimistic," but "merely realistic" and preparing for all possible contingencies, but, like Bradley, he was covering his backside. Patton was also sceptical, telling his staff on 16 April: "No question in my mind now that we can establish a beachhead. Had some doubts but none now. Only question now is what happens after we get [a] foothold." The point was made more bluntly by Ike's Chief of Staff, Gen. Walter Bedell Smith. On 12 May he rated the "chances of holding the beachhead" at "only fifty-fifty."[17]

Monty was an exception and he paid for his optimism later, when the battle of Normandy became bogged down. Of course, Monty was vain and opinionated, and his manner caused offence. Yet his imperious surveys of Overlord at the major briefings on 7 April and 15 May have to be understood against the background of widespread doubt. All who attended, American and British, were impressed by these performances in St. Paul's School (where Monty himself had sat, without distinction, as a schoolboy some forty years before). Bradley recalled him tracing the plan "with rare skill" on a huge relief model of Normandy, tramping about "like a giant through Lilliputian France." Churchill's military secretary Hastings Ismay remembered that his line was that this was "a perfectly normal operation which is certain of success." To men haunted by Dunkirk and Anzio his confidence and his insistence on speedy breakout was invigorating. Eisenhower was also an inspirational figure, though in a different vein. His first talk to senior SHAEF staff was done "in a charming way with a smile and a sense of humor," according to the American diplomat William Phillips, who considered it "the best presentation of Anglo-American relations that I have heard for a long time." Ike sounded equally relaxed about the impending invasion, telling Bradley's staff in January that there was "no possibility of failure." His own short address on 15 May reassured all but inveterate sceptics like Brooke. "Before the warmth of his quiet confidence the mists of doubt dissolved," recalled Admiral Morton L. Deyo.[18]

But what Ike and Monty knew as the weeks passed, with plans still in turmoil and staffs still bickering, was that success would depend largely on the ordinary soldiers. They were the human battering rams that must crack the Atlantic Wall and drive fast into occupied France.

Most of the army planning for Overlord concentrated on these assault divisions. In the American, British, and Canadian armies massing in England there was a serious shortage of combat veterans. Bradley faced particular problems. Before his arrival "the 29th Division had staked out squatters' rights on Omaha Beach" by virtue of its longevity in England. When the front was enlarged, Utah was given to the 4th Division, which had arrived in Devon in January 1944. Yet neither of these units had seen combat before and Bradley had particular doubts about ex–National Guard units such as the 29th. So he turned to the 1st Division—the "Big Red One"—veterans of North Africa and Sicily, to help on Omaha, conscious that this would be the third landing for many of its men but convinced he had no choice.[19] The revised Omaha Beach plan called for two regimental combat teams, one from the 1st and one from the 29th, stiffened further by two battalions of Rangers, under temporary 1st Division command. The rest of the two divisions would come in behind. There were worries, too, about the airborne divisions, particularly as Leigh-Mallory's gloom deepened. The 82nd had seen tough fighting in Sicily and at Salerno, but the 101st would be jumping in action for the first time. These airborne operations were reduced in scope as German strength in the Cotentin grew during May.

Eisenhower and Bradley were also anxious about their subordinates. When Ike arrived in January 1944, there were three U.S. corps commanders in the UK, none of whom had any real combat experience. Although regarded by Marshall as a "good man" but not "a driver," Gerow held on to V Corps, mainly because of his close friendship with Ike. But Eisenhower and Bradley wanted hardened leaders for the other two First U.S. Army (FUSA) corps, the VIIth and follow-up XIXth, and Marshall sent over Pacific veterans J. Lawton Collins and Charles H. Corlett. There were also worries about Gerhardt, commander of the key 29th Division, whom Gerow considered prone to sudden and autocratic decisions. In February, Ike told Gerow that if Gerhardt did not shape up he should be sent home, adding "I will take the responsibility." Ike's final preinvasion assessment of his commanders did not exude confidence. On 21 May he cabled Marshall: "I am quite satisfied with all my commanders down to include Corps; while I have my fingers crossed in the case of two or three Division commanders, I believe that they ought to come through."[20]

This shortage of combat talent helps explain why Ike persevered with George Patton. In addition to his deception role in Kent, Patton was to head the follow-up Third U.S. Army (TUSA) after FUSA had established itself in France. That spring TUSA HQ was located at Peover Hall, about fifteen miles south of Manchester, commanding troops in northwest England and Northern Ireland. On 25 April Patton was obliged to make an impromptu speech at the opening of a British Welcome Club for GIs in the nearby town of Knutsford. He extolled the value of these clubs, and remarked light-heartedly that "since it is evident destiny of the British and the Americans, and, of course, the Russians, to rule the world, the better we know each other, the better job we will do." Next day papers all across the United States carried front-page quotes from what was billed as Patton's first public speech in England, and the references to who should "rule the world" caused a political furore. Ike was now fed up with Patton's "lifelong habit of posing and of self-dramatization which causes him to break out in these extraordinary ways." But Marshall left the matter in his hands and eventually Eisenhower decided to retain him—a decision based, as he put it, "solely upon my convictions as to the effect upon OVER-LORD." When they met on 1 May Patton ate humble pie but also told Ike bluntly that "this attack is badly planned and on too narrow a front and may well result in an Anzio, especially if I am not there." Ike's reply is revealing: "Don't I know it, but what can I do?" Keeping Patton seemed a part of the answer.[21]

Conscious that so much depended on the men and their leaders, all the Overlord commanders visited the combat divisions assiduously that spring. Monty set the ball rolling on 14 January with a five-day tour of FUSA units. As usual, he struck an informal note, addressing groups of several hundred men from a jeep or other prominent position. The first time he spoke to an American unit he was very nervous. He told them he was keen to visit the United States but did not know whether to start in the North or South. From the back a GI called out, "What the hell are you trying to do? Start another war?" Despite Monty's self-importance and his high-pitched English accent, many GIs were impressed that a senior commander should take the trouble to address them. The CO of the 3rd Armored was still enthusing about his visit two weeks later.[22]

Eisenhower also spent days on the road, visiting twenty-six divisions and twenty-four airfields between 1 February and 1 June. Following Monty's practice, he told the men to break ranks and gather round, but his manner was less stagey than that of his British subordinate. Ike was particularly impressive one-to-one, asking GIs about their families, civilian jobs, and postwar plans. "Where are you from, soldier?" was always his first question and he was particularly delighted when he met a fellow Kansan. (In April 1944 Pfc. Walter Thorpe secured a ten-minute interview with the Supreme Commander simply by walking up to sentries at SHAEF HQ and saying, "Tell him I'm from Abilene, Kansas.") Ike's aide, Harry Butcher, greatly admired his "method of talking personally with individual soldiers or to small groups of them. It creates a bond of understanding which quickly spreads by word of mouth to other soldiers"—though Ike was always angry when his words appeared in the press. "To him," noted Butcher, "his personal tie with the GI is virtually sacred."[23]

The training of the assault divisions received particular attention in the final months before D-Day. That was why the Americans had been so insistent on obtaining unfettered use of the area around Slapton Sands (chapter 8). This Devon training ground has become notorious because of the tragedy during exercise Tiger—a simulation of the Utah assault involving the 4th Infantry and the 82nd and 101st Airborne divisions. In the early hours of 28 April an "invasion flotilla" of eight Landing Ships, Tank (LSTs) was moving slowly through Lyme Bay en route westwards to Slapton Sands, some forty miles away, when it was attacked by nine German torpedo boats from Cherbourg. Two LSTs exploded and sank, another was seriously damaged, and at least 639 men were lost, mostly engineers whose expertise was vital to service the beaches. Part of the blame adhered to the Royal Navy, who because of a mixup, failed to provide a replacement escort for the rear of the straggling convoy after the destroyer originally designated had been damaged the previous day. This aspect of exercise Tiger has become well known, despite accusations of an official coverup. But journalist Nigel Lewis has argued that there may have been an earlier tragedy on the morning of 27 April, when the naval commander Admiral Don P. Moon postponed H-Hour for sixty minutes because of delays in the arrival of landing craft. Lewis has suggested that certain units of the 4th Division did not receive the message and landed at the original time, ten minutes before naval vessels offshore began softening-up fire. Certainly several officers on Royal Navy warships independently recalled reports soon after, that they had shelled GIs and inflicted heavy casualties. An earlier and separate tragedy of this sort might explain why the U.S. Navy and Army estimates of the death toll for Tiger diverge (639 and 749) and why some bodies were buried at Slapton (forty miles from where the convoy was attacked). If British vessels were implicated in *two* fatal errors, this may also help explain why official secrecy was retained for so long.[24]

Whether some deaths were caused by "friendly fire" remains speculation (and the secret VII Corps critique of the exercise makes no mention of it), but the fatalities of exercise Tiger have become a cause célèbre. This preoccupation has distracted from a more general point about Tiger, glossed over in the Army's official history, namely that almost *everything* went wrong with this putative "combined operation." Gen. Collins said caustically afterwards that "the infantry was fighting one battle and the supporting weapons another." Air cooperation was minimal, since the 9th AAF was still unready to cooperate, while naval gunfire was patchy because of the confusion over H-Hour. If a few GIs were shelled by their own side, most received no cover at all. Moreover, the task force close to shore would have been an easy target for German batteries. There was also what the engineers called "wild confusion" on the beach, with troops and vehicles arriving in the wrong order and causing serious jams. Under enemy fire, this chaos could have been disastrous, especially when exacerbated, as it was during Tiger, with troops moving up and down the beach having landed in the wrong places. There was chronic communication failure at all levels and between all arms, of which the "friendly fire" disaster, if it occurred, was only the most upsetting manifestation. And the soldiers themselves also performed poorly, coming in overloaded (even with bedrolls) and then milling around aimlessly on the beach, often indifferent to supposed minefields. "We are completely devoid of mine consciousness," 4th Division Commander "Tubby" Barton told his men, "and a hell of a lot of us are going to be killed." Even when under way, the GIs tended to straggle out across country, oblivious to the need for cover, with junior officers failing to establish discipline or direction.[25]

The exercise was observed by Eisenhower and his staff. Ike's aide, Harry Butcher, was particularly concerned about

> the absence of toughness and alertness of the young American officers whom I saw on this trip. They seem to regard war as one grand maneuver in which they are having a happy time. They are as green as growing corn. . . . A good many of the full colonels also give me a pain. They are fat, gray and oldish. . . . We should have a more experienced division for the assault than the 4th which has never been in a fight in this war.

To add to Ike's worries, it was clear from the E-boat attack that the Germans had located the exercise and could easily infer its real target. For a time there were even (unfounded) fears that officers briefed on the Overlord plan had been captured. And the loss of the three LSTs had eliminated Ike's reserve of landing ships. Little wonder the invasion commanders left Devon very depressed. Bradley called it "more like a peacetime maneuver than a dress rehearsal of an assault against the continent."[26]

In fact, Tiger had shown up the same deficiencies as earlier exercises. As Bradley said, they were really extensions of peacetime manouevres, with no defending fire and often not even notional defenders. One experienced British observer remarked on "the unrealities" of exercise Duck I in January: It "did not, of course, represent a feasible 'Operation of War.' "[27] Obviously, lessons were being learnt all the time and one might hope that real war would galvanize all concerned, but general officers—all students of military history—knew that the shock of battle was literally shock, inducing paralysis and anomie in all but the most seasoned troops. And, as they kept brooding, with the exception of the 1st Division, these were *not* seasoned troops.

Tiger was VII Corps' dress rehearsal for Utah. The six Fabius exercises that followed in early May provided final runs for the other beaches. Fabius I for Omaha on 3 May was smoother than Tiger and had few fatalities, but familiar problems recurred, notably in interservice cooperation, traffic control, communications, and navigation. But by now the time for training was over. The invasion, provisionally scheduled at the Teheran conference for 1 May 1944, had been postponed one month to allow extra preparation. Further delay would be problematic, because the necessary conjunction of light and tidal conditions occurred on only about three days in a month—low tide for locating beach obstacles, early daylight to enable accurate naval and air bombardment, and a moonlit night beforehand for the airborne drop. And any slippage beyond June would imperil sychronization with the Russian summer offensive and truncate the campaigning season on the Continent. For Ike the burden was enormous. There was little doubt that preparations for this hazardous operation left much to be desired, yet he could wait no longer. With Fabius over, the final troop movements began.

Theoretically, there were three stages to "mounting" the invasion. First the assault troops, previously packaged out across southern England, moved to assembly areas for reconstitution as operational units. Excess administrative personnel were shed at this point, equipment was packed, and vehicles waterproofed. The units then moved into the marshaling areas, where the SOS took over responsibility for their food and quarters, and final preparations for invasion were made. From Portsmouth westward there were 95 marshaling camps with capacity for 187,000 troops and 28,000 vehicles. Dorset, where the 1st Division and supporting "29ers" were preparing for Omaha (Force O), included several large military camps, taken over from the British and capable of quick expansion, where assembly and marshaling could be done in the same place. Farther west the 4th Division was concentrated around Torbay (Force U) and most of the 29th westward along from Plymouth to Falmouth (Force B). In these coastal areas of Devon and Cornwall large camps were rare and assembly and marshaling occurred separately. For the latter, special "sausages" were created— elongated areas of some five to ten miles in length where up to twenty-five hundred men congregated in a dozen or more small tented encampments. From here the third and final stage was when the troops moved down to embarkation points, usually only a few miles away. For the airborne divisions the whole process was truncated into one. Regiments of the 101st, which had been based in Wiltshire and Berkshire, were assembled and marshaled at nearby airfields such as Greenham Common and Upottery, which they had used for final training and from which they would depart for D-Day. Likewise, the 82nd assembled at airfields in Lincolnshire, Nottinghamshire, and Leicestershire.[28]

It was only in the marshaling areas that men seemed "to fully grasp the vast scope of what lay in store for them." Ground troops were issued with life belts, seasickness pills, and some "occupation French francs"—many of which were gambled away in a frenzy of card games. Another ominous sign was the sudden improvement in the food. David K. Webster of the 101st recalled a profusion of "such luxuries as fried chicken, fruit cocktail, white bread with lots of butter. The realization that we were being fattened up for the slaughter didn't stop us from going back for seconds." Movies were also available in abundance. Davey Jones of San Francisco was waiting at Folkingham airfield in Lincolnshire with his unit of the 82nd Airborne. "I was just nineteen at the time and I cried all the way through the film, not because it was a sad movie but because I thought that this would be the last film I would ever see." At the end of May field officers and then noncoms were given details of their impending operation, using sand tables, relief maps, and photos. At this point the camps were sealed off. Lyle Groundwater, a lieutenant with the 4th Division, recalled two lines of barbed wire being placed around his camp near Abergavenny in south Wales. English soldiers patroled the exterior, Americans the interior. "We had no telephone or wireless, or radio connections with the outside at all. Any messages that were sent to us were brought by messengers who came in and had to remain in the camp." Finally the men were briefed, given passwords, and issued with live ammunition.[29]

Officially the English were to know nothing about this marshaling process. VII Corps headquarters was at Breamore, south of Salisbury, where Lady Normanton loaned some English history books to Gen. Collins. On 19 July 1944 the general sent an apologetic note from France: "I am sorry I was unable to return your books personally, but that might have given away the fact that we were on the move." Some GIs were equally discreet. On one of a line of empty bell tents "somewhere in England" after D-Day was chalked the message, "Sorry Jean HAD to Go, Johnny." Even for those with less romantic attachments,

parting was indeed "sweet sorrow." Just three weeks before the invasion "Mac" McIntyre of the 4th Division had sat with his friends the
Prince family, staring pensively into the flames of their fire. Mrs. Prince
handed him a cup of tea. "France must be lovely at this time of year,"
she murmured, unthinkingly expressing what was on everyone's
mind. "It hit me smack in the eyes," Mac recalled. When he saw the
Princes for a final visit, they laid on sandwiches of tongue and roast
beef washed down by Bass ale spiked with port. He had brought gifts
of tobacco, cigarettes, candy, and oranges. At the end of an hilarious
evening nothing was said directly, but "Mr. Prince all but broke my
hand when we parted, and Mum's eyes were misty. The boys were
silent, but the expression on their faces spoke louder than words."[30]

Even for those English people who did not have such rich relations
with the Yanks, May 1944 put the American occupation in a different
perspective. The GI buildup of the previous months had been partly
concealed by the packaging out of troops in camps, barracks, and
billets all over the country. Marshaling for the invasion made clear the
scale of the American presence. Transport centres like Cheltenham,
Cirencester, and Oxford became almost endless traffic jams, with long
convoys of trucks halted or crawling along. The environs of Plymouth,
Poole, or Southampton were vast vehicle parks, and quaysides such as
Brixham in Devon disappeared under mounds of equipment ready for
loading.

In these last weeks American technology was on display as never
before. Its impact is recalled by English historian John Keegan, then a
schoolboy in rural Somerset:

> How different they looked from our own jumble-sale champions,
> beautifully clothed in smooth khaki, as fine in cut and quality as a
> British officer's . . . and armed with glistening, modern, automatic
> weapons, Thompson sub-machine-guns, Winchester carbines, Ga-
> rand self-loading rifles. More striking still were the number, size and
> elegance of the vehicles in which they paraded about the country-
> side in stately convoy. The British army's transport was a sad collec-
> tion of underpowered makeshifts, whose dun paint flaked from their
> tinpot bodywork. The Americans travelled in magnificent, gleaming,
> olive-green, pressed-steel, four-wheel-drive juggernauts, decked
> with what car salesmen would call optional extras of a sort never
> seen on their domestic equivalents—deep-treaded spare tyres,
> winches, towing cables, fire-extinguishers. There were towering
> GMC six-by-sixes, compact and powerful Dodge four-by fours and
> . . . tiny and entrancing jeeps, caparisoned with whiplash aerials and
> sketchy canvas hoods. . . . And, as spring became summer in 1944,

. . . they brought a new wave of equipment, half-track scout cars, amphibious trucks and gigantic transporters, laded with tanks and bulldozers—a machine previously unknown in Britain . . .

Keegan and his friends—"relentlessly patriotic little prep-school boys" convinced of "the paramountcy of the British empire"—were both awed and charmed. "There was something in particular about jeeps, and the way they were driven with one high-booted leg thrust casually outside the cab, which softened even the most chauvinist ten-year-old heart."[31]

What this huge modernistic mustering also signaled was that, at last, the GIs were going to war. Among many Britons outside East Anglia, there was still the feeling, expressed by diarists like Cecil King, that the Americans were doing little for the war and that their troops would never be great fighters. But William E. Jones of the 4th Infantry Division recalled a different atmosphere when marching into Plymouth for embarkation. "The townspeople were all lined up along the sidewalks, something they had never done before . . . they knew that we were going for the real thing this time. They would say 'Good luck boys' and all that stuff." Bob Sheehan, a lieutenant of an ordnance unit, had a similar experience as he and his vehicles crawled down to their embarkation point. Late in the day the convoy

had stopped before a row of houses. Here a group of men, women and children all stood watching the never-ending columns of tanks and trucks manned by their sweating crews. They waved now and then, but truth to tell, they were waved out. Overcome by the awesome sight of this enormous cavalcade, they just stood still. We somehow became aware of their anxiety and feeling for us. It was as if we had assumed the object of all their hopes and fears for the coming struggle.

Then from the house to our left emerged a mother-figure with bowls of strawberries and cream. She handed them to me and gave a gulpy kiss to my forehead. "Good luck," she said. "Come back safe."

The rest of the onlookers were then galvanized into action. Figures hurried down to waiting vehicles and the crews were invited to come in for a hurried wash and, in some cases, shave. Yet others brought out tea or lemonade. There was a kind of togetherness that I had never seen before. A sharing of spirit. It was no longer them and us. We were family and danger was afoot.

It was a great consolation to us that these ordinary people cared. They didn't know us, had never met us, and would never see us again. But for that magic moment in time we were all allies. We left the bowls in a neat pile on the roadside. The vehicles ahead moved on and as we in our turn did so, a little girl ran out of the house and gathered up the bowls in her arms. She shyly turned her face upwards and I kissed her goodbye. That little girl was my last personal contact with the people of Great Britain on their own soil.[32]

The last weekend of May 1944 was Whitsun Bank Holiday in Britain and Britons reveled in the hottest days of the year to date. On Sunday 28 May seven thousand citizens of Nottingham (half of them "young ladies") flocked to the Notts County soccer ground to see two teams from the 82nd U.S. Airborne playing baseball. "The Red Devils" beat "The Panthers" 18–0, mainly thanks to Forrest Brewer, a former professional with the Washington Senators. The following day twenty-five thousand people packed Lord's cricket ground ("London's equivalent of Yankee Stadium," as it was described to one GI) to see England beat Australia. Although the England team included heroes such as Wally Hammond and Len Hutton, its opponents were actually Australian airmen (who had won an earlier game on Saturday). On the Tuesday, as Britons returned to work in still beautiful weather, the invasion force began boarding—Force U on 30 May, Force O on 31 May, and Force B (the follow-up regiments for Omaha) on 1 June. Loading was complete by Saturday 3 June—just as the weather broke.[33]

The three American task forces amounted to some twenty-five hundred vessels. The total invasion fleet comprised nearly five thousand ships and upwards of 200,000 men. Most of the troops were on large transports or LSTs ready to debouch later into smaller landing craft. The ships were crammed full, with little room to sit, let alone sleep, as they waited in the swelling seas. Abiding memories were the smell of diesel oil, vomit, and backed-up toilets. The food was still good—even ice cream—but appetites had faded and the crap games had become mechanical. Although some GIs derided "fox-hole religion," the religious services on ship, as in the marshaling areas, were well attended. Young men in their early twenties confronted, often for the first time, the fact of their own mortality. Warren R. Lloyd, a West Virginian preparing for Utah, tried to imagine what combat would be like. "My mind couldn't cope with that. I finally decided I would just have to wait until the time came." Increasingly GIs' thoughts turned to families back home. Most wrote several letters while they waited—to parents, wives, siblings, friends. Not all were pensive, however. On the transport *New Amsterdam*, off Weymouth, Lt. George Kerchner was censoring his men's mail. Staff Sgt. Larry Johnson had written a letter that simply could not be sent through Army channels. "Larry," said Kerchner, "you'd better post this yourself—after you get to France." Johnson had written to a girl asking for a date in early June. She lived in Paris. Kerchner found such crazy optimism deeply reassuring.[34]

Books also helped while away the time. Lt. Edward Yarberry from Colorado was reading *A Tree Grows in Brooklyn*. Looking back, he recalled, "it seems that my uppermost worry at the time was whether or not I was going to get to finish the book before we went in." And senior officers kept working over the final pep talks they would deliver. On the British boats snatches of Shakespeare's *Henry V* were much favoured—probably because of Laurence Olivier's recent film. But GI Bruce Bradley recalled only that "we were told we were expendable in the first wave. I remember nobody responded to those chilling words." On 5 June Gen. Leland S. Hobbs, commander of the follow-up 30th Division, told his men:

> War is a series of three things. Remember it. Long, hard waits, just waiting. Relatively short, hard fighting. And quite short, pleasant rest. That is the cycle. That is the way it goes. Wait, fight, rest, fight, wait, and around it goes. The hardest part is the waiting, and the time when you will most have to apply your discipline and your courage is in that waiting period.[35]

By then two and half million men were waiting—for Eisenhower. On him alone lay responsibility for deciding whether the invasion could go ahead in the now stormy and unpredictable weather. His optimum dates were 5, 6, and 7 June. Meeting at Southwick House, overlooking Portsmouth Harbour, on the evening of Saturday the 3rd, Ike decided to let Forces O and U sail on schedule, while deferring a final decision. The following morning he called them back and postponed H-Hour for twenty-four hours. At 9:30 that Sunday evening he met senior commanders again in the library of Southwick House. Rain was pouring down and window frames rattled in the storm. SHAEF meteorologists were divided but there was some hope of thirty-six hours of fairly clear weather with moderate winds. The airmen— Tedder and Leigh-Mallory—were not happy, but Monty was categorical when asked: "I would say—Go!" Ike, pacing the room, had to weigh it all up. The weathermen would not predict how long the window of opportunity would last. On the other hand, the Russians were waiting, tidal conditions would not be right again before 19 June, and delay until then would be a logistical nightmare and a shattering letdown for troop morale. "The question," said Ike, was "just how long you can hang this operation on the end of a limb and let it hang there." At 9:45 he announced his decision, albeit in halting phrases expressing the inner anguish. "I'm quite positive we must give the order . . . I don't like it, but there it is . . . I don't see how we can possibly do anything else." Admiral Ramsay left the room to set five thousand vessels in motion for France. Even then it was still not too late to call it off. Around dawn the following morning, Monday 5 June, there was a final review. Although the Channel might get rough again on 7 June, the weather *was* beginning to clear. Eisenhower pondered for a moment, then said firmly, "Okay, let's go." In a moment the room was empty as his subordinates hurried to their command posts. Millions had waited for Eisenhower. Now he had to wait on them.[36]

Ike occupied himself on 5 June by visiting some British troops at Portsmouth, briefing the press and playing checkers and swapping yarns with Harry Butcher. After dinner he decided to visit Newbury airfield, where part of the 101st Airborne was preparing to embark on the big C-47 transports. The 101st was dropping into combat for the first time and on his mind weighed Leigh-Mallory's warning that the paratroops would take 70 percent casualties. He wandered unannounced through the groups of men, with their shaven heads and blackened faces, stepping over packs and guns. His opening gambit was now famous: "Where are you from, soldier?" Back came the answers—"Missouri, Sir," "Kansas, Sir," "Texas, Sir." There was cheering as the list of states unfolded like a political convention, or a "roll of battle honors," one observer recalled. Afterwards Ike drove to the 101st HQ and watched the transports fly overhead. Those standing with him saw tears in his eyes. In his wallet, unknown to them, was a draft press release that he had scrawled earlier in the day—just in case. It read:

> Our landings in the Cherbourg-Havre area have failed to gain a satisfactory foothold and I have withdrawn the troops. My decision to attack at this time and place was based upon the best information available. The troops, the air and the Navy did all that Bravery and devotion to duty could do. If any blame or fault attaches to the attempt it is mine alone.[37]

21

Overlord
and Under Ike

★ ★ ★

EISENHOWER'S POIGNANT DRAFT WAS NEVER NEEDED. BY NIGHTFALL ON 6 June 156,000 Allied troops were in France, at a cost of some ten thousand casualties—two-thirds of them American. On Utah the landings were virtually unopposed: In the 4th Division only 197 men were killed, wounded or missing, less than one-third of its losses in the Tiger dress rehearsal on Slapton Sands. The U.S. airborne divisions suffered twenty-five hundred casualties but they kept open the causeways off Utah Beach and held at bay German reinforcements. On most of the three Anglo-Canadian beaches the landings did not meet heavy resistance. Only at the western end of Gold and especially on adjacent Omaha were the landings bitterly contested. Even on Omaha, where the 1st and 29th Divisions sustained over two thousand casualties, a narrow beachhead had been secured by nightfall.[1]

It was the start of a campaign in which nothing went according to plan, except the final outcome. Compared with expectations, the landings were easy, the breakout hard, the pursuit breathtakingly quick, and the kill frustratingly slow. The ebb and flow of Allied fortunes washed back across the Channel, shaping the last year of the American occupation of Britain in equally unforeseen ways, as we shall see in the next chapter. And, in the process, the balance of the Anglo-American alliance shifted irrevocably away from the British. By the spring of 1945, victory in the West was overwhelmingly an American triumph and that also had an effect on how the U.S. Army was perceived and remembered. At the centre of this story is the person of Dwight D. Eisenhower.

★ ★ ★

The D-Day landings repeated many of the mistakes made on Slapton Sands (not least because most of the planning had been done by February 1944 and could not be adjusted to take account of lessons learnt in the exercises).[2] The heavy swell and spring tides drove landing craft hundreds of yards off target, with results that were fortuitous on Utah but disastrous on Omaha. Where the enemy was well established, beach obstacles and defending fire proved as deadly as the Tiger umpires had predicted. The airborne troops were even more disrupted by cloud, weather, and flak—the 101st was scattered over some four hundred square miles. And, despite repeated after-exercise reports, ground and airborne troops carried far too much equipment and many drowned in shallow water offshore or in the swamps of the Cotentin.

What made the difference, overall, between success and failure were three factors. First, the Allies enjoyed overwhelming air superiority. Opinions remain divided on the merits of the interdiction bombing campaign that spring, but the Luftwaffe itself had been driven from the skies over the Channel in the previous few months. This was partly the result of numerical superiority. The 8th AF increased its bomber and fighter strength by almost 50 percent between January and June 1944; the 9th more than fivefold. Equally important was the advent of long-range fighters that not only protected the bombers but also sought out enemy fighters. By May they had forced the Luftwaffe back to defend Germany. On D-Day there were fifty Allied sorties for every one by the Germans in the invasion area.[3]

Second, the bad weather proved a blessing in disguise. It may have driven Eisenhower and his colleagues close to despair, it certainly left thousands of soldiers chronically seasick, and it also contributed to the failure to reach Caen on D-Day (because of delays on the beaches and the lack of tactical air support). But it did persuade senior German commanders that invasion was not imminent. Rommel, in charge of Army Group B along the French coast, left for home early on 4 June and did not return until the evening of D-Day. The German Navy made no changes in dispositions and only five German aircraft flew along the Channel on routine sorties on 5 June, when the invasion fleet was already at sea. One of the Allied minesweeping flotillas was actually in sight of the French coast for the last three hours of daylight. Contrary to all the expectations of Ike, Monty, and their subordinates, despite weeks of leaks and rumours, they did achieve a remarkable degree of tactical surprise.[4]

Most important of all for the success of Overlord, the Allies also achieved strategic surprise. Von Rundstedt was anticipating an attack on Normandy, even if he was temporarily knocked off balance by its timing. But he still did not believe it was the *main* thrust, which he expected to come from Dover. Four weeks after D-Day, to quote official historian Sir Michael Howard, "the German High Command was still completely convinced" of the existence of "Army Group Patton" and had some twenty-two divisions waiting to repel its attack. The Fortitude deception did not prevent the Germans moving powerful reinforcements into Normandy piecemeal, but it helped ensure that a massed counterattack never materialized in the crucial first ten days.[5]

Tiger and the other chaotic exercises on the Devon coast had in many ways been an accurate pointer to the Overlord landings. The fears of the Allied commanders had been justified. But for the absence of German aircraft, the pervasive bad weather, and the success of the deception plans, all the Allied beaches might have been like "Bloody Omaha."

Lt. Ray Nance landed at the western end of Omaha, near the road up to Vierville. He was the only officer of A Company, 116th Infantry Regiment, to make it across the beach. But he was wounded three times, and could only move using his carbine as a crutch. Fifty years later he still recalled those initial moments of D-Day. When the ramp came down, he was first off the landing craft, jumping into waves up to his hips. He waded to the beach and dropped down on the sand. Then he looked about him. "There was nobody in front: not a soul. I turned around and I didn't see anybody coming. I got away before the fire came on that ramp." That was why Nance was the only one of seventeen GIs on his landing craft who survived. Along the beach, the 16th Infantry also suffered heavy casualties. But these were men from all over the United States, unlike the 116th, nearly half of whom were former National Guardsmen from Appalachian Virginia. Four others on Nance's boat came from his hometown of Bedford, where Company A had been based. In all, nineteen men from Bedford were killed on D-Day, including two sets of brothers. News of the fatalities started to arrive on Wednesday 19 July. By the end of that week, Bedford (five thousand population) was in shock. Families stood outside the Western Union Office waiting for the next telegram of condolence from the Pentagon.[6]

What went wrong? Why did the 16th and 116th, and the other follow-up regiments of the 1st and 29th Divisions, suffer so heavily? Some historians have depicted Omaha as a fatal miniature of the American predilection for a "head-on, power-drive strategy," for a "direct assault" on enemy strongpoints.[7] But this is too neat. Stated simply, what went right for the Allies elsewhere on D-Day went wrong on Omaha. Admittedly, there was no threat from the Luftwaffe, but on this beach both intelligence and weather worked much more than elsewhere to the Allies' disadvantage.

The critical intelligence failure was the assumption that the beach was held only by weak and overstretched elements of the "static" 716th Infantry Division. On board ship Capt. Walter Schilling had told D Company of the 116th that only one or two of the twenty-two German bunkers on Vierville Beach would be occupied, and these "only by Polish and Russian volunteers and over-age Home Guard" who would not prove fanatical defenders. In fact the GIs hit troops from the 352nd Division, mobile and battle-hardened, who were believed to be some twenty miles inland. Eisenhower's grandson has suggested that Ike and Gerow knew of the true deployment but concealed it from the Omaha commanders, apparently to avoid damaging morale, but there seems to be no evidence to substantiate this claim. The 21st Army Group's last appraisal, on 4 June, speculated that the 352nd might have pushed one regiment up to the beach but this report did not reach the commanders before the assault force sailed and the security blanket came down. Even if news had reached them, it would have made no difference at that stage to the plan.[8]

Omaha also suffered most from the appalling weather. The British beaches were somewhat better protected thanks to the Calvados Reef. In addition, the landing craft for Omaha were launched eleven miles out to sea (compared with seven miles for the British beaches) to keep the big troopships beyond the range of the massive German coastal battery at Pointe du Hoc. It was the heavy seas that caused most of the boats carrying the 116th's artillery to founder offshore, swamped by vast waves as they sat low in the water. Such was the storm that the 16th Infantry lost all but two of the twenty-nine DD tanks that tried to "swim" ashore; previously a total of thirty thousand had been launched in training in England with only one fatality. All along Omaha the tides and wind drove troops onto unfamiliar beaches and separated the carefully coordinated boat crews of weapons-men and engineers, leaving the infantry unable to penetrate the obstacles and the engineers defenceless as they tried to blow paths through them. The 116th suffered a particular shortage of engineers because of the strong eastward current. Those who landed near Vierville had lost the boats carrying their explosives. Not until mid-afternoon did they have enough TNT to blow the German defences barring the road off the beach.[9]

The bad weather therefore contributed to the lack of heavy firepower available on Omaha Beach. It also played havoc with aerial support. Over Omaha this was in the hands of heavy bombers from the

8th AF, who had to bomb by instruments through the cloud. With Ike's concurrence, they deliberately delayed release by a few seconds to ensure that they did not hit the invading troops. Consequently, the 13,000 bombs dropped by 329 B-24s missed the beach completely and landed as far as three miles inland. The main casualties were Normandy cows, though the French inhabitants of Colleville village suffered heavily as well. Over Utah, by contrast, air support came from medium bombers flying under the cloud and bombing visually, to much greater effect. As for the naval gunfire, here Omaha was the victim of time and tides. The Army would only permit a forty-minute prebombardment, to maximize surprise. This began at 0550. But the British Army allowed its task force to start up at 0530, which, because of the later tide on their coast, meant two hours' firing or even more before the assault troops went in. The potential value of such softening-up was demonstrated the hard way later on D-Day morning. About 1030 two American destroyers, venturing within one thousand yards of shore, blasted the area around the St. Laurent exit, allowing troops to flush out enemy defences and engineers to clear a way off the beach. This was crucial for the advance in that area. Little wonder that the 115th Regiment's after-action report emphasized the importance of close cooperation with naval gunfire.[10]

A combination of bad weather, faulty intelligence, and mistaken planning left the GIs on Omaha with inadequate firepower. Whether that would have mattered but for the unexpected German strength is unanswerable, but it is significant, as Russell Weigley, Max Hastings, and other historians have remarked, that where the British faced elements of the same 352nd Division their progress was also very slow.[11] This was the experience of the the the 50th Northumbrian Division at Le Hamel, on neighbouring Gold Beach. In these tough circumstances, what mattered was the coolness and courage of individuals under fire. Omaha was preeminently a story of small-unit actions, fought by men like Ray Nance without equipment, commanders, or direction.

The whole Normandy campaign failed to go according to plan. The 1st, 4th, and 29th Divisions, and those who followed them across the Channel, were totally unprepared for the kind of warfare they faced beyond the beachhead in the small fields, tight hedges, and high banks of the *bocage*. The restrictions on training in Britain were partly to blame. Areas of Devon, Cornwall, or County Fermanagh would have offered tolerable simulation, *if* the U.S. Army had been able to range freely. More important, however, was the fact that Allied strategists did not expect a tenacious defence of Normandy. They assumed Rommel would mount an early counteroffensive against the beachhead. If that failed, then the Germans would probably make an orderly retreat to the Seine and Loire, which would become their main line of defence. Few anticipated Hitler's determination to contest every hedgerow. Seven weeks after D-Day, the Americans had sustained seventy-three thousand casualties and the British-Canadians forty-nine thousand. The beachhead was nowhere more than thirty miles in depth.[12]

The breakout, when it came, was another surprise, despite Montgomery's later insistence that the battle of Normandy was "fought exactly as planned before the invasion." First, it had been expected that the strongest thrust would come from the Anglo-Canadian forces around Caen, who enjoyed the bulk of the Allied armour and the best tank country. Monty's slowness in taking Caen led to bitter recriminations. In consequence, weight was shifted to Bradley's 12th Army Group in the *bocage*, whose successful operation Cobra (25–28 July) made possible the unleashing of Patton's 3rd Army and the spectacular American drive east across central France. The GIs reached Paris and the Seine by 24 August and the German border by 11 September. This, too, was not planned. The main American objective in Overlord had always been the capture of the Brittany ports, from Brest to St.-Nazaire. The decision to swing east on 3 August, leaving only minimal forces to seize the Breton Peninsula, was a dramatic shift that "changed the entire course of the campaign." It gained spectacular successes but also led directly to the logistical crisis that followed.[13]

Overlord was intended not as a race to Berlin but as a ninety-day campaign to secure "a lodgement on the Continent from which further offensive operations can be developed." Crucial to that lodgement were ports of sufficient capacity to handle the vast supply needs of modern, motorized armies. That is why Cherbourg and the Breton ports were the main American objectives of Overlord: Bradley was looking west not east. The overall aim was to secure northwestern France to the Seine and Loire by D plus ninety, with full port capacity, and then pause for a month to build a logistic base from which to move east of the Seine. Instead, that new campaign was begun without any pause and it advanced far beyond any notional targets. The Americans took nineteen days to move from the Seine to the German border—instead of the 260 that had been allowed. Having been a month behind "schedule" just before the breakout, by 11 September 1944 the GIs were on a line they "should not" have reached until 21 May 1945. "Should not," that is, in the lexicon of those trying to supply them. Even if Allied logistics had been faultless (which they were not), all the efforts of the "Red Ball Express"—and its rail equivalent, the "Toot Sweet Specials"—could not have kept up with such an erratic yet ultimately swift advance.[14]

Eisenhower and his lieutenants knew this, of course. But they were capitalizing on the tactical opportunities that had opened up and gambling on a German collapse akin to that of autumn 1918. When the American offensive started running out of gas (literally) in September, Ike gambled again by agreeing to Monty's plan for a combined airborne drop and armoured thrust to get across the Rhine—operation Market-Garden on 17 September, which led to the tragedy of Arnhem. In his preoccupation with pursuit, Ike had not ignored the ports completely. Both in August, over Brittany, and in September, in the campaign to clear the Scheldt River above Antwerp, he (like Bradley and Montgomery) assumed that only limited forces were required. In both cases they proved gravely mistaken. When the port of Brest finally fell, it had been systematically destroyed by the Germans. And by the time the first Allied supply ship docked in Antwerp on 28 November, eighty-three days after the city itself had been captured, winter had set in. Eisenhower had three great Allied Army Groups ranged along the German border: Monty's Anglo-Canadians in the north, Bradley's GIs in the middle, and Devers's mix of Americans and French in the south. But now the war of movement had become a struggle of attrition.

If both breakout and then breakdown were surprising, the scale of the German counteroffensive in mid-December came as a total shock. Nothing on the scale and savagery of the Nazi thrust into Bradley's troops in Ardennes had been anticipated and for a few days a frisson of panic ran through Washington. Was this a repeat of Ludendorff's March 1918 onslaughts, which had almost sliced through the Allied front? But Ike's nerve held, as did that of most of his troops. The 101st's epic defence of Bastogne, together with the speed of Patton's counter-attack, strangled the German Bulge and opened the way to renewed advance. As in the autumn, Ike favoured a general offensive all along the front, but with most weight being placed on the northern route around the Ruhr, using Monty's 21st Army Group reinforced by the U.S. 9th Army. Yet Patton's men, further south, were actually first across the Rhine on 22–23 March. It was, to quote American historian Charles B. MacDonald, "a pattern already made familiar in Sicily and again in Normandy: Montgomery's troops attracted German reserves, while American troops broke through and rapidly exploited the gains."[15]

April 1945 was a repeat of August 1944, with 300,000 Germans surrendering in the Ruhr pocket and a whole army group eliminated.

Ike made his last thrust not across northern Germany, as the British wanted, but in the centre towards Dresden, using Bradley's 12th Army Group. His aim was to end the remaining German resistance and not, despite Churchill's chagrin, to enter the Reich's capital before the Russians. Germany surrendered on 8 May, over three weeks ahead of the 1 June date that Allied logistic planners had guestimated back in mid-1944. Staff officers took pride in their predictions after the war.[16] But, as we have seen, the route and the timing by which the Allied armies got to that point most certainly did not go according to plan.

After the war, the reasons for their successes and setbacks turned, in the United States, into debates about the relative merits of Allied and Axis soldiers and of American and British strategies. Reflection on both of these issues sheds considerable light on the U.S. Army in the last year of the war and on how it was perceived in Britain.

The GIs' performance in North Africa had been chequered, while the campaign in Italy, for all its grimness, was often dismissed as a sideshow. Normandy was therefore anxiously awaited as the GIs' real test in Europe, a stern one indeed for a green army. On 30 June 1944 *The New York Times* carried a special editorial to celebrate the fall of Cherbourg entitled "The American Soldier." It noted the "theme of enemy propaganda that the American soldiers are homesick, jazz-crazed, immature boys who do not know what they are fighting for" and admitted that, "even in uniform they are still primarily civilians and normal human beings, with normal instincts and desires, and they make no secret of this." But, said the *Times*, the last few weeks had shown that "the American Army has come of age and now ranks with the best in the world in fighting prowess, in battle skills and in generalship." In support it cited a tribute from the London *Sunday Express* (a Beaverbrook paper not renowned for its affection towards the United States) that the Americans had "proved themselves to be a race of great fighters in the very front rank of men at arms."[17]

This was a typical sentiment in Britain. After two years of waiting, the Yanks were finally fighting, and feelings warmed towards them. In the spring press mogul Cecil King had still been busily noting anti-American gossip in London. Reports from Italy, he said, showed that, although American matériel, transport, and engineering were "of the very highest order," the "value of American troops in action is almost nil." But on 26 June King observed that the "Americans seem to be fighting better in France and are certainly very much more popular in this country than they were earlier." This was also the judgement of official reports. A BBC listener survey in February observed that British people were shocked at the "slovenly appearance" of GIs and this made "a very great many doubt whether the American soldier will ever be the equal of the British." But on 3 August, the Ministry of Information's weekly survey of British opinion found that comment on the GIs was "more generally favourable than at any time since they arrived in this country. Their work in Normandy, especially at Cherbourg, is the factor most widely reported to have increased their prestige."[18]

Historians have not been as ready as contemporaries to praise the GIs, however. After the war S.L.A. Marshall claimed that his postcombat interviews for the Army in the Pacific and Europe suggested that, at very most, 25 percent of GIs fired their weapons during an average firefight. In the 1970s Col. Trevor N. Dupuy tabulated seventy-eight engagements in 1943–44 and calculated that German soldiers consistently inflicted casualties at a 50 percent higher rate than they incurred from GIs. In the hands of historian Martin van Creveld this became a general argument about the superiority of German "fighting power." Van Creveld contended that, whatever their weaknesses in strategy and logistics, the Germans were better fighters than the Americans on the ground. Units were more cohesive, officers and particularly NCOs were superior leaders, and German doctrine stressed individual initiative rather than drilled obedience. This was not simply a criticism of the GIs. Dupuy's figures included the British as well, and "the central theme" of Max Hastings's study of the Normandy campaign "was that when Allied troops met Germans on anything like equal terms, the Germans always prevailed."[19]

These arguments remain controversial. "Slam" Marshall's famous statistic accords with the anecdotage of battle but it was probably a guestimate, with no clear evidence to back it up. Dupuy's complex formulae actually rest on some highly intuitive attempts to quantify the advantages of artillery, air support, and defensive positions. Assign different values for these variables and his argument can be turned on its head to favour the GIs. Nor were British and American deficiencies identical. The casualty replacement system was one of the U.S. Army's greatest disasters. Reflecting the principle of interchangeable parts, it led to men being fed into the line piecemeal. This was the most demoralizing way to experience one's baptism of fire; many "repples" were dead before the rest of the squad knew their names. The British regimental system and the practice of unit replacements helped overcome this morale problem, but regimentalism had its own vices, such as a fragmented training programme. And, as we have seen, it was widely observed that the pervasive hierarchies of English life accentuated barriers between officers and men, not to mention tank crews and infantry.[20]

Although the intricacies of this debate lie beyond the scope of this book, three general points should be made. First, the Allied armies in Normandy comprised largely green troops. Only five men of the fifteen thousand in the American 29th Division on Omaha Beach had been in combat before. Even "veteran" divisions from the Mediterranean, such as the U.S. 1st or the British 51st, included numerous untested replacements. Against them were ranged a number of crack Panzer and SS Divisions. Second, Britain was an awful place for training. Assault troops were well schooled in amphibious landings at Woolacombe and Slapton, but most of the follow-up divisions had no room for realistic training. Field craft and manoeuvre had to be learnt the hard way in Normandy by GIs who had spent much of their time on the roads. Tank crews had little opportunity to work with infantry and aircraft, or even to practice live-fire operations on their own. In fact, Gen. Marshall commented later that troops who had been in Britain for some time actually went backwards in training, and were always inferior in preparation to units entering battle direct from the United States. Third, however, the Americans were quick learners. As Michael Doubler has argued, what stands out from the *bocage* campaign is not just the U.S. Army's unpreparedness but also the speed with which it adapted—improvising hedgerow tactics and refining combined-arms cooperation between infantry, tanks, and aircraft. At Yalta in February 1945 Marshall finally let rip at what he deemed Sir Harold Alexander's patronizing attitude to the GIs. "Yes," he admitted, "American troops start out and make every possible mistake. But after the first time, they do not repeat their mistakes. The British troops start in the same way and continue making the same mistakes over and over for a year." Whatever the truth of his aspersions on the British, the theme of Yankee flexibility recurs in German accounts.[21]

What emerged from the finishing school of Normandy was a distinctive way of warfare. Whether or not the best Germans outclassed the best British, American, or Canadian troops in "fighting power," the Allies' superiority in firepower was unquestioned. Once this was harnessed to a proper combined-arms doctrine, the effects were shattering, as Germans trapped in the Falaise pocket discovered. One precondition was bringing the airmen down to earth. Their fixation with strategic bombing meant that tactical airpower was still in its infancy on the Allied side in 1944, despite the campaigns in the Mediterranean. Gen. Lesley J. McNair, the great trainer of the American Army, was only the most famous fatality from USAAF "friendly fire" in Normandy, while air-ground coordination was being learnt the hard way. But by late 1944 German attacks had little chance of success, except, as in the Ardennes, when bad weather grounded Allied planes. The other ingredient of firepower was the systematic use of artillery—in Russell Weigley's words "the sovereign American remedy for battle problems," which "impressed friend and foe alike as the outstanding combat branch of the American ground forces." By 1944 the artillery was in a different league from that of 1940. Better ammunition and fuses, plus improved weaponry (notably the 105mm howitzer) were all important. But the crux was communication. Instead of indiscriminate barrages, vintage 1918, observers with FM radios and Piper Cub spotter planes made it possible to select a few targets and call down massive fire upon them. Using timed fuses, all the shells, from whatever distance, would explode simultaneously. "On Time, On Target"—TOT for short—was one of the great military revolutions of the war.[22]

The other distinctive element of the American way of warfare was mobility. Many GIs still remember their surprise in Normandy to see, from the debris along the roadside, that the Germans were using horses and carts to supply their troops. It has been justly claimed that "no other single item of equipment—weapon or otherwise—influenced the course of World War II more than American trucks." The jeep and the 2½-tonner were not merely prodigies of American technology, to be gaped at by English schoolboys such as the young John Keegan. They were war-winning weapons, for instance in Patton's spectacular dash across central France in August or his sudden about-turn in December into the Ardennes. In the first week of the Bulge Ike moved 250,000 men and 50,000 vehicles into the fray. "Not even in Vietnam, not even in the 1991 Gulf War," observed Stephen Ambrose, "was the U.S. Army capable of moving so many men and so much equipment so quickly." By the spring of 1945 every American division was able to motorize all its infantry.[23]

The British, it should be acknowledged, shared in the firepower revolution, through the Royal Artillery on the ground and the "artillery of the air." But in the number of guns and the sophistication of the communications net, American artillery was far ahead. And the mobility of the U.S. Army was quite unique. When Churchill learnt on 7 August 1944 that twelve U.S. divisions were well through the Avranches gap, he exclaimed "Good heavens, how do you feed them?" Bradley told him that they were running trucks up to the front "bumper to bumper, 24 hours a day." In the prime minister's letter of congratulation to Ike in March 1945 on the "destruction of all the

Germans west of the Rhine," he remarked particularly that "no one who studies war can fail to be impressed by the admirable speed and flexibility of the American Armies." Perhaps, as Russell Weigley has argued, the U.S. Army never harmonized firepower and mobility in a coordinated military doctrine, but by 1945 it had undoubtedly pushed combined-arms operations to a level of effectiveness far beyond that of the Wehrmacht in 1940.[24]

What made possible American firepower and mobility were the vast resources, both material and human, of the United States—now almost fully mobilized. In 1944 America produced about 40 percent of the world's armaments and 60 percent of the combat munitions of the Allies. Britain had reached the apogee of its, much smaller, productive effort in 1942. And although both countries faced acute shortages of combat infantrymen in 1944, the American problem was miscalculation and mismanagement, whereas the British were scraping the bottom of the barrel. The caution for which Montgomery was denounced in the United States, both in 1944–45 and after the war, was only partly due to his passion for a properly "teed-up" offensive. The underlying problem, as he admitted privately in 1946, was that "we had not the manpower to replace heavy casualties. The War Office told me a week before D-Day that it could guarantee replacements only for the first month. After that I would have to break up divisions of ancillary troops." As the campaign dragged on, the numbers game told remorselessly against the British. At the end of April 1945 there were 5.1 million Allied troops under Eisenhower. Of these 60 percent (3 million) were American and just over 25 percent (1.3 million) British. Of the eight Allied armies in Ike's command, five were American and only one British. Monty's 21st Army Group, comprising the 2nd British and 1st Canadian armies, required the attachment of American units (particularly the 9th Army) to be operationally effective in the latter stages of the war. Similarly, in Italy after summer 1944, the shift of most American units to southern France left the remaining forces, largely British, incapable of major offensives. These were signs that the weight of the alliance had now shifted overwhelmingly in America's favour. In North Africa in 1943 the British Army could cite superior numbers as well as experience to justify taking the lead. By 1945 the U.S. Army had indeed come of age, both in size and maturity. Britain was definitely the junior partner.[25]

Statistics of manpower and output were known only to a few in wartime Britain. Where the transatlantic transfer of power became public was in the row about strategy and command. This became personalized in the figures of Montgomery and Eisenhower: Which of them should run the war in Europe?

Despite his success in North Africa, Ike remained on the margins of British public opinion when he returned to London in 1944. The popular press had noted his humble origins, though usually focusing on Texas (where he was born) rather than Kansas (where he grew up) because that fitted more conveniently into movie stereotypes of America. One London paper described him with spectacular inaccuracy as "a Texan and former cowboy himself when he worked his way through the University of Texas"! Ike's informal manner and broad grin also attracted comment and a British correspondent described his first press conference at SHAEF in January 1944 as "one of the happiest, least formal military conferences that I have ever attended." But Ike was still seen in Britain, to quote the *Daily Mail*, as "a masterly organiser and co-ordinator" rather than as a real general. The War Cabinet felt in December 1943 that British opinion would be "surprised and rather uneasy" at Ike's appointment. Felix Branham, a GI spending Christmas with a British family, recalled the "total silence" that ensued when the BBC announced the news. "The atmosphere," he said, "went very cool."[26]

What eased matters, initially, was the appointment of Monty as commander of land forces during the invasion itself. Ike would have preferred Alexander, but Churchill told FDR: "I feel the Cabinet are right that Montgomery is a public hero and will give confidence among our people, not unshared by yours." With the naval and air commanders also British, it was a repeat of the government's "stratosphere" ploy of 1942–43, leaving Ike in charge of diplomacy while the Brits ran the war. But Monty's command was only intended to be temporary. By mid-August American papers were complaining that Ike was only a "figure-head" for "British dominance," and Marshall urged him to move to France and take direct command of the land forces. This he did on 1 September, making Monty coequal with Bradley as an Army Group commander. While serious London papers such as *The Times* found the move "desirable in the circumstances," given the size of the U.S. contingent and the clamour from American opinion, the popular press portrayed it as a "demotion" for Monty. The *Daily Mail* (motto "For King and Empire") editorialized that "there is bound to be disappointment in this country" where Monty was placed in "a very special category" on account of "his military genius." Effective 1 September, Churchill therefore elevated Monty to field marshal. He told Ike that this was "necessary from the point of view of the British nation with whom Montgomery's name is a household word." Although public reaction was one of "delight," according to MOI reports, there was also suspicion that the new rank was "a sop for his recent demotion."[27]

As the Allied armies raced across France, criticism abated. Success is always uncontroversial. But argument renewed when the campaign lost momentum that autumn. Behind the scenes Monty wanted SHAEF to concentrate resources on a northern thrust (led by himself), whereas Ike preferred a more general advance, though with a bias to the northern flank. Twice in three months Ike was forced to present this as a resignation issue to Monty (either you or me) before his subordinate backed off. But what really hit the headlines were the command changes during the German Ardennes counteroffensive. Two of Bradley's armies were north of the Bulge, almost cut off from his command post to the south in Luxembourg, and Ike decided to shift them, temporarily, to Montgomery. Even Bradley admitted that "if Monty's were an American command" this "would be the logical thing to do." But, with a furore developing in Washington about who was to blame for the early success of the German offensive, Bradley was sensitive to anything that might discredit him or the U.S. Army.[28]

The setbacks had also revived British press demands for a separate ground commander. Although some commentators in London were ready to see the job go to an American, in view of the preponderance of U.S. forces in France, even this involved criticism of Ike as someone "constantly preoccupied with problems that arise behind the front." When news of Monty's enlarged command leaked out (through the American press), the more jingoistic British papers were jubilant. "A British Field-Marshal was called in at the moment of greatest crisis to handle two American armies," exulted *The Mail*. Further American leaks suggested that British troops were also playing a major role in the battle. When Monty gave a press conference about how this was "one of the most interesting and tricky battles I have ever handled," Bradley blew his top. He gave his own account to correspondents, making clear that the command changes were temporary, and he told Ike that he would resign rather than serve under Monty. Patton felt the same way about that "tired little fart."[29]

In retrospect this row was slightly artificial on both sides. Bradley's hypersensitive HQ were most angered by a triumphalist "BBC statement" about Monty, which later turned out to be a German propaganda broadcast. With a virtual news blackout, the British press made far too much of (American) leaks about the British contribution, and most backed off rather shamefacedly when the truth was known. It should also be noted that both Monty and the British press paid warm tributes during the battle to the courage and resolution of the American soldiers. Behind the lines, said Stanley Baron, a war correspondent for the *News Chronicle*, the GI looks like "a civilian in disguise"— informal, irreverent, and unsoldierly in manner. But, in the Ardennes, he said, one sees the other half, "the soldier half" of the GI, who "fights, and if need be dies . . . with bravery as utterly complete and selfless as any man, anywhere, can fight and die." In similar vein, the *Mail*'s correspondent, John Hall, expressed his "admiration for the combat GIs" and their "magnificent" middle-level officers. He also extolled the "remarkable feats of swift American organisation," concluding that, although the details could not yet be revealed, "in half a dozen ways American mobility outsmarted the Hun blitz in this affair." It was left to Churchill, in the Commons on 18 January 1945, to make clear that this had not been "an Anglo-American battle" and that U.S. troops had "done almost all the fighting" and had "suffered almost all the losses," on a scale equivalent to both sides at Gettysburg. It was, said Churchill, "the greatest American battle of the war" and would be "regarded as an ever famous American victory."[30]

Behind the scenes in 1945, the British continued to press their strategic arguments and Churchill made a further bid for a British ground commander, this time Alexander. But neither effort had much success. The epic of the Bulge had demonstrated to the British public what British policymakers had realized for some time. Germany's defeat in the West was, fundamentally, an American victory.

It was one of Ike's great achievements that he prevented this from poisoning Anglo-American relations. Monty may have been right in strategic terms (though this is arguable) but his position was diplomatically untenable. To concentrate on a northern thrust would have meant placing many U.S. troops under British command and leaving the rest kicking their heels. This was politically impossible in the United States, even if Monty had been an emollient man. Equally, Ike understood that Monty was not only an able commander but also a hero in Britain. Dismissing him, or even marginalizing him, were not options, either. The so-called broad-front advance was therefore as much diplomacy as strategy. Eisenhower "could not let either a British or an American general win the war single-handedly," observed historian Martin Blumenson; "both British and Americans had to win together." Ike also ensured, in the words of Eric Larrabee, "that American armies stood forth at the close in proportion to their numbers and their contribution to the fighting, but without denigration to their comrades in arms." This balancing act was a remarkable accomplishment, which those, like Patton and Spaatz, who groused that "we have paid a hell of a price for the supreme command," failed to appreciate. And in the last months of the war, Ike finally overcame the doubts about whether he was truly a military commander, rather than merely an allied supremo. During the Bulge, it was he who made the crucial decisions to reinforce Bastogne and turn Patton northward, insisting that the German offensive was not a disaster but an opportunity. If, as Churchill averred, this was one of the great American victories of the war, credit at the command level was undoubtedly Eisenhower's.[31]

In February 1944, Patton told Ike's staff that their boss was about to become "the greatest general of all time—including Napoleon." This was just duplicitous Georgie trying to curry favour. As historian James A. Huston observed, the apt analogy is with George Washington not Napoleon Bonaparte: "As Washington held together the military effort of disparate colonies, Eisenhower held together the forces of divergent Allies to common triumph in Europe." And, like Washington, his triumph made Ike a celebrity. At home, he was already talked about for the White House (in the summer of 1945 *President* Truman privately offered to support an Eisenhower campaign in 1948!). Abroad, as biographer Stephen Ambrose has remarked, the sudden deaths of Roosevelt and Hitler in April had made Ike "one of the three best-known men in the world, just behind Stalin and Churchill." British leaders were well aware of this. In late 1944 the Foreign Office had been pulling strings to obtain a Cambridge honorary degree for Ike, partly as compensation for putting up with Monty, but also "to cause pleasure to a man who might quite possibly some day be a Presidential candidate." But Churchill wanted to secure more prestigious honours. On 12 June 1945 Ike received the Freedom of the City of London and the Order of Merit, Britain's highest award.[32]

Even the bitter election campaign in Britain did not overshadow Ike's London triumph. Most newspapers paid tribute in lead editorials (though not the *Daily Mail*). THE MAN FROM TEXAS A LONDONER NOW proclaimed the banner headline on the front page of the *Evening Standard* on 12 June. The writer of the paper's "Londoner's diary," had "never known a more cheerful London crowd." Even that on VE day "did not surpass it in high spirits and good humour." When Ike slipped out of his hotel for some fresh air, he was mobbed by autograph hunters and had to be rescued by police. To receive the Freedom of the City he drove in open carriage through the debris and destruction around St. Paul's to the bomb-scarred Guildhall, entering it in procession behind a six-hundred-year-old mace. After the ceremony, Ike had to respond—the first formal speech of any length he had ever given in public. He worked so hard on drafts that he found he had committed them to memory. The result was what veteran CBS commentator Ed Murrow called "the finest utterance of any soldier of our day."[33]

Ike's Guildhall address struck all the right notes. There was the Old World/New World polarity, flatteringly expressed: "Abilene, Kansas, and Denison, Texas, would together equal in size possibly one five-hundredth of a part of great London . . . whose name stands for grandeur and size throughout the world." But also the community of values:

> To preserve his freedom of worship, his equality before the law, his liberty to speak and act as he sees fit, subject only to provisions that he trespass not upon similar rights of others—a Londoner will fight. So will a citizen of Abilene. When we consider these things, then the valley of the Thames draws closer to the farms of Kansas and the plains of Texas.

Ike paid extended tribute to the fortitude of the British war effort and to London's lonely defiance of Hitler: "The Battle of Britain will take its place as another of your deathless traditions." He acknowledged that "you had been more than two years in war" before America joined in. In his speech (and in remarks afterwards) he also said "a word of thanks for your hospitality to my soldiers, who came to your country in great numbers, often to your great inconvenience, if not irritation." And he represented the award as a tribute to all GIs and to the unparalleled Allied teamwork. "If we keep our eyes on this guidepost, then no difficulties along our path of mutual co-operation can ever be insurmountable."[34]

What a contrast with Woodrow Wilson in 1918! Both men had come to London triumphantly at the end of a great war, incarnating their country for the British and articulating its philosophy. But Wilson was a statesman, Ike a soldier. The former stood forth as the scholar-preacher (Keynes's Presbyterian minister thundering commandments like Moses from Sinai); the latter as a humble representative of small-town America (even an ex-cowboy, if the British press was to be believed). When Wilson addressed the state banquet at Buckingham Palace (chapter 1), he made no mention of British achievements in a war in which America had been marginal. When Eisenhower spoke at the end of a conflict that had made America a superpower, he paid extended tribute to British efforts. And where Wilson stressed the moral distance between Old World and New, Ike's theme was teamwork and shared values.

One should not, of course, make over-much of two speeches, thirty-seven years apart. Wilson was tactless and self-righteous, Ike a natural politician—their words reflect their characters. But, taken together, the two men symbolize the distance Anglo-American relations had traveled in those four decades. America's preeminence was now a matter of deeds not words—testimony to economic and military potential that, this time, had been fully mobilized. But it had been mobilized through an alliance that entangled the two countries far more completely than that of 1917–18. And, unlike World War One, the extended presence of American soldiers in Britain on a large scale had brought America, literally, home to Britons in a new way. The general whom GIs nicknamed "Private First Class Eisenhower" was truly what Ralph Waldo Emerson would have called a "representative man."

22

"Returning Britain
to the British"

★ ★ ★

WHILE WAR ON THE CONTINENT WAS RESHAPING THE ALLIANCE AND BRIT-
ish opinions about the GIs, in 1944–45 the American occupation of
Britain took on a different character. The year after D-Day is often
dismissed as a brief postscript to the story of the GIs and the British. If
U.S. Army planners had had their way, that would indeed have been
the case. On 1 September 1944, the day Ike moved his HQ to France,
a new UK Base Section was established. Its task, in the words of an
internal history, was that of "returning Britain to the British." Its
intended legacy, stated Commanding General Egmont F. Koenig in
March 1945, was "to leave behind the memory of well-disciplined
troops, and an honest, clean, decent operating organization." Like so
much in 1944–45, however, things did not go according to plan.[1]

In 1942–44, to quote Churchill, Britain became the great "assembly
base for the war against Hitler," from which airmen and eventually
soldiers ventured across the Channel.[2] But, as we have seen, the
cramped little island was hardly ideal for this purpose and both governments were anxious to reduce the American occupation as soon as
room in France became available. The rundown plan, first issued on
3 May 1944, was variously known as Rhumba or Reverse Bolero. Its
object was to return property and land to the British quickly, because
of the political sensitivity of American occupation and the insecurity
of vacated camps, where supplies were being stolen and buildings
damaged.

Some accommodation could easily be released. The 100,000 private
billets were no longer needed, and many of the hotels, apartments,

schools, and the like that had accommodated 650,000 GIs in the spring could be returned. There was also no need for most of the marshaling camps along the coast west of the Solent, and forty-eight of these had been vacated by 23 June. It was particularly important to hand back areas used for special training by the invasion troops, notably around Slapton Sands in Devon where hasty eviction had been so resented in December 1943. The bitterness had been sharpened by reports of large-scale damage caused not merely by live fire but by GI vandals. In an effort at reassurance, the Army allowed British reporters into the area during February, but these were carefully chaperoned affairs. Confidential Army reports indicated considerable "wilful damage" by bivouacking troops—windows smashed, stair rails used for firewood, and excrement left in buildings. It was not until the autumn that the residents, some 750 households, were allowed to return. (A few did not bother, having "sampled for the first time in their lives the pleasures of electric light, water on tap, gas cooking and fitted bathrooms.") Given free rein, locals and newsmen found that the situation was "not as bad as feared"—superficial damage rather than wholesale devastation. But some buildings were rubble—the hotel on Slapton Beach had been a target for U.S. naval gunfire. Farmers complained that it would take years to decontaminate the fields, and those with smallholdings, shops, and pubs had often been ruined.[3]

It was estimated that one-third of households had suffered significant financial hardship. Compensation was to come from the British government, via Reverse Lend-Lease, but Whitehall claimed that the Compensation (Defence) Act of 1939 did not cover loss of income. Irritation about all this was directed at the Americans. Ambassador Winant was particularly concerned, since he had personally gone to Churchill to secure Slapton Sands for the U.S. Army. In early 1944 he badgered ETO to help these hardship cases. The matter took months to resolve, because the Army feared the gesture could boomerang if known in America, where similar cases were not compensated, but in May 1944 Gen. J.C.H. Lee allocated £6,000 for the Slapton hardship fund. This money eased the return of the evacuees—though it was not the end of the Slapton saga (as we shall see in chapter 25).[4]

The policy of handing Britain back to the British depended on sending the Americans over to France. As the beachhead expanded in Normandy, so bases and airfields could be established there and more combat divisions inserted into an expanding front line. In late summer, events seemed to be progressing satisfactorily (table 22.1), with the activation of Patton's 3rd Army in August and Simpson's 9th Army in September—both of whom had been waiting in Britain. The 82nd and

22.1 U.S. ARMY TROOP STRENGTH IN THE UNITED KINGDOM, MAY 1944 TO APRIL 1945

Date	Total	Field Forces	Air Forces	Communications Zone (service troops)	Nonoperating[a]	GFRS[b]	Division
31 May 44	1,526,965[c]	640,635	426,819	366,310	93,201	[d]	20
30 June 44				Figures unavailable			
31 July 44	910,196	161,621	339,567	244,603	144,405	[e]	4[f]
31 August 44	829,580	144,823	347,660	180,537	82,488	81,086	6
30 September 44	687,944	33,741	309,985	171,516	72,936	99,766	1
31 October 44	630,561	97,668	280,888	147,044	71,240	33,721	7
30 November 44	682,542	144,840	273,837	147,553	83,087	33,225	5
31 December 44	676,718	118,202	265,483	143,830	119,747	29,456	3
31 January 45	650,013	68,928	261,232	134,872	132,666	52,315	0
28 February 45	606,000	58,000	224,000	126,000	115,000	63,000	0
31 March 45	498,000	16,000	244,000	104,000	93,000	41,000	0
30 April 45	431,860	270	223,535	108,774	58,111	41,170	0

[a]Mainly hospital patients.
[b]Ground Force Replacement System
[c]Does not include 14,430 men in Iceland on 31 May 1944.
[d]Included in nonoperating total for this date.
[e]Breakdown unavailable.
[f]Includes 82nd and 101st Airborne Divisions, returned to England.

Source: Rupp., 2: p. 288.

101st Airborne, having returned to Britain after a few weeks in Normandy, departed for good in mid-September to land in Holland, leaving the 17th Airborne as the only U.S. combat division in the country. Most of the 9th Air Force departed for the Continent in September and, of the ETO's supply personnel (now renamed Communications Zone, or ComZ), only a quarter (171,000) remained in Britain by the end of that month. The 8th Air Force, still 300,000 strong, was left as the major U.S. organization in Britain. By 30 September there were under 700,000 U.S. soldiers in Britain, less than half the D-Day peak of over 1.5 million, and UK Base was actually slightly ahead of schedule. Keeping in time with Rhumba seemed easier than staying in step with Bolero.[5]

One phone call on 30 September changed all that. Base Commander Brig. Gen. Harry B. Vaughan was told that the 84th Infantry Division and the 12th Armored were waiting offshore to be unloaded and accommodated. Without even the foretaste of a rumour, his staff had thirty-six hours to prepare for more than thirty thousand unexpected guests! Their arrival was one consequence of the Allied failure to seize the French ports—there were no facilities to discharge them on the Continent. Contrary to Vaughan's initial information, this was not a unique event. With Brittany bypassed and the Scheldt still sealed, the saga of the "diverted divisions" dragged on into the winter. Between October 1944 and April 1945 (see Appendix 1), room had to be found for nine infantry divisions, three armored divisions, three Corps HQs and one Army HQ, some 155,000 troops, plus other field units of sub-division size and three hundred service units who were also originally destined for direct shipment to France. In all, some 300,000 men were involved.[6]

Making space for this new crop of GIs caused serious delays to the programme of handing Britain back to the British. Vaughan had hastily to reappropriate camps, depots, and training areas that he had just relinquished, such as Tenby in south Wales and particularly in the southern triangle around Dorchester, Chippenham, and Winchester. Having said good-bye to the 2nd Armored just after D-Day, Tidworth hosted four more Armored Divisions between June 1944 and New Year 1945. In consequence, Wiltshire, and not the 8AF heartland of Norfolk and Suffolk, remained the most densely occupied county of England through the winter of 1944–45 (see maps 22A and 22B).

Most of the diverted divisions stayed only three to five weeks. The longest visit was that of the 11th Armored, which spent two months from early October 1944 around Warminster in Wiltshire, before being rushed to the Ardennes. This gave the GIs involved opportunity only for superficial impressions of England—the view through a beer glass rather than across a tea table, with time only for pubs and perhaps London rather than for making friends with a British family. The same was true of another significant group of itinerants—the replacements being held in British depots before being sent to the front. There were nearly 100,000 men in "repple depples" at the end of September 1944, and although the average fell to around 30,000 in the autumn, it rose to 63,000 in February and remained at around 41,000 for the rest of the war (table 22.1). These men also spent only a few weeks in Britain and for many it was coloured by the draconian regime of Col. Kilian's 10th Replacement Depot, often known as "Stalag Lichfield."

The war on the Continent also slowed up other aspects of Rhumba. In June and July sixty-five thousand wounded GIs were evacuated to Britain, but, as the front expanded in France, it was intended to shift more medical facilities there, reserving Britain for serious cases requiring more than thirty days hospitalization. But the movement of medical units was delayed by the lack of French ports and so the second half of 1944 also saw a large number of what might be called diverted doctors in Britain, staying for periods ranging from a few hours to two months. And then, in the winter of 1944–45, the number of GIs hospitalized in Britain rose close to capacity. One reason was the Battle of the Bulge, in which twenty thousand GIs were wounded. But even more potent than Field Marshal von Rundstedt was "General Winter." In November and December twenty-three thousand GIs (nearly all combat infantry) succumbed to trench foot—equivalent to the riflemen strength of five divisions. Pneumonia, frostbite, and other winter ailments also took their toll. The conjunction of these two crises around Christmas and New Year strained the limited hospital capacity on the Continent. Throughout January an average of 125,000 GIs were hospitalized in Britain, reaching a peak of 129,000 on 7 February. Although the figure declined rapidly in the spring, a total of 381,433 GIs were evacuated to Britain between D-Day and VE day. Not all were permanently lost to the Army, however. Between November 1944 and January 1945 alone, 100,000 GIs returned to the Continent from hospitals in Britain. These walking wounded were other itinerant visitors to Britain.[7]

Also flocking in from the Continent were GIs on leave—the purest (or impurest?) of all the military tourists. Most aimed for London. After the restrictions of the invasion period, troops started arriving there in large numbers during the autumn and caused serious problems. In Italy and France the U.S. Army established rest areas and leave centres

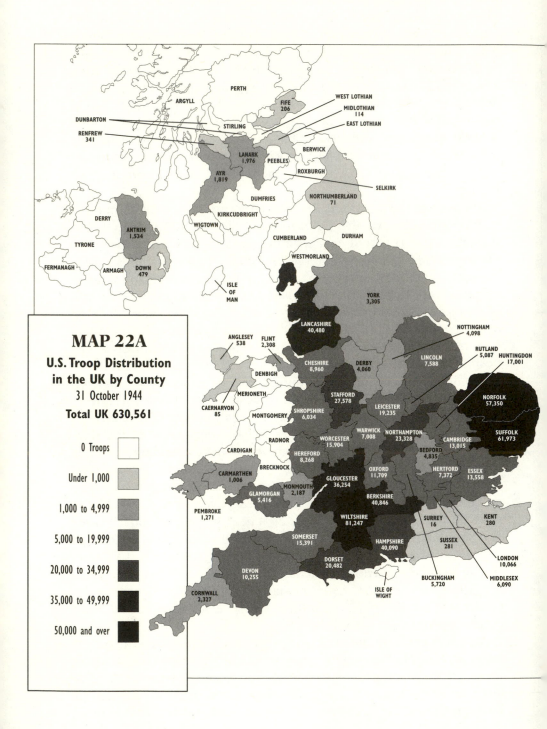

MAP 22A

**U.S. Troop Distribution
in the UK by County**

31 October 1944

Total UK 630,561

0 Troops	
Under 1,000	
1,000 to 4,999	
5,000 to 19,999	
20,000 to 34,999	
35,000 to 49,999	
50,000 and over	

PERTH

ARGYLL

FIFE
206

WEST LOTHIAN

MIDLOTHIAN
114

DUNBARTON

STIRLING

EAST LOTHIAN

RENFREW
341

LANARK
1,976

PEEBLES

BERWICK

AYR
1,819

ROXBURGH

SELKIRK

DUMFRIES

NORTHUMBERLAND
71

KIRKCUDBRIGHT

DERRY

WIGTOWN

ANTRIM
1,534

CUMBERLAND

DURHAM

TYRONE

WESTMORLAND

FERMANAGH

ARMAGH

DOWN
479

ISLE
OF
MAN

YORK
3,305

ANGLESEY
538

FLINT
2,308

LANCASHIRE
40,480

NOTTINGHAM
4,098

RUTLAND
5,087

HUNTINGDON
17,001

DENBIGH

CHESHIRE
8,960

DERBY
4,060

LINCOLN
7,588

MERIONETH

STAFFORD
27,578

NORFOLK
57,350

CAERNARVON
85

SHROPSHIRE
6,034

LEICESTER
19,235

MONTGOMERY

WARWICK
7,008

NORTHAMPTON
23,328

CAMBRIDGE
13,015

SUFFOLK
61,973

RADNOR

WORCESTER
15,904

BEDFORD
4,835

CARDIGAN

HEREFORD
8,268

HERTFORD
7,372

ESSEX
13,558

BRECKNOCK

OXFORD
11,709

CARMARTHEN
1,006

GLOUCESTER
36,254

MONMOUTH
2,187

BERKSHIRE
40,846

GLAMORGAN
5,416

SURREY
16

KENT
280

PEMBROKE
1,271

WILTSHIRE
81,247

SUSSEX
281

LONDON
10,066

SOMERSET
15,391

HAMPSHIRE
40,090

DEVON
10,255

DORSET
20,482

BUCKINGHAM
5,720

MIDDLESEX
6,090

CORNWALL
2,327

ISLE OF
WIGHT

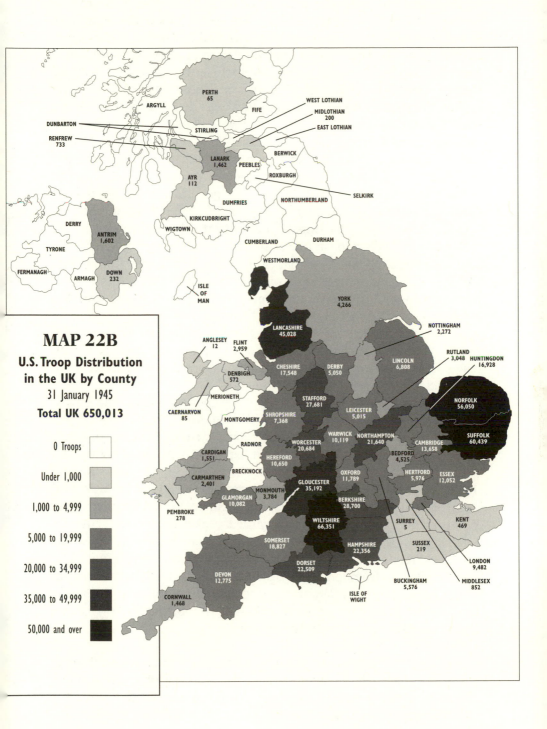

MAP 22B

U.S. Troop Distribution
in the UK by County
31 January 1945

Total UK 650,013

0 Troops

Under 1,000

1,000 to 4,999

5,000 to 19,999

20,000 to 34,999

35,000 to 49,999

50,000 and over

PERTH
65

ARGYLL

FIFE

WEST LOTHIAN

MIDLOTHIAN
200

EAST LOTHIAN

DUNBARTON

STIRLING

RENFREW
733

LANARK
1,462

PEEBLES

BERWICK

AYR
112

ROXBURGH

SELKIRK

DUMFRIES

NORTHUMBERLAND

KIRKCUDBRIGHT

WIGTOWN

DERRY

ANTRIM
1,602

TYRONE

FERMANAGH

ARMAGH

DOWN
232

CUMBERLAND

DURHAM

WESTMORLAND

ISLE
OF
MAN

YORK
4,266

NOTTINGHAM
2,272

ANGLESEY
12

FLINT
2,959

LANCASHIRE
45,028

RUTLAND
3,048

HUNTINGDON
16,928

DENBIGH
572

CHESHIRE
17,548

DERBY
5,050

LINCOLN
6,808

MERIONETH

STAFFORD
27,681

LEICESTER
5,015

NORFOLK
56,050

CAERNARVON
85

SHROPSHIRE
7,368

WARWICK
10,119

NORTHAMPTON
21,640

CAMBRIDGE
13,658

SUFFOLK
60,439

MONTGOMERY

WORCESTER
20,684

BEDFORD
4,525

CARDIGAN
1,551

RADNOR

HEREFORD
10,650

OXFORD
11,789

HERTFORD
5,976

ESSEX
12,052

CARMARTHEN
2,401

BRECKNOCK

GLOUCESTER
35,192

BERKSHIRE
28,700

SURREY
5

KENT
469

GLAMORGAN
10,082

MONMOUTH
3,784

PEMBROKE
278

WILTSHIRE
66,351

SUSSEX
219

LONDON
9,482

SOMERSET
18,827

HAMPSHIRE
22,356

BUCKINGHAM
5,576

MIDDLESEX
852

DORSET
22,509

DEVON
12,775

CORNWALL
1,468

ISLE OF
WIGHT

for its troops, but in Britain it still relied on the American Red Cross to provide its "hotel" service. During September alone the ARC was forced to double its bed capacity in the capital to over nine thousand. Finding that accommodation was harder than ever, because, since June, London had been the prime target for German V-1s and V-2s. By October twenty-three thousand houses had been destroyed and one million damaged, and the housing stock was depleted further by the need for hostels for some 100,000 repair workers. In August the cabinet placed London out of bounds to all British troops on leave, unless they lived there, but Eisenhower refused to accept a ban on American troops. Both he and Ambassador Winant argued that GIs (unlike Tommies) had nowhere else to go. They took it up with Churchill personally, insisting on a quota of twelve thousand beds in London. Eventually, the British government relented, helped by an informal quid pro quo at the beginning of December whereby Ike allocated three thousand combat engineers to repair work in London. In view of the manpower crisis on the Continent, this aroused some adverse comment in the American press but Ike continued it until the New Year when, he told Churchill, "the exigencies of battle permit no other decision." Not only had it been a humanitarian act and good public relations, the gesture also helped keep London open to GIs on leave. In the last weeks of the war a daily average of seventeen thousand U.S. troops were on pass in the city.[8]

The period from 1944–45 was therefore no mere coda to the American occupation of Britain. Nor was the rundown smooth and rapid. Although U.S. Army strength had dropped steadily in the summer of 1944, the problems on the Continent kept it at between 600,000 and 700,000 until March 1945, and on VE day the figure was still over 400,000. There were still GIs aplenty right to the end of the war. But, and this is equally important, few of them remained for very long. Whether diverted divisions and rattled replacements en route for France, or hospital patients and leave personnel coming from the opposite direction, these regimented tourists had a very different experience of Britain from long-time residents such as the flyboys and their ground crews, or the 29ers who waited twenty months for D-Day. In fact, the last year of the occupation had a pronounced in-out rhythm: more the hokey-cokey than the rhumba.

One of these fleeting visitors was Cliff Hope, the twenty-year-old son of a Kansas congressman, who arrived in Liverpool with his artillery observer battalion on 30 June 1944. Awaiting transfer to France, the battalion spent the first two weeks in the Herefordshire town of Leominster. Hope, a long-standing Anglophile, found it "as I had always imagined England would be." He was enchanted by the "picture-postcard town" and the "green, green countryside" around it. In southwest Kansas the towns had been built no more than seventy years before, when the railroad arrived; at nearby Mortimer's Cross the church dated back to 1304 and Yorkists and Lancastrians had fought their civil war four centuries before Unionists and Confederates. Hope also discovered the true home of the Hereford cattle so common in western Kansas, having previously assumed that they originated in Hereford, Texas! Although he spent a good deal of spare time in the Black Swan pub (usually known as the Dirty Duck), through the local Congregational church he did pay a few visits to the home of the Hammond family. He remembered their hospitality with gratitude, but it was only a brief glimpse of English home life, confirming his *Mrs. Miniver* stereotype, and he never saw the Hammonds again—as, he said, "was the case with most wartime friends." On 14 July the battalion moved to Lopcombe Corner in Wiltshire, a battered British Army camp where the GIs lived in Nissen huts and had their "honey buckets" emptied daily by a man in a horsedrawn wagon—"straight out of a Thomas Hardy novel." Every evening a "middle-aged hooker" whom they dubbed Ten-Shilling Annie stood at the gate, but the nearest Hope got to Anglo-American relations was "romping" in a haystack (and only romping) with a fun-loving girl called Diane whom he met at a dance. On 15 August the battalion left Wiltshire for France.[9]

Cliff Hope had time in those six weeks for only a few brief glimpses of English life. Hospital patients from France had better opportunities because they were often in England for longer and, with normal demands of military training and discipline relaxed, convalescents were allowed a great deal of free time on pass. Take the case of another Kansan, Chuck Neighbor, who had been sent as a replacement to the 29th Division in February 1944. He arrived at Bridestowe in Devon with little more than seventeen weeks basic training, and such was the intensity of the preinvasion regime at Woolacombe, Slapton, and on the moors that Neighbor had little time for tourism. Only once was his whole company given a pass to nearby Okehampton and, in the four months before D-Day, he never saw London.

By late July, however, Chuck Neighbor was back in Britain. Wounded in the back near St.-Lô on 13 July, he was airlifted out and spent four months in the Midlands, mostly at the 52nd General Hospital near Kidderminster. Once on his feet, there was time for sightseeing. Two-thirds of the rehabilitation groups were allowed out each evening and Neighbor did plenty of "pubbing" and walking, as well as dating a couple of girls from Ireland. He returned to his company in December only to be wounded in the leg on 3 January when he stumbled over a German booby trap. Because of the shortage of beds on the Continent during the Bulge, Neighbor was shipped back to Blandford Hospital in Dorset. During that time he finally saw London on a whirlwind forty-eight-hour pass and enjoyed a week in Edinburgh visiting a pen pal from his teenage years in Kansas. Including two spells in Lichfield replacement depot awaiting shipment back across the Channel, Chuck Neighbor spent roughly seven months in Britain in the period July 1944 to February 1945. He saw far more of the country *after* D-Day than beforehand.[10]

Americans visiting Britain from across the Channel often reacted very positively. That was not simply because hospital patients and GIs on leave were freer of normal military restraints. Like those who arrived via Tunisia and Sicily in 1943, they had different criteria to GIs straight from America. Britain might have looked pinched, primitive, and foreign to men fresh from the bright(ish) lights of Manhattan, but it seemed wonderfully agreeable compared with the hazardous hedgerows of Normandy or the frozen mud of the Roer Valley. "I finally got off that quarrelsome continent for the first time in nearly a year," GI Frank Gurley wrote his parents from London in September 1945. "We live in large Red Cross–sponsored apartment houses with clean sheets every day and a heeuge [sic] bathtub." It was also a relief to be able to communicate again. Betty Magnuson, a WAC from Minnesota, had a week in London in July 1945 after months in France. "Strange, indeed, it was to be again in an English speaking world," she wrote: "to understand a play, to read a newspaper without consulting one's foreign language dictionary; even to understand overheard conversations on the street!" She was not alone. Many GIs would have echoed Ike's remark at a London theatre in May 1945: "It's nice to be back in a country where I can *almost* speak the language." Most of all, Britain, though battered, still had a sense of normalcy about it. Exposure to death and destruction had sobered many young GIs, giving them a new appreciation of family life. The director of the ARC's Home Hospitality service in London noted in January 1945 that over the previous year the "outlook of the American soldier has changed . . . on returning now from the combat area he no longer wishes for just excitement and gaiety—he wants the comfort and quietness of home life." In the spring of 1945 half the GIs coming to Britain on leave were visiting British homes.[11]

As usual, such close personal contact had a profound effect on

soldiers' reactions to Britain. One can see this in the story of Mike, a
GI from the Deep South, who was sent to England from the Continent
in March 1945 with a minor wound. Once the immediate surgery had
been accomplished, Mike had plenty of time to explore his surroundings. At first, everything looked grim. The weather was awful, the beer
no better than a diuretic, and his hospital near Coventry could be
called "convalescent" in name only. Mike felt a keen desire to get back
to his buddies at the Front and to share what they were going through.
But by May spring had come and he had fallen in love with an English
girl named Anne, aged nineteen, the daughter of a Coventry factory
worker. Everything about England now seemed different. He felt that
he would just as soon be out on the town with a group of Tommies as
with a crowd of GI's, most of whom seemed cocky, profane, and
aggressive. He felt he could easily settle in Coventry. A month later he
and Anne were engaged.[12]

Part of what impressed Mike about Coventry was the fortitude of a
city incinerated in the notorious German air raid in November 1940.
On 13 May 1945 Coventry Cathedral was the venue for a special
Mother's Day service for GIs like Mike from convalescent hospitals in
the area. It was held in the roofless shell of the cathedral, rubble all
around, set in a city centre whose shattered roofs, ruined walls, and
empty lots bore witness to numerous visits by the Luftwaffe.

The Battle of Britain—to which so many U.S. soldiers paid tribute,
from Ike downwards—was no mere fact of history. On 13 June 1944,
a week after D-Day, the first V-1 flying bombs landed near London. By
late June the Germans were firing more than a hundred a day and the
V-1 had pushed Normandy off most of the front pages. "Hitler'll get
hisself disliked if he goes on like this," groused one London woman to
her greengrocer. On 8 September the V-2 rocket offensive began. With
their longer range, these weapons could be launched from Germany
itself and the attacks continued until the last weeks of the war. Between June 1944 and the end of March 1945 over thirty-five hundred
V-weapons landed in England, killing nearly nine thousand civilians
and seriously injuring almost twenty-five thousand. This was much
less than wartime casualties from "orthodox" bombing (113,000), but
the destruction of buildings was immense and these random, daylight
attacks inflicted considerable psychological damage. The sounds of the
V-1, variously known as the buzz bomb or doodlebug, were particularly unnerving: first a noise like a spluttering motorbike, then ominous silence after the engine cut out, and finally a hoarse roar as the
V-1 crashed to earth.[13]

No American in London in the summer of 1944 could ignore the

V-weapons. Fifty military police were killed on 2 July when a V-1 landed on them standing in formation, about to get into trucks. In June 1944 Eisenhower's HQ in Bushy Park, on the southwest edge of London, was near the centre of the heaviest concentration of V-1s. Ike's aide, Harry Butcher, noted in his diary that "most of the people" he knew were "semi-dazed from loss of sleep" and had "the jitters" whenever a door banged or a motorcycle was heard. On the night of 19–20 June alone Butcher counted twenty-five explosions between 7 P.M. and 1 A.M. Many Americans were struck by the phlegmatic demeanour of Londoners. Col. Joseph Darnall, the U.S. Army's hospital supremo in Britain, noted two alerts while he was in the cinema on 17 June, "but the show went on and no one left." Another moviegoer was airman John L. Moore, who recalled the romantic climax of *Lady in the Dark*. Just as the hero took the heroine in his arms, the noise of a V-1 could be heard. Then it cut out. From the balcony, a voice yelled out: "For God's sake KISS HER before it's too late!" The audience was still laughing when the building rocked from the explosion.[14]

If Americans were impressed by Londoners' fortitude under fire, the assistance of U.S. engineers on repairs was applauded in return. Five hundred GIs who had helped were entertained at a reception by London County Council on 18 January. Papers the next day showed the chairman of the LCC gingerly eating a "hot dog"—the quotation marks indicating the novelty of such Americana, even after three years of occupation. Yet more impressive was the flow of American wounded back across the Channel. To people near the ports of Weymouth and Southampton, or hospital centres such as Malvern or Kidderminster, this was incontrovertible evidence that the Yanks were fighters as well as talkers. One Glasgow housewife had a letter to her "adopted" Yank returned from France with the word *Deceased* rubber-stamped on it. A woman in Solihull, near Birmingham, was appalled when their GI Joe returned on leave to see the family. He "came in and collapsed. His nerves were completely shattered. He could not even cross the road alone. He had gone out a happy laughing boy and came back a complete wreck."[15]

In 1944–45 the realities of war on both sides of the Channel often enhanced mutual respect between GIs and British. But there was another, seedier side to that last year of the American occupation. The constant ebb and flow of short-term visitors was particularly difficult to control. In any case, the U.S. Army command was focusing most of its attention and manpower on the Continent. It proved very hard to create the legacy that Gen. Koenig wanted to leave behind—"the

memory of well-disciplined troops, and an honest, clean, decent operating organization.''

Some disciplinary problems were insoluble. The two airborne divisions, the 82nd and 101st, spent a couple of months back in England
after fighting in Normandy before they dropped into Holland. On their
return, they needed an emotional release. The 101st arrived back in
Southampton on 13 July. The men were taken back to their old billets,
issued new uniforms, two months back pay, and seven-day passes for
London. ''It's the only time I ever saw the Army do anything right,''
said paratrooper Gordon Carson. Right, even necessary, it may have
been from the morale standpoint, but it was a nightmare for the U.S.
military police in London. Although many paratroops simply had a
very good time, there was also an orgy of drunkenness, fights, and
vandalism. The head of the SOS's London base section, Gen. Pleas B.
Rogers, told the 82nd's commander, Maxwell Taylor, that twenty-four
hours after his men hit town the MPs asked to double their patrols
from two to four, because paratroops ganged up on them when making arrests. Even sober men were often egregiously ill-dressed: not just
''one pocket unbuttoned, but all the buttons on their blouses unbuttoned'' and no jackets, hats, or ties. ''These men feel that now they
have been in combat they are beyond uniform regulations,'' Rogers
complained. And it was hard to answer the remark of one unbuttoned
corporal: ''the last time I saw my brother in Normandy *he* didn't have
a blouse on.''[16]

London was at the centre of another disciplinary headache of
1944–45: the renewed increase in venereal disease among GIs.
Before D-Day the incidence of VD had dropped to the equivalent of
twenty cases per thousand men per annum (twenty-five was considered a ''satisfactory'' level and thirty ''excessive''). This reflected the
lack of passes and intense work schedules in the weeks before the
invasion. By October 1944 the annual rate was fifty-three per thousand and although declining to around forty in the winter, it reached
new peaks of sixty-two in May 1945 and sixty-six in June. Although
the increase was partly caused by infected troops from the Continent
on leave, Gen. Vaughan, the UK Base commander, also noted other
familiar problems: lack of information about health and prophylaxis
and inadequate recreation facilities, particularly during the winter
months. Strenuous efforts were made to improve the situation. On 2
December 1944, for instance, the weekly troop educational leaflet,
''Army Talks,'' was devoted to VD. There was also a crackdown by
police and magistrates on brothel-keeping in 1944–45, particularly
in London but also in other cities such as Birmingham. But the offi-

cial British attitude to prostitution remained anomalous—brothels were illegal yet streetwalkers flourished—and it was impossible in Britain to follow the practice of many commanders on the Continent and discreetly licence a few whorehouses (such as the 29th Division's notorious "Riding School" in Rennes). As for Piccadilly, where the interaction of prostitutes, thieves, and drunken GIs remained a concern to the end of the war, it was felt that little more could be done. Speaking for the U.S. Embassy, Herbert Agar shrugged it off as "a situation brought about by the war and true in every large city."[17]

In any case, the root problem, as before, was not professional prostitutes but good-time girls. And it was in the last month of the war that the sexual-social problems of the American occupation were most acute. As we saw earlier (chapter 16), what seems to have increased dramatically during the war was not immorality but illegitimacy. Compared with the late 1930s many fewer children conceived out of wedlock were legitimized by the subsequent marriage of their parents. This was particularly because soldier-fathers—British, American, and others—were moved on by their armies. The problem got worse as the war progressed and in 1945 the percentage of such extramarital conceptions that were regularized by marriage fell to a nadir of 37 percent. This compared with around 70 percent before the war and 60 percent by 1950 (table 16.1). In absolute numbers illegitimate births in England and Wales in 1945 reached a 1940s peak of nearly sixty-five thousand. Exactly how many had American fathers is impossible to say, but in August 1948 *Life* magazine suggested that in wartime Britain twenty-two thousand children were born out of wedlock to white U.S. soldiers. Certainly, it is clear that many Anglo-American affairs, especially before D-Day and in the last heady months of the war, ended with the GI back stateside and the British woman holding the baby.[18]

The majority of these mothers were younger women, because that is the prime period of fertility. But in 1945 the percentage of conceptions outside wedlock among fifteen- to twenty-year-old girls was almost the same as before the war, and the rate among twenty- to twenty-five-year-olds not much higher (table 22.2). In the age bracket twenty-five to thirty, however, the rate was 75 percent up on 1939; for those aged thirty to thirty-five it was more than double. This was not necessarily the result of "spinsters kicking over the traces as they neared middle age." One-third of all illegitimate children in Birmingham during the last two years of war, for instance, were born to married women. Nor was that always a sign of in-

22.2 EXTRAMARITALLY CONCEIVED MATERNITIES PER 1,000 UNMARRIED WOMEN IN ENGLAND AND WALES, 1938-45

Age of Mother	1938	1939	1940	1941	1942	1943	1944	1945	1940–1945 Average
15–	12.0	12.1	11.4	10.1	10.4	10.7	11.4	12.4	11.1
20–	37.1	36.5	36.2	32.3	34.0	34.9	38.4	43.3	36.5
25–	27.6	26.6	28.1	28.6	30.5	33.4	43.0	46.5	35.0
30–	16.0	15.8	16.1	18.0	20.5	23.5	29.9	33.2	23.5
35–	10.6	10.0	9.7	10.7	11.9	13.2	15.6	17.2	13.0
40–	4.2	4.0	4.0	4.7	5.1	5.7	5.9	5.9	5.2
15–45	19.8	19.0	18.9	17.9	19.0	20.2	23.3	25.8	20.9
Ratio to 1938									
Crude[a]	1.00	.96	.95	.90	.96	1.02	1.18	1.30	1.05
Standardized[b]	1.00	.98	.98	.92	.98	1.04	1.18	1.32	1.07

[a]Crude birth rates.
[b]Crude birth rates adjusted to take account of changes in the age distribution of the population.

Source: *The Registrar General's Statistical Review of England and Wales for the Six Years 1940–1945*, text, vol. II, civil (London, 1951), p. 82.

fidelity. Of the 520 illegitimacy cases recorded in the city in 1945, nearly half the mothers were divorced, widowed, or separated. Similar statistics were reported elsewhere. In numerous such cases, affairs with GIs were an attempt to establish new partnerships by women (often mothers) whose earlier marriage bonds had been severed by death or frayed by separation.[19]

Whatever the reasons for the rise in illegitimacy, its penalties fell most heavily on the offspring. By the spring of 1945 the American government had agreed to remit paternity payments due from GI fathers into a special fund in Britain, which would help keep the child until the age of fourteen. But this only applied where American paternity had been proved in law and while the father was in U.S. Army service. After his discharge, enforcement would be a matter for state courts in the United States. In some cases of marital infidelity, the British father, returning from war, agreed eventually to legitimize the child as his own. In other cases, the GI "did the decent thing," willingly or otherwise. Even when neither of these resolutions occurred, the mother might eventually contrive a new life elsewhere, fabricating the impression of wartime widowhood to cloak the stigma of illegitimacy. Although this did not address the psychological pain for such children—a point to which I shall return in the last chapter—it did ease the social pressures upon them.[20]

It was not possible, however, to blur into the background if you were the "brown baby" of a white mother and a black GI. Irresponsible press reports suggested figures of ten thousand or even twenty thousand. In 1946 a survey by the League of Coloured Persons in Britain located 544 such children, but this was acknowledged to be partial, and authoritative estimates in the late 1940s produced figures of twelve hundred or seventeen hundred. The children were concentrated in the West Country, East Anglia, and the northwest, where black GIs had been most evident. Of the thirty-seven in Somerset in December 1945, twenty-seven were children of married women, but all were living in residential nurseries because surrendering the child was often the only way for the wife to secure a reconciliation with her British husband. Although the U.S. consul in Manchester believed that "sooner or later such children should be shipped to the United States" and the Foreign Office explored that possibility, few of them crossed the Atlantic. The colour bars in many American states made fostering mixed-race children a sensitive issue. Instead, they usually grew up in children's homes in Britain or with foster parents, though some were eventually adopted by British families.[21]

Less tragic than the "brown babies" but more worrying for the authorities was the black market. By the winter of 1944–45, with victory in sight, people had become weary of austerity and rationing. Despite wartime taxation, there was much more money available than prewar, particularly for working-class households where both husband and wife were in industrial jobs. At Christmas 1944 the money supply was 25 percent up on the previous year, but, to quote the *Daily Mail,* "in the shops there is virtually nothing to buy between essentials and fantastically priced luxuries." At the same time, however, there existed a huge, separate system of goods and services associated with the armed forces, of which the American was particularly opulent. As we have seen, this was established partly to create an Americanized ethos for GIs, but also to keep their massive spending power out of the British civilian market. By 1944 the pay problem was under control, thanks to savings schemes, but it was proving impossible to keep American goods out of desperate British hands. The black market flourished more or less openly all over the country, especially in what police called the "L triangle" of London, Liverpool, and Leeds. In a front-page exposé in January 1945, the *News Chronicle* announced that "you can buy almost anything you want in the Leeds black market"—from hams to cosmetics, from whisky to petrol.[22]

American PXs and quartermaster depots were a major source of scarce or luxury items, such as sugar, cigarettes, or cosmetics. After D-Day there was also a steady supply of items "liberated" from the Continent. In one instance, U.S. airmen flew one thousand bottles of champagne (worth $20,000 on the black market) to an air base in Essex. Not only luxuries were involved. In February 1945 U.S. military police cracked a ring of six GIs and eight British civilians who had stolen six thousand sheets from the Medical Corps. In late 1945 the Army even rescinded authority for GIs visiting British homes to take some rations with them because of what Gen. Lee called "certain unfortunate black market practices where men took improper advantage of this privilege."[23]

Sometimes, however, the problem was not systematic crime but looting when GIs moved out. The day after the 4th Armored Division left Chippenham in July 1944, the farmer for whom Avice Wilson worked sent her down to one of his fields "to clear up the left-overs." She salvaged three cartloads of wood, makeshift chairs and tables, and shower partitions, as well as a fifty-pound bag of precious white flour and part of a crate of tomatoes. Later in the day local schoolkids found boxes of condoms, which they used as balloons. "The farm laborers laughing at them were in a dilemma," Avice recalled. "If they were to stop the children playing with them, they would have to give a reason

why. And that might cause questions at home. So they said nothing."
The balloons were durable and remained in evidence for weeks afterwards.[24]

The U.S. Army issued strict instructions to prevent this kind of thing,
but thereby created other problems. British papers in the summer of
1944 and again the following spring contained reports of wholesale
destruction of food and supplies by U.S. troops, and indignant questions were asked in the House of Commons. When the 8th Infantry
Division left Omagh in June 1944 the Northern Ireland government
investigated reports that sheets, towels, stationery, and timber had
been among the items burnt and that tinned food, razor blades, and
cooking utensils had been thrown on the city dump. In June 1945 the
author J. B. Priestley stated publicly that when a large American
military hospital in the West Country was closed, thousands of sheets
had been burnt, seven grand pianos smashed, and tons of crockery
deliberately run over by a steamroller. Churchill was particularly upset
by a press report from Warwickshire about the destruction of several
thousand U.S. Army parcels that had been damaged or had lost their
labels. Supposedly watches, whisky, leather wallets, tons of fruit, and
thousands of cigars and cigarettes had been destroyed. To make matters worse the work was done, under supervision, by German prisoners
of war, who were allowed to "gorge" themselves before burning the
rest. The prime minister said that "with recent ration cuts the people
would not stand for this sort of thing."[25]

The U.S. Army strenuously denied such allegations. A complaint
about the Omagh case reached Roosevelt himself and he asked the
War Department to check it out. Secretary Stimson reported that
special investigators sent by Eisenhower had concluded that the reports were all "hearsay" and that "no property of salvageable or
useable value was destroyed or burnt." The custodian of the city dump
assured them: "If there had been anything any good I would have
taken it myself." Likewise, Gen. Koenig, the commander of UK Base,
stated in June 1945 that "any rumours that we are burning uniforms
or equipment, destroying things deliberately, are false." To cover himself completely, he added that "if such acts have been committed they
have been done by saboteurs." But the British authorities were not so
sure. In the Omagh case, the Northern Ireland government judged
that "in the end there were some failures to obey orders on the part
of units" and Churchill was told in June 1945 that, among the parcels
destroyed by German POWs, "undoubtedly there were some articles of
a useable nature." While it is clear that such rumours *were* exaggerated—not least because they fitted British stereotypes of careless

American abundance—it is also evident that this kind of thing did go on and that no one involved had any reason to admit as much to U.S. Army investigators![26]

The spate of such complaints in the spring of 1945 was a sign that operation Rhumba, the American pullout, was now getting into its stride. The diverted divisions had moved on to the Continent, the winter wave of wounded had subsided, and the war was virtually won. During March 1945 the total number of GIs dropped below the 600,000 level that had been fairly stable through the winter and by VE day there were little more than 400,000 in Britain (table 22.1). Those who remained shared to the full in the celebrations all over Britain on 8 May. In Piccadilly the Union Jack, the Stars and Stripes, and even the Hammer and Sickle flapped in the breeze as civilians and soldiers clogged the nearby streets and scaled the still-boarded statue of Eros. Similar scenes were enacted around the country. Christen T. Jonassen, a wounded GI from the 2nd Division, had been hospitalized in Sherborne, Dorset. On 9 May he wrote home that the town "probably never had a night like last night, since it was founded hundreds of years ago." Every cottage, it seemed, flew an Allied flag and every pub was full. Jonassen and his buddy were called into one by a crowd of British servicemen and women: "Hey Yanks! Come in here and have one on us." After bawling out a medley of English and American songs, punctuated by toasts from mugs of beer, they surged outside to join the crowds lurching around the ancient market town in "dance-like marching." Men and women, GIs, Brits, and other Allied servicemen

> all marched and sang, linked tightly together. The feeling was infectious, the strain had lifted. Years of control, black out, bombardment, sacrifice and hardship were over. One seems to lose consciousness of the "I" and became one with the other, and like one joyous, free being went sweeping through the streets of old Sherborne.[27]

With the war over in Europe, the Army's priority was to redeploy men and matériel against Japan. Between mid-May and early July 1945 most of the 8th Air Force left East Anglia—a vast airborne exodus of over 2,100 heavy bombers and 41,500 crew, with ground personnel following by sea. On 31 July only 175,000 GIs remained in the United Kingdom and the figure was down to 62,000 by the end of November 1945 (table 22.3).[28]

22.3   U.S. ARMY TROOP STRENGTH IN THE UNITED KINGDOM, MAY TO NOVEMBER 1945

Date	Total*
31 May	347,812
30 June	231,325
31 July	175,723
31 August	148,530
30 September	101,759
31 October	77,527
30 November	62,000

*These figures are for assigned strength and do not include temporarily attached personnel, unlike table 22.1. The difference for 30 April 1945, for instance, was 12,000 men.

Source: NA RG 332 ETO Adm 443, 445, 447, 448—TSFET Progress Reports, G-1 section, June, August, October, November 1945.

Maintaining discipline among those who were left became ever more difficult. Education seemed one answer. Since 1943 selected GIs had been attending week-long special courses for Allied service personnel at fifteen British universities. By January 1944 over sixteen thousand American service personnel had been involved. Airman Harry Crosby spent a fascinating week at Balliol College, Oxford, in February 1944 engaged in lectures and discussions ranging from Shakespeare to the "English and American Characters." All through the week, however, they "kept returning to two knotty problems, disharmony among the Allies and too much harmony between the genders." With the war nearing its end, the U.S. Army sought to extend this scheme as leave opportunities for men in Britain and on the Continent. Ambitious plans were concocted for short courses, particularly at the British Army's Educational Centre at Shrivenham in Wiltshire, and even for British and American soldiers to attend the other country's universities. There was also considerable enthusiasm in the British-American Liaison Board for an "opposite numbers" scheme, whereby GIs could be attached to businesses and industries of their choice for up to three weeks. For the U.S. Army this was another way to keep GIs occupied, while the Foreign Office considered it "a golden opportunity" to foster Anglo-American relations. But these postwar education schemes never got going on a large scale and by May 1946 only fourteen thousand GIs had been involved. The British had hoped for continued

American largesse, but the U.S. government's priorities were not educational. As Roosevelt told Winant in October 1944: "After the surrender of Germany it is my intention to return from Europe to the United States as many of our troops as possible and at the earliest practicable dates."[29]

Even in the final months of the war, however, GIs could still educate British people about America. To placate black pressure groups at home, the Roosevelt administration decided to send a token unit of black members of the Women's Army Corps (WACs) overseas. On 12 February 1945 the 6888th Central Postal Battalion started arriving at King Edward's School in Birmingham. Their first task was to clear the school hall, packed almost to the ceiling with damaged or misdirected mail. This was no easy task, with some seven million men in the European Theater and, for instance, more than seventy-five hundred Robert Smiths on file. But the 850-strong unit took seriously the motto "no mail, low morale" and worked three eight-hour shifts, seven days a week, up to VE day, averaging sixty-five thousand pieces of mail each shift. The WACs faced the usual problems of segregation. The American Red Cross told the unit's commander, Major Charity Adams, that they thought "your colored girls would be happier if they had a hotel all to themselves" in London, but Adams and her WACs declined on principle. They visited London for day trips or stayed with English families. The WACs also made little use of the Silver Birch Club created for them by the Ministry of Information because such clubs were intended for blacks only. But, as the MOI noted, the unit was also "inundated with offers of private hospitality and entertainment." Many WACs recalled their welcome with gratitude and locals were also impressed. One local paper remarked that they

> speak extremely good English—much better than the average native. They have lively minds and an interest in historical England which is insatiable. They seem to know a great deal more about the Shakespeare country than most Midlanders. In fact, these WACs are very different from the coloured women portrayed on the films where they are usually either domestics of the old-retainer type or sloe-eyed sirens.[30]

But the black WACs were only birds of passage, staying in Birmingham three months before they departed for France. And by this time British attention was shifting from war to peace. The government-sponsored hospitality campaign had peaked in mid-1944. By November only seventy-three of the original two hundred Welcome Clubs for

GIs were still operating, and the Foreign Office reported that the British-American Liaison Board had "been dying since August." Although much good work was done during the winter in U.S. Army hospitals and in schemes such as the "Opposite Numbers" programme, British funds and American interest were both in decline. Enthusiasts for the special relationship still dreamed dreams—one civil servant proposed a permanent Anglo-American Alliance Board in Whitehall; the U.S. consul in Manchester wanted a network of American cultural attachés around Britain—but these were officials on the periphery of policy making. In July 1945, the MOI's American Forces Liaison Division observed that "the tide of American invasion is receding. Hospitals are closing down. . . . Farewell parties are reported from all the regions." The division itself was wound up on 31 October, two weeks after the London edition of the GI newspaper, *Stars and Stripes.* In early 1946 only one U.S. air base remained, at Honington in Suffolk. On 26 February the Stars and Stripes were lowered there for the last time on a suitably rain-swept parade ground and the keys of the station handed back to the RAF. By mid-1946, to quote one official report, the U.S. Army's "only major activity in the United Kingdom was the shipment of war brides."[31]

23

Happily Ever After?

★ ★ ★

UNTIL 1944 THE NUMBER OF GI BRIDES WAS RELATIVELY SMALL. ACCORDING to Eisenhower's headquarters, on 16 February 1944 there were "4,093 United States military personnel married to individuals residing in the United Kingdom." Nor had many brides already gone west—only 218 wives of U.S. citizens were given entry visas to the United States in 1942 and 1943. However, 14,290 Canadian servicemen had married British women by the end of 1943. The contrast between the American and Canadian statistics reflects the limited scale of the U.S. presence until late 1943 and the ETO policy of discouraging GI marriages (chapter 13). The real spate of Anglo-American marriages did not come until the last year of the war—with a surge in the spring of 1944 and an even bigger one in the spring of 1945. And the consequences of those marriage booms took years to unfold.[1]

The first of these surges was closely linked to D-Day. The vast American buildup brought 1.65 million Yanks to Britain by June 1944. Canadian and other Allied contingents also reached their peak. And soldiers and their girlfriends knew that the waiting for war was nearly over and that, soon, many men were going to die. "My God, but it was easy to fall in love in those two months before D-Day," exclaimed one Canadian soldier twenty years later, remembering the warm evenings and the smell of flowers that seemed to be everywhere in London, even the bomb sites and the slums.

There was a feeling that these were the last nights men and women would make love, and there was never any of the by-play or persuading that usually went on. People were for love, so to speak. It was so easy to fall in love. . . . I won't describe the scenes or sounds of Hyde Park or Green Park at dusk and after dark. They just can't be described. You can just imagine, a vast battlefield of sex.

In units waiting in Cheshire in late June, Robert Easton considered that "from officers to privates we're obsessed by sex, and much the same seems true of the civilian population. Nature's way of compensating, I suppose, for all the death. The more life is threatened, the more it asserts itself. Prune back a tree and you see the same result."[2]

But it was not merely sex. Many relationships, often of brief duration, were consecrated as well as consummated in the weeks before soldiers crossed the Channel. The need to be wanted, to know that someone was *bound* to wait for you, was particularly intense as young men faced (often for the first time) their mortality. Some of these marriages worked; others did not—here are two contrasting examples.

The story of Bill and Lottie is documented incompletely but poignantly from his surviving letters. They had met while his unit was based in England in the summer of 1944. Writing from France in August he waxed nostalgic: "I wish we could have that last day over again." But there was also a note of anxiety: "Did you go and see a doctor yet?" In due course Lottie confirmed that she was pregnant. Bill then offered to marry her and secured his CO's permission to do so when furloughs became available. They were married in November and had five days honeymoon, thanks to loans from his buddies. Lottie then returned to her parents' home in London as her due-date drew near. By January Bill's tone was peeved: "Surely you can average better than two letters a month if you try?" In April he was jubilant at news of the birth. "Words can't express my feelings, darling. How are you feeling, all right? I wish I could have been there. . . . By the way, you didn't tell me the baby's name." The correspondence then dried up completely on her side. On 30 August 1945 he wrote for the last time from southern France:

> Well, darling, I don't know what to think about you. I haven't had a word for three months now. Down in your heart do you really think you're being fair. Where you are concerned at least I think I have done my share. I was man enough to go to a lot of trouble and expense to come all the way from France to marry you. I certainly didnt have to do that if I didnt want to. All I ask is that you be decent enough to let me know what you want to do. I dont believe that is asking too much. I dont imagine you care to go to the States with me and live, if not what do you want to do? Are you going to get a

divorce? . . . I'm to leave for home, if nothing happens, in a few days. Please write soon and let me know what your plans are, thats all I ask of you and it isn't much. I'll admit I wasnt much of a husband but I didnt have much chance to be one either.[3]

Leo Boyle, from Oregon, was a paratrooper with the 101st Airborne based in the Wiltshire village of Aldbourne that spring. Aged thirty, he was older than most of his buddies. His mother was a devout Methodist and one Sunday he decided to go to the local chapel, mostly to please her, intending that then he would write to tell her. After the evening service one of the church members introduced himself. He had two boys, about Boyle's age, in the British Army in Egypt and missed their company. He invited the GI back to his home for a meal. It was there that he met the man's niece, Wynifred Hawkins, who, coincidentally, he had seen earlier in the day and noted as "a charming young lady."

At first the two dated casually—they felt an affinity for each other but had nothing like marriage in mind. It was after Wyn's invalid aunt told them "you two are in love with each other" that their relationship developed into courtship and engagement. Boyle was lucky in having a sympathetic CO, Lt. Dick Winters, who readily gave permission. But the day he tried to go into the nearby town of Marlborough to secure a marriage licence was a day on which the Military Police were having a crackdown on deserters. With the aid of his prospective father-in-law (a local councilman) Boyle took a bus into Marlborough, secured the precious document, and was smuggled back to his quarters in a relative's car, using up part of the scarce petrol allowance.

The wedding took place in the Methodist chapel at Aldbourne on 20 May 1944. The couple spent their honeymoon at Wyn's sister's home in Slough, west of London. Boyle secured a three-day pass, though he had to phone the unit orderly room morning and evening. As soon as he returned, the 101st moved into secure areas prior to the Normandy drop. On 13 June, near Carentan, Boyle received a bullet wound in the left knee. He was shipped back to England and hospitalized in Malvern. Wyn had friends nearby and visited him regularly. Patched up in time for the 101st's next drop into Holland, in September, Boyle was wounded much more severely when a shell smashed his left thigh and tore away most of the flesh. A much longer period of hospitalization followed, this time in Cirencester, which was within bus distance from Wyn's home in Aldbourne. But in early 1945 Boyle was shipped back to the United States, for what turned out to be months of surgery and skin grafts in the hospital at Santa Barbara, California. It was a year before Wyn could get transportation to join him.[4]

Such marriages were fraught with uncertainty. Not only for the couples, but for their families. British parents like the Hawkins could usually meet and vet their prospective son-in-law. But the GI's parents rarely met the bride before the wedding or even before she had made them grandparents. John Sullivan and Elsie Williams became engaged early in 1944. He was on the USAAF public relations staff in Grosvenor Square, London, where she worked as a secretary. By mail, they tried to win over his family in Rutherford, New Jersey. John's sister Irma was "delighted to have an English sister-in-law. It lends such a dashing international flavor to the family." John's father put a brave face on the news: "Of course it was a great surprise to hear of your engagement. Now that it has been announced I can only say that I am greatly pleased about it and of course very anxious to welcome Elsie to our family." The biggest worry was Mrs. Sullivan, a devout Roman Catholic. "Mom, I hope you'll like Elsie," wrote John on 22 June. "I'm sure you will—of course, I'd prefer that she were Catholic, but she says she'll think about converting when we both get back to the States." Six days later he wrote again: "I'm still sweating out your reaction to Elsie's and my engagement." Elsie, too, sent letters and needlework to her prospective in-laws, trying to give them a sense of herself and her family. On 1 July she added a postscript: "I'm rather anxious to know how you feel about it. Not badly I hope, 'cos we are very happy about it."

Her letter crossed one from Mrs. Sullivan sending her "love and blessing" to them both. "At first," she told Johnnie, "I felt bad to think my youngest son would go miles overseas and I would not be there to see you get married. But then I realize those are the fortunes of war." John and Elsie were married on 23 August 1944 at the Catholic church near Elsie's home in Anerley, south London. (Being on a headquarters staff helped him cut through the red tape, though a honeymoon was only possible because a sympathetic officer ordered him to Torquay for a week "for the purpose of carrying out instructions of the Theater Commander.") All John's mother could do was to arrange for a wedding cake to be shipped to them, but it did not arrive until September. John and Elsie lived in London for another year, before John was sent back to the United States and discharged. Not until March 1946, after a miscarriage and five months' separation, did Elsie arrive in New Jersey and meet her in-laws.[5] The couple lived with John's parents until they moved into an apartment next door.

There was a second and larger surge of GI brides in 1945. With Germany defeated, U.S. Army obstacles to marriage weakened. And the future seemed open and hopeful once again. Edith Heap, a British WAAF officer on the RAF bomber base at Bourn, near Cambridge, recalled how the spirits of all servicemen lifted in early 1945. "The boys felt they might survive after all and from now on, until the end of it all, I received a dozen offers of marriage, some very surprising, for I had no idea of any particular interest. I hadn't even been out with them except in a group to Cambridge, etc." She rejected all her suitors, sure that their impulsiveness was "the result of a new hope for a future, and because I was there and spoke the same language." Something of this was undoubtedly true of many Anglo-American matches of 1945, with peace and spring in the air. But others were the considered outcome of long-standing relationships, as GIs got leave from the Continent or from other parts of the UK to wed British girlfriends. When Bridget Goodlace and airman Ralph Johnson were married in St. Margaret's, Middlesex, in June 1945 it was some three years from the day they first met on a Cambridge fairground and a year since their engagement.[6]

Whether end-of-war affairs or cautiously planned alliances, the surge of GI marriages in 1945 came at the worst possible time for the U.S. government. By law dependents of GIs were entitled to shipment to the United States but from April 1945 virtually no shipping space was available because the Army's priority was to bring the boys home as soon as possible. After Japan surrendered in August 1945 the clamour from soldiers, families, and Congress alike for rapid discharge became overwhelming. There was even an undercurrent of antagonism in America towards war brides. A Gallup poll in April 1946 found 36 percent of respondents disapproving of GIs marrying "English girls." Shipping for these women was therefore bottom priority. In the first eight months of 1945, 94 percent of passengers transported to America from all over the world on U.S. military vessels were service personnel and only 1.33 percent (some twenty thousand) were civilians. Four percent of passengers were actually Axis prisoners of war.[7]

Inevitably there was a backlash in Britain. The American Red Cross Clubs in London had 1,670 applications in May alone for accommodation for GI families. On 16 June ETO announced that it might be ten or twelve months before GI brides could obtain a free passage and this intensified public and press agitation. The U.S. embassy was mobbed by desperate wives and, according to its in-house history, the "atmosphere in the Consular section for many months actually resembled an infants' clinic." The British Foreign Office also began to worry about the diplomatic implications of the marriage boom, estimated at anything up to 100,000. The embassy in Washington advised that "whatever the total number may prove to be, it is clear that these women will prove an increasingly important factor in Anglo-American relations," and warned the FO that "there is a growing volume of evidence to show that, for various reasons, these marriages are not working out well."[8]

Matters came to a head in October 1945. About a thousand GI brides held a noisy protest meeting in Caxton Hall, Westminster, on the evening of the 11th before marching to the U.S. embassy with cries of "we want our husbands" and "we want transport." They received little joy from harassed embassy officials. Next day the *News Chronicle* reported the story under the headlines: G.I. BRIDES ARE TOLD THEY MUST WAIT. NO REPLY TO CRY OF WHAT ABOUT THE FILM STARS. But, behind the scenes, conferences in London and Paris on 11–12 October hammered out a plan for transporting the brides and their children starting in January 1946 and also resolved the procedural responsibilities of the Army and State Department. The situation was further eased when Congress passed the War Brides Act on 28 December 1945. This enabled all "alien spouses" and "alien children" of U.S. citizens serving in or honourably discharged from the armed forces to sidestep many normal immigration requirements. These included the need for entry visas and observance of the national quotas established in 1924, which, in the UK case, would have restricted entries to six thousand per month. A special team of immigration officials was sent over to simplify the paperwork, reducing thirty-seven questions on the normal steamship manifest down to a checklist of names, ages, and identity numbers.[9]

Even so, the processing of the war brides was no easy task. Two staging areas were established in England: at the Carlton Hotel in Bournemouth and at Tidworth Barracks, in which some of the brides' husbands had lived during their service in Britain. In January 1946, just as the programme was about the begin, there was a manpower crisis when GIs detailed to staff the staging areas protested that this work was delaying their discharge. The Army hurriedly utilized more British staff and also German prisoners of war (POWs). Brides and their children were summoned to Bournemouth or Tidworth four or five days before the intended departure from Southampton. There the paperwork was completed, tickets issued, currency exchanged, and British ration cards surrendered. Further orientation was given about the journey and medical inspections conducted.[10]

For many women these few days in limbo were some of the worst of their lives. Leaving home to take the special train to Tidworth was traumatic. With transatlantic travel beyond the dreams and the pocket of most British people, families naturally felt they were saying good-bye forever. Maureen Roth's father broke down—she had never seen him cry before—and said that, if she were unhappy, he would send her a return ticket (the equivalent of two months' pay). Vicky Blackmore, by then Mrs. DiNaro with twin boys, found that her brother had left for work early on the day of her departure—he could not bear to say farewell. She was taken by taxi to Waterloo station in London by a friendly neighbour. On the journey she repeatedly panicked, shouting to the driver, "Stop, I'm going back." The neighbour kept urging the driver on. "I wouldn't have made it without her," Vicky admitted years later. Many of the brides recalled Tidworth station in bleak mid-winter, snow on the platform, struggling with bags and screaming children. At the barracks some GIs could not conceal their resentment at this unwelcome duty, which was delaying their return home. Mary Coffman never forgot the opening of a "welcome" speech from one officer: "You may not like conditions here, but remember no one asked you to come." At first there were no cribs for the babies, until one inventive officer obtained file drawers and footlockers that he lined with pillows and rubber mattresses. Washing facilities were rudimentary, food often abysmal, and the obligatory physical exam proved a public humiliation. Women stood naked on the stage of the camp theatre while a doctor shone a flashlight between their legs to check for VD, watched from the back by a crowd of American officers.[11]

By the spring, after protests from wives and their stateside husbands, conditions had improved. Facilities for babies were much better and nightly movies and a welcoming Red Cross Club made the wait more tolerable. But nothing could calm the undercurrent of anxiety. Avice Grasso (née Wilson) from Chippenham found three other women in her room at Tidworth: "None had more than a week with her husband nor had seen him for a year." How would they get on when they met again? She also recalled that "some girls neglected their children shamefully, others didn't know how to take care of them." A few even went out in the evenings with German POWs, though those who were caught (it was rumoured) never got to the United States.[12]

The first special shipment of war brides left Southampton on 26 January 1946 aboard the S.S. *Argentina*, a 1930s passenger liner that had transported some 200,000 troops during the war. Onboard were 452 brides (thirty of them pregnant), 173 children, and one bridegroom, whose WAC wife awaited him in New York. The women had husbands in forty-five of the forty-eight American states and were aged from sixteen to forty-four. On 5 February the *Queen Mary* followed, with nearly twenty-three hundred wives and children among its passengers. One veteran steward, who had witnessed all the indignities inflicted on the *Queen* by wartime GIs, could not get over the sight of the huge indoor swimming pool, drained and full of hundreds of nappies (diapers) laid out to dry. "What is the world coming to?" he asked. Although the *Queen Mary* did several runs, many war brides traveled in much lowlier accommodations, such as the hospital ship *Bridgeport* and the *Santa Paula,* which looked like a tugboat alongside the *Queen.* But almost any shipping space was better than further delays. In the fourteen months between VE day and 30 June 1946, the Army shipped 38,723 dependents from the United Kingdom to the United States—28,299 adults and 10,424 children—in what the American press dubbed "Operation Diaper Run."[13]

Just how many war brides were there in all? It is surprisingly difficult to give a simple answer. Some historians have suggested 70,000; others 100,000—even claiming that 30,000 of these were shipped secretly during the war. The internal history of the London embassy's consular section reckoned "between 50,000 and 60,000" of whom "the vast majority desired their wives to go to the United States."[14] Even this is probably too high. The obscurity lies in the fact that until the 1950s the U.S. Immigration and Naturalization Service (INS) did not publish its annual reports and so the evidence has to be gleaned from its unpublished statistics. These show that 34,528 "alien wives" entered the United States from the United Kingdom under the War Brides Act between 28 December 1945 and 30 June 1950. (There were also forty-two UK husbands of female GIs.)[15] Since the act did not cover pre-1946 entrants and not all spouses in 1946–50 entered under its provisions, it is more appropriate to use the overall INS figures for those entering as alien wives of U.S. citizens. These are set out in table 23.1 and show that 37,879 "alien wives of U.S. citizens" were admitted from the UK between July 1941 and June 1950. Of these 27,094 arrived in 1945–46 and 7,160 in 1946–47. Not all would have been brides of GIs (as opposed to American civilians or diplomatic staff and some married GIs who came to Britain during the Cold War), but it gives us an upper figure. These statistics also belie stories of a massive influx during the war (only 627 alien wives were admitted from the UK in 1941–45).

INS statistics are, however, little use for estimating the number of children, mainly because the offspring of a U.S. citizen could immediately be registered as a citizen and therefore did not figure on immigration returns (unlike the British mother). The best guide is therefore the statistics of dependents shipped to America at U.S. government expense. These give a figure of 14,078 children from the UK up to February 1948, over half being under the age of one. On the other hand, 458 were aged five to nine and nearly three hundred were teenagers—newly adopted offspring from earlier marriages. The mothers of these older children were middle-aged—several hundred being in their forties—but the bulk of the brides were young. Over half were aged twenty to twenty-four and a further one-fifth were under the age of twenty. War brides, the INS noted, were younger than the average immigrant of the 1930s and 1940s. They also settled all over the States and not mainly in the metropolitan areas. In the year from July 1946 through June 1947, for instance, 27,212 war brides and children arrived in the United States from all over the world (a quarter of them from the UK). Only 40 percent went to cities of over 100,000, of which New York (nearly 2,600) far outstripped the rest. One-third of war brides and children were destined for towns with populations of between 2,500 and 100,000, and another quarter for settlements of less than 2,500.[16]

23.1   WOMEN FROM THE UK ADMITTED TO THE UNITED STATES AS WIVES OF CITIZENS, JULY 1941 TO JUNE 1950

Year (1 July–30 June)	English Wives	Total UK Wives
1941–42	81	114
1942–43	71	104
1943–44	66	118
1944–45	151	291
1945–46	23,197	27,094
1946–47	5,894	7,160
1947–48	1,544	1,843
1948–49	734	914
1949–50	190	241
1941–50	31,928	37,879

Source: U.S. Dept. of Justice, Immigration and Naturalization Service, unpublished annual reports, 1942–50 (INS Library, Washington, DC).[17]

All these statistics can only be approximate. We do not know, for instance, how many couples elected to stay in Britain, but anecdotal evidence suggests that the figure was small. Nor is it clear how many GI marriages ended in early divorce in Britain. In March 1946 the Married Women's Association in London had record of two hundred women who were threatened with divorce proceedings by GI husbands. Another statistical gap is that some women were admitted to the United States as GI fiancées rather than as brides, but that amounted to only 112 in the four years from July 1946. All in all, an estimate of forty thousand GI brides would seem reasonable, and forty-five thousand an outside limit. This is much less than generally thought. It is also interesting to compare the figures for Canadian war brides. Although less numerous in toto (500,000 as against three million), the Canadian troops, as we have seen, were around much longer (from Christmas 1939) and were more fully integrated into British life. In all, 44,886 Canadian service personnel were married in Britain in 1940–46 and they produced 21,358 offspring during that time. In some cases, both partners were Canadians or one might be from another Allied force, but the bulk of the weddings were Anglo-Canadian. Overall, 40,353 wives and 19,678 children were shipped to Canada at government expense up to March 1948, compared with figures of 33,849 and 14,078 in the American case over virtually the same period.[18] Such statistics should be used with caution, but they suggest that although the Canadian forces in Britain were roughly one-sixth the size of the American, they married about the same number of British women. The restrictive policies of the U.S. Army seem to have had some success.

The war brides represented the ebb tide of the American invasion of Britain. They flowed back across the Atlantic, sometimes along the route that their husbands had taken a few years before, with Tidworth Barracks and the *Queen Mary* among the markers. Like their husbands, they left family and friends to make a turbulent crossing of the Atlantic into the unknown. But the differences were more significant than the similarities. For most of the soldiers, their transatlantic odyssey began a relatively brief if traumatic parenthesis in their American lives; for their British brides it was intended as the start of a new life in the New World. The GIs who sailed up the Clyde or the Mersey were welcomed, if at all, impersonally and anonymously. The young women whose ships passed the Statue of Liberty and drew into the Hudson River expected a very personal welcome. Expected? Hoped for, longed for, prayed for, it would be more accurate to say. Many, as they scanned the quayside, fought back the fear that there might be no one there. Others tried to recall their husband's face. Sheila Ochocki, from London, saw a husband (not hers) walking up the gangplank in a zoot suit. "Oh God," she thought, "I hope mine doesn't look like that."[19] Some brides did not expect to be met, except by Traveller's Aid personnel. For them the reunion would only come after a long rail journey into the American heartland. And on most ships, as the turmoil abated, a few distraught women were left, facing up to the bleak reality that *he* was not coming.

Reunion was only the beginning of building a relationship with a man you hardly knew. Many of the marriages were characterized by a whirlwind courtship and then a long separation. Often pregnancy had forced a decision or at least confirmed a half-spoken engagement. Now the woman, as wife and mother, had to live with a man who often seemed less impressive when stripped of his American uniform. Many brides were also acutely homesick. The extremes of climate were enervating, the bustle of urban life overwhelming. The vast emptiness of rural America, not to mention its poverty and primitiveness, came as a shock to girls used to the intense communalism of an English village or small town. Some were the victims of outright deception. Stories were legion about brides who discovered that life stateside was not all that their husband had promised (or insinuated—for brides often filled in the gaps from their movie image of America). Instead of a splendid ranch there was a squalid cabin with no plumbing. "Chains of gasoline stations" translated into proprietorship of a single pump. A solicitor's daughter from Cheltenham married a Greek-American whose father, supposedly, had a string of smart restaurants in New York. She came home after finding that the "restaurants" were peanut stands outside baseball grounds and that she was expected to serve on one.[20]

For some GIs, Anglo-American relations looked different when viewed from the other side of the Atlantic. Eisenhower's friendship with Kay Summersby cooled in the last months of the war, as he began thinking of his return to Washington and of resuming life with Mamie. Since Kay was not a U.S. citizen, this enabled Ike to terminate her position on his staff. In a businesslike letter of explanation, he said he was "personally much distressed that an association that has been so valuable to me has to be terminated in this particular fashion." Similar farewells occurred lower down the Army. Mike, the Southern GI mentioned in the previous chapter, arrived back in America regretfully in August 1945. He was still in love with Anne in Coventry and had no desire to return home. The Old World continued to cast its spell upon him and he would have liked another year to roam around Europe. Two months later, however, he told his mother he was writing to Anne to postpone any formal engagement because he was not ready to settle down. He thought he might remain in the Army for a while. In any case, he had been going out with a nurse from New England whom he liked a lot. Anne, like old England, faded into history. The two had been entangled together in his affections.[21]

These relationships had not been formalized, but they give an intimation of the change of mood that often led to the breakdown of a war bride's marriage. Here is the story of one divorce, as told from the vantage point of the bride, nearly forty years later, after her ex-husband's death. Irene was herself the product of a broken home. She was brought up by foster parents in Sutton, south of London, and worked during the war in Wiltshire, like many future war brides, as a member of the Women's Land Army. There she met Andrew, a tall, lean, rather taciturn GI, who asked her to wait for him when he was shipped off to France. She was much in love. They became engaged and submitted the necessary paperwork. Permission was granted. One day he simply appeared at the door of the farm where she was working and announced, "I've come on leave to get married." At short notice the wedding took place under special licence at a church in Sutton on 5 June 1945.

Andrew was sent back to the United States in August. He was an erratic correspondent and, with papers full of stories about GI divorces and a baby due in February 1946, Irene grew despondent. Before the child was born she wrote Andrew and asked directly whether he wanted her to come over. He immediately replied that he did and arrangements were made. Irene and her son arrived in New York on 29 May 1946. When her name was called, she came up on deck. "Here was Andrew. A feeling of relief swept over me to see that he had really come for me." In his Buick they drove across country to Michigan, staying in motels along the way. Since her engagement, Irene had corresponded with her future mother-in-law and "Andy had told me that his mother and father were divorced but it wasn't until I arrived at Port Huron that I came to realize what a mixed-up affair it all was." Andrew lived with his mother and her new partner in a cramped and untidy apartment over a furniture store. Mother was sociable and generous, but disorganized. The sink always seemed full of dirty dishes, the laundry was done spasmodically, and the household was chronically in debt.

Eventually Irene and Andrew were able to move into rented accommodation a few miles away but, after news that a second child was on the way, Andrew went completely into his shell. Meals were eaten in silence and Irene became deeply depressed. Although things were patched up for the birth of their second son in May 1947, Andy only came to the hospital once in a week. During this time he had shifted from job to job. In the summer of 1948 he decided to rejoin the Army and disappeared to Fort Jackson, South Carolina, leaving her living out of town, unable to drive an automobile, with two small boys. Finally her brother-in-law drove the family down to South Carolina and obliged Andy to find accommodation for them all in the city of Columbia.

It was clear, however, that he was seeing other women and soon he announced he was going to live on base. Asked why, he replied: "I don't know, it's not your fault, I just don't want the responsibility of a wife and children." Forty years later that moment was still vivid in Irene's memory:

> I don't think there are any words to describe how it feels to know you are no longer wanted. A terrible blankness descends over your mind, coupled with a deep anxiety and despair. What on earth are you going to do, two small boys barely two and three years old and in a foreign country as well. You feel totally stunned, later reaction sets in. You go through the day's chores mechanically. It's only when bathing the boys ready for bed, putting their night clothes on, making their milk drinks, the whole unhappy situation becomes a reality, the tears begin to trickle slowly down your face, you tuck the children into their beds, kiss them goodnight, then go away and have a good weep.

Within weeks Andrew was back, but simply to say he wanted a divorce. These were quick and easy to obtain across the state line in Georgia and she was too numb to do anything but sign. She could not have made ends meet but for meals and money from friends and she recalled Christmas 1948 as "the saddest one I have ever known. Walking round Woolworths in the week before Christmas I was overcome with grief as I watched soldiers with their children laughing and talking together as they bought gifts and Christmas decorations." She had to move in with friends. That was impossible for long, so she took the boys back to Michigan and did the rounds of the in-laws and remote family friends, lodging with each for a few weeks. Finally, through the British Council, she was able to borrow the £126 necessary to return to England on the *Queen Mary*. Most of her belongings had been sold long before, but even to buy suitcases to transport those that remained required the help of friends. Irene and the two boys took a Greyhound bus to Detroit at the end of October 1950 and then an overnight train to New York. The boys fell asleep but she dozed fitfully.

> Thoughts kept drifting through my mind of the past four years, and always the question of why it had turned out this way, what had gone wrong that a journey across the ocean to this New Life had ended in this way, and as always there seemed no reasonable answer to these questions.[22]

Where a marriage failed, most brides, like Irene, had no choice but to go back to Britain, endure the humiliation ("I told you so"), and pick up the threads as best they could. Most, but not all. Avice Wilson was a jeweler's daughter in Chippenham, Wiltshire, aged seventeen as the war ended in 1945, who worked as a government milk-tester. For two years the town had played host to a succession of American armoured divisions, training on the nearby downs, and it was almost de rigueur for a local girl to have a GI boyfriend. Avice saw Johnnie for the first time on VJ day, leading the conga line through Chippenham market square. He proved gregarious, cheerful, and generous—the classic GI. He was also a man of enterprise, both on- and off-duty, and took her all over southern England—to dances, restaurants, even the seaside. "As a family," Avice recalled,

> I think we were impressed with the "action" of the G.I.s. Something needed doing or getting? Right, we had it as soon as possible. Admittedly, the Americans had greater resources than we had at that time, but it was a combination of drive and confidence that never failed to dazzle us.

Ironically, one of Johnnie's last jobs was arranging supplies at Tidworth, where Avice had many opportunities to observe the war brides. In May 1946 it was his turn to leave. Two months before, she had rebuffed his proposal of marriage. Now she succumbed. "I decided I couldn't bear life without Johnnie (or was it Chippenham without Johnnie?) so we married." He went to the States in June and she followed in July, getting VIP treatment from his former buddies at Tidworth. Her new home was a steel town on the edge of Buffalo, upstate New York. Although Avice managed the adjustment to an Italian-American family (her mother-in-law spoke no English at all) and she sensed no resentment that Johnnie had married outside the clan, she found it harder to cope with her husband. "I found Johnnie had an Italian temperament which I had never seen in him when we were together in England. He was quick to lose his temper and quick to make up. I could not react fast enough." Work also drew them apart. He supervised the unloading of iron-ore boats at the steel mill. She found an absorbing job running a control lab for a manufacturer of dairy products. She left Johnnie in 1951 and the marriage was annulled. Yet Avice stayed in America. As she wrote thirty years later:

> I have never wanted to live in England permanently, life for a woman of my age is much freer in the States. I dislike English weather, the food, the reliance on traditions to solve problems, and the class system. Yet I go to my family almost every year and I feel I will always be a woman of Wiltshire soil.[23]

Her reflections capture something of the ambivalence of many GI brides—love of an American was often reinforced by restlessness about Britain. In marriage, no less than in his other relationships, each GI was both a person and a symbol.

Just how many marriages ended in divorce is unclear. Newspapers naturally found the breakdowns rather than the successes to be better copy and there are no official statistics. The British Home Office, coordinating the problems of divorced brides and their dependents, estimated in August 1946 that thirty thousand British women had married GIs. "We have no means of ascertaining how many of these marriages are unsuccessful," an official wrote, "but having regard to the circumstances of the time, it would be surprising if this figure were less than 1,000." The government's legal aid scheme for wives still in Britain whose GI husbands started divorce proceedings against them in the U.S. courts helped 503 cases between March 1947 and the end of 1950. Other brides, like Irene, were divorced in America, where the English-Speaking Union took a particular interest in their welfare. Using information from its one hundred local committees, the ESU reckoned in January 1947 that "not more than five per cent of the marriages had been unsuccessful" and compared this figure with the current American divorce rate of 33 percent. Again, we have to be wary of official statistics. American divorce laws varied from state to state—the British consul general in Chicago described them as being in "chaotic condition with no semblance of equity or justice, or even decency"—and many cases probably never came to the notice of the British authorities. But none of these statistics confirms some gloomy contemporary predictions that most of the marriages would fail. The Home Office guess of roughly 3 percent and the ESU estimate of 5 percent are fairly close.[24]

We should not, therefore, end the story of the war brides with the divorcées. Those whose marriages survived showed equal fortitude, even though their accounts of it are less vivid and detailed because the pain has been absorbed and absolved in a rewarding partnership. An extreme case is a woman from Brighton whose marriage began with her husband losing a leg in combat and the death of her baby. She migrated to Appalachian Virginia and raised four children but said three decades later that, once she and her husband were reunited stateside, "nothing spectacular has happened."[25]

Take the story of Wyn Boyle, who had to wait a year to be reunited with her wounded paratrooper husband, Leo, in California. Early in 1946 she traveled on the *Queen Mary* to New York. With a group of brides she made the long train journey, another three thousand miles, across the continent to rejoin her husband. She had never been to America before and knew it only from the movies. The strong young soldier she had married before D-Day was now a semi-invalid. It had taken months to patch up his shattered leg. He was discharged from the Army with a 30 percent disability (later raised to 50 percent). He tried working as a railroad brakeman, but his legs were not strong enough. Nor were they up to the job of a post office sorter. Leo eventually found his métier as a high school teacher, working with disabled students in Salem, Oregon. But this was after years of struggle and he could never have done it without her help. "She took it very well," he reflected fifty years later. "A real trouper." Then, quietly and unselfconsciously: "I think it's something called love."[26]

One of the most equal partnerships was that between Grace Chawe and Alva Reinecke. Grace was the daughter of an Anglo-Chinese couple who lived in Shepherd's Bush, London. Her father served in the British Merchant Navy and died at sea. Alva was an Army medic from Black Earth, Wisconsin, whom Grace met late in 1942 in Evesham, where she worked as a Land Girl. They became engaged in January 1944, but "we did not marry in England as he wanted me to see his home and family. He wanted me to be sure it was forever."

Alva was shipped home in October 1945. Grace and her sister, engaged to a GI from Chicago, booked passages on the *Argentina* (as fiancées they could not travel at Uncle Sam's expense) and sailed for New York in August 1946. When Alva finally met her in Madison, Wisconsin, it was the first time she had seen him in civilian clothes. "I must say it was like meeting a stranger." But they married the following month. She was one of four GI brides from Britain in the area (though only their marriage survived). They took over the family farm and "were considered very good farmers." But "Alva had promised me we would spend part of our life in the U.S. and part in England." This they did, living their later years near Salisbury. When their son married, "he paid us a great compliment," Grace wrote. At the reception he said: "My mother and father, because of their love for each other, have shown me what happiness a good marriage can bring."[27]

Following the GI brides across the Atlantic (and sometimes back again) has taken us well beyond 1945. But that is only right if we seek a rounded assessment of the American occupation of Britain. For its significance cannot be measured within the confines of those four years, 1942–45. The last two chapters of the book consider its long-term impact, first for the two countries and then for some of the men and women involved.

Part VI

HISTORY AND MEMORY

24

Americanization
and Its Discontents

★ ★ ★

IN JANUARY 1944 THE BRITISH JOURNALIST KINGSLEY MARTIN CALLED THE
American presence "one of the great social experiments of the war."
But what were its results? For Churchill it was a catalyst of the new
"special relationship" between the two "English-speaking peoples."
Commending the idea that British troops should join GIs in celebrating
the Fourth of July 1944, he minuted: "It was a very good thing that
America got independent of us and a still better thing that she has
come back into the family." With hindsight, others have seen it as the
beginning of a progressive Americanization of Britain. According to
one rhapsodic British newspaper article in 1993: "It is fifty years since
the American way of life arrived in Britain, borne by hundreds of
thousands of GIs here in preparation for the invasion of Europe.... We
liked them so much we bought the whole way of life. Half a century
on, like a dominant gene, it has taken over."

But terms like *special relationship* and *Americanization* must be handled with caution. The former was British myth as much as international reality, as closer examination of the postwar years shows. And
Americanization is a crude concept that glosses over the complexities
of British society. Moreover, it conceals the fact that the United States
was not as "American" as movie-mad Britons imagined. We need to
reflect on the Americanization of America as well.[1]

To consider these themes, we should begin by pulling out some of the
threads of this book and tying them into a larger tapestry. For the
Yanks in Britain were only part of a vast American diaspora during
1942–45. In a truly world war (unlike 1914–18), GIs were based from

Iceland to Iran, from New Guinea to Nova Scotia. Seen globally, the American wartime presence in Britain has most in common with that in Australia. Both were Allies (not enemies like Germany or liberated countries like France); both were base areas where soldiers were fretfully waiting for war; and in each the community of language and culture made hosts extremely accessible to guests.

Australia witnessed many of the same patterns as Britain. Soldiers got on worst: Yanks and Diggers fought about women and about who was winning the war, with the GIs' superior pay, rations, and uniforms a constant aggravation. Americans complained of chronic overcharging, and the Australian black market was kept well supplied, courtesy of Uncle Sam. GIs quipped that the cheapest thing in Australia was the girls while some Australian church leaders condemned the soldiers and their "jazz philosophy" for wartime moral decadence. On the other hand, there was much cheerful hospitality, black GIs were generally well treated, and several thousand war brides eventually migrated to the United States. The similarities continue even down to the conduct of the American Red Cross. In both Australia and Britain, unlike almost every other U.S. war theatre, the ARC was asked to run a "hotel chain" for soldiers' leave accommodation. Such work as an Army welfare agency was regarded by many Australian Red Cross officials as a flagrant breach of the Geneva convention under which the organization was supposed to serve only the sick, wounded, and prisoners of war.[2]

The main differences between the American presence in these two English-speaking countries were intensity and duration. In December 1942 there were only 100,000 GIs in Australia and the wartime peak was probably no more than 150,000. Of course, this was in a population of only seven million, and around places such as Brisbane the impact of the GIs was intense. But, overall, it was not difficult to make space: Australia was the size of the continental United States. And the GIs were present in significant numbers for a shorter time than in Britain. The peak years were 1942–43; rundown was rapid in 1944 as the Japanese tide ebbed back across the Pacific.[3]

The American visitation of the British Isles was larger and longer. Of the eighty-nine combat divisions sent overseas by the Pentagon during the war, forty passed through the UK (Appendix 1). Between January 1942 and September 1945 a total of 2,914,843 members of the U.S. Army and Army Air Forces disembarked in the United Kingdom. Admittedly, some of these were two-timers, such as wounded GIs from the Continent or the 1st Infantry Division, which was at Tidworth from August to October 1942 and in Dorset from November

1943 until D-Day. On the other hand, this total does not include those arriving by air, who totaled eighty thousand by D-Day alone. Nor does it count U.S. Navy personnel, nearly 122,000 strong on D-Day. It is therefore reasonable to say that about three million American service-men and women passed through the United Kingdom in 1942–45. This is over 18 percent of the total number of Americans who served in the U.S. armed forces during the war (16.35 million) and a quarter of those posted overseas. Judged from the receiving end, GIs were the equivalent of 7 percent of the prewar population of England, Wales, and Northern Ireland (roughly 42 million).[4]

The American occupation of Britain was therefore distinctive. But any estimate of the impact has to take account of its partiality because we are not talking about three million GIs in residence across the whole country for more than three years. The detailed patterns of occupation set out in earlier chapters may be summarized in four phrases: ups and downs, ins and outs, to and fro, and hit and miss.

Ups and downs, in that the three million Americans did not come and go in the steady crescendo/diminuendo of the Bolero and Rhumba orchestrations. Numbers grew in the spring and summer of 1942, peaking at 228,000 before the invasion of North Africa, but in early 1943 there were little more than 100,000 GIs in the United Kingdom. From mid-1943 a second surge began, culminating in perhaps 1.65 million American service personnel on the eve of D-Day. Thereafter numbers dropped again, but American strength remained between 600,000 and 700,000 through the winter of 1944–45 and even at the end of the war 400,000 were still left.

The ins and outs of the story lie in the way that troops often arrived and departed in short order, notably the "diverted divisions" routed via Britain to France 1944–45. This caused considerable disruption but allowed little time to make close contact with the natives. At the other extreme were some ground crew on the air bases, who put down deep roots in East Anglia, and the twenty-month visit by the 29th Division. Even where units remained, however, men came and went. Over half the 29ers on Omaha Beach were not the original National Guardsmen from Virginia and Maryland but replacements. Many had spent only a few months in Britain.

GIs also shifted to and fro. Again airmen were something of an exception, with the 306th Bomb Group clocking up a record thirty-eight months at Thurleigh in Bedfordshire. More typical were combat units such as the 2nd Infantry Division, which had six months around the Ulster city of Armagh and then two more at Tenby on the south Wales coast before landing in Normandy on D plus one. Service personnel in construction or trucking units were particularly peripatetic. They often had to make do with a series of small, isolated, and ill-provisioned bases. The consequent morale and discipline problems were exacerbated by the fact that a disproportionate number of these men were black, and suffered from limited education, poor officers, and chronic racial discrimination.

The GIs' impact on the United Kingdom was also hit and miss. Some areas, notably mid-Wales, the extreme north of England, and most of Scotland, were home to very few GIs. Polish troops, for instance, made a much greater impression in Perthshire and Angus than did the Americans. The biggest enclaves of Yanks were in the flyboy country of Norfolk and Suffolk, the southern triangle from Dorset and Devon up into the Midlands, and the northwest supply corridor thence to Liverpool and Manchester. Although numerically much smaller, the density of American occupation in Ulster, especially in early 1944, was also significant. These four areas saw large concentrations of resident GIs. In addition, big cities, above all London, "welcomed" many Americans on leave. There the impact was often much more negative, for hosts and guests, than in "residential" areas.

The patchiness of the American occupation, both in time and space, must make us wary of postulating dramatic consequences, particularly when we remember the polls showing how many GIs never crossed the doorstep of a British home. The American consul in Manchester, George Armstrong, was a close observer of grass-roots patterns. He observed in September 1944 that the "average British civilian has barely touched the outer fringe of the American invasion."[5]

So, what was the wartime impact of the GIs? A BBC Listener Research report observed in February 1944: "Two years ago the sight of an American soldier anywhere in the country would have been a source of immediate comment and interest; today the United States uniform is, in many parts of Great Britain, as familiar as, if not more familiar, than our own." Clearly millions of British people met an American for the first time during the years 1942 to 1945. Some got to know individual GIs quite well. Pollsters found that, in consequence, the percentage of "don't knows" in surveys about America diminished. There was also a marked decline in the "cousin" image of America: British people increasingly recognized it as a foreign country rather than as a former colony. Overall, surveys showed a definite increase in favourable feeling about the United States as the war progressed. Sir Godfrey Haggard, head of American Forces liaison in the British Ministry of Information, judged in September 1945 that "a noticeably more intelligent and less critical attitude towards the Americans exists among the people of this country than when they arrived," and that among the young "an unmistakeable interest in America has been aroused."[6]

But familiarity did not necessarily breed affection, as diplomats in London had hoped. One middle-aged countrywoman remarked: "Every time I see an American soldier slouching along, hands in his pockets, shoulders hunched, chewing gum, I'm glad I'm not an American." And opinion analysts reckoned that, although a majority of Britons still felt in 1944 that American political institutions were "more truly democratic" than their own, this view was *less* prevalent than in 1942. In the previous two years many people had "actually seen the colour bar in operation."[7]

In fact, personal contact, pleasant or otherwise, did not automatically affect national images, as the propagandists had also hoped. The extreme right and extreme left remained antagonistic to the United States; the old tended to be more sceptical than the young. Many respondents to a survey in March 1945 expressed "their liking for individual Americans but their dislike of them en masse." Mass-Observation suggested that attitudes to GIs were "often close to those shown towards Jews by anti-semites, who will specifically excuse from their antagonism Jews they know (and like) as *individuals*." M-O also believed that the focus of the British stereotype of America remained "youthfulness." Those favourably disposed mentioned traits such as energy, enterprise, generosity, and efficiency. Those who basically disliked the United States cited boastfulness, immaturity, materialism, and immorality—what M-O called "the less pleasing qualities of adolescence." Individual Americans could be grist to either mill. In April 1947 Mass-Observation concluded that the "impact of reality, in the shape of the G.I. in Britain, might have been expected to have modified people's preconceived ideas" about America and Americans. "In fact," claimed M-O, "the American soldier appears to have had relatively little effect on them."[8]

We need to remember that, when Mass-Observation was questioning its panel in early 1947, the Marshall Plan and the North Atlantic Alliance were still unimagined. In 1944–45, there were widespread fears in the British government and press, reflected in opinion surveys, that America would revert to an uncooperative nationalism, as in the interwar years. American troops were withdrawn quickly from Europe and in 1945–46 it was London, not Washington, that was taking a firm line against Soviet expansion in Europe and the Middle East. A Gallup poll in March 1945 showed that, when the "average Englishman" considered transatlantic relations, his "greatest fears are of potentially disastrous economic competition with the United States." And with Britain (and much of continental Europe) swinging leftwards after the defeat of fascism, there was a sense of ideological distance as well. In March 1946, the Labour government's foreign secretary, Ernest Bevin, called Britain "the last bastion of social democracy" not only against "the Communist dictatorship of Soviet Russia" but also "the red tooth and claw of American capitalism."[9]

The patchiness of the wartime American presence and the "widening" of the Atlantic that occurred immediately after the war should make us wary of postulating any continuous process of Americanization. Despite the common language, basic differences remained between the two countries—those abiding verities of time and space that have run through this book. American influences on Britain, after the war as during it, took shape within a society whose own traditions remained entrenched and whose geography was always constricting. And the sense of "Britishness" was intense. In October 1943 a Gallup poll indicated that, for 20 percent of the population, America was the country they would most like to visit after the war—putting it top of the list. Yet only 4 percent wanted to migrate there and two-thirds of the population had absolutely no desire to live anywhere else than Britain. Moreover, some profound postwar trends owed nothing to America or the GIs. From the late 1940s Britain's major cities absorbed thousands of nonwhite immigrants from the empire, whose children grew up knowing no other home. The welcome generally offered to black GIs and the strenuous British objections in wartime to any "colour bar" were no guides to how these nonwhite Britons were treated. The segregation and hostility apparent in prewar Cardiff and Liverpool became widespread in the 1950s and 1960s. Guests were one thing, residents another.[10]

These qualifications must be remembered whenever we talk of the special relationship or of the Americanization of Britain. What, fifty years on, makes for the impression of continuity, however, is the effect of the Cold War. For one thing, that brought GIs back to Britain. The numbers involved were small by comparison with 1942–45: no more than forty-six thousand during the early 1950s peak and well under thirty thousand for most of the time thereafter. The troops were also highly localized: East Anglia around Mildenhall, the Oxford-Reading area around Greenham Common, and at Burtonwood in Lancashire, plus, from the 1960s, the Polaris submarine base at Holy Loch on the Clyde. Moreover, most GIs in Britain in the 1950s were not single or at least alone, but brought their families with them. In December 1952 there were forty-five thousand servicemen, ten thousand wives, and about the same number of children. The married GI posed fewer disciplinary problems than his wartime counterpart, but the presence of families often accentuated the "isolationism" and self-sufficiency of American bases. Nevertheless, the GIs again personified the American way of life, albeit with more limited impact than in 1942–45.[11]

Thus, the wartime American occupation, like the wartime Anglo-American alliance, might have been of transitory importance, but for the way both were confirmed by the Cold War. For most of that half-century epoch of a divided and dangerous Europe, Britain tended to look west—for defence and dollars, for mores and models. It is within this long-term pattern that the impact of the GIs must be understood. There are at least four ways in which the American occupation *worked with* other prewar, wartime, and postwar trends to shape or sharpen British images of the United States.

Preeminent was the impression of American wealth. Perhaps it was a GI bearing gifts to a British home or lavishing his monthly pay on his girlfriend. It might be the riches of Army "surplus" slipping into the black market or the technological sophistication of a mechanized army that dazzled British schoolboys. The GI's superior uniform had a similar effect, as did the image of such amenities as the three-bin washing-up system that British soldier Tom Tateson remembered years after D-Day. Few Britons realized that, thanks to George C. Marshall, most GIs were living far better in the wartime Army than they had in Depression America. What struck home was simply American abundance, confirming the glittering movie images. The GI therefore played a part in the promotion of what came to be known as "consumerism"—the endless production of goods and labour-saving devices, with demand encouraged by advertizing. This has now become a phenomenon of the developed world as a whole, with America no longer the predominant supplier. Today, as historian Carol Gluck has observed, Hollywood still provides the software but Sony provides the hardware. In Britain, however, from the 1920s through the 1960s, America was the acme of modernity.[12]

Material wealth also fostered cultural values. Margaret Mead rightly suggested that in wartime, as before, British evaluations of American life varied sharply by age and class. Younger, less-educated, and working-class Britons were more likely to praise America's material and technological advantages. Older Britons and those with more education tended to be censorious of American materialism. In August 1944 the director general of the BBC, William Haley, instructed that "the amount of American material" being broadcast should not be increased further without reference to him. He feared that the BBC's growing use of recorded American series, such as Bob Hope and Jack Benny, might "become a Frankenstein." In 1947, G. M. Trevelyan, England's most revered historian, bemoaned "an age that has no culture except American films and football pools." The "advent of real democracy, coinciding with two world wars, has done it—cooked the goose of civilisation." But to those who loved American music and movies, the age of mass culture was a delight. The GIs—jitterbugging and gum-chewing—accentuated a trend that began during the Jazz Age of the 1920s and continued on via the gyrations of Elvis Presley to the present day.[13]

But the GI was a soldier as well as an American. By the end of the war he had also come to embody American power. As Gen. Marshall noted in 1956, underlying the British opposition to an early Second Front were doubts that fun-loving America could mass-produce quality soldiers to match Hitler's Wehrmacht. In the winter of 1942–43 the British victory at Alamein and the American reverses in Tunisia served to confirm British prejudices. And the rowdy way in which the Americans waited for war in Britain led many locals, not to mention acidulous diarists such as Cecil King, to assume that the GIs could brag, drink, and fornicate, but not fight. That is why the year from June 1944 had such an impact—the truly awesome sight of American power wending its way down to the ports of southern England; the news coming back from Normandy and the Ardennes to show that GIs were real soldiers; the growing evidence, dramatized by Monty's "demotion," that America was the dominant partner in the alliance. These were all signs that a superpower (the neologism coined in 1944) was in a different league from even a great power. The need for Britain to shelter under the American nuclear umbrella during the Cold War rammed the point home. It was not an agreeable truth and from the 1960s a stream of protesters denounced Britain's role as what George Orwell called America's "Airstrip One." But, whether they housed Flying Fortresses or cruise missiles, bases like Greenham Common were durable symbols of American power.[14]

What made that power palatable for the majority of the population was a sense of affinity. Ike had touched a chord in June 1945 when he spoke about the underlying community of values between Abilene and London. Sure, there were differences—a short acquaintance with GIs was enough to persuade most British people of that. But, judged against fascism and communism, the similarities between Americans and Britons seemed far more significant than the differences—democracies against totalitarians, the West against the rest. Unquestionably, it was much better to have GIs "over here" than the Wehrmacht or the Red Army. Moreover, this British conception of a special relationship (it was always much more a British idea than an American) served to differentiate the "English-speaking peoples" from continental Europe—ravaged by war and wracked by political turmoil. In the 1950s most Britons reposed little trust in failed allies like France and former enemies like Germany, particularly against the Soviet threat. The United States had much more to offer in power, wealth, and ideology. Britain's abstention from the European Economic Community until the 1970s reflected this pervasive sense that the Atlantic was narrower than the Channel.

Again the cultural elite squirmed with distaste. In 1953 Harold Nicolson—writer, landowner, and snob—lamented that "the destinies of the world should be in the hands of a giant with the limbs of an undergraduate, the emotions of a spinster and the brains of a pea-hen." But that was why the GI proved such a potent symbol. Truly the youth of America, he incarnated its wealth, materialism, and new-found power. This was part of the fascination or irritation he evoked so strongly in wartime Britain.[15]

And the other side of the story? What did Britain mean to the GI? Again, we cannot discuss this in isolation from larger concurrent trends, particularly the end of the Depression, the GI's experience of military service in general, and the emergence of America as a super-power.

Six out of every ten Americans serving in the armed forces in World War Two had been born in the decade 1918–27. Wartime GIs were overwhelmingly children of the Depression, whose formative years coincided with American's gravest economic crisis. By 1943, however, less than 2 percent of the workforce was unemployed. Between 1939 and 1945 GDP rose in real terms by 70 percent, thanks to war orders and the consumer boom. Even allowing for wartime inflation, families with more than one wage earner often enjoyed incomes unimaginable during the Depression. Sure, there were squalid camps around boom-towns like Mobile, Alabama. Undoubtedly, soaring levels of VD and juvenile crime evoked concern. But the basic point is clear: GIs returned home to a country that was booming as never before in their adult lifetimes.[16]

America's first experience with long-term wartime conscription played a crucial part in this economic transformation. The draft continued, with much greater success, the efforts of the New Deal to regain full employment. As historian Robert Higgs has written, "during the war the government pulled the equivalent of 22 percent of the prewar labor force into the armed forces. Voilà," said Higgs, "the employment rate dropped to a very low level." And at the end of the war, the Servicemen's Readjustment Act of 1944 (better known as the GI Bill of Rights) cushioned their return to the civilian workforce. Despite the gratitude of veterans, and although there was "a small but significant percentage of boys from poor families for whom the GI Bill spelled opportunity," most of those who entered college or university under its provisions (some 80 percent) were "boys who would have gone on to higher education anyway." In fact, noted historian Keith Olson, the GI Bill was "more an antidepression measure than an expression of gratitude to veterans." Fearing a postwar slump, the government wanted to delay the soldiers' return to the workforce. Fortunately for the Truman administration, postwar prosperity (and Cold War demand for munitions and draftees) prevented a return to prewar levels of unemployment.[17]

The idea that military service generated civilian benefits was not new. After the Civil War the scope of veterans' pensions was gradually enlarged (to woo voters) until they constituted over 40 percent of federal outlays in the early 1890s. In 1913 two-thirds of native white males over sixty-five outside the South were drawing federal veterans benefits. But enactments like Civil War pensions or the GI Bill were examples of how warfare bred welfare *after* the fighting was over. In George Marshall's "army of democracy" this process occurred *during* the conflict as well. The Chief of Staff believed that "coddling the soldiers" was essential for morale, when GIs were under compulsion to serve and had been sent far from home for a somewhat nebulous cause. Hence the insistence on levels of pay, food, and facilities that caused friction with most host countries. The Army also provided many of these children of the Depression with their first steady job, not to mention free housing and medical care. Glen H. Elder's life-course studies are suggestive here. In a small but unique sample of three hundred men from the San Francisco Bay area who were questioned regularly from the 1920s, he found that those whose families had suffered in the 1930s and who were drafted young (before marriage and full-time civilian employment) were very likely to view military service as a positive turning-point in their lives. Even in the Army, for those who survived, 1941–45 was a good war.[18]

A feeling of well-being is usually relative rather than absolute. You feel better than before, or better off than someone else. For GIs the sense of improvement in their circumstances compared with the Depression was reinforced by observation of the countries they visited. In continental Europe, the ravages of war and destruction particularly enhanced that feeling. But we saw (chapter 15) how it occurred in Britain as well. In London the bombed ruins and the Piccadilly commandos conveyed an impression of physical and moral decadence, all the more powerful because one was at the heart of a supposedly great empire. Outside the metropolis, in towns and villages, the ubiquitous evidence of rationing and the eager, not to say demeaning, passion of kids and young women for American largesse also left their mark. And Britain was always glimpsed from an Americanized cocoon, whether on base or in American Red Cross "hotels." Okay, there was the mud, the damp, and the brussels sprouts—the GI's lot was not a happy one. But most concluded, objectively as well as emotionally, that it was much better to be a Yank than a Limey.

The sense of well-being was not simply material. The Depression had been psychological as much as economic. "The morale of our society is weak," observed literary critic Edmund Wilson in 1931, arguing that "what we have lost" was "not merely our way in the economic labyrinth but our conviction of the value of what we are doing." In similar vein, it has been claimed, the most significant achievement of the war economy was that it "broke the back of the pessimistic expectations almost everybody had come to hold during the seemingly endless Depression. . . . People began to think: if we can produce all these planes, ships and bombs, we can also turn out prodigious quantities of cars and refrigerators." Moreover, others were crying out for that production. In 1945, with most of the developed countries in ruins, the United States was generating half the world's manufactured output. And the world needed not just American goods, it seemed, but also American values and power. Throughout America in 1945 there was a sense of prodigious achievement. "The Great Republic has come into its own," declared the *New York Herald Tribune;* "it stands first among the peoples of the earth." According to the nationalist *Chicago Tribune* it was the "good fortune of the world" that "power and unquestionable intentions go together." Of course, there was still communist Russia, whose power and questionable intentions were already suggesting the Manichean worldview of Cold War America. But American opinion no longer took *Great* Britain seriously. By the end of the war it was recognized in the British Foreign Office that the "Big Three" concept had been replaced in American minds by the idea of "a world that rotates in two orbits of power"—leaving Britain, one senior diplomat noted ruefully, like "Lepidus in the triumvirate with Mark Antony and Augustus."[19]

Postwar America, to quote one baby boomer, therefore seemed like a new nation, "conceived in victory." GIs came to share in that general superiority complex. When Col. Hans von Luck's men captured men from the 34th Division in Tunisia in 1943, they were struck not only by their excellent rations but also by the printed slip enclosed with each package:

> You are the best paid and best equipped soldier in the world. We have given you the best weapons in the world. Whether you are also the best fighter is now for you to prove.

In war nothing succeeds like success. By 1945 the U.S. Army had won, and victory was taken as proof of superiority. Knowing nothing of the magnitude of the Russian war effort (the Soviets' operation Bagration in mid-1944 was an even greater triumph than the battle of Normandy), GIs had little doubt that *they* had defeated the Wehrmacht. The élan of the breakout across France, the fortitude shown in the Battle of the Bulge, the remarkable American firepower and mobility—all these were compelling pieces of evidence. What they saw of the British Army (and few looked closely) confirmed their sense that "we had won the war." Contrary to the hopes of publicists, war service abroad "had not after all provided an education in internationalism." Summing up the data generated by Army pollsters, Samuel A. Stouffer judged that familiarity with the British and other Allies had not bred affection or respect. "Though our armies crossed the seas and lived on all the continents," Stouffer concluded, the GIs "came home, as they went out, indubitably American."[20]

In fact, one might hazard the view that they returned *even more* American than when they departed. Nineteen thirties America had a keen sense of regionalism and the first effect of Army life was often to enhance the GI's awareness of sectional and ethnic identity. In the training camps of Dixie, Northerners discovered the distinctiveness of Southern values. In their squads or aircrews, Irish met Pole, Italian mixed with Jew, New Englanders rubbed shoulders with men from Texas or Wyoming. But in the British Isles, they were almost always treated as "Yanks"—the occasional Jewish seder or a St. Patrick's Day with distant relatives notwithstanding. The uniform, of course, created an impression of uniformity: American soldiers all looked the same. But many GIs, I think, came to accept that they *were* all Yanks—overseas, the similarities outweighed the differences. Compared with the British (let alone the French or Germans) they were better paid and better fed. Their wealth could cut through the class barriers of the Old World, enabling them to buy a meal at London's best restaurants where no English private would get past the doorman. And this status was all because they were citizens and soldiers of the United States. For those children of the Depression who survived the war with body and mind intact, the experience of seeing the world from the cocoon of Uncle Sam's Army must have left most with a new sense of the wealth and power of the United States. In a new way, they were American and proud of it.

What of black GIs? Although many also benefited materially from military service, those from the North found the Army a humiliating introduction to Southern etiquette. Segregation often consigned blacks to work below their abilities and discrimination usually meant that they enjoyed inferior facilities to their white counterparts. Some even found they were treated worse than their enemies. Staff Sgt. David Cason, Jr., was a GI in the all-black 92nd Division—one of the few black combat units. Traveling home by train for a furlough he had a stopover at El Paso, Texas. The only place that would serve him some food was "a dingy, dinky place" near the station. But the station restaurant

> was doing a rush business with white civilians and German prisoners of war. There sat the so-called enemy comfortably seated, laughing, talking, making friends, with the waitresses at their beck and call. If I had tried to enter that dining room the ever-present MPs would have busted my skull, a citizen soldier of the United States. . . . Nothing infuriated me as much as seeing those German prisoners of war receiving the warm hospitality of Texas.

Such stories were not uncommon. By contrast, many black GIs found that "overseas duty compared to camp life stateside was a lark," to quote Sgt. Lester D. Simons of Ann Arbor, Michigan. Particularly in Britain and continental Europe they benefited from the absence of a formal colour bar and, in many cases, found local people genuinely hospitable. As we have seen, plenty of prejudice lurked close to the surface, but the basic point was clear: outside "the land of the free," Jim Crow was not the norm.[21]

Black GIs who had served in Europe therefore returned to America feeling much more ambivalent than their white counterparts. Timuel Black had been so impressed with his treatment in Europe that he briefly considered staying on after the war, but he was close to his parents and wanted to get home to Chicago. As his troopship sailed up the Hudson River, white GIs were standing on deck, talking excitedly about the Statue of Liberty, but Black stayed below, confused and bitter. Then, suddenly, he found himself in tears. "Glad to be home, proud of my country, as irregular as it is. Determined it could be better. . . . I could no longer push my loyalty back, even with all the bitterness that I had." But Joseph Curtis, of Washington, D.C., recalled a negative reaction on his ship as it berthed in New York on 29 August 1945. On the dock girls were shouting and waving. White GIs shouted back. But the black soldiers looked on, silent and pensive. One of them voiced what the others were thinking: "Now we're niggers again."[22]

As Curtis put it forty years later, service in Europe "made me realize what was possible." Thereafter he and other black veterans could always say to themselves: "when we were overseas, it wasn't like this." Some channeled this feeling into the black political protest that had gained momentum during the war. Returning black veterans were in the forefront of voter registration drives in the South. The state of Mississippi, under the aegis of Senator Theodore Bilbo, was notorious for racial discrimination. The white primary, poll tax, literacy tests, and general intimidation ensured that only twenty-five hundred adult blacks in the state registered in 1944 out of a possible 350,000. On returning to Mississippi black GIs, such as the young Medgar Evers, made a point of trying to register, often appearing in uniform complete with medals. They were also prominent in testifying before a special Senate committee inquiry in December 1946. By 1950 registration in the state had risen by twenty thousand and the political action helped mobilize younger blacks. Evers became state field secretary of the NAACP, until killed by a sniper in June 1963.[23]

But behind the "Magnolia Curtain" things remained much the same in Mississippi. And as World War gave way to Cold War and McCarthyism, all forms of political protest were liable to the charge of subversion. It seems likely, therefore, that although military service made blacks more impatient with discrimination, most sought individual rather than group advancement. This is the conclusion of Prof. John Modell and his collaborators. Of those black men who were in their twenties when they entered the Army, by 1950 over half were living in a region of the country different from that of their birth. This compares with about one-third of blacks who did not serve and less than a quarter of white veterans. Black Southerners were particularly likely to find the Army a "modernizing" experience, breaking them out of the old mould and prompting a new start elsewhere. And the GI Bill gave them a chance to be educated outside the poor negro colleges of the South. This mobility is related to deeper trends, of course, including the decline of Southern agriculture and the general migration of blacks into Northern cities. But one may infer that the impact of wartime service overseas on black GIs was indirect. After the initial wave of militancy, it inspired a drive for *economic* rather than *political* advancement. Yet the more prosperous, urbanized black community that black veterans helped create was an essential seedbed for the political activists of their children's generation.[24]

During World War Two the GI became a symbol of American wealth, values, and power. His brief but intense stay in Britain contributed there to longer-term patterns of Americanization. Service overseas helped Americanize him as well, particularly if he was white. But we cannot push this historical sociology too far. Not only is the evidence lacking, or only just being investigated. There is also a danger of ascribing too much to a passing moment. Britain was never crudely Americanized, the overwhelming majority of Americans did not serve overseas, and, even for those Yanks and Limeys who formed rich relationships, life did not stand still. What has endured most of all are the memories.

25

Remembering,
with Advantages

★ ★ ★

THIS BOOK HAS RESTED ON THREE PILLARS OF EVIDENCE: OFFICIAL PAPERS OF the period; the more personal documentation provided by wartime letters and diaries; and the belated testimony offered by memoirs and interviews. The first two of these are the familiar props of professional historians. The last is more controversial. How far can one trust people's memories of events four or five decades ago? Are we simply listening to party pieces, rehearsed in the same words on innumerable occasions?

In the early 1970s, Tom Harrisson, founder of the British survey group Mass-Observation, dusted off the old observer reports of the Blitz and compared some of them with the current memories of their authors. The discrepancies were substantial. One man, author of a vivid report on Coventry, could not recall being in the city at all. This is a reminder of the fallibility of memory. Yet the attraction of "oral history" is that the past is still alive: One can keep on asking, probing, teasing out more of what happened. Survivors can fill in the gaps in the written record, telling of things so mundane and obvious that no one bothered to write them down. This is particularly true for GIs in wartime Britain—many surviving U.S. Army unit records, for instance, begin in earnest only with 6 June 1944: What was prologue is past forever. As Tom Harrisson concluded, "writing this sort of social history" involves "an unceasing conflict between the recollection and the record," and an acknowledgement of "the inadequacy of both."[1]

Coping with the potentials and the pitfalls of memory has been one fascination of this book. Not only because it put me in touch with the past, via some remarkable and hospitable people, but because it showed how that past lives on powerfully in the present. In the process, I also realized how little we historians understand about the nature of memory, although it is at the heart of our profession. (Even the neurophysiologists and biochemists, for all their intricate experiments on the brains of chicks, rats, or sea slugs, are far from a holistic understanding.) Conventionally we think of the vicissitudes of memory in photographic terms: a record of the past that fades with age. We need to keep in mind the contrary words of Sir Frederic Bartlett, one of the pioneers of modern experimental psychology, that remembering is "an imaginative reconstruction, or construction, built out of the relation of our attitude towards a whole active mass of organized past reactions or experience." But even that is insufficient. We need to push further the truism that memory is selective. Consider the stories of two wartime GIs.[2]

It took Leon Standifer forty years to remember that he had killed a German in hand-to-hand combat. Standifer had been raised in a small college town in Mississippi where the Baptist church held sway. On his own admission "a young, idealistic, religious boy," he wrestled as a rifleman in the 94th Infantry Division with the ethics of taking life. In the whole war he fired his rifle three times in action. "One shot was a deliberate miss, and two were probable leg wounds." Standifer himself was hit in the leg and hospitalized during the Brittany campaign, but in January 1945 he rejoined his platoon near Nennig, on the Siegfried Line. The front was static; the GIs lived in foxholes in the icy ground. Frequently they would stumble over decaying corpses hidden by the snow. Standifer was sent out alone on patrol one night, although he was running a high fever. Squatting beside a tree, he suddenly felt a tap on his shoulder. He swung round and glimpsed the silhouette of a German helmet. What happened next was a mixture of instinct and training. Standifer jumped up, reaching for the knife concealed in his boot. Then he stepped to one side, thrust his knee into the German's back, grabbed his chin, and slid the knife across his throat—just as his instructor at Fort Benning had taught. There was no sound at all, but the blood gushed all over his glove. Standifer took the soldier's wallet and his belt buckle. Then, shivering with cold and shock, he made his way back to the American lines. Two days later he was hospitalized with pneumonia.

Lying in bed, exhausted and feverish, he had nightmares of putrefying bodies and blood running over his hands. By day he tried to remember what had happened. Sometimes he thought he had killed a man, comforting himself that he had completed his patrol and fulfilled his mission. Other times he was sure the fight had been just another nightmare (but then why did he have an SS buckle?). After a month Standifer was sent to a convalescent hospital near Hereford in England, where the tranquil beauty of the Wye Valley and the sympathy of a British woman ATS driver helped exorcize the demons. After six weeks there, Standifer felt he was beginning to make peace with himself. "I could still smell the decaying men and remember blood seeping through my gloves." But "I hadn't killed anyone—by now I had convinced myself of it—except indirectly, by calling down artillery." By the time he was fit for action again, the war was over.

Afterwards Standifer went to graduate school and ended up as a professor of horticulture at Louisiana State University. There were still occasional dreams of blood all over his hands but, most of the time, he remained convinced that they were nightmares not memories. In 1961 he and his wife visited Nennig and tried to locate his unit's positions. But the ghosts of friends proved too strong, the smell of decaying bodies too oppressive. His wife helped him back to the car, numb and frightened. It was only after he started attending divisional reunions in 1978, having avoided them for years, that the story was gradually pieced together. In 1986 he put the question directly to his former platoon leader. "Jim, I think I killed a man with a knife, but I'm not sure it wasn't a nightmare." Jim Westmoreland filled him in on the story of the young GI returning from patrol, covered with blood, his nerves close to breaking point. At last the dreams, nightmares, and memories came into some kind of focus.[3]

Jack Crowley saw his daughter Shirley for the first time when she was forty-one. They met in the airport at Sacramento, California, in May 1987, some six thousand miles from Birmingham, England, where she had been born and raised. During the winter of 1944–45 Jack was a sergeant from the 35th Infantry Division who was recuperating at Pheasey Farm camp near Birmingham. A land mine had exploded near him in France, leaving him concussed and, for a time, nearly deaf, with two broken eardrums. He was also suffering combat exhaustion and spent much time anguishing over the memory of dying comrades. Like Leon Standifer, and many other GIs, he found recuperation in England deeply therapeutic. He enjoyed visiting sights like Stratford and Oxford and, although something of a loner, liked the occasional drink in a pub. But he was no dancer and it was only in search of a drink that he walked into the Masque Ballroom in Birmingham one Saturday night in November 1944. Instead, he met Lily Ross.

Soon this handsome, gentle, courteous American was a regular at

Lily's two-up, two-down house in Long Street. Her widowed mother took to him, as did her friends and neighbours. He became part of the family and bought her a ring from the local jeweler. There was some mention of a wife back home who wanted a divorce, but Lily was too much in love to ask many questions. Then suddenly, one evening in May 1945, Jack failed to turn up for a date. This had never happened before. The days passed and no news came. Lily's other worry was confirmed by a visit to the doctor: She was five months pregnant. A formidable aunt marched her up to Jack's base, only to find a handful of men left closing it up. The American Red Cross told her it was not their policy to help trace fathers. Eventually Lily and her mother decided adoption was out of the question. They would bring up the baby themselves. Shirley was born in September 1945 and took her mother's name. The space on the birth certificate for "father" was left blank.

How she tracked down her father is another story, to be told later in this chapter. It was not until the spring of 1986, in a transatlantic phone call, that Shirley told Jack, "I've got some news for you. I think I'm your daughter." He was still somewhat deaf: "You're what?" She repeated the words. "Your daughter." There was a pause. "Oh, my God." Jack was married for a second time, with two grown-up sons. His first reactions were shock and disbelief. But he did not put the phone down. He was friendly and reassuring. Letters and phone calls were followed by visits, with Jack accepting Shirley fully as part of his family. He readily agreed that his name be added to her birth certificate. But during that first phone call, and afterwards, he could not remember anything about Lily Ross. Even when Shirley sent him a photo, all he could say was that she looked familiar. Her mother "was understandably shattered, and very, very annoyed. The man who'd been the love of her life couldn't even remember her." This had not been a one-night stand, but a close, loving relationship lasting more than six months, in which Jack had been a regular visitor in her home and a part of the family. Yet the whole period had become a blank spot. As Shirley acknowledged, the shock and concussion had perhaps affected memory as well as hearing. "My father recalls very little about the war and his part in it."[4]

The stories of Leon Standifer and Jack Crowley expose the deeper mysteries of memory. Each of these GIs had managed to blot out one of the most momentous events of his life, permanently in Crowley's case. That was a psychological legacy of combat trauma. For each, a period in Britain also played a decisive part in the curative process of amnesia. Peace, tranquility, and female company were all part of the flight from horrific reality across the Channel. These are extreme cases, but they highlight a basic point. Not only do old men forget, they also remember with advantages—the words Shakespeare put in the mouth of Henry V before Agincourt capture a fundamental truth of human psychology, especially in wartime. Memory is about therapy as well as remembrance. Its function is as much to forget the past as to record it. What GIs recall about their sojourns in wartime Britain is inextricably tied up with what they want to remember *and* forget about the war itself.

In 1945 no therapy was available. The object of the government (and the soldiers) was to get the boys home as soon as possible. They flooded back across the ocean, into the port of entry (usually New York), and then to a separation centre. Curtis Moore, a jeep driver who had gone the whole distance with the 29th Division in Britain, France, and Germany, was discharged at Fort Meade, Maryland, where he had arrived as a draftee in the spring of 1941. With $200 in his pocket, he set out for home in Roanoke, Virginia:

> I walked out of there—a big army base. I had my uniform on and all. I turned round and looked back at it. And there I was by myself. I had to catch a bus to Washington and catch a train to go home. And I'd had four-and-a-half years service and people telling me what to do and when to be back and when to eat. And I stood there for about fifteen minutes and thought about that thing and I said, "I'm free to do anything I want to do."

Free at last! It was almost like the slaves walking off the plantations at the end of the Civil War. Simply to do what one wanted—for most GIs that was the initial, overwhelming feeling after discharge. Curtis Moore spent his first week back in Roanoke partying.[5]

But the glow of homecoming soon wore off. The war could not be shrugged off as a parenthesis in normal living. Men had been changed by what they had seen and done overseas. Glad though they were to be home, it quickly became apparent that most family and friends could not comprehend what the GIs had gone through. Those who could were other soldiers, particularly one's buddies. Many veterans spent a lot of time in 1945–46 out drinking with other soldiers. There one could swap stories—and anaesthetize the pain. This pain was the underlying problem because nothing had been done, perhaps could be done, to help GIs come to terms with the death and destruction they had witnessed and often inflicted. Psychologists warned that the effect of combat was "not like the writing on a slate that can be erased, leaving the slate as before. Combat leaves a lasting impression on men's minds, changing them as radically as any crucial experience through which they live." But the treatment of combat stress, insofar as it existed at all, was regarded as a short-term expedient—to get men back into action—rather than a phased programme of readjustment into civilian life. Bob Slaughter, another 29er from Roanoke, has remained angry at the Army's failure:

> They transformed us from a civilian into a soldier. They transformed us from a civilized person into an uncivilized person. A civilized person could never have been a combat soldier. They made an animal out of you. And then, when the war's over, they said, "OK, you're now a civilian. We'll take your uniform. Here's your bus pass. Go home. . . . And be normal." But it didn't work like that. You're still the animal that you were back in Normandy.[6]

Many veterans "never did get civilized," Slaughter recalled. Some drank themselves into an early grave.

> The ones that survived just had to take hold of themselves. When I got married and had my first child, I decided I . . . was ruining myself, my wife, my kid. There was too much at stake. So I cut out the beer joints, I quit drinking, and I got away from it.

Such family responsibilities helped readjustment. So did education. Murphy Scott, another 29er from Virginia, had already completed a semester of college before the war. He arrived home in October 1945 and reenrolled at Virginia Polytechnic Institute in Blacksburg for the second semester the following January. This was a new focus for his life.[7]

Increasingly, silence seemed best. Betty Bayse Hutchinson had been an Army nurse at Menlo Park, California, specializing in plastic surgery cases. Her husband had served in the South Pacific. Both put "blinders on the past. . . . That's the way we lived in suburbia, raising our children, not telling them about the war. I don't think it was just me. It was everybody. You wouldn't fill your children full of these horror stories, would you?" The same was true of collective memory. Although many combat units established their own associations and held well-attended annual reunions in the first years after 1945, interest then began to slacken. Bob Slaughter had little to do with the 29th Association. In his own words, he "went dormant" about the war for a quarter-century. Reliving it seemed pointless: "You'd talk to people and they didn't know what you were saying." Furthermore, "it didn't do any good. I could see it was hurting my health to re-create these vivid terrible things," often in gruesome nightmares about Omaha Beach. And, like many GIs, raising a young family and holding down a job were full-time occupations. The past was dead; life lay in the present and future.[8]

This was not a surprising pattern. The aftermath of America's greatest conflict, in 1861–65, had been similar. Of course, this had been a civil war, and many hoped that time and silence would help heal the nation's self-inflicted wounds. But the basic psychology of veterans was the same after both conflicts. Gen. Robert E. Lee, the instigator of triumphs like Chancellorsville and tragedies like Pickett's Charge at Gettysburg, would read nothing about the war: "I do not wish to awaken memories of the past." In the 1870s little was published about the Civil War and veterans' associations atrophied. It was not until the following decade that the trend was reversed. Between 1878 and 1890 membership of the Grand Army of the Republic, the leading Northern veterans group, soared from 30,000 to 428,000.[9]

Similarly, it was about a quarter-century after 1945 that associations of World War Two veterans really began to flourish. Take the case of the 8th Air Force's 100th Bomb Group, which had been stationed at Thorpe Abbotts in Norfolk during the war. There had been two group reunions back in 1947 and 1952, but these were just isolated events. In 1968 Irv Waterbury, a Midwest developer who had played in the group's dance band, came east to run in the Boston Marathon and took the opportunity to track down some other members of the 100th. Out of the networking he set in motion came a 1969 reunion at Andrews Air Force Base near Washington. This set up a proper group organization and a quarterly newsletter, edited by Harry Crosby, former group navigator turned professor of writing.

Other unit associations were also born, or took on new life, around this time. In some cases, the Vietnam War may have been a reason. The controversy it engendered in America in the early 1970s sparked interest in (and defences of) the "good war" of 1941–45. But Harry Crosby reckoned that, for the 100th at least, what mattered was "biological not historical rhythm." By 1970 former GIs were mostly around the age of fifty. Established in work and with families raised, they had both the leisure and emotional security to look back. Later, retirement from full-time employment added a further stimulus. By 1993 the 100th had a mailing list of some fifteen hundred former GIs (out of seven thousand who served with the group during the war) and around one thousand attend reunions. Such success is partly due to the fame of the "Bloody Hundredth" and the quality of its newsletter, "Splasher Six" (named after the homing beacon at Thorpe Abbotts). But it exemplifies, in striking form, what many associations have experienced.[10]

In the 1990s their activities became especially important to survivors. A major reason was the creeping barrage of fiftieth-anniversary celebrations from 1991 to 1995. In 1992–93 airmen returned to England in droves to commemorate their units' arrivals a half-century before. In June 1994 GIs flocked back to Normandy. But again, in Harry Crosby's phrase, biology matters as much as history. These are men in the evening of life. The future is no longer open and enticing: familiarity (and a sort of novelty) lie in reexploring the past. Old places, and especially old faces, assume new importance. For many there is also the need to tie up those loose ends that were hurriedly buried in a tangled bundle after the war. Now the past has to be put into sequence with the present, ghosts must be exorcized, death faced in the past as well as in the future. Talking about the war is still painful, but also therapeutic. Studies have shown that periodic reunions and sympathetic spouses can be vital in coping with the long-term trauma of combat. For many veterans, writing their memoirs (published or not) is particularly valuable. "Instead of keeping it in, you're letting it out," said Bob Slaughter. "It makes you feel a little bit *cleaner*—I guess that's the word." For Harry Crosby, writing his autobiography was "a kind of catharsis."[11]

From the 1940s to the 1990s, memory has been a form of therapy for ex-GIs—an extended effort to make peace with the war. For all its enormity, this is, in the end, a facet of the universal aging process: coming to terms with life in the face of death. In lines from a poem by John Sparrow, an Oxford academic:

> Insensibly, ere we depart,
>   We grow more cold, more kind;
> Age makes a winter in the heart,
>   An autumn in the mind.[12]

Memory, then, is not merely fragile and fallible; it is inextricably tied up with a person's psychological health. But this is not to deny its potential validity, as Alice and Howard Hoffman have shown. He was a GI who served in Italy, France, and Germany in a chemical mortar battalion. Discharged in 1945 at the age of twenty, he became a distinguished academic psychiatrist. His wife was a pioneer of the oral history movement in America, who, in the 1970s, decided to test out his recollections of World War Two. In 1978 she conducted an extensive series of free-recall interviews, allowing him to reminisce at will about the war. She repeated the process in 1982. In the interim Howard as far as possible avoided situations that might encourage recall or rehearsal (such as films about the war). After the second set of interviews they used unit records, photographs, and site visits, as well as reunions, to check his memories against what they could best establish as fact.[13]

This was obviously an unusual project. Few are in a position to engage in such an extensive process of recall and corroboration. Moreover, both subject and observer were trained to think about the processes of learning and memory. Nevertheless, the Hoffmans' results are instructive. On the positive side they established that what Howard did remember was both broadly stable over time (between 1978 and 1982) and also accurate with regard to the events of 1944–45. They postulated that within people's long-term memory there is a subset that they called "archival memory" because of its relative immutability and permanence. Depending on the orientation of the person, the memories can be either visual or verbal. Howard Hoffman's memories were mostly in images. (Harry Crosby, by contrast, called himself "a word man," with an essentially audio-memory.) Whether in images or words, the Hoffmans suggested, this archival memory has the character of a photographic scrapbook. It comprises recollections that have been rehearsed (to self and others) and are thereby ordered and consolidated. They are also easily recalled and they have been selected for preservation over a lifetime. The Hoffmans also judge that the process of selection and rehearsal usually occurred at or soon after the event itself. Some archival memories were free-floating episodes, but most were arranged in a fixed sequence. They might be unique happenings, such as the death of a buddy, or the initial occurrence of some significant routine, such as basic training or the first sound of gunfire. Either way, they usually derive from events that are highly emotional and are regarded as turning points in life. They are central to our idea of who we are and what our life has signified. Archival memory is the core of every person's unwritten autobiography.

But the Hoffmans also revealed the fallibility of memory. Some important events could not be remembered at all, in one case even with the cue of a photo showing that Howard had been there. Although his mental archive was arranged in sequence, it was often weak about exact time and place. And there was a tendency to telescope events. Some brief but vivid memories such as the battle of

Cassino were recalled in great detail, whereas the more routine but longer period of six months he spent in the occupation of Germany figured very little. We are back again with the conjunction of remembering and forgetting. Although Howard Hoffman did not visit wartime Britain, the lessons of his story can be used to understand better the memories of GIs who served there. Of particular importance are the polarities between combat and occupation, between the notable and the routine.

"I live D-Day a little bit every day," confessed Felix Branham, a 29er, in September 1993. "I don't let it bother me that much, but . . ." In 1990, Charles Cawthon, a company commander in the 29th on Omaha Beach, reckoned that "the image of no one—loved, admired, or disliked—remains more vivid" than the "white face, staring eyes, and open mouth of the first soldier I witnessed struck in battle." Yet even a unique day like 6 June 1944 leaves only fragments. Cawthon admitted that, although that morning was etched forever in his memory, "the afternoon and night of D-day are a tapestry in which scenes emerge from a generally gray background and then fade or run together, or change position until it is difficult to fix them in time and place." These men had spent twenty months in England waiting for war, but their memories, like their unit records, are fuller and more vivid after 6 June 1944 than before. Recollections of England are shadowy, more episodic. What sticks, to borrow the Hoffman's framework, are dramatic moments, such as the *Queen Mary* slicing an English cruiser in two on the transatlantic crossing, or vignettes of what became routine, such as route marches around Stonehenge or training on desolate Dartmoor.[14]

The airmen are a somewhat different case—for most of them England *was* a combat theatre. To revisit their old bases causes pain that is absent for ex-GIs from Army ground units. When John Comer returned to his first airfield at Ridgewell, Essex, in 1972, he found that little was left. The site had reverted to arable land and two old hangars were used for farm machinery. In a fine drizzle he stood remembering men with whom he flew his early missions. "During those months together we formed bonds of friendship I have never experienced before or since." Many of those men did not return. "My wife and two close friends were with me but they could not participate in my nostalgia. Nor did they try. To me, it represented the most intensely lived year of my life. To me this was ground as hallowed as Lincoln's Gettysburg."[15]

For many, the emotion is more intense because so little now remains. As Hiram Drache, once of the 457th Bomb Group, neared his old base at Glatton, south of Peterborough, his "heart began to throb." Catching sight from the car of old landmarks such as the water tower and church spire, "it seemed like nothing had changed, but within a few minutes I realized that . . . except for the main runway, it was all gone." In his mind's eye the squadron office was still clear. He could visualize the huts where he and his friends had lived. But now there was only an open field. He kicked the grass, looked up among the trees, "in search of one small token of those days." There was nothing. "I was speechless and hurt to realize that except for those who actually lived there, few will know . . . what was once there." Such present desolation seems an affront to the fullness of memory. It was "like the place existed only in fiction," said one returning veteran. "But," he added defiantly, "I was really there."[16]

The airmen's war memories are much more rooted in England than those of other GIs. But even for them, it is the missions that were etched so clearly. What happened between is much dimmer. Most recollections centre on the base itself. As with other GIs, the pubs, the local people, even the superbenders in London are all more of a blur. And these are the memories of aircrew, who, Harry Crosby noted, are the most enthusiastic participants in reunions and return visits. "The forgetting was done by the people who didn't think they'd done any-thing that mattered. The ground echelons—the so-called paddlefeet—had terrible inferiority complexes." Crosby reckoned that people tend to remember the triumphs: "if we weren't heroic, that's what we put behind." This fits with the idea of archival memory as reinforcement of one's own self-image.[17]

As Crosby and other former flyboys will testify, they were totally reliant on the dedication and skill of their paddlefeet. But the low self-esteem of many service personnel, on air bases or supporting the Army, may be a further reason for the haziness of their memories of Britain. They were not fighting, life was mostly boring routine, and many did not think they were doing anything significant. This meant fewer memories worth preserving for the archives.

For service personnel, as for combat GIs and aircrew, what sticks in mind most are the people. Most GIs had close friends during the war and their stories of Britain revolve to a large extent around other GIs. Not entirely, however. There are often warm memories of British families who extended hospitality. In particular, most can recall British girlfriends, often with fading black-and-white photos as mementos. The "oversexed" stereotype, to some extent, stems from the bias of their own reminiscing.

What, then, *do* GIs tend to remember about wartime Britain? As always, we must take account of the number and diversity of those involved. But, speaking broadly, I believe that three observations may be made. First, those memories are often partial, both in extent and clarity. Service in Britain was boring routine for most GIs. They tend to recall occasional dramas, interesting people, leisure on leave or in pubs, rather than the daily drudgery of keeping occupied as an army of occupation. Second, those memories of Britain tend to assume a rosy hue. This is not to deny that most GIs have some bad stories to tell. But the mud, the rain, the weak beer, the rip-offs, even the brussels sprouts have lost their sour taste. They are recollected with amusement rather than with irritation. For combat troops, Britain was the calm before (or after) the storm, standing in stark contrast with war on the Continent. For the aircrews that duality was all the more powerful because it was experienced every day they flew a mission. Even for service troops, the negatives have been filtered away. And that is because, third, these are the memories of youth. I don't mean just inevitable nostalgia for days when one was fit, young, and hopeful. There is also a deeper recognition, that good or bad, life burned in the war years with a peculiar, unrepeated, yet unforgettable intensity. After 1945, most fled from its heat. In later years they are drawn back, like moths to a candle. The fascination and the poignancy are summed up by Richard M. Prendergast—in war a GI in the 106th Infantry Division smashed in the Bulge after a few weeks in Britain, in peace a successful Chicago businessman. "At that young age, we hit the climax. . . . We shot the last act in the first reel."[18]

There are Brits, too, who share something of that feeling. For many women who were then in their teens and twenties, the war years stand out as a time of emancipation, between prewar parental restraints and postwar marital domesticity. In the ATS, the Land Army, or the munitions factories they enjoyed unprecedented income and independence. Of course, wartime also meant tedium, privations, and destruction. Most can recall vividly their own brushes with death in the Blitz or during the V-bomb attacks. But, for many, the negatives were relieved by the American presence. As stressed earlier (chapter 16), this is not merely the memory of romances and affairs. It is also testimony to youth—to the energy, fun, and dancing that were associated with the GIs. For Margaret Whiting, then a teenager in Cambridge, they still evoke a warm glow forty years later. "To go to one of their bases was absolutely fantastic because there was no shortage of anything. Each base was a little America, with plenty of food and drink and fantastic great iced cakes. Every night you could, you were out. All the girls were doing it. It was a lovely atmosphere." In the wistful words of one Suffolk woman: "I still remember the Yanks almost more than I do the war."[19]

On others, too, the Yanks left an indelible impression. There were many little boys in 1941–45 who begged gum or watched, riveted, as the "Forts" and Liberators took wing. For most it was a passing fad, but in some it developed into a deep and abiding fascination. In 1943 Roger Freeman was an "aeroplane-mad youth" in wartime Suffolk, ecstatic when an American air base was carved out of farmland a mile from his home. In later life he became the doyen of 8th Air Force historians, to whose meticulous studies all others are indebted. Mike Harvey's passion developed postwar, as a construction contractor engaged in the demolition of wartime runways and their return to farmland. In the late 1960s he worked at Thorpe Abbotts. Looking down from the crumbling control tower he mused about its past, and when the 100th Bomb Group Association purchased the tower and surrounding buildings in 1977, Mike and other British volunteers restored them and created a vivid museum, attracting thousands of visitors each year.[20]

For Ken Small, a submerged Sherman tank became a similar obsession. He was a Yorkshireman who bought a guest house at Slapton Sands in 1968. Distressed to learn of Exercise Tiger in April 1944, when hundreds of GIs were killed in the German E-boat attack, he became determined to purchase and raise the tank, rusting in sixty feet of water offshore. His single-minded, decade-long battle against military bureaucrats in Whitehall and Washington was finally successful, though at the cost of Small's marriage. In 1984 a memorial area was established by the beach road, with the tank at its centre, to commemorate the GIs who died practicing for war.[21]

There are other Brits for whom the past is even more personal. It was only in the summer of 1993 that Jane _____ discovered that she had *two* fathers in the Normandy invasion. One was the British soldier who, for years, Jane believed was her dad; the other was an American GI who, she learned at age forty-eight, was in fact her natural father. The truth only came out after her mother's death, when an aging aunt gave her the bare bones of the story. In the 1930s Jane's parents had lived in London. To escape the air raids, her mother had been evacuated down to the West Country with her two children. While living and working there, she met this GI, fell deeply in love, and Jane was conceived just before his unit left for Normandy. Her British husband crossed the Channel at the same time with his own unit. While he was fighting in Holland that winter, his wife wrote asking for a divorce. She said she wanted to take all her children to the United States. On the advice of friends, her husband told her to wait until he got home and then they would sort things out. By the time he returned, the idea had been dropped and Jane's birth certificate carried his name as father. This remained the family story until Jane's mother died.

Although Jane had entertained occasional suspicions, the true story came as a shock. Most of all she resented the concealment—everybody in the family knew, it seemed, except herself. "We wanted to spare you," said her British father, who, she admitted, had been a "wonderful" parent. But she did not wish to be spared. Within weeks she began a quest for the facts about her father. Was he still alive? If so, could she locate him fifty years later? Or had he died on the Continent? That might explain her mother's change of heart in 1944–45. For Jane the research was of more than academic interest. "I want my identity," she said simply.[22]

In 1993 Jane was only just starting down a path that many others had followed before her. Shirley McGlade, the end of whose odyssey was mentioned at the beginning of this chapter, had lived with the lack of her American father all her life. As a child, she was told that he had been a brave GI who had married her mother and had then been killed in the Normandy invasion. When she was five, her mother married a divorcé who proved a brutal stepfather. To feed her own daydreams, and fob off her classmates, Shirley found a face she liked in the *Picturegoer* annual, clipped it out, and stuck it in a plastic wallet. Movie star Jeff Chandler became Dad, at least to satisfy the kids in the playground. Despite mysterious outbursts at times from her stepfather about a "bloody Yank's leftovers," this fiction survived until the age of eleven. Then Shirley saw her birth certificate with the blank where her father's name should have been. At fifteen she moved out—home was too grim to bear—and was soon pregnant. Fortunately, history did not repeat itself. Her boyfriend became a loyal and supportive husband.

For some years her new family was all consuming. It was only when she discovered from her seven-year-old son that D-Day had occurred in June 1944, and not a year later as she had thought, that she dragged the truth out of her mother. Her father had not died heroically a few months before her birth; he had simply disappeared. Attempts to locate Jack Crowley through official channels met with obfuscation. The Pentagon claimed that relevant records could not be released because of privacy legislation. (One suspects that an additional, undeclared reason was to cover the truth about U.S. Army marriage policy. We saw in chapters 13 and 16 that American officers frequently separated GIs and their British lovers, even if the latter were pregnant, and that this contributed to the rise in illegitimate births during the war.) It was not until the mid-1980s, helped by the media, that Shirley McGlade finally found her dad.[23]

Jane and Shirley are not lone stories. Transatlantic Children's Enterprise (TRACE), founded by former war bride Pamela Winfield in 1986, has helped nearly five hundred GI children. Shirley McGlade set up her own group, War Babes. With the aid of the Public Citizen Litigation Group, a civil liberties lobby in Washington, it even took the U.S. government to court in the late 1980s and secured significant concessions in official practice. Henceforth a designated contact person at the National Personnel Records Center in St. Louis would release details of the city and state in which the ex-GI lived. Had this information been available to Shirley McGlade, she might have found her father in fourteen weeks rather than the fourteen years it actually took.[24]

In Shirley's case the search ended happily. Often GIs, after initial shock and embarrassment, have been pleased to fill in this part of their own past. In some cases, veterans have initiated the contacts themselves. Walter Comer, a widower from Philadelphia, was a black GI in Britain during the war who returned to Britain in May 1992 to seek the daughter he fathered a half-century before. He had her baby photo but had lost contact with her mother after his return to the States. "Maybe they are both dead by now," he said, "maybe they wouldn't want to see me even if I could find them. But I wouldn't feel right if I didn't try because I keep thinking, maybe they could use my help."[25]

The search does not always have a happy ending. It was not until 1988 that Virginia Sims finally prised the name of her GI father out of her mother and tracked him down via the Alabama driver's licence bureau. By then, she discovered, James W. Delmar had been dead for two years. Another example is Howard B. who was brought up in Nottinghamshire by his grandmother. It was many years before he found out that "Auntie" was actually his mother. After finally obtaining his GI father's name from wartime letters, and with the help of TRACE, he went through endless American telephone directories, writing letters to likely names. Eventually he tracked his father down in Colorado, but, after some friendly phone conversations and the promise of letters, the man changed his phone number and became "unlisted." Even so, the quest was not wasted. "It gave me a great feeling," wrote Howard, "peace of mind, knowing I have a father, not just an image, even if he is out of reach." Likewise, it helped David E. to discover in his forties, after a traumatic childhood with his stepfather, that he was in fact the son of a legendary B-17 pilot who had died in a crash in February 1944. His mother had idolized the American as a teenager and remained faithful to his memory over the years.[26]

★ ★ ★

Memory lives on, above all, at the memorials. Every year 1.5 million visitors tour the Normandy American Cemetery at Colleville, on the bluffs above Omaha Beach. Two million paid their respects in the fortieth anniversary year of 1984. The 9,386 war dead buried there range from the anonymous to the famous: from 307 "unknown" graves to the remains of Gen. Lesley J. McNair, trainer of the wartime Army, who was killed by "friendly fire" outside St.-Lô. Thousands of these men waited for war in Britain at Tidworth, Dartmoor, or Slapton Sands. In the United Kingdom itself, the official resting place is the American Cemetery at Madingley, near Cambridge, where the university donated thirty acres, looking out over the East Anglian farmland. The cemetery was established on 7 December 1943, the second anniversary of Pearl Harbor, though its landscaping was not completed for more than a decade. At Madingley 3,811 wartime GIs are buried in seven concentric rows fanning out down the hill. The majority are airmen who served in East Anglia, and on a clear day one of their wartime landmarks, the tower of Ely Cathedral, can be discerned sixteen miles away to the northeast. Not all these men were "war heroes," though. Some died from illness, others from motor crashes or accidents during training—reminders of the "routineness" of much of the American occupation of Britain.

Elsewhere stand other memorials: a stained-glass window in the cathedral at Lichfield, or a playground presented by GIs to the village of Freckleton in Lancashire to commemorate a tragic air crash. Across East Anglia, the vanished air bases are recalled in roadside plaques as well as evocative museums such as Thorpe Abbotts or Framlingham. Norwich Central Library contains a memorial library, established by members of the 2nd Air Division as a continuing witness to comrades who did not survive. The Swan in Lavenham, Suffolk, an old GI haunt, cherishes a picture of Gen. Frederick Castle, lost while leading the biggest 8th Air Force mission to date on Christmas Eve 1944. And along Slapton Sands in Devon stand two memorials—an obelisk erected by the U.S. government in 1954 to thank the British villagers who were evicted and Ken Small's Sherman tank, a 1984 memorial to the forgotten GI dead of exercise Tiger.

For the survivors of these years, such silent memorials have unquestioned eloquence. But they speak also to younger generations, evoking what G. M. Trevelyan called the "poetry" of history. "The dead were and are not. Their place knows them no more and is ours today. Yet they were once as real as we, and we shall to-morrow be shadows like them." That is the message of any war memorial. Those to the GIs in

Britain have the added poignancy of young men living life to the full as they waited for war.[27]

February 1993. Mid-winter hangs heavy on Madingley Cemetery. Looking up the hill, white crosses (and occasional Stars of David) blur into grey mist and frosted grass. Yet the eye is caught by a floral tribute against one of the crosses—an anniversary remembrance from a British woman for a young American flyer who was killed in February 1944. Yellow and deep red it stands, at once memorial to one man and symbol of the GIs and the British in their wartime moment—a splash of colour in a bleached landscape, an irregular shape amid the strict geometry, an exclamation of life to punctuate the sentence of death. And on it a note:

> All my love
>   As Always.
> And thank you, Michael.
>   Mary.

Appendix 1:
U.S. Combat Divisions in the United Kingdom

★ ★ ★

NOTE: DATES AND LOCATIONS ARE FOR THE DIVISIONAL COMMAND POST. ELEMENTS of the division often arrived/departed over a longer period and were quartered over a wide area. Dates are by day, month, year. AB = Airborne Division; AR = Armored Division.

Division	Arrive UK	Depart UK	Main Divisional Command Posts
34	26/1/42	12/42	Omagh, Northern Ireland (NI)
1AR	16/5/42	25/11/42	Castlewellan, NI
1	7/8/42	22/10/42	Tidworth, Wiltshire
	7/11/43	6/6/44	Blandford, Dorset
29	11/10/42	6/6/44	Tidworth, Wiltshire (to 27/5/43); Tavistock, Devon
5	9/8/43	9/7/44	Tidworth, Wiltshire (to 22/10/43); Bryansford, NI
3AR	15/9/43	25/6/44	Bruton, Somerset
101AB	15/9/43	6/6/44	Newbury, Berkshire
	15/7/44	17/9/44	Newbury, Berkshire
28	18/10/43	24/7/44	Tenby, Pembroke (to 15/4/44); Chiseldon, Wiltshire
2	19/10/43	7/6/44	Armagh, NI (to 19/4/44); Tenby, Pembroke (to 15/5/44); St. Donat's Castle, Glamorgan
2AR	24/11/43	9/6/44	Tidworth, Wiltshire
9	27/11/43	10/6/44	Winchester, Hampshire
82AB	9/12/43	6/6/44	Castle Dawson, NI (to 14/2/44); Braunstone Park, Leicester
	13/7/44	17/9/44	Braunstone Park, Leicester
8	15/12/43	30/6/44	Belfast, NI (to 26/1/44); Knockmore, NI (to 1/3/44); Omagh, NI

Division	Arrive UK	Depart UK	Main Divisional Command Posts
4AR	8/1/44	13/7/44	Chippenham, Wiltshire
4	28/1/44	6/6/44	Tiverton, Devon (to 15/5/44); Southbrent, Devon
30	22/2/44	14/6/44	Chichester, Sussex (to 1/4/44); Chesham, Buckinghamshire
5AR	23/2/44	23/7/44	Chiseldon, Wiltshire (to 15/4/44); Ogbourne St. George, Wiltshire (but Division in Devon and Cornwall)
6AR	25/2/44	19/7/44	Batsford, Oxfordshire
90	5/4/44	8/6/44	Birmingham, Warwickshire (K. Edward's School); Cardiff, Glamorgan (from 31/5/44)
79	17/4/44	14/6/44	Pettypool Hall, Cheshire; Tiverton, Devon (from 1/6/44)
83	19/4/44	25/6/44	Keele Hall, Staffordshire; Southampton, Hampshire (from 17/6/44)
35	1/5/44	8/7/44	Okehampton, Devon (to 31/5/44); Tavistock, Devon
7AR	13/6/44	7/8/44	Tidworth, Wiltshire
80	13/6/44	3/8/44	Pettypool Hall, Cheshire (most of Division arrived 7/7/44); Salisbury, Wiltshire (from 31/7/44)
9AR	31/7/44	25/9/44	Tidworth, Wiltshire (most of Division arrived 28/8/44)
94	11/8/44	8/9/44	Chippenham, Wiltshire
95	-17/8/44	15/9/44	Winchester, Hampshire
17AB	25/8/44	24/12/44	Chiseldon, Wiltshire
84	1/10/44	1/11/44	Winchester, Hampshire
12AR	2/10/44	17/11/44	Tidworth, Wiltshire
11AR	5/10/44	3/12/44	Warminster, Wiltshire
99	10/10/44	9/11/44	Blandford, Dorset
75	20/10/44	13/12/44	Tenby, Pembroke
87	22/10/44	3/12/44	Knutsford, Cheshire (most of Division arrived 13/11/44)
78	25/10/44	22/11/44	Bournemouth, Dorset
106	1/11/44	26/11/44	Batsford Park, Oxfordshire
8AR	21/11/44	4/1/45	Tidworth, Wiltshire
66	26/11/44	26/12/44	Dorchester, Dorset
69	13/12/44	26/1/45	Winchester, Hampshire
76	21/12/44	17/1/45	Bournemouth, Dorset

Source: *ETO Order of Battle: Divisions* (TS. Paris, 1945), copy in MHI Library, supplemented by Divisional histories.

Appendix 2: Abbreviations

★ ★ ★

AA	Antiaircraft
AAC	Army Air Corps (U.S.)
AAF	Army Air Forces (U.S.)
AARC	Anglo-American Relations Conference/Committee
AB	Airborne Division
ABCA	Army Bureau of Current Affairs (UK)
AEF	American Expeditionary Force
AFHQ	Allied Force Headquarters (Mediterranean)
AFLD	American Forces Liaison Division (MOI)
AFN	American Forces [Radio] Network
AFS	*Armed Forces and Society*
AG	Adjutant General
AGCT	Army General Classification Tests (U.S.)
AGF	Army Ground Forces (U.S.)
AHR	*American Historical Review*
AIPO	American Institute of Public Opinion
AJS	*American Journal of Sociology*
AR	Armored Division
ARC	American Red Cross
AS	Samuel A. Stouffer, et al., *The American Soldier*, (2 vols., Princeton, NJ, 1949).
ASF	Army Service Forces (U.S.); successor to SOS.
ATS	Auxiliary Territorial Service (UK, women)
AWC	U.S. Army War College
AWOL	Absent without leave
BALB	British-American Liaison Board
BBC	British Broadcasting Corporation

BBCWAC	BBC Written Archives Centre, Caversham Park, Reading
BC	Bomber Command
BEF	British Expeditionary Force, France
BIPO	British Institute of Public Opinion (Gallup polls)
BS	Base Section
BTNI	British Troops in Northern Ireland
CAB	Cabinet (UK)
Calder	Angus Calder, *The People's War: Britain, 1939–1945* (pbk. ed., London, 1971).
CBO	Anglo-American Combined Bomber Offensive
CBS	Columbia Broadcasting System
C&C	Wesley F. Craven and James L. Cate, *The Army Air Forces in World War II* (7 vols., Chicago, 1948–58).
CCC	Civilian Conservation Corps (New Deal program)
CCS	Combined Chiefs of Staff
CG	Commanding General
C-in-C	Commander in Chief
CIGS	Chief of the Imperial General Staff (UK)
CO	Commanding Officer
CO	Colonial Office (UK)
ComZ	Communications Zone (ETO ASF in 1944–45)
COS	Chiefs of Staff (UK)
C-R	Warren F. Kimball, ed., *Churchill and Roosevelt: The Complete Correspondence* (3 vols., Princeton, NJ, 1984).
CSW	Combat Support Wing (AAF)
DD	Duplex-drive amphibious tanks
D-Day	Allied landings in Normandy, 6 June 1944.
DDEL	Dwight D. Eisenhower Library, Abilene, Kansas
Desp.	Despatch
DR	Defence Regulations (UK)
ED	Board of Education (UK)
EP	Alfred D. Chandler, Jr., ed., *The Papers of Dwight David Eisenhower: The War Years* (5 vols., Baltimore, 1970).
ETOUSA	European Theater of Operations, U.S. Army (often ETO)
FCH	Field Censor, Home
FDRL	Franklin D. Roosevelt Library, Hyde Park, New York
FO	Foreign Office (UK)
FRUS	U.S. Department of State, *Foreign Relations of the United States* (Washington, DC, 1861–).
FUSA	First U.S. Army

GB	Great Britain
GCML	George C. Marshall Research Library, Lexington, Virginia
GCMP	Larry I. Bland and Sharon Ritenour Stevens, eds., *The Papers of George Catlett Marshall* (3 vols. to date, Baltimore, 1981–91).
GHQ	General Headquarters
GI	Government Issue
Gilbert	Martin Gilbert, *Road to Victory: Winston S. Churchill, 1941–1945* (London, 1986).
GNP	Gross National Product
GOC	General Officer Commanding
GPO	Government Printing Office, Washington, D.C.
G-1	Asst. Chief of Staff for personnel (U.S.)
G-2	Asst. Chief of Staff for intelligence (U.S.)
G-3	Asst. Chief of Staff for operations (U.S.)
G-4	Asst. Chief of Staff for supply (U.S.)
G-5	Asst. Chief of Staff for civil affairs (U.S.)
HC	House of Commons, *Debates*, 5th series.
HI	Home Intelligence
HJFRT	*Historical Journal of Film, Radio and Television*
HMG	His Majesty's Government (UK)
HQ	Headquarters
HSTL	Harry S. Truman Library, Independence, Missouri
IG	Inspector General
IHR	*International History Review*
Ind	Indorsement
INF	MOI papers
INS	U.S. Immigration and Naturalization Service
IRA	Irish Republican Army
IWM	Imperial War Museum, London
JA	Judge Advocate
JAG	Judge Advocate General
JAH	*Journal of American History*
JAS	*Journal of American Studies*
JCS	Joint Chiefs of Staff (U.S.)
JEH	*Journal of Economic History*
JFH	*Journal of Family History*
JMH	*Journal of Military History*
JSS	*Journal of Strategic Studies*
KCL	Liddell Hart Centre for Military Archives, King's College, London

King	William Armstrong ed., *With Malice Toward None: A War Diary by Cecil H. King* (London, 1970).
KP	Kitchen Police
LAB	Ministry of Labour (UK)
LC	Library of Congress, Washington, D.C.
LCC	London County Council
LCI	Landing Craft, Infantry
LCP	League of Coloured Persons (UK)
LCT	Landing Craft, Tank
LCVP	Landing Craft, Vehicle and Personnel
LSI	Landing Ship, Infantry
LST	Landing Ship, Tank
MA	*Military Affairs*
M&D	B. R. Mitchell, with Phyllis Deane, *Abstract of British Historical Statistics* (Cambridge, 1962).
MGM	Metro-Goldwyn-Mayer
MHI	U.S. Army Military History Institute, Carlisle, Pennsylvania
MI	Larry I. Bland, ed., *George C. Marshall Interviews and Reminiscences for Forrest C. Pogue* (2nd ed., Lexington, VA, 1991).
M-O	Mass-Observation
MOI	Ministry of Information (UK)
MP	Member of Parliament (UK)
MP	Military Police (U.S.)
MR	Map Room papers (FDRL)
M&S	Maurice Matloff and Edwin M. Snell, *Strategic Planning for Coalition Warfare, 1941–1942* (Washington, DC, 1953).
NA	National Archives, Washington, D.C.
NAACP	National Association for the Advancement of Colored People (U.S.)
NAC	National Archives of Canada, Ottawa
NCO	Noncommissioned Officer (noncom in U.S.)
NHC	Naval Historical Center, Navy Yard, Washington, D.C.
NI	Northern Ireland
OAFH	Office of Air Force History, Bolling AFB, D.C.
OCS	Officer Candidate School
OPD	Operations Division, U.S. War Department
Orwell	Sonia Orwell and Ian Angus, eds., *The Collected Essays, Journalism and Letters of George Orwell*, vols. 2 and 3 (London, 1968).
OSS	Office of Strategic Services (U.S.)
OWI	Office of War Information (U.S.)

PM	Provost Marshal
PMG	Provost Marshal General
Pogue	Forrest C. Pogue, *George C. Marshall* (4 vols., New York, 1963–86).
POW	Prisoner of War
PPF	President's Personal Files (FDRL)
PREM	Prime Minister's Files (PRO)
PreMed	U.S. Army Medical Depart., *Preventive Medicine in World War II*, vol. 5 and vol. 8 (Washington, DC, 1960 and 1976).
PRO	Public Record Office, London
PRONI	Public Record Office, Northern Ireland
PSF	President's Secretary's File (FDRL)
PX	Post Exchange (U.S.)
QMG	Quartermaster General (WO)
RAF	Royal Air Force
RCAF	Royal Canadian Air Force
RCT	Regimental Combat Team
RG	Record Group (NA and NAC)
RIO	Regional Information Officer (MOI)
RN	Royal Navy
Rupp.	Roland G. Ruppenthal, *Logistical Support of the Armies* (2 vols., Washington, D.C., 1953–59)
SAC	Supreme Allied Commander
SHAEF	Supreme Headquarters, Allied Expeditionary Force (Northwest Europe)
SOS	Services of Supply, U.S. Army
SPOBS	U.S. Army Special Observer Group in London (1941–42)
TC	U.S. Army Transportation Corps
Terkel	Studs Terkel, *"The Good War": An Oral History of World War Two* (London, 1985)
TS	Typescript
TUSA	Third U.S. Army
UK	United Kingdom of Great Britain and Northern Ireland
UN	United Nations
UNO	University of New Orleans, Eisenhower Center
USAFBI	United States Army Forces in the British Isles
USFET	United States Forces, European Theater
USN	U.S. Navy
USSTAF	U.S. Strategic Air Forces

VD	Venereal Disease
VE Day	Victory in Europe Day, 8 May 1945 (Also known as VD Day)
VJ Day	Victory over Japan Day, 15 August 1945
V-1	German flying bombs
V-2	German long-range rockets
WAAC	Women's Army Auxiliary Corps (predecessor of WAC)
WAC	Women's Army Corps (U.S.)
WLA	Women's Land Army (UK)
WM	War Cabinet minutes (UK)
WO	War Office
WP	War Cabinet memoranda (UK)
WSC	Winston S. Churchill, *The Second World War* (6 vols., London, 1948–54).
WVS	Women's Voluntary Service (UK)

Appendix 3: Code Names

★ ★ ★

Anvil	Original name for 1944 landings in southern France.
Arcadia	First Roosevelt-Churchill Washington conference (12/41–1/42).
Beaver	Slapton Sands exercise for Neptune (end 3/44).
Bodyguard	Original name of deception plan for Overlord (later Fortitude).
Bolero	Buildup of U.S. forces in United Kingdom.
Cobra	U.S. breakout near St.-Lô (end 7/44).
Dragoon	Allied landings in southern France (8/44).
Duck	Slapton Sands exercises for Neptune (1–2/44).
Fabius	Six rehearsal exercises for Neptune (5/44).
Fortitude	Deception plan for Overlord suggesting main attack on Pas de Calais.
Fox	Slapton Sands exercise for Neptune (3/44).
Gold	Western British beach on D-Day.
Gymnast	Early plans for invading French Northwest Africa (1941–42).
Jubilee	Dieppe raid (19 August 1942).
Juno	The Canadian beach on D-Day.
Magnet	Movement of U.S. forces into Northern Ireland (1/42).
Market Garden	Allied land/paratroop operation in Netherlands to establish bridgehead across Rhine (9/44).
Neptune	Assault phase of Overlord (6/44).
Omaha	Eastern U.S. beach on D-Day (1st/29th Divisions).
Overlord	Establishment of Allied "lodgement" in France (6–8/44).
Pointblank	Combined bomber offensive from UK (43–44).
Rhumba	Rundown of American presence in UK (44–45).
Roundup	Plan for major Allied invasion of France in 1943.

Rutter   Original name for Dieppe raid (later Jubilee).
Sledgehammer   Plan for limited invasion of France in 1942.
Sword   Eastern British beach on D-Day.
Symbol   Roosevelt-Churchill conference in Casablanca (1/43).
Torch   Allied invasion of French Northwest Africa (11/42).
Trident   Roosevelt-Churchill conference in Washington (5/43).
Utah   Western U.S. beach on D-Day (4th Division).

Essay on Sources

★　★　★

A COMPREHENSIVE BIBLIOGRAPHICAL LIST WOULD FURTHER LENGTHEN AN ALREADY substantial book, while providing little guidance for researchers. What follows is therefore a general indication of the major archives and volumes that I have found especially useful. The endnotes for each chapter provide specific citations. Abbreviations are indicated in parentheses (see also Appendix 2).

DOCUMENTS: UNITED STATES

The starting point is the National Archives (NA) in Washington, D.C. Anyone working there after 1994 will benefit from the consolidation of most relevant documents in the new "Archives II" complex at College Park, Maryland, which brings together collections previously housed in the main building downtown on Pennsylvania Avenue and in the Washington National Records Center in Suitland, Maryland.

The core collection is that of the U.S. Army's European Theater of Operations (ETO) in Record Group (RG) 332. The unpublished "Administrative History" of ETO and the related Administrative History Files (ETO Adm) synthesize much valuable material, but the raw files of the ETO's subordinate sections are also essential, particularly those of the Adjutant General (AG). RG 330, entry 94, contains an invaluable set of opinion polls of GIs in Britain—a project set in motion by Ike in 1942. Also useful is RG 331, the records of the Supreme Headquarters, Allied Expeditionary Force (SHAEF) in 1944–45. Additional material can be found in various War Department collections, such as RG 107 (Assistant Secretary of War), RG 165 and 319 (General and Special Staffs), RG 247 (Chaplains), and RG 338 (Army commands). RG 407 includes the records of subordinate units, particularly corps and divisions, though these are limited in quantity and quality before D-Day. All this material is classified under decimal filing systems, usually that of the War Department itself. Thus 250.1 deals with morale, 291.1 with marriages, 685 with training areas, and so on.

The National Archives also hold State Department records. Its main decimal file in RG 59 was of limited use for this project, but the records of overseas posts in RG 84 contained numerous detailed reports from U.S. consuls around Britain about the local conditions. The "post" files for London, Manchester, Birmingham, and Belfast are particularly rich. There is also a good deal in the papers of the London outpost of the Office of War Information (OWI) in RG 208, and some snippets in the RG 181 collection of naval districts and shore establishments. RG 200 contains the voluminous records of the American Red Cross—a very important source for Army welfare activities in Britain. RG 120 contains comparative material on the U.S. Army in Britain, 1917–19.

In studying the Army Air Force I relied on the decimal files held by the Office of Air Force History (OAFH) at Bolling Air Force Base (AFB) on the southeast of Washington. These are microfilms of the originals at Maxwell AFB in Alabama. Case 500 on the European Theater was particularly important. Bolling also has private diaries and letters of various airmen, as does the Library of Congress (LC). At the latter, the papers of Generals Ira C. Eaker and Carl Spaatz were especially useful. LC, of course, holds an enormous number of nonmilitary manuscript collections. Of these I benefited particularly from the papers of anthropologist Margaret Mead and the National Association for the Advancement of Colored People (NAACP). At the Naval Historical Center, Washington Navy Yard (NHC), the papers of Admiral Harold R. Stark and the Administrative History of U.S. Naval Forces Europe were helpful. At the Immigration and Naturalization Service (INS) Library I found (at last!) statistical material on war brides.

Beyond the Beltway, I have spent weeks over the years at the U.S. Army Military History Institute (MHI) at Carlisle Barracks, Pennsylvania. The Archives there house an ever-growing number of collections of retired officers and men, as well as useful oral histories. These helped flesh out the official documents. I also made use of MHI's extensive questionnaires that it encourages veterans to fill in about their military careers. Several thousand have been returned for World War Two alone. At the other end of the building the MHI Library was essential, providing, on open stacks, a unique collection of books, journals, and official documents, ranging from unit histories to the Observers Reports on ETO in 1944–45. The latter are available in RG 332 but can be consulted much more easily at MHI.

Another essential repository was the Dwight D. Eisenhower Library (DDEL) in the president's hometown of Abilene, Kansas. Despite the excellent published series of Eisenhower papers, there is still much unused material in his prepresidential 1916/1952 file (16/52). Equally, there is far more in the diary and papers of his aide Harry C. Butcher than appeared in the expurgated (and doctored) publication, *My Three Years with Eisenhower* (New York, 1946). The DDEL also contains the papers of many of Ike's military colleagues. Most yielded only marginalia, but the Norman Cota collection and the microfilm of

Jacob Devers's papers were more useful. In addition, the DDEL (like MHI) has been soliciting letters and unpublished memoirs from ordinary GIs, and these revealed many vignettes of "real life."

The other significant presidential library for my purposes was the Franklin D. Roosevelt Library at Hyde Park, New York, next to the old family home on bluffs above the Hudson River. Although FDR delegated most GI-related problems to the Army, useful evidence is scattered through the Map Room (MR) papers, the President's Secretary's File (PSF), the President's Personal File (PPF), and the Official File (OF). Eleanor Roosevelt took a keen interest in the welfare of GIs, and the diary of her visit to Britain in the autumn of 1942 is very useful. The papers of Ambassador John G. Winant and presidential confidant Harry L. Hopkins were also helpful.

At the George C. Marshall Library in Lexington, Virginia, the general's own Pentagon Office files provide rich pickings, especially for the later part of the war, which the excellent published edition of Marshall Papers has not yet reached. Also valuable were microfilm and photocopies of material from the War Department records that Forrest C. Pogue accumulated for his biography of Marshall. Thanks to these, what would take hours to track down in Washington can be located in minutes in Lexington. The photo collection is also especially well indexed. At nearby Staunton, Virginia, the 116th Infantry Regiment (part of the 29th Division) has an interesting museum and archive.

In the Eisenhower Center at the University of New Orleans, Professor Stephen Ambrose and his colleagues have accumulated an enormous collection of transcripts from taped recollections by GIs (and also some by British and Canadian soldiers). Although these concentrate on D-Day, they do contain many revealing insights into life in Britain.

A few other archives should be mentioned. At the Hoover Institution in Stanford, California, there were a number of small collections, particularly relating to Ulster, as well as the memoirs of Gen. J.C.H. Lee. The diary of Patton's aide Robert S. Allen at the Wisconsin State Historical Society in Madison provided some snippets, as did that of diplomat William Phillips in the Houghton Library at Harvard.

DOCUMENTS: UNITED KINGDOM

Here the nodal point is the Public Record Office at Kew. Although the Ministry of Information (MOI) had primary responsibility for arranging hospitality for GIs, most of its working papers on American Forces Liaison have apparently been destroyed, leaving only some in-house histories and peripheral material in INF 1/327. A few other MOI files are useful, notably the fascinating weekly home intelligence reports in INF 1/292. Similar lacunae exist in the War Office papers, although the origins and development of the interattachment scheme between the two armies is well documented in WO 32/10266–8 and in the morale committee papers in WO 163/161–2 and /222. There is also some material scattered in the Home Forces papers in WO 199. WO 219 contains copies of the SHAEF papers also available in RG 331 in the NA.

Because of these gaps, the Foreign Office General Political Correspondence (FO 371) provides the fullest indicator of governmental action (the FO being determined to keep tabs on anything foreign-related in Whitehall). Its extensive files for 1943–45 on American troops (1942 suffered badly from the weeders) contain copies of MOI and WO reports on public attitudes to GIs as well as policy material on hospitality arrangements. Postwar FO 371 files are useful on war brides and their dependents. There are also nuggets in Eden's private office papers in FO 954.

The other main PRO collection is that of the Cabinet Office. The War Cabinet minutes and memoranda (CAB 65 and CAB 66) record some top-level discussion, especially on black GIs in 1942. Of various cabinet committees, the Chiefs of Staff's Committee (CAB 79–80) and the Bolero panel in CAB 81/48–52 are important, and other useful CAB papers include those of the Lord President's Secretariat in CAB 123. The well-indexed prime minister's operational and confidential papers (PREM 3 and 4) contain some significant documents, as do those of the Chief of the Air Staff (AIR 8). The Home Office has suffered badly from the weeders, but important files remain in the "War" section of HO 45.

The other official archive I visited was the Public Record Office of Northern Ireland (PRONI) in Belfast, where the Cabinet Secretariat's civil defence files (CAB 9CD) are the most useful. The Imperial War Museum (IWM) in south London, like MHI in America, has accumulated an outstanding collection of private papers and unpublished memoirs, many by "ordinary" people, on which I have drawn frequently for colour and detail. In the extensive Liddell Hart Archive at King's College, London (KCL), the papers of Adam, Alanbrooke, and Ismay, as well as Liddell Hart himself, repaid study. There is much fascinating material in the Mass-Observation Archive at the University of Sussex, near Brighton (M-O), and in the BBC Written Archives Centre at Caversham Park, near Reading (BBCWAC). On a smaller scale, I also found material in the collections of Nancy and Waldorf Astor at Reading University, in Lord Halifax's Hickleton papers at the Borthwick Institute, York, and the Altrincham (Edward Grigg) papers at the Bodleian Library in Oxford. At the Churchill College Archive Centre in Cambridge, the wartime papers of P. J. Grigg and Churchill himself were useful—though the latter are mostly copies of material in the PREM files in the PRO, arranged by date rather than by topic.

DOCUMENTS: CANADA

As I stress in the book, the Canadians were the largest Allied contingent in Britain after the GIs (indeed they exceeded them until mid-1943). The National Archives of Canada (NAC) in Ottawa have a mass of material in Record Group (RG) 24. This throws light not only on the Canadians' problems (see chapter 9) but also on relations with GIs and with British troops and civilians. There are also additional insights in Mackenzie King's diary (available on microfilm).

BOOKS

Anyone studying the U.S. Army in World War Two must start with the series of official histories of that name (the so-called green books, now ninety in all), which were written by staff at the Center of Military History (CMH). They are mines of information on Army organization and training, as well as on individual campaigns. Roland G. Ruppenthal's first volume on *Logistical Support of the Armies* (1953) is the most detailed on Britain (abbreviated as Rupp.).

Although pathbreaking in their time, the green books were generally monographic military or organizational histories. Studies that address broader issues of war and society include Martin Van Creveld's comparison of the American and German armies, *Fighting Power* (1982), and, from a less critical standpoint, John Sloan Brown, *Draftee Division* (1986)—despite its pietas, a rare example of a unit history (on the 88th) that examines combat in the light of mobilization and training. Lee Kennett, *G.I.* (1987) offers an excellent overview of the social history of the American soldier during the war. Geoffrey Perret, *There's a War to Be Won* (1991) is an up-to-date history of the wartime Army, while Robert K. Griffith, Jr., *Men Wanted for the U.S. Army* (1982) provides the background on the interwar years. Samuel A. Stouffer, et al., *The American Soldier* (2 vols., 1949) remains essential (abbreviated as AS), even though the polls and the raw data on which it was based are now available in NA RG 330/94.

My thinking about soldiering in general has been influenced by classics such as John Keegan, *The Face of Battle* (1976); John English, *On Infantry* (1984); and Paul Fussell's acute, if cynical, *Wartime* (1989); as well as by John Ellis's compendious *World War II: The Sharp End* (2nd ed., 1990) and Brian Loring Villa's innovative and fascinating study *Unauthorized Action: Mountbatten and the Dieppe Raid* (1990). I have also benefited from Omer Bartov's extensive work, much of it summed up in *Hitler's Army* (1991), as well as that of Etienne Dejonghe on the German occupation of France—see for example, "Etre 'occupant' dans le Nord," *Revue du Nord*, 65 (1983), 707–45. For those wishing to look at the American occupation of other lands, the volumes on Australia by John H. Moore and by Daniel and Annette Potts, cited at the beginning of the notes for chapter 24, are particularly useful. Highly revealing as well as essential for comparison is C. P. Stacey and Barbara M. Wilson, *The Half-Million: The Canadians in Britain, 1939–1946* (1987), based on the rich material in the Canadian archives.

On GIs in Britain Norman Longmate, *The G.I.s* (1975) remains basic; Juliet Gardiner's more recent and livelier *"Over Here"* (1992) is indebted to it. On the airmen in Britain, Roger A. Freeman, *The Peaceful Invasion* (1992) is short, readable, and well illustrated. All three rely heavily on the recollections of survivors. Freeman's own research is essential on the 8th Air Force, notably *The Mighty Eighth* (2nd ed., 1986) and *Airfields of the Eighth: Then and Now* (6th ed., 1992). Among other lavishly illustrated if nostalgic books on the airmen are Philip Kaplan and Rex Alan Smith, *One Last Look* (1983) and

D. A. Lande, *From Somewhere in England* (1991). None of these, however, really gets to grips with the mass of archival material on either side of the Atlantic, particularly in America. The only exception on a smaller scale is Graham Smith's carefully researched study of the black GIs in Britain, *When Jim Crow Met John Bull* (1987).

American unit histories, despite the post–D-Day focus, usually have a few pages on their prehistory in Britain. I worked through these most easily in the MHI library. Among the better covered are the stories of the 34th Division in Northern Ireland in 1942 and the 82nd and 101st Airborne in England in 1944. On a company from the latter, Stephen E. Ambrose, *Band of Brothers* (1992), is vivid and revealing. But the most important division for these purposes is the 29th, derisively nicknamed "England's Own" because of its twenty-month sojourn in 1942–44, and I spent much time on Joseph E. Ewing's postwar unit history *29 Let's Go!* (1948) and Joseph Balkoski, *Beyond the Beachhead* (1989) on the division in and before Normandy. Veterans of the 29th were also one of my main targets for interview.

The biographies of senior commanders also repay careful study, notably Forrest C. Pogue on Marshall (4 vols., 1963–87) and Stephen E. Ambrose on Eisenhower (2 vols., 1983–84). Ambrose's older study of Ike's war years *The Supreme Commander* (1970) contains some material not used in the biography. A selection of Ike's wartime papers (EP) was published in five volumes under the general editorship of Alfred D. Chandler (1970), while the equally meticulous *Papers of George Catlett Marshall* (GCMP) is progressing under the care of Larry I. Bland. (For both these valuable projects scholars are indebted to Johns Hopkins University Press.) Mention should also be made of the transcripts of Forrest Pogue's extensive background interviews with Marshall in 1956–57 (MI), revised ed., 1991. *The Patton Papers*, vol. 2, edited by Martin Blumenson (1974) are interesting on Britain, on Ike, and on Patton's paranoia.

For D-Day I used Gordon A. Harrison's green-book official history, *Cross-Channel Attack* (1951), and the shorter accounts *Omaha Beachhead* (1945) and *Utah Beach to Cherbourg* (1948), published by CMH after the war; I also spent several days walking the beaches and the surrounding area. For the Normandy campaign, four more recent studies by leading military historians stand out: Russell F. Weigley, *Eisenhower's Lieutenants* (1981) on the American side; Carlo D'Este, *Decision in Normandy* (1983) on the "Monty" question; Max Hastings, *Overlord* (1984); and John Keegan, *Six Armies in Normandy* (1984). Each has much to say, directly or by implication, about the readiness of the men for the battle. I also learnt a great deal from Nigel Hamilton's official biography of *Monty*, especially vol. 2 (1983). The fiftieth anniversary biblio-deluge appeared in 1994, after this book was completed, but two volumes with the title *D-Day* stand out—Stephen E. Ambrose's epic narrative of 6 June itself and the stimulating collection of scholarly essays edited by Theodore A. Wilson.

On the American home front I have been helped by Richard Polenberg,

War and Society: The United States, 1941–1945 (1972) and John M. Blum, *V Was for Victory* (1976). For life in wartime Britain, all scholars are indebted to Angus Calder's pathbreaking *The People's War* (1971), to his more recent *The Myth of the Blitz* (1991), and to Arthur Marwick, *The Home Front* (1976), as well as to the latter's general work on war and social change. Norman Longmate, *How We Lived Then* (1971) contains a wealth of anecdotal detail on the trials and tribulations of daily life in wartime Britain.

Postwar strands can be traced in Simon Duke, *U.S. Bases in the United Kingdom* (1987) and in the personal stories of war brides and war babes told in three books: Elfrieda Berthiaume Shukert and Barbara Smith Scibetta, *War Brides of World War Two* (1988); Pamela Winfield, *Bye Bye Baby* (1992); and Shirley McGlade, with Mary McCormack, *Daddy, Where Are You?* (1992). The broader contours of Anglo-American relations may be followed in David Dimbleby and David Reynolds, *An Ocean Apart* (1988) and William Roger Louis and Hedley Bull, eds., *The "Special Relationship"* (1986).

Notes

★ ★ ★

UNLESS THE RESULT IS PONDEROUS OR CONFUSING, I GIVE A SINGLE SET OF CITATIONS for the whole paragraph, identifying specific references within squared brackets where necessary. Some frequently cited books and journals are abbreviated throughout (see list of abbreviations, Appendix 2, for full details).

Introduction

1. Halifax diary, 12 May 1943, Hickleton papers, Borthwick Institute, York, A7/8/12; author's interview with Sandy Conti, 17 May 1994; *Daily Express*, 5 September 1979, p. 15; *Time*, 28 May 1984, p. 33.
2. Marc Hillel, *Vie et moeurs des G.I.s en Europe, 1942–1947* (Paris, 1981), pp. 83–4; Geoffrey Perret, *There's a War to Be Won: The United States Army in World War Two* (New York, 1991), p. 470.
3. For these figures see discussion in chapter 24, esp. note 4.
4. Robert S. Raymond, *A Yank in Bomber Command*, ed. Michael Moynihan (Newton Abbot, Devon, 1977), p. 46.
5. Payne Templeton, TS. memoirs, MHI, quoting p. 18.
6. Author's interview with Robert W. Coakley, 16 June 1983.
7. Author's interview with Joseph O. Curtis, 23 April 1983.
8. CM ETO 1161, in JAG, ETO Branch History, 1942–45 (TS. 1946), vol. II, appendix 83, NA RG 332, ETO Adm. 559A.
9. Doris N. Amsbaugh, memoirs, IWM.
10. Author's interview with John Ray, 20 September 1986.
11. Norman Longmate, *The GIs: The Americans in Britain, 1942–1945* (London, 1975); Juliet Gardiner, *"Over Here": The GIs in Wartime Britain* (London, 1992); and Roger A. Freeman, *The Friendly Invasion* (Lavenham, 1992). The exception is Graham Smith, *When Jim Crow Met John Bull: Black American Soldiers in Britain during World War II* (London, 1987).

12. Cf. Akira Iriye, "Culture and International History," in Michael J. Hogan and Thomas G. Paterson, eds., *Explaining the History of American Foreign Relations* (New York, 1991), pp. 214–25. See also the pioneering work of Christopher Thorne, e.g. *The Far Eastern War: States and Societies, 1941–45* (London, 1986).

13. Omer Bartov, "The Missing Years: German Workers, German Soldiers," *German History*, 8 (1990), p. 52; cf. Richard H. Kohn, "The Social History of the American Soldier: A Review and Prospectus for Research," AHR, 86 (1981), pp. 553–67.

14. Lawrence Stone, "The Revival of Narrative: Reflections on a New Old History," *Past and Present*, 85 (November 1979), p. 10; Theda Skocpol, *States and Social Revolutions: A Comparative Analysis of France, Russia, and China* (New York, 1979), introduction, esp. p. 29.

15. For a fascinating example of what can be done see Sarah A. Fishman, *We Will Wait: Wives of French Prisoners of War, 1940–1945* (New Haven, 1991).

Chapter 1: "Never Again"

1. David Kennedy, *Over Here: The First World War and American Society* (Oxford, 1980), p. 144.

2. William J. Wilgus, *Transporting the A.E.F. in Western Europe, 1917–1919* (New York, 1931), p. 455 [total troops]; A.J.P. Taylor, *Beaverbrook* (Harmondsworth, 1974), p. 197; "History of the Operations of Base Section No. 3," pp. 636–43, NA RG 120/2473; *The Times*, 5 July 1918, pp. 7–8; PRO FO 395/225, 134898/112490/N/45 and 120952/120937/N/45.

3. JA Report, 3 February 1919, in NA, RG 120/2498, AEF, SOS, BS 3, JAG, Reports (Monthly).

4. Report of the Labor Bureau, AEF, SOS, BS 3, 13 January 1919, in NA, RG 120/2474, SOS, BS 3, Historical—"report of purchasing agent" [blacks]; JA report, 3 February 1919, para. 7; History of Base Section 3, p. 84 [arrests].

5. Edward B. Parsons, *Wilsonian Diplomacy: Allied-American Rivalry in War and Peace* (St. Louis, 1978), p. 25 [Sims]; Dean C. Allard, "Anglo-American Naval Differences during World War I," *Military Affairs*, 44 (1980), pp. 75–81; John J. Pershing, *My Experiences in the World War* (2 vols., London, 1931), vol. II, p. 28.

6. Lloyd C. Gardner, *Safe for Democracy: The Anglo-American Response to Revolution, 1913–1923* (New York, 1984), pp. 2–3.

7. Inaugural address, 4 March 1801, in James D. Richardson, ed., *A Compilation of the Messages and Papers of the Presidents*, vol. I (Washington, DC, 1896), p. 323.

8. Thomas Jones, *Whitehall Diary*, ed. Keith Middlemas, vol. II (London, 1969), p. 177 [Baldwin]; Churchill memo for cabinet, 20 July 1927, in Martin Gilbert, *Winston S. Churchill*, companion vol. 5, part 1 (London, 1979), p. 1033.

9. Quoted in Cushing Strout, *The American Image of the Old World* (New York, 1963), p. 205.

10. Vansittart, minute of 5 February 1934, in Norman Rose, *Vansittart: Study of a Diplomat* (London, 1978), pp. 126–27; Neville Chamberlain to Hilda, 17 December 1937, Chamberlain papers, NC 18/1/1032, Birmingham University Library.

11. Neville Chamberlain to Ida, 27 January 1940, NC 18/1/1140.

12. David Reynolds, "1940: Fulcrum of the Twentieth Century?" *International Affairs*, 66 (1990), pp. 328–29.

13. Memo of 3 September 1940, PRO CAB 66/11, WP (40) 352.

14. Memo of 25 May 1940, PRO CAB 66/7, WP (40) 168.

15. Warren F. Kimball, *The Juggler: Franklin Roosevelt as Wartime Statesman* (Princeton, NJ, 1991), p. 7 ["juggler"]; Halifax to Churchill, 11 October 1941, PRO PREM 4/27/9.

16. Lindsay to Halifax, 20 September 1938, PRO FO 371/21527, A7504/64/45; Henry L. Stimson diary, 25 September 1941, Sterling Library, Yale University; PRO CAB 99/18, COS(R) 12, II/5 [Hopkins]; David Reynolds, *The Creation of the Anglo-American Alliance, 1937–1941: A Study in Competitive Co-operation* (London, 1981), pp. 35, 42, and 212 [Boston speech].

17. Pogue, *Marshall*, 1: 324 [Hyde Park]; Mark A. Stoler, *George C. Marshall: Soldier-Statesman of the American Century* (Boston, 1989), p. 78.

18. Christopher Thorne, *The Far Eastern War: States and Societies, 1941–1945* (pbk ed. London, 1986), pp. 211–12; Ed Cray, *General of the Army: George C. Marshall, Soldier and Statesman* (New York, 1990), p. 158.

19. J. Garry Clifford and Samuel R. Spencer, Jr., *The First Peacetime Draft* (Lawrence, KS, 1986), pp. 232–33 [extension]; Theodore A. Wilson, *The First Summit: Roosevelt and Churchill at Placentia Bay, 1941* (2nd ed., Lawrence, KS, 1991), pp. 183–86, quoting Hopkins on p. 186.

20. Churchill to Smuts, 8 November 1941, PRO PREM 3/476/3; C-R 1: p. 283; PRO CAB 65/25, WM 8 (42) 1 [Churchill quoting FDR].

21. PRO CAB 99/17, WW 2nd mtg., 23 December 1941 [FDR]; cf. WO 193/331.

22. Stoler, *Marshall*, p. 91; MI, p. 358.

23. "Notes on My Life," Alanbrooke papers, 3/A/V, p. 325, KCL; John Colville, *The Fringes of Power: Downing Street Diaries, 1939–1955* (London, 1985), p. 624 ["lover"].

24. D. Cameron Watt, *Succeeding John Bull: America in Britain's Place, 1900–1975* (Cambridge, 1984), pp. 21–2.

Chapter 2: The Barrier of a Common Language

1. Statistics for this chapter are drawn from B. R. Mitchell with Phyllis Deane, *Abstract of British Historical Statistics* (Cambridge, 1962); U.S. Bureau of the Census, *Historical Statistics of the United States: Colonial Times to 1970* (Washington, DC, 1975). Also useful were David C. Marsh, *The Changing*

Social Structure of England and Wales, 1871–1961 (London, 1965), and Jim Potter, *The American Economy between the World Wars* (London, 1974).

2. Philip S. Bagwell and G. E. Mingay, *Britain and America: A Study of Economic Change, 1850–1939* (London, 1970), p. 60.

3. Paul Bairoch, "Europe's Gross National Product: 1800–1975," *Journal of European Economic History*, 5 (1976), p. 285 [GNP]; Gavin Wright, "The Origins of America's Industrial Success, 1879–1940," *American Economic Review*, 80 (1990), p. 661 [minerals]; David M. Potter, *People of Plenty: Economic Abundance and the American Character* (Chicago, 1954).

4. Alfred D. Chandler, Jr., and Herman Daems, eds., *Managerial Hierarchies: Comparative Perspectives on the Rise of the Modern Industrial Enterprise* (Cambridge, MA, 1980), chs. 1 and 2, statistics from p. 42.

5. David Cannadine, *The Decline and Fall of the British Aristocracy* (London, 1990), pp. 8–25.

6. Maris A. Vinovskis, ed., *Towards a Social History of the American Civil War: Exploratory Essays* (Cambridge, 1990), p. 7; Richard Polenberg, *One Nation Divisible: Class, Race and Ethnicity in the United States since 1938* (Harmondsworth, 1980), p. 15.

7. Stephen Skowronek, *Building a New American State: The Expansion of National Administrative Capacities, 1877–1920* (New York, 1982), ch. 1; Michael J. Hogan, ed., *The End of the Cold War: Its Meanings and Implications* (New York, 1992), p. 218 [May].

8. Maldwyn A. Jones, *American Immigration* (Chicago, 1960), p. 1; James Stuart Olson, *The Ethnic Dimension in American History* (New York, 1979), p. 346 [British heritage].

9. John M. Blum, *V was for Victory: Politics and American Culture during World War II* (New York, 1976), p. 151.

10. Steven F. Lawson, *Black Ballots: Voting Rights in the South, 1944–1969* (New York, 1976), p. 22.

11. Memo, August 1942, PRO CO 876/14, p. 4. Generally I have used James Walvin, *Passage to Britain: Immigration in British History and Politics* (Harmondsworth, 1984), esp. chs. 4–5.

12. A. H. Halsey, *Change in British Society* (Oxford, 1978), chs. 2–3.

13. John Stevenson, *British Society, 1914–45* (Harmondsworth, 1984), p. 472; Orwell, 2: p. 68; cf. Morton Keller, "Anglo-American Politics, 1900–1930, in Anglo-American Perspective," *Comparative Studies in Society and History*, 22 (1980), pp. 458–77.

14. On wealth distribution see Stevenson, *British Society*, p. 330, and Anthony J. Badger, *The New Deal: The Depression Years, 1933–1940* (London, 1984), p. 104. Arthur Marwick, *Class: Image and Reality in Britain, France and the USA since 1930* (London, 1981), pp. 105–7 [*Fortune*].

15. Robert Wiebe, *The Segmented Society: An Introduction to the Meaning of America* (New York, 1975), esp. ch. 2.

16. Ernest R. May, "Comment," AHR, 82 (1977), p. 603.

17. Jim Potter, *American Economy*, pp. 69, 95, and 137.

18. James T. Patterson, *America's Struggle against Poverty, 1900–1980* (Cambridge, MA, 1981), p. 16 [Brookings]; Peter Fearon, *War, Prosperity and Depression: The U. S. Economy, 1917–45* (London, 1987), pp. 101–7.

19. Badger, *New Deal*, p. 311.

20. Frank Freidel, *FDR: Launching the New Deal* (Boston, 1973), p. 202 [inaugural]; Gerald D. Nash, *The Great Depression and World War II: Organizing America, 1933–1945* (New York, 1979), p. 8 ["bewilderment"].

21. John Modell and Duane Steffey, "Waging War and Marriage: Military Service and Family Formation, 1940–1950," JFH, 13 (1988), pp. 196–97 [birth statistics]; Robert S. McElvaine, ed., *Down and Out in the Great Depression: Letters from the "Forgotten Man"* (Chapel Hill, NC, 1983), p. 10 ["hard times"]; Jack C. Gray interview, UNO Orals, 1st Inf. Div.

Chapter 3: Transatlantic Reflections

1. William Brock, "The Image of England and American Nationalism," JAS, 5 (1971), pp. 225–45; Henry Steele Commager, ed., *Britain through American Eyes* (New York, 1974), p. xxviii [Lowell].

2. D. P. Crook, *The North, the South, and the Powers, 1861–1865* (New York, 1974), p. 216.

3. Edward P. Crapol, *America for Americans: Economic Nationalism and Anglophobia in the Late Nineteenth Century* (London, 1973), p. 4.

4. Bruce M. Russett, *Community and Contention: Britain and America in the Twentieth Century* (Cambridge, MA, 1963), pp. 131–33 [school statistics]; Ray Allen Billington, *The Historian's Contribution to Anglo-American Misunderstanding* (London, 1966), p. 28 [quotation].

5. Hadley Cantril, ed., *Public Opinion, 1935–1946* (Princeton, NJ, 1951), p. 485 [AIPO poll, April 1936]; Jeffrey Richards, *The Age of the Dream Palace: Cinema and Society in Britain, 1930–1939* (London, 1984), ch. 2; David Dimbleby and David Reynolds, *An Ocean Apart: The Relationship between Britain and America in the Twentieth Century* (London, 1988), pp. 113–15.

6. Russett, *Community and Contention*, p. 103; "American Attitudes toward the British," OWI Surveys Div., memo 65, 21 August 1943, pp. 13–15, Philleo Nash papers, HSTL, box 6.

7. Thomas Lamont to Lord Lothian, 7 August 1940, Lamont papers 105–12 (Harvard University Business School, Baker Library); Frank Gillard, "Goodnight, and Good Luck," *The Listener*, 1 May 1975, p. 565 [MacLeish].

8. *The New York Times*, 24 July 1940, p. 20.

9. Samuel Grafton, *An American Diary* (New York, 1943), p. 5 ["old-school-tie"]; *The New York Times*, 20 September 1940, p. 22, and 21 September, p. 2 [Reston].

10. David Reynolds, "Roosevelt, the British Left, and the Appointment of John G. Winant as United States Ambassador to Britain in 1941," IHR, 4 (1982), pp. 406–7.

11. Cantril, ed., *Public Opinion*, pp. 1109, 1155 [war efforts]; OWI Survey of

Intelligence materials, 32, 16 July 1942, pp. 19–20, FDRL PSF 173: OWI Intelligence reports.

12. *Hansard's Parliamentary Debates*, 3rd ser., 183: 103–4, 27 April 1866 [Disraeli]; W. T. Stead, *The Americanisation of the World* (London, 1902); G. Lowes Dickinson, *Appearances: Being Notes of Travel* (London, 1914), p. 160.

13. On the sources see Ian McLaine, *Ministry of Morale: Home Front Morale and the Ministry of Information in World War II* (London, 1979), pp. 51–3, and Calder, pp. 13–14.

14. LR/815, 15 April 1942, BBCWAC R9/9/6; MOI HI Special Report 8, 23 February 1942, pp. 1–2, PRO INF 1/293.

15. LR/296, 8 July 1941, BBC R9/9/5; MOI HI special 8 [6 percent]; Cantril, ed., *Public Opinion*, pp. 957, 958 [polls].

16. MOI HI special 8, pp. 1 and 7; John Dizikes, *Britain, Roosevelt and the New Deal: British Opinion, 1932–1938* (New York, 1979), p. 138.

17. M-O 1095, 16 February 1942, p. 11, M-O Archive, Sussex University Library, Brighton.

18. David Reynolds, *The Creation of the Anglo-American Alliance, 1937–1941* (London, 1981), p. 11 [Nicolson]; MOI HI special 32, 16 October 1942, PRO INF 1/293.

19. Richards, *Age of the Dream Palace*, esp. pp. 11–15, 67–9; Peter Stead, "Hollywood's Message for the World: The British Response in the Nineteen Thirties," HJFRT, 1 (1981), p. 22 [manager].

20. *Daily Express*, 18 March 1927, p. 6; *The Times*, 16 January 1935.

21. Richards, *Age of the Dream Palace*, p. 24 [courting]; Dimbleby and Reynolds, *An Ocean Apart*, p. 106 [Evans]; M-O 1095, 16 February 1942, p. 16.

22. *The Times*, 19 May 1939, p. 18; Kennedy to Harry Cohn, 17 November 1939, copy in FDRL PSF 53: Kennedy.

23. Sigmund Skard, *American Studies in Europe: Their History and Present Organization* (2 vols., Philadelphia, 1958), 1: p. 59 ["experiments"]; Richard H. Heindel, *The American Impact on Great Britain, 1898–1914* (Philadelphia, 1940), pp. 15–18 [survey]; cf. *Planning*, no. 148, 30 May 1939.

24. M-O 523B, 10 December 1940; Churchill to Foreign Secretary, 20 December 1940, PRO PREM 4/25/8.

25. Calder, pp. 266–67; M-O 999, 15 December 1941; speech by Health Minister Ernest Brown, 4 July 1941, copy in PRO FO 371/26257, A 5212/2643/45; MOI HI 35, 28 May–4 June 1941, PRO INF 1/292; LR/296, 8 July 1941, BBCWAC R9/9/5, and LR/586, 22 January 1942, R/9/9/6.

26. Frank Darvall, minutes, 31 December 1941, PRO INF 1/915; M-O 1095, 16 February 1942, pp. 5–7; M-O 1569, 22 January 1943, pp. 6–7.

27. M-O 1095, 16 February 1942, p. 1.

Chapter 4: "Don't You Know There's a War On?"

1. Terkel, p. vi; Mark H. Leff, "The Politics of Sacrifice on the American Home Front in World War II," JAH, 77 (1991), p. 1296.
2. Richard R. Lingeman, *Don't You Know There's a War On?: The American Home Front, 1941–1945* (New York, 1970), p. 169. Other basic overviews are Richard Polenberg, *War and Society: The United States, 1941–1945* (Philadelphia, 1972) and John Morton Blum, *V Was for Victory: Politics and American Culture During World War Two* (New York, 1976).
3. Peter Fearon, *War, Prosperity and Depression: The U.S. Economy, 1917–45* (London, 1987), esp. pp. 273–74, 278.
4. Lingeman, *Don't You Know*, pp. 67–9; Gerald D. Nash, *The American West Transformed: The Impact of the Second World War* (Bloomington, IN, 1985), chs. 2–5; Pete Daniel, "Going Among Strangers: Southern Reactions to World War II," JAH, 77 (1990), pp. 886, 898.
5. Blum, *V Was for Victory*, p. 92; Robert Higgs, "Wartime Prosperity?: A Reassessment of the U.S. Economy in the 1940s," JEH, 52 (1992), pp. 49–53; Fearon, *War*, p. 279 ["dreams"]; Harold G. Vatter, *The U.S. Economy in World War Two* (New York, 1985), p. 19.
6. Fearon, *War*, p. 265.
7. Blum, *V Was for Victory*, p. 115; Lingeman, *Don't You Know*, p. 65 [corporations]; Fearon, *War*, pp. 273, 283 [spending]; Polenberg, *War and Society*, p. 237.
8. I am adapting the argument of Higgs, "Wartime Prosperity?" pp. 42–4. See also Fearon, *War*, p. 278, and U.S. Bureau of the Census, *Historical Statistics of the United States: Colonial Times to 1970* (Washington, DC, 1975), pp. 1140–41.
9. Ross Gregory, *America 1941: A Nation at the Crossroads* (New York, 1989), p. 292; Terkel, p. 244.
10. Arthur Marwick, *The Home Front: The British and the Second World War* (London, 1976), p. 75 ["concern"]; Calder, p. 20 ["grooves"]; David Cannadine, "British History: Past, Present—and Future?" *Past and Present*, 116 (August 1987), p. 183 ["happened"].
11. Norman Longmate, *The GIs: The Americans in Britain, 1942–1945* (London, 1975), p. 70 [Avonmouth]; Kurt Gabel, *The Making of a Paratrooper: Airborne Training and Combat in World War II* (Lawrence, KS, 1990), p. 146; Basil Collier, *The Defence of the United Kingdom* (London, 1957), pp. 311, 528 [statistics].
12. Norman Longmate, *How We Lived Then: A History of Everyday Life during the Second World War* (London, 1971), ch. 4, quoting from p. 45.
13. W. K. Hancock and M. M. Gowing, *British War Economy* (2nd ed., London, 1975), pp. 357 and 500.
14. Lord Birkenhead, *Halifax: the Life of Lord Halifax* (London, 1965), p. 508. The discussion of rationing draws particularly on Longmate, *How We Lived Then*, chs. 13, 21–22, and Lingeman, *Don't You Know*, ch. 7. I have also used the detailed "Memos on Daily Difficulties" prepared by Lady

Reading for Mrs. Roosevelt, November 1942, in FDRL, Eleanor Roosevelt papers, box 2974.

15. Hancock and Gowing, *British War Economy*, p. 351 [armed forces]; Sheila Ferguson and Hilde Fitzgerald, *Studies in the Social Services* (2nd ed., London, 1978), p. 4 [addresses].

16. Richard M. Titmuss, *Problems of Social Policy* (2nd ed., London, 1976), pp. 355–56, 562 [statistics]; John Macnicol, "The Evacuation of School-children," in Harold L. Smith, ed., *War and Social Change: British Society in the Second World War* (Manchester, 1986), p. 27 ["trauma"]; cf. Travis L. Crosby, *The Impact of Civilian Evacuation in the Second World War* (London, 1986).

17. Harold L. Smith, "The Effect of the War on the Status of Women," in Smith, ed., *War and Social Change*, p. 211 [1931]; for all other statistics see Penny Summerfield, *Women Workers in the Second World War: Production and Patriarchy in Conflict* (London, 1984), esp. pp. 29–31, 34.

18. Alan S. Milward, *War, Economy and Society, 1939–1945* (Berkeley, CA, 1977), pp. 63, 67; Hancock and Gowing, *British War Economy*, p. 551 [national wealth]; Paul Kennedy, *The Rise and Fall of the Great Powers: Economic Change and Military Conflict from 1500 to 2000* (London, 1988) p. 368 [U.S. GNP].

19. King, p. 162 [Bracken]; Calder, p. 263 [Bowen].

20. Lingeman, *Don't You Know*, pp. 253, 254, 263.

Chapter 5: Occupational Hazards

1. S.L.A. Marshall, *Men against Fire* (Washington, DC, 1947), p. 42; Edward A. Shils and Morris Janowitz, "Cohesion and Disintegration in the Wehrmacht during World War II," *Public Opinion Quarterly*, 12 (1948), pp. 280–315; John Baynes, *Morale: A Study of Men and Courage* (London, 1967).

2. Omer Bartov, *Hitler's Army: Soldiers, Nazis, and War in the Third Reich* (New York, 1991), esp. pp. 28–58; Elliot P. Chodoff, "Ideology and Primary Groups," AFS 9 (1983), p. 588 [quotation]; Anthony Kellett, *Combat Motivation: The Behavior of Soldiers in Battle* (Boston, 1982), pp. 101–4.

3. Roger J. Spiller, "Isen's Run: Human Dimensions of Warfare in the 20th Century," *Military Review*, 68/5 (May 1988), p. 28 ["victory"]; AS 1: p. 431.

4. Denis Winter, *Death's Men: Soldiers of the Great War* (pbk. ed., London, 1979), p. 171; Bartov, *Hitler's Army*, p. 98; John Ellis, *World War II: The Sharp End* (2nd ed., London, 1990), p. 191 ["deference"]; Paul Fussell, *Wartime: Understanding and Behavior in the Second World War* (pbk. ed., New York, 1989), p. 81 ["inspections"].

5. J. Glenn Gray, *The Warriors: Reflections on Men in Battle* (2nd ed., New York, 1970), p. 51; Gerald F. Linderman, *Embattled Courage: The Experience of Combat in the American Civil War* (New York, 1987), p. 75; John Keegan, *The Face of Battle* (pbk. ed., Harmondsworth, 1978), p. 333; Winter, *Death's Men*, pp. 179–81.

6. Sam C. Sarkesian, ed., *Combat Effectiveness: Cohesion, Stress, and the Volunteer Military* (Beverly Hills, CA, 1980), p. 34 [Clark]; Ellis, *Sharp End*, p. 251.

7. Keegan, *Face of Battle*, p. 175.

8. Loren W. Gast, 1st Division questionnaires, MHI; Kellett, *Combat Motivation*, p. 59 [1860s]; Martin Van Creveld, *Supplying War: Logistics from Wallenstein to Patton* (Cambridge, 1977), pp. 233–34; John A. English, *On Infantry* (New York, 1984), p. 139 [ratios].

9. James L. Robertson, Jr., *Soldiers Blue and Gray* (pbk. ed., New York, 1991), p. 97 [whisky]; Linderman, *Embattled Courage*, p. 124 ["spoiling"]; Alistair Horne, *To Lose a Battle: France 1940* (Harmondsworth, 1979), p. 138 ["ennui"]; V. Rostowsky, "La vie quotidienne des civils ardennais pendant 'la drole de guerre,'" in Maurice Vaisse, ed., *Ardennes 1940* (Paris, 1991), esp. pp. 181–82.

10. Geoffrey Parker, *The Army of Flanders and the Spanish Road, 1567–1659: The Logistics of Spanish Victory and Defeat in the Low Countries' Wars* (Cambridge, 1972), pp. 179–80; Winter, *Death's Men*, p. 143.

11. MOI report, 1 January 1940 ["quinze francs"], and Robert Nichols to Philip Nichols, 14 February 1940 ["All classes"], PRO FO 371/24308, C949/ and C2935/65/17; Campbell to Halifax, desp. 405, 9 April 1940, PRO FO 371/24299, C5331/9/17 ["opulence"]; PRO CAB 63/144 (AG, BEF); M. Rousseau, "Douai pendant la seconde guerre mondiale, 1939–1945," *Revue du Nord*, 61 (1979), p. 478.

12. Fussell, *Wartime*, p. 108.

13. Parker, *Army of Flanders*, pp. 175–76; J. M. Brereton, *The British Soldier: A Social History from 1661 to the Present Day* (London, 1986), pp. 37–8 [marriage]; Vernon L. Kellogg, *Military Selection and Race Deterioration* (Oxford, 1916), p. 194 [VD rates]; Byron Farwell, *Armies of the Raj: From the Mutiny to Independence, 1858–1947* (London, 1990), ch. 10; Winter, *Death's Men*, p. 152 [Rouen].

14. Manfred Messerschmidt, "German Military Law in the Second World War," in Wilhelm Deist, ed., *The German Military in the Age of Total War* (Leamington, 1985), p. 324; Bartov, *Hitler's Army*, p. 68 [12th Infantry]; Omer Bartov, *The Eastern Front, 1941–45: German Troops and the Barbarisation of Warfare* (London, 1985), pp. 126–29 [women]; Richard Cobb, *French and Germans, Germans and French: A Personal Interpretation of France under Two Occupations, 1914–1918/1940–1944* (Hanover, NH, 1983), pp. 66–7 [dependents].

15. Bartov, *Hitler's Army*, p. 72; Etienne Dejonghe, "Etre 'occupant' dans le Nord (vie militaire, culture, loisirs, propagande)," *Revue du Nord*, 65 (1983), 707–45, quoting (my translation) from p. 714.

16. Winter, *Death's Men*, p. 165 [Noakes]; Bartov, *Eastern Front*, p. 91 [remote control].

17. Robertson, *Soldiers Blue and Gray*, pp. 48 [private] and 123 [Belknap]; J. G. Fuller, *Troop Morale and Popular Culture in the British and Dominion Armies, 1914–1918* (Oxford, 1990), p. 78 ["Divisional Rest"].

18. English, *On Infantry*, pp. 157–63; Meirion and Susie Harries, *Soldiers of the Sun: The Rise and Fall of the Imperial Japanese Army, 1868–1945* (London, 1991), pp. 313–14; Field Marshal Sir William Slim, *Defeat into Victory* (London, 1956), p. 184; *The Memoirs of Field-Marshal the Viscount Montgomery of Alamein, K.G.* (London, 1958), p. 84.

19. Montgomery, *Memoirs*, p. 84; Harries, *Soldiers of the Sun*, chs. 32, 42, and 43, quoting from p. 361; Leonard V. Smith, "The Disciplinary Dilemma of French Military Justice, September 1914–April 1917: The Case of 5ᵉ Division d'Infanterie," JMH, 55 (1991), p. 67; and, on similar lines, Fuller, *Troop Morale*, pp. 26–9.

20. Brereton, *British Soldier*, p. 62 [quote]; Winter, *Death's Men*, pp. 230–31 [1914].

21. Colin Jones, "The Welfare of the French Foot-Soldier," *History*, 65 (1980), p. 211.

Chapter 6: Citizen Soldiers

1. Arthur Miller, *Situation Normal . . .* (New York, 1944), p. 3; Lee Kennett, *G.I.: The American Soldier in World War II* (pbk. ed., New York, 1989), p. 72.

2. John Whiteclay Chambers II, *To Raise an Army: The Draft Comes to Modern America* (New York, 1987), esp. pp. 1, 52–3, 62; Robert K. Griffith, Jr., *Men Wanted For the U.S. Army: America's Experience with an All-Volunteer Army between the World Wars* (Westport, CT, 1982), ch. 7, esp. pp. 179–80.

3. W. K. Hancock and M. M. Gowing, *British War Economy* (2nd ed., London, 1975), pp. 314, 370–71; John Modell and Duane Steffey, "Waging War and Marriage: Military Service and Family Formation, 1940–1950," JFH 13 (1988), p. 199 [deferment statistics]; George Q. Flynn, *Lewis B. Hershey: Mr. Selective Service* (Chapel Hill, NC, 1985), pp. 109–10 ["fathers"].

4. Flynn, *Hershey*, p. 77 [quotation]; cf. Chambers, *To Raise an Army*, pp. 250, 253.

5. Chambers, *To Raise an Army*, p. 27; Morris Janowitz, *Military Conflict* (Beverley Hills, CA, 1975), p. 78 ["service"].

6. John K. Mahon, *History of the Militia and the National Guard* (New York, 1983), chs. 12–13, esp. p. 194.

7. Terkel, p. 301 [Wax]; AS 1: p. 59 [education].

8. Robert H. Berlin, "U.S. Army World War II Corps Commanders: A Composite Biography," JMH 53 (1989), p. 150. Also Pogue, vol. 2, chs. 4–5.

9. Marshall, memos of 1 and 22 October 1942, GCMP 3: pp. 377, 400 ["dig"]; Martin van Creveld, *Fighting Power: German and US Army Performance, 1939–1945* (Westport, CT, 1982), chs. 10–11; AS 1: p. 391 ["command"].

10. Richard H. Kohn, "The Social History of the American Soldier: A Review and Prospectus for Research," AHR 86 (1981), p. 563.

11. This paragraph draws on Kennett, *G.I.*, chs. 2–3; Edwin P. Hoyt, *The GI's War: American Soldiers in Europe during World War II* (New York, 1991), chs. 1–2; Kurt Gabel, *The Making of a Paratrooper: Airborne Training and Combat in World War II* (Lawrence, KS, 1990), ch. 2 ["Army Way"].

12. Kennett, *G.I.*, p. 40 [Texan]; Terkel, pp. 561–62 [black GI]; AS 1, ch. 4, esp. pp. 125, 144.

13. *Life*, 18 August 1941, p. 17; Railey, "Morale in the U.S. Army," 29 September 1941, pp. 15, 18–20, MHI; AS 1: p. 59 [education]. See also Stephen D. Wesbrook, "The Railey Report and Army Morale, 1941: Anatomy of a Crisis," *Military Review*, 60/6 (June 1980), pp. 11–24.

14. "Old Sarge," *How to Get Along in the Army* (New York, 1942), p. 111 ["humiliation"]; AS 1: p. 371 ["children"]; John A. Thompson, *Reformers and War: American Progressive Publicists and the First World War* (Cambridge, 1987), p. 52 [Croly].

15. Ross Gregory, *America 1941: A Nation at the Crossroads* (New York, 1989), p. 36; E. B. Sledge, *With the Old Breed at Peleliu and Okinawa* (Novato, CA, 1981), p. 100; cf. Lawrence Ingraham and Frederick Manning, "American Military Psychiatry," in Richard A. Gabriel, ed., *Military Psychiatry: A Comparative Perspective* (New York, 1986), pp. 58–9.

16. Howard Brotz and Everett Wilson, "Characteristics of Military Society," AJS 51 (March 1946), p. 375; Miller, *Situation Normal*, p. 172 [Pyle].

17. OWI intelligence report 54, 18 December 1942, FDRL PSF 174.

18. Pogue, 3: p. 585.

19. Pogue, 2, ch. 13; David Brinkley, *Washington Goes to War* (pbk. ed., New York, 1989), pp. 73–4 ["Madam"].

20. WO, "Monthly Notes on the Army of the United States," July 1942, NAC RG 24/12538, 4/NOTES/4; Dill to Brooke, 5 May 1942, Alanbrooke papers, KCL, 14/38; GCMP 3: p. 536.

21. Pogue, 3: p. 83 [*Time*]; E. J. Kahn, *McNair: Educator of an Army* (Washington, 1945), p. 8; GCMP 2: p. 347 [steak]; AS 1: pp. 10–13 [polls].

22. Griffith, *Men Wanted*, pp. 66–9, 98–9, 200–1, 237–38 [pay]—note that an "unclassified" draftee started out at a lower rate for his first four months of training—$21 on the 1940 scale; GCMP 3: p. 358 ["squeakings"].

23. Clella Reeves Collins, *When Your Son Goes to War* (New York, 1943), p. 142 [milk]; Kennett, *G.I.*, p. 93 ["happy"]; Wesbrook, "Railey Report," pp. 22–3.

24. Alvin Bridges in Terkel, p. 388.

25. Morris J. MacGregor, Jr., *Integration of the Armed Forces, 1940–1965* (Washington, DC, 1981), pp. 3–7; Gerald W. Patton, *War and Race: The Black Officer in the American Military, 1915–1941* (Westport, CT, 1981), pp. 168–69.

26. Ulysses Lee, *The Employment of Negro Troops* (Washington, DC, 1966), pp. 17–18 [92nd]; Arthur E. Barbeau and Florette Henri, *The Unknown Sol-*

diers: Black American Troops in World War I (Philadelphia, 1974), ch. 8; AS 1: p. 492 [scores].

27. Edward M. Coffman and Peter F. Herrly, "The American Regular Officer Corps between the World Wars," AFS 4 (1977), pp. 55–6, 60.

28. AGWAR memo, 16 October 1940, in Morris J. MacGregor and Bernard C. Nalty, eds., *Blacks in the United States Armed Forces: Basic Documents* (Wilmington, DE, 1977), 5: pp. 32–3; MacGregor, *Integration*, p. 24; Lee, *Negro Troops*, p. 211 [officers]; Alan M. Osur, *Blacks in the Army Air Forces during World War II: The Problem of Race Relations* (Washington, DC, 1977), chs. 2–3.

29. AGWAR memo, 16 October 1940 and Marshall, memo, 1 December 1941, in MacGregor and Nalty, eds., *Blacks*, 5: pp. 32, 114.

30. The military inefficiency of racial discrimination is stressed in MacGregor, *Integration*, pp. 23–34, and Richard M. Dalfiume, *Desegregation of the U.S. Armed Forces: Fighting on Two Fronts, 1939–1953* (Columbia, MO, 1969), pp. 2–3, 104.

31. J. Garry Clifford and Samuel R. Spencer, Jr., *The First Peacetime Draft* (Lawrence, KS, 1986), p. 3 [No. 158]; Terkel, p. 39 [Rasmus]; Morton Sosna, "The GIs' South and North-South Dialogue during World War II," in Winfred B. Moore, Jr., et al., eds., *Developing Dixie: Modernization in a Traditional Society* (New York, 1988), p. 318 [Mississippi accent]; Leon C. Standifer, *Not in Vain: A Rifleman Remembers World War II* (Baton Rouge, LA, 1992), pp. 43–4.

32. This paragraph draws heavily on Sosna's article, "The GIs' South," pp. 311–25, quoting from p. 319 [Bronx]. I have, however, revised his figure for the number of outsiders passing through the South (pp. 312–13), because 16.3 million served in the armed forces during the war, not 12.5 million as he suggested (that being peak strength in 1945).

33. Terkel, pp. 279–80 [Black]; AS 1: pp. 490, 563, 595 [stereotype quotes].

34. Meyer H. Maskin and Leon L. Altman, "Military Psychodynamics: Psychological Factors in the Transition from Civilian to Soldier," *Psychiatry*, 6 (1943), p. 265; Kent Roberts Greenfield, et al., *The Organization of Ground Combat Troops* (Washington, DC, 1947), pp. 203 [ASF], and 337 [thirty-two thousand].

35. Maurice Matloff, "The 90-Division Gamble," in Kent Roberts Greenfield, ed., *Command Decisions* (Washington, DC, 1960), p. 380.

36. W. Edgar Gregory, "The Idealization of the Absent," AJS 50 (1944), pp. 53–4; AS 2: p. 593; Marshall to Watson, 3 November 1942, GCMP 3: pp. 419–20 [medals]; other quotes from Pogue, 3: pp. 81–2.

37. John Hersey, *Into the Valley: A Skirmish of the Marines* (rev. ed., New York, 1991), p. 59.

Chapter 7: Marking Time

1. Mollie Panter-Downes, *London War Notes, 1939–1945*, William Shawn, ed. (New York, 1971), p. 239.

2. See Richard M. Leighton, "OVERLORD Revisited: An Interpretation of American Strategy in the European War, 1942–1944," AHR 68 (1963), pp. 919–37.

3. Marshall memo, 23 December 1941, GCMP 3: p. 32.

4. Generally see Rupp. 1: pp. 19–31; C&C 1: ch. 17.

5. WWI (Final), 20 January 1942, in PRO CAB 80/33, COS (42) 75. This paper, dated 18 December 1941, is reproduced almost verbatim in WSC 3: pp. 582–84.

6. Henry L. Stimson diary, 5 and 8 March 1942 (Sterling Library, Yale University). Cf. Churchill tel., 5 March 1942, in C-R 1: pp. 381–84.

7. Eisenhower, note, 22 January 1942, in EP I: p. 66; the U.S. plan is reprinted in J.R.M. Butler, *Grand Strategy*, vol. III, part 2 (London, 1964), appendix III.

8. DC (O), 10th mtg., 14 April 1942, copy in PRO PREM 3/333/6 [Churchill and Eden]; M&S, p. 191 ["superficial"].

9. Rupp. 1: 56 ["wishful"]; Richard M. Leighton and Robert W. Coakley, *Global Logistics and Strategy, 1940–1943* (Washington, DC, 1955), p. 362 ["SLEDGEHAMMER's"].

10. Ernie Pyle, *Brave Men* (New York, 1944), p. 207; cf. Capt. A. H. Hastie, memoirs, IWM, p. 165.

11. Rupp. 1: ch. 1, esp. pp. 27–8; Dwight D. Eisenhower, *Crusade in Europe* (New York, 1948), pp. 49–50; Charles L. Bolte interview, 9 December 1971, p. 77, MHI [Eaker]; Spaatz, memo for Arnold, May 1942, GCML reel 383/5698/52; EP 1: pp. 165–66, 295–96, 315, 320, 334–35 [8 June].

12. Pogue, 2: ch. 15, n. 50.

13. Eisenhower diary, 5 January, 5 February 1942, DDEL; memo for file by Gen. Edward C. Betts, 12 July 1944, EM 16/52: box 11, Betts, DDEL; Stephen E. Ambrose, *Eisenhower* (2 vols, New York, 1983–84), 1: p. 186 ["fanatic," "SOB"].

14. Brooke, diary, 20 January 1943, copy in Alanbrooke papers, KCL, 3A/ VIII, p. 608.

15. FDR to Churchill, 31 May 1942, C-R, 1: p. 503; M&S, p. 234.

16. PRO CAB 79/56, COS (42) 51st mtg. (O), 8 June 1942.

17. CCS (42) 28th mtg., 20 June 1942, and CCS (42) 83, 21 June 1942, PRO CAB 99/20; Stimson diary, 21 June, p. 2.

18. Pogue, 2: 340–41; for Marshall doubts see Stimson diary, 38: 13, 59, and Mark A. Stoler, *George C. Marshall: Soldier-Statesman of the American Century* (Boston, 1989), pp. 99–100.

19. Marshall memo, 23 December 1941, GCMP 3: 34—punctuation slightly amended; Richard W. Steele, "American Popular Opinion and the War against Germany: The Issue of a Negotiated Peace, 1942," JAH, 65 (1978), p. 705. Marshall admitted after the war (Pogue, 2: p. 330): "We failed to see that the leader in a democracy has to keep the people entertained. (That may sound like the wrong word, but it conveys the

thought.) The people demand action. We couldn't wait to be completely ready."

20. Joseph L. Strange, "The British Rejection of Operation SLEDGEHAMMER: An Alternative Motive," MA 46 (1982), pp. 10, 12; Lord Moran, *Winston Churchill: The Struggle for Survival, 1940–1965* (pbk. ed., London, 1968), p. 63.

21. Robert E. Sherwood, *Roosevelt and Hopkins: An Intimate History* (New York, 1948), p. 611 [quote]; M&S, pp. 249–50, 279.

22. Meeting of 30 May 1942, FRUS, 1942, 3: p. 577; Churchill, aide-mémoire, 14 August 1942, in Gilbert, 7: p. 190.

23. Rupp., 1: pp. 87–113; also C&C, 2: pp. 600, 619.

24. M&S, p. 323 ["balanced"]; Eaker to Eubank, 19 February 1943, Ira C. Eaker papers, LC, box 17.

25. Harry C. Butcher diary, 21 July 1942, DDEL; Marshall to Eisenhower, 26 and 28 September 1942, GCMP 3: pp. 367–68.

26. Pogue, 3: pp. 31, 202 [Sledgehammer]; GCMP 3: p. 270 [GCM and King]; COS (42) 70th mtg. (O), 10 July 1942, PRO CAB 79/56 [Brooke]; M&S, pp. 276, 282 [FDR and WSC].

27. Pogue, 3: p. 22; Mark A. Stoler, *The Politics of the Second Front: American Military Planning and Diplomacy in Coalition Warfare, 1941–1943* (London, 1977), p. 77 [Wedemeyer]; WSC, 2: p. 6.

28. Albert C. Wedemeyer, *Wedemeyer Reports!* (New York, 1958), p. 168 ["trap"]; Leighton and Coakley, *Global Logistics*, pp. 662 ["Army forces"], 715, 718.

29. Eric Larrabee, *Commander in Chief: Franklin Delano Roosevelt, His Lieutenants, and Their War* (New York, 1988), pp. 155, 187 [King]; Mark A. Stoler, "The 'Pacific-First' Alternative in American World War II Strategy," IHR 2 (1980), pp. 449–50 ["sideshow"].

30. Figures from C&C, 2: pp. 639–41.

31. Pickering to Stark, 30 April 1945, in Harold L. Stark papers, NHC, box 3; Admin. History, USN Forces in Europe, 1940–46, (TS., London, 1946), part V, ch. XI (NHC).

32. Ira C. Eaker, oral history, 1972, MHI, sec. 3, pp. 20–1.

33. MI, pp. 565, 627; Geoffrey Perret, *There's a War to Be Won: the United States Army in World War II* (New York, 1991), pp. 98, 103.

34. Lee, Service Reminiscences, TS (1956), pp. 81–93, J.C.H. Lee papers, Hoover Library, Stanford, CA: *Time,* 25 September 1944, pp. 21–2; EP 1: pp. 474, 566–68, 591, and Butcher diary, 18 and 20 September 1942 and 27 January 1944, DDEL [Dep. Commander]; Perret, *There's a War,* pp. 303–4 [Sears]; NA RG 332 ETO Adm 16 [train]; *New York Herald Tribune,* 12 September 1947, pp. 1, 7.

Chapter 8: Making Space

1. Marshall to McNair, 21 January 1942, Marshall papers, GCML, 76/32; Martin Blumenson, *Patton: The Man behind the Legend, 1885–1945* (pbk.

ed., New York, 1987), pp. 160–61; Geoffrey Perret, *There's a War to Be Won*, (New York, 1991), p. 101.

2. USP (42) 2nd mtg., 12 April 1942, copy in DDEL 16/52 file, box 152: Bolero ["towns"].

3. PRO CAB 81/48, BC(L) (42) 8, 8 May 1942.

4. Philip Kaplan and Rex Alan Smith, *One Last Look: A Sentimental Journey to the Eighth Air Force Heavy Bomber Bases of World War II in England* (New York, 1983), p. 36 [Vermont].

5. John W. Blake, *Northern Ireland in the Second World War* (London, 1956), esp. pp. 287–88.

6. Diary, 5 April 1944, John J. McCloy papers, Amherst College, DY1/13. Troop distribution data in NA RG 332 ETO Adm 345–47.

7. UK population figures from M&D, pp. 22–3.

8. NA RG 332 ETO Adm 266, Provost Marshal's traffic accident report and statistics, May 1944; cf. M&D, p. 230.

9. Bruce Jacobs, "It Seems Like Only Yesterday . . . Omaha Beach," *The National Guardsman*, 23/6 (June 1969), p. 3.

10. Author's interview with J. Robert Slaughter, 24 August 1993; UNO/29 orals: Erik Juleen, p. 3, Robert M. Miller, pp. 1 and 4, Sidney Bingham to Thomas Eagan, 11 January 1947 [Xmas].

11. Rupp. 1: pp. 81–3, 159–71, 195–200.

12. See NA RG 332 ETO AG 685 (Maneuver Grounds), esp. Eaker to CG USAFBI, 3 March 1942; Harry C. Butcher diary, DDEL, 25 September 1942 [RING].

13. Graham A. Cosmas and Albert E. Cowdrey, *Medical Service in the European Theater of Operations* (Washington, DC, 1992), pp. 36–44, 80–2.

14. See Joseph R. Darnall, "Hospitalization in the European Theater of Operations, US Army, World War II," *The Military Surgeon*, 103 (December 1948).

15. C&C 1: p. 631 and 2: pp. 647–48; Roger A. Freeman, *The Friendly Invasion* (Lavenham: 1992), p. 7 [175]; Freeman, *Airfields of the Eighth: Then and Now* (6th ed., London, 1992), p. 8.

16. Joseph R. Darnall, memoirs, MHI, pp. 82–3.

17. Cosmas and Cowdrey, *Medical Service in ETO*, pp. 83–6; C. M. Kohan, *Works and Buildings* (London, 1952), pp. 260–77; Robert S. Arbib, *Here We Are Together: The Notebook of an American Soldier in Britain* (London, 1946), p. 52 [Debach].

18. Maurice Moynihan, ed., *Speeches and Statements by Eamon de Valera, 1917–73* (Dublin, 1980), p. 465; Welles, memo, 6 February 1942, FRUS 1942, I: pp. 755–56.

19. Harold L. Ickes, MS Diary, LC, 7 February 1942 [FDR]; *A Pocket Guide to Northern Ireland* (Washington, DC, 1942), pp. 10–11; Joseph T. Carroll, *Ireland in the War Years* (Newton Abbot, 1975), ch. 9, quoting p. 146.

20. Mark Willcox, Jr., memo, "Irish situation," [October 1942], Hoover Inst., Stanford University, TS Ireland W 667; PRO CAB 122/650, WW (JPC)

7, 10 January 1942; intell. summary, 29 August–13 September 1942, Martin M. Philipsborn papers, MHI: N. Africa box; Halifax secret diary, 14 June 1942, Hickleton papers, A 7.8.19, Borthwick Institute, York [Hopkins]; Parker W. Buhrman, desp. 39, 22 June 1942, p. 2, NA RG 84 Belfast: 800 Confdntl.

21. Lt. Comndr. Robert E. Vining, report, 26 April 1943, p. 51, Hoover Institution, TS Ireland V 785 [Falls Road]; Buhrman, report 65, 8 September 1942, NA RG 84, 800 Conf.; D. K. McNair, report, 27 December 1942, NA RG 181/775 Londonderry, A 7-2, Censorship [Donegal]; Carolle J. Carter, "Ireland: America's Neutral Ally, 1939–1941," *Eire-Ireland*, 12 (Summer 1977), p. 6 [Dublin]; USSTAF History, vol. II, ch. 2, pp. 134–35, OAFH, USSTAF 519.01 [Langford Lodge].

22. Carroll, *Ireland in the War Years*, p. 160 [Hitler]; John Bowman, *De Valera and the Ulster Question, 1917–1973* (Oxford, 1982), pp. 241–42 ["sympathies"]; Robert Fisk, *In Time of War: Ireland, Ulster and the Price of Neutrality* (pbk. ed., London, 1985), pp. 233–44; Gray to Stark, 22 April 1943, Harold R. Stark papers, NHC, box 1: corr.

23. Fisk, *In Time of War*, pp. 327–30; T. Ryle Dwyer, *Irish Neutrality and the USA, 1939–1947* (Dublin, 1977), pp. 156–59. Instructions in Arnold to 8AF, 26 March 1943, OAFH, USSTAF 519.955-1: Neutral Countries.

24. Diary notes, Jacob L. Devers papers, DDEL, microfilm reel 6: pp. 863–68.

25. Para. mostly based on WO memo, "The Use of Land for Military Purposes," May 1943, NA RG 332, ETO AG 685 (Training Grounds); also WO AG, Notes for Estimates speech, February 1943, Sir Ronald Adam papers, KCL, IV; *Sunday Dispatch*, 20 May 1945, p. 2.

26. Capt. Littlewood, lecture, 26 June 1941, NAC RG 24/13692, WD, DA, and QMG; Censors' Report CR 24, p. 5, NAC RG 24/12319, 4/CENSORS/4/6 [Horsham].

27. Julia White, memoirs, IWM, pp. 9–14.

28. Col. Thomas J. Heavey, report on ETO visit, 13 October 1942 to 13 January 1943, p. 6, in ETO Observers' reports, MHI, vol. 6; Andrews to Marshall, 26 February 1943, Marshall papers 56/27, GCML; UNO/29, Edwin P. Young oral, p. 1; Devers, report on mission to ETO, January 1943, Devers papers, DDEL, reel 6, p. 828; Hawley, directive 22, 1 September 1943, MHI Med. History Unit Collctn., Hawley, box 2; author's interview with Melvin Sherr, 4 September 1993.

29. Quoted in Joseph Balkoski, *Beyond the Beachhead: The 29th Division in Normandy* (Harrisburg, PA, 1989), p. 55.

30. CO 115th to CO 2/115th, 12 August 1943, NA RG 332, ETO AG 685 (Training Grounds); Thrasher to CG SOS, 10 November 1942, NA RG 332, ETO AG 684 (Target Ranges).

31. Heavey, Obs. Rpt., p. 6; George F. Hofmann, *The Super Sixth* (Louisville, KY: 1975), p. 44; Romie L. Brownlee and William J. Mullen III, *Changing an Army: An Oral History of Gen. William E. DePuy* (Washington, DC, 1988), p. 14; Haislip to McNair, 31 January 1944, Wade H. Haislip

papers, box 1, Hoover Inst., Stanford, box 1; *Combat History of the Second Infantry Division in World War II* (Baton Rouge, LA, 1946), p. 18.

32. Hamilton Howze, "Senior Officers Debriefing Program," 20 November 1972, no. 2, p. 46, MHI; Ward quoted from draft biography, ch. 2, p. 29, Orlando Ward papers, MHI; Eisenhower to Bradley, 16 April 1943, EP 2: 1093; Richard W. Stewart, "The 'Red Bull' Division: The Training and Initial Engagements of the 34th Infantry Division, 1941–43," *Army History*, no. 25 (winter 1993), pp. 1–10.

33. PRO CAB 65/36, WM 141 (43) 2; CAB 66/41, WP (43) 429 and 431.

34. Rupp. 1: 340–45.

35. Winant to Lee, 13 May 1944, NA RG 332, ETO G-1, 091.711; Barker to Stewart, 12 October 1943, NA RG 332, ETO AG 685 (Training Grounds); PRO PREM 3/454/2, esp. Attlee to Churchill, 5 November 1943, and COS (43) 659.

36. Gen. Norman Cota to CG ETO, 9 November 1943, ETO AG 685 (Trng Grnds); Fred Houck, poltcl. rpts. 19 and 21, 15 November and 15 December 1943, NA RG 84 Plymouth, 800: PO Reports.

37. Nigel Lewis, *Channel Firing: The Tragedy of Exercise Tiger* (pbk. ed., London, 1990), p. 15 [font]; *Daily Express*, 13 December 1943 [notice].

Chapter 9: A Day Trip to Dieppe

1. Nigel Hamilton, *Monty* (3 vols., pbk. ed., London, 1987), 1: p. 518. Basic accounts are Ronald Atkin, *Dieppe 1942: The Jubilee Disaster* (London, 1980); T. Murray Hunter, *Canada at Dieppe* (Ottawa, 1982); and Brian Loring Villa, *Unauthorized Action: Mountbatten and the Dieppe Raid* (Toronto, 1990)—a highly stimulating if not totally persuasive reappraisal.

2. PRO CAB 65/30, WM (42) 73, 11 June 1942 [Churchill]; Villa, *Unauthorized Action*, p. 160 [air battle]; David Eisenhower, *Eisenhower: At War, 1943–1945* (New York, 1986), p. 96.

3. WSC 4: p. 459; Mountbatten, address, 28 September 1973, IWM Misc. 4/55; John Keegan, *Six Armies in Normandy* (Harmondsworth, 1983), p. 124. Soon after D-Day, journalists (clearly briefed) were discussing the lessons learnt from Dieppe: see *The Times*, 5 August 1944, p. 5.

4. Philip Ziegler, *Mountbatten: The Official Biography* (London, 1986), pp. 194, 196; Hamilton, *Monty*, 1, pt. 4: ch. 16, esp. pp. 516 [quote] and 524–25; Villa, *Unauthorized Action*, pp. 202–8, 237–39.

5. Gilbert, pp. 180–81, 198; Mollie Panter-Downes, *London War Notes, 1939–1945*, William Shawn, ed. (New York, 1971), p. 231—column for 20 June 1942.

6. Villa, *Unauthorized Action*, pp. 193–97, 245 [quote].

7. "Weekly Strength Cdn Army UK," 31 March 1944, RG 24/18688, 133.065 (D223) UK (National Archives of Canada—henceforth NAC)—also the source for other such statistics. See also generally C. P. Stacey and Barbara M. Wilson, *The Half-Million: The Canadians in Britain, 1939–1946* (Toronto, 1987)—the basic background for what follows. There is also

useful material in the wartime volume [C. P. Stacey and George Stanley], *The Canadians in Britain, 1939–1944* (Ottawa, 1945).

8. John Swettenham, *McNaughton* (3 vols., Toronto, 1968–69), 2: pp. 111–12, 182 ["willingness"], 246–47 ["decentralized"]; C. P. Stacey, "Canadian Leaders of the Second World War," *Canadian Historical Review*, 66 (1985), 65 ["acid test"]; Villa, *Unauthorized Action*, pp. 218–20.

9. W.A.B. Douglas and Brereton Greenhous, *Out of the Shadows: Canada in the Second World War* (Toronto, 1977), pp. 103–4.

10. Villa, *Unauthorized Action*, pp. 222–31. In *A Date with History: Memoirs of a Canadian Historian* (Ottawa, 1982), p. 95, C. P. Stacey suggested that Crerar was much keener on the raids than McNaughton, but, as Villa showed, McNaughton also pressed the case.

11. Stacey and Wilson, *Half-Million*, pp. 33–7; Reginald H. Roy, *For Most Conspicuous Bravery: A Biography of Major-General George R. Pearkes, VC, Through Two World Wars* (Vancouver, 1977), pp. 138–39 [pavilion]; CMHQ to 1st Div., 5 February 1940, NAC RG 24/12714, 20/1 DIV/1 ["short changed"]; C. P. Stacey, *Six Years of War: I, The Army in Canada, Britain and the Pacific* (Ottawa, 1955), p. 419 [mail, Crerar].

12. Hardy-Syms, memo, 19 December 1940, NAC RG 24/10088, 14/BILLETS/2, p. 107B; Howard Clegg, *A Canuck in England: Journal of a Canadian Soldier* (London, 1942), pp. 102, 105.

13. Clegg, *Canuck in England*, pp. 99 ["relief"], 126 [bathrooms]. On Aldershot see Peter Holt, "The Local Community: Aldershot—A Case Study," in John Sweetman, ed., *Sword and Mace: Twentieth-Century Civil-Military Relations in Britain* (London, 1986), pp. 79–105.

14. Report in NAC RG 24/12714, p. 23B; Stacey and Wilson, *Half-Million*, p. 40.

15. McNaughton memo, "Discipline," 15 October 1940, NAC RG 24/13692, WD DA and QMG; Mackenzie King diary, 14 September 1940, NAC.

16. Roy, *Pearkes*, pp. 155, 158–9, 161–63; Stacey, *Six Years*, 1: p. 253; Stacey and Stanley, *Canadians in Britain*, ch. II.

17. John A. English, *The Canadian Army and the Normandy Campaign: A Study of Failure in High Command* (New York, 1991), p. 75; Montgomery to Crerar, 28 June 1942, NAC RG 24/10771, 222 C1 (D270); Douglas and Greenhous, *Out of the Shadows*, p. 36 [Breadliner].

18. Terry Copp and Bill McAndrew, *Battle Exhaustion: Soldiers and Psychiatrists in the Canadian Army, 1939–1945* (Montreal, 1990), pp. 11–13, 18, and 59.

19. NAC RG 24/12318, 4/CENSOR/4/3: pp. 20–1 [mutinies], 73 [Russia], 80 [meals], 121 [Aldershot], and 289 ["Heaven"].

20. Stacey, *Six Years*, 1: p. 418 [command]; Copp and McAndrew, *Battle Exhaustion*, pp. 18, 32–3; FCH/CR 15, pp. 2, 5, in NAC RG 24/12318, 4/CENSOR/4/4 [fights].

21. See NAC RG 24/10752, 220 C1 .009 (D47) MORALE.

22. Roy, *Pearkes*, pp. 160, 172; Swettenham, *McNaughton*, p. 184 [Crerar];

Crerar to Commanders, 5 February 1942, NAC RG 24/10771, 222 C1 (D270); Crerar to Montgomery, 5 February 1942, NAC RG 24/10768, 222 C1 (D189). Cf. J. L. Granatstein, *The Generals: The Canadian Army's Senior Commanders in the Second World War* (Toronto, 1993), p. 102.

23. Lord Moran, *The Anatomy of Courage* (London, 1945), p. 145; FCH/CR 35, 4–19 August 1942, p. 2, in NAC RG 24/12319, 4/CENSOR/4/8.
24. Ibid., FCH/CR 36, p. 2 [survivor], and CR 37, p. 2.
25. New York *Daily News*, 20 August 1942, p. 1; *The New York Times*, 20 August 1942, p. 1, and 22 August, p. 4; McNaughton to Ralston, 1 September 1942, NAC RG 24/12329, 4/DIEPPE/1; Eisenhower to Marshall, 20 August 1942, EP 1: pp. 483–84.

Chapter 10: U.S. and Them

1. Baily, report, 20 September 1943, Spaatz papers, LC, box 70: A-Am rels/2; Gilbert, p. 493; Churchill to Attlee, 14 September 1943, PRO FO 954/22A, p. 197.
2. Radcliffe, memo, 5 June 1942, PRO CAB 80/36, COS (42) 295.
3. A. V. Dicey, *Law of the Constitution* (9th ed., London, 1939), p. 300. On the background see Arthur L. Goodhart, letter in *The Times*, 11 August 1942, p. 2, and his article "The Legal Aspect of the American Forces in Great Britain," *American Bar Association Journal*, 28 (November 1942), pp. 762–65.
4. On 1917–18 see JA report in NA RG 120/2473, History of Base Section 3, SOS, AEF, pp. 93–6, and papers in HO 45/19314. The 1933 and 1940 acts are *Public General Acts and Measures*, 23 Geo. 5, c.6 and 3 and 4 Geo. 6, c.51.
5. Attorney General, minute, 20 November 1941, HO 45/19314.
6. Winant to Hull, tel. 3009, 29 May 1942, NA RG 59 811.203/130 (confidential file).
7. PRO CAB 66/23, WP (42) 151; cf. CAB 65/26, WM 50 (42) 5.
8. See NAC RG24/12383, 4/PRO/17, and RG24/12771, 29/US FORCES/1.
9. *The Times*, 3 August 1942, p. 5; CAB 65/27, WM 96 (42) 11, 27 July 1942 [Home Sec.]; cf. report of ETO Theater JA, 1942–6, pp. 6–7, Ray W. Barker papers, 2/4, DDEL.
10. *Daily Telegraph*, 11 August 1942, p. 3; *Time*, 24 August 1942, pp. 62, 64. See also cuttings in HO 45/19315, file 52.
11. Quoting ARC, "Military Relief in Great Britain," November 1918, NA RG 200, ARC (1917–34), 941.08 Reports ["objected"]; History of Base Section 3, p. 336–37, NA RG 120/2473.
12. Rupp., 1: 25–6, 83–4, 254–55; memo of meeting on 6 February 1942, p. 4, NA RG 59, Acheson papers, box 3: British L-L Agreement; Ismay to Churchill, 20 November 1942, PRO PREM 4/26/10, p. 1157 [tea]; Harold L. Ickes MS. diary (LC), 7 February 1942, p. 6328 [FDR]; Somervell to Eisenhower, 19 July 1942, and reply, 27 July, in 16/52 file: box 110, DDEL; John J. McCloy diary, 10 August 1942, McCloy papers DY1/6

(Amherst Coll., MA). See also USFET Gen. Board rpt. 128, "Logistical Build-up in the British Isles," p. 8, MHI.

13. PRO CAB 65/41, WM 13 (44) 5, 31 January 1944; Llewellin report, 16 February 1944, PRO CAB 123/81. Cf. GCMP 3: 615–16.

14. Southern Command conf., 13 July 1942, PRO WO 199/1664; PRO CAB 81/48, BC(L) (42), meetings 10/2, 13/13 and 14/4; WO memo, 15 September 1942, NA RG 332, ETO Adm 270 [Major].

15. Report from Region 10, January 1943, PRO FO 371/34123, A1867/33/45.

16. FCH/CR 15, 5–19 January 1942, p. 1, NAC RG 24/12318, 4/CENSOR/4/4; FCH/CR 66, 21 May–5 June 1943, p. 5, NAC RG 24/12321, 4/CENSOR REPS/1/2.

17. Col. A. H. Killick, min., 20 July 1942, PRO WO 32/10477.

18. HC 377: 1376, 10 February 1942; Kingsley Wood to Churchill, 15 July 1942, PRO PREM 4/12/4.

19. Crerar to Montgomery, 14 July 1942, NAC RG 24/10771, 222C1 (D293) PAY.

20. Kingsley Wood to Cripps, 23 June 1942, and enclosures, PRO CAB 127/62.

21. ETO-1, NA RG 330/94, box 1014; ETO HQ gen. release 1931, 1 June 1944, NA RG 332 ETO Adm 23, doc. 43; SHAEF AGWAR to commanders, AG 123, 14 July 1944, PRO WO 219/1353.

22. PRO WO 163/161, MC/M 3 (43) 25ii; White to Marshall, 22 April 1943, NA RG 165, WD GS G-1, entry 43, 240; Llewellin, report, 16 February 1944, PRO CAB 123/81; Winant to FDR, tel. 4705, 22 August 1942, NA RG 59, 740.0011 EW1939/23712(C); FDR to Winant, 10 September 1942, FDRL PSF 53: GB, Winant.

23. Bernard S. Carter to Norman Davis, tel. 545, 5 February 1942, NA RG 200 ARC 1935–46, 900.616 ETO: Recrtn., 1942–43.

24. Quotations and most statistics from Gibson to Davis, 25 January 1943, NA RG 200 900.08 ETO: Gibson rpt. See also SAF-GB-F, 6 January 1943, attachment 2, in 900.031 ETO: Field Service Letters; Gibson to Eleanor Roosevelt, 14 November 1942, Eleanor Roosevelt papers, FDRL, box 2964: ARC; and report of military observers, 10 December 1943, para. 8d, Robert P. Patterson papers, LC, box 135: GB.

25. On the historical background see NA RG 200 ARC decimal file .004; also monograph in NA RG 332 ETO Adm 538. The WW2 authorization is in Marshall to Davis, 19 December 1941, RG200 900.616 All Theatres (AT): Charges.

26. Also in Australia. See Richard Allen to Chairman, 6 April 1945, NA RG 200 900.616 AT: Recrtn. See also ch. 24.

27. Quotations from USAFBI to AGWAR, tel. 788, 15 March 1942, NA RG 332 ETO AG GR CGC 080: ARC, April–September 1942. Cf. Joseph E. Hayden, report, 16 December 1942, NA RG 200 900.616 ETO: Recrtn., 1942–43 [b&b charges].

28. Carter to Allen, tel. 506, 16 February 1942, NA RG 332 ETO AG GR CGC 080: ARC 1942 [quoting Chaney].

29. NA RG 332 ETO Adm 20: ARC, esp. Stimson to Davis, 20 March 1942; also Stimson diary, 13 April 1942, Sterling Library, Yale University.

30. Robert C. Lewis, report, 13 June 1942, NA RG 200 900.06 ETO: Visits [Londonderry]; AARC mtgs. 1–3 and 6, min. 15, PRO WO 32/10267 [Salisbury].

31. See esp. PRO CAB 123/176, quoting Bracken to Anderson, 23 July 1942; also Altrincham Papers, Bodleian Library, Oxford: esp. Eden to E. Grigg, 27 March 1942 and E. Grigg to Bracken 6 November 1942.

32. Bracken to P. J. Grigg, 6 August 1942, PRO WO 32/10266 ["interfering"]; Eisenhower to AGWAR, 9 August 1942, NA RG 332 ETO 336.2 ["agent"]; Butcher diary, DDEL, 9 July 1942 [Stevenson]; Katherine Lewis, memo, 30 September 1942, NA RG 200 900.616 AT: Recrtn.; History of Amcn. Forces Liaison Div., 1942–45, p. 7, PRO INF 1/327B.

33. Hazard to Gregg, 14 February 1945, RG332 ETO Adm 20 [employees]; Denis Judd, *Lord Reading* (London, 1982), p. 249 [sayings]; Calder, pp. 224–25 [WVS hat, etc.]; Lady Reading, WVS circular, July 1942, enclsd. with Reading to Butcher, 27 July 1942, Butcher papers, DDEL, box 1.

34. Butcher diary, DDEL, 18, 27–8 July 1942; cf. NA RG 200 900.42 ETO: Clothing; Allen to Mrs Davis, 31 October 1942, 900.616 AT: Recrtn. [Bracken].

35. Richard F. Allen (Vice-Chairman ARC, Washington), in Allen-Carter transcript, 20 March 1942, NA RG 200 900.08 ETO: phone convrstns. [on Lady Reading]; Gibson to Lee, 7 April 1943, NA RG 332 ETO AG GR CGC 080: ARC March 43–January 44.

36. Warburg to Eisenhower, 19 August 1942, Butcher papers, DDEL, box 1; cf. Butcher diary, same date.

37. Orders of 19 July and 25 August 1942, EP 1: 396–99 [homes] and 496–97 [propaganda]; Eisenhower to AGWAR, 9 August 1942, NA RG 332 ETO AG 336.2 (NA); Butcher diary, 9 July 1942; Winant to Eisenhower, 12 December 1944, DDEL 16/52 file: box 124.

38. Huxley to Pulsifer, 28 October and 4 November 1942, NA RG 332 ETO AG CGC 080: Clubs, 1942.

39. PRO INF 1/327B, esp. pp. 1, 2, and 9. The account of MOI work for GIs in Ian McLaine's generally valuable book, *Ministry of Morale: Home Front Morale and the Ministry of Information in World War II* (London, 1979), pp. 263–73, is brief and somewhat inaccurate.

Chapter 11: Hearts and Minds

1. Hohler, min., 25 February 1943, PRO FO 371/34123, A1867/33/45.

2. 2nd ind., HQ II Corps to CG AFHQ, 23 November 1942, NA RG 332 ETO AG 250.1: Morals and Conduct, 1942; Hopkins to Churchill, tel., 2 April 1942, FDRL MR, box 13: Hopkins; Spaatz to commanders, 29 September 1942, Spaatz papers, LC, box 322: Eaker.

3. Arnold, notes on Harper to Arnold, 4 January 1943, p. 24, Arnold papers, LC, box 39: US-British problems; Marshall, statement, 18 April 1942, printed in GCMP 3: 165; Butcher diary, DDEL, 14 August 1942.

4. FDR to Churchill, 6 October and reply, 7 October 1942, in C-R 1: pp. 619–20, 625; Winant to FDR, 5 October 1942, FDRL MR, box 12/1A; Marshall to FDR, 8 October 1942, FDRL PPF 8113: S&S. On publishing details see the New York Public Library checklists compiled by C. E. Dornbusch, *Stars and Stripes* (New York, 1948) and *Yank, The Army Weekly* (New York, 1950).

5. Adams, memo, "American Output," 29 July 1942, BBCWAC R34/188; notes of mtg., 29 July 1942, and Cockburn, memo, 24 July 1942 ["lousy"], R34/912/1. The reporter was Frederick R. Kuh, Londonderry, article enclsd. with Stark to Knox, 1 July 1942, Stark papers, NHC, box 1: ComNavEu corr.

6. Calder, pp. 413–22; "A Man in the Street," *Meet the Americans* (London, 1943), pp. 11–12 [CBS]; BBC Cairo to Rendall, 16 May 1942, BBCWAC R34/373/2.

7. See BBCWAC R34/270/1, esp. Rendall, min., 27 March 1941, and Adams, report, 22 December 1942 [Canadians]; BBCWAC R34/907, esp. Adams to Graves, 31 July 1942 [quote], and summary memo, "Broadcasts for American Troops," May 1943.

8. Ryan to Adams, 21 June 1943, and Adams's reply, 25 June 1943, BBC WAC R34/907 [cricket]; Adams to C(P), 20 March 1943, R34/270/2 ["sore"]. On CFN see R34/390.

9. William Phillips diary, vol. 28, 5 August 1942, Houghton Library, Harvard Univ.; Eisenhower to AGWAR 5 August 1942, EP 1: p. 443; Butcher diary, DDEL, 20 August 1942; HQ ETO to commands, 24 August 1942, NA RG 332 ETO AG CGC 091.711: Foreign Armies, 1943.

10. Ibid., G-1 to AG, 11 March 1943 [commendation]; AS 1: pp. 12–13, 18–19, 24.

11. ETO-1, NA RG 330/94, box 1014. Ike's comments are in Butcher diary, DDEL, 9 July 1942.

12. RG 330/94, box 1014: esp. ETO-3 [recreation], ETO-5 [talks], and ETO-8 [ARC].

13. Astor to Andrews, 10 February, and Andrews to Astor, 13 February 1943, Waldorf Astor papers, Reading Univ. Library Ms. 1066/1/217: "American Army Edctn."

14. Penelope Summerfield, "Education and Politics in the British Armed Forces in the Second World War," *International Review of Social History*, 26 (1981), pp. 133–58; S. P. Mackenzie, *Politics and Military Morale: Current-Affairs and Citizenship Education in the British Army, 1914–1950* (Oxford, 1992), chs 4–6, quoting from pp. 86 [Grigg] and 119 [Adam]. Cf. Robert H. Ahrenfeldt, *Psychiatry in the British Army in the Second World War* (London, 1958), pp. 24–5, 38–9.

15. See generally summary memo by Thurman, "Army Talks," NA RG 332 ETO Adm 30 [including Arter quote]; monograph, "Andrews period," pp.

97–106, ETO Adm 499 [quoting Barker and ETO COS Col. Barth on p. 105]; Osborn to Agar, 4 October 1943, NA RG 332 ETO G-1 350: Education, Misc. [Pentagon]

16. Reinhold Niebuhr, "England Teaches Its Soldiers," *The Nation*, 21 August 1943, pp. 208–10; *Time*, 6 September 1943, p. 42.

17. Arter to C/Adm., 21 September 1943, and Lawrence to C/Adm, 17 September 1943, NA RG 332 ETO G-1 350: Education, Misc.; *The New York Times*, 12 October 1943, p. 5.

18. G-1 ETO to Dep. CG, 10 March 1944, NA RG 332 ETO G-1 350 file; RG 332 ETO, *The Administrative and Logistical History of ETOUSA*, pt. XI, vol. II, ch. VII, p. 7 ["genitals"].

19. Eisenhower to AGWAR, 9 August 1942, NA RG 332 ETO AG 336.2; *A Short Guide to Great Britain* (Washington, DC, 1943), pp. 2, 10, 29; *A Pocket Guide to Northern Ireland* (Washington, DC, 1942), p. 2.

20. HQ 8 AFSC, "Indoctrination Program," 10 September 1943, NA RG 332 ETO AG CGC 250.1: Inter-racial reltns., 1943.

21. *A Welcome to Britain*, copy in FDRL Audiovisual, 201–2594-3. Cf. Sir Ronald Adam, TS. memoirs, ch. 10, KCL.

22. "Current Affairs," nos. 22 (18 July 1942) and 26 (12 September 1942)—quoting from the latter.

23. "Current Affairs," 64, 11 March 1944; "Army Talks," vol. II, no. 11, 15 March 1944; Weybright to Mead, 18 January 1944, and Lady Reading to Mead, 22 May 1944, Margaret Mead papers, LC, Organizations file, box E155, folders 3 and 5; Dudley to Weybright, 1 March 1944, PRO FO 371/38623, AN1023.

24. LR/296, 8 July 1941, BBCWAC R9/9/5; PRO INF 1/312, esp. RIO conf., 4 July 1941, min. 4, and Sir Kenneth Clark, "Publicity about USA," 21 June 1941; Sir David Scott to Murray, 22 February 1941, PRO FO 371/26228, A1092/591/45. For fuller detail on what follows see David Reynolds, "Whitehall, Washington and the Promotion of American Studies in Britain during World War Two," JAS 16 (1982), pp. 165–88.

25. Board of Educ. memos, "The Schools in Wartime" series, nos. 26 [quotations] and 28, PRO ED 138/27. On the books see generally PRO ED 121/3 and FDRL Winant papers, box 191: Clarendon Press.

26. PRO ED 121/4, quoting R. A. Butler, min., 18 November 1941, and Adams, report on courses 1941–42, February 1943. Also memo, August 1944, PRO ED 121/102 [statistics].

27. NA RG 84, Manchester Post File, 842, esp. report on Blackley, 18 July 1942; Louis MacNeice, *Meet the US Army* (London, 1943), p. 6; cf. PRO FO 371/34118, A6944/32/45; Moss to Eaker, 23 November 1942, in Spaatz papers, LC, box 322.

28. Tino Balio, ed., *The American Film Industry* (Madison, WI, 1976), p. 394.

29. For what follows see the reports on "Motion Pictures" from U.S. Consuls in Cardiff, 15 February, Birmingham, 23 March, and Manchester, 23 March 1943, in their respective "post files," NA RG 84, 840.6.

30. Eliot to Kuhn, 27 March 1943, NA RG 208/361, box 135: Policy/

London/General; Clayton R. Koppes and Gregory D. Black, *Hollywood Goes to War: How Politics, Profits, and Propaganda Shaped World War II Movies* (New York, 1987), esp. pp. vii [*Manual*], 14–5, 64–71.

31. Gould, memo, 10 August 1944, NA RG 208/567, box 3515: *Arsenic*; Roberts to Mooney, 31 December 1943, ibid., box 3511: "Frontier Outlaws"; Michelle, memo, 2 November 1944, ibid., box 3524: *Meet Me*; Kuhn, memo, 7 January 1943, NA RG 208/566, box 3509: "Kuhn"; also Koppes and Black, *Hollywood*, ch. 6.

32. Kuhn to Ulric Bell, 17 February 1943, NA RG 208/566/3509: "Kuhn"; Cunningham to Revnes, 18 March 1944, box 3517: "Picture of Dorian Gray"; Kaye, review, 16 April 1943, box 3515: *Spitfire*; cf. K.R.M. Short, " 'The White Cliffs of Dover': Promoting the Anglo-American Alliance in World War II," HJFRT 2 (1982), pp. 3–25.

33. Agar to Sherwood, 30 November 1942, and note by Elmer Davis, NA RG 208/573/834: "British Div." On "Young America" see London OWI report, April 1944, NA RG 208/361/130 [quoting p. 27]; and Riley, report, 17 March 1945, PRO ED 121/77.

34. OWI London, report, 5 August 1943, NA RG 208/6/74: London office; Achilles, memo, 22 January 1942, NA RG 59 811.42741/120; cf. Frank A. Ninkovich, *The Diplomacy of Ideas: U.S. Foreign Policy and Cultural Relations 1938–1950* (New York, 1981), ch. 2.

35. Buhrman to Brownell, 5 February 1942, and Buhrman to SecState, 5 August 1942, NA RG 84 Belfast, 841; on Armstrong see RG 84 Manchester, 842 (1942–45).

Chapter 12: Friends and Relations

1. PRO FO 371/34117, A5706; PRO CAB 81/48, BC(L) (43) 17, BC(L) 2 (43) 6; Southern Report, Oct.–Dec. 1943, PRO FO 371/38623, AN394; Baker to Abbey, 16 November 1943, NA RG 84, Bristol, 800 Poltcl; PRO INF 1/327B, p. 7 ["experiment"].

2. Eaker to commands, 14 July 1943, Eaker papers, LC, box 18; RSLO Cambridge, rpt., 12 August 1943, PRO FO 371/34126, A7443; *Time*, 6 December 1943, pp. 36, 39.

3. Margaret S. Carroll, draft memo, 28 December 1943, p. 2, NA RG 84, London, Winant papers, box 4; W. J. Gallman to Hull, desp. 13212, 11 January 1944, NA RG 59, 811.24541/8; Orwell, 3: pp. 55 and 77.

4. Rowe, memo, 22 August 1942, PRO CAB 123/214; Rowe to N. Butler, 10 May 1943, PRO FO 371/34116, A4003.

5. AAR/M (43) 1, min. 4, 4 August 1943, PRO WO 163/222; PRO FO 371/34126, A6417, A6423, A6424; PRO FO 371/34119, A7670, esp. Adam, min., 10 August, and A7757.

6. FRUS: Washington and Quebec, 1943, p. 932; FO min. on PRO FO 954/2, p. 53b, and Eden, note, FO 371/34119, A7670, p. 11.

7. Eden to Dill, 24 August 1943, and Marshall to Dill, 6 September 1943, Marshall papers, GCML, 64/33; AGWAR to London, R-2512 and 2513, 1 September 1943, NA RG 332 ETO AG CGC 091.711.

8. Eaker to Devers, 2 September 1943, Eaker papers, LC, box 18; Devers to Marshall, 3 September 1943, ETO AG CGC 091.711.

9. Rowe to Scott, 7 September 1943, and Rowe to N. Butler, 29 September 1943, PRO FO 371/34119, A7670, A8805; min. by Mason, 14 September on A8461 ["salutary"].

10. WO 163/222, esp. AAR/M 4 (43) 30, 21 October 1943 [terms of ref.]; David Reynolds, "GI and Tommy in Wartime Britain: The Army 'Inter-Attachment' Scheme of 1943–44," JSS 7 (1984), 412–14, 420 [statistics, quotes].

11. Letters from Bovenschen, 9 October, PRO WO 32/10268, and from Devers, 15 October 1943, RG 332 ETO AG CGC box 474 091.711.

12. FO 371/34119: Butler to Campbell, 15 October 1943, A8805; Law, min., 31 August and Law to Davis, 3 September 1943, A7670; cf. Davis to Stimson, 4 September 1943, NA RG 200 ARC 900.91 (ETO).

13. FO 371/38596, esp. Wright to Butler, 14 February 1944, AN 759 ["Cola"] and Campbell to Butler, 7 March 1944, AN1034 [Allen]; FDR to Davis, 8 January 1944, NA RG 200 ARC 900.616 (AT) Recrtn.

14. Allen to Mrs. Dwight Davis, 7 April 1944, and Gibson to Allen, 31 May 1944, NA RG 200 900.91 ETO; memos from Falk and Hazard to Gregg, both 14 February 1945, NA RG 332 ETO Adm. 20 [statistics]; *Leicester Mercury*, 2 May 1944, p. 8; *The New York Times*, 16 March 1944, p. 5, 17 March, p. 9, and 24 March, p. 6; PRO FO 371/38596, esp. Malcolm, min., 7 April 1944, AN1381.

15. NA RG 200 ARC: esp. Gibson to Allen, 31 May 1944, 900.91 (ETO) Criticism; Bracken to Gibson, 26 March 1943, 900.616 (ETO) Recreation; Allen to Gibson, 27 May 1944, 900.91 (AT) Charges ["Allied armies"] and Allen to O'Connor, 10 August 1944, 900.616 (AT) Policies, ETO ["standards"].

16. PRO FO 371/38596: mins. by Alan Dudley, 25 February 1944, AN759; Sir David Scott, 21 March, AN1034 ["canteens"]; and Angus Malcolm, 2 April, AN1283 ["Stalin"].

17. Bracken to Grigg, 30 December 1943, Altrincham Papers, Bodleian Library, Oxford, Ms 1006; INF 1/327B, pp. 9, 28, 68; NA RG 332 ETO Adm. 23 Classfd.: regional reports (3/-5/44).

18. Law, min., 31 December 1943, FO 371/34121, A10601; Ganoe, min., 19 February 1944, RG 332 ETO Adm 23 Classfd. ["agitation"]; Dudley, mins., 16 and 21 February 1944, FO 371/38506, AN 886, AN887.

19. PRO INF 1/150, esp. Haggard, min., 23 October 1944; also Dudley, min., 1 March 1944, FO 371/38506, AN887.

20. See FO 371/38504, AN218; FO 371/38506, AN 886, 887; and FO 371/38507, AN1024, AN1238; also Matthews to Winant, tel. 1642, 9 March 1944, NA RG 59 811.24541/9, Confdntl.

21. PRONI CAB 9CD/225/19, esp. minutes of 10 September 1942 and Stronge/Adams memo, 4 March 1943; Brian Barton, *Brookeborough: The Making of a Prime Minister* (Belfast, 1988), pp. 192–93; MOI report on

U.S. forces, 21 April 1943, in Hoover Library, Stanford Univ., TS. Ireland V 785.

22. Report of mtg., 25 October 1943, and MOI NI hospty. report, June 1944, PRONI CAB 9CD/225/19; PRO INF 1/327B, pp. 85–7.

23. NA RG 332 ETO Adm. 23 Clas.: Ganoe to Lee, 22 March 1944.

24. Minutes of RIO conference on relations in Birmingham, 25 August 1944, INF 1/326; INF 1/327B, esp. pp. 5, 7, 74, and 76.

25. PRO FO 371/38508, AN1643.

26. Parker to RIOs, 10 December 1943, and Butler to Parker, 18 December, FO 371/34122, A11276; Reading letter, 25 January 1944, Eleanor Roosevelt papers, FDRL, box 1739; INF 1/327B, pp. 33–6.

27. INF 1/327B, pp. 33–6, 62–3.

28. Dudley, min., 19 June 1944, FO 371/38596, AN 2298.

29. Gibson to Allen, 31 May 1944, pp. 8–9, ARC 900.91 (ETO) Criticism; de Paula, report, 31 January 1945, ETO Adm. 20B.

30. Statements by DOMG and AG, MC/M 4 (44) 32, 21 April 1944, PRO WO 163/162; INF 1/327B, p. 64 [Willert].

31. BALB 12/126, 4 August 1944, FO 371/38511, AN3143.

32. Ike to Taylor, 24 January 1944, and to Lee, 19 February, EP 3: 1683, 1741; cf. Ike to Sayler, 25 February 1944, Henry B. Sayler papers, DDEL, box 4/7: ETO corr.

33. MOI Hospitality Rpt., 31 October 1944, FO 371/38625 AN3129.

34. Huxley, reports on Oxford, 22/23 February 1944, Northampton, 9 March, Southampton, 10 March, in NA RG 332 ETO Adm. 23 Clas.

35. MOI HI Report 192, 8 June 1944, PRO INF 1/292.

Chapter 13: Male and Female

1. Graham A. Cosmas and Albert E. Cowdrey, *Medical Service in the European Theater of Operations* (Washington, DC, 1992), pp. 118–19; Mattie E. Treadwell, *The Women's Army Corps* (Washington, DC, 1954), p. 772. See generally D'Ann Campbell, *Women at War with America: Private Lives in a Patriotic Era* (Cambridge, MA, 1984), and Campbell, "Servicewomen of World War II," AFS 16 (1990), 251–70.

2. Treadwell, *Women's Army Corps*, pp. 380–409; "History of USSTAF," vol. II, p. 157, OAFH 519.01.

3. Hartle to subordinates, 20 January 1943, NA RG 332 ETO AG 250.1 1943, vol. 1; John Costello, *Love, Sex and War: Changing Values, 1939–1945* (London, 1985), p. 314 [Birmingham]; Edwin R. W. Hale and John Frayn Turner, eds., *The Yanks Are Coming* (New York, 1983), pp. 26–7 [Roesler].

4. Robert Arbib, *Here We Are Together* (London, 1946), p. 86.

5. Joan Blewitt Cox, memoirs, IWM, pp. 497–98; PM to SOS HQ, 12 February 1943, RG 332 ETO AG 250.1 SOS (1943–44) [Cheltenham]; PMG to JA, 26 February 1943, ibid., AG 250.1 1943, vol. 2.

6. Moore, report, 19 August 1943, in PreMed 8: p. 400.

7. PreMed 5: pp. 141–43, 155–79; Philip J. Funigello, *The Challenge to Urban*

Liberalism: Federal-City Relations during World War II (Knoxville, TN, 1978), pp. 144–50.

8. Richard L. Blanco, "The Attempted Control of Venereal Disease in the Army of Mid-Victorian England," *Journal of the Society for Army Historical Research,* 45 (1967), pp. 234–41; Judith R. Walkowitz, *Prostitution and Victorian Society: Women, Class and the State* (Cambridge, 1980); Suzann Buckley, "The Failure to Resolve the Problem of Venereal Disease among the Troops in Britain during World War I," in Brian Bond and Ian Roy, eds., *War and Society: A Yearbook of Military History,* vol. 2 (London, 1977), pp. 65–85.

9. PreMed 5: p. 253; meeting of 29 October 1942, PRO FO 371/34124, A2283/33/45.

10. HC 385: pp. 1807–88; *Time,* 28 December 1942, pp. 23–4.

11. M-O 1573 and 1599 [quotes], 26 January and 23 February 1943.

12. AARC 8th meeting, 1 February 1943, WO 32/10267; Rowe, memo, 26 January 1943, and FO minutes, FO 371/34124, A2283.

13. Minutes of meeting, 16 April 1943, FO 371/34125, A4483; PreMed 5: pp. 237–38, 240–41; Joint Commt. on VD, Interim Report, 29 September 1943, p. 7, copy in NAC RG24/12612, 11/HYG VD/5.

14. *The New York Times,* 2 June 1943, p. 9, and 4 June, p. 4; PRO FO 371/34125, A5268, A5869 [quoting Frankfurter in Wright to Butler, 11 June 1943], and FO 371/34126, A7065.

15. See papers in FO 371/34126, A11600, quoting R. H. Parker (MOI) from mins. of mtg., 7 December 1943; "Talk for meeting at NCSS Bristol," 25 October 1943, [quoting GI on p. 2], Waldorf Astor papers, Ms. 1066/1/636, Reading Univ. Library; Lady Reading to E. Roosevelt, 25 January 1944, Eleanor Roosevelt papers, FDRL, box 1739.

16. PreMed 5: pp. 196–204 [p. 201 on PRO-KIT], 227–28, 232–34.

17. NA RG 332 ETO Adm. History, part XI, vol. I, p. 139; Winant to Marshall, 24 February 1944, Marshall papers, 90/31, GCML; Ike to Marshall, 6 April 1944, and reply, 9 April, NA RG 331 SHAEF 726.1 VD Control.

18. PreMed 5: pp. 254, 256; Gen. Luton to DGMS, Ottawa, 21 September 1944, NAC RG 24/12613, 11/HYG VD/8, p. 48.

19. Keith Sword, et al., *The Formation of the Polish Community in Britain, 1939–50* (London, 1989), p. 404, n. 14; C. P. Stacey and Barbara M. Wilson, *The Half-Million: The Canadians in Britain, 1939–1946* (Toronto, 1987), p. 138.

20. Quotations from "Marriages of Soldiers," AWC Historical Study 6, July 1942, pp. 1–2, AWC Curricular Archives, MHI.

21. AR 600–750, para. 14, and War Dept. Circ. 57, 26 February 1942, MHI Library.

22. William F. Sprague, monograph, "The Problem of Marriages in the ETO," April 1944, pp. 4–5, NA RG 332 ETO Adm 518.

23. Sprague, p. 6; Dep. CG to C/S 10 March 1943, RG 332 ETO AG GR CGC 291.1.

24. Copies of both circulars in ETO AG GR CGC 291.1: HQ SOS.

25. Statistics and quotation from G-1 (Abbott) to C/S, 5 April 1943, ETO AG GR CGC 291.1.

26. ETO AG GR CGC 291.1 HQ SOS: esp. C/S to AG, 25 November 1942, Lee annotation on AG to C/S, 18 December 1942, "Marriage policy of CG, SOS," 30 January 1943.

27. ETO AG GR CGC 291.1: esp. Carrier sheet: "Marriage in UK," March 1943, and Andrews to commanders, 13 April 1943; Hartle to Andrews, 20 April 1943, and Andrews, 1st ind., 22 April 1943, RG 332 ETO Adm 392: Andrews Corr. For an example of deliberate pregnancy see Thurber, report, April 1943, NA RG 200 ARC 1935–46, 900.11/6121 ETO (GB) Camp AU, GB 1041.

28. Elfrieda B. Shukert and Barbara S. Scibetta, *War Brides of World War II* (Novato, CA, 1988), pp. 20–21; AGWAR, memo, 24 November 1943, and inds., NA RG 332 ETO Adm 200.

29. General Registry Office, Edinburgh, circular 11/1942, 30 December 1942, "Marriage with Members of the Forces of the Dominions and Allied Nations"; for the War Dept. exchange with the Canadians see Gen. Guy Henry to John D. Hickerson, 23 February 1944, and M. Wernhof to J. G. Parsons, 1 February 1944, NA RG 59, 811.22/374 and 373 respectively.

30. Quotations from Hartle to Andrews, 20 April 1943, ETO Adm. 392.

31. PRO HO 45/23126 [bigamy]; SW Region reports, September [quotations], October and November 1942, FO 371/34123, A866/33/45 [Elles]; PRO FO 371/30680, A6833/, A7713/990/45, esp. Ward, min., 14 August 1942 in A7713; HC 383: pp. 1745–46, 15 October 1942; and *Birmingham Post*, 16 October 1942; Lang to Devers, 18 May 1943, RG 332 ETO AG GR CGC 291.1.

32. E. L. Davies to Dominions Office, 13 September 1943, PRO HO 45/23126, file 827, 371/24; JA to G-1, 31 December 1943, ETO AG GR CGC 291.1.

33. Sprague, monograph, p. 21, ETO Adm 518.

Chapter 14: Black and White

1. This chapter draws on material deployed in more detail in David Reynolds, "The Churchill Government and the Black American Troops in Britain during World War II," *Transactions of the Royal Historical Society*, 5s, 35 (1985), pp. 113–33. See also Graham Smith, *When Jim Crow Met John Bull: Black American Soldiers in World War II Britain* (London, 1987); and Christopher Thorne, "Britain and the Black GIs: Racial Issues and Anglo-American Relations in 1942," in *Border Crossings: Studies in International History* (Oxford, 1988), pp. 259–74.

2. Henry L. Stimson diary, 13 January 1942, Sterling Library, Yale Univ.; Stimson annotations on Eisenhower to Marshall, 25 March 1942, NA RG 165, OPD 291.21.

3. F. E. Evans, min., 22 January 1942, PRO FO 371/26206, A10036/257/45.

4. PRO 79/20, COS 126 (42) 11, 21 April 1942; Chaney to AGWAR, tel. 1151, 17 April 1942, and Marshall to Chaney, tel. 769, 19 May 1942, NA RG 165, OPD 291.21.

5. Ulysses Lee, *The Employment of Negro Troops* (Washington, 1966), p. 433; CAB 81/49, MPS (42) 22 [beds]; HDE(B) (42) 1, para. 7, in HO 45/19314, file 26 [Betts]; Harry L. Hopkins papers, FDRL, box 136: Colored Troops; PRO CAB 65/27, WM 119 (42) 6; R. I. Campbell to FO, tel. 4086, 12 August 1942, PRO FO 954/30A, p. 151; FDR to Marshall, 25 August, Marshall to FDR, 9 September and FDR to Winant, 10 September 1942, FDRL, PSF 106. Eden's remarks to Winant about climate in Eden to Halifax, tel. 692, 1 September 1942, FO 954/298, US/42/158. This document was kept closed for fifty years, perhaps because of the embarrassing spuriousness of its arguments.

6. Stimson diary, 24 September and 2 October 1942; James P. Warburg to Elmer Davis, 1 September 1942, NA RG 107/47, ASW 291.2 [Sulzberger]; Spaatz to CG ETO, 24 July 1942, Spaatz papers, LC, box 322: Eaker.

7. Eisenhower to Gen. Surles, 10 September 1942, Harry C. Butcher papers, box 1, DDEL.

8. White to Davis 18 August and 16 December 1942, NAACP papers, LC, II/A/24: ARC Service Clubs; PRO FO 371/30680, A11660, A11903/990/45, quoting min. by Angus Malcolm, 28 December 1942; Eleanor Roosevelt to Stimson, 22 September 1942, in Morris J. MacGregor and Bernard C. Nalty, eds., *Blacks in the United States Armed Forces: Basic Documents*, vol. V (Wilmington, DE, 1977), p. 170; Stimson diary, 2 October 1942.

9. Stark to Knox, 1 July 1942, Harold L. Stark papers, NHC, box 1: ComNavEu correspondence.

10. Butcher diary, 15 August 1942; Eisenhower press conf., 14 July 1942, p. 11, and Eisenhower to Daniell, 17 August 1942, Butcher papers, box 1.

11. ETO HQ, "Policy on Negroes," 16 July 1942, printed in full in Lee, *Negro Troops*, pp. 623–24.

12. Eisenhower to Lee, 5 September 1942, EP 1: pp. 544–45.

13. Draft History of USSTAF, vol. II, ch. 2, table XV, OAFH 519.01; HQ V Corps to CG SOS, 19 August 1942, and encls., NA RG 332, ETO AG CGC 291.2: August 42–October 43, item 326.

14. Carter, rpt., September 1942, NA RG 247, 201 file, Carter, Edwin R., Jr.; Davis diary, 2 October 1942, and Davis to Sadie Davis, 25 and 30 September and 4 October 1942 in Benjamin O. Davis, Sr., papers, MHI.

15. Davis, Antrim report, 10 October 1942, Davis papers, MHI, box T-11: Inspctn. tours, Europe, 1941–45; RG 332, ETO AG CGC 291.2: August

42–October 43: esp. Gaige to G-1, 23 July, Montgomery to Lee, 26 August, and Lee to Plank, 28 September.

16. Ibid.: Landon, memo, 7 August 1942 ["pride"]; Montgomery to Lee, 5 August 1942; G-1, memo for the records, 24 August 1942 [Carter's brief]; Davis to CG ETO, 25 October 1942; Marvin E. Fletcher, *America's First Black General: Benjamin O. Davis, Sr., 1880–1970* (Lawrence, KS, 1989), p. 104 [OCS].

17. Winant to FDR, tel. 4705, 22 August 1942, NA RG 59 740.0011 EW1939/23712; Martha S. Putney, *Blacks in the Women's Army Corps during World War II* (Metuchen, NJ, 1992), p. 97; Gibson, statement 16, 8 September 1942, NA RG 332 ETO AG GR CGC 080: ARC, ETO, April–September 1942; Beinecke, in SOS Staff Conf., 30 August 1943, ETO Adm 20: ARC [negro staff clubs]. Cf. ARC statement, 23 December 1942, that the Duchess St. club in London "will be used exclusively for Negro troops" (OAFH 519.7022).

18. RG332 ETO AG GR CGC 080: ARC SOS (June 42–December 43), item 8, quoting SS Section to AG SOS, 7 November 1942, and G-1 to AG, 11 November 1942; cf. Rupp., 1: 154–59 [on G-25].

19. HO letter, 4 September 1942, printed in PRO CAB 66/29, WP (42) 456; Dahlquist to Newsam, 3 September 1942, RG 332 ETO AG GR CGC 291.2: (1943) Negroes.

20. See PRO CO 876/14, esp. WO draft paper, 8 September 1942 [on 5 August mtg.] and Dowler's notes.

21. RIO, Manchester, 23 July 1942, PRO CAB 123/176 [Chester]; BC(L) (42) Misc. 3, 12 August 1942, CO 876/14; BBC West Regional Director, memo, 14 August 1942, BBCWAC, R 34/912/1; *Sunday Pictorial*, 6 September 1942, p. 3 [Worle].

22. *Daily Herald*, 7 September 1942, cf. Plank to Eisenhower, 9 October 1942, in NA RG 332 ETO AG CGC 291.2: August 42–October 43; *New Statesman and Nation*, 22 August 1942, p. 121, and 19 September 1942, p. 184; Commons, *Debates*, 5s, 383: p. 670, 29 September 1942; CO 876/14, esp. J. L. Keith, min., 12 September, WO draft paper, 8 September 1942 and final version WP 441.

23. Memo by Cranborne, 3 October 1942, CAB 66/29, WP (42) 442; David Dilks, ed., *The Diaries of Sir Alexander Cadogan, OM, 1938–1945* (London, 1971), p. 483.

24. PRO CAB 65/28, WM 140 (42) 4, 13 October 1942; minute by Sir Arthur Dawe [quotation] and letter from Col. Rolleston, WO, 31 October 1942, CO 876/14.

25. Law, min., 5 October 1942, and Eden, notes, FO 371/30680, A9731/990/45; John Harvey, ed., *The War Diaries of Oliver Harvey 1941–1945* (London, 1978), p. 141; PREM 4/26/9, p. 864 [Eisenhower]; CAB 66/30, WP (42) 473; CAB 65/28, WM 143 (42) 3; "Current Affairs," 32 (5 December 1942), p. iii.

26. Lee, *Negro Troops*, p. 433; Statistical summaries, 31 January and 10 July

1944, NA RG 332, ETO Adm 424; Negro morale report, 16–30 April 1944, ETO Adm 218; Dehra Parker to Robert Gransden, 3 January 1944, PRONI 9CD/225/19.

27. PRO CAB 66/29, WP (42) 459, 12 October 1942 [Bracken]; Grigg to Churchill, 21 October 1943, PRO PREM 4/26/9; PRO FO 371/34126, A10199, esp. Haig, memo, 6 September 1943 and minute by Donnelly, 16 November 1943.

28. Butler, min., 24 November 1943, ibid., A10199; Butler to Wright, 14 March 1944, PRO FO 371/38609, AN 587 ["friends"]; cf. H. G. Nicholas, ed., *Washington Despatches, 1941–1945* (Chicago, 1981), p. 345 [Patton].

29. All quotations from reports in PRO FO 371/34126, A6556, except Leicester, which is from FO 371/38624, AN2089.

30. Riddell, mtg. of 10 June 1943, min. 6, PRO FO 371/34117, A5706, and SOS order, 13 January 1944, NA RG 332 ETO Adm. 270 [billeting]; AAR/M 2 (44) 10, 16 February 1944, PRO WO 163/222 [exchanges]; PRO INF 1/327B, pp. 36–7, and BALB 2/13, 17 March 1944, PRO FO 371/38507, AN1301 [Welcome Clubs].

31. Quotations from SOS Staff conference, 20 September 1943, pp. 9 [Plank], 14 [Lee], NA RG 332 ETO Adm. 455.

32. Depositions by Farrell, 27 November and Leslie, 29 November 1943, in 8AFSC IG report, 3 December 1943, NA RG 332 ETO AG CGC 250.1: Interracial relations, 1943.

33. William A. Weaver, *Yankee Doodle Dandy* (Ann Arbor, MI, 1958), p. 365.

34. IG to G-1, 7 January 1944, NA RG 332 ETO AG GR CGC 291.1; cf. *Reynolds News*, 9 February 1947 [Davenport].

35. Harbaugh, memo, 29 August 1944, and 4th ind. on Anderson case, 8 January 1945, OAFH, USSTAF 519.765-1.

36. See papers in USSTAF 519.765.1 (quoting Celia ____ to HQ USSTAF, 29 November 1944) and 519.7071-1; cf. BALB 15 (1944) 168, 26 September 1944, PRO FO 371/38513, AN3827. Surnames have been omitted to respect personal privacy.

37. White, Observations on ETO, 11 February 1944, p. 11, NAACP papers, LC, II/A/587; ETO JA History, 1: pp. 13, 237–41, NA RG 332 ETO Adm 559A; Gunnar Myrdal, *An American Dilemma: The Negro Problem and American Democracy* (2 vols., New York, 1944), p. 550.

38. HC 399: 1875–76, 400: 2132, 401: 42, 1415–27, 10 May, 15 and 20 June, 6 July 1944 [Davies, col. 1875]; cf. FO 371/38623, AN1847, AN1879.

39. All legal discussion of the trial comes from U.S. Army, JAGO, CM 264262 (CM ETO 2863). I have omitted the names of the two people involved.

40. Ibid., review by XIX Corps JA, 2 June 1944.

41. *Daily Mirror*, 30 May and 2 June 1944; King, 3 June 1944, p. 255; Dean, min., 17 June 1944, PRO FO 371/38624, AN2244; *Tribune*, 9 June 1944, pp. 9–11; see also NA RG 407, AG 291.2 file for June 1944.

42. JAGO, CM 264262, review by ETO asst. staff judge advocate, 17 June 1944, with concurrence by Betts and statement by Eisenhower.

43. Ibid., draft memo, no date, by XIX Corps JA; Ganoe to O'Donnell, 21 June 1944, NA RG 332 ETO Adm 218.

44. DTPM and TPM, 1 June 1944, NA RG 332 ETO PR Sec. 291.2; Lawrence to Agar 19 June 1944, ETO AG GC 092; PRO FO 371/38510, AN2591, BALB 84/10, 23 June 1944; HQ UK Base to CG Com Z, 21 November 1944 [quote] and reply, 7 December, NA RG 332 ETO AG 250.1 1944, vol. 2.

45. See NA RG 332 ETO AG GR GC 291.2, 1944 vol. 2: quoting Lawrence to DTC, 22 June 1944 and Betts to G-1, 28 June.

Chapter 15: Yanks

1. Orwell, 3: p. 54.

2. Rupp., 1: pp. 233–34 [*Queens*]; William E. Jones, 4th Inf., UNO Orals. These paragraphs are a mosaic of many fragments of evidence, particularly from MHI and UNO oral histories. Only direct quotations will be specifically cited.

3. "Arrival of American Troops in Northern Ireland, 27/1/42" and "American Troop Interviews, 30/1/42," in BBCWAC, Talks: Denis Johnston.

4. George E. McIntyre, memoirs, MHI, p. 88 ["curious"]; William S. Weston, memoirs, MHI, p. 32 ["subway"]; Evelyn Waugh, *Put Out More Flags* (pbk. ed., London, 1943), p. 215.

5. Joseph B. Mittelman, *Eight Stars to Victory: A History of the Veteran Ninth U.S. Infantry Division* (Washington, DC, 1948), p. 51; Chester B. Hansen, War Diaries, MHI, September 1943; Omar N. Bradley, *A Soldier's Story* (New York, 1951), pp. 170–71.

6. ETO-1 supplementary report, 2 November 1942, p. 18, NA RG 330/94, box 1014; cf. AS 1: pp. 365, 369.

7. ETO SOS Research report 9, 13 September 1943, NA RG 332 ETO AG 250.1, 1943, vol. 3.

8. UNO orals: 101st A/B, Walter Gordon, tape 4, p. 5, and 29th Div., Harold Baumgarten, p. 2 [tents]; MHI, WW2 questionnaires, 29th Div.: Baumgarten, p. 21 ["Jew"].

9. On 8AF see, e.g., Eaker to McGinnis, 31 May 1942, and to 8BC commanders, 29 September 1942, Spaatz papers, box 322: Eaker corr. (LC); ETO-2, RG 330/94, box 1014, pp. 4–5; mid-1943 figures from "What the Soldier Thinks," 2 (August 1943), p. 65, Philleo Nash papers, HSTL, box 34.

10. Stephen E. Ambrose, *Band of Brothers* (New York, 1992), p. 47 [Webster]; AARC report on U.S. Troops, 8 March 1943, copy in NA RG 332 ETO AG CGC 250.1 SOS.

11. Cf. Paul Fussell, *Wartime: Understanding and Behavior in the Second World War* (New York, 1990), ch. 9; Henry Elkin, "Aggressive and Erotic Tendencies in Army Life," AJS 51 (1946), pp. 408–13.

12. Ted Fossieck to Janice Fossieck, 26 December 1943 and 9 January 1944, Theodore H. Fossieck papers, MHI.

13. See his diary, quoting from 4 September and 2 November 1943, 2 January and 17 April 1944 (Yale Divinity School, Ms Gp. 30, box 264).

14. Kay Summersby Morgan, *Past Forgetting: My Love Affair with Dwight D. Eisenhower* (New York, 1975), esp. pp. 171–74; Stephen E. Ambrose, *Eisenhower* (2 vols., New York, 1983), esp. 1: pp. 188–90, 277–78, 415, 418 [quotation].

15. Richard R. Lingeman, *Don't You Know There's A War On?: The American Home Front, 1941–1945* (New York, 1976), p. 93.

16. Ted Fossieck to Janice Fossieck, 12 March 1944, MHI.

17. "Doughboy Ambassador: Letters from Dick Murray to Herbert Kubly," *Common Ground*, V/2 (Winter 1945), p. 94.

18. NA RG 330/94, ETO-2 survey, pp. 5–6.

19. William S. Weston, "History of Battery B, 459th AAA AW Bn.," 1: 41, MHI WW2 surveys, 29th Div.; WO DQMG(L), "Digest of November [1942] Reports," PRO WO 32/10267 [Chester].

20. NA RG 84 London post files, 814.2 ARC, U.S. Forces, Gen. (1942): quoting from Armstrong, supplementary memo, 22 July 1942, p. 3, and Wilkinson to Abbey, 13 June and 2 December 1942.

21. Wilkinson to Abbey, 23 June 1942, NA RG 84 Birmingham, 814.2 ARC; Mittelman, *Eight Stars to Victory*, p. 155.

22. Margaret Mead, "A GI View of Britain," *The New York Times Magazine*, 19 March 1944, p. 18.

23. ETO-1, RG 330/94 [spending]; John P. Downing, *At War with the British* (Daytona Beach, FL, 1980), pp. 29–32 [1st Div.].

24. Gen. Rogers to CG SOS, 10 June 1943, NA RG 332 ETO AG 250.1 1943, vol. 3; author's interview with Curtis C. Moore, 24 August 1993; *Daily Mirror*, 1 January 1944, p. 3.

25. Letter to Beatrice, 11 August 1942, in Martin Blumenson, *The Patton Papers* (2 vols., Boston, 1972–74), 2: p. 82; Leland D. Baldwin diary, OAFH 168.7163, pp. 44 [ruins] and 52 [coffee].

26. M-O 1657, 2 April 1943, p. 13.

27. Buhrman, desp. 150, 11 September 1942, NA RG 84 Belfast, 823 Conf., and report 65, 8 September 1942, ibid., 800 Conf.; M-O 1306, 8 June 1942, p. 1.

28. Bettman, report, February 1944, pp. 37–40, PRO INF 1/327A; Armstrong, "Social Relations" report, 14 April 1944, pp. 1 and 3, NA RG 84 Manchester: 800, Spec. Pol. Reports; Margaret Mead, "As Johnny Thinks of Home He Learns Little in England," *Social Action*, 10/3, 15 March 1944, pp. 7–13.

29. 8AF PM, report, 10 November 1943, Spaatz papers, LC, box 70.

30. ETO-13 and -17, 14 December 1943, 21 March 1944, NA RG 330/94; Devers to Eaker, 22 December 1943, Spaatz papers, box 324.

31. MOI HI Special Report 40, 11 March 1943, p. 3, PRO INF 1/293; Mail Censorship Report 104, PRO FO 371/44601, AN147.
32. Spry to Butler, 4 May 1943, PRO FO 371/34116, A4003.
33. Daniel Glaser, "The Sentiments of American Soldiers Abroad Toward Europeans," AJS 51 (March 1946), p. 438.

Chapter 16: Gals

1. *Daily Mirror*, 20 December 1943, p. 5.
2. Margaret Mead, "A GI View of Britain," *The New York Times Magazine*, 19 March 1944, p. 34.
3. Bridget A. Johnson (née Goodlace), memoir, IWM, p. 2.
4. A. H. Halsey, ed., *Trends in British Society since 1900* (London, 1972), p. 559; Avice R. Wilson, memoir, IWM, p. 1.
5. Shirley Joseph, *If Only Their Mothers Knew: An Unofficial Account of Life in the Women's Land Army* (London, 1946), p. 47.
6. Norman Longmate, *How We Lived Then: A History of Everyday Life during the Second World War* (London, 1971), p. 419.
7. IWM 90/10/1, pt. 2, p. 66.
8. Norman Longmate, *The G.I.s* (London, 1975), p. 257; author's interview with Harry Crosby, 3 September 1992.
9. *Current Affairs*, 64 (11 March 1944), pp. 11–14; cf. Margaret Mead, "What Is a Date?," *Transatlantic*, June 1944, pp. 54–60.
10. Roger A. Freeman, *The Friendly Invasion* (Lavenham, 1992), p. 74; Ganoe, talk with Miss Farrand, 17 November 1943, NA RG 332 ETO Adm 212 [ARC quote]; Longmate, *G.I.s*, p. 261.
11. Juliet Gardiner, *"Over Here"* (London, 1992), p. 116 [Bing].
12. Richard M. Titmuss, *Problems of Social Policy* (London, 1976 ed.), p. 562; Evelyn Waugh, *Put Out More Flags* (London, 1943), p. 80; W. K. Hancock and M. M. Gowing, *British War Economy* (London, 1975 ed.), p. 351; Penny Summerfield, *Women Workers in the Second World War: Production and Patriarchy in Conflict* (London, 1984), pp. 31, 62.
13. Quotations from Sheila Ferguson and Hilde Fitzgerald, *Studies in the Social Services* (London, 1978 ed.), pp. 97–8.
14. Longmate, *How We Lived Then*, pp. 337, 341.
15. King, p. 288; M-O 2022, 16 February 1944, p. 8.
16. M-O 1635, 1835 [quotation], 1836 and 1970, 30 March, 11 and 23 June, 8 December 1943.
17. Summerfield, *Women Workers*, chs. 3–4, quoting p. 131.
18. Summerfield, *Women Workers*, p. 97 [child care]; memo on "Service Pay and Allowances," 20 March 1944, GEN 31/7, in PRO CAB 78/20; Ferguson and Fitzgerald, *Studies in the Social Services*, pp. 21–2; Harold D. Smith, ed., *War and Social Change: British Society in the Second World War* (Manchester, 1986), pp. 196–97 [debt]; Eliot Slater and Moya Woodside, *Patterns of Marriage: A Study of Marriage Relationships in the Urban Working Classes* (London, 1951), pp. 216–17.

19. Ferguson and Fitzgerald, *Studies in the Social Services*, pp. 23 [Army MO], 98 [Birmingham], and 99 [probation officer]; *The Registrar General's Statistical Review of England and Wales, 1940–1945* (London, 1951), text, vol. II, civil, p. 24 [marriages]; Slater and Woodside, *Patterns of Marriage*, p. 215 [London woman].

20. Slater and Woodside, *Patterns of Marriage*, pp. 220–21; Colin and Eileen Townsend, eds., *War Wives: A Second World War Anthology* (London, 1990), pp. 109–12.

21. O. R. McGregor, *Divorce in England: A Centenary Study* (London, 1957), pp. 41, 43–4 [quote]; Jane Waller and Michael Vaughan-Rees, *Women in Wartime: The Role of Women's Magazines, 1939–1945* (London, 1987), pp. 75–6.

22. Registrar General, *Statistical Review, 1940–5*, pp. 54, 80.

23. McGregor, *Divorce in England*, ch. 1; *The Registrar General's Statistical Review of England and Wales, 1946–1950* (London, 1954), text, civil, p. 90.

24. Quoting from *The Registrar General's Statistical Review of England and Wales, 1938–1939* (London, 1947), text, p. 192 ["revelation"]; *Statistical Review, 1940–5*, pp. 79–80.

25. *Statistical Review, 1940–5*, p. 81.

26. Jeffrey Weeks, *Sex, Politics and Society: The Regulation of Sexuality since 1800* (London, 1981), pp. 60–5; Peter Laslett and Karen Oosterveen, "Long-term Trends in Bastardy in England: A Study of the Illegitimacy Figures in the Parish Registers and in the Reports of the Registrar General, 1561–1960," *Population Studies*, 27 (1973), esp. p. 270; N.F.R. Crafts, "Illegitimacy in England and Wales in 1911," *Population Studies*, 36 (1982), pp. 327–31; Peter Laslett, Karla Oosterveen, and Richard M. Smith, eds., *Bastardy and Its Comparative History* (London, 1980), esp. pp. 53–65.

27. Eustace Chesser, *The Sexual, Marital and Family Relationships of the English Woman* (London, 1956), pp. 311, 355.

28. Derek Thompson, "Courtship and Marriage in Preston between the Wars," *Oral History*, 3/2 (Autumn 1975), pp. 42–3; cf. Slater and Woodside, *Patterns of Marriage*, pp. 94–5.

29. Avice Wilson, memoirs, IWM, p. 3; Longmate, *G.I.s*, p. 272 [journalist]; Longmate, *How We Lived Then*, p. 420 [Bournemouth girl]; *Time*, 10 August 1942, p. 44.

30. Private information.

31. *Current Affairs*, 11 March 1944, p. 14.

32. Joan Blewitt Cox, memoirs, IWM, pp. 492–512.

33. Barbara Wace to Lady Astor, 19 April 1944, Nancy Astor papers, Reading University Library, MS 1416/1/1/1642; John Warren to Elizabeth Warren, 22 April 1944, in Michael E. Stevens, ed., *Letters from the Front, 1898–1945* (Madison, WI, 1992), pp. 86–7.

34. Calder, pp. 363–64 [quotation]; background in Longmate, *How We Lived Then*, ch. 15.

35. AAR/M (44) 8 annex, WO 163/222 [AAF parties]; Clinton Reams, UNO orals, 1st Div., pp. 20–1.

36. M-O 1657, 2 April 1943, p. 12 [begging]; diary entries for 20, 22, 23, 25 October and 13 December 1943, Ms Gp. 30, box 264 (Yale Divinity School Library).

37. George E. McIntyre, memoirs, MHI, pp. 91–6.

38. MOI HI Spec. Rpt. 40, 11 March 1943, p. 2, PRO INF 1/293.

Chapter 17: Flyboys

1. R. J. Overy, *The Air War, 1939–1945* (London, 1980), p. 102; Max Hastings, *Bomber Command* (London, 1979), p. 349.

2. Roger A. Freeman, *The Mighty Eighth: A History of the Units, Men and Machines of the US 8th Air Force* (London, 1986 ed.), p. 51; D. A. Lande, *From Somewhere in England: The Life and Times of 8th AF bomber, fighter and ground crews in World War II* (London, 1991), p. 47 [Stone]. Mission statistics here and elsewhere are taken from Roger A. Freeman, *The Mighty Eighth War Diary* (London, 1991 ed).

3. Roger A. Freeman, *The American Airman in Europe* (London, 1991), p. 56.

4. Roger A. Freeman, *Airfields of the Eighth: Then and Now* (London, 1978), p. 160 [Mendlesham].

5. Author's interview with Harry Crosby, 3 September 1992; John Comer, *Combat Crew* (London, 1978), p. 42.

6. Lande, *From Somewhere*, pp. 28–30.

7. Harry H. Crosby, *A Wing and a Prayer: The "Bloody 100th" Bomb Group of the U.S. Eighth Air Force in Action Over Europe in World War II* (New York, 1993), pp. 140–41; Lande, *From Somewhere*, p. 62 [Bieck]; Juliet Gardiner, *"Over Here"* (London, 1992), p. 177 [navigator]; USSTAF Surgeon, "Report on morale of combat crew of 8AF," 31 August 1944, para. 8, OAFH 519.701 (1944–46).

8. Comer, *Combat Crew*, pp. 251, 258.

9. Freeman, *Airfields*, p. 29 [Bassingbourn]; Lande, *From Somewhere*, p. 24 [Attlebridge].

10. Comer, *Combat Crew*, p. 205.

11. Freeman, *Airfields*, p. 16 [Alconbury]; Freeman, *American Airman*, p. 115 [Gjelhaug]; Lande, *From Somewhere*, p. 62 [Schroepfer]; USSTAF Surgeon, "Report on morale of combat crew of 8AF," 31 August 1944, App. B.

12. USSTAF Surgeon, "Report on morale of combat crew of 8AF," 31 August 1944, para. 8; ETO Research Branch, "Attitudes of Combat Crews," 8 July 1944, OAFH 519.701 (1944–45).

13. Freeman, *Mighty Eighth*, pp. 63–6 [Blitz Week]; Richard Le Strange, *Century Bombers: The Story of the Bloody Hundredth* (Thorpe Abbotts, 1989), pp. 15–19.

14. Freeman, *Mighty Eighth War Diary*, p. 89; Comer, *Combat Crew*, pp. 42–54.

15. Crosby interview.

16. K.A.H. Murray, *Agriculture* (London, 1955), p. 20 [Slump]; Ronald Blythe, *Akenfield: Portrait of an English Village* (Harmondsworth, 1972), p. 316 [McIver]. "Akenfield" is actually Debach, a village north of Ipswich, which hosted an 8AF base during the war.

17. Calder, p. 488.

18. Blythe, *Akenfield*, p. 320.

19. Memo, "Aerodrome Programme," May 1942, PRO PREM 3/333/7, p. 386; R. Douglas Brown, *East Anglia 1942* (Lavenham, 1988), p. 170 [Ridgewell].

20. *The Times*, 17 August 1942, p. 2; cf. PRO CAB 81/48, BC(L) (42) 83 and BC(L) 18 (42) 6.

21. Freeman, *Airfields*, p. 84 [Eye]; Le Strange, *Century Bombers*, pp. 8, 64–6; Norman Longmate, *The G.I.'s* (London, 1975), pp. 156–57 [Polebrook].

22. Roger A. Freeman, *The Peaceful Invasion* (Lavenham: 1992), pp. 31; Freeman, *Mighty Eighth*, pp. 243–44, 248–50.

23. King, pp. 194, 216, 230–31.

24. PreMed 5: p. 255; Freeman, *Peaceful Invasion*, pp. 12, 66; C. P. Stacey and Barbara M. Wilson, *The Half-Million: The Canadians in Britain, 1939–1946* (Toronto, 1987), p. 151 [Bomber Command].

25. Michael J. F. Bowyer, *Action Stations: The Military Airfields of Cambridge-shire* (Wellingborough, 1987), p. 23; cf. Freeman, *Mighty Eighth War Diary*, p. 89; Longmate, *G.I.'s*, p. 150; Lande, *From Somewhere*, p. 62 [Kranz].

26. Longmate, *G.I.'s*, p. 151 [ARC woman]; Lande, *From Somewhere*, pp. 16, 85–6 [Kupferman];

27. Andrews to Marshall, 20 January 1943, NA RG 332, ETO Adm 392; Portal to Evill for Arnold, 19 February 1943, copy in Spaatz papers, LC, box 323: Eaker; Maurice Matloff, *Strategic Planning for Coalition Warfare, 1943–1944* (Washington, DC, 1959), p. 28.

28. On this "broker" diplomacy see Alex Danchev, *Very Special Relationship: Field-Marshal Sir John Dill and the Anglo-American Alliance, 1941–44* (London, 1986), ch. 6. On how precise was American "precision bombing" see Ronald Schaffer, "American Military Ethics in World War II: The Bombing of German Civilians," and the ensuing exchange in JAH, 67 (1980), pp. 318–34, and 68 (1981), 85–92.

29. John Terraine, *The Right of the Line: The Royal Air Force in the European War, 1939–1945* (London, 1988), pp. 513–14; C&C 2: 373–75 ["complementary," p. 374]; Hastings, *Bomber Command*, p. 187.

30. Sir Charles Webster and Noble Frankland, *The Strategic Air Offensive Against Germany* (4 vols., London, 1961), 2: p. 5.

Chapter 18: Negroes

1. Army Mail Censorship Report no. 64, 26 March–10 April 1943, p. 2, PRO FO 371/34124, A2391. The fullest study of the topic is Graham A. Smith, *When Jim Crow Met John Bull: Black American Soldiers in World War II Britain* (London, 1987).
2. See John O'Regan, ARC Field Director, report for August 1943, NA RG 200, 900.11/6121 ETO (GB) Camp AY, GB-1045.
3. MOI regional reports, 2–9 March 1943, PRO FO 371/34123, A1609; Rowe, report, 8 March 1943, copy in NA RG 332 ETO AG CGC, 250.1: SOS.
4. *New Statesman and Nation*, 26 September 1942, p. 202; Leland D. Baldwin MS diary, p. 28 (OAFH 168.7163); R. Douglas Brown, *East Anglia, 1942* (Lavenham, 1988), p. 165 [Vicar].
5. Regional Commissioners' Reports, August 1942, in PRO FO 371/34123, A866; MOI HI Weekly, no. 102, PRO INF 1/292.
6. Norman Longmate, *The G.I.'s* (London, 1975), p. 129; Smith, *Jim Crow*, p. 198; Haig, memo, 6 September 1943, PRO FO 371/34126, A10199.
7. Smith, *Jim Crow*, p. 118; Poynton, min., 17 March 1944, PRO CO 537/1223 ["blimpish"]; figures from Keith, min., 20 November 1944, PRO CO 537/1223, and memo in PRO CO 876/14, doc. 4.
8. CO LBC to CO ETO, 10 March 1943, NA RG 332 ETO AG GR CGC 291.2 (1943); Constantine to Watson, 12 January 1943, PRO CO 876/15, which also contains details of the Waldron case.
9. Buccleuch to Macmillan, 30 September 1942, PRO CO 876/41; Petherick to Eden, 16 August 1942, 17 July and 4 December 1943, PRO FO 954/30A; Keith, min., 28 August 1942, PRO CO 876/14 [on WVS]; Ann Meader, diary, 4 October 1942, Hoover Inst., Stanford.
10. Smith, *Jim Crow*, p. 202; WO Q(AL), memo, 13 November 1942, copy in NA RG 332 ETO AG 336.2.
11. Anthony H. Richmond, *Colour Prejudice in Britain: A Survey of West Indian Workers in Liverpool, 1941–1951* (London, 1954), quoting pp. 20, 78; K. L. Little, "Loudoun Square: A Community Survey," *The Sociological Review*, 34 (1942), pp. 12–33, 119–46, quoting p. 27; and Little, "The Psychological Background of White-Coloured Contacts in Britain," ibid., 35 (1943), pp. 12–28, quoting p. 28.
12. Little, "Psychological Background," pp. 14, 18.
13. 8AF Provost Marshal, report, 10 November 1943, Spaatz papers, LC, box 70: A-Am. Rels.
14. Richmond, *Colour Prejudice*, p. 84; Graham A. Smith, "Jim Crow on the Home Front," *New Community*, 8/3 (1980), p. 322 [Constantine]; I. G. Cummings, "Colour Discrimination in the United Kingdom," May 1946, PRO CO 537/1224.
15. Memo from HQ 4th District EBS SOS, 25 September 1943, copy in NA RG 107/91, box 204: "ETO: Racial Relations"; Chief Constable, Leicester, to N. Midland Regional Office, 4 February 1943, copy in NA RG 332 ETO AG CGC, 250.1 (1943, vol. 1).

16. Baker to Abbey, 14 September 1942, NA RG 84 Bristol 800: Confidential [strike]; M-O 1569, 22 January 1943, quoting pp. 33–4. On December 1942 see Goodman to Lee, 21 December 1942, NA RG 332 ETO AG 312.1: Lee; and IWM, 90/10/1, pt.2, pp. 53–4.

17. Alexander, memos, 22 January and 11 April 1944, NA RG 332 ETO PRO box 3, 291.2: Alexander reports; Col. James A. Day, "Report of Investigation," 27 February 1944, tabs G and H, NA RG 332, entry 11080, ETO AG CGC 291.2; cf. Day to CG ETO, 27 February 1944, para 7a, in NAACP papers, LC, IIA/587: White, Erpn. tour, 1944.

18. PRO LAB 26/55, esp. report by Arnold Watson, 18 December 1943, and Gater to Leggett, 23 June 1944; Richmond, *Colour Prejudice*, pp. 86–90, quoting p. 88 ["We the Negroes"]; Janet Toole, "GIs and the Race Bar in Wartime Warrington," *History Today*, July 1993, pp. 22–28.

19. ETO-1, Supplementary, 2 November 1942, Sta. K, NA RG 330/94.

20. Leon C. Standifer, *Not In Vain: A Rifleman Remembers World War II* (Baton Rouge, LA, 1992), p. 15; MOI HI special report no. 40, 11 March 1943, p. 5, PRO INF 1/293.

21. See NA RG 332 ETO PRO, 322: Negro Chorus, quoting PRO SOS to CG ETO, 2 July 1943; and Asst. PRO Plans to PRO ETO, 16 February 1944, in ibid., 020: Bureau of PR.

22. George W. Goodman, "The Englishman Meets the Negro." *Common Ground*, 5/1 (Autumn 1944), esp. 3–4; William H. Simons to Ruth E. Simons, 14 September 1943, Simons papers; author's interview with William H. Simons, 26 April 1983.

23. W. H. Simons to R. E. Simons, 4 October 1943; ETO B-2, 7 February 1944, NA RG 330/94.

24. Mary Penick Motley, ed., *The Invisible Soldier: The Experience of the Black Soldier, World War II* (Detroit, 1975), pp. 110, 266.

25. Goodman to White, 11 October 1943, NAACP papers, LC, II/A/24: ARC—White; Goodman to Lee, 21 December 1942, NA RG 332 ETO AG CGC 312.1: Lee; Eddy to Collins, 24 February 1944, and IG to CG, 9th Inf. Div., 23 February 1944, in J. Lawton Collins papers, DDEL, box 3: 201 personal letters; Camille K. Jones to Harvey Gibson, [July 1944], NA RG 332 ETO Adm 20A.

26. See reports in OAFH USSTAF 519.765-1, esp. Chief Constable, Sheffield to CO, Wortley, 10 September 1942, and enclosed CID report 9 September 1942. See also Smith, *Jim Crow*, pp. 97–100.

27. OAFH USSTAF 519.765-1: quotation in CS 8AFSC report, 13 October 1942.

28. OAFH 519.01, USSTAF History, 1945, vol. II, p. 166; PreMed 5: p. 264.

29. Maj. Nathan E. Guyer to CG 8AFSC, 27 March 1943, OAFH USSTAF 519.765-1.

30. PreMed 5: p. 196.

31. The fullest account is in Kenneth P. Werrell, "Mutiny at Army Air Force Station 569: Bamber Bridge, England, June 1943," *Aerospace Historian*, 22/4 (December 1975), pp. 202–9; see also Alan M. Osur, *Blacks in the*

Army Air Forces during World War II (Washington, DC, 1977), pp. 99–102. My interpretation differs somewhat from these.

32. Miller to CG 8AF, 26 June 1943, Spaatz papers, LC, box 323: Eaker corr; Eaker ind., 29 June 1943, in Eaker papers, LC, box 18: 8AF Commands; Miller to CG ETO, 13 July 1943, OAFH USSTAF 519.771-1.

33. Miller to CG 8AF, 20 July 1943, Spaatz papers, LC, box 323; Miller, 1st ind., 26 July 1943, on Grubb letter of 22 July, OAFH USSTAF 519.765-1.

34. Meeting, 10 July 1943, Eaker papers, LC, box 20: staff mtgs.; Eaker to CG ETO, 10 August 1943, OAFH USSTAF 519.201–25.

35. Report of Grubb's inspection tour, 8 November 1943, NA RG 332 ETO Adm 218/2; Carrel to Hicks, 7 and 8 October 1943, OAFH USSTAF 519.765-1 [officers]; Knerr to CG 8AF, 6 December 1943, 1st ind. on Grubb to Knerr, 27 November, OAFH USSTAF 519.201–25.

36. Interview with Grubb, 5 July 1944, History, vol. V, ASC: Docs., item 244, OAFH USSTAF 519.01; Goodall to JAG WD, 3 October 1944, NA RG 107/47, box 124, ASW: Gen. Corr., 291.2.

37. Meader diary, 31 October 1942 (Hoover Inst., Stanford); BALB 11 (44) 119, 21 July 1944, PRO FO 371/38511, AN3006.

38. 8AF Provost Marshal report, 10 November 1943, p. 5, Spaatz papers, LC, box 70: A-Am. collabtn.

39. Regional Commissioner 10, report, January 1943, PRO FO 371/34123, A1867; Base Censor 1, morale report, 16 December 1942, NA RG 332 ETO AG CGC 250.1 (1942, vol. 2).

40. Joseph O. Curtis to Josephine Simons, 29 January and 19 March 1944; author's interview with Joseph Curtis, 23 April 1983.

Chapter 19: Allies

1. WO Q(AL), conclusions from recent reports, 13 November 1942, p. 7, copy in NA RG 332 ETO AG 336.2.

2. On prices see Robert S. Raymond, Diary, IWM, 28 May and 8 June 1943; Brunskill, report, [mid-December 1943], PRONI CAB 9CD/229/19.

3. PRO INF 1/292, HI 100, p. 6 [saluting]; see also Shelby Stanton, *U.S. Army Uniforms of World War II* (London, 1991), esp. ch. 1, and François Bertin, *American Soldiers in Europe in 1944*, tr. Angela Moyon (La Guerche-de-Bretagne, 1988).

4. WO Q(AL) report, 13 November 1942 ["our country," "dresses"]; Army Mail Censorship reports, 61 and 64 [ATS], PRO FO 371/34124, A2391; Norman Longmate, *The G.I.'s* (London, 1975), p. 108 [medals]; NA RG 332 ETO AG 250.1, 1942, vol. 1, 18.

5. E.g., Lord Davies to Eaker, 14 July 1943, Ira C. Eaker papers, box 17: 8AF HQ (LC).

6. Basil Collier, *The Defence of the United Kingdom* (London, 1957), p. 297; Walter S. Dunn, Jr., *Second Front Now—1943* (University AL, 1980), pp. 217–20.

7. Robert H. Ahrenfeldt, *Psychiatry in the British Army in the Second World*

War (London, 1958), p. 273 [desertions]; AG's serial letter, "Administration of Discipline," March 1943, p. 20, Sir Ronald Adam papers, KCL, V/3.

8. M-O 686, "Report on Education in the Armed Forces," 5 May 1941; James Lucas, *Experiences of War: The British Soldier* (London, 1989), pp. 32–3 [Bombardier].

9. Joseph L. Strange, "The British Rejection of Operation SLEDGEHAMMER, An Alternative Motive," MA 46/1 (February 1982), esp. 9–13 [including Dill and Cadogan]; Brooke, diary, 31 March 1942, Alanbrooke papers, KCL, 5/5.

10. Nigel Hamilton, *Monty* (3 vols., pbk. ed., London, 1987), 1: p. 493 [Churchill and Brooke]; *Hitler's Table Talk, 1941–1944,* trs. Norman Cameron and R. H. Stevens (Oxford, 1988), pp. 573–74.

11. Carlo D'Este, *Decision in Normandy* (New York, 1991), pp. 503–4; Hamilton, *Monty,* 1: pp. 372–515.

12. James J. Sadkovich, "Understanding Defeat: Reappraising Italy's Role in World War II," *Journal of Contemporary History,* 24 (1989), pp. 45–7; Hamilton, *Monty,* 2: p. 276 [theatre].

13. Teheran to MOI, Empax 307, 8 July 1942, PRO FO 371/31417, E4542 ["Bolsheviks"]; Fraser to HQ 10th Army, 11 July 1942, quoting Chargé d'Affaires, Teheran ["allies"], FO 371/31418, E5595; Army Commander personal memo, 29 November 1942, Sir James Gammell papers, IWM 73/14/1; Patricia Ledward and Colin Strang, eds., *Poems of This War by Younger Poets* (Cambridge, 1942), p. 21 [Neal].

14. Tonie and Valmai Holt, *The Visitor's Guide to the Normandy Landing Beaches* (Ashbourne, Derbyshire, 1989), p. 151 [3rd]; B. R. Mullaly, *The South Lancashire Regiment: The Prince of Wales's Volunteers* (Bristol, 1953), pp. 373–74, 400–1; John Keegan, *Six Armies in Normandy* (Harmondsworth, 1983) p. 170.

15. Wally Littlewood, memoirs, IWM, p. 123; Harold Foster, memoirs, IWM, p. 117; Hamilton, *Monty,* 1: pp. 388, 420; Brian Horrocks, *A Full Life* (pbk. ed., London, 1962), p. 86 ["problems"].

16. Quarterly Morale Report, 25 September 1942, PRO WO 163/161.

17. David Fraser, *And We Shall Shock Them: The British Army in the Second World War* (London, 1983), p. 98.

18. John Ellis, *World War II: The Sharp End* (2nd ed., London, 1990), pp. 192 [Sandhurst], 226 [Anzio]; Calder, *People's War,* p. 285 [Bingham].

19. *The Memoirs of Field-Marshal the Viscount Montgomery of Alamein, K.G.* (London, 1958), p. 185; Calder, *People's War,* p. 350.

20. Coordinator of Information, R&A Branch, British Empire section, "Morale in the British Armed Forces," 21 March 1942, NA RG 208/366A/237.

21. John A. English, *The Canadian Army and the Normandy Campaign: A Study of Failure in High Command* (New York, 1991), p. 163; Shelford Bidwell and Dominick Graham, *Fire-Power: British Army Weapons and Theories of*

War, 1904–1945 (London, 1982), pp. 227–28; cf. Keegan, *Six Armies*, pp. 193–97.

22. MC/P (43) 8, morale report, 19 June 1943, p. 8, PRO WO 163/161; CO I, 513th QM Truck Regt., report, 23 December 1943, NA RG 332 ETO AG CGC 092 [Belfast]; 17th Signal Op. Bn., report, 24 January 1944, NA RG 338 FUSA AG GC 092/50 [High Wycombe].

23. MI12 report on U.S. soldiers' mail, 1–20 September 1943, PRO FO 371/ 34126, A9114 ["Bergman"]; entry for 4 November 1943, Yale Univ. Divinity School Library, Ms Gp. 30, box 264.

24. David Reynolds, "GI and Tommy in Wartime Britain: The Army 'Inter-Attachment' Scheme of 1943–44," JSS 7 (1984), p. 415; GCMP, p. 619 [Marshall].

25. Reynolds, "GI and Tommy," pp. 415–16; verse quoted in MHI Vignettes of Military History, no. 172.

26. Robert S. Raymond, *A Yank in Bomber Command*, ed. Michael Moynihan (Newton Abbot, Devon, 1977), p. 151.

27. Ted Fossieck to Janice, 26 February 1944, p. 4, MHI; Raymond, diary, IWM, p. 291; Tom Tateson, memoirs, IWM, p. 3.

28. WO AG, "Notes for Estimates Speech," February 1943, p. 2, Adam papers, KCL, box IV; C. P. Stacey, *Six Years of War* (Ottawa, 1955), vol. I, p. 426; NAC RG 24/18683, 133.065 (D216) UK.

29. Ackroyd, "Notes" [May 1943], NAC RG 24/12383, 4/PRO/17, f. 205; CR 88, 6–20 April 1944, p. 5, NAC RG 24/12322, 4/CENS/1/5; English, *Canadian Army*, p. 289 [diary].

30. MC/P (43) 10, App. A, PRO WO 163/161 ["Germans"]; cf. NAC RG 24/10725, 219 C1.009 (D52) Morale-Cdns in UK, esp. McNaughton to Adam, 20 July 1943, and draft, 18 September 1943.

31. CR 52, 6–20 January 1943, p. 3, NAC RG 24/12321, 4/CENS/1/1; English, *Canadian Army*, p. 159.

32. CR 37, 20 August–3 September 1942, p. 3, NAC RG 24/12319, 4/CENS/ 4/8; CR 53, 21 January–5 February 1943, p. 5, and CR 67, 6–21 June 1943, p. 5, NAC RG 24/12321, 4/CENS/1/1 and 1/2; MOI RIO 10 report, 23 July 1942, PRO CAB 123/176.

33. CR 34, 19 July–3 August 1942, p. 3, NAC RG 24/12319, 4/CENS/4/7; intercept, 7 September 1942, ibid., 4/CENS/4/8 [Worthington]; CR 81 23 December 1943–6 January 1944, NAC RG 24/12321, 4/CENS/1/3.

34. Charles J. V. Murphy, "The First Canadian Army," *Fortune*, January 1944, p. 106.

35. CR 88, 6–20 April 1944, p. 14, NAC RG 24/12322, 4/CENS/1/5; Gen. Benjamin O. Davis Sr. diary, MHI, 27 October 1942; cf. Robin W. Winks, *The Blacks in Canada: A History* (New Haven, 1971), esp. pp. 487, 493.

36. Nye to Bourne, 21 May 1942, PRO WO 216/81; Kenneth Young, ed., *The Diaries of Sir Robert Bruce Lockhart, vol. 2* (London, 1980), p. 191.

37. GCMP 3: pp. 176–77, 180–81, 188, 225–26, 232–33, 250–51; MI, pp. 587–88, 619; Churchill to Stimson, 25 June 1942, PRO PREM 3/459; "Note by Lord Ismay," 23 March 1950, Ismay papers, KCL, II/3/209;

Mountbatten to Marshall, 10 June 1942, Marshall papers, GCML, 77/8; Alanbrooke diary, KCL, 5/5, 24 June 1942; Dill to Brooke, 5 May 1942, Alanbrooke papers, KCL, 14/38.

38. Butcher diary, DDEL, 23 February 1943; Montgomery to Brooke, 23 February and 4 April 1943, IWM, BLM 49/18 and 49/25.

39. Alexander to Brooke, 3 April 1943, Alanbrooke papers, KCL, 14/63.

40. PM to Dill, 29 April, PM to CIGS, 30 April, and Dill to PM. 30 April 1943, Alanbrooke papers, KCL, 14/38; Reginald Winn, memoir, pp. 5–6, GCML; MI, p. 616.

41. MI, p. 582; "Notes on My Life," 20 January 1943, Alanbrooke papers, KCL, 3A/VIII; *Sunday Telegraph*, 9 February 1964, p. 4.

42. Martin Blumenson, *The Patton Papers* (2 vols., Boston, 1972–74), 2: pp. 116, 186; Montgomery to Brooke, 4 April 1943, Montgomery papers, IWM, BLM 49/25.

43. Carlo D'Este, *Bitter Victory: The Battle for Sicily, 1943* (London, 1988), pp. 558–60; Eisenhower to Marshall, 18 August 1943, EP 2: p. 1342.

44. Martin Blumenson, *Mark Clark* (London, 1985), p. 119 [McNair]; Blumenson, *Patton Papers*, 2: p. 218.

45. Daniel D. Holt, "An Unlikely Partnership: Dwight Eisenhower, Mark Clark and the Philippines," *Kansas History*, 13/3 (Autumn 1990), pp. 151, 157–62; Blumenson, *Patton Papers*, 2: pp. 14–15, 61, 144, 153, 220.

46. Blumenson, *Patton Papers*, 2: pp. 254, 306; Hamilton, *Monty*, 2: p. 353; Carlo D'Este, *Fatal Decision: Anzio and the Battle for Rome* (London, 1991), pp. 408–412; Dominick Graham and Shelford Bidwell, *Tug of War: The Battle for Italy 1943–1945* (London, 1986), p. 37 ["paranoia"]; Blumenson, *Clark*, p. 202 ["Rome"].

47. Stephen E. Ambrose, *The Supreme Commander: The War Years of General Dwight D. Eisenhower* (New York, 1970), pp. 79–81, 293–94, 298–99, 305; Blumenson, *Patton Papers*, 2: p. 220; Ike to Handy, 28 January 1943, and to Marshall, 5 April 1943, EP 2: pp. 928, 1071; Brooke, diary, 1 April 1945, Alanbrooke papers, KCL, 5/10 ["allies"].

48. Stephen E. Ambrose, *Eisenhower* (2 vols., New York, 1983–84), 1: pp. 194–95 ["botched"], 272 ["prima donnas"]; Pogue 3: p. 321 ["sleep"]; Dwight D. Eisenhower, *Crusade in Europe* (New York: 1948), p. 207 ["Overlord"].

Chapter 20: Countdown to D-Day

1. *News Chronicle*, 17 January 1944, p. 1; MOI HI report 188, 11 May 1944, PRO INF 1/292; OWI London, weekly public opinion report, 25 May 1944, NA RG 208/35/109: GB Cables; *Daily Telegraph*, 4 May 1944, p. 1; *Daily Mail*, 5 June 1944, p. 3.

2. Cornelius Ryan, *The Longest Day* (pbk. ed., New York, 1959), pp. 46–8; David Eisenhower, *Eisenhower: At War, 1943–1945* (New York, 1986), pp. 208, 239, 241, 242–43.

3. Robert S. Allen diary, 10 April 1944 (Wisconsin State Historical Soc.,

Madison); *The New York Times*, 28 February 1944, pp. 1 and 4; *Daily Mail*, 10 April 1944, p. 2; Liddell Hart papers, KCL, 11/1944/7 and /15.

4. *Daily Telegraph*, 18 May 1944, p. 6; Michael Howard, *Strategic Deception in the Second World War* (pbk. ed., London, 1992), ch. 6.

5. PRO CAB 65/33, WM 34 (43) 1 ["safeguard"]; Brooke diary, 9 February 1944, Alanbrooke papers, KCL, 5/8; Churchill to Ismay, 5 February 1944, PRO PREM 3/345/4 ["knock"]; Eisenhower to Hollis, 6 March 1944, EP 3: pp. 1761–62; PRO CAB 65/45, WM 31 (44) 2 CA, 10 March 1944 [Churchill]. See generally F. H. Hinsley and C.A.G. Simkins, *British Intelligence in the Second World War, vol. 4* (London, 1990), pp. 249–55.

6. D. Eisenhower, *Eisenhower: At War*, p. 108; Theodore A. Wilson, ed., *D-Day 1944* (Lawrence, KS, 1994), pp. 77–78.

7. This account of invasion planning draws heavily on the official U.S. history by Gordon A. Harrison, *Cross-Channel Attack* (Washington, DC, 1951), esp. ch. 5.

8. Omar N. Bradley, *A Soldier's Story* (New York, 1951), p. 234 [Leigh-Mallory]; Eisenhower to Marshall, 19 February 1944, EP 3: p. 1738.

9. Eisenhower, memo, 22 March 1944, EP 3: p. 1783.

10. Harry Butcher diary, 25 January 1944, DDEL ["private war"]; Harrison, *Cross-Channel Attack*, pp. 193–94.

11. Bradley, *Soldier's Story*, p. 249; John Terraine, *The Right of the Line: The Royal Air Force in the European War, 1939–1945* (pbk. ed., London, 1988), p. 621 ["own"].

12. See generally Stephen E. Ambrose, *The Supreme Commander: The War Years of Dwight D. Eisenhower* (Garden City, NY, 1969), pp. 363–76; Max Hastings, *Overlord: D-Day and the Battle for Normandy* (pbk. ed., London, 1984), pp. 47–54. Also Stephen E. Ambrose, *Eisenhower* (2 vols., 1983–84), 1: p. 290, and Omar N. Bradley, with Clay Blair, *A General's Life* (London, 1983), p. 230.

13. Roosevelt to Churchill, 11 May 1944, C-R 3: p. 127; Eisenhower to Marshall, 28 January 1944, and Marshall to Eisenhower, 7 February, EP 3: pp. 1693, 1708.

14. Max Hastings, *Bomber Command* (London, 1979), pp. 271–73; Michael Howard, *The Mediterranean Strategy in the Second World War* (London, 1968), p. 57 ["chauvinism"]; Churchill to MacArthur, 12 March 1944, Churchill papers, CHAR 20/137B, Churchill College, Cambridge; Eisenhower to Marshall, 21 March 1944, EP 3: p. 1777.

15. Brooke diary, 15 May 1944, Alanbrooke papers, KCL, 5/8.

16. Gilbert, pp. 534, 670, 760; Dwight D. Eisenhower, *Crusade in Europe* (Garden City, NY, 1948) p. 245; cf. Carlo D'Este, *Decision in Normandy* (pbk. ed., New York, 1991), p. 87; McCloy diary, 20 April 1944, John J. McCloy papers, DY1/13, Amherst College, MA; Brooke diary, KCL, 5/9, 5 June 1944.

17. Leigh-Mallory to Eisenhower, 29 May 1944, DDEL 16/52 file, box 71; Harry C. Butcher diary, DDEL, 28 April [Gerow], 12 May [Smith] and 30

May 1944 ["record"]; McCloy diary, 17 April 1944 [Bradley]; Robert S. Allen diary, 16 April 1944 [Patton].

18. Quotations from Nigel Hamilton, *Monty* (3 vols., pbk. ed., London, 1987), 2: pp. 549–53, 570–78; D'Este, *Decision in Normandy*, p. 84 [Ismay]; Bradley, *Soldier's Story*, p. 239 [Monty and Ike]; William Phillips diary, vol. 30, 19 January 1944, Houghton Library, Harvard Univ.; Warren Tute, et al., *D-Day* (pbk. ed., London, 1975), p. 97 [Deyo].

19. Bradley, *Soldier's Story*, p. 236.

20. MI, p. 614; Butcher diary, DDEL, 7 February 1944 [Gerhardt]; Eisenhower to Marshall, 21 May 1944, EP 3: p. 1878.

21. Eisenhower to Marshall, 30 April and 3 May 1944, EP 3: pp. 1841, 1846; Martin Blumenson, *The Patton Papers* (2 vols., Boston, 1972–74), vol. 2, ch. 24, quoting Ike from Patton diary, 1 May, on p. 450.

22. Hamilton, *Monty*, 2: pp. 497–98, 528; cf. notes on "American Forces," p. 4, Liddell Hart papers, KCL, LH 11/1944/7.

23. Ambrose, *Supreme Commander*, p. 400; Ambrose, *Eisenhower*, 1: p. 294; D. Eisenhower, *Eisenhower: At War*, p. 222 [Thorpe].

24. Nigel Lewis, *Channel Firing: The Tragedy of Exercise Tiger* (pbk. ed., London, 1990), chs. 17–18 and postscript, esp. pp. 263–65. Other accounts, focusing on the E-boat attack, include Edwin P. Hoyt, *The Invasion before Normandy: The Secret Battle of Slapton Sands* (pbk. ed., London, 1988), and Ken Small, with Mark Rogerson, *The Forgotten Dead* (pbk. ed., London, 1989). See also Charles B. MacDonald, "Slapton Sands: The 'Cover-Up' That Never Was," *Army*, 38/6 (June 1988), pp. 64–7.

25. Transcript of 5 May 1944 critique of *Tiger*, quoting pp. 19, 38, 47, in NA RG 407 207-3.0 April 44, Collins file; cf. Rupp., 1: pp. 351–52.

26. Butcher Diary, DDEL, 28 April 1944; Hoyt, *Invasion Before Normandy*, p. 129 [Bradley].

27. Col. R. Henriques, notes, 11 January 1944, NA RG 407, 329-3.01 Lessons—DUCK.

28. On 'mounting' the invasion see Rupp., 1: ch. IX.

29. 8th Inf. Regt. after-action report, 21 July 1944, in DDEL, U.S. Army unit records, box 791, 4th Div.; Stephen E. Ambrose, *Band of Brothers* (New York, 1992), p. 60 [Webster]; David J. Pike, *Airborne in Nottingham: The Impact of an Elite American Parachute Regiment on an English City in World War II* (Nottingham, privately printed, n.d.), p. 50 [Jones]; Lyle Groundwater, UNO 90th Div. oral, p. 1.

30. Collins to Lady Army Normanton, 19 July 1944, J. Lawford Collins papers, DDEL, box 3, 201 file: personal letters; Edgar R. Winters, UNO 101st Div. oral, p. 115; George E. McIntyre, memoirs, MHI, pp. 114–15.

31. John Keegan, *Six Armies in Normandy* (Harmondsworth, 1983), pp. 11–12, 13–14.

32. PRO INF 1/292, HI 175, appendix, para. 7, 11; William E. Jones, UNO 4th Div. oral, p. 7; Edwin R. W. Hale and John Frayn Turner, eds., *The Yanks Are Coming* (New York, 1983), pp. 161–62 [Sheehan].

33. Pike, *Airborne in Nottingham*, pp. 23 and 49; *Daily Telegraph*, 29 and 30 May 1944; Harrison, *Cross-Channel Attack*, p. 272.

34. Warren R. Lloyd, UNO 90th Div. oral, p. 5; Ryan, *Longest Day*, pp. 68–9 [including Kerchner].

35. Quotations from UNO 4th Div. orals by Edward Yarberry, p. 2 and Bruce D. Bradley, p. 3; Hobbs address, 5 June 1944, Leland S. Hobbs papers, DDEL, box 2.

36. Harrison, *Cross-Channel Attack*, pp. 272–74; Ambrose, *Supreme Commander*, pp. 417–18; cf. Hamilton, *Monty*, 2: pp. 599–601. A censorship report on letters from British assault troops before D-Day found that "a minority showed strong resentment" of their incarceration in sealed camps and concluded that "a postponement of the operation might have had serious consequences." See 21AG CR, 1–14 June 1944, copy in NAC RG 24/12322, 4/CENS REPS/2.

37. D. Eisenhower, *Eisenhower: At War*, p. 253 [101st]; cf. Ambrose, *Eisenhower*, 1: p. 309; note, 5 June 1944, EP 3: p. 1908.

Chapter 21: Overlord and Under Ike

1. Cornelius Ryan, *The Longest Day* (pbk. ed., New York, 1959), p. 303; Gordon A. Harrison, *Cross-Channel Attack* (Washington, DC, 1951), p. 330. Royce L. Thompson, who made a detailed study of the statistics for the official army history, observed in 1968: "I doubted then and now that compilation of an accurate set of invasion statistics is feasible." Letter to Eugenia Lejeune, 16 October 1968, with memo of 27 May 1968, in Royce L. Thompson papers, GCML.

2. Maj. Carl W. Plitt, S-3 16th Inf., memo, 30 June 1944, NA RG 407, 301-INF(16)-3.01: Lessons, Fox, Fabius, Neptune.

3. Alfred Goldberg, "Air Campaign OVERLORD: To D-Day," in Eisenhower Foundation, *D-Day: The Normandy Invasion in Retrospect* (Lawrence, KS, 1971), pp. 58–9, 62.

4. On the weather see F. H. Hinsley, et al., *British Intelligence in the Second World War, vol. III, pt. 2* (London, 1988), pp. 126, 131–32.

5. Michael Howard, *Strategic Deception in the Second World War* (London, 1992), p. 191.

6. Author's interview with E. Ray Nance, Bedford VA, 24 August 1993; Stephen E. Ambrose, *D-Day* (New York, 1994), pp. 497–98.

7. Chester Wilmot, *The Struggle for Europe* (London, 1952), pp. 264–65; Russell F. Weigley, *Eisenhower's Lieutenants: The Campaigns of France and Germany, 1944–1945* (London, 1981), p. 89.

8. Hinsley, *British Intelligence*, vol. 3, pt. 2, pp. 130, 842–43; cf. David Eisenhower, *Eisenhower: At War, 1943–1945* (New York, 1986), pp. 239, 278.

9. George M. Elsey, "Naval Aspects of D-Day in Retrospect," in Eisenhower Foundation, *D-Day*, p. 181–82, and S. W. Roskill, *The War At Sea, 1939–1945*, vol. III, pt. 2 (London, 1961), pp. 47–8; Harrison, *Cross-Channel Attack*, pp. 309, 313, 317; Higham, "Technology and D-Day," p. 231 [DDs]; author's interview with Gen. Robert Ploger, 4 September 1993.

10. Harrison, *Cross-Channel Attack*, pp. 300–1, 325; Roskill, *War at Sea*, III/2, p. 47; Elsey, "Naval Aspects," pp. 181–86; 29th Div. After Action Report, June 1944, 115th Inf., p. 2 (C&GSC R-11408).

11. Weigley, *Eisenhower's Lieutenants*, pp. 89, 91; Max Hastings, *Overlord: D-Day and the Battle for Normandy* (pbk. ed., London, 1984), pp. 116, 120–21.

12. Rupp., 1: p. 481; John Keegan, *Six Armies in Normandy* (Harmondsworth, 1983), pp. 260–61.

13. Carlo D'Este, *Decision in Normandy* (New York, 1983), ch. 28, quoting Monty from p. 488; Martin Blumenson, *Breakout and Pursuit* (Washington, DC, 1961), p. 432 ["campaign"].

14. The logistical crisis is summarized in Roland G. Ruppenthal, "Logistic Planning for OVERLORD in Retrospect," in Eisenhower Foundation, *D-Day*, pp. 87–103, quoting p. 88.

15. Charles B. MacDonald, *The Mighty Endeavor: The American War in Europe* (2nd ed., New York, 1986), pp. 474–75.

16. Forrest C. Pogue, *The Supreme Command* (Washington, DC, 1954), p. 257.

17. *The New York Times*, 30 June 1944, p. 20.

18. King, pp. 253–54, 263; PRO INF 1/292, HI 175, Appendix, p. 3 [BBC], and HI 200, p. 8.

19. S.L.A. Marshall, *Men Against Fire: The Problem of Battle Command in Future Warfare* (2nd ed., Gloucester, MA, 1978), p. 54; T. N. Dupuy, *Numbers, Predictions and War: Using History to Evaluate Combat Factors and Predict the Outcome of Battles* (New York, 1979), p. 104; Martin van Creveld, *Fighting Power: German and U.S. Army Performance, 1939–1945* (Westport, CT, 1982); Hastings, *Overlord*, p. 369.

20. Roger J. Spiller, "S.L.A. Marshall and the Ratio of Fire," *RUSI Journal*, 133/4 (Winter 1988), pp. 63–71; John Sloan Brown, *Draftee Division: The 88th Division in World War II* (Lexington, KY, 1986), pp. 168–75 [Dupuy]. See also the essays on the American and British armed forces in Allan R. Millett and Williamson Murray, eds., *Military Effectiveness* (3 vols, Boston, 1988), vol. 2, esp. pp. 64–84, 107–30.

21. Charles H. Gerhardt memoirs, p. 54, DDEL [29th]; MI, pp. 469, 588 [training]; Michael D. Doubler, *Busting the Bocage: American Combined Arms Operations in France, 6 June–31 July 1944* (Ft. Leavenworth, KS, 1988), pp. 65–6; Carlo D'Este, *Bitter Victory: The Battle for Sicily, 1943* (London, 1988), p. 323 [Yalta].

22. Weigley, *Eisenhower's Lieutenants*, pp. 127 [quotes], 151–54, 164–66, 381; Geoffrey Perret, *There's A War To Be Won: The United States Army in World War II* (New York, 1991), pp. 89–93 [TOT].

23. John Desch, "The 1941 German Army/the 1944–45 U.S. Army: A Comparative Analysis of Two Forces in Their Primes," *Command Magazine*, 18 (September–October 1992), 63; Stephen E. Ambrose, *Band of Brothers* (New York, 1992), p. 177.

24. Shelford Bidwell and Dominick Graham, *Fire-Power: British Army Weapons and Theories of War, 1904–1945* (London, 1982), chs. 14–16; Omar

N. Bradley, *A Soldier's Story* (New York, 1951), pp. 368–69; Churchill to Eisenhower, 9 March 1945, DDEL 16/52, box 22; Weigley, *Eisenhower's Lieutenants*, pp. 727–30.

25. Alan S. Milward, *War, Economy and Society, 1939–1945* (Berkeley, 1977), pp. 67, 70; D'Este, *Decision in Normandy*, ch. 15, quoting p. 250 [Monty]; L. F. Ellis, *Victory in the West* (2 vols., London, 1962–68), 2: p. 406 [statistics].

26. Dwight D. Eisenhower, *At Ease: Stories I Tell to Friends* (London, 1968), p. 258; *Daily Telegraph*, 18 January 1944, p. 6; *Daily Mail*, 17 January 1944, p. 2; Sec. War to CIGS, 15 December 1943, PRO PREM 3/336/1; author's interview with Felix Branham, 4 September 1993.

27. C-R 3: p. 624; Butcher diary, DDEL, 19 August 1944; Pogue, *Supreme Command*, pp. 263–64; *Times*, 1 September 1944, p. 5; *Daily Mail*, 1 September 1944, p. 2; Churchill to Eisenhower, 31 August 1944, DDEL 16/52, box 22; PRO INF 1/292, HI 205, p. 1, and 206, p. 2.

28. Bradley, *Soldier's Story*, ch. 21, quoting p. 476; Ambrose, *Eisenhower*, 1: chs. 18–19.

29. *Sunday Dispatch*, 31 December 1944, p. 4 ["preoccupied"]; *Daily Mail*, 6 January 1945, p. 1; Ambrose, *Eisenhower*, 1: p. 380 [Bradley, Patton].

30. *News Chronicle*, 21 December 1944, p. 2; *Daily Mail*, 29 December 1944, p. 2; Ellis, *Victory*, 2: pp. 425–28 [Monty]; HC 407: cols. 415–16.

31. D'Este, *Decision in Normandy*, p. 470 [Blumenson]; Eric Larrabee, *Commander in Chief: Franklin Delano Roosevelt, His Lieutenants, and Their War* (New York, 1987), p. 507; cf. Ambrose, *Supreme Commander*, pp. 570, 588; Patton diary, 3 February 1944, in Robert S. Allen papers, box 15/11, Wisconsin State Historical Soc., Madison.

32. Butcher diary, DDEL, 11 February 1944; Eisenhower Foundation, *D-Day*, p. 144 [Huston]; Dwight D. Eisenhower, *Crusade in Europe* (New York, 1948), p. 444 [Truman]; Ambrose, *Eisenhower*, 1: p. 409; PRO FO 371/38515, A4648, esp. minute by Nevile Butler, 14 November 1944.

33. *Evening Standard*, 12 June 1945, pp. 1–2; Eisenhower, *At Ease*, pp. 298–300; *New York Herald Tribune*, 28 April 1946, Section VII, p. 2 [Murrow].

34. *At Ease*, pp. 388–90; *Evening Standard*, 12 June, p. 1.

Chapter 22: "Returning Britain to the British"

1. NA RG 332, ETO Adm. 602: "History of UK Base," TS., pp. 24, 68, 116—a prime source for this chapter, as is ETO Adm. History, part XI, vol. I, pp. 136–49. Cf. Norman Longmate, *The G.I.'s* (London, 1975), ch. 28, and Juliet Gardiner, *"Over Here"* (London, 1992), ch. 18.

2. Churchill to Roosevelt, 31 October 1942, C-R 1: p. 650.

3. NA RG 84, Plymouth 800 political report, February 1944; Maj. Chris T. Den Ouden, deposition, 17 May 1944 in RG 332 ETO AG GC 250.1, 1944, v. 2 [Torcross]; *News Chronicle*, 4 August 1944, p. 3 ["sampled"]; *Western Morning News*, 4 August ["feared"].

4. See NA RG 332 ETO Adm. 131, esp. Medd to Ganoe, 27 January 1944, Ganoe to Winant, 9 March, and Winant to Lee, 13 May.

5. History of UK Base, esp. pp. 97–9.

6. Ibid., ch. VI.

7. Graham A. Cosmas and Albert E. Cowdrey, *Medical Service in the European Theater of Operations* (Washington, DC, 1992), esp. pp. 90, 257, 395, 442, 481, 494, 618; also RG 332 ETO Adm. History, pt. XI, vol. I, pp. 93–5.

8. RG 332 ETO, UK Base Section Historical Reports: Special Services, and PM Section, 8 May 1945; PRO CAB 65/43, WM 126 (44) 4, and FO 371/38626, AN3729, 4171, 4646; EP docs. 2147 and 2214, quoting Eisenhower to Churchill, 1 January 1945.

9. Cliff Hope, *Growing Up in the Wartime Army: A GI in the 1940s* (Manhattan, KS, 1985), pp. 53–9.

10. Author's interview with Charles H. Neighbor, Roanoke, VA, 28 August 1993.

11. Letter to parents, 9 September 1945, Franklin I. Gurley papers, MHI; Betty Magnuson Olson, memoirs, MHI, pp. 501, 585; Stephen Ambrose, *Eisenhower* (2 vols., New York, 1983–84), 1: p. 410; Agnes de Paula, ARC Home Hospitality Report for January 1945, NA RG 332 ETO Adm. 20B; PRO FO 371/44625, AN1571, BALB progress report, 15 May 1945.

12. Private information. The names are pseudonyms.

13. Basil Collier, *The Defence of the United Kingdom* (London: 1957), chs. 24–5 and appendices 45 and 49–50; King, p. 265 ["Hitler"].

14. Harry C. Butcher diary, DDEL, 20 June 1944; Joseph R. Darnall, memoirs, MHI, pp. 107–11, 124; Roger A. Freeman, *The Friendly Invasion* (Lavenham, 1992), p. 83 [Moore].

15. *Daily Mail*, 19 January 1945, p. 4; Longmate, *The G.I.'s*, pp. 313–14.

16. Stephen E. Ambrose, *Band of Brothers* (New York, 1992), p. 108; Rogers to Taylor, 24 July 1944, copy in Matthew B. Ridgway papers, MHI, box 3, personal file.

17. PreMed 5: pp. 254, 262–63; Vaughan to District commanders, 19 November 1944, NA RG 332 ETO UK Base historical reports, box 6 (Surgeon); Edward Smithies, *Crime in Wartime: A Social History of Crime in World War II* (London, 1982), pp. 144–49; PRO FO 371/44625, AN1690, BALB 26/274, 18 May 1945 [Agar].

18. *Life*, 23 August 1948, p. 41.

19. *The Registrar General's Statistical Review of England and Wales, 1940–1945*, text, vol. II, civil (London, 1951), p. 82; Sheila Ferguson and Hilde Fitzgerald, *Studies in the Social Services* (2nd ed., London, 1978), p. 98; Angus Calder, *The People's War* (London, 1971), p. 361 ["spinsters"].

20. On paternity payments see BALB 25/260(2), in PRO FO 371/44625, AN 1540.

21. LC NAACP II/A/631, "Brown Babies, 1945–9" file, esp. LCP report by Sylvia McNeill (1946) and George Padmore, TS article, 24 April 1947; *Ebony*, IV/5 (March 1949), pp. 19–22; NA RG 84 Manchester, 800

(Confdtl.) Monthly Political Report, February 1945, p. 4; PRO 371/51617, AN 34 [Somerset]; PRO FO 371/61021, AN 3823.

22. *Daily Mail*, 20 December 1944, p. 3; *News Chronicle*, 11 January 1945, p. 1.

23. RG 332 UK Base Historical, box 4, PM reports, 1 February and 1 March 1945; Lee to Winant, 25 November 1945, John G. Winant papers, FDRL, box 205; Smithies, *Crime in Wartime*, ch. 4.

24. Avice Wilson, memoirs, IWM, p. 4A.

25. Gransden to Brunskill, 7 July 1944, PRONI CAB 9CD/225/14; PRO FO 371/44601, AN 2038 and 2042; PRO PREM 4/27/10, p. 783 [Churchill].

26. Stimson to Pa Watson, 4 October 1944, FDRL PSF 104: War Dept.; *Manchester Guardian*, 28 June 1945, p. 3 [Koenig]; Brunskill to Gransden, 15 July 1944, PRONI 9CD/225/14; Ismay to Colville, 8 June 1945, PRO PREM 4/27/10, pp. 778–79.

27. Christen Jonassen, "Letter Written on V-E Day 1945," in MHI, Columbus Round Table collection.

28. Roger A. Freeman, *The Mighty Eighth* (2nd ed., London, 1989), p. 232.

29. Clarence Linton, outline history, 10 January 1944, p. 6, NA RG 332 ETO Adm. 320; author's interview with Harry H. Crosby, 29 June 1992; Crosby, *A Wing and a Prayer* (New York, 1993), ch. 15; on education see PRO FO 371/44492-3; on "Opposite Numbers" see FO 371/44625-6 (quoting Law to Bracken, 26 April 1945, AN 1383); FDR to Winant, 8 October 1944, FDRL, MR, box 11.

30. Charity Adams Earley, *One Woman's Army: A Black Officer Remembers the WAC* (College Station, TX, 1989), pp. 137–70, quoting p. 163; Martha S. Putney, *Blacks in the Women's Army Corps during World War II* (Metuchen, NJ, 1992), pp. 104–5, quoting *Birmingham Sunday Mercury;* Midland Region Report on American Liaison, 20 October 1945, PRO INF 1/327B, p. 72.

31. PRO 371/38513, AN4176, minute by Alan Dudley, 23 November 1944; FO 371/38514, AN4428, memo by Dep. RIO, Cambridge, November 1944; FO 371/38515, AN4499, BALB 17/187 [Clubs]; FO 371/44626, AN2352, MOI AFL Div. report, 20 July 1945; George A. Armstrong, memo on "A Cultural Program," 5 February 1945, NA RG 84 Manchester 842 file; Freeman, *Mighty Eighth,* p. 234; EuCom Chief Historian, "War Brides and the Shipment to the United States" (1947), p. 38, MHI Library.

Chapter 23: Happily Ever After?

1. Eisenhower to AGWAR, E-41109, 9 August 1944, NA RG 331, SHAEF SGS, 291.1 [4,093]; INS, unpublished annual reports, 1942–43, table 20b (INS Library, Washington, DC); Canadian figures from NAC RG 24/12444, 6/BIRTHS/1.

2. Barry Broadfoot, ed., *Six War Years, 1939–1945: Memories of Canadians at*

Home and Abroad (Toronto, 1974), p. 179; Robert and Jane Easton, *Love and War: Pearl Harbor through V-J Day* (Norman, OK, 1991), p. 210.

3. IWM 82/32/1, quoting from letters of 21 August 1944, 8 January, 22 April, and 30 August 1945. The names are pseudonyms.

4. UNO/101/Malarkey tape, pp. 31–5; author's interview with Leo and Wyn Boyle, 12 September 1993.

5. John H. Sullivan letters collection, DDEL, quoting pp. 197, 210, 213, 215–18, 230; letter to author, 20 April 1994.

6. Edith M. Kup (née Heap), memoirs, IWM, p. 89; Bridget A. Johnson, memoirs, IWM, pp. 2–4.

7. Hadley Cantril, ed., *Public Opinion, 1935–1946* (Princeton, 1951), p. 805; ASF Control Div., *Statistical Review, World War II* (TS., 1946), pp. 126–27 (MHI Library).

8. Richard A. Johnson, "American Embassy," p. 18, NA RG 59, War History Branch, box 29: London ["clinic"]; PRO FO 371/44657, AN 1988, AN 1989 and AN 2405 (Gore-Booth to FO, 30 June 1945).

9. *News Chronicle*, 12 October 1945; Ernest E. Salisbury, "The Immigration of G.I. Brides," *INS Monthly Review*, May 1946, pp. 305–8.

10. For background see the TS. monograph by the Office of the Chief Historian, European Command (EuCom), *War Brides and the Shipment to the United States* (Frankfurt, 1947), in the series "Occupation Forces in Europe" (MHI Library).

11. Elfrieda Berthiaume Shukert and Barbara Smith Scibetta, *War Brides of World War II* (Novato, CA, 1988), pp. 50–2.

12. Avice R. Wilson, diary, 27 July 1946, and memoirs, p. 9 (IWM).

13. Shukert and Scibetta, *War Brides*, pp. 57–64 [voyages]; EuCom, *War Brides*, p. 57 [statistics].

14. Longmate, p. 345, proposes seventy thousand as "the number of women needing transport"; his figure is used by Juliet Gardiner, *"Over Here"* (London, 1992), p. 204. Shukert and Scibetta, *War Brides*, pp. 2, 39–40, 277, suggest thirty thousand (wartime) plus seventy thousand (postwar), which seems to be based on a misreading of Longmate. Cf. Henry E. Stebbins, "Consular Section," p. 4, NA RG 59 War History Branch box 30: London.

15. INS Annual Report, 1950, table 9A.

16. Wives are listed by country of birth. A woman born in England whose family emigrated to Australia where she later married a GI would, on this criterion, be counted as a UK war bride. In some years INS also tabulated the bride's country of last permanent residence. Comparison of the two figures suggests that the difference was not great: In 1946–47, the totals were 7,160 (birthplace) and 7,149 (residence).

17. N. H. Carrier and J. R. Jeffrey, eds., *External Migration: A Study of the Available Statistics, 1815–1950* (London, 1953), p. 40 [children, ages]; INS Annual Reports for 1946, p. 14, and 1947, table 12A.

18. *The Star*, 4 March 1946, p. 3 [200]; INS Annual Report, 1950, table 9B

[fiancées]; C. P. Stacey and Barbara M. Wilson, *The Half-Million: The Canadians in Britain, 1939–1946* (Toronto, 1987), pp. 138–41; Carrier and Jeffery, eds., *External Migration*, pp. 39–40.

19. Shukert and Scibetta, *War Brides*, p. 75.
20. Quotations from Longmate, pp. 361–3.
21. Ambrose, 1: pp. 389, 416–17; private information.
22. Irene's story from IWM 88/50/1, chs. 9–21, quoting esp. from pp. 30, 33, 53–4, 56–7, 64.
23. Wilson, memoirs, IWM, quoting pp. 8, 9, 14–15.
24. Macassey (HO) to Gage, 1 August 1946, PRO FO 371/51621, AN 2306; Law Soc. report for 1950, FO 371/91009, AU 1832/1; ESU press release, 9 January 1947, FO 371/61017, AN 304; memo by W. H. Gallienne, Chicago, 23 March 1946, FO 371/51619, AN 1227.
25. Longmate, pp. 341–42, 365.
26. Author's interview with Leo and Wyn Boyle, 12 September 1993.
27. Grace Eva Reinecke, memoirs, IWM 88/43/1.

Chapter 24: Americanization and Its Discontents

1. "U.S. Army in England," TS. 28 January 1944, Kingsley Martin papers, box 30/1, Sussex Univ. Library, Brighton; Churchill to Ismay, 19 June 1944, PRO PREM 4/27/10, p. 1193; Mick Brown, "American Love Affair," *Telegraph Magazine*, 6 November 1993, pp. 16, 20, 23; similarly Richard Gott in *The Guardian*, 26 March 1994, p. 29.
2. See John Hammond Moore, *Over-Sexed, Over-Paid, and Over Here: Americans in Australia, 1941–1945* (London, 1981); E. Daniel Potts and Annette Potts, *Yanks Down Under, 1941–1945: The American Impact on Australia* (Melbourne, 1985).
3. Potts, pp. 11–12, 26, 29–30; Moore, pp. 52–3.
4. NA RG 332, ETO Adm. 452, TC Progress Report, 30 September 1945, table 1; U.S. Census Bureau, *Historical Statistics of the United States* (Washington, DC, 1975), p. 1140.
5. NA RG 84 Manchester, 800 Monthly Political Report (Confidential), September 1944, p. 4.
6. BBC Listener Research report, "America," 17 February 1944, PRO INF 1/292, HI 175, appendix; Haggard to Broadmead, 27 September 1945, PRO FO 371/44601, AN3040; cf. Mass-Observation report 2454, 26 January 1947, M-O Archives, Univ. of Sussex.
7. M-O 2222, March 1945, p. 3; BBC report, 17 February 1944.
8. M-O 2222, p. 4; M-O Bulletin, April 1947.
9. BIPO survey, March 1945, PRO INF 1/327A ["fears"]; Robin Edmonds, *Setting the Mould: The United States and Britain, 1945–1950* (Oxford, 1986), p. 28 [Bevin].
10. BIPO poll, 7 October 1943, in PRO INF 1/292, HI 160, app., p. 5; James Walvin, *Passage to Britain: Immigration in British History and Politics* (Harmondsworth, 1984), pp. 95–9.

11. Simon Duke, *US Defence Bases in the United Kingdom* (London, 1987), esp. ch. 6; PRO FO 371/97607, esp. Sec. State for Air to PM, 5 December 1952; George Kent, "Report on Our GIs in Britain," *Readers' Digest,* September 1953, pp. 1–6.

12. Carol Gluck, quoted in David Reynolds, "The American Occupations of Germany, Austria and Japan: Towards a Comparative Framework," in G. Mai et al., eds., *The American Occupations of Germany, Austria and Japan* (Baton Rouge, LA, forthcoming).

13. Mead to Winant, 18 October 1943, copy in OWI London October 1943 report, NA RG 208/361/130; memo by Haley, 16 August 1944, BBCWAC R34/188; David Cannadine, *G. M. Trevelyan: A Life in History* (London, 1992), p. 175.

14. MI, pp. 587, 602, 619; George Orwell, *Nineteen Eighty-Four* (London, 1949), p. 7.

15. Harold Nicolson, *Diaries and Letters, 1945–1962,* ed. Nigel Nicolson (London, 1968), p. 243.

16. John Modell and Duane Steffey, "Waging War and Marriage: Military Service and Family Formation, 1940–1950," JFH 13 (1988), p. 196; Peter Fearon, *War, Prosperity and Depression: The U.S. Economy, 1917–45* (London, 1987), pp. 272–80.

17. Robert Higgs, "Wartime Prosperity? A Reassessment of the U.S. Economy in the 1940s," JEH 52 (1992), p. 43; Robert J. Havighurst, et al., *The American Veteran Back Home: A Study of Veteran Readjustment* (New York, 1951), p. 120; Keith W. Olson, *The G.I. Bill, the Veterans, and the Colleges* (Lexington, KY, 1974), pp. 24, 109.

18. David R. Segal, *Recruiting for Uncle Sam: Citizenship and Military Manpower Policy* (Lawrence, KS, 1989), pp. 7–8, 80–3; MI, p. 481; Glen H. Elder, Jr., Cynthia Gimbel, and Rachel Ivie, "Turning Points in Life: The Case of Military Service in War," *Military Psychology,* 3 (1991), pp. 215–31.

19. Charles C. Alexander, *Nationalism in American Thought, 1930–1945* (Chicago, 1969), p. 2 [Wilson]; Higgs, "Wartime Prosperity?" pp. 56–7; Christopher Thorne, *Allies of a Kind: The United States, Britain, and the War Against Japan, 1941–1945* (London, 1978), p. 503 [press]; Washington desp. 1038, 9 August 1945, and min. by Sir Orme Sargent, 1 October 1945, PRO FO 371/44557, AN2560.

20. Terkel, p. 584 [baby boomer]; *Panzer Commander: The Memoirs of Colonel Hans von Luck* (pbk. ed., New York, 1991), p. 142; M. B. Smith, "Did War Service Produce International-Mindedness?" *Harvard Educational Review,* 15 (1945), p. 257 ["education"]; AS 2: p. 644.

21. Mary Penick Motley, ed., *The Invisible Soldier: The Experience of the Black Soldier, World War II* (Detroit, 1975), pp. 49 [Simons], 61, 162, 266 [Cason]; E. T. Hall, Jr., "Race Prejudice and Negro-White Relations in the Army," AJS 52 (1947), pp. 401–9.

22. Terkel, p. 282; author's interview with Joseph O. Curtis, 23 April 1983.

23. Curtis interview; Steven F. Lawson, *Black Ballots: Voting Rights in the South, 1944–1969* (New York, 1976), pp. 101–15, 296.

24. John Modell, Marc Goulden, and Sigurdur Magnusson, "World War Two in the Lives of Black Americans: Some Findings and An Interpretation," JAH 76 (1989), pp. 838–48; Olson, *G.I. Bill*, pp. 74–5.

Chapter 25: Remembering, with Advantages

1. Tom Harrisson, *Living Through the Blitz* (2nd ed., London, 1990), pp. 321–27, quoting from p. 327.

2. Frederic C. Bartlett, *Remembering: A Study in Experimental and Social Psychology* (Cambridge, 1932), p. 213; cf. Steven Rose, *The Making of Memory: From Molecules to Mind* (London, 1992).

3. Leon C. Standifer, *Not in Vain: A Rifleman Remembers World War II* (Baton Rouge, LA, 1992), esp. chs. 14–16.

4. Shirley McGlade, with Mary McCormack, *Daddy, Where Are You?: The Moving Story of a Daughter's Search for her GI Father* (London, 1992), esp. pp. 4–11, 101–2.

5. Author's interview with Curtis C. Moore, 24 August 1993.

6. R. R. Grinker and J. Spiegel, *Men Under Stress* (Chicago, 1945), p. 371 ["slate"]; author's interview with J. Robert Slaughter, 24 August 1993.

7. Interviews with Slaughter and Murphy Scott, 24 August 1993.

8. Terkel, p. 133 [Hutchinson]; Slaughter interview.

9. Gerald F. Linderman, *Embattled Courage: The Experience of Combat in the American Civil War* (New York, 1987), pp. 266–77.

10. Richard Le Strange, *Century Bombers: The Story of the Bloody Hundredth* (Thorpe Abbotts, Norfolk, 1989), pp. 211–18; author's interview with Harry H. Crosby, 18 August 1993.

11. Slaughter and Crosby interviews; Glen H. Elder, Jr., and Elizabeth C. Clipp, "Wartime Losses and Social Bonding: Influences Across 40 Years in Men's Lives, *Psychiatry*, 51 (May 1988), pp. 177–98.

12. John Sparrow, *Grave Epigrams and Other Verses* (Burford, Oxon., 1981), p. 16.

13. Alice M. and Howard S. Hoffman, *Archives of Memory: A Soldier Recalls World War II* (Lexington, KY, 1990).

14. Author's interview with Felix Branham, 4 September 1993; Charles R. Cawthon, *Other Clay: A Remembrance of World War II Infantry* (pbk ed., New York, 1991), pp. xvii, 58, 66.

15. John Comer, *Combat Crew* (London, 1988), pp. xi–xii.

16. D. A. Lande, *From Somewhere in England* (Shrewsbury, 1991), p. 13.

17. Harry H. Crosby, *A Wing and a Prayer* (New York, 1993), p. 140; author's interview with Crosby.

18. Terkel, p. 58.

19. David Dimbleby and David Reynolds, *An Ocean Apart* (London, 1988), p. 151 [Whiting]; Juliet Gardiner, *"Over Here,"* (London, 1992), p. 213.

20. E. Anglian Tourist Board, *The Reunion, 1942–1992* (Hadleigh, Suffolk,

1992), pp. 74–7 [Freeman]; 100th Bomb Gp. Museum brochure; *Splasher Six*, 24/1 (spring 1993), pp. 8–10.

21. Ken Small, with Mark Rogerson, *The Forgotten Dead* (London, 1988).

22. Author's interview.

23. McGlade, *Daddy, Where Are You?*; cf. *Guardian Weekly*, 31 December 1989, p. 16.

24. Author's interview with Pamela Winfield, 3 January 1994; McGlade, *Daddy Where Are You?*, ch. 15.

25. *The New York Times*, 20 May 1992, p. A4 [Comer].

26. "GI Baby," *After the Battle*, 64 (1989), pp. 45–9 [Sims]; Pamela Winfield, *Bye Bye Baby: The Story of the Children the GIs Left Behind* (London, 1992), pp. 28–32, 89–91.

27. George Macaulay Trevelyan, *Clio, A Muse, and Other Essays* (2nd ed., London, 1930), p. 196.

Index

★ ★ ★

In denoting individuals, ranks and titles are omitted, since these often changed several times during the War.

Permissions Acknowledgments

★ ★ ★

GRATEFUL ACKNOWLEDGMENT IS MADE TO THE FOLLOWING FOR PERMISSION TO PRINT UNPUB-lished material:

BBC WRITTEN ARCHIVES CENTRE: Excerpts from papers held at the Written Archives Centre, Caversham Park, Reading. Used by permission.

I. M. CORRY: Excerpts and a photo from memoirs held at the Imperial War Museum, London. Used by permission.

JOAN BLEWITT COX: Excerpts from her unpublished manuscript held at the Imperial War Museum. Copyright © Joan Blewitt Cox. Used by permission.

JOSEPH O. CURTIS: Excerpts from his wartime letters. Used by permission.

CURTIS BROWN GROUP LTD., LONDON: Approximately 651 words from reports in the Mass-Observation Archive at the University of Sussex. Copyright © the Trustees of the Mass-Observation Archive at the University of Sussex. Reproduced by permission of the Curtis Brown Group Ltd., London.

THEODORE H. FOSSIECK, COLONEL, M.I. (RETIRED): Excerpts from four letters to his wife held at the U.S. Army Military History Institute, Carlisle Barracks, Pennsylvania. Used by permission.

GODWIN BREMRIDGE & CLIFTON, SOLICITORS: Excerpt from the memoirs of Miss Julia M. White held at the Imperial War Museum. Used by permission.

MARY E. HAIGHT: Extract from the memoirs of Payne Templeton, held at the U.S. Army Military History Institute. Used by permission.

CHESTER B. HANSEN: Excerpts from his diary from September, 1943, held at the U.S. Army Military History Institute. Used by permission.

THE CONTROLLER OF H.M. STATIONERY OFFICE: Crown copyright documents in the Public Record Office, London. Used by permission.

BRIDGET A. JOHNSON: Excerpts from her memoir held at the Imperial War Museum. Used by permission.

CHRISTEN T. JONASSEN: Excerpt from a letter written on VE Day. Used by permission.

EDITH KUP: Excerpt from her memoirs held at the Imperial War Museum. Used by permission.

LIDDELL HART CENTRE FOR MILITARY ARCHIVES: Excerpts from the Alanbrooke and Ismay papers held at the Liddell Hart Centre for Military Archives, King's College, London. Used by permission.

ELNORA D. MCLENDON AND GENERAL BENJAMIN O. DAVIS, JR.: Excerpts from the papers of General Benjamin O. Davis, Sr., held at the U.S. Army Military History Institute. Used by permission.

VISCOUNT MONTGOMERY OF ALAMEIN: Excerpts from letters by his father, Field Marshal Montgomery. Used by permission.

ALLEN REINECKE: Excerpts from the memoirs of his mother, Grace Eva Reinecke, held at the Imperial War Museum. Used by permission.

WILLIAM H. SIMONS: Excerpts from his wartime letters. Used by permission.

JOHN H. SULLIVAN: Excerpts from "V . . . — Letters from London" by John H. Sullivan, held at the Dwight D. Eisenhower Library, Abilene, Kansas. Copyright © John H. Sullivan. Used by permission.

TOM TATESON: Excerpts from his memoirs held at the Imperial War Museum. Used by permission.

Grateful acknowledgment is made to the following for permission to reprint previously published material:

LEO COOPER LTD.: Excerpts from *Combat Crew* by John Comer. Copyright © 1988 by John Comer. Reprinted by permission.

CYGNET PRESS: Excerpt from poem on page 16 of *Grave Epigrams and Other Verses* by John Sparrow. Reprinted by permission of Cygnet Press and Simon Rendall.

HARCOURT BRACE & COMPANY AND A. M. HEATH & COMPANY LIMITED: Excerpt from "The Lion and the Unicorn" from *The Collected Essays, Journalism and Letters of George Orwell, Vol. II: My Country Right or Left, 1940–1943* and an excerpt from *The Collected Essays, Journalism and Letters of George Orwell, Vol. III: As I Please, 1943–1945* edited by Sonia B. Orwell and Ian Angus. Copyright © 1968 by Sonia Brownell Orwell. Rights throughout the world excluding the United States are controlled by A. M. Heath & Company Limited. Published in the United Kingdom by Martin Secker and Warburg. Reprinted by permission of Harcourt Brace & Company and A. M. Heath & Company Limited.

HIPPOCRENE BOOKS AND DAVID AND CHARLES PUBLISHERS: Excerpts from *A Yank in Bomber Command* by Robert S. Raymond. Rights throughout the United States are controlled by Hippocrene Books. Reprinted by permission.

MIDAS BOOKS: Excerpt from *The Yanks Are Coming* by Edwin R. W. Hale and John Frayn Turner (1983). Reprinted by permission of Midas Books, Parapress Ltd., Publishers, 12 Dene Way, Speldhurst, Tunbridge Wells, Kent TN3 0NY, England.

MIRROR GROUP NEWSPAPERS: Excerpt from an article from the December 20, 1943, issue of the *Daily Mirror*. Reprinted by permission.

THE NEW YORK TIMES: Excerpt from an editorial from July 24, 1940, from two articles by "Scotty" Reston from September 20 and September 21, 1940, and from an editorial from June 30, 1944. Copyright © 1940, 1944 by The New York Times Company. Reprinted by permission.

THE STATE HISTORICAL SOCIETY OF WISCONSIN: Excerpt from p. 86 of *Letters from the Front, 1898–1945*, edited by Michael E. Stevens. Reprinted by permission.

TIMES NEWSPAPERS LIMITED: Excerpts from *With Malice Towards None: A War Diary* by Cecil King (Sidgwick & Jackson, 1970); an excerpt from the leading article on cinema audiences in *The Times* (January 16, 1935) and an excerpt from "US Air Force Settle in All-American Airfields" in *The Times* (August 17, 1942). Copyright © 1935, 1942, 1970 by Times Newspapers Limited. Reprinted by permission.

UNIVERSITY PRESS OF KANSAS: Excerpt from *The Making of a Paratrooper* by Kurt Gabel. Copyright © 1990 by the University Press of Kansas. All rights reserved. Reprinted by permission.

ABOUT THE AUTHOR

DAVID REYNOLDS is a fellow of Christ's College, Cambridge University, and is one of Britain's leading historians of international relations. In the last twenty years, he has traveled, researched, and lectured all over the United States, including two periods as a visiting fellow at Harvard. His first book, *The Creation of the Anglo-American Alliance, 1937–1941*, was awarded the Bernath Prize in 1982. His second, *An Ocean Apart: The Relationship Between Britain and America in the Twentieth Century*, accompanied the BBC/PBS television series for which he was historical adviser. His other works include a new interpretation of modern British foreign policy, *Britannia Overruled*, and two edited volumes entitled *The Origins of the Cold War in Europe* and *Allies at War: The Soviet, American and British Experience, 1939–1945*.